Sociology
Themes and Perspectives

Michael Haralambos

with Robin Heald

D1102559

University Tutorial Press

Published by University Tutorial Press Limited
842 Yeovil Road, Slough, SL1 4JQ

ISBN 0 7231 0793 9 (limp)
ISBN 0 7231 0812 9 (full bound)

Published 1980, reprinted 1980, 1981 (six times)
1982 (twice), 1983

Printed in Great Britain by
Richard Clay (The Chaucer Press) Ltd,
Bungay, Suffolk

To
Pauline and Kate
Helen and Emma

Preface

This book aims to provide a systematic introduction to sociology for GCE Advanced level students, undergraduates and the general reader. It attempts to strike a balance between theory and research findings. The major theoretical perspectives are introduced in the first chapter and examined critically and in detail in the final chapter. Much of the material in the main body of the book is structured in terms of these perspectives. The emphasis on theory is balanced by detailed consideration of the findings of a range of empirical studies. A separate chapter is devoted to methodology – the study of the methods used to obtain and interpret data and of the general assumptions which underlie the study of man and society.

In recent years increasing emphasis has been given to the relationship between ideology and sociology. Sociologists are concerned about the possibility that their theories and findings may be influenced by their own attitudes, values and political beliefs. The book attempts to reflect this concern. The concept of ideology is introduced in the first chapter. In addition, Chapters 2 to 11, which cover the main substantive areas in sociology, close with an interpretation of the ideological basis of the views expressed within them.

The book is organized in the following way. Aspects of sociological theory are introduced in Chapter 1. Since they form the basis of the material which follows, an initial awareness of theory is essential. Chapters 2 to 11 cover areas of society which sociologists have considered important. Chapter 12 deals with methodology and refers to issues and research findings examined in previous chapters. There is an argument for reading this chapter after the introduction since without an appreciation of methodology, the student is not fully prepared to evaluate research. The book closes with a detailed examination of aspects of sociological theory. This chapter aims to tie together various arguments which have been developed throughout the book. It is important that it be read in conjunction with the previous chapter because of the integral relationship between methodology and theory.

The division of labour for writing the book was as follows. All the chapters were written by Michael Haralambos with the exception of Chapter 7 which was written jointly by Michael Haralambos and Robin Heald.

A book involves the work of many people. The manuscript was typed

Preface

by Barbara Grimshaw, Pauline Haralambos and Jean Buckley. Their assistance is appreciated. Particular thanks are due to Barbara Grimshaw who did the bulk of the typing, met deadlines often at short notice, yet always produced the highest quality typescript. The help of librarians is essential for a book of this kind. The assistance of the staffs of W R Tuson College Library, Preston Polytechnic Library and Lancashire County Library, Corporation Street, Preston is gratefully acknowledged. Special thanks are due to William Dickey and the staff of W R Tuson Library whose help went well beyond what would normally be expected from the services of a library. Writing a book requires support, interest and constructive criticism from friends and colleagues. In this regard, thanks are due to Christine Robinson, Frances Smith, Peter Adamson, Dave Beddow, Maurice Gavan, James O'Gorman and Terry Richards. James O'Gorman's interest and support is particularly appreciated. The skill and understanding of an editorial staff are essential for the completion of a manuscript. In this respect the work of Chris Kington who guided the early stages of the book and Simon Boyd who saw it through to completion is gratefully acknowledged. Particular thanks go to Josephine Warrior who edited the manuscript with tact, skill and precision.

This book could not have been completed without the help of the authors' wives. Robin Heald thanks Helen for her support and patient understanding. I should like to thank Pauline for her unwavering support and encouragement over some four years. She took over many of the responsibilities of running the home and remained cheerful and optimistic when it seemed as though the book would never be completed. Her contribution is immeasurable.

Michael Haralambos
January 1980

Contents

Contents

Contents

Contents

Contents

10 Deviance 406

Contents

Contents

1 The sociological perspective

'Man learns his behaviour and uses his intelligence whereas animals simply act on instinct.' Like most common-sense notions, this idea has an element of truth but reality is far more complex.

The regimented society of social insects such as ants and bees is an object lesson in order and organization. Every member has clearly defined tasks in a co-operative enterprise. Thus in a beehive the worker bees, depending on their age, will either feed the young, stand guard and repel strangers, forage for food or ventilate the hive by beating their wings. The behaviour of insects is largely instinctive. It is based on programmes contained in the genes which direct their actions. However, it would be a mistake to assume that the behaviour of insects is based solely on instinct. Experiments have indicated that at least some have the ability to learn. For example, ants are able to memorize the path through a maze and are capable of applying this learning to other mazes.

Moving from insects to reptiles to mammals, the importance of learned, as opposed to genetically determined, behaviour gradually increases. Studies of macaque monkeys on islands in northern Japan provide some indication of the importance of learned behaviour. On one island the macaques lived in the forested interior. Japanese scientists attempted to discover whether they could change the behaviour patterns of the troupe. They began by dumping potatoes in a clearing in the forest. Gradually the macaques changed their eating habits and became largely dependent on potatoes, a food previously unknown to them, as their staple diet. The scientists slowly moved the food dumps towards the shoreline and the troupe followed. The potatoes were then regularly placed on the beach which now became the normal habitat for the macaques. In the following months, without any encouragement from the scientists, a number of new behaviour patterns emerged in the troupe. Firstly, some members began washing the potatoes in the sea before eating them. Others followed suit until it became standard practice in the group. Then some of the younger macaques began paddling in the sea and eventually took the plunge and learned how to swim. They were imitated by their elders and again, the novel behaviour of the few became the accepted behaviour of the group. Finally, some adventurous youngsters began diving off low rocky outcroppings on the shoreline, a practice which was copied by other members of the troupe.

The Japanese macaques had learned new behaviour patterns and these

1

patterns were shared by members of the group. The simple generalization that animal behaviour is genetically determined whereas the behaviour of man is learned is clearly incorrect. However, the range and complexity of learned behaviour in man is far greater than in any other species. This is shown by experiments with man's nearest living relative, the chimpanzee. For a few years chimpanzees raised in human households learn as well as human infants of the same age, but they soon reach the limit of their ability and are rapidly overtaken by human youngsters. Compared to mammals other than man, chimpanzees have a considerable learning capacity. They can solve simple problems to obtain food, they can learn a basic sign language to communicate with humans and even ape their more intelligent cousins in the famous chimpanzee tea party. Yet despite this capacity to learn, the behavioural repertoire of chimpanzees is rudimentary and limited compared to man.

More than any other species, man relies for his survival on behaviour patterns which are learned. Man has no instincts, that is genetically programmed directives to behave in particular ways. An instinct involves not only the impulse to do something, but also specific instructions on how to do it. Birds have an instinct to build nests. They have an impulse for nest building and all members of a particular species are programmed to build nests in the same way. The range and variety of dwellings constructed by man clearly shows the absence of directives based on instinct. The following examples from nineteenth-century North America provide an illustration. In the Arctic, the Eskimos constructed igloos from rectangular blocks cut from closely compacted snow. On the northwest coast of the USA and the west coast of Canada, tribes such as the Nootka built oblong houses with a framework of cedar logs, walled and roofed with planks. On the opposite side of the subcontinent, in the eastern woodlands, the Iroquois also lived in oblong dwellings, known as 'long houses', but they substituted birchbark for planks. On the prairies, the easily transportable conical tipi made from long saplings covered in buffalo hides provided shelter for tribes such as the Sioux and Cheyenne. Further south, the Apache of Arizona and New Mexico lived in domed wickiups made from brushwood and scrub. In the same area, tribes such as the Zuñi and the Hopi built the first apartment houses in the USA. Even today many members of these tribes live in multi-occupation dwellings made from sun-dried mud bricks known as adobe. These examples show clearly that man's genetic code does not contain specific instructions to behave in a particular way.

Culture and society

To all intents and purposes a newborn human baby is helpless. Not only is it physically dependent on older members of the species but it also lacks the behaviour patterns necessary for living in human society. It relies primarily on certain biological drives such as hunger and the charity of its elders to satisfy those drives. The infant has a lot to learn. In order to survive, it must learn the skills, knowledge and accepted ways of behaving of the society into which it is born. It must learn a way of life; in sociological terminology, it must learn the culture of its society.

Ralph Linton states that, 'The culture of a society is the way of life of its members; the collection of ideas and habits which they learn, share and transmit from generation to generation'. In Clyde Kluckhohn's elegant phrase, culture is a 'design for living' held by members of a particular society. Since man has no instincts to direct his actions, his behaviour must be based on guidelines which are learned. In order for a society to operate effectively, these guidelines must be shared by its members. Without a shared culture, members of society would be unable to communicate and cooperate, and confusion and disorder would result. Culture therefore has two essential qualities: firstly it is learned, secondly it is shared. Without it there would be no human society.

To a large degree culture determines how members of a society think and feel, it directs their actions and defines their outlook on life. Members of society usually take their culture for granted. It has become so much a part of them that they are often unaware of its existence. The following example given by Edward T. Hall provides an illustration. Two individuals, one from North America, the other from South America are conversing in a hall forty foot long. They begin at one end of the hall and finish at the other end, the North American steadily retreating, the South American relentlessly advancing. Each is trying to establish the 'accustomed conversation distance' defined by his culture. To the North American, his South American counterpart comes too close for comfort whereas the South American feels uneasy conversing at the distance his partner demands. Often it takes meetings such as this to reveal the pervasive nature of culturally determined behaviour.

Culture defines accepted ways of behaving for members of a particular society. Such definitions vary from society to society. This can lead to considerable misunderstanding between members of different societies as the following example provided by Otto Klineberg shows. Amongst the Sioux Indians of South Dakota, it is regarded as incorrect to answer a question in the presence of others who do not know the answer. Such behaviour would be regarded as boastful and arrogant, and, since it reveals the ignorance of others, it would be interpreted as an attempt to undermine their confidence and shame them. In addition the Sioux regard it as wrong to answer a question unless they are absolutely sure of the correct answer. Faced with a classroom of Sioux children, a White American teacher, who is unaware of their culture, might easily interpret their behaviour as a reflection of ignorance, stupidity or hostility.

Every society has certain common problems to deal with, for example the problem of dependent members such as the very young and the very old. However, solutions to such problems are culturally determined: they vary from society to society. The solutions provided in one society may well be regarded as indefensible by members of other societies. Under certain circumstances, infanticide – the killing of infants – and geronticide – the killing of old people – have been practised by certain groups of Australian aborigines, Eskimos and Caribou Indians. Particularly in the more arid parts of Australia, female infanticide was practised to reduce the population in times of famine, and occasionally the baby was eaten. In Tasmania aborigine hunters led a nomadic life to take advantage of the seasonal food supply in different regions. The old and infirm who were too feeble to keep up with the band were left behind to die. The Caribou Indians, who lived to the west of Hudson Bay in Canada, were dependent for their food supply on the caribou herds. Sometimes, in winter, the herds failed to appear. To prevent the starvation of the whole community, the following priorities were established. First the active male adults were fed because if they were to weak to hunt, nobody would eat. Next, their wives were fed since they could bear more children. Male infants were considered more important than female because they would grow up to become hunters. Old people were the most expendable and in times of famine they committed suicide by walking naked into the snow. If there were no old people left, girl babies would be killed. The practices of infanticide and geronticide are culturally defined behaviour patterns designed to ensure the survival of the group in times of extreme food shortages. Like many of the customs of non-Western societies, they appear strange and even heartless to Western man, but in the context of the particular society, they are sensible, rational and an accepted part of life.

The above examples of culturally defined behaviour have been selected because they differ considerably from behaviour patterns in Western society. It is easier to appreciate the idea that human behaviour is largely determined by culture with the use of examples which appear strange to Western man.

Socialization

The process by which individuals learn the culture of their society is known as socialization. Primary socialization, probably the most important aspect of the socialization process, takes place during infancy, usually within the family. By responding to the approval and disapproval of its parents and copying their example, the child learns the language and many of the basic behaviour patterns of its society. In Western society, other important agencies of socialization include the educational system, the occupational group and the peer group – a group whose members share similar circumstances and are often of a similar age. Within its peer group, the young child, by interacting with others and playing childhood games, learns to conform to the accepted ways of a social group and to appreciate the fact that social life is based on rules. Socialization is not, however, confined to childhood. It is a lifelong process. At the beginning of their working lives, the young bricklayer, teacher and accountant soon learn the rules of the game and the tricks of the trade. Should they change jobs in later life, they will join a different occupational group and may well have to learn new skills and adopt different mannerisms and styles of dress.

Without socialization, an individual would bear little resemblance to any human being defined as normal by the standards of his society. The following examples, though they lack the reliability demanded by today's standards of reporting, nevertheless provide some indication of the importance of socialization. It is reported that Akbar, who was an emperor in India from 1542 to 1602, ordered that a group of children be brought up without any instruction in language, to test the belief that they would eventually speak Hebrew, the language of God. The children were raised by deaf mutes. They developed no spoken language and communicated solely by gestures. There is an extensive, though somewhat unreliable, literature on children raised by animals. One of the best documented cases concerns the so-called 'wolf-children of Midnapore'. Two females, aged two and eight, were reportedly found in a wolf den in Bengal in 1920. They walked on all fours, preferred a diet of raw meat, they howled like wolves and lacked any form of speech. Whether these children had been raised by wolves or simply abandoned and left to their own devices in the forest is unclear. However, such examples indicate that socialization involving prolonged interaction with adults is essential not only for fitting new members into society but also to the process of actually becoming human.

Norm and value

Every culture contains a large number of guidelines which direct conduct in particular situations. Such guidelines are known as norms. A norm is a specific guide to action which defines acceptable and appropriate behaviour in particular situations. For example, in all societies, there are norms governing dress. Members of society generally share norms which define acceptable male and female apparel and which specify appropriate dress for different age groups. For example, in British society, a seventy year old grandmother dressed as a teenager would contravene the norms for her age group. Norms of dress provide guidelines for what to wear on particular occasions. A formal dance, a funeral, a day out on the beach, a working day in the bank, on the building site or in the hospital – all these situations are governed by norms which specify appropriate attire for the occasion. Norms of dress vary from society to society. A missionary presented with bare-breasted African females in his congregation provides an example. Flushed with embarrassment, he ordered a consignment of brassières. The ladies could make little sense of them in terms of their norms of dress. From their point of view, the most reasonable way to interpret these strange articles was to regard them as headgear. Much to the dismay of the missionary, they placed the two cups on the top of their heads and fastened the straps under their chins.

Norms are enforced by positive and negative sanctions, that is rewards and punishments. Sanctions can be informal, such as an approving or a disapproving glance, or formal, such as a fine or a reward given by an official body. Continuing the example of norms of dress, an embarrassed silence, a hoot of derision or a contemptuous stare will make most members of society who have broken norms of dress change into more conventional attire. Usually the threat of such negative sanctions is sufficient to enforce normative behaviour. Conversely an admiring glance, a word of praise or an encouraging smile provide rewards for conformity to social norms. Certain norms are formalized by translation into laws which are enforced by official sanctions. In terms of laws governing dress, the nude bather on a public beach, the 'streaker' at a sporting event and the 'flasher' who exposes himself to an unsuspecting individual are subject to official punishments of varying severity. Like informal sanctions, formal sanctions may be positive or negative. In terms of norms associated with dress, awards are made by official bodies such as tailors' organizations to the best-dressed men in Britain.

To summarize, norms define appropriate and acceptable behaviour in specific situations. They are enforced by positive and negative sanctions which may be formal or informal. The sanctions which enforce norms are a major part of the mechanisms of social control which are concerned with maintaining order in society.

Unlike norms, which provide specific directives for conduct, values provide more general guidelines. A value is a belief that something is good and desirable. It defines what is important, worthwhile and worth striving for. It has often been suggested that individual achievement and materialism are major values in Western industrial society. Thus the individual believes it is important and desirable to come top of the class, to win a race or reach the top of his chosen profession. Individual achievement is often symbolized and measured by the quality and quantity of material possessions that a person can accumulate. In the West, the value of materialism motivates individuals to invest time and energy producing and acquiring material possessions. Like norms, values vary from society to society. For example, the Sioux Indians placed a high value on generosity. In terms of Sioux values, the acquisitive individual of Western society would at best be regarded as peculiar and more probably would be condemmed as grasping, self-seeking and antisocial.

Many norms can be seen as reflections of values. A variety of norms can be seen as expressions of a single value. In Western society the value placed on human life is expressed in terms of the following norms. The norms associated with hygiene in the home and in public places reflect a concern for human life. Norms defining acceptable ways for settling an argument or dispute usually exclude physical violence and manslaughter. The array of rules and regulations dealing with transport and behaviour on the highway are concerned with protecting life and limb. The same applies to safety regulations in the workplace, particularly in mining and manufacturing industries. Thus the variety of norms concerned with the health and safety of members of society can be seen as expressions of the value placed on human life.

Many sociologists maintain that shared norms and values are essential for the operation of human society. Since man has no instincts, his behaviour must be guided and regulated by norms. Unless norms are shared, members of society would be unable to cooperate or even comprehend the behaviour of others. Similar arguments apply to values. Without shared values, members of society would be unlikely to cooperate and work together. With differing or conflicting values they would often be pulling in different directions and pursuing incompatible goals. Disorder and disruption may well result. Thus an ordered and stable society requires shared norms and values. This viewpoint will be considered in greater detail in a later section.

Status and role

All members of society occupy a number of social positions known as statuses. In Western society, an individual will usually have an occupational status such as bus driver, clerk or solicitor; family statuses as son or daughter, father or mother; and a gender status as male or female. Statuses are culturally defined, despite the fact they may be based on biological factors such as sex or race. For example, skin colour assigns individuals to racial statuses such as Black and White but this merely reflects the conventions of particular societies. Other biological characteristics such as hair colour have no connection with an individual's status and, in future societies, skin colour may be equally insignificant.

Some statuses are relatively fixed and there is little an individual can do to change his assignment to particular social positions. Examples of such fixed or ascribed statuses include gender and aristocratic titles. On rare occasions, however, ascribed statuses can be changed. Edward VIII was forced to abdicate for insisting on marrying an American divorcée. Anthony Wedgewood-Benn renounced his peerage in order to stand for election to the House of Commons. Revolutions in America and Russia abolished the ascribed status of members of the aristocracy. Ascribed statuses are usually fixed at birth. In many societies occupational status has been or still is transmitted from father to son and from mother to daughter. Thus in the traditional Indian caste system, a son automatically entered the occupation of his father. Statuses which are not fixed by inheritance, biological characteristics, or other factors over which the individual has no control, are known as achieved statuses. An achieved status is entered as a result of some degree of purposive action and choice. In Western society an individual's marital status and occupational status are achieved. However, as the following chapter will indicate, the distinction between ascribed and achieved status is less clear cut than has so far been suggested.

Each status in society is accompanied by a number of norms which define how an individual occupying a particular status is expected to act. This group of norms is known as a role. Thus the status of husband is accompanied by the role of husband, the status of solicitor by the role of solicitor and so on. As an example, a solicitor is expected to possess a detailed knowledge of certain aspects of the law, to support his client's interests and respect the confidentiality of his business. His attire is expected to be sober, his manner restrained, confident yet understanding, his standing in the community beyond reproach. Playing or performing roles involves social relationships in the sense that an individual plays a role in relation to other roles. Thus the role of doctor is played in relation to the role of patient, the role of husband in relation to the role of wife. Individuals therefore interact in terms of roles.

Social roles regulate and organize behaviour. In particular, they provide means for accomplishing certain tasks. It can be argued, for example, that teaching can be accomplished more effectively if teacher and student adopt their appropriate roles. This involves the exclusion of other areas of their lives in order to concentrate on the matter in hand. Roles provide social life with order and predictability. Interacting in terms of their respective roles, teacher and student know what to do and how to do it. With a knowledge of each other's roles they are able to predict and comprehend the actions of the other. As an aspect of culture, roles provide an important part of the guidelines and directives necessary for an ordered society.

This section has introduced some of the basic concepts used by many sociologists. In doing so, however, it has presented a somewhat one-sided view of man in society. Man has been pictured rather like an automaton who simply responds to the dictates of his culture. All members of a particular society appear to be produced from the same mould. They are all efficiently socialized in terms of a common culture. They share the same values, follow the same norms and play a variety of roles, adopting the appropriate behaviour for each. Clearly this picture of conformity has been overstated and the pervasive and constraining influence of culture has been exaggerated. There are two reasons for this. Firstly, overstatement has been used to make the point. Secondly, many of the ideas presented so far derive from a particular perspective in sociology which has been subject to the criticisms noted above. This perspective, known as functionalism, will now be examined.

Theories of society

This section will examine three theories of society. A theory is a set of ideas which claims to explain how something works. A sociological theory is therefore a set of ideas which claims to explain how society or aspects of society work. The theories in this section represent only a selection from the range of sociological theories. They have been simplified and condensed to provide a basic introduction. Since they are applied to various topics throughout the text, an initial awareness is essential. Criticism of the theories has been omitted from this chapter for the sake of simplicity. It will be dealt with throughout the text and in detail in the final chapter. Again for simplicity, each theory is presented as though there were no disagreement about its nature. For example, functionalism, the first theory examined is presented as if there were only one version of the theory whereas in fact there are several.

Functionalism

Functionalism was the dominant theoretical perspective in sociology during the 1940s and 1950s. From the mid 1960s onwards, its popularity steadily declined due partly to damaging criticism, partly to competing perspectives which appeared to provide superior explanations, and partly to changes in fashion. The key points of the functionalist perspective may be summarized by a comparison drawn from biology. If a biologist wanted to know how an organism such as the human body worked, he might begin by examining the various parts such as the brain, lungs, heart and liver. However, if he simply analysed the parts in isolation from each other, he would be unable to explain how life was maintained. To do this, he would have to examine the parts in relation to each other since they work together to maintain the organism. Thus he would analyse the relationships between the heart, lungs, brain and so on to understand how they operated and appreciate their importance. From this viewpoint, any part of the organism must be seen in terms of the organism as a whole. Functionalism adopts a similar perspective. The various parts of society are seen to be interrelated and taken together, they form a complete system. To understand any part of society, such as the family or religion, the part must be seen in relation to society as a whole. Thus where a biologist will examine a part of the body, such as the heart, in terms of its contribution to the maintenance of the human organism, the functionalist will examine a part of society, such as the family, in terms of its contribution to the maintenance of the social system.

9

Functionalism begins with the observation that behaviour in society is structured. This means that relationships between members of society are organized in terms of rules. Social relationships are therefore patterned and recurrent. Values provide general guidelines for behaviour and they are translated into more specific directives in terms of roles and norms. The structure of society can be seen as the sum total of normative behaviour – the sum total of social relationships which are governed by norms. The main parts of society, its institutions, such as the family, the economy, the educational and political systems are major aspects of the social structure. Thus an institution can be seen as a structure made up of interconnected roles or interrelated norms. For example, the family is made up of the interconnected roles of husband, father, wife, mother, son and daughter. Social relationships within the family are structured in terms of a set of related norms.

Having established the existence of a social structure, functionalist analysis turns to a consideration of how that structure functions. This involves an examination of the relationship between the different parts of the structure and their relationship to society as a whole. From this examination, the functions of institutions are discovered. At its simplest, function means effect. Thus the function of the family is the effect it has on other parts of the social structure and on society as a whole. In practice the term function is usually used to indicate the contribution an institution makes to the maintenance and survival of the social system. Thus a major function of the family is the socialization of new members of society. This represents an important contribution to the maintenance of society since order, stability and cooperation largely depend on learned, shared norms and values.

In determining the functions of various parts of the social structure, functionalists are guided by the following ideas. Societies have certain basic needs or requirements which must be met if they are to survive. These requirements are sometimes known as functional prerequisites. For example, a means of producing food and shelter may be seen as a functional prerequisite since without them members of society could not survive. A system for socializing new members of society may also be regarded as a functional prerequisite since without culture social life would not be possible. Having assumed a number of basic requirements for the survival of society, the next step is to look at the parts of the social structure to see how they meet such functional prerequisites. Thus a major function of the economic system is the production of food and shelter. An important function of the family is the socialization of new members of society.

From a functionalist perspective, society is regarded as a system. A system is an entity made up of interconnected and interrelated parts. From this viewpoint, it follows that each part will in some way affect every other part and the system as a whole. It also follows that if the system is to survive, its various parts must have some degree of fit or compatibility. Thus a functional prerequisite of society involves a minimal degree of integration between the parts. Many functionalists argue that this integration is based largely on 'value consensus', that is on agreement about values by members of society. Thus if the major values of society are expressed in the various parts of the social structure, those parts will be integrated. For example, it can be argued that the value of materialism integrates many parts of the social structure in Western industrial society. The economic system produces a large range of goods and ever increasing productivity is regarded as an important goal. The educational system is partly concerned with producing the skills and expertise to expand production and increase its efficiency. The family is an important unit of consumption with its steadily increasing demand for consumer durables such as washing machines, televisions and three-piece suites. The political system is partly concerned with improving material living standards and raising productivity. To the extent that these parts of the social structure are based on the same values, they may be said to be integrated.

One of the main concerns of functionalist theory is to explain how social life is possible. The theory assumes that a certain degree of order and stability are essential for the survival of social systems. Functionalism is therefore concerned with explaining the origin and maintenance of order and stability in society. Many functionalists see shared values as the key to this explanation. Thus value consensus integrates the various parts of society. It forms the basis of social unity or social solidarity since individuals will tend to identify and feel kinship with those who share the same values as themselves. Value consensus provides the foundation for cooperation since common values produce common goals. Members of society will tend to cooperate in pursuit of goals which they share. Having attributed such importance to value consensus, many functionalists then focus on the question of how this consensus is maintained. Indeed the American sociologist Talcott Parsons has stated that the main task of sociology is to examine 'the institutionalization of patterns of value orientation in the social system'. Emphasis is therefore placed on the process of socialization whereby values are internalized and transmitted from one generation to the next. In this respect, the family is regarded as a vital part of the social structure. Once learned, values must be maintained. In particular those who deviate from society's values must be brought back into line. Thus the mechanisms of social control discussed earlier in the chapter, are seen as essential to the maintenance of social order.

In summary, society, from a functionalist perspective, is a system made up of interrelated parts. The social system has certain basic needs which must be met if it is to survive. These needs are known as functional prerequisites. The function of any part of society is its contribution to the maintenance of society. The major functions of social institutions are those which help to meet the functional prerequisites of society. Since society is a system, there must be some degree of integration between its parts. A minimal degree of integration is therefore a functional prerequisite of society. Many functionalists maintain that the order and stability they see as essential for the maintenance of the social system are largely provided by value consensus. An investigation of the source of value consensus is therefore a major concern of functionalist analysis.

Marxism

Marxian theory offers a radical alternative to functionalism. It became increasingly influential during the 1970s, due partly to the decline of functionalism, partly to its promise to provide answers which functionalism failed to provide and partly because it was more in keeping with the tenor and mood of the times. Marxism takes its name from its founder, the German-born philosopher, economist and sociologist, Karl Marx (1818–83). The following account represents a simplified version of Marxian theory. It must also be seen as one interpretation of that theory. Marx's extensive writings have been variously interpreted and, since his death, several schools of Marxism have developed.

Marxian theory begins with the simple observation that in order to survive, man must produce food and material objects. In doing so he enters into social relationships with other men. From the simple hunting band to the complex industrial state, production is a social enterprise. Production also involves a technical component known as the forces of production which includes the technology, raw materials and scientific knowledge employed in the process of production. Each major stage in the development of the forces of production will correspond with a particular form of the social relationships of production. Thus the forces of production in a hunting economy will correspond with a particular set of social relationships. Taken together, the forces of production and the social relationships of production form the economic base or infrastructure of society. The other aspects of society, known as the superstructure, are largely shaped by the infrastructure. Thus the political, legal and educational institutions and the belief and value systems are primarily determined by economic factors. A major change in the infrastructure will therefore produce a corresponding change in the superstructure. Marx maintained that, with the possible exception of the societies of prehistory, all historical societies contain basic contradictions which means that they cannot survive forever in their existing form. These contradictions involve the exploitation of one social group by another. For example in feudal society, lords exploit their serfs, in capitalist society, employers exploit their employees. This creates a fundamental conflict of interest between social groups since one gains at the expense of another. This conflict of interest must ultimately be resolved since a social system containing such contradictions cannot survive unchanged.

The points raised in this brief summary of Marxian theory will now be examined in greater detail. The major contradictions in society are between the forces and relations of production. The forces of production include land, raw materials, tools and machinery, the technical and scientific knowledge used in production, the technical organization of the production process and the labour power of the workers. The relations of production are the social relationships which men enter into in order to produce goods. Thus in feudal society they include the relationship between the lord and vassal and the set of rights, duties and obligations which make up that relationship. In capitalist industrial society they include the relationship between employer and employee and the various rights of the two parties. The relations of production involve the relationship of social groups to the forces of production. Thus in feudal society, land, the major force of production, is owned by the lord whereas the serf has the right to use land in return for services or payment to the lord. In Western industrial society, the forces of production are owned by the capitalist whereas the worker owns only his labour which he hires to the employer in return for wages.

The idea of contradiction between the forces and relations of production may be illustrated in terms of the infrastructure of capitalist industrial society. Marx maintained that only labour produces wealth. Thus wealth in capitalist society is produced by the labour power of the workers. However, much of this wealth is appropriated in the form of profits by the capitalists, the owners of the forces of production. The wages of the workers are well below the value of the wealth they produce. There is thus a contradiction between the forces of production, in particular the labour power of the workers which produces wealth, and the relations of production which involve the appropriation of much of that wealth by the capitalists. A related contradiction involves the technical organization of labour and the nature of ownership. In capitalist society, the forces of production include the collective production of goods by large numbers of workers in factories. Yet the forces of production are privately owned, the profits are appropriated by individuals. The contradiction between the forces and relations of production lies in the social and collective nature of production and the private and individual nature of ownership. Marx believed that these and other contradictions would eventually lead to the downfall of the capitalist system. He maintained that by its very nature, capitalism involves the exploitation and oppression of the worker. He believed that the conflict of interest between capital and labour, which involves one group gaining at the expense of the other, could not be resolved within the framework of a capitalist economy.

Marx saw history as divided into a number of time periods or epochs, each being characterized by a particular mode of production. Major changes in history are the result of new forces of production. Thus the change from feudal to capitalist society stemmed from the emergence, during the feudal epoch, of the forces of production of industrial society. This resulted in a contradiction between the new forces of production and the old feudal relations of production. Capitalist industrial society required relations of production based on wage labour rather than the traditional ties of lord and vassal. When they reach a certain point in their development, the new forces of production lead to the creation of a new set of relations of production. Then, a new epoch of history is born which sweeps away the social relationships of the old order. However, the final epoch of history, the communist or socialist society which Marx believed would eventually supplant capitalism, will not result from a new force of production. Rather it will develop from a resolution of the contradictions contained within the capitalist system. Collective production will remain but the relations of production will be transformed. Ownership of the forces of production will be collective rather than individual and members of society will share the wealth that their labour produces. No longer will one social group exploit and oppress another. This will produce an infrastructure without contradiction and conflict. In Marx's view this would mean the end of history since communist society would no longer contain the contradictions which generate change.

In view of the contradictions which beset historical societies, it appears difficult to explain their survival. Despite its internal contradictions, capitalism has continued in the West for over 200 years. This continuity can be explained in large part by the nature of the superstructure. In all societies the superstructure is largely shaped by the infrastructure. In particular, the relations of production are reflected and reproduced in the various institutions, values and beliefs that make up the superstructure. Thus the relationships of domination and subordination found in the infrastructure will also be found in social institutions. In Marx's words, 'The existing relations of production between individuals must necessarily express themselves also as political and legal relations'. The dominant social group or ruling class, that is the group which owns and controls the forces of production, will largely monopolize political power and its position will be supported by laws which are framed to protect and further its interests. In the same way, beliefs and values will reflect and legitimate the relations of production. Members of the ruling class 'rule also as thinkers, as producers of ideas'. These ideas justify their power and privilege and conceal from all members of society the basis of exploitation and oppression on which their dominance rests. Thus under feudalism honour and loyalty were 'dominant concepts' of the age. Vassals owed loyalty to their lords and were bound by an oath of allegiance which encouraged the acceptance of their status. In terms of the dominant concepts of the age, feudalism appeared as the natural order of things. Under capitalism, exploitation is disguised by the ideas of equality and freedom.

The relationship between capitalist and wage labourer is defined as an equal exchange. The capitalist buys the labour power which the worker offers for hire. The worker is defined as a free agent since he has the freedom to choose his employer. In reality, equality and freedom are illusions. The employer–employee relationship is not equal. It is an exploitive relationship. The worker is not free since he is forced to work for the capitalist in order to survive. All he can do is exchange one form of 'wage slavery' for another. Marx refers to the dominant ideas of each epoch as 'ruling class ideology'. Ideology is a distortion of reality, a false picture of society. It blinds members of society to the contradictions and conflicts of interest which are built into their relationships. As a result they tend to accept their situation as normal and natural, right and proper. In this way a 'false consciousness' of reality is produced which helps to maintain the system. However, Marx believed that ruling class ideology could only slow down the disintegration of the system. The contradictions embedded in the structure of society must eventually find expression.

In summary, the key to understanding society from a Marxian perspective involves an analysis of the infrastructure. In all historical societies there are basic contradictions between the forces and relations of production and there are fundamental conflicts of interest between the social groups involved in the production process. In particular, the relationship between the major social groups is one of exploitation and oppression. The superstructure derives largely from the infrastructure and therefore reproduces the social relationships of production. It will thus reflect the interests of the dominant group in the relations of production. Ruling class ideology distorts the true nature of society and serves to legitimate and justify the status quo. However the contradictions in the infrastructure will eventually lead to a disintegration of the system and the creation of a new society.

Interactionism

Although functionalism and Marxism provide very different perspectives on society, they have a number of factors in common. Firstly, they offer a general explanation of society as a whole and as a result are sometimes known as macro-theories. Secondly, they regard society as a system, hence they are sometimes referred to as systems theories. Thirdly, they tend to see man's behaviour as shaped by the system. In terms of Talcott Parsons's version of functionalism, behaviour is largely directed by the norms and values of the social system. From a Marxian viewpoint, behaviour is ultimately determined by the economic infrastructure. Interactionism differs from functionalism and Marxism on these three points. It focusses on small-scale interaction rather than society as a whole. It usually rejects the notion of a social system. As a result it does not regard human action as a response or reaction to the system.

Interactionism, as used in this chapter and in the main part of the book, covers a number of related perspectives. These perspectives will be differentiated and examined in detail in the chapter on social theory. As its name suggests, interactionism is concerned with interaction which means action between individuals. The interactionist perspective seeks to understand this process. It begins from the assumption that action is meaningful to those involved. It therefore follows that an understanding of action requires an interpretation of the meanings which actors give to their activities. Picture a man and a woman in a room and the man lighting a candle. This action is open to a number of interpretations. The couple may simply require light because a fuse has blown or a power cut has occurred. Or, they may be involved in some form of ritual in which the lighted candle has a religious significance. Alternatively, the man may be trying to create a more intimate atmosphere as a prelude to a sexual encounter. Finally the couple may be celebrating a birthday, a wedding anniversary or some other red-letter day. In each case a different meaning is attached to the act of lighting a candle. To understand the act it is therefore necessary to discover the meaning held by the actors.

Meanings are not fixed entities. As the above example shows, they depend in part on the context of the interaction. Meanings are also created, developed, modified and changed within the actual process of interaction. For example, a pupil entering a new class may initially define the situation as threatening and even hostile. This definition may be confirmed, modified or changed depending on his perception of the interaction which takes place in the classroom. The pupil may come to perceive his teacher and fellow pupils as friendly and understanding and so change his assessment of the situation. The way in which an actor defines a situation has important consequences. It represents his reality in terms of which he structures his action. For example, if the pupil maintained his definition of the classroom as threatening and hostile, he may keep to himself and speak only when spoken to. Conversely if he changed this definition, there would probably be a corresponding change in his actions in that context.

The actions of the pupil in the above example will depend in part on his interpretation of the way others see him. For this reason many interactionists place particular emphasis on the idea of the self. They suggest that an individual develops a self-concept, a picture of himself, which has an important influence on his actions. A self-concept develops from interaction processes since it is in large part a reflection of the reactions of others towards the individual. Hence the term 'looking glass self' coined by Charles Cooley. An actor tends to act in terms of his self-concept. Thus if he is consistently defined as disreputable or respectable, servile or arrogant he will tend to see himself in this light and act accordingly.

Since interactionists are concerned with definitions of situation and self, they are also concerned with the process by which those definitions are constructed. For example, how does an individual come to be defined in a certain way? The answer to this question involves an investigation of the construction of meaning in interaction processes. This requires an analysis of the way actors interpret the language, gestures, appearance and manner of others and their interpretation of the context in which the interaction takes place. The definition of an individual as a delinquent provides an example. Research has indicated that police are more likely to perceive an act as delinquent if it occurs in a low-income inner city area. The context will influence the action of the police since they typically define the inner city as a 'bad area'. Once arrested, a suspect is more likely to be defined as a juvenile delinquent if his manner is interpreted as aggressive and uncooperative, if his appearance is seen as unconventional or slovenly, if his speech is defined as ungrammatical or slang and if his posture gives the impression of disrespect for authority or arrogance. Thus the jive-talking Black American from the inner city ghetto with his cool, arrogant manner and colourful clothes is more likely to be defined as a delinquent than the White 'all-American boy' from the tree-lined suburbs.

Definitions of individuals as certain kinds of persons are not, however, simply based on preconceptions which actors bring to interaction situations. For example, the police will not automatically define the Black juvenile involved in a fight as delinquent and the White juvenile involved in a similar activity as non-delinquent. A process of negotiation occurs from which the definition emerges. Often negotiations will reinforce preconceptions but not necessarily. The young Black may be able to convince the policeman that the fight was a friendly brawl which did not involve intent to injure or steal. In this way he may successfully promote an image of himself as a high spirited teenager rather than a malicious delinquent. Definitions and meanings are therefore constructed in interaction situations by a process of negotiation.

The idea of negotiation is also applied to the concept of role. Like functionalists, the interactionists employ the concept of role but they adopt a somewhat different perspective. Functionalists imply that roles are provided by the social system and the individual enacts his role as if he were reading off a script which contains explicit directions for his behaviour. Interactionists argue that roles are often unclear, ambiguous and vague. This lack of clarity provides actors with considerable room for negotiation, manoeuvre, improvisation and creative action. At most, roles provide very general guidelines for action. What matters is how they are employed in interaction situations. For example, two individuals enter marriage with a vague idea about the roles of husband and wife. Their interaction will not be constrained by these roles. Their definition of what constitutes a husband, a wife, and a marital relationship will be negotiated. It will be fluid rather than fixed, changeable rather than static. Thus, from an interactionist perspective, roles, like meanings and definitions of the situation, are negotiated in interaction processes.

In summary, interactionism focusses on the process of interaction in particular contexts. Since all action is meaningful, it can only be understood by discovering the meanings which actors assign to their activities. Meanings both direct action and derive from action. They are not fixed but constructed and negotiated in interaction situations. From their interaction with others, actors develop a self-concept. This has important consequences since the individual tends to act in terms of his definition of self. Understanding the construction of meanings and self-concepts involves an appreciation of the way actors interpret the process of interaction. This requires an investigation of the way in which they perceive the context of the interaction and the manner, appearance and actions of others. While interactionists admit the existence of roles, they regard them as vague and imprecise and therefore as open to negotiation. From an interactionist perspective, action proceeds from negotiated meanings which are constructed in ongoing interaction situations.

Positivism and phenomenology

The previous section has briefly examined three theoretical perspectives in sociology. These perspectives will now be considered in terms of one of the major debates within the discipline: the positivist versus the phenomenological approach to the study of man and society. Many of the founding fathers of sociology believed that it would be possible to create a science of society based on the same principles and procedures as the natural sciences such as chemistry and biology. This approach is known as positivism. Auguste Comte (1798–1857), who is credited with inventing the term sociology and regarded as one of the founders of the discipline, maintained that the application of the methods and assumptions of the natural sciences would produce a 'positive science of society'. He believed that this would reveal that the evolution of society followed 'invariable laws'. It would show that the behaviour of man was governed by principles of cause and effect which were just as invariable as the behaviour of matter, the subject of the natural sciences.

In terms of sociology, the positivist approach makes the following assumptions. The behaviour of man, like the behaviour of matter, can be objectively measured. Just as the behaviour of matter can be quantified by measures such as weight, temperature and pressure, methods of objective measurement can be devised for human behaviour. Such measurement is essential to explain behaviour. For example, in order to explain the reaction of a particular chemical to heat, it is necessary to provide exact measurements of temperature, weight and so on. With the aid of such measurements it will be possible to accurately observe the behaviour of matter and produce a statement of cause and effect. This statement might read A + B = C where A is a quantity of matter, B a degree of heat and C a volume of gas. Once it has been shown that the matter in question always reacts in the same way under fixed conditions, a theory can be devised to explain its behaviour. From a positivist viewpoint such methods and assumptions are applicable to human behaviour. Observations of behaviour based on objective measurement will make it possible to produce statements of cause and effect. Theories may then be devised to explain observed behaviour.

The positivist approach in sociology places particular emphasis on behaviour that can be directly observed. It argues that factors which are not directly observable, such as meanings, feelings and purposes, are not particularly important and can be misleading. For example if the majority of adult members of society enter into marriage and produce children, these facts can be observed and quantified. They therefore form reliable data. However, the range of meanings that members of society give to these activities, their purposes for marriage and procreation are not directly observable. Even if they could be accurately measured, they may well divert attention from the real cause of behaviour. One individual may believe he entered marriage because he was lonely, another because he was in love, a third because it was the 'thing to do' and a fourth because he wished to produce offspring. Reliance on this type of data for explanation assumes that individuals know the reasons for marriage. This can obscure the real cause of their behaviour.

The positivists' emphasis on observable 'facts' is due largely to the belief that human behaviour can be explained in much the same way as the behaviour of matter. Natural scientists do not inquire into the meanings and purposes of matter for the obvious reason of their absence. Atoms and molecules do not act in terms of meanings, they simply react to external stimuli. Thus if heat, an external stimulus, is applied to matter, that matter will react. The job of the natural scientist is to observe, measure, and then explain that reaction. The positivist approach to human behaviour applies a similar logic. Men react to external stimuli and their behaviour can be explained in terms of this reaction. For example they enter into marriage and produce children in response to the demands of society. Society requires such behaviour for its survival and its members simply respond to this requirement. The meanings and purposes they attach to this behaviour are largely inconsequential.

It has often been argued that systems theory in sociology adopts a positivist approach. Once behaviour is seen as a response to some external stimulus, such as economic forces or the requirements of the social system, the methods and assumptions of the natural sciences appear appropriate to the study of man. Marxism has often been regarded as a positivist approach since it can be argued that it sees human behaviour as a reaction to the stimulus of the economic infrastructure. Functionalism has been viewed in a similar light. The behaviour of members of society can be seen as a response to the functional prerequisites of the social system. These views of systems theory represent a considerable oversimplification of complex theories. However, it is probably fair to say that systems theory is closer to a positivist approach than the views which will now be considered.

Phenomenological perspectives in sociology reject many of the assumptions of positivism. They argue that the subject matter of the social and natural sciences is fundamentally different. As a result the methods and assumptions of the natural sciences are inappropriate to the study of man. The natural sciences deal with matter. To understand and explain the behaviour of matter it is sufficient to observe it from the outside. Atoms and molecules do not have consciousness. They do not have meanings and purposes which direct their behaviour. Matter simply reacts 'unconsciously' to external stimuli; in scientific language it behaves. As a result the natural scientist is able to observe, measure, and impose an external logic on that behaviour in order to explain it. He has no need to explore the internal logic of the consciousness of matter simply because it does not exist.

Unlike matter, man has consciousness – thoughts, feelings, meanings, intentions and an awareness of being. Because of this, his actions are meaningful, he defines situations and gives meaning to his actions and those of others. As a result, he does not merely react to external stimuli, he does not simply behave, he acts. Imagine the response of early man to fire caused by volcanoes or spontaneous combustion. He did not simply react in a uniform manner to the experience of heat. He attached a range of meanings to it and these meanings directed his actions. For example he defined fire as a means of warmth and used it to heat his dwellings; as a means of defence and used it to ward off wild animals; and as a means of transforming substances and employed it for cooking and hardening the points of wooden spears. Man does not just react to fire, he acts upon it in terms of the meanings he gives to it. If action stems from subjective meanings, it follows that the sociologist must discover those meanings in order to understand action. He cannot simply observe action from the outside and impose an external logic upon it. He must interpret the internal logic which directs the actions of the actor.

Max Weber (1864–1920) was one of the first sociologists to outline this perspective in detail. He argued that sociological explanations of action should begin with 'the observation and theoretical interpretation of the subjective "states of minds" of actors'. As the previous section indicated, interactionism adopts a similar approach with particular emphasis on the process of interaction. Where positivists emphasize facts and cause and effect relationships, interactionists emphasize insight and understanding. Since it is not possible to get inside the heads of actors, the discovery of meaning must be based on interpretation and intuition. For this reason objective measurement is not possible and the exactitude of the natural sciences cannot be duplicated. Since meanings are constantly negotiated in ongoing interaction processes it is not possible to establish simple cause and effect relationships. Thus some sociologists argue that sociology is limited to an interpretation of social action and phenomenological approaches are sometimes referred to as 'interpretive sociology'.

A number of sociologists have argued that the positivist approach has produced a distorted picture of social life. They see it as tending to portray man as a passive responder to external stimuli rather than an active creator of his own society. Man is pictured as reacting to various forces and pressures, to economic infrastructures and the requirements of social systems. Peter Berger argues that society has often been viewed as a puppet theatre with its members portrayed as 'little puppets jumping about on the ends of their invisible strings, cheerfully acting out the parts that have been assigned to them'. Society instils values, norms and roles, and men dutifully respond like puppets on a string. However, from a phenomenological perspective man does not merely react and respond to an external society, he is not simply acted upon, he acts. In his interaction with others he creates his own meanings and constructs his own reality and therefore directs his own actions.

The distinction between positivist and phenomenological approaches is not as clear cut as this section has implied. There is considerable debate over whether or not a particular theory should be labelled positivist or phenomenological. Often it is a matter of degree since many theories lie somewhere between the two extremes. The debate will be dealt with throughout the text and examined in detail in the closing chapters.

Sociology and ideology

The positivist approach assumes that a science of society is possible. It therefore follows that objective observation and analysis of social life are possible. An objective view is free from the values, moral judgments and ideology of the observer. It provides facts and explanatory frameworks which are uncoloured by the observer's feelings and opinions. An increasing number of sociologists argue that a value-free science of society is not possible. They maintain that the values of the sociologist directly influence every aspect of his research. They argue that the various theories of society are based, at least in part, on value judgments and ideological positions. They suggest that sociological perspectives are shaped more by historical circumstances than by objective views of the reality of social life.

Those who argue that an objective science of society is not possible maintain that sociology can never be free from ideology. The term ideology refers to a set of ideas which present only a partial view of reality. An ideological viewpoint also includes values. It involves not only a judgment about the way things are but also the way things ought to be. Thus ideology is a set of beliefs and values which provides a way of seeing and interpreting the world which results in a partial view of reality. The term ideology is often used to suggest a distortion, a false picture of reality. However there is considerable doubt whether reality and ideology can be separated. As Nigel Harris suggests, 'Our reality is the next man's ideology and vice versa'.

Ideology can be seen as a set of beliefs and values which express the interests of a particular social group. Marxists use the term in this way when they talk about the ideology of the ruling class. In this sense ideology is a viewpoint which distorts reality and justifies and legitimates the position of a social group. Karl Mannheim uses the term in a similar way. He states that ideology consists of the beliefs and values of a ruling group which 'obscures the real condition of society both to itself and others and thereby stabilizes it'. Mannheim distinguishes this form of ideology from what he calls 'utopian ideology'. Rather than supporting the status quo, the way things are, utopian ideologies advocate a complete change in the structure of society. Mannheim argues that such ideologies are usually found in oppressed groups whose members want radical change. As their name suggests, utopian ideologies are based on a vision of an ideal society, a perfect social system. Mannheim refers to them as 'wish-images' for a future social order. Like the ideologies of ruling groups, he argues that utopian ideologies are a way of seeing the world which prevents true insight and obscures reality.

Mannheim's ideas will now be applied to two of the major theoretical perspectives in sociology, Marxism and functionalism. It has often been argued that Marxism is largely based on a utopian ideology, functionalism on a ruling ideology. Marxism contains a vision and a promise of a future ideal society – the communist utopia. In this society the forces of production are communally owned and as a result oppression and exploitation disappear. The communist utopia provides a standard of comparison for present and past societies. Since they inevitably fall far short of this ideal, their social arrangements will be condemned. It has been argued that the communist utopia is not a scientific prediction but merely a projection of the 'wish-images' of those who adopt a Marxian position. Utopian ideology has therefore been seen as the basis of Marxian theory.

By comparison, functionalism has often been interpreted as a form of ruling class ideology. Where Marxism is seen to advocate radical change, functionalism is seen to justify and legitimate the status quo. With its emphasis on order and stability, consensus and integration, functionalism appears to adopt a conservative stance. Rapid social change is not recommended since it will disrupt social order. The major institutions of society are justified by the belief that they are meeting the functional prerequisites of the social system. Although functionalists have introduced the concept of dysfunction to cover the harmful effects of parts of the system on society as a whole, the concept is rarely employed. In practice, functionalists appear preoccupied with discovering the positive functions, the beneficial effects of social institutions. As a result, the term function is associated with the idea of useful and good. This interpretation of society tends to legitimate the way things are. Ruling class ideology has therefore been seen as the basis of functionalist theory.

This section has provided a brief introduction to the question of the relationship between sociology and ideology. It is important to note that the above interpretation of the ideological basis of Marxism and functionalism is debatable. However, a case can be made to support the view that both perspectives are ideologically based. The relationship between ideology and sociology will be considered in detail throughout the text. Each chapter in the main section of the book will conclude with an interpretation of the ideological basis of the views it covers.

2 Social stratification

Men have long dreamed of an egalitarian society, a society in which all members are equal. In such a society men will no longer be ranked in terms of prestige. No one will experience the satisfaction of occupying a high social status; no one will suffer the indignity of being relegated to a position which commands little respect. No longer will high status evoke deference and admiration or envy and resentment from those in less worthy positions. Wealth will be distributed equally amongst the population. The rich and poor, haves and have-nots will be a thing of the past. Words such as privilege and poverty will either change their meaning or disappear from the vocabulary. In an egalitarian society, the phrase 'power to the people' will become a reality. No longer will some have power over others. Positions of authority and the obedience they command will disappear. Exploitation and oppression will be concepts of history which have no place in the description of contemporary social reality. Men will be equal both in the sight of God and in the eyes of their fellow men.

Clearly the egalitarian society remains a dream. All human societies from the simplest to the most complex have some form of social inequality. In particular, power and prestige are unequally distributed between individuals and social groups. In many societies there are also marked differences in the distribution of wealth. Power refers to the degree to which individuals or groups can impose their will on others, with or without the consent of those others. Prestige relates to the amount of esteem or honour associated with social positions, qualities of individuals and styles of life. Wealth refers to material possessions defined as valuable in particular societies. It may include land, livestock, buildings, money and many other forms of property owned by individuals or social groups. This chapter is concerned with the study of the unequal distribution of power, prestige and wealth in society.

It is important at the outset to make a distinction between social inequality and social stratification. The term social inequality simply refers to the existence of socially created inequalities. Social stratification is a particular form of social inequality. It refers to the presence of social groups which are ranked one above the other, usually in terms of the amount of power, prestige and wealth their members possess. Those who belong to a particular group or stratum will have some awareness of common interests and a common identity. They will share a similar life style which to some degree will distinguish them from members of other social strata. The Indian caste system provides an example of a social stratification system.

Hindu society in traditional India was divided into five main strata: four varnas or castes, and a fifth group, the outcaste, whose members were known as untouchables. Each caste is subdivided into jatis or sub-castes, which in total number many thousands. Jatis are occupational groups – there are carpenter jatis, goldsmith jatis, potter jatis, and so on. Castes are ranked in terms of ritual purity. The Brahmins or priests, members of the highest caste, personify purity, sanctity and holiness. They are the source of learning, wisdom and truth. Only they can perform the most important religious ceremonies. At the other extreme, untouchables are defined as unclean, base and impure, a status which affects all their social relationships. They must perform unclean and degrading tasks such as the disposal of dead animals. They must be segregated from members of the caste system and live on the outskirts of villages or in their own communities in the middle of paddy fields. Their presence pollutes to the extent that even if the shadow of an untouchable falls across the food of a Brahmin it will render it unclean. In general, the hierarchy of prestige based on notions of ritual purity is mirrored by the hierarchy of power. The Brahmins were custodians of the law, and the legal system which they administered was based largely on their pronouncements. Inequalities of wealth were usually linked to those of prestige and power. In a largely rural economy, the Brahmins tended to be the largest landowners and the control of land was monopolized by members of the two highest castes.

As exemplified by caste, social stratification involves a hierarchy of social groups. Members of a particular stratum have a common identity, like interests and a similar life style. They enjoy or suffer the unequal distribution of rewards in society as members of different social groups. Social stratification, however, is only one form of social inequality. It is possible for social inequality to exist without social strata. For example, some sociologists have argued that it is no longer correct to regard Western industrial society, particularly the USA, as being stratified in terms of a class system. They suggest that social classes have been replaced by a continuous hierarchy of unequal positions. Where there were once classes, whose members had a consciousness of kind, a common way of life and shared interests, there is now an unbroken continuum of occupational statuses which command varying degrees of prestige and economic reward. Thus it is suggested that a hierarchy of social groups has been replaced by a hierarchy of individuals. Although many sociologists use the terms social inequality and social stratification interchangeably, the importance of seeing social stratification as a specific form of social inequality will become apparent as the chapter develops.

Before looking at some of the major issues raised in the study of social stratification, it is necessary to examine certain aspects of stratification systems. There is a tendency for members of each stratum to develop their own subculture, that is certain norms, attitudes and values which are distinctive to them as a social group. When some members of society experience similar circumstances and problems which are not common to all members, a subculture tends to develop. For example, it has often been suggested that distinctive working-class and middle-class subcultures exist in Western industrial societies. Similar circumstances and problems often produce similar responses. Members of the lowest stratum in stratification systems which provide little opportunity for the improvement of status tend to have a fatalistic attitude towards life. This attitude becomes part of their subculture and is transmitted from generation to generation. It sees circumstances as largely unchangeable; it sees luck and fate rather than individual effort as shaping life and therefore tends to encourage acceptance of the situation. An attitude of fatalism may be seen in typical phrases from traditional low-income Black American subculture such as, 'I've been down so long that down don't bother me', 'I was born under a bad sign' and 'It's an uphill climb to the bottom'. Members of a social group who share similar circumstances and a common subculture will be likely to develop a group identity. They tend to have a consciousness of kind, a feeling of kinship with other group members. They will therefore tend to identify with their particular stratum and regard themselves, for example, as middle or working class.

Strata subcultures tend to be particularly distinctive when there is little opportunity to move from one stratum to another. This movement is known as social mobility. Social mobility can be upward, for example moving from the working to the middle class, or downward. Stratification systems which provide little opportunity for social mobility may be described as 'closed', those with a relatively high rate of social mobility as 'open'. In closed systems an individual's position is largely ascribed. Often it is fixed at birth and there is little he can do to change his status. Caste provides an example of a closed stratification system. An individual automatically belongs to the caste of his parents and, except in rare instances, spends the rest of his life in that status. By comparison, social class, the system of stratification in capitalist industrial society, provides an example of an open system. Some sociologists claim that an individual's class position is largely achieved. It results from his personal qualities and abilities and the use he makes of them rather than ascribed characteristics such as the status of his parents or the colour of his skin. By comparison with the caste, the rate of social mobility in class systems is high.

A person's position in a stratification system may have important effects on many areas of his life. It may enhance or reduce his 'life chances', that is his chances of obtaining those things defined as desirable and avoiding those things defined as undesirable in his society. Referring to Western society Gerth and Mills state that life chances include, 'Everything from the chance to stay alive during the first year after birth to the chance to view fine arts, the chance to remain healthy and grow tall, and if sick to get well again quickly, the chance to avoid becoming a juvenile delinquent and very crucially, the chance to complete an intermediary or higher educational grade'. A comparison of Blacks and Whites in the USA provides an illustration of the effect of one stratification system on life chances. Blacks and certain other ethnic minority groups form the base of the stratification system. The rate of infant mortality among Blacks is twice that of Whites and the proportion of Black mothers dying during childbirth is four times that for Whites. Compared to Whites, Blacks are less likely to acquire educational qualifications, their marriages are more likely to end in separation or divorce and they are more likely to have a criminal record. Many sociologists would see these differences in life chances as a direct consequence of social stratification.

Social versus natural inequalities

Many stratification systems are accompanied by beliefs which state that social inequalities are biologically based. Such beliefs are often found in systems of racial stratification where, for example, Whites claim biological superiority over Blacks and see this as the basis for their dominance. The question of the relationship between biologically based and socially created inequality has proved extremely difficult to answer. The French philosopher Jean-Jacques Rousseau provided one of the earliest examinations of this question. He refers to biologically based inequality as 'natural or physical, because it is established by nature, and consists in a difference of age, health, bodily strength, and the qualities of the mind or the soul'. By comparison, socially created inequality 'consists of the different privileges which some men enjoy to the prejudice of others, such as that of being more rich, more honoured, more powerful, or even in a position to exact obedience' (quoted in Bottomore, 1965, pp. 15–16). Rousseau believed that biologically based inequalities between men were small and relatively unimportant whereas socially created inequalities provide the major basis for systems of social stratification. Most sociologists would support this view.

However, it could still be argued that biological inequalities, no matter how small, provide the foundation upon which structures of social inequality are built. This position is difficult to defend in the case of certain forms of stratification. In the caste system, an individual's status is fixed by birth. A person belongs to his parents' jati and automatically follows the occupation of the jati into which he was born. Thus no matter what the biologically based aptitudes and capacities of an untouchable, there is no way he can become a Brahmin. Unless it is assumed that superior genes are permanently located in the Brahmin caste, and there is no evidence that this is the case, then there is probably no relationship between genetically based and socially created inequality in traditional Hindu society. A similar argument can be advanced in connection with the feudal or estate system of medieval Europe. Stratification in the feudal system was based on landholding. The more land an individual controlled, the greater his wealth, power and prestige. The position of the dominant stratum, the feudal nobility, was based on large grants of land from the king. Their status was hereditary, land and titles being passed on from father to son. It is difficult to sustain the argument that feudal lords ultimately owed their position to biological superiority when a son, no matter what his biological make-up, inherited the status of his father.

The most stubborn defence of the biological argument has been provided for systems of racial stratification. In the USA, Black Americans, who make up 12% of the population, have traditionally formed a distinct social stratum at the base of the stratification system. The majority of Blacks occupied the most menial and subservient occupational statuses, being employed as agricultural labourers and as unskilled and semi-skilled manual workers in industry. In the mid 1960s, the average income for Black families was only 54% of the average for White families. Blacks had little political power being scarcely represented in local and national government: in 1962, in the southern states, only six Blacks were elected to public office. This system of racial stratification has often been explained in terms of the supposed genetically based inferiority of Blacks. In particular, it has been argued that Blacks are innately inferior to Whites in terms of intelligence. 'Scientific' support for this view has been provided by intelligence tests which indicate that on average Blacks score fifteen points below Whites.

However, most sociologists would argue that systems of racial stratification have a social rather than a biological basis. They would maintain that systematic discrimination against Blacks, made possible by the power of the dominant stratum, accounts for the system of racial stratification in the USA. Thus Blacks have been excluded from high status occupations because of lack of power rather than the quality of their genes. Support for this view is provided by evidence from the late 1960s and 1970s. During the mid 1960s, in the USA, laws were passed banning racial discrimination in areas such as employment, politics and education. Blacks are now moving out of the lowest stratum in ever increasing numbers. By 1971, seventy Blacks were elected to public office in the southern states. Although the figure is small, it represents a dramatic increase. Black family income is slowly approaching the White average. From 1960 to 1970, the percentage of Blacks employed in professional, managerial and technical occupations rose steadily and in some cases doubled. This evidence suggests that social rather than biological mechanisms were responsible for the traditional status of Blacks in the USA.

The question of the relationship between intelligence and social inequality is particularly difficult to answer. The average intelligence quotient of Blacks in America is still significantly below that of Whites. In addition, Blacks are still disproportionately represented in the lower levels of the stratification system. Since it is generally agreed that intelligence has a genetic component, can it not be argued that social inequality has a biological basis? This question will be examined in detail in the chapter on education. (See pps. 189–93.) However, a few preliminary remarks can be made to refute this view. Firstly, intelligence is based on both genetic and environmental factors; the two are inseparable. Thus an individual's social background will affect his performance in an IQ test. In particular, the deprivations he experiences as a member of a low social stratum will reduce his IQ score. Secondly, many researchers argue that intelligence tests are based on White middle-class knowledge and skills and are therefore biased against Blacks. Thirdly, the tests measure only a small part of the range of mental abilities. Most sociologists would therefore conclude that the social status of Blacks in the USA is the result of a social rather than a biological mechanism.

So far the question of what exactly constitutes biological inequality has not been answered. It can be argued that biological differences become biological inequalities when men define them as such. Thus André Béteille states that, 'Natural inequality is based on differences in quality, and qualities are not just there, so to say, in nature; they are as human beings have defined them, in different societies, in different historical epochs'. Biological factors assume importance in many stratification systems because of the meanings assigned to them by different cultures. For example, old age has very different meanings in different societies. In traditional aborigine societies in Australia it brought high prestige and power since the elders directed the affairs of the tribe. But in Western societies, the elderly are usually pensioned off and old age assumes a very different meaning. Even with a change of name to senior citizen, the status of old age pensioner commands little power or prestige. So-called racial characteristics are evaluated on the basis of similar principles, that is values which are relative to time and place. The physical characteristics of Blacks in America were traditionally defined as undesirable and associated with a range of negative qualities. However, with the rise of Black Power during the late 1960s, this evaluation was slowly changed with slogans such as 'Black is beautiful'. It can therefore be argued that biological differences become biological inequalities only to the extent that they are defined as such. They form a component of some social stratification systems simply because members of those systems select certain characteristics and evaluate them in a particular way. André Béteille argues that the search for a biological basis for social stratification is bound to end in failure since the 'identification as well as the gradation of qualities is a cultural and not a natural process'.

Beliefs which state that systems of social stratification are based on biological inequalities can be seen as rationalizations for those systems. Such beliefs serve to explain the system to its members: they make social inequality appear rational and reasonable. They therefore justify and legitimate the system by appeals to nature. In this way a social contrivance appears to be founded on the natural order of things.

Social stratification – a functionalist perspective

Functionalist theories of stratification must be seen in the context of functionalist theories of society. When functionalists attempt to explain systems of social stratification, they set their explanations in the framework of larger theories which seek to explain the operation of society as a whole. They assume that there are certain basic needs or functional prerequisites which must be met if society is to survive. They therefore look to social stratification to see how far it meets these functional prerequisites. They assume that the parts of society form an integrated whole and thus examine the ways in which the social stratification system is integrated with other parts of society. Functionalists maintain that a certain degree of order and stability are essential for the operation of social systems. They will therefore consider how stratification systems help to maintain order and stability in society. In summary, functionalists are primarily concerned with the function of social stratification, with its contribution to the maintenance and well-being of society.

Talcott Parsons

Like many functionalists, Talcott Parsons believes that order, stability and cooperation in society are based on value consensus, that is a general agreement by members of society concerning what is good and worthwhile. Parsons argues that stratification systems derive from common values. It follows from the existence of values that individuals will be evaluated and therefore placed in some form of rank order. In Parsons's words, 'Stratification, in its valuational aspect, then, is the ranking of units in a social system in accordance with the common value system'. Thus those who perform successfully in terms of society's values will be ranked highly and they will be likely to receive a variety of rewards. At a minimum they will be accorded high prestige since they exemplify and personify common values. For example, if a society places a high value on bravery and generosity, as in the case of the Sioux Indians, those who excel in terms of these qualities will receive a high rank in the stratification system. The Sioux warrior who successfully raids the Crow and Pawnee, the traditional enemies of his tribe, captures horses and distributes them to others, may receive the following rewards. He may be given a seat on the tribal council, a position of power and prestige. His deeds will be recounted in the warrior societies and the squaws will sing of his exploits. Other warriors will follow him in raids against neighbouring tribes and the success of these expeditions may lead to his appointment as a war chief. In this way excellence in terms of Sioux values is rewarded by power and prestige. Since different societies have different value systems, the ways of attaining a high position will vary from society to society. Parsons argues that American society values individual achievement, efficiency and 'puts primary emphasis on productive activity within the economy'. Thus the successful business executive who has achieved his position through his own initiative, ability and ambition, and runs an efficient and productive business will receive high rewards.

Parsons's argument suggests that stratification is an inevitable part of all human societies. If value consensus is an essential component of all societies, then it follows that some form of stratification will result from the ranking of individuals in terms of common values. It also follows from Parsons's argument that there is a general belief that stratification systems are just, right and proper, since they are basically an expression of shared values. Thus the American business executive is seen to deserve his rewards because members of society place a high value on his skills and achievements. This is not to say there is no conflict between the haves and have-nots, the highly rewarded and those who receive little reward. Parsons recognizes that in Western industrial society, 'There will be certain tendencies to arrogance on the part of some winners and to resentment and to a "sour grapes" attitude on the part of some losers'. However, he believes that this conflict is kept in check by the common value system which justifies the unequal distribution of rewards.

Functionalists tend to see the relationship between social groups in society as one of cooperation and interdependence. Particularly in complex industrial societies, different groups specialize in particular activities. As no one group is self-sufficient it cannot meet the needs of its members. It must, therefore, exchange goods and services with other groups, and so the relationship between social groups is one of reciprocity. This relationship extends to the strata in a stratification system. To present an oversimplified example, it can be argued that many occupational groups within the middle class in Western society plan, organize and coordinate the activities of the working class. Each class needs and cooperates with the other since any large-scale task requires both organization and execution. In societies with a highly specialized division of labour, such as industrial societies, some members will specialize in organization and planning, others will follow their directives. Talcott Parsons argues that this inevitably leads to inequality in terms of power and prestige. Referring to Western society, he states that, 'Organization on an ever increasing scale is a fundamental feature of such a system. Such organization naturally involves centralization and differentiation of leadership and authority; so that those who take responsibility for coordinating the actions of many others must have a different status in important respects from those who are essentially in the role of carrying out specifications laid down by others'. Thus those with the power to organize and coordinate the activities of others will have a higher social status than those they direct.

As with prestige differentials, Parsons argues that inequalities of power are based on shared values. Power is legitimate authority in that it is generally accepted as just and proper by members of society as a whole. It is accepted as such because those in positions of authority use their power to pursue collective goals which derive from society's central values. Thus the power of the American business executive is seen as legitimate authority because it is used to further productivity, a goal shared by all members of society. This use of power therefore serves the interests of society as a whole.

Parsons sees social stratification as both inevitable and functional for society. It is inevitable because it derives from shared values which are a necessary part of all social systems. It is functional because it serves to integrate various groups in society. Power and prestige differentials are essential for the coordination and integration of a specialized division of labour. Without social inequality, Parsons finds it difficult to see how members of society could effectively cooperate and work together. Finally, inequalities of power and prestige benefit all members of society since they serve to further collective goals which are based on shared values. Parsons has been strongly criticized on all these points. Other sociologists have seen stratification as a divisive rather than an integrating force. They have seen it as an arrangement whereby some gain at the expense of others. They have questioned the view that stratification systems derive ultimately from shared values. These criticisms will be examined in detail in later sections.

Kingsley Davis and Wilbert E. Moore

The most famous functionalist theory of stratification was first presented in 1945, in an article by the American sociologists Davis and Moore entitled, *Some Principles of Stratification*. Davis and Moore begin with the observation that stratification exists in every known human society. They attempt to explain 'in functional terms, the universal necessity which calls forth stratification in any social system'. They argue that all social systems share certain functional prerequisites which must be met if the system is to survive and operate efficiently. One such functional prerequisite is effective role allocation and performance. This means that firstly, all roles must be filled, secondly that they be filled by those best able to perform them, thirdly that the necessary training for them be undertaken and fourthly that the roles be performed conscientiously. Davis and

Moore argue that all societies need some mechanism for insuring effective role allocation and performance. This mechanism is social stratification which they see as a system which attaches unequal rewards and privileges to the different positions in society.

If the people and positions which make up society did not differ in important respects there would be no need for stratification. However, people differ in terms of their innate ability and talent. Positions differ in terms of their importance for the survival and maintenance of society. Certain positions are more 'functionally important' than others. They require special skills for their effective performance and there are a limited number of individuals with the necessary ability to acquire such skills. A major function of stratification is to match the most able people with the functionally most important positions. It does this by attaching high rewards to those positions. The desire for such rewards motivates people to compete for them and in theory the most talented will win through. Such positions usually require long periods of training which involve certain sacrifices such as loss of income. The promise of high rewards is necessary to provide an incentive to encourage people to undergo this training and to compensate them for the sacrifice involved. It is essential for the well-being of society that those who hold the functionally most important positions perform their roles diligently and conscientiously. The high rewards built into these positions provide the necessary inducement and generate the required motivation for such performance. Thus Davis and Moore conclude that social stratification is a 'device by which societies insure that the most important positions are conscientiously filled by the most qualified persons'.

Davis and Moore realise that one difficulty with their theory is to show clearly which positions are functionally most important. The fact that a position is highly rewarded does not necessarily mean it is functionally important. They suggest that the importance of a position can be measured in two ways. Firstly by the 'degree to which a position is functionally unique, there being no other positions that can perform the same function satisfactorily'. Thus it could be argued that a doctor is functionally more important than a nurse since his position carries with it many of the skills necessary to perform a nurse's role but not vice versa. The second measure of importance is the 'degree to which other positions are dependent on the one in question'. Thus it may be argued that managers are more important than routine office staff since the latter are dependent on direction and organization from management.

To summarize, Davis and Moore regard social stratification as a 'functional necessity' for all societies. They see it as a solution to a problem faced by all social systems, that of 'placing and motivating individuals in the social structure'. They offer no other means of solving this problem and imply that social inequality is an inevitable feature of human society. They conclude that differential rewards are functional for society, that they contribute to the maintenance and well-being of social systems.

Melvin M. Tumin

Davis and Moore's views provoked a long debate. Tumin, their most famous opponent, has produced a comprehensive criticism of their theory. He begins by questioning the adequacy of their measurement of the functional importance of positions. Davis and Moore have tended to assume that the most highly rewarded positions are indeed the most important. However, many occupations which afford little prestige or economic reward can be seen as vital to society. Thus, Tumin argues that '*some* labour force of unskilled workmen is as important and as indispensable to the factory as *some* labour force of engineers'. In fact a number of sociologists have argued that there is no objective way of measuring the functional importance of positions. Whether one considers lawyers and doctors as more important than farm labourers and refuse collectors is simply a matter of opinion.

Tumin argues that Davis and Moore have ignored the influence of power on the unequal distribution of rewards. Thus differences in pay and prestige between occupational groups may be due to differences in their power rather than their functional importance. For example, the difference between the wages of farm labourers and coal miners can be interpreted as a result of the bargaining power of the two groups. This point will be examined in detail in later sections.

Davis and Moore assume that only a limited number of individuals have the talent to acquire the skills necessary for the functionally most important positions. Tumin regards this as a very questionable assumption. Firstly, as the chapter on education will indicate, an effective method of measuring talent and ability has yet to be devised. Secondly, there is no proof that exceptional talents are required for those positions which Davis and Moore consider important. Thirdly, the chapter on education will suggest that the pool of talent in society may be considerably larger than Davis and Moore assume. As a result, unequal rewards may not be necessary to harness it.

Tumin also questions the view that the training required for important positions should be regarded as a sacrifice and therefore in need of compensation. He points to the rewards of being a student – leisure, freedom and the opportunity for self-development. He notes that any loss of earnings can usually be made up during the first ten years of work. Differential rewards during this period may be justified. However, Tumin sees no reason for continuing this compensation for the rest of an individual's working life.

According to Davis and Moore, the major function of unequal rewards is to motivate talented individuals and allocate them to the functionally most important positions. Tumin rejects this view. He argues that social stratification can, and often does, act as a barrier to the motivation and recruitment of talent. This is readily apparent in closed systems such as caste and racial stratification. Thus the ascribed status of untouchables prevented even the most talented from becoming Brahmins. Until recently, the ascribed status of Blacks in the USA blocked all but a handful from political office and highly rewarded occupations. Thus closed stratification systems operate in exactly the opposite way to Davis and Moore's theory.

Tumin suggests, however, that even relatively open systems of stratification erect barriers to the motivation and recruitment of talent. As the chapter on education will show, there is considerable evidence to indicate that the class system in Western industrial society limits the possibilities of the discovery and utilization of talent. In general, the lower an individual's class position, the more likely he is to leave school at the minimum leaving age and the less likely he is to aspire to and strive for a highly rewarded position. Thus the motivation to succeed is unequally distributed throughout the class system. As a result social class can act as an obstacle to the motivation of talent. In addition, Tumin argues that Davis and Moore have failed to consider the possibility that those who occupy highly rewarded positions will erect barriers to recruitment. Occupational groups often use their power to restrict access to their positions, so creating a high demand for their services and increasing the rewards they receive. Tumin claims that the American Medical Association has been guilty of this practice. By its control of entry into the profession, it has maintained a shortage of doctors and so ensured high rewards for medical services. In this way the self-interested use of power can restrict the recruitment of talented individuals to highly rewarded positions.

Tumin concludes that stratification, by its very nature, can never adequately perform the functions which Davis and Moore assign to it. He argues that those born into the lower strata can never have the same opportunities for realizing their talents as those born into the higher strata. Tumin maintains that, 'It is only when there is a genuinely equal access to recruitment and training for all potentially talented persons that differential rewards can conceivably be justified as functional. And stratification systems are apparently *inherently antagonistic* to the development of such full equality of opportunity'.

Finally, Tumin questions the view that social stratification functions to integrate the social system. He argues that differential rewards can 'encourage hostility, suspicion and distrust among the various segments of a society'. From this viewpoint, stratification is a divisive rather than an integrating force. Stratification can also weaken social integration by giving members of the lower strata a feeling of being excluded from participation in the larger society. This is particularly apparent in systems of racial stratification. For example, the saying 'On the outside looking in', is a typical phrase from traditional Black American subculture. By tending to exclude certain groups from full participation in society, stratification 'serves to distribute loyalty unequally in the population' and therefore reduces the potential for social solidarity. Tumin concludes that in their enthusiastic search for the positive functions of stratification, the functionalists have tended to ignore or play down its many dysfunctions.

Michael Young

Many of the criticisms of Davis and Moore's views have been based on evidence which indicates that no stratification system operates as their theory argues. Even in the relatively open systems of Western industrial societies, there is considerable evidence to suggest that large numbers of able and talented individuals remain in the lower strata. Research has also indicated that many members of the upper strata owe their position primarily to the fact that they have been born into those strata and have capitalized on the advantages provided by their social background. In a brilliant satire entitled *The Rise of the Meritocracy*, Michael Young imagines a future British society in which talent and social roles would be perfectly matched, in which the most able individuals would fill the functionally most important positions. Social status would be achieved on the basis of merit in a society where all members have an equal opportunity to realize their talents. Following Michael Young's usage of the term, such a system of role allocation has come to be known as a meritocracy.

Despite removing the most obvious criticism of Davis and Moore's theory, Young questions the proposition that a stratification system based on meritocratic principles would be functional for society. He notes the following dysfunctional possibilities. Firstly, members of the lower strata may become totally demoralized. In all previous stratification systems they have been able to divert blame from themselves for their lowly status by providing reasons for their failure. They could claim that they never had the opportunity to be successful whereas those who filled the top jobs owed their position to their relatives, friends and the advantages of birth. However, in a meritocracy, those at the bottom are clearly inferior. As a result they may become demoralized since, as Young states, 'Men who have lost their self-respect are liable to lose their inner vitality'. Since all members of a meritocracy are socialized to compete for the top jobs and instilled with ambition, failure could be particularly frustrating. Young argues that, 'When ambition is crossed with stupidity it may do nothing besides foster frustration'. In a meritocracy, talent and ability are efficiently syphoned out of the lower strata. As a result these groups are in a particularly vulnerable position because they have no able members to represent their interests.

Members of the upper strata in a meritocracy deserve their position;

their privileges are based on merit. In the past they had a degree of self-doubt because many realized that they owed their position to factors other than merit. Since they could recognize 'intelligence, wit and wisdom' in members of the lower strata, they appreciated that their social inferiors were at least their equal in certain respects. As a result they would accord the lower orders some respect and the arrogance which high status tends to encourage would be tempered with a degree of humility. All this may change in a meritocracy. Social inferiors really are inferior, those who occupy the top positions are undoubtably superior. Young argues that this may result in an upper stratum free from self-doubt and the restraining influence of humility. Its members may rule society with arrogance and haughty self-assurance. They may despise the lower strata whose members may well find such behaviour offensive. This may result in conflict between the ruling minority and the rest of society.

Although Young's picture of a meritocracy is fictional, it indicates many of the possible dysfunctional elements of such a system. It suggests that a society based on meritocratic principles may not be well integrated. It indicates that a stratification system which operates in this way may, on balance, be dysfunctional. Young's ideas are important because they cast serious doubt on liberal views of a just society. As the chapter on education will illustrate, many liberal reforms have aimed to create greater equality of opportunity, to give every member of society an equal chance of becoming unequal. Michael Young's picture of a fully operative meritocracy suggests that the liberal dream of a fair and just society may produce a far from perfect reality.

Eva Rosenfeld

So far, criticism of functionalist theories has been concerned with the view that stratification is functional. This section turns to the functionalists' claim that stratification is inevitable. The chapter began by posing the possibility of an egalitarian society, a society without social inequality. An example of one attempt to translate this idea into reality is provided by the Israeli Kibbutzim system. In Israel about 4% of the population live in some 240 kibbutzim. These communities have an average population of between 200 and 700 and an economic base of agriculture plus some light industry. Many kibbutzim are founded on the Marxist principle of 'from everyone according to ability – to everyone according to need', the guiding ideal being the creation of an egalitarian society. Property such as machinery, buildings and produce is communally owned. Commodities such as clothing, shoes and toiletries are distributed to members according to their need. Services such as cooking, laundry and the education of children are freely available to all. Wages as such and therefore wage differentials do not exist in many kibbutzim.

Stratification in terms of wealth is thus absent. All major decisions are taken by a general assembly in which each adult member of a kibbutz has the right to vote. It would therefore appear that power to the people has become a reality.

Despite these arrangements designed to create an egalitarian society, social inequality exists in the kibbutzim. From her research, Eva Rosenfeld had identified two distinct social strata which are clearly recognized by members. The upper stratum is made up of 'leader–managers', who are elected by members of the kibbutz and are responsible for the day-to-day running of the community. The lower stratum consists of the 'rank and file', the agricultural labourers and machine operatives. Authority and prestige are not equally distributed. The right to organize and direct the activities of others is built into the role of leader–manager. In addition the status itself carries high prestige. Rosenfeld notes that leader–managers are 'respected for their contribution to the communal enterprise as leaders, organizers, managers of farms and shops'. Rosenfeld also identifies an 'unequal distribution of seemingly crucial emotional gratifications'. Managers obtain more satisfaction from their work than the rank and file. In the words of one old-timer, members of the rank and file sometimes ask, 'What the hell am I breaking my neck for? What do I get out of this?' There is evidence of a conflict of interest between the two strata. Managers call for 'ever greater effort and self-sacrifice' whereas the rank and file are often apathetic to such exhortations and concerned with more immediate rises in their living standards. Managers are sometimes accused of not knowing 'what kibbutz life tastes like' while they in turn sometimes accuse the rank and file of insufficient effort and failing to appreciate the long-term goals of the kibbutz.

Rosenfeld's study lends some support to the functionalist claim that social stratification, at least in terms of power and prestige, is inevitable in human society. The position of leader–manager in the kibbutz carries authority and commands high prestige. Those who occupy such positions form a fairly distinct social stratum. Talcott Parsons has argued that any division of labour requires an authority structure to organize and coordinate the various specialized tasks involved. He also maintains that in order to operate effectively, positions of authority must carry higher prestige than positions subject to that authority. Despite the logic of these arguments and the evidence which supports them, they do not prove that social stratification is inevitable. Simply because the egalitarian society has yet to become a reality does not mean it is not possible.

Social stratification – a Marxian perspective

Marxian perspectives provide a radical alternative to functionalist views of the nature of social stratification. They regard stratification as a divisive rather than an integrative structure. They see it as a mechanism whereby some exploit others rather than a means of furthering collective goals. They focus on social strata rather than social inequality in general. Functionalists such as Parsons and Davis and Moore say little about social stratification in the sense of clearly defined social strata whose members have shared interests. However, this view of social stratification is central to Marxian theory.

Marx's views will first be briefly summarized and then examined in more detail.

In all stratified societies, there are two major social groups: a ruling class and a subject class. The power of the ruling class derives from its ownership and control of the forces of production. The ruling class exploits and oppresses the subject class. As a result, there is a basic conflict of interest between the two classes. The various institutions of society such as the legal and political systems are instruments of ruling class domination and serve to further its interests. Only when the forces of production are communally owned will classes disappear, thereby bringing an end to the exploitation and oppression of some by others.

From a Marxian perspective, systems of stratification derive from the relationships of social groups to the forces of production. Marx used the term class to refer to the main strata in all stratification systems, though most modern sociologists would reserve the term for strata in capitalist society. From a Marxian view, a class is a social group whose members share the same relationship to the forces of production. Thus during the feudal epoch, there are two main classes distinguished by their relationship to land, the major force of production. They are the feudal nobility who own the land and the landless serfs who work the land. Similarly, in the capitalist era, there are two main classes, the bourgeoisie or capitalist class which owns the forces of production and the proletariat or working class whose members own only their labour which they hire to the bourgeoisie in return for wages.

Marx believed that Western society had developed through four main epochs: primitive communism, ancient society, feudal society and capitalist society. Primitive communism is represented by the societies of prehistory and provides the only example of a classless society. From then on, all societies are divided into two major classes: masters and slaves in ancient society, lords and serfs in feudal society and capitalists and wage labourers in capitalist society. During each historical epoch, the labour power required for production was supplied by the subject class, that is by slaves, serfs and wage labourers respectively. The subject class is made up of the majority of the population whereas the ruling or dominant class forms a minority. The relationship between the two major classes will be discussed shortly.

Classes did not exist during the era of primitive communism when societies were based on a socialist mode of production. In a hunting and gathering band, the earliest form of human society, the land and its products were communally owned. The men hunted and the woman gathered plant food, and the produce was shared by members of the band. Classes did not exist since all members of society shared the same relationship to the forces of production. Every member was both producer and owner, all provided labour power and shared the products of their labour. Hunting and gathering is a subsistence economy which means that production only meets basic survival needs. Classes emerge when the productive capacity of society expands beyond the level required for subsistence. This occurs when agriculture becomes the dominant mode of production. In an agricultural economy, only a section of society is needed to produce the food requirements of the whole society. Thus many individuals are freed from food production and are able to specialize in other tasks. The rudimentary division of labour of the hunting and gathering band was replaced by an increasingly more complex and specialized division. For example, in the early agricultural villages, some individuals became full-time producers of pottery, clothing and agricultural implements. As agriculture developed, surplus wealth, that is goods above the basic subsistence needs of the community, was produced. This led to an exchange of goods and trading developed rapidly both within and between communities. This was accompanied by the development of a system of private property. Goods were increasingly seen as commodities or articles of trade to which the individual rather than the community had right of ownership. Private property and the accumulation of surplus wealth form the basis for the development of class societies. In particular, they provide the preconditions for the emergence of a class of producers and a class of non-producers. Some are able to acquire the forces of production and others are therefore obliged to work for them. The result is a class of non-producers which owns the forces of production and a class of producers which owns only its labour power.

From a Marxian perspective, the relationship between the major social classes is one of mutual dependence and conflict. Thus in capitalist society, the bourgeoisie and proletariat are dependent upon each other. The wage labourer must sell his labour power in order to survive since he does not own a part of the forces of production and lacks the means to produce goods independently. He is therefore dependent for his livelihood on the capitalists and the wages they offer. The capitalists, as non-producers, are dependent on the labour power of wage labourers, since without it, there would be no production. However, the mutual dependency of the two classes is not a relationship of equal or symmetrical reciprocity. Instead, it is a relationship of exploiter and exploited, oppressor and oppressed. In particular, the ruling class gains at the expense of the subject class and there is therefore a conflict of interest between them. This may be illustrated by Marx's view of the nature of ownership and production in capitalist society.

The basic characteristics of a capitalist economy may be summarized as follows. Capital may be defined as money used to finance the production of commodities for private gain. In a capitalist economy goods, and the labour power, raw materials and machinery used to produce them, are given a monetary value. The capitalist invests his capital in the production of goods. Capital is accumulated by selling those goods at a value greater than their cost of production. In Raymond Aron's words, 'The essence of capitalist exchange is to proceed from money to money by way of commodity and end up with more money than one had at the outset'. Capitalism therefore involves the investment of capital in the production of commodities with the aim of maximizing profit. Capital is privately owned by a minority, the capitalist class. However, in Marx's view, it is gained from the exploitation of the mass of the population, the working class. Marx argued that capital, as such, produces nothing. Only labour produces wealth. Yet the wages paid to the workers for their labour are well below the value of the goods they produce. The difference between the value of wages and commodities is known as 'surplus value'. This surplus value is appropriated in the form of profit by the capitalists. Since they are non-producers, the bourgeoisie are therefore exploiting the proletariat, the real producers of wealth. Marx maintained that in all class societies, the ruling class exploits and oppresses the subject class.

From a Marxian perspective political power derives from economic power. The power of the ruling class therefore stems from its ownership and control of the forces of production. Since the superstructure of society – the major institutions, values and belief systems – is seen to be largely shaped by the economic infrastructure, the relations of production will be reproduced in the superstructure. Thus the dominance of the ruling class in the relations of production will be reflected in the superstructure. In particular, the political and legal systems will reflect ruling class interests since, in Marx's words, 'The existing relations of production between individuals must necessarily express themselves also as political and legal relations'. For example, the various ownership rights of the capitalist class will be enshrined in and protected by the laws of the land. Thus the various parts of the superstructure can be seen as instruments of ruling class domination and as mechanisms for the oppression of the subject class. In the same way, the position of the dominant class is supported by beliefs and values which are systematically generated by the infrastructure. As noted in the previous chapter, Marx refers to the dominant concepts of class societies as ruling class ideology since they justify and legitimate ruling class domination and project a distorted picture of reality. For example, the emphasis on freedom in capitalist society, illustrated by phrases such as 'the free market', 'free democratic societies' and 'the free world', is an illusion which disguises the wage slavery of the proletariat. Ruling class ideology produces 'false class consciousness', a false picture of the nature of the relationship between social classes. Members of both classes tend to accept the status quo as normal and natural and are largely unaware of the true nature of exploitation and oppression. In this way the conflict of interest between the classes is disguised and a degree of social stability produced but the basic contradictions and conflicts of class societies remain unresolved.

Class and social change

Marx believed that the class struggle was the driving force of social change. He states that, 'The history of all societies up to the present is the history of the class struggle'. A new historical epoch is created by the development of superior forces of production by a new social group. These developments take place within the framework of the previous era. For example, the merchants and industrialists who spearheaded the rise of capitalism emerged during the feudal era. They accumulated capital, laid the foundations for industrial manufacture, factory production and the system of wage labour, all of which were essential components of capitalism. The superiority of the capitalist mode of production led to a rapid transformation of the structure of society. The capitalist class became dominant, and although the feudal aristocracy maintained aspects of its power well into the nineteenth century, it was fighting a losing battle.

The class struggles of history have been between minorities. For example, capitalism developed from the struggle between the feudal aristocracy and the emerging capitalist class, both groups in numerical terms forming a minority of the population. Major changes in history have involved the replacement of one form of private property by another and of one type of production technique by another. For example, capitalism involved the replacement of privately owned land and an agricultural economy by privately owned capital and an industrial economy. Marx believed that the class struggle which would transform capitalist society would involve none of these processes. The protagonists would be the bourgeoisie and the proletariat, a minority versus a majority. Private property would be replaced by communally owned property. Industrial manufacture would remain as the basic technique of production in the society which would replace capitalism.

Marx believed that the basic contradictions contained in a capitalist economic system would lead to its eventual destruction. The proletariat would overthrow the bourgeoisie and seize the forces of production, the source of power. Property would be communally owned and, since all members of society would now share the same relationship to the forces of production, a classless society would result. Since history is the history of the class struggle, history would now end. The communist society which replaces capitalism will contain no contradictions, no conflicts of interest, and will therefore be unchanging. However, before the dawning of this utopia, certain changes must occur.

Marx distinguished between a 'class in itself' and a 'class for itself'. A class in itself is simply a social group whose members share the same relationship to the forces of production. Marx argues that a social group only fully becomes a class when it becomes a class for itself. At this stage its members have class consciousness and class solidarity. Class consciousness means that false class consciousness has been replaced by a full awareness of the true situation, by a realization of the nature of exploitation. Members of a class develop a common identity, recognize their shared interests and unite, so producing class solidarity. The final stage of class consciousness and class solidarity is reached when members realize that only by collective action can they overthrow the ruling class and when they take positive steps to do so.

Marx believed that the following aspects of capitalist society would eventually lead to the proletariat developing into a class for itself. Firstly capitalist society is by its very nature unstable. It is based on contradictions and antagonisms which can only be resolved by its transformation. In particular, the conflict of interest between the bourgeoisie and the proletariat cannot be resolved within the framework of a capitalist economy. The basic conflict of interest involves the exploitation of workers by the capitalists. Marx believed that this contradiction would be highlighted by a second, the contradiction between social production and individual ownership. As capitalism developed, the workforce was increasingly concentrated in large factories where production was a social enterprise. Social production juxtaposed with individual ownership illuminates the exploitation of the proletariat. Social production also makes it easier for workers to organize themselves against the capitalists. It facilitates communication and encourages a recognition of common circumstances and interests.

Apart from the basic contradictions of capitalist society, Marx believed that certain factors in the natural development of a capitalist economy will hasten its downfall. These factors will result in the polarization of the two main classes. Firstly the increasing use of machinery will result in a homogeneous working class. Since 'machinery obliterates the differences in labour' members of the proletariat will become increasingly similar. The differences between skilled, semi-skilled and unskilled workers will tend to disappear as machines remove the skill required in the production of commodities. Secondly, the difference in wealth between the bourgeoisie and the proletariat will increase as the accumulation of capital proceeds. Even though the real wages and living standards of the proletariat may rise, its members will become poorer in relation to the bourgeoisie. This process is known as pauperization. Thirdly, the competitive nature of capitalism means that only the largest and most wealthy companies will survive and prosper. Competition will depress the intermediate strata, those groups lying between the two main classes, into the proletariat. Thus the 'petty bourgeoisie', the owners of small businesses, will 'sink into the proletariat'. At the same time the surviving companies will grow larger and capital will be concentrated into fewer hands. These three processes – the obliteration of the differences in labour, the pauperization of the working class and the depression of the intermediate strata into the proletariat – will result in the polarization of the two major classes. Marx believed he could observe the process of polarization in nineteenth-century Britain when he wrote, 'Society as a whole is more and more splitting into two great hostile camps . . . bourgeoisie and proletariat'. Now the battle lines were clearly drawn, Marx hoped that the proletarian revolution would shortly follow and the communist utopia of his dreams would finally become a reality.

Marx's work on class has been examined in detail for the following reasons. Firstly, many sociologists claim that his theory still provides the best explanation of the nature of class in capitalist society. Secondly much of the research on class has been inspired by ideas and questions raised by Marx. Thirdly, many of the concepts of class analysis introduced by Marx have proved useful to Marxists and non-Marxists alike. And, as T. B. Bottomore writing in 1965 notes, 'For the past eighty years Marx's theory has been the object of unrelenting criticism and tenacious defence'. This observation remains true today.

Social stratification – a Weberian perspective

The work of the German sociologist Max Weber (1864–1920) represents one of the most important developments in stratification theory since Marx. The similarities and differences of their approaches will become apparent as Weber's ideas are examined.

Like Marx, Weber sees class in economic terms. He argues that classes develop in market economies in which individuals compete for economic gain. He defines a class as a group of individuals who share a similar position in a market economy and by virtue of that fact receive similar economic rewards. Thus in Weber's terminology, a person's 'class situation' is basically his 'market situation'. Those who share a similar class situation also share similar life chances. Their economic position will directly affect their chances of obtaining those things defined as desirable in their society, for example access to higher education and good quality housing.

Like Marx, Weber argues that the major class division is between those who own the forces of production and those who do not. Thus those who have substantial property holdings will receive the highest economic rewards and enjoy superior life chances. However, Weber sees important differences in the market situation of the propertyless groups in society. In particular the various skills and services offered by different occupations have differing market values. For example, in capitalist society, managers, administrators and professionals receive relatively high salaries because of the demand for their services. Weber distinguished the following class groupings in capitalist society.

1 The propertied upper class
2 The propertyless white-collar workers
3 The petty bourgeoisie
4 The manual working class

In his analysis of class, Weber has parted company with Marx on a number of important issues. Firstly, factors other than the ownership or non-ownership of property are significant in the formation of classes. In particular, the market value of the skills of the propertyless varies and the resulting differences in economic return are sufficient to produce different social classes. Secondly, Weber sees no evidence to support the idea of the polarization of classes. Although he sees some decline in the numbers of the petty bourgeoisie, the small property owners, due to competition from large companies, he argues that they enter white-collar or skilled manual trades rather than being depressed into the ranks of unskilled manual workers. More importantly, Weber argues that the white-collar 'middle class' expands rather than contracts as capitalism develops. He maintains that capitalist enterprises and the modern nation state require a 'rational' bureaucratic administration which involves large numbers of administrators and clerical staff. (Weber's views on bureaucratic administration are outlined in Chapter 7, pp. 279–86.) Thus Weber sees a diversification of classes and an expansion of the white-collar middle class rather than a polarization. Thirdly, Weber rejects the view, held by some Marxists, of the inevitability of the proletarian revolution. He sees no reason why those sharing a similar class situation should necessarily develop a common identity, recognize shared interests and take collective action to further those interests. For example, Weber suggests that the individual manual worker who is dissatisfied with his class situation may respond in a variety of ways. He may grumble, work to rule, sabotage industrial machinery, take strike action or attempt to organize other members of his class in an effort to overthrow capitalism. Weber admits that a common market situation may provide a basis for collective class action but he sees this only as a possibility. Finally Weber rejects the Marxian view that political power necessarily derives from economic power. He argues that class forms only one possible basis for power and that the distribution of power in society is not necessarily linked to the distribution of class inequalities.

While class forms one possible basis for group formation, collective action and the acquisition of political power, Weber argues that there are other bases for these activities. In particular, groups form because their members share a similar 'status situation'. Whereas class refers to the unequal distribution of economic rewards, status refers to the unequal distribution of 'social honour'. Occupations, ethnic and religious groups and most importantly styles of life are accorded differing degrees of prestige or esteem by members of society. A status group is made up of individuals who are awarded a similar amount of social honour and therefore share the same status situation. Unlike classes, members of status groups are almost always aware of their common status situation. They share a similar life style, identify with and feel they belong to their status group and often place restrictions on the ways in which outsiders may interact with them. Weber argues that status groups reach their most developed form in the caste system of traditional Hindu society in India. Castes and sub-castes are formed and distinguished largely in terms of social honour. Life styles are sharply differentiated and accorded varying degrees of prestige. Barriers are set up to social intercourse between status groups, such as the ban on intercaste marriage. Weber sees status distinctions as the basis of group formation in caste societies.

In many societies class and status situations are closely linked. Weber notes that, 'Property as such is not always recognized as a status qualification, but in the long run it is, and with extraordinary regularity'. However, those who share the same class situation will not necessarily belong to the same status group. For example the *nouveaux riches* (the newly rich) are sometimes excluded from the status groups of the privileged because their tastes, manners and dress are defined as vulgar. Status groups may create divisions within classes. In a study of Banbury, conducted in the 1950s, Margaret Stacey found that members of the manual working class distinguished three status groups within that class: the 'respectable working class', the 'ordinary working class' and the 'rough working class'. Economic factors influenced the formation of these groups, for example the 'roughs' were often in the lowest income bracket, but they did not determine status since the income of many 'roughs' was similar to that of members of other status groups. Status groups can also cut across class divisions. In the USA, Blacks, no matter what their class situation belong to the same status group. This can form the basis for collective political action. For example in the 1960s and 1970s many middle and working-class Blacks united in various organizations under the banner of the Black Power movement.

Weber's observations on status groups are important since they suggest that in certain situations status rather than class provides the basis for the formation of social groups whose members perceive common interests and a group identity. In addition, the presence of different status groups within a single class and of status groups which cut across class divisions can weaken class solidarity and reduce the potential for class consciousness. These points are illustrated by Weber's analysis of 'parties'.

Weber defines 'parties' as groups which are specifically concerned with influencing policies and making decisions in the interests of their membership. In Weber's words parties are concerned with 'the acquisition of social "power"'. Parties include a variety of associations from the mass political parties of Western democracies to the whole range of pressure or interest groups which include professional associations, trade unions, the Automobile Association and the RSPCA. Parties often represent the interests of classes or status groups, but not necessarily. In Weber's words, 'Parties may represent interests determined through "class situation" or "status situation" . . . In most cases they are partly class parties and partly status parties, but sometimes they are neither'. The combination of class and status interests can be seen in the various Black Power organizations in the USA. They represent a status group but they also represent class interests. The majority of Blacks are working-class and many Black organizations are directly concerned with improving their class situation. Weber's view of parties suggests that the relationship between political groups and class and status groups is far from clear cut. Just as status groups can both divide classes and cut across class boundaries, so parties can divide and cut across both classes and status groups.

Weber's analysis of classes, status groups and parties suggests that no single theory can pinpoint and explain their relationship. The interplay of class, status and party in the formation of social groups is complex and variable and must be examined in particular societies during particular time periods. Marx attempted to reduce all forms of inequality to social class and argued that classes formed the only significant social groups in society. Weber argues that the evidence provides a more complex and diversified picture of social stratification.

Class in capitalist society

The two previous sections have examined Marxian and Weberian views of social stratification in general and class in capitalist society in particular. This section is concerned with more recent views of class in capitalist society. It attempts to answer the following questions. What is the class structure of capitalist society? How has it changed? What factors have shaped the class structure? Are classes important social groups in capitalist society?

Like Marx and Weber, most modern sociologists use economic factors as the basic criteria for differentiating social classes. Thus the British sociologist Anthony Giddens identifies three major classes in advanced capitalist society. They are an upper class based on the 'ownership of property in the means of production', a middle class based on the 'possession of educational or technical qualifications' and a lower or working class based on the 'possession of manual labour-power'. These classes are distinguished by their differing relationship to the forces of production and by their particular strategies for obtaining economic reward in a capitalist economy. In the competitive bargaining situation of capitalism, the bargaining strength of the three classes, as measured in terms of economic reward, differs significantly. However, as the following section will indicate, social class involves more than simply a collection of individuals who share a similar economic position.

Recent studies of social class have focussed on the white-collar non-manual middle class and the blue-collar manual working class. These classes are often subdivided into various levels in terms of occupational categories. A typical classification is given below.

Middle class	Higher professional, managerial and administrative
	Lower professional, managerial and administrative
	Routine white-collar and minor supervisory
Working class	Skilled manual
	Semi-skilled manual
	Unskilled manual

Frank Parkin provides the following justification for using occupational classifications of social class. He claims that, 'The backbone of the class structure, and indeed the entire reward system of modern Western society, is the occupational structure'. Thus the rewards attached to occupations form the basis of the system of social inequality in capitalist society.

Now that the broad outlines of the class structure have been drawn, the next task is to explain the differences in occupational reward. From a functionalist perspective it may be argued that the reward system matches the functional importance of occupations. Thus, in terms of Davis and Moore's theory, the manager is more highly rewarded than the factory worker because of the greater functional importance of his position. It is more important because the labour force is dependent on management direction whereas the reverse is not the case. In addition, the manager's position is 'functionally unique' since the manager can change roles with the factory worker but not vice versa. In view of the functional importance of the manager's position, high rewards are attached to managerial status to insure that it is filled by able and resourceful individuals. In terms of Talcott Parsons's theory, the rewards attached to occupations will reflect priorities established by society's values. In modern industrial societies a high value is placed on 'productive activity'. Thus managerial occupations are more highly rewarded than manual jobs because they make a greater contribution to production. The problems with functionalist explanations of differential reward have already been discussed. In particular it is difficult, if not impossible, to show that highly rewarded positions are functionally most important to society. Moreover, whether or not they make a greater contribution to translating society's values into reality is a matter of opinion.

An alternative explanation argues that power rather than the functional requirements of society determines differential occupational rewards. Thus managers receive higher rewards than factory workers because they have greater power. However, as Frank Parkin observes, the next question is why are some occupational groups more powerful than others? Parkin argues that in modern capitalist societies, the power to acquire rewards is directly related to the demands of the market for occupational skills. He claims that 'marketable expertise is the most important single determinant of occupational reward'. In general the rewards for skills are determined by the 'law' of supply and demand. Compared to unskilled workers, there is a high demand and a short supply of skilled manual workers. As a result skilled workers are able to command a higher economic return for their services.

The supply of and demand for various skills can be controlled to some degree by particular occupational groups. In this way such groups can increase their market power and therefore their economic rewards. Parkin notes that many professional bodies, such as doctors and lawyers, restrict the supply of new members by imposing strict entrance requirements to the profession and insisting upon lengthy and expensive training, much of which he believes 'is of little practical value'. Skilled manual groups employ similar strategies, controlling entry into trades by means of long apprenticeships. The high wages of printers are due partly to this practice. In general, the more skilled and highly rewarded an occupational group, the greater its ability to control its market position in its favour. Unskilled groups find it difficult to create an 'artificial' scarcity since their jobs are easily and quickly learned and the supply of unskilled labour is fairly plentiful. Parkin concludes that occupational reward is due to the demand in the market for skills and expertise, a demand which can be controlled in varying degrees by different occupational groups.

Many studies have shown that the hierarchy of occupational reward in capitalist society is similar to the hierarchy of occupational prestige. Thus professional and managerial occupations are more highly rewarded in both economic and status terms than manual jobs. Frank Parkin argues that occupational prestige derives primarily from class. He claims that the occupational status hierarchy arises from 'the moral judgments of those who occupy dominant positions in the class structure'. Those highly placed in the class structure largely control important agencies of socialization such as schools and the mass media. It is therefore likely that their ideas of occupational prestige will be adopted by society as a whole. Since their jobs entail long training periods, high academic qualifications, expertise and responsibility, occupations of this type will be awarded considerable social honour. Those in dominant positions promote these views in order to justify and legitimate their high economic rewards. According high prestige to an occupation implies that its economic rewards are deserved. Thus Parkin concludes that class inequalities generate prestige inequalities, that high occupational prestige derives primarily from high occupational reward.

This section has attempted to provide a profile and explanation of the class structure in advanced capitalist society. The following two sections examine the working and middle classes in greater detail.

The working class in capitalist society

Marx predicted an increasing homogeneity within the industrial working class. He assumed that technical developments in industry would remove the need for manual skills. As a result craftsmen and tradesmen would steadily disappear and the bulk of the working class would become un-skilled machine minders. The growing similarity of wages and circumstances would increase working class solidarity. Marx argued that, 'The interests and life situations of the proletariat are more and more equalized, since the machinery increasingly obliterates the differences of labour and depresses the wage almost everywhere to an equally low level'. While there may have been a tendency for many industrial workers to become unskilled during the nineteenth century, many sociologists have argued that this trend was reversed in the present century.

The German sociologist Ralf Dahrendorf argues that contrary to Marx's prediction, the manual working class has become increasingly heterogeneous or dissimilar. He sees this resulting from changes in technology arguing that 'increasingly complex machines require increasingly qualified designers, builders, maintenance and repair men and even minders'. Dahrendorf claims that the working class is now divided into three distinct levels: unskilled, semi-skilled and skilled manual workers. Differences in economic and prestige rewards are linked to this hierarchy of skill. Thus skilled craftsmen enjoy higher wages, more valuable fringe benefits, greater job security and higher prestige than semi-skilled and unskilled workers. Dahrendorf argues that in place of an homogeneous proletariat 'we find a plurality of status and skill groups whose interests often diverge'. This divergence of interest is recognized by many manual groups. For example, craftsmen jealously guard their wage differentials against claims for pay increases by the less skilled. In view of the differences in skill, economic and status rewards and interests within the ranks of manual workers, Dahrendorf claims that 'it has become doubtful whether speaking of the working class still makes much sense'. He believes that during the twentieth century there has been a 'decomposition of labour', a disintegration of the manual working class.

Whether or not it still makes sense to talk about a manual working class is a matter of judgment. Many sociologists would disagree with Dahrendorf. They would argue that the inequalities and conflicts of interest within the working class are relatively insignificant compared to those which divide manual workers from the rest of society. This view will now be examined.

There are significant differences between the market situations of manual and non-manual workers. Table 1 compares the average gross weekly earnings, including overtime pay, of the two groups. It refers to men over twenty-one in full-time employment in Great Britain.

Table 1

	1970	1971	1974	1975	1976
Manual	£26.8	£29.4	£43.6	£55.7	£65.1
Non-manual	£35.8	£39.1	£54.4	£68.4	£81.6

(Source: *Social Trends*, 1977, p. 102).

Comparisons of gross weekly earnings do not, however, reveal a number of important market advantages held by many white-collar occupational groups. In general, blue-collar workers, despite their lower earnings, work longer hours than their white-collar counterparts. This is particularly true for manual workers whose earnings approach the white-collar average. Westergaard and Resler note that in 1971, more than half of the highest paid manual workers worked over fifty hours per week. A second market advantage of white-collar workers concerns the differences in income careers between manual and non-manual employees. The wages of manual workers rise gradually during their twenties, peak in their early thirties and then slowly but steadily fall to levels well below those of their twenties. This drop in wages often begins when the financial demands on the male worker are greatest – wives have left paid employment and dependent children must be supported. By comparison, the earnings of many white-collar workers rise sharply during the first half of their working lives, peak during their forties or later and then decline slightly to a level nearly twice that reached during their twenties. Their occupations provide a career structure and incremental payments which, for many, result in a steady increase in earnings and living standards. Manual workers have relatively few opportunities for promotion and their pay structure is unlikely to include incremental increases. A third white-collar market advantage involves security of earnings and employment. Compared to non-manual workers, manual workers have a greater risk of redundancy, unemployment, lay-offs and short-time. Finally, the gross weekly earnings of white and blue-collar workers do not reveal the economic value of fringe benefits. Such benefits include company pension schemes, paid sick leave, the use of company cars, meals and entertainment which are paid for in part or in total by the employer. Again white-collar workers enjoy a market advantage. Fringe benefits increase in value as occupational earnings rise. One study estimates that they add a further 11% to the salaries of junior management and a further 31% to the salaries of higher executives (discussed in Westergaard and Resler, 1976, p. 87). A survey of the terms and conditions of employment of six occupational groups in various manufacturing industries, conducted in 1968 by Dorothy Wedderburn and Christine Craig, reveals important differences in the fringe benefits of manual and non-manual employees. The results of this survey are given in table 2.

Table 2   Selected differences in terms and conditions of employment

| | Percentage of establishments in which the condition applies | | | | | |
	Opera-tives	Fore-men	Clerical workers	Tech-nicians	Middle managers	Senior managers
Holiday: 15 days +	38	72	74	77	84	88
Choice of holiday time	35	54	76	76	84	88
Normal working 40+ hours per week	97	94	9	23	27	22
Sick pay – employers' scheme	57	94	98	97	98	98
Pension – employers' scheme	67	94	90	94	96	96
Time off with pay for personal reasons	29	84	83	86	91	93
Pay deductions for any lateness	90	20	8	11	1	0
Warning followed by dismissal for persistent lateness	84	66	78	71	48	41
No clocking on or booking in	2	46	48	45	81	94

(Source: Wedderburn, 1970, p. 593, and the Department of Employment and Productivity Survey 1969)

In terms of fringe benefits in particular and conditions of employment in general, the position of white-collar workers is significantly better than that of blue-collar employees. Summarizing the results of the study, Wedderburn states, 'Our survey shows a big gulf between manual workers on the one hand and non-manual workers on the other'.

The above evidence suggests that the market situation of manual workers is substantially inferior to that of white-collar workers. This provides support for the proposition that manual workers form a social class. Further evidence to support this view is provided by a comparison of the life chances of manual and non-manual groups. White-collar workers generally enjoy higher standards of health compared to their blue-collar counterparts. They have lower rates of infant mortality, a lower incidence of long-standing illness and a longer life expectancy. The levels of educational attainment of the two groups differ significantly. Children from white-collar backgrounds generally obtain higher educational qualifications than the children of manual workers. Measured in terms of material goods, white-collar workers enjoy a superior quality of life. Their houses are more spacious and more likely to be equipped with amenities such as central heating. White-collar families are more likely to benefit from consumer durables such as washing machines, freezers, food mixers and vacuum cleaners. Compared to manual workers, nonmanual workers have a greater chance of experiencing those things defined as desirable and of avoiding those things defined as undesirable in Western industrial society.

Many sociologists would argue that social class involves more than a similar market situation and similar life chances. In order to become a social class, a collection of similarly placed individuals must to some degree form a social group. This involves at least a minimal awareness of group identity and some appreciation of and commitment to common interests. It also involves some similarity of life style. Members of a social group will usually share certain norms, values and attitudes which distinguish them from other members of society. Finally, belonging to a social group usually means that a member will interact primarily with other members of his group. Manual workers will now be examined in terms of these criteria for class formation.

A number of studies conducted over the past thirty years in Britain indicate that the vast majority of the population believe that society is divided into social classes. These studies show that most manual workers describe themselves as working-class, most white-collar workers see themselves as middle-class. However, there are a number of problems with this type of evidence. As Kenneth Roberts observes, 'because individuals are prepared to label themselves as middle or working class when invited by sociologists, it does not necessarily follow that they ordinarily think in these terms'. Thus class identification may have little significance to those concerned. Secondly, the labels middle and working-class may mean different things to different people. In a survey conducted in 1950, F. M. Martin found that 70% of manual workers regarded themselves as working-class. The remaining 30% who defined themselves as middleclass did so partly because of the meanings they attached to the term working-class. They saw the working class as a group bordering on poverty and defined its members as lazy and irresponsible, hence their desire to dissociate themselves from this classification. A third problem with this type of evidence is that identification with a particular class says little about an individual's overall view of the nature of the class structure and how it operates. Research on this topic will be examined shortly. However, despite the above problems, the fact that most manual workers define themselves as working-class indicates at least a minimal awareness of class identity.

Research on political attitudes and voting behaviour provides evidence which may indicate some awareness of and commitment to class interests. Approximately two-thirds of manual workers regularly vote for the Labour Party. The most common reason given is that Labour represents the interests of the working man. Those manual workers who identify themselves as working-class are more likely to vote Labour than those who see themselves as middle-class. This type of evidence may be interpreted as an indication of some degree of awareness and commitment to collective class interests. (The relationship between social class and voting behaviour will be examined in detail in the following chapter, pp. 129–34.)

From his observations of the working class in nineteenth-century England, Engels wrote, 'The workers speak other dialects, have other thoughts and ideals, other customs and moral principles, a different religion and other politics than those of the *bourgeoisie*. Thus they are two radically dissimilar nations . . .' (quoted in Parkin, 1972, p. 79). Few, if any, sociologists would suggest that the gulf between the classes is as great today. However, many would argue that the norms, values and attitudes of the working and middle classes differ to some degree. They would therefore feel justified in talking about working-class subculture and middle-class subculture. As a result it has been argued that manual and non-manual workers form social groups distinguished by relatively distinct subcultures.

The description of working-class subculture that follows is taken mainly from studies of what has come to be known as the traditional working class. The traditional worker lives in close-knit working-class communities and is employed in long-established industries such as mining, docking and ship-building. There is evidence that such communities are breaking up and that the industries referred to are either declining or substantially reducing their workforce. As a result, traditional working-class subculture may well be disappearing. Evidence to support this view will be examined shortly. Firstly, however, traditional working-class subculture will be described.

The traditional worker's attitude to life is one of fatalism. From this perspective there is little the individual can do to alter his situation and changes or improvements in his circumstances are due largely to luck or fate. In view of this life must be accepted as it comes. Since there is little chance of individual effort changing the future, long-term planning is discouraged in favour of present-time orientation. There is a tendency to live from day to day and planning is limited to the near future. As a result, there is an emphasis on immediate gratification. There is little pressure to sacrifice pleasures of the moment for future rewards; desires are to be gratified in the present rather than at a later date. This attitude to life may be summarized by the following everyday phrases: 'what is to be will be'; 'take life as it comes'; 'make the best of it'; 'live for today because tomorrow may never come.' By comparison, middle-class subculture is characterized by a purposive approach to life. Man has control over his destiny and with ability, determination and ambition can change and improve his situation. Associated with this attitude is an emphasis on future time orientation and deferred gratification. Long-term planning and deferring or putting off present pleasures for future rewards are regarded as worthwhile. Thus the individual is encouraged to sacrifice money and or leisure at certain stages of his life to improve his career prospects.

In so far as he sees a possibility of improving his situation, the traditional worker tends to adopt a collective strategy. There is an emphasis on mutual aid and group solidarity rather than individual achievement. In particular, collective action in trade unions is seen as the means for improving wages and working conditions. There are close bonds between individuals both at work and in leisure activities. The traditional worker frequently socializes with his workmates, many of whom are also his neighbours, in the pub or working man's club. This emphasis on group loyalty and solidarity tends to discourage individual achievement. Those who aspire to middle-class status and occupations may be accused of putting on airs and graces and regarding themselves as a cut above the rest. Partly because of this, parents tend to confine their hopes for their children's future to 'good', 'steady' working-class trades. By comparison, middle-class subculture emphasizes an individual rather than a collective strategy. A high value is placed on individual achievement and the route to success is seen in terms of individual effort. Parents have high aspirations for their children and look forward to them achieving a higher social status than themselves.

In addition to particular values and attitudes, members of society usually have a general image or picture of the social structure and the class system. These pictures are known as 'images of society' or more particularly, 'images of class'. Some sociologists have argued that there is a marked contrast between the images of society held by the traditional working class and the middle class. The traditional worker tends to perceive the social order as sharply divided into 'us' and 'them'. On one side are the bosses, managers and white-collar workers who have power, and on the other, the relatively powerless manual workers. There is seen to be little opportunity for individual members of the working class to cross the divide separating them from the rest of society. This view of society is referred to as a 'power model' and those who hold it as 'proletarian traditionalists'. Research has indicated that traditional workers may hold other images of society and their perceptions of the social order are not as simple and clear cut as the above description suggests. However, the power model appears to be the nearest thing to a consistent image of society held by a significant number of traditional workers. By comparison, the middle-class image of society resembles a ladder. There are various strata or levels differentiated in terms of occupational status and life styles of varying prestige. Given ability and ambition, opportunities are available for individuals to rise in the social hierarchy. This view of the social order is known as a 'status' or 'prestige model'.

The above account of traditional working-class subculture is based mainly on the work of British sociologists John H. Goldthorpe and David Lockwood. Although various studies of working-class life provide support for their views, not all sociologists admit the existence of a distinctive working-class subculture. This contrary view will be examined in later chapters. (In particular see Chapter 4, pp. 154–60 and Chapter 5, pp. 195–6.)

This section began with Dahrendorf's argument that in view of the heterogeneity and conflicts of interest which divided them, it made little sense to consider manual workers as a social class. The main part of this section has presented argument and evidence in support of the proposition that manual workers form a social class, a view held by many sociologists. It has been suggested that manual workers share a similar market situation and similar life chances, that they have some awareness of class identity, at least a minimal commitment to common class interests and a subculture which distinguishes them from other groups in society. As such, it may be argued that manual workers form a social group, in particular a working class.

Embourgeoisement

Writing in the nineteenth century, Marx predicted that the intermediate strata would be depressed into the proletariat. During the 1950s and early 1960s, a number of sociologists suggested that just the opposite was happening. They claimed that a process of embourgeoisement was occurring whereby increasing numbers of manual workers were entering the middle stratum and becoming middle-class. During the 1950s there was a general increase in prosperity in advanced industrial societies and, in particular, amongst a growing number of manual workers whose earnings now fell within the white-collar range. These highly paid 'affluent workers' were seen to be increasingly typical of manual workers. This development, coupled with studies which suggested that poverty was rapidly disappearing, led to the belief that the shape of the stratification system was being transformed. From the triangle or pyramid shape of the nineteenth century, with a large and relatively impoverished working class at the bottom and a small wealthy group at the top, it was argued that with an increasing proportion of the population falling into the middle range, the stratification system was changing to a diamond or pentagon shape. In this 'middle mass society', the mass of the population was middle rather than working-class.

The theory used to explain this presumed development was a version of economic determinism. It was argued that the demands of modern technology and an advanced industrial economy determined the shape of the stratification system. The American sociologist Clark Kerr claimed that advanced industrialism requires an increasingly highly educated, trained and skilled workforce which in turn leads to higher pay and higher status occupations. In particular skilled technicians are rapidly replacing unskilled machine minders. Jessie Bernard argued that working-class affluence is related to the needs of an industrial economy for a mass market. In order to expand, industry requires a large market for its products. Mass consumption has been made possible by high wages, which in turn have been made possible because large sectors of modern industry have relatively low labour costs and high productivity. Bernard claimed that there is a rapidly growing 'middle market' which reflects the increased purchasing power of affluent manual workers. Home ownership, and consumer durables such as washing machines, refrigerators, televisions and motor cars are no longer the preserve of white-collar workers. With reference to the class system, Bernard states, 'The "proletariat" has not absorbed the middle class but rather the other way round . . . In the sense that the class structure here described reflects modern technology, it vindicates the Marxist thesis that social organization is "determined" by technological forces' (quoted in Goldthorpe and Lockwood, 1969, p. 9). Thus Bernard suggests that Marx was correct in emphasizing the importance of economic factors but wrong in his prediction of the direction of social change.

The supporters of embourgeoisement argued that middle-range incomes led to middle-class life styles. It was assumed that the affluent worker was adopting middle-class norms, values and attitudes. For example, in Britain, it was believed that affluence eroded traditional political party loyalties and that increasing numbers of manual workers were now supporting the Conservative Party. The process of embourgeoisement was seen to be accelerated by the demands of modern industry for a mobile labour force. This tended to break up traditional close-knit working-class communities found in the older industrial areas. The geographically mobile, affluent worker moved to newer, suburban areas where he was largely indistinguishable from his white-collar neighbours.

Despite the strong support for embourgeoisement, the evidence on which it was based was largely impressionistic. As such, embourgeoisement remained an hypothesis, a process that was assumed to be occurring, but which had not been adequately tested. In a famous study entitled, *The Affluent Worker in the Class Structure*, Goldthorpe, Lockwood, Bechhofer and Platt present the results of research designed to test the embourgeoisement hypothesis. They attempted to find as favourable a setting as possible for the confirmation of the hypothesis. Thus if embourgeoisement was not taking place in a context which offered every opportunity, then it would probably not be occurring in less favourable contexts. They chose Luton, a prosperous area in southeast England with expanding industries. A sample of 229 manual workers was selected plus a comparative group of 54 white-collar workers drawn from various grades of clerks. The study was conducted from 1963 to 1964 and examined workers from Vauxhall Motors, Skefko Ball Bearing Company and Laporte Chemicals. Nearly half the manual workers in the survey had come from outside the southeast area in search of stable, well paid jobs. All were married and 57% were house owners or buyers. Relative to other manual workers they were highly paid and their wages compared favourably with those of many white-collar workers. Although the Luton study was not primarily concerned with economic aspects of class, Goldthrope and Lockwood argue, like many of the opponents of the embourgeoisement thesis, that similarity of earnings is not the same thing as similarity of market situation. Relative to affluent manual workers, white-collar workers retain many of their market advantages. These include, 'continuity of employment, fringe benefits, long-term income prospects and promotion chances'. The Luton study tested the embourgeoisement hypothesis in four main areas: attitudes to work; interaction patterns in the community; aspirations and social perspectives; and political views. If affluent workers were becoming middle-class they should be largely indistinguishable from white-collar workers in these areas.

The affluent workers define their work in 'instrumental' terms, as a means to an end rather than an end in itself. Work is simply a means of earning money to raise living standards. Largely because of this 'instrumental orientation' they derive little satisfaction from work. They do not compensate for this lack of job satisfaction by building up rewarding social relationships with their workmates. Few have close friends at work or participate in the social clubs provided by their firms. Since they define work as simply a place to make money, they do not see it as a context for making friends. Most affluent workers accept their position as manual wage earners as more or less permanent. They feel that there is little chance for promotion and that supervisory jobs imply too great a degree of involvement with and commitment to the company. They are concerned with making a 'good living' *from* their firms rather than a 'good career' *within* their firms. Like the traditional worker, affluent workers see improvement in terms of wages and working conditions resulting from collective action in trade unions rather than individual achievement. However their attitude to unions differs from traditional working-class collectivism which was based largely on class solidarity, on strong union loyalty and the belief that members of the working class ought to stick together. The affluent worker joins with his workmates as a self-interested individual to improve his wages and working conditions. He has no apparent commitment to the ideal of working-class solidarity and regards trade unions in instrumental terms, as a means to personal ends. Thus the 'solidaristic collectivism' of the traditional worker has largely been replaced by the 'instrumental collectivism' of the affluent worker.

By contrast, white-collar workers do not define work in purely instrumental terms. They expect and experience a higher level of job satisfaction. They make friends at work and the firms' social clubs have a largely white-collar membership. Promotion for the white-collar worker is a desired objective, even a 'moral expectation'. He feels an obligation to put his ability into the firm and in return expects long-term security and career opportunities. However, because promotion prospects are increasingly slim for many lower-grade white-collar workers, they are adopting a strategy of instrumental collectivism and joining trade unions in order to improve their market situation. In general, though, Goldthorpe and Lockwood conclude that in the area of work, there are significant differences between affluent manual workers and white-collar workers. In this respect, the embourgeoisement hypothesis is not confirmed. Affluent workers are not becoming middle-class.

Supporters of the embourgeoisement thesis argued that once the affluent worker left the factory gates, he adopted a middle-class life style. His friendship patterns followed middle-class norms and he associated with his white-collar neighbours as frequently and freely as with persons of his own occupational status. Goldthorpe and Lockwood found little support for this view. Affluent workers drew their friends and companions from kin and neighbours and in this respect they follow traditional working-class norms. By comparison, white-collar workers mix more with friends made at work and with persons who are neither kin nor neighbours. Despite the fact that many of their neighbours were white-collar workers, affluent workers nearly always befriended fellow manual workers. They show no desire to mix with members of the middle class and there is no evidence that they either value or seek middle-class status. In one respect there is a convergence between the life styles of the affluent worker and the lower middle class. Both tend to lead a 'privatized' and home-centred existence. The affluent worker's social relationships are centred on and largely restricted to the home. His time is spent watching television, gardening, doing jobs around the house and socializing with his immediate family. There is no evidence of the communal sociability of the traditional working class but apart from the similarity of the privatized and family-centred life of affluent workers and the lower middle class, Goldthorpe and Lockwood argue that the affluent worker has not adopted middle-class 'patterns of sociability'. In particular, he has not, nor shows any desire to become assimilated into middle-class society.

In terms of their general outlook on life, affluent workers differ in important respects from the traditional worker. Many had migrated to Luton in order to improve their living standards rather than simply accepting life in their towns of origin. In this respect, they have a purposive rather than a fatalistic attitude. As previously noted, however, the means they adopt to realize their goals – instrumental collectivism – are not typical of the middle class as a whole. In addition their goals are distinct from those of the middle class in that they focus simply on material benefits rather than a concern with advancement in the prestige hierarchy. This emphasis on materialism is reflected in the affluent workers' images of society. Few see society in terms of either the power model based on the idea of 'us and them' which is characteristic of the traditional worker, or in terms of the prestige model which is typical of the middle class. The largest group (56%) sees money as the basis of class divisions. In terms of this money or pecuniary model, they see a large central class made up of the majority of the working population. Only a minority made up of the extremes of wealth, that is the very rich and the poor, fall outside this class. The manual/non-manual distinction is not seen as forming a significant division in the class system. Although differing from the traditional worker, the affluent worker's outlook on life and image of society do not appear to be developing in a middle-class direction.

Finally, Goldthorpe and Lockwood found little support for the view that affluence leads manual workers to vote for the Conservative Party. In the 1959 election, 80% of the affluent worker sample voted Labour, a higher proportion than for the manual working class as a whole. Some evidence of an awareness of class interests is indicated. Goldthorpe and Lockwood note that 'by far the most common kind of reason given for attachment to the Labour Party was one couched in "class terms": Labour was typically seen as the party *of* the working class, as the party for which the manual worker would naturally vote'. However, support for the Labour Party, like support for trade unions, was often of an instrumental kind. There was little indication of the strong loyalty to Labour which is assumed to be typical of the traditional worker.

Goldthorpe and Lockwood tested the embourgeoisement hypothesis under conditions favourable to its confirmation, but found it was not confirmed. They conclude that it is therefore unlikely that large numbers of manual workers are becoming middle-class. Despite this the Luton workers differ in significant respects from the traditional working class. In view of this, Goldthorpe and Lockwood suggest that they may form the vanguard of an emerging 'new working class'. While the new working class is not being assimilated into the middle class, there are two points of 'normative convergence' between the classes. These are privatization and instrumental collectivism. Finally Goldthorpe and Lockwood argue that the results of their study represent a rejection of economic determinism. The affluent worker has not simply been shaped by economic forces. Instead, 'class and status relationships' have 'an important degree of autonomy, and can thus accommodate considerable change in this infrastructure without themselves changing in any fundamental way'. Thus the life style and outlook of the affluent worker are due in large part to the adaptation of traditional working-class norms to a new situation; they are not simply shaped by that situation.

An important study of London dockers conducted in the early 1970s by Stephen Hill suggests that the new working class might not be as new as Goldthorpe and Lockwood believed. The 139 dock labourers in Hill's survey were remarkably similar to the Luton workers. Judging from past studies, the docks are one of the heartlands of proletarian traditionalism. Strong working-class solidarity, long-standing loyalties to unions and the Labour Party, close bonds between workmates, communal leisure activities, an emphasis on mutual aid and a power model of society have been seen as characteristic of dock workers. Either this picture has been exaggerated or there have been important changes in dockland life. There is probably some truth in both these points. David Lockwood, writing in 1975, admits that the differences between the traditional and new worker have probably been exaggerated. The system of casual labour in the docks was abolished in 1967 and replaced by permanent employment. The constant threat of underemployment entailed in the casual labour system tended to unite dock workers. The change to permanent employment may have reduced the traditional solidarity of dockland life.

Like the Luton workers, the dockers in Hill's study defined their work primarily in instrumental terms. Their main priority was to increase their living standards. Only a minority made close friends at work and only 23% reported seeing something of their workmates outside work. Most dockers lived a privatized life style and leisure activities were mainly home and family-centred. Like the Luton workers, dockers regarded collective action in trade unions as essential for economic improvement. Over 80% of dockers voted Labour, the most common reason for this being an identification with Labour as the party of the working class. Again these findings are very similar to those of the Luton study. In terms of their views of society, the dockers belied their proletarian traditionalist image. Only 14% saw the class structure in terms of a power model whereas 47%, the largest group subscribing to one particular view, saw society in terms of a money model. In this respect they are again similar to the Luton workers. Hill concludes that, 'The evidence of dock workers strongly suggests that the working class is more homogeneous than has been allowed for: those who wish to divide it into old and new greatly exaggerate the divisions which actually occur within the ranks of semi-skilled and unskilled workers'.

The working class – a class for itself?

Many Marxist sociologists argue that the contradictions of capitalism will eventually lead to a class conscious proletariat. Class consciousness involves a full awareness by members of the working class of the reality of their exploitation, a recognition of common interests, the identification of an opposing group with whom their interests are in conflict and a realization that only by collective class action can that opponent be overthrown. When practical steps are taken in pursuit of this goal, the working class becomes a class for itself. Evidence from a variety of studies suggests that the working class is a long way from becoming a class for itself.

It has often been argued that the image of society held by proletarian traditionalists contains certain elements of class consciousness. The power model with its emphasis on 'us and them' implies some recognition of common class interests, an indication of class solidarity and at least a vague awareness of an opponent with whom the workers are in conflict. However the money model, which, judging from the studies of Goldthorpe and Lockwood and Hill, is the dominant image of society held by workers in Britain, suggests that the working class is becoming less rather than more class conscious. Further evidence from these studies supports this view. Nearly 70% of the Luton workers believed that the inequalities portrayed in their images of society were a necessary and inevitable feature of industrial society. They were concerned with improving their position in the existing society rather than trying to create a new social order. Given the fact that they had improved their economic position, they had some commitment to the existing order. Marxists have often argued that the road to revolution involves an alliance between the trade union movement and a radical political party. Workers must see the politics of the workplace and society as one and the same. The Luton workers typically saw the union as an organization limited to advancing their economic interests in the workplace. In fact 54% of the Luton trade unionists expressed clear-cut disapproval of the link between trade unions and the Labour Party. In general the Luton workers saw little opposition between themselves and their employer, 67% agreeing with the statement that at work, 'teamwork means success and is to everyone's advantage'. They were largely indifferent to 'exploitation' at work, home and family concerns being their central life interest.

This picture of harmony must not be overdrawn. As Goldthorpe and Lockwood state, the employer-employee relationship is not free from 'basic oppositions of interest'. Workers are concerned with maximizing wages, employers with maximizing profits. The teamwork image of industrial relations held by the majority of workers did not prevent a bitter strike in 1966 at the Luton branch of Vauxhall Motors. Despite the apparent acceptance of the social order by the Luton workers, their responses to a number of questions indicate some resentment about social inequality: 75% agreed with the statement that there is 'one law for the rich and another for the poor' and 60% agreed that big business has 'too much power'.

The dock labourers in Stephen Hill's study expressed similar attitudes to those of the Luton workers. They showed no great hostility to employers or management, the majority being 'fairly indifferent' towards them.

Most were opposed to the link between trade unions and the Labour Party. Hill states that, 'The dock workers I interviewed were certainly hostile to the traditional alliance between unionism and Labour, refusing to accept the view that these formed the industrial and political wings of an integrated labour movement'. However, despite the lack of radicalism in the workers' views of employers and of the link between trade unions and political parties, Hill did find evidence of left-wing opinions. Over 80% of the dockers agreed with the statements that there is 'one law for the rich and another for the poor' and 'big business has too much power' and nearly 75% agreed that 'the upper classes prevent fair shares'. Thus, like the Luton workers, the dockers appear to hold apparently conflicting radical and conservative views. Possible reasons for this will be discussed shortly.

The studies by Hill and Goldthorpe and Lockwood may be interpreted as indicating a reduction of the potential for class consciousness. It appears that the proletarian traditionalist has been replaced by the privatized worker who is preoccupied with home and family and largely indifferent to wider political issues. John Westergaard, however, takes a rather different view. Firstly, he argues that the relatively self-contained working-class communities of the proletarian traditionalist encouraged a parochial outlook. Workers tended to have a narrow identification with their occupational group rather than with the working class as a whole. Westergaard argues that the break up of traditional working-class communities may be necessary to provide 'larger conceptions of class identity and wider social vision'. Secondly, since the privatized worker defines his work in instrumental terms, his sole attachment to work is the 'cash-nexus' or money connection. As such, his attachment to work is single-stranded. It is not strengthened by pride in work, friendships at work or loyalty to the employer. A single-stranded connection is brittle. It can easily snap. If the privatized worker's demands for high wages and rising living standards are not met, for example in times of economic depression, the cash-nexus may well snap and there will be nothing else to hold him to his job and make him accept the situation. In such circumstances the privatized worker may become increasingly radical and recognize that his interests lie in collective class action. Thirdly, Westergaard argues that the seeds of class consciousness are already present even in the apparently conservative Luton workers. He sees evidence of this from their views on the power of big business and the workings of the legal system, views echoed by the London dockers. Westergaard claims, 'There are patent signs here, as from other evidence, of widespread, indeed routine, popular distrust; of a common sense of grievance, a belief that the dice are loaded against ordinary workers, which involves at the very least a rudimentary diagnosis of power and a practical conception of conflicts of interest between classes'.

Before proceeding, it is important to examine some of the methodological problems involved in obtaining workers' images of society and political attitudes. The usual method used to elicit images of society is the unstructured interview. This involves a general discussion about views on class with the respondent being encouraged by the interviewer to indicate such things as his own class position, the number of classes he sees and the main determinants of class position. The information is then analysed, interpreted and classified into images of society. Two problems are immediately apparent. Firstly, the interviewer may steer the respondent into areas which are of interest and concern to the sociologist rather than himself. Secondly, the classification owes a great deal to those who interpret the results of the interview. Jennifer Platt, one of the co-authors of the Luton study, has since argued that the data on affluent workers' images of society are open to alternative interpretation and classification. Information on images of society is sometimes obtained from questionnaires, as are data on political attitudes. Respondents are often asked to agree or disagree with particular statements such as, 'In Britain today there are basically two main classes, bosses and workers'. There are many problems associated with this method which will be discussed in detail in the chapter on methodology (pp. 507–15). In particular, the same question may mean different things to different people and simple yes/no answers to questions framed by sociologists may reveal little about the respondent's real views. However, there is a more general problem with data on images of society and political attitudes, no matter what method is used to obtain them. This concerns their salience to the respondents. Are they important, relevant and meaningful to the respondents in their everyday lives or are they of little significance and simply produced to satisfy inquisitive sociologists?

There is a tendency to assume that workers do hold a clear, consistent and coherent image of society and a tendency to mould data into neat, tidy categories. The Luton workers are usually discussed in terms of their money model of society yet only 54% held that model, while 26% had images which fitted neither power, prestige or money models and 7% had 'no communicable image'. Hill's study revealed that only 47% of dockers held a money model and he was impressed with 'the *range* of different images which people within one group can embrace'. More emphasis might well be given to the variety and diversity of workers' images of society. In addition, there is evidence which indicates that many workers do not hold clear and consistent views on society. Hill found that the dockers' fairly radical opinions on the power of big business, the workings of the law and the maintenance of inequality by the upper classes were inconsistent with their relatively conservative views on the role of trade unions and the nature of employment. He notes that they 'appeared to have their views fairly well compartmentalized'. As a result the dockers seemed to have no problem with holding apparently contradictory views. Similar findings were produced from a study of the ideology of 951 unskilled manual workers in Peterborough, conducted in 1970/1 by R. M. Blackburn and Michael Mann. They found that both right and left-wing views co-existed in the workers' ideology and concluded that they do not possess 'consistent and coherent images of society'. In fact Blackburn and Mann suggest that there is every reason to expect that this should be the case. The workers' experience of subordination and exploitation in the workplace will tend to produce a power model of society and radical attitudes which demand a change in the status quo. However, the workers are also exposed to the ideology of the dominant class broadcast by the mass media and transmitted by the educational system and various other institutions. This ideology is conservative: it supports the existing social arrangements and states that the relationship between capital and labour is right, natural and inevitable. As a result, workers 'remain confused by the clash between conservatism and proletarianism, but touched by both'.

This section began by asking whether the working class in capitalist society was moving in the direction of class consciousness. Certainly strands of radical opinion exist in the British working class but it is a long way from becoming a class for itself. Compared to the proletarian traditionalist, the workers in Hill's and Goldthorpe and Lockwood's studies appear less radical and less likely to see society in conflict and oppositional terms. Blackburn and Mann's study shows that where radical opinions exist, they are tempered by conservative viewpoints. However, from a Marxian view, much of the preceding discussion may be largely inconsequential. In Marx's words, 'It is not a question of what this or that proletarian or even the whole proletariat momentarily *imagines* to be the aim. It is a question of what the proletariat *is* and what it *consequently* is historically compelled to do' (quoted in Mann, 1973, p. 45). Many Marxists believe that class consciousness will eventually be generated by the contradictions of capitalism and that the proletarian revolution is the destiny of the working class. Many non-Marxist sociologists would regard this outcome as a possibility but a very unlikely one. They would tend to agree with Kenneth Roberts' summary of the situation, 'Given the continuing blue-collar predicament, being paid visibly and considerably less than managers and professional people, the flat career pattern and limited access to housing and related life chances outside the work situation, there is going to remain a working class that can never be organized into total acquiescence. For society at large, therefore, the working class remains an unstable and continuing challenge but not a revolutionary threat'.

The middle class in capitalist society

During this century, one of the most significant changes in the occupational structure of advanced industrial societies has been the growth of the white-collar sector. This includes clerical, technical and scientific, administrative, managerial and professional occupations. In Britain in 1975, 37·4% of the male labour force was employed in non-manual jobs. Many sociologists argue that this large and expanding white-collar group has formed a middle class which lies between the manual working class and the upper class. Critics of Marx have argued that this development has largely invalidated his theory. They claim that it no longer makes sense to see society as divided into two opposing classes. Rather than a polarization of classes, the middle class is seen to bridge the gap between capital and manual labour. A later section will consider whether or not the middle class can be accommodated in terms of Marxian theory but first various groups within the middle class will be examined.

The lower middle class – routine white-collar workers

Clerical workers and sales staff compose the main occupational groups in the lower middle class. By the early 1970s in Britain, this group accounted for about 33% of the male white-collar labour force. Sociological research has concentrated on low-grade clerical workers – clerks who are employed to deal with routine administrative tasks. This occupational group has grown steadily. In 1851 clerks formed less than 1% of the labour force, by 1901, 4%, by 1951 over 10% and by 1971, 14%. It has been argued that this growth is due to the increase in size and complexity of industrial and commercial enterprises and the expansion of local and national government, particularly in such areas as education, social welfare and public administration. These developments involve a complex administrative structure which requires large numbers of clerical staff.

In a study entitled *The Blackcoated Worker*, published in 1958, David Lockwood makes the following observations on the class position of the clerk. Since the mid 1930s the market situation of the clerk has deteriorated relative to manual workers. From 1900 until the mid 1930s clerks' earnings were similar to those of skilled manual workers but they have since dropped below the skilled manual average. Table 3 illustrates this process.

In other respects, though, the clerk has certain market advantages compared to manual workers. His job is more secure and he is less likely to be laid off or made redundant. He works shorter hours and is likely to have longer holidays. His fringe benefits, such as company pension schemes and sickness pay, are superior to those of many manual workers. Finally, he has a greater chance of rising to supervisory and managerial positions. However, recent evidence suggests that the clerk's opportunities for promotion have become increasingly slim.

Lockwood suggests that the increasing similarity of clerical and manual

Table 3   Earnings of male clerks in relation to manual workers' earnings from 1913/14 to 1960 and 1971

Occupational group (men only)	Indices of earnings – occupational group average expressed as a percentage of average for all male manual workers in the same period					
	1913/14	1922/4	1935/6	1955/6	1960	1971
Clerks	122	122	122	99	102	96
Skilled manual workers	122	121	124	118	119	106
Semi-skilled manual workers	85	85	83	89	87	99
Unskilled manual workers	78	86	82	83	80	87
All manual workers	100	100	100	100	100	100

(Note: No direct comparison can be made between the 1971 figures and the earlier ones since different methods of assessment are used).

(Source: Westergaard and Resler, *Class in a Capitalist Society*, 1976, p. 76, reprinted by permission of Penguin Books Ltd)

earnings is due to a rise in manual earnings resulting in part from a growth in overtime and bonus payments. Other researchers have given the following reasons for the deterioration in the clerk's market situation. The improvement in educational standards which has resulted in near universal literacy and basic numeracy has reduced the scarcity of skills required for clerical work. The supply of potential clerks has grown rapidly with the increasing numbers of women demanding entry into the labour market. Clerical work is regarded as suitable for women and they accounted for 60% of clerks in 1951. The potential supply of clerks has been further increased by a de-skilling of many clerical jobs, a process which will be examined shortly. Despite a steady growth in the demand for clerks, these factors may well have led to the supply exceeding the demand which has resulted in a depression of earnings. Finally, it has been argued that the reduction of promotion opportunities is due to the fact that academic qualifications, rather than long-service and experience, are increasingly demanded for recruitment to managerial positions. Many routine clerks left school at the minimum-leaving age and lack the necessary qualifications.

In response to a decline in earnings and promotion prospects, more and more clerks have turned to trade unions to improve their market situation. This is typical working-class strategy, but Lockwood argues that it does not necessarily mean that clerks are becoming more closely associated with manual workers. He observes that clerical unions have tended to maintain a separate identity rather than seeing themselves as part of the trade union movement and the labour movement as a whole. Kenneth Roberts makes a similar point arguing that rather than joining the working class to fight for a common cause, clerical unions are concerned with staying ahead of them. The view that manual unions are involved in a struggle to represent the interests of the working class as a whole must not be exaggerated, however. As the Luton study indicated, as far as the motives of the members were concerned, instrumental collectivism appears common to both clerks and manual workers.

Lockwood argues that the status situation of the clerk has become increasingly ambiguous. In terms of housing and living standards, the relative decline in his income has made it difficult for him to distinguish himself from manual workers. In addition, changes in the clerk's work situation have brought him closer to manual workers. In the past, clerks tended to work closely with management in small offices and this personal contact with higher authority produced 'reflected prestige'. In the large modern office there is less personal contact and management and clerical grades are increasingly separated. Clerical work itself has become more similar to factory work. It is routine, repetitive and fragmented into small, relatively simple operations. Each worker specializes in one operation, for example filing or checking invoices. This process has been accompanied by increased supervision, organization and coordination of the clerk's work by management staff. In terms of the nature of his work tasks and subordination to authority, the clerk is coming closer to manual workers. Lockwood argues that the clerk's 'original claim to middle-class status has been slowly undermined during the rise of the modern office'. Yet compared with manual workers, clerks still cooperate more closely with management and office staff are physically separated from the factory floor. These factors discourage clerks from identifying with manual workers.

The ambiguity of the clerk's status and class situations are reflected in his class identification and political attitudes. Various surveys conducted in the 1950s indicate that about 25% of clerks defined themselves as working class. Later evidence suggests this proportion has increased, due possibly to the fact that a growing number of clerks are recruited from manual backgrounds. Compared to other sections of the middle class, clerks are more likely to support the Labour Party. Surveys have indicated that at various times between 30 and 50% of clerks vote Labour. In terms of these factors it is difficult to place the clerk squarely in the middle class.

Lockwood concludes that, 'Strictly speaking the clerk belongs neither to the middle class nor the working class'. In view of his market, work and status situations, the position of the clerk is ambiguous. The majority of clerks regard themselves as middle class and do not identify with manual workers. Lockwood rejects the Marxian view that this is simply an indication of false class consciousness. Many Marxists would argue that the clerk is a member of the proletariat since he does not own the forces of production, is propertyless, and therefore obliged to sell his labour power in order to make a livelihood. Lockwood, however, maintains that the clerk's middle-class identification cannot be dismissed as false consciousness since it reflects real differences between the situations of clerical and manual workers.

A number of sociologists have suggested that clerks and routine white-collar workers in general are undergoing a process of proletarianization. They are becoming, for all intents and purposes, working class. Certainly in terms of earnings, this process has already occurred. Westergaard and Resler, who support the proletarianization thesis, note that with respect to earnings, 'male clerks and shopworkers are now firmly among the broad mass of ordinary labour; and indeed often well down towards the bottom of the pile'. They argue that it makes little sense to label routine white-collar workers as middle class. Indeed, they suggest that the bulk of the working population, despite changes in the occupational structure, remain basically working class. Westergaard and Resler claim that 'If routine non-manual work is bracketed with manual work with which it now has so many conditions in common, at least three in every four men and five in every six women are in jobs of an essentially wage-earning character. There is little in this to support the notion that the occupational structure has been fundamentally recast in a "middle class" mould'.

The professions in the class structure

In recent years, the professions have been the fastest growing section of the occupational structure. In the USA, the proportion of professionals in the male labour force increased threefold between 1950 and 1970. By 1970, they accounted for 15% of the US labour force, though the proportion is smaller in other Western societies. The following reasons have been given for the rapid growth of the professions. The increasing complexity of trade and commerce demands financial and legal experts such as accountants and lawyers. The growth of industry requires increasingly specialized scientific and technical knowledge which results in the development of professions such as science and engineering. The creation of the welfare state and the expansion of local and national government has produced a range of 'welfare professions', and has resulted in the growth of the medical and teaching professions and the increasing employment of professionals in government bureaucracies. Professionals have been seen both as producers and products of industrialization. Their skills and knowledge are regarded as essential for the development and expansion of industrial economies. In turn, the wealth produced by this development has provided the means to pay for the specialized services which the professionals supply.

In terms of their market situation, the professionals can be divided into two groups, the higher and lower professionals. The higher professionals include judges, barristers, solicitors, architects, planners, doctors, dentists, university lecturers, accountants, scientists and engineers. The lower professionals include school teachers, nurses, social workers and librarians. As table 4 indicates, there are significant differences in earnings between the two groups.

Table 4　Relative earnings of main occupational groups from 1913/14 to 1960: male earners only

Occupational group (men only)	Indices of earnings – occupational group average expressed as a percentage of average for all men in the same period				
	1913/14	1922/24	1935/36	1955/56	1960
Higher professionals	357	326	341	244	253
Managers and administrators	217	269	237	234	230
Lower professionals	169	179	165	97	105
Foremen	123	150	147	124	126
Clerks	108	102	103	82	85
Skilled manual workers	108	101	105	98	99
Semi-skilled manual workers	75	70	72	74	72
Unskilled manual workers	69	72	70	69	67
All non-manual workers	142	158	152	144	145
All manual workers	88	83	85	83	82
All men	100	100	100	100	100

(Source: Westergaard and Resler, *Class in a Capitalist Society*, 1976, p. 74 reprinted by permission of Penguin Books Ltd)

Measured in terms of earnings, the market situation of lower professionals is not substantially superior to that of skilled manual workers. However, compared to skilled manual workers, lower professionals have a number of market advantages which include greater security of employment, wider promotion opportunities, annual salary increments and more valuable fringe benefits.

Various explanations have been advanced to account for the occupational rewards of professionals. These explanations are influenced by the sociologist's theoretical perspective and his evaluation of the services provided by professionals. Bernard Barber offers a functionalist view of the role and rewards of higher professionals. He argues that professionalism involves 'four essential attributes'. Firstly, a body of systematic and generalized knowledge which can be applied to a variety of problems. Thus doctors have a body of medical knowledge which they apply to diagnose and treat a range of illnesses. Secondly, professionalism involves a concern for the interests of the community rather than self-interest. Thus the primary motivation of professionals is public service rather than personal gain. For example, doctors are concerned primarily with the health of their patients rather than with lining their own pockets. Thirdly, the behaviour of professionals is strictly controlled by a code of ethics which is established and maintained by professional associations and learned as part of the training required to qualify as a professional. Thus doctors take the Hippocratic oath which lays down the obligations and proper conduct of their profession. Should they break this code of conduct, their association can strike them from the register and ban them from practising medicine. Finally, the high rewards received by professionals, which includes the prestige accorded to professional status as well as earnings, are symbols of their achievements. They denote the high regard in which professionals are held and reflect the value of their contribution to society.

Barber argues that the knowledge and skills of professionals provide them with considerable power and it is therefore essential for the well-being of society that this power be used for the benefit of all. He accepts the view that professionals are primarily concerned with service to the community and believes they use their expertise for public benefit. He claims that professionals make important contributions to the functional well-being of society and in addition, their services are highly regarded in terms of society's values. As a result, professionals are highly rewarded.

Functionalist explanations of the role and rewards of professionals have been strongly criticized. They make the following assumptions, all of which are questionable. Firstly, professionals make important contributions to the well-being of society as a whole. Secondly, they serve all members of society rather than particular groups. Thirdly, they are concerned with service to the community rather than with self-interest. These assumptions will now be questioned.

In recent years, there has been increasing criticism of the view that professionals provide valuable services to society. Architects have been denounced for building houses and flats which are unfit to live in; planners have been condemned for producing urban chaos; teachers have been attacked for crushing originality and stifling creativity in their pupils; and lawyers have been accused of mystifying the legal system to the point where the layman finds it largely unintelligible. In *Medical Nemesis*, a savage attack on the medical profession, Ivan Illich provides an example of this type of criticism. He claims that, 'The medical establishment has become a major threat to health'. Contrary to the view promoted by the medical profession, Illich argues that the environment, in particular food, working conditions, housing and hygiene, rather than medical provision, is the main determinant of the health of a population. He notes that the incidence of diseases such as tuberculosis, cholera, dysentery, typhoid and scarlet fever declined rapidly long before medical control. He attributes this decline to changes in the environment rather than to antibiotics and widespread immunization. In the same way, Illich argues that much of the illness in contemporary society is due to the environment. He claims that industrial society is characterized by boring and monotonous work, lack of freedom for the individual to control his own life and a compulsion to acquire material possessions, directed by the mistaken belief that they bring happiness and fulfilment. These 'ills' of industrial society are responsible for much of the illness experienced by its members. In claiming to diagnose and treat this illness doctors can do more harm than good. In Illich's view, such treatment 'is but a device to convince those who are sick and tired of society that it is they who are ill, impotent and in need of repair'. By claiming exclusive rights to the diagnosis of illness, doctors obscure its real source. By treating the individual rather than the environment, doctors not only do little to prevent illness but also direct attention away from measures which could prove more effective. Space prevents a full summary of Illich's closely reasoned attack on the medical profession but his views suggest that the functionalist argument that the higher professionals confer positive benefits on society is at least questionable. (See Chapter 5 for Illich's criticisms of the teaching profession pp. 187–9.)

The functionalist view that the professions serve society as a whole rather than sectional interests has also been called into question. It has been argued that the higher professions primarily serve the interests of the wealthy and powerful. Thus accountants and lawyers are employed in the service of capital, architects build for the wealthy and doctors and psychiatrists in private practice care for their physical and mental needs. The American sociologist C. Wright Mills makes the following observations on the law profession in the USA. Rather than being guardians of the law for the benefit of all, lawyers have increasingly become the servants of the large corporation. They are busily employed 'teaching the financiers how to do what they want within the law, advising on the chances they are taking and how to best cover themselves'. Lawyers draw up contracts, minimize taxation, advise on business deals and liase between banks, commercial and industrial enterprises. In the service of the corporation, the 'leading lawyer is selected for skill in the sure fix and the easy out-of-court settlement'. The lucrative business open to members of the legal profession means that members of low-income groups are largely unable to afford their services. Mills suggests that the rewards of the professions are directly related to the demand for their services by the rich and powerful. Since lawyers increasingly serve 'a thin upper crust and financial interests' they are highly rewarded. This view sees professionals as employed largely in the service of sectional interests. It rejects the functionalist argument that the rewards of professionals are related to the functional importance of their role for society as a whole.

The functionalist claim that the professions are concerned with public service rather than personal gain has also been called into question. Rather than attempting to define professionals in terms of the nature of their work, a number of sociologists have argued that professionalism is simply a strategy employed by particular occupational groups to improve their market situation. Thus Noel and José Parry define professionalism as 'a strategy for controlling an occupation in which colleagues set up a system of self-government'. The occupation is controlled primarily in the interests of its members. From this perspective, professionalism involves the following factors. Firstly, restriction of entry into the occupation, which is provided by the profession's control of the training and qualifications required for membership and of the numbers deemed necessary to provide an adequate service. By controlling supply, professionals can maintain a high demand for their services and so gain high rewards. Secondly, professionalism involves an association which controls the conduct of its members, 'in respects which are defined as relevant to the collective interests of the profession'. In particular, professional associations are concerned with promoting the view that professional conduct is above reproach and that professionals are committed to public service. This serves to justify high occupational rewards. By claiming the right to discipline their own members, professional associations largely prevent public scrutiny of their affairs and so maintain the image which they project of themselves. Thirdly, professionalism involves a successful claim that only members are qualified to provide particular services. This claim is often reinforced by the law. Thus in Britain, a series of laws have guaranteed solicitors a monopoly on particular services. These monopolies are jealously guarded. For example, the Law Society has prosecuted unqualified individuals for performing services which are defined as a legal monopoly of the law profession. In this way professions can control rival occupational groups which might threaten their dominance of a section of the market. Parry and Parry conclude that by adopting the strategy of professionalism, certain occupational groups are able to extract high rewards from the market.

Viewing professionalism as a market strategy provides an explanation for the differing rewards of various so-called professions. Some of the occupational groups which claim professional status lack many of the attributes of professionalism. In terms of Parry and Parry's definition, they are professions in name only. They have little control over their market situation and as a result receive lower rewards than occupational groups which are more fully professionalized. Parry and Parry illustrate this point by a comparison of doctors and teachers. They claim that doctors receive higher rewards than teachers because they are more fully professionalized. This is due largely to the fact that doctors were able to organize themselves into a professional group before the state intervened in medicine and became a major employer of medical practitioners. The British Medical Association was founded in 1832 and the Medical Registration Act of 1858 granted doctors a monopoly on the practice of medicine and gave them important powers of self-government. Once established as a professional body, doctors had considerable control over their market situation. Teachers, however, failed to achieve professionalism before state intervention in education. Since the state was largely responsible for initiating and paying for mass education, it was able to establish greater control over teachers. In particular, the state controlled both the supply of teachers and standards for entry into the occupation. Since they lack the market control which professionalism provides, teachers have turned to trade unionism to improve their market situation. Parry and Parry conclude that the differences in occupational reward between doctors and teachers are attributable to the degree of professionalization of the two groups.

A fragmented middle class

The previous sections have examined two of the main groups within the middle class: routine white-collar workers and professionals. This section will briefly examine other white-collar occupational groups. It will also question the proposition that non-manual occupations may be grouped together and seen to form a relatively cohesive middle class.

Since the nineteenth century, there has been a steady decline in the numbers of the petty bourgeoisie, the owners of small businesses. In Britain the proportion of 'employers and proprietors' declined from 5% of the total working population in 1951 to 2·6% in 1971. Most of this decline is due to a reduction in the number of small businesses. This development has been seen as a result of competition from large businesses and government fiscal measures, particularly in the area of taxation, which have imposed heavy financial burdens on the small business.

Related to the decline of the small business is the rise of the salaried manager. In Britain, from 1951 to 1971, the proportion of 'managers and administrators' increased from 5·5% to 8·6% of the working population. In the early years of industrialization, the roles of manager and owner were usually combined. The owner of the company was directly involved in the day-to-day running of his business. Since the second half of the nineteenth century, the joint stock company has become the typical form of capitalist enterprise. Individual ownership has been replaced by joint ownership which involves a relatively large number of people owning stocks or shares in the company. Shareholders are not directly involved in the day-to-day running of the company which has been taken over by salaried managers. This process is sometimes referred to as the separation of ownership and control. It has been argued that joint stock companies are largely controlled by salaried managers rather than owners. However, it is important not to exaggerate this separation as the following chapter will indicate. (See pp. 122–3.)

The development of the joint stock company has been accompanied by an increase in the size and complexity of industrial and commercial firms. It has been argued that a large management hierarchy is essential to plan, organize, coordinate and control the multitude of complex and specialized tasks involved in a modern corporation. A similar argument has been advanced for the rapid growth in the numbers of administrators employed in local and national government. The expansion of public administration in areas such as taxation, education, health and social services has resulted in the growth of large organizations. It has been argued that the administrator in government bureaucracies performs a similar function to the manager in the large business corporation. As previous sections have indicated, both managers and administrators, in terms of their earnings and fringe benefits, are highly placed in the middle class. (See table 2, p. 52 and table 4, p. 70.)

In view of the diverse occupational groups within the middle class, a number of observers have questioned the idea that white-collar workers do indeed form a single class. With respect to earnings and fringe benefits, inequalities within the middle class are significantly greater than those within the manual working class. In addition, the market strategies of white-collar groups vary considerably: routine white-collar workers and lower professionals rely increasingly on trade unions; higher professionals adopt a strategy of professionalism; top managers often negotiate salaries directly with their employers; while the petty bourgeoisie depend on the sale of the goods and services which their businesses offer. Whether these groups share similar interests in the market is debatable. Some awareness of common white-collar interests may be indicated by the fact that the majority of non-manual workers in Britain vote Conservative. Yet whether this can be seen as an awareness of common class interests is questionable, as the following chapter will show. Some indication of a common class identification may be drawn from the fact that the majority of white collar workers define themselves as middle-class. However, this classification means different things to different people, a point which will now be examined.

From a study of images of class, Roberts, Cook, Clark and Semeonoff claim that, 'The days when it was realistic to talk about *the* middle class are gone'. They argue that the middle class is increasingly divided into a number of different strata, each with a distinctive view of its place in the stratification system. Roberts *et al* base these observations on a survey, conducted in 1972, of the class images of a sample of 243 male white-collar workers. They found a number of different images of class, the four most common of which will now be briefly described. Some 27% of the white-collar sample had a 'middle mass' image of society. They saw themselves as part of a middle class made up of the bulk of the working population. This middle mass lay between a small, rich and powerful upper class and a small, relatively impoverished, lower class. No division was drawn between most manual and non-manual workers and within the large central class, 'no basic ideological cleavages, divisions of interest or contrasts in life-styles' were recognized. Those who held a middle mass image of society were likely to be in the middle range income bracket for white-collar workers.

The second most common image, held by 19% of the sample, was that of a 'compressed middle class'. Those who subscribed to this view saw themselves as members of a narrow stratum which was squeezed between two increasingly powerful classes. Below them, the bulk of the population formed a working class and above them was a small upper class. Small businessmen typically held this compressed middle-class image. They felt threatened by what they saw as an increasingly powerful and organized working class and by government and big business which showed little inclination to support them.

A third group of white-collar workers saw society in terms of a finely graded ladder containing four or more strata. Although this is assumed to be the typical middle-class image of society, it was subscribed to by only 15% of the sample. Those who saw society in these terms tended to be well educated with professional qualifications and relatively highly paid. Though they described themselves as middle-class, they indicated no apparent class loyalty and often rejected the whole principle of social class.

Finally, 14% of the white-collar sample held a 'proletarian' image of society. They defined themselves as working class and located themselves in what they saw as the largest class at the base of the stratification system. They saw themselves as having more in common with manual workers than with top management and higher professionals. Those who held a proletarian image were usually employed in routine white-collar occupations with few promotion prospects and relatively low wages.

The wide variation in white-collar class imagery leads Roberts *et al* to conclude that, 'The trends are towards fragmenting the middle class into a number of distinguishable strata, each with its own view of its place in the social structure'. The diversity of class images, market situations, market strategies and interests within the white-collar group suggests that the middle class is becoming increasingly fragmented. Indeed, the proposition that white-collar groups form a single social class is debatable.

Class and capitalism – a Marxian perspective

This section examines Marxian views on the nature of class in contemporary capitalist society. As previous sections have indicated, the class system appears very different from Marx's predictions. Critics of Marx argue that there is no evidence of a polarization of classes. Indeed they suggest that just the opposite has occurred. A large and growing middle class has emerged between the traditional proletariat and bourgeoisie. Rather than a polarization of classes, there is a continuum of inequality, with, at best, blurred dividing lines between strata.

John Westergaard and Henrietta Resler

In a comprehensive study of class in modern Britain, Westergaard and Resler maintain that the nature of class in contemporary capitalist society can best be explained in terms of a Marxian framework. They argue that the private ownership of capital provides the key to explaining class divisions. They see little change in the structure of inequality during this century and claim that, 'Property, profit and the market – the key institutions of a capitalist society – retain their central place in social arrangements and remain the prime determinants of inequality'. In detail the class system is complex but in essence it is simple. The major division is still between capital and labour. Sociologists who focus on the details of class, for example the differences between manual and routine white-collar workers, merely obscure the overall simplicity of the system. Such differences are insignificant compared to the wide gulf which separates the capitalists from the bulk of the wage and salary earning population.

To support their argument, Westergaard and Resler point to the concentration of wealth in the hands of a small minority. They argue that, 'Possession of property – of capital in the means of production in particular – remains the crucial source of wealth, and the most potent cause of inequality of income'. Table 5 shows trends in the distribution of private property. Figures for 1911 to 1960 and those for 1961 and 1971 are calculated on a different basis and so cannot be directly compared. The former probably overstate the concentration of property, the latter are probably an understatement.

Table 5 The distribution of private property, from 1911 to 1960 and for 1961 and 1971

Groups within adult population (aged 25+) owning stated proportions of aggregate personal wealth	Estimated proportion of aggregate personal wealth						
	Period 1911–1960 (common basis)					Period 1961–1971 (common basis)	
	1911/13 %	1924/30 %	1936/38 %	1954 %	1960 %	1961 %	1971 %
Richest 1% owned	69	62	56	43	42	32	26
Richest 5% owned	87	84	79	71	75	55	47
Richest 10% owned	92	91	88	79	83	*	*
Hence:							
Richest 1% owned	69	62	56	43	42	32	26
Next 2–5% owned	18	22	23	28	33	23	21
Next 6–10% owned	5	7	9	8	8	*	*
95% owned only	13	16	21	29	25	45	53
90% owned only	8	9	12	21	17	*	*

(Source: Westergaard and Resler, 1976, p. 112, *ibid*)

Westergaard and Resler state, 'The retention of a massive share in all wealth by the top 5 or 10 per cent of the population is very striking'. The most significant shift in property ownership is within the richest 10%. Westergaard and Resler argue that redistribution within this wealthy group is largely the result of an attempt by the most wealthy to escape death duties by transferring property to relatives and friends. They see any increase in the share of property of those outside the most wealthy 10% as due mainly to the spread of home ownership. However, the ownership of capital in private industry remains concentrated in the hands of a small minority. In 1970, only about 7% of all adults aged twenty-five and over owned shares in private companies. The majority of shareholders are 'small-holders' – over half own less than £1 000 of stock. Reviewing the distribution of private property over the past sixty years, Westergaard and Resler conclude that, 'There is nothing here to affect property ownership in its crucial form: ownership of the means of production'.

Westergaard and Resler argue that private ownership of capital is the major determinant of inequalities in income. The role of the state and the labour market are secondary, and in any case are largely influenced by the power of capital. Via taxation and welfare provision, the state has done little to redistribute income. The benefits gained from the Welfare State by the working class are largely paid for by taxes from its members. What at first sight the wealthy appear to lose from taxation, they largely regain in tax concessions on private insurance policies, payments to company pension schemes, mortgages and the like. Income differences which arise from the operation of the labour market are relatively small compared to those which result from the ownership and non-ownership of the forces of production. Table 6 shows trends in income distribution. Data on income are usually derived from tax returns, which provide only a very rough estimate and tend to understate high incomes. For example, they do not include various fringe benefits, nor of course do they account for income gained from tax evasion which Westergaard and Resler guess is substantial. Westergaard and Resler have therefore adjusted the figures provided by the Inland Revenue to include various sources of 'hidden' income.

In terms of the adjusted figures, the richest 1% received as much income as the poorest 30%, the richest 5% as much as the poorest 50%. There was a trend towards greater income equality from 1938 to 1949, which slowed from 1949 to 1954 and then virtually ceased. Westergaard and Resler conclude that, 'There are no indications of an inherent and continuing trend towards substantial redistribution of income within the capitalist economy of Britain'.

Westergaard and Resler argue that the maintenance of inequalities of wealth and income is due to the power of the capitalist class. They see evidence of this power from the fact that the dominance of capital is not

Table 6   Share of top income recipients in personal income after direct taxes, from 1938 to 1959/60, before and after adjustment for certain omissions

Groups of 'income units'	Estimated percentage share of total value of all personal income received by the richest 1% (5%, 10%) of all 'income units'				
	1938 %	1949 %	1954 %	1957 %	1959/60 %
Before adjustment					
The richest 1% received	11½	6½	5½	5	5
After adjustment					
The richest 1% received	15	10½	9½	9	10
The richest 5% received	*	*	*	*	20½
The richest 10% received	*	*	*	*	30

(Source: Westergaard and Resler, 1976, p. 42, *ibid*)

exposed to 'serious challenge'. They maintain that, 'The favoured group enjoys effective power, even when its members take no active steps to exercise power. They do not need to do so – for much of the time at least – simply because things work that way in any case'. The free market economy of capitalism ensures that the owners of the forces of production receive a disproportionate share of income. It is generally taken for granted, by members of society and governments alike, that investments should bring profit and that the living standards of the propertyless should be based on the demands of the market for their skills. In general, governments have favoured the interests of capital, assuming that the well-being of the nation is largely dependent on the prosperity of private industry. The relationship between the state and capital will be examined in detail in the following chapter.

Westergaard and Resler claim that the class divisions in British society are systematically generated by a capitalist economic system. They identify two major classes. The dominant class is made up of perhaps 5% and at most 10% of the population. It includes the major owners of the forces of production, company directors, top managers, higher professionals and senior civil servants, many of whom are large shareholders in private industry. The subordinate class consists of the bulk of the wage and salary earning population. Westergaard and Resler reject the view that the so-called separation of ownership and control in the joint stock company results in the rise of salaried managers who should properly be placed in a middle class. They argue that 'directors and top executives, in whose hands the major strategic policy decisions lie, are, in fact, owners of large stockholdings themselves'. Like the 'absentee owners', their main concern is the maximization of profit. As such the interests of owners and controllers are largely similar.

The general profile of inequality drawn by Westergaard and Resler is supported by a large body of evidence but their explanation for this inequality is open to a number of criticisms. They insist that private property is the basic determinant of class inequality. However, as Frank Parkin notes, this leaves unexplained the privileged position of top professionals and higher civil servants, many of whom are propertyless. What, asks Parkin, is the significance of private property in determining the high rewards of doctors and the low rewards of nurses, the large salaries of higher civil servants and the relatively small salaries of lower civil servants? Westergaard and Resler do not provide an answer. The view that private property is the primary determinant of the distribution of rewards in capitalist society may be questioned by evidence from socialist societies where the forces of production are communally owned. As a later section will indicate, there are marked social inequalities in East European communist societies. (See pp. 91–95.) Westergaard and Resler fail to show that inequality in capitalist societies is generated by mechanisms which are distinct from those which operate in socialist societies. This throws some doubt on their claim that the key to the class system in capitalist society is the private ownership of the forces of production.

Harry Braverman

In *Labor and Monopoly Capital*, the American Marxist Harry Braverman examines the changing nature of class in the USA over the past 100 years. He argues that classes are 'not fixed entities but rather ongoing processes, rich in change, transition, variation'. From this point of view, classes in capitalist society are constantly developing and it therefore makes little sense to attempt to place the population into neatly defined strata at one point in time. Instead the process of class formation must be examined. Braverman argues that this process is largely directed by changes in the nature of work in capitalist society. Capitalism involves the maximization of profit which results in the accumulation of capital. In pursuit of this end, the labour process has been transformed over the past 100 years. This transformation has important consequences for the formation of classes.

The relations of production in capitalist society are those of dominance and subordinacy. Workers are subject to the authority of employers and their work is controlled from above. Braverman sees this as the hallmark of the proletarian condition and from this viewpoint claims that there has been a progressive proletarianization of the workforce in the USA. He maintains that the bourgeoisie, in which he includes top management, has steadily tightened its control over the workers. As a result, the gulf between the bourgeoisie and proletariat is widening rather than narrowing. Braverman gives the following reasons for this process. Skill, initiative and control are steadily removed from work with the development of mechanized and automated production. These qualities and powers are now built into the machine. In a detailed analysis of manual work, Braverman rejects the view held by many sociologists that the skill requirements of manufacturing industry have increased during this century. In addition, the labour process has been increasingly 'rationalized' in capitalist society. Tasks are broken down into simple operations and directed and organized from above. As a result, the worker controls less and less of the work process which now requires more and more coordination from management. Again skill and initiative are steadily removed from work. This development applies not only to manufacturing industry, but to work in general. The net results of these changes are a de-skilling of the labour force, a reduction of its control over the work process and in particular, a cheapening of labour power. The costs of labour are reduced because the de-skilled worker can be easily replaced and he no longer has the bargaining power which scarce skills provide. Control over the workforce is therefore strengthened and in terms of the relationship of dominance and subordinacy, the gulf between the classes grows wider.

This development has been accompanied by the transformation of the bulk of the population into employees of capital. In the USA of today the vast majority of the workforce is either directly employed by private industry or by the state, which Braverman regards as an agent of capital. The self-employed craftsman, the farmer who owns his own smallholding and the independent professional in private practice are steadily disappearing and entering the ranks of wage earning and salaried employees. The goods and services required for subsistence are increasingly supplied by capitalist enterprises, and the population is less and less able to supply its own needs outside the capitalist market. As a result, the worker must sell his labour power in order to subsist and therefore becomes increasingly dependent upon capital and forced to submit to its control.

Braverman now examines the consequences of these developments for the process of class formation. First he argues that some 70% of the labour force in the USA now fits squarely into the proletariat. These workers are forced to sell their labour power in order to subsist. Their work has undergone a process of degradation which involves the removal of skill, responsibility and control and the work process is dominated by the employer and management. Labour power has been cheapened by de-skilling which results in members of the proletariat receiving low returns for their labour. For example clerical workers in the USA were paid twice as much as the average manual wage in 1870 whereas by 1971 their wages were below those of all grades of manual workers. Braverman claims that this is due in large part to the rationalization and subsequent de-skilling of office work. At present, the proletariat proper consists of manual workers, clerks, those employed in the lower levels of retail sales work and service occupations which mainly involve cleaning and building care and kitchen work and food service.

Between the bourgeoisie and the proletariat is an intermediate group made up of between 15 and 20% of the labour force. This group consists of the lower levels of management, marketing and financial specialists, engineers, technicians and scientists and state employees such as teachers and administrators. Since they are sellers of labour power, this group could be seen as part of the proletariat which Braverman defines as 'that class which, possessing nothing but its power to labour, sells that power in return for its subsistence'. However, Braverman notes that in certain respects, the intermediate group does not conform to the proletarian condition. Firstly the economic returns of its members are significantly greater than those of the working class. Secondly, although they are subject to the authority and control of top management, they themselves exercise authority, albeit delegated from above, over lower ranks of workers. As a result the intermediate stratum shares characteristics of both proletariat and bourgeoisie – it receives 'its petty share in the prerogatives and rewards of capital, but it also bears the mark of the proletarian condition'. Whether it will be fully submerged into the proletariat, only time will tell. Braverman regards this as a distinct possibility, arguing that the same processes which resulted in the proletarianization of clerks may eventually lead to the proletarianization of the intermediate stratum.

Braverman has argued that the class system in the USA has been shaped by the principal driving force of capitalism, the accumulation of capital. The labour process has been transformed by the drive for greater productivity, greater control, cheaper labour power and therefore higher profit. These developments have largely shaped the process of class formation. Yet it could be argued that similar processes are occurring in socialist societies. Braverman admits that the nature and organization of work in the Soviet bloc countries share many similarities with work in capitalist society. However, he argues that this is simply because these countries have imitated the capitalist model in their drive to increase productivity. This model is a product of capitalism not of socialism. Braverman hopes that it represents a transitional stage in the development of communist societies and that socialist principles will eventually lead to a change in the nature of the labour process.

Social mobility in capitalist society

This section examines the nature of social mobility in capitalist society. It is generally agreed that the rate of social mobility – the amount of movement from one stratum to another – is significantly higher in industrial as compared to pre-industrial societies. Industrial societies are therefore described as 'open', as having a relatively low degree of 'closure'. In particular, it is argued that status in pre-industrial societies is largely ascribed whereas in industrial societies, it is increasingly achieved. As a result, ascribed characteristics such as class of origin, sex, race and kinship relationships have less and less influence on an individual's social status. Status is seen to be increasingly achieved on the basis of merit. Thus talent, ability, ambition and hard work are steadily replacing ascribed characteristics as the criteria for determining a person's position in the class system. Indeed, a number of sociologists have suggested that this mechanism of social selection is built into the values of industrial society. Thus Talcott Parsons argues that achievement is one of the major values of American society. Individuals are judged and accorded prestige in terms of their occupational status which is seen to be largely achieved by their own effort and ability.

Sociologists are interested in social mobility for a number of reasons. Firstly, the rate of social mobility may have an important effect on class formation. For example, Anthony Giddens suggests that if the rate of social mobility is low, class solidarity and cohesion will be high. Most individuals will remain in their class of origin and this will 'provide for the reproduction of common life experiences over generations'. As a result distinctive class subcultures and strong class identifications will tend to develop. Secondly, a study of social mobility can provide an indication of the life chances of members of society. For example, it can show the degree to which a person's class of origin influences his chances of obtaining a high status occupation. Thirdly, it is important to know how people respond to the experience of social mobility. For example, do the downwardly mobile resent their misfortune and form a pool of dissatisfaction which might threaten the stability of society? Before considering these issues, it is necessary to examine the nature and extent of social mobility in capitalist society.

Sociologists have identified two main types of social mobility. The first, intragenerational mobility, refers to social mobility within a single generation. It is measured by comparing the occupational status of an individual at two or more points in time. Thus, if a person begins his working life as an unskilled manual worker and ten years later is employed as an accountant, he is socially mobile in terms of intragenerational mobility. The second type, intergenerational mobility, refers to social mobility between generations. It is measured by comparing the occupational status of sons with that of their fathers. Thus, if the son of an unskilled manual worker becomes an accountant, he is socially mobile in terms of intergenerational mobility. This section will focus on intergenerational mobility, the type of social mobility most frequently studied by sociologists.

There are many problems associated with the study of social mobility. Occupation is used as an indicator of social class and researchers use different criteria for ranking occupations. Many researchers classify occupations in terms of the prestige associated with them, others place more emphasis on the economic rewards attached to them. As a result, occupational classifications differ and the results of various studies are not strictly comparable. A further problem arises from the fact that it is not possible to identify many members of the bourgeoisie on the basis of their occupations. A person's occupation does not necessarily say anything about the extent of his investments in private industry. In view of these problems, the findings of social mobility studies must be regarded with caution.

The first major study of intergenerational mobility in England and Wales was conducted by David Glass and his associates in 1949. The main findings of this study are summarized in table 7.

Table 7

		Sons' status category in 1949							
		1	2	3	4	5	6	7	Total
Fathers' status category	1	**38.8** / **48.5**	14.6 / 11.9	20.2 / 7.9	6.2 / 1.7	14.0 / 1.3	4.7 / 1.0	1.5 / 0.5	100.0 / (129)
	2	10.7 / 15.5	**26.7** / **25.2**	22.7 / 10.3	12.0 / 3.9	20.6 / 2.2	5.3 / 1.4	2.0 / 0.7	100.0 / (150)
	3	3.5 / 11.7	10.1 / 22.0	**18.8** / **19.7**	19.1 / 14.4	35.7 / 8.6	6.7 / 3.9	6.1 / 5.0	100.0 / (345)
	4	2.1 / 10.7	3.9 / 12.6	11.2 / 17.6	**21.2** / **24.0**	43.0 / 15.6	12.4 / 10.8	6.2 / 7.5	100.0 / (518)
	5	0.9 / 13.6	2.4 / 22.6	7.5 / 34.5	12.3 / 40.3	**47.3** / **50.0**	17.1 / 43.5	12.5 / 44.6	100.0 / (1 510)
	6	0.0 / 0.0	1.3 / 3.8	4.1 / 5.8	8.8 / 8.7	39.1 / 12.5	**31.2** / **24.1**	15.5 / 16.7	100.0 / (458)
	7	0.0 / 0.0	0.8 / 1.9	3.6 / 4.2	8.3 / 7.0	36.4 / 9.8	23.5 / 15.3	**27.4** / **25.0**	100.0 / (387)
	Total	100.0 / (103)	100.0 / (159)	100.0 / (330)	100.0 / (459)	100.0 / (1 429)	100.0 / (593)	100.0 / (424)	(3 497)

Status categories

No   Description
1   Professional and high administrative
2   Managerial and executive
3   Inspectional, supervisory and other non-manual (higher grade)
4   Inspectional, supervisory and other non-manual (lower grade)
5   Skilled manual and routine grades of non-manual
6   Semi-skilled manual
7   Unskilled manual

(Source: Glass, *Social Mobility in Britain*, Routledge & Kegan Paul, 1954, p. 183)

The percentages in the horizontal rows (in the top right-hand corner of each cell) compares the status of sons with the status of their fathers. Thus, taking all the sons whose fathers were in status category 1, 38.8% of these sons are themselves in category 1, 14.6% in category 2 and so on through to category 7 in which only 1.5% of sons born into category 1 are located. The figures in bold print, going diagonally across the table, indicate the extent to which sons share the same status as their fathers. For example, 27.4% of all sons whose fathers were in category 7 are themselves in that same category in 1949.

The percentages in the vertical columns (in the bottom left-hand corner of each cell) refer to the parental status of the men found in each category in 1949. For example, of all the men in status category 1 in 1949, 48.5% have fathers who were in that category, 15.5% have fathers who were in category 2 and so on. The bold figures show the percentage of men in each category who have the same status as their fathers. For example, 25% of all the men in category 7 are the sons of fathers from that category.

Overall, the table indicates a fairly high level of intergenerational mobility. Nearly two-thirds of the men interviewed in 1949 were in a different status category from that of their fathers. Roughly one third moved upwards and one third downwards. However, for the most part, the change in status is not very great. Most mobility is short range, sons generally moving to a category either adjacent or close to that of their fathers. There is little long range mobility either from top to bottom or vice versa. In the higher status categories there is a considerable degree of self-recruitment – a process by which members of a stratum are recruited from the sons of those who already belong to that stratum. The way the figures are presented tends to disguise the degree of self-recruitment. From the table it appears that the highest level of self-recruitment is in category 5. Thus in 1949, 50% of the members of category 5 are the sons of fathers who were in that same category, but since category 5 is by far the largest group, a relatively high degree of self-recruitment is to be expected. By comparison, category 1 is a very small group made up of just over 3.5% of the sample. Yet in 1949, 48.5% of the members of category 1 are the sons of fathers who were in that same category. This is over thirteen times greater than would be expected by chance. If parental occupation had no influence on a person's status, only some 3.5% of the sons in category 1 would have fathers in that category. Family background appears to have an important influence on life chances. The higher the occupational status of the father, the more likely the son is to obtain a high status position. Most men are likely to stay at roughly the same level as their fathers and this is particularly true at the top end of the scale. Glass's study therefore reveals a significant degree of inequality of opportunity.

Any conclusions drawn from this study must, however, be tentative.

85

The research methodology has been the subject of lengthy criticism. In particular, it has been argued that Glass's findings do not reflect changes in the occupational structure before 1949. For example, a comparison of the actual numbers of sons born into the first four status categories (shown in the right-hand vertical column of the table) with the number found in those categories in 1949 (shown in the horizontal row across the bottom) suggests a contraction of white-collar occupations. However, as Payne, Ford and Robertson note, there was a 16% expansion of these occupations during the thirty years preceding 1949. This throws doubt on the validity of Glass's sample. It suggests that his findings may seriously underestimate the rate of social mobility and in particular the degree of long range upward mobility (for a detailed criticism of Glass's methodology see Payne, Ford and Robertson, 1977).

After 1949, the next major study of social mobility in England and Wales was conducted in 1972. Known as the Oxford Mobility Study, it was undertaken by a group of sociologists at Nuffield College, Oxford. The results cannot be compared in detail with those of the 1949 study since different criteria were used as a basis for constructing the various strata. Where Glass used a classification based on occupational prestige, the Oxford study categorized occupations largely in terms of their market rewards. Table 8 summarizes the main findings on intergenerational mobility from the Oxford survey.

One of the most striking differences between the 1972 and 1949 surveys is the amount of long range mobility, particularly mobility out of the manual working class. For example, table 8 shows that 7.1% of the sons of class 7 fathers are in class 1 in 1972. However, despite the relatively high rate of long range upward mobility, a large proportion (45.7%) of the sons of class 1 fathers are themselves in class 1 in 1972. The combination of a fairly high degree of inheritance of privileged positions and a relatively high rate of long range upward mobility is probably due to the fact that there is literally more room at the top. The occupations which make up class 1 expanded rapidly in the twenty or so years before 1972. They have grown at such a rate that they can only be filled by recruitment from below. Class 1 fathers simply do not produce sufficient sons to fill class 1 occupations in the next generation.

The figures in the vertical columns, which refer to the class of origin of those found in each class in 1972, also differ significantly from the 1949 study. For example, figures showing the composition of class 1 in 1972 indicate that each of the other classes contributed at least 10% of its members. Even so, 25.3% of class 1 is made up of the sons of class 1 fathers. This level of self-recruitment is over three times greater than would be expected by chance. By comparison, 28.5% of class 1 is made up of the sons of manual workers which is about half the proportion which would be expected by chance. Clearly inequality of opportunity exists, but the way to the top is by no means closed.

Table 8

		Sons' class in 1972							
		1	2	3	4	5	6	7	Total
Fathers' class	1	**45.7**	19.1	11.6	6.8	4.9	5.4	6.5	100.0
		25.3	12.4	9.6	6.7	3.2	2.0	2.4	(680)
	2	29.4	**23.3**	12.1	6.0	9.7	10.8	8.6	100.0
		13.1	**12.2**	8.0	4.8	5.2	3.1	2.5	(547)
	3	18.6	15.9	**13.0**	7.4	13.0	15.7	16.4	100.0
		10.4	10.4	**10.8**	7.4	8.7	5.7	6.0	(687)
	4	14.0	14.4	9.1	**21.1**	9.9	15.1	16.3	100.0
		10.1	12.2	9.8	**27.2**	8.6	7.1	7.7	(886)
	5	14.4	13.7	10.2	7.7	**15.9**	21.4	16.8	100.0
		12.5	14.0	13.2	12.1	**16.6**	12.2	9.6	(1 072)
	6	7.8	8.8	8.4	6.4	12.4	**30.6**	25.6	100.0
		16.4	21.7	26.1	24.0	31.1	**41.8**	35.2	(2 577)
	7	7.1	8.5	8.8	5.7	12.9	24.8	**32.2**	100.0
		12.1	17.1	22.6	17.8	26.7	28.0	**36.6**	(2 126)
	Total	100.0	100.0	100.0	100.0	100.0	100.0	100.0	
		(1 230)	(1 050)	(827)	(687)	(1 026)	(1 883)	(1 872)	(8 575)

Classes

No	Description

1 Higher professionals, higher grade administrators, managers in large industrial concerns and large proprietors
2 Lower professionals, higher grade technicians, lower grade administrators, managers in small businesses and supervisors of non-manual employees
3 Routine non-manual – mainly clerical and sales personnel
4 Small proprietors and self-employed artisans
5 Lower grade technicians and supervisors of manual workers
6 Skilled manual workers
7 Semi-skilled and unskilled manual workers

(Adapted from Goldthorpe, 1980, pp. 44 and 48)

The Oxford survey indicates that England and Wales are considerably more open than previous studies have suggested. In particular, it shows that there is not a high degree of closure at the top. However, class 1 is a fairly large group which includes about 10 to 15% of the male working population. Studies which concentrate on small elite groups within class 1 reveal a much higher degree of closure. The process by which members of wealthy and powerful groups are drawn from the sons of those who already belong to such groups, is known as elite self-recruitment. The following studies indicate the degree of elite self-recruitment in Britain. A study by Willmott and Young conducted in 1970 in the London area, included a sample of 174 managing directors. It revealed that 83% were the sons of professionals and managers. A survey by Stanworth and Giddens designed to investigate the social origins of company chairmen revealed a high degree of elite self-recruitment. Out of 460 company chairmen in 1971, only 1% had manual working-class origins, 10% had middle-class backgrounds and 66% came from the upper class which is defined as 'industrialists, landowners, (and) others who possess substantial property and wealth' (there were insufficient data to classify the remaining 23%). Studies of the social background of top civil servants reveal a wider basis of recruitment but significantly less than the Oxford survey would suggest. A study by Halsey and Crewe shows that in 1967, only 17% of the higher administrative grades in the civil service were filled with individuals from manual working-class backgrounds. Thus the Oxford study, while showing a relatively high rate of mobility into class 1, does not indicate the degree of elite self-recruitment. Though class 1 as a whole appears fairly open, elite groups within that class are relatively closed.

The following reasons have been given to account for the rate of social mobility in industrial society. Firstly, there is considerable change in the occupational structure. For example, in Britain, the proportion of manual workers in the male labour force has declined from 70% in 1921 to 55% in 1971. Thus, for each succeeding generation, there are more white-collar and fewer blue-collar jobs available. This helps to account for the finding of the Oxford study that upward mobility considerably exceeds downward mobility. Secondly, manual and non-manual fertility rates differ. In particular, working-class fathers have generally had more children than middle-class fathers. This differential fertility can also be seen as a reason for the relatively high rate of upward mobility. As the Oxford study indicated, class 1 fathers did not produce sufficient sons to fill the rapidly growing numbers of class 1 occupations. As a result, recruitment from lower strata was essential to fill those positions. Thirdly, many sociologists have argued that occupational status in industrial society is increasingly achieved on the basis of merit. Jobs are allocated in terms of talent and ability rather than through family and friendship connections. Education is seen to play a key part in this process. The educational system grades people in terms of ability, and educational qualifications have a growing influence on occupational status and reward. Since educational opportunities are increasingly available to all young people, no matter what their social background, the result is a more open society and a higher rate of social mobility. This view however, has been strongly criticized. The arguments involved are complex and will be discussed in detail in Chapter 5.

The nature and extent of social mobility in Western industrial societies pose a number of questions concerning class formation and class conflict.

Marx believed that a high rate of social mobility would tend to weaken class solidarity. Classes would become increasingly heterogeneous as their members ceased to share similar backgrounds. Distinctive class sub-cultures would tend to disintegrate since norms, attitudes and values would no longer be passed from generation to generation within a single stratum. Class identification and loyalty would weaken since it would be difficult for mobile individuals to feel a strong consciousness of kind with other members of the class in which they found themselves. As a result, the intensity of class conflict and the potential for class consciousness would be reduced.

Ralf Dahrendorf believes that this situation has arrived in modern Western societies. He argues that as a result of the high rate of social mobility, the nature of conflict has changed. In an open society, there are considerable opportunities for individual advancement. There is therefore less need for people to join together as members of a social class in order to improve their situation. In Dahrendorf's words, 'Instead of advancing their claims as members of homogeneous groups, people are more likely to compete with each other as individuals for a place in the sun'. As a result class solidarity and the intensity of specifically class conflict will be reduced. Dahrendorf then goes a step further and questions whether the rather loose strata of mobile individuals can still be called social classes. But he stops short of rejecting the concept of class, arguing that, 'although mobility diminishes the coherence of groups as well as the intensity of class conflict, it does not eliminate either'.

In an article based on the Oxford Mobility Study, John H. Goldthorpe and Catriona Llewellyn make the following observations on the relationship between social mobility and class formation. The findings of the Oxford study indicate that the highest degree of homogeneity in terms of social background is found in the manual working class. Around 70% of its members in 1972 are the sons of manual workers. If present trends continue, this level of self-recruitment will increase. Goldthrope and Llewellyn claim that this 'offers a very favourable basis for strategies of solidarity'. In other words, the similarity of origins and experience of the majority of manual workers provides a basis for collective action in pursuit of common interests. The Oxford study indicates a high rate of mobility out of the working class. As Dahrendorf suggests, this might encourage individual rather than collective strategies. However, since upward mobility is substantially greater than downward mobility, relatively few people move down into the working class. Goldthorpe and Llewellyn argue that collective strategies may well be encouraged by 'decreasing mobility into the working class, which must make for a steadily greater homogeneity of origins among its members and thus, one might suppose, for a greater potential for solidarity'. By comparison, the middle class is increasingly heterogeneous in terms of the social background of its members. In Goldthorpe's words, it is 'a class of low classness' (quoted in Bourne, 1979, p. 291). It lacks coherence and class solidarity, an observation which matches Kenneth Roberts's picture of a 'fragmentary' middle class.

A number of sociologists have attempted to assess the effects of mobility on social order. Frank Parkin has seen the relatively high rate of upward mobility as a 'political safety-valve'. It provides opportunities for many able and ambitious members of the working class to improve their situation. As a result, the frustration which might result, if opportunities for upward mobility were absent, is prevented from developing. To some degree this will weaken the working class. The upwardly mobile have found individual solutions to the problems of low status and low pay. If they remained within the working class, they might well join with other members in collectivist strategies which might benefit the class as a whole. In addition those who move out of the working class show little desire to improve the lot of their class of origin. Research from a number of Western societies indicates that upwardly mobile individuals tend to take on the social and political outlooks of the class into which they move. American studies in particular suggest that those who move upward into the middle class often become more conservative than those born into it. Thus the upwardly mobile pose no threat to social stability. Indeed, they can be seen to reinforce it.

Similar conclusions have been drawn from studies of downward mobility. American sociologists Harold Wilensky and Hugh Edwards examined the response of 'skidders' – persons moving down into the working class – to the experience of social demotion. They found that the downwardly mobile tend to be more politically conservative than those born into and remaining within the working class. The experience of downward mobility did not lead them to reject the social order and so threaten the stability of society. Instead they clung to middle-class values, anticipating upward mobility and a restoration of their former status. Their presence in the working class tends to weaken that class since they are not really a part of it. Wilensky and Edwards state that, 'Skidders, along with other workers who escape from working-class culture psychologically or actually, function to reduce working-class solidarity and social criticism from below – and therefore slow down the push towards equality'. Thus both upward and downward mobility tend to reinforce the status quo. Both introduce conservative elements into social strata, both appear to weaken working-class solidarity and therefore reduce the intensity of class conflict.

This section closes the examination of class in capitalist society. The subject of class has been and still is a dominant concern of European sociologists. It is probably the most difficult and confused area within sociology, not least because there is no general agreement about what constitutes class. The subject will be returned to in the following chapters when the relationship between social class and various aspects of society and behaviour will be considered. The last part of this chapter will now examine the nature of stratification in socialist societies.

Stratification in socialist societies

Socialist or communist societies are societies in which the forces of production are communally owned. The information in this section will be drawn mainly from the USSR and Eastern European countries such as Poland and Czechoslovakia. Since there are important differences between these societies, conclusions about stratification under communism will be on a very broad and general level.

Marx believed that public ownership of the forces of production is the first and fundamental step towards the creation of an egalitarian society. This would abolish at a stroke the antagonistic classes of capitalist society. Classes, defined in terms of the relationship of social groups to the forces of production, would disappear. All members of society would now share the same relationship – that of ownership – to the forces of production. Social inequality would not, however, disappear overnight. There would be a period of transition during which the structures of inequality produced by capitalism would be dismantled. Marx was rather vague about the exact nature of the communist utopia which should eventually emerge from the abolition of private property. He believed that the state would eventually 'wither away' and that the consumption of goods and services would be based on the principle of 'to each according to his needs'. Whether he envisaged a disappearance of all forms of social inequality, such as prestige and power differentials, is not entirely clear. One thing that is clear, though, is that the reality of contemporary communism is a long way from Marx's dreams.

Eastern European communism has not resulted in the abolition of social stratification. Identifiable strata, which can be distinguished in terms of differential economic rewards, occupational prestige and power, are present in all socialist states. Frank Parkin identifies the following strata in East European communist societies.

1 White-collar intelligentsia (professional, managerial and administrative positions)
2 Skilled manual positions
3 Lower or unqualified white-collar positions
4 Unskilled manual positions

Although income inequalities are not as great as in capitalist societies, they are still significant. For example, the average monthly earnings in 1966 in the USSR for engineering and technical workers were 150 rubles; for technically unqualified manual workers, 104 rubles; and for routine white-collar workers, 88 rubles (source: Lane, 1970, p. 402). Mervyn Matthews has estimated that in the early 1970s, the basic earnings of the small occupational elite in Russia (about one employed person in 500) were roughly four times the average wage and in some cases considerably higher. If various 'extras' or fringe benefits are included, they add at least 50 to 100% to top incomes. Studies of occupational prestige in communist societies produce generally similar results to those from capitalist societies. Top administrators, managers and professionals are accorded the highest prestige with unskilled manual workers forming the base of the prestige hierarchy. Frank Parkin argues that, as in the West, there is a fairly close correspondence between inequalities of occupational reward, hierarchies of occupational prestige and levels of skill and expertise.

The Polish sociologist Wlodzimierz Wesolowski presents the following analysis of social inequality in communist societies. Although social stratification exists, the disappearance of classes in the Marxian sense has removed the basic source of conflict. No longer does a small minority exploit the mass of the population. There are no serious conflicts of interest between the various strata since the forces of production are communally owned and everybody is working for the benefit of society as a whole. Although economic inequalities remain, they are determined (and justified) by the principle, 'to each according to his work'. Wesolowski claims that 'the share of the individual in the division of the social product is determined by the quality and quantity of his work . . . wages are a function of the quality of work, that is, they are a function of the level of skill and education necessary for carrying out a given job'. While admitting the difficulty of measuring such factors, Wesolowski argues that they form the basis on which governments fix wage differentials. This argument is similar to the views of Western functionalists and is open to many of the same criticisms.

Wesolowski explains power differentials in communist society in the following way. Social life, particularly in large, complex societies, would be impossible without 'positions of command and subordination'. This inevitably involves power differentials, 'For as soon as the positions of authority are filled, those who occupy the positions have the right (and duty) to give orders, while the others have the duty to obey them'. Wesolowski implies that in communist societies, those in positions of authority use their power for the benefit of society as a whole. Again his arguments are similar to those applied by Western functionalists to the analysis of capitalist society.

A very different picture is presented by the Yugoslavian writer, Milovan Djilas. He argues that those in positions of authority in communist societies use power to further their own interests. He claims that the bourgeoisie of the West have been replaced by a new ruling class in the East. This 'new class' is made up of 'political bureaucrats', many of whom are high ranking officials of the Communist Party. Although in legal terms, the forces of production are communally owned, Djilas argues that in practice they are controlled by the new class for its own benefit.

Political bureaucrats direct and control the economy and monopolize decisions about the distribution of income and wealth. In practice, the result is, 'He who has power grabs privileges and indirectly grabs property'. Wide income differentials separate the new class from the rest of society. Its members enjoy a range of privileges which include high quality housing at modest rents, the use of cars which are in short supply, *haute cuisine* food in exclusive restaurants at subsidized rates, the right to purchase scarce goods in special shops, excellent holiday accommodation in state-run resorts, special medical facilities, access to the best schools for their children and a variety of cash payments over and above their basic salaries. In this way Djilas claims that members of the new class 'handle material goods on behalf of their own interests'.

If anything, Djilas sees the new class as more exploitive than the bourgeoisie. Its power is even greater because it is unchecked by political parties. Djilas claims that in a single party state political bureaucrats monopolize power. In explaining the source of their power, Djilas maintains the Marxian emphasis on the forces of production. He argues that the new class owes its power to the fact it controls the forces of production. Others have reversed this argument claiming that in communist societies economic power derives from political power. Thus T. B. Bottomore argues that the new class 'controls the means of production because it has political power'.

There are, however, important differences between the new class and the bourgeoisie of the West. In the West property can be passed from father to son whereas in the East, members of the new class have no legal claim to property. Their privilege rests largely on political office which cannot be passed directly to their offspring. In addition, the new class appears considerably more open than the bourgeoisie. Frank Parkin provides the following evidence. A Hungarian study conducted in 1963 showed that nearly 77% of managerial, professional and administrative posts were filled by individuals from manual and peasant families. In Yugoslavia, the 1960 census indicated that nearly 62% of managerial and administrative positions were filled by individuals with manual backgrounds but this is due partly to the rapid expansion of these types of occupations. The rate of downward mobility is low and Parkin notes that, 'the offspring of privileged status groups can usually bank on reproducing their parents' status'. Recruitment from below may well taper off if the expansion of top positions slows down. Under such circumstances, the new class may be able to largely reproduce itself from generation to generation.

In certain respects, the overall picture of stratification in communist societies is similar to that of the West. A number of American sociologists have argued that stratification systems in all industrial societies, whether capitalist or communist, are becoming increasingly similar. This view, sometimes known as 'convergence theory', argues that modern industrial economies will necessarily produce similar systems of social stratification. In particular, modern industry requires particular types of workers. In the words of Clark Kerr, one of the main proponents of convergence theory, 'The same technology calls for the same occupational structure around the world – in steel, in textiles, in air transport'. Kerr assumes that technical skills and educational qualifications will be rewarded in proportion to their value to industry. Since the demands of industry are essentially the same in both East and West, the range of occupations and occupational rewards will become increasingly similar. As a result the stratification systems of capitalist and communist societies will converge.

Convergence theory has been the subject of strong criticism. Firstly, it has been argued that there are important differences between the stratification systems of East and West. Secondly, the factors which shape the two systems have been seen as basically different. Thirdly, it has been argued that the view that economic forces shape the rest of society ignores other important sources of change. Thus John H. Goldthorpe claims that convergence theory fails to consider the influence of political and ideological forces. In the West market forces are the main factors generating social stratification. By comparison, in the East, social inequality is far more subject to political regulation. Frank Parkin makes a similar point, seeing the bases of stratification in capitalist and communist societies as qualitatively different. He argues that in the East, 'the rewards system is much more responsive to manipulation by the central authority than it is in a market based economy'. Parkin also notes a number of specific differences between the stratification systems of East and West. Firstly, income inequalities are considerably smaller in the East. Secondly the manual/non-manual distinction seems less marked in communist societies. In particular skilled manual workers are relatively highly placed and routine white-collar workers do not share the prestige and fringe benefits of their Western counterparts. Thirdly, the rate of upward mobility is higher in the East. In particular, there is far more recruitment from below to elite positions. However, convergence theory does not argue that the stratification systems of East and West are the same, only that they will become increasingly similar. On this particular point, only time will provide the final answer.

So far, communism has failed to live up to the expectations of many of its supporters. It may be that Eastern European societies are still in the process of transition and are indeed moving towards an egalitarian goal. There is some evidence of a decline in income inequality within the mass of the population during the 1960s and early 1970s. However, there is little indication of a reduction in the privileges of the elite. From his study of elite life styles in the USSR, Mervyn Matthews concludes that not only is privilege accepted at the top, but it is 'actively promoted'. It is built into administrative practices and so institutionalized. While communal ownership of the forces of production may be essential for the creation of an egalitarian society, other changes are clearly necessary.

Sociology, ideology and social stratification

It is evident from this chapter that sociologists are not neutral, dispassionate observers of the social scene. Like everybody else, they see the world in terms of their values and attitudes. To some degree this will affect their analysis of society. Their commitment to a particular set of values will influence what they see, what they look for, what they consider important, what they find and how they interpret their findings. Some sociologists have carried this argument a stage further and claimed that not only are the views of particular sociologists value based, but also the major theoretical perspectives within the discipline. Thus, as the previous chapter indicated, functionalism and Marxism have been seen as ideologically based. It has been argued that functionalism is founded on a conservative ideology, Marxism on a radical ideology. This argument can be illustrated from theories of social stratification.

At first sight, functionalist views on stratification appear value free. The language of the functionalists is sober and restrained and their analyses have a scientific ring to them. However, functionalist theories of stratification have been strongly attacked for what many see as their right-wing, conservative bias. On this basis, Alvin Gouldner criticizes Davis and Moore's assertion that social stratification is inevitable in all human societies. Gouldner claims that this statement is little more than an article of faith. He sees it as based ultimately on the conservative doctrine that 'the social world is for all time divided into rulers and ruled'. This implies that attempts to fundamentally change or eradicate systems of social stratification will be harmful to society. As a result, it can be argued that functionalist views provide support and justification for social inequality. Gouldner claims that the logical conclusion of functionalist theories is that 'equality is a dream'. By suggesting that an egalitarian society is an illusion, the functionalists direct research away from alternatives to social stratification. This again encourages acceptance of the status quo rather than demands for radical change. Finally, Gouldner argues that the basic assumptions of functionalist theory are essentially conservative. Functionalism is concerned with explaining the basis of social order. In pursuit of this aim, it focusses on the contributions of the various parts of society to the maintenance of order. Since stratified societies often provide evidence of order and stability, functionalism leads sociologists to assume that social stratification contributes to this situation. Since order and stability are assumed to be 'good' for society, any attempts to dismantle systems of social stratification will be seen as harmful to society. In Gouldner's words, the functionalist position implies that 'only "evil" – social disorder, tension or conflict – can come from efforts to remove the domination of man by man or to make fundamental changes in the character of authority'. In this way Gouldner claims that functionalism advocates the maintenance of the status quo.

By comparison, Marxian theories are openly radical. They advocate fundamental social change in many contemporary societies. They begin from the value judgment that some form of communist system is the only just and fair social arrangement. From this standpoint they evaluate various forms of social stratification. This often results in a passionate condemnation of social inequality, particularly of class systems in capitalist society. The ideological basis of Marxian theory is clearly revealed with the use of value laden terms such as exploitation and oppression. Indeed Marxists usually make no secret of their political views. For example, the British sociologist John Westergaard openly condemns the concentration of power and wealth in capitalist society. Writing with Henrietta Resler in the early 1970s, he argues that private property is increasingly threatened in Britain and adds, 'We ourselves hope that this threat will become a reality'.

It has often been argued that Marxian views of the contours of the class system are ideologically based. Starting from the judgment that capitalist society is divided into exploiters and exploited leads to the idea of a two class system. Many non-Marxists argue that this view ignores other important divisions in society. Thus David Lockwood attacks those Marxists who dismiss the clerks' middle-class identification as false class consciousness. Lockwood argues that this identification is based on real differences between the position of clerks and manual workers. He claims that Marxists who dismiss these differences as insignificant are allowing their political views to influence their judgment. Marxists often respond in the same vein. They accuse sociologists who focus on divisions within and between the so-called middle and manual working classes of a conservative bias. They claim that this directs attention away from the concentration of wealth and power at the top and, in doing so, protects privilege. Marxists have levelled similar accusations against studies of social mobility. For example, the Russian sociologist Alexandrov accuses American 'bourgeois sociologists' of using the concept of social mobility to disguise the real nature of class exploitation under capitalism. The results of social mobility studies give the impression of an open society with considerable opportunity for upward mobility but Alexandrov maintains that nearly all mobility occurs within the proletariat, not across 'real' class boundaries. In particular, there are minimal opportunities for workers to enter the bourgeoisie. The picture of a relatively open society presented by mobility studies disguises this situation and so conceals the extent to which the bourgeoisie maintains its wealth and power.

This section has shown that it is possible to argue that theories of stratification are based ultimately on ideology. Indeed many sociologists accept this view and make no secret of their commitment to particular values. For example, Ralf Dahrendorf's position is clear when he approvingly quotes Kant to the effect that social inequality is 'a rich source of much that is evil, but also of everything that is good'. From the author's viewpoint, however, there is much more to applaud in Melvin Tumin's statement that, 'The evidence regarding the mixed outcomes of stratification strongly suggests the examination of alternatives. The evidence regarding the possibilities of social growth under conditions of more equal rewarding are such that the exploration of alternatives seems eminently worthwhile'. It may be that only a commitment to a more egalitarian society will lead to the kind of research that Tumin advocates.

3 Power and politics

Max Weber has defined power as, 'the chance of a man or a number of men to realize their own will in a communal action even against the resistance of others who are participating in the action'. Power is therefore an aspect of social relationships. An individual or group do not hold power in isolation, they hold it in relation to others. Power is therefore power over others. In terms of Weber's definition, it is simply the degree to which an individual or group can get its own way in a social relationship. This is a very broad definition of power since it enters into every aspect of social life. It extends from parents assigning domestic chores to their children to teachers enforcing discipline in the classroom, from a manager organizing his workforce to a political party enacting legislation. In each case, an individual or group have power to the degree to which others comply with their will. Many sociologists argue that 'political sociology' is the study of power in its broadest sense. Thus Dowse and Hughes state that 'politics is about "power", politics occurs when there are differentials in power'. In terms of this definition, any social relationship which involves power differentials is political. This is a long way from the traditional study of politics which has concentrated on the state and the various institutions of government such as Parliament and the judiciary. The emphasis upon the state and the machinery of government remains important in political sociology, but they are examined in relation to society as a whole rather than in isolation.

Sociologists often distinguish between two forms of power, authority and coercion. Authority is that form of power which is accepted as legitimate, that is as right and just, and therefore obeyed on that basis. Thus if members of British society accept that Parliament has the right to make certain decisions and they regard those decisions as lawful, Parliamentary power may be defined as legitimate authority. Coercion is that form of power which is not regarded as legitimate by those subject to it. Thus from the point of view of the Republicans in Northern Ireland, the power of the British government may be defined as coercion. However, the distinction between authority and coercion is not as clear-cut as the above definitions suggest. It has often been argued that both forms of power are based ultimately on physical force and those who enforce the law are able to resort to physical force whether their power is regarded as legitimate or not.

This chapter is mainly concerned with the nature and distribution of power in modern industrial societies. It examines who holds power: is it concentrated in the hands of a small minority or widely distributed throughout society? It examines how power is used: is it used to further the interests of the powerholders or for the benefit of society as a whole? Answers to these questions depend in part on the ways in which power is defined and measured. As a result, various views of the nature of power will be examined, as will the methodology used to measure power.

Power – a functionalist perspective

Weber's definition of power implies that those who hold power do so at the expense of others. It suggests that there is a fixed amount of power and therefore if some hold power, others do not. This view is sometimes known as a 'constant-sum' concept of power. Since the amount of power is constant, power is held by an individual or group to the extent that it is not held by others. Weber's definition also implies that the powerholders will tend to use power to further their own interests. As later sections will indicate, this interpretation of the nature and use of power has been adopted by many sociologists. They argue that power is used to further the sectional interests of the powerholders which are in conflict with the interests of those subject to that power. They therefore see power used mainly for the exploitation and oppression of some by others.

Arguing from a functionalist perspective, Talcott Parsons rejects the constant-sum concept of power and the view that power is employed in the furtherance of sectional interests. Rather than seeing power as something which some hold at the expense of others, Parsons regards it as something possessed by society as a whole. As such, power is 'a generalized facility or resource in the society'. In particular, it is 'the capacity to mobilize the resources of the society for the attainment of goals for which a general "public" commitment has been made'. In this sense, the amount of power in society is measured by the degree to which collective goals are realized. Thus, the greater the efficiency of a social system for achieving the goals defined by its members, the more power exists in society. This view is sometimes known as a 'variable-sum' concept of power, since power in society is not seen as fixed or constant. Instead it is variable in the sense it can increase or decrease.

Parson's view of power is developed from his general theory of the nature of society. He begins from the assumption that value consensus is essential for the survival of social systems. From shared values derive collective goals, that is goals shared by members of society. For example, if materialism is a major value of Western industrial society, collective goals such as economic expansion and higher living standards can be seen to stem from this value. The more able Western societies are able to realize these goals, the greater the power that resides in the social system. Steadily rising living standards and economic growth are therefore indications of an increase of power in society.

Parsons's view of power differentials within society also derives from his general theory. Since goals are shared by all members of society, power will generally be used in the furtherance of collective goals. As a result, both sides of the power relationship will benefit and everybody will gain by the arrangement. For example, politicians in Western societies will promote policies for economic expansion which, if successful, will raise the living standards of the population as a whole. Thus, from this viewpoint, the exercise of power usually means that everybody wins. This forms a basis for the cooperation and reciprocity which Parsons considers essential for the maintenance and well-being of society.

As the previous chapter indicated, Parsons regards power differentials as necessary for the effective pursuit of collective goals. If members of society pool their efforts and resources, they are more likely to realize their shared goals than if they operate as individuals. Cooperation on a large scale requires organization and direction which necessitates positions of command. Some are therefore granted the power to direct others. This power takes the form of authority. It is generally regarded as legitimate since it is seen to further collective goals. Thus some are granted authority for the benefit of all.

Parsons's views may be illustrated by the following examples. One of the major goals of traditional Sioux Indian society was success in hunting. This activity involved cooperation and power relationships. During the summer months the buffalo, the main food supply of the tribe, were gathered in large herds on the northern plains of North America. The buffalo hunt was a large-scale enterprise under the authority and control of marshals who were appointed by the warrior societies. An effective hunt required considerable organization and direction and was strictly policed. In particular, the marshals were concerned to prevent excitable young warriors from jumping the gun and stampeding the herd which might endanger the food supply of the entire tribe. Marshals had the authority to beat those who disobeyed the rules and destroy their clothes and the harness of their horses. Thus, by granting power to the marshals, by accepting it as legitimate, and obeying it on that basis, the whole tribe benefitted from the exercise of their authority.

Parsons's analysis of the basis of political power in Western democracies provides a typical illustration of his views on the nature of power. He argues that, 'Political support should be conceived of as a generalized grant of power which, if it leads to electional success, puts elected leadership in a position analogous to a banker. The "deposits" of power made by constituents are revocable, if not at will, at the next election'. Just as money is deposited in a bank, members of society deposit power in political leaders. Just as the depositor can withdraw his money from the bank, so the electorate can withdraw its grant of power from political leaders at the next election. In this sense power resides ultimately with members of society as a whole. Finally, just as money generates interest for the depositor, so grants of power generate benefits for the electorate since they are used primarily to further collective goals. In this way power *in* society can increase.

Many sociologists have argued that Parsons's views of the nature and application of power in society are naive. They suggest that he has done little more than translate into sociological jargon the rationalizations promoted by the powerholders to justify their use of power. In particular, they argue that Parsons has failed to appreciate that power is frequently used to further sectional interests rather than to benefit society as a whole. These criticisms will be examined in detail in the following sections.

Power – a Marxian perspective

A Marxian analysis of power provides a radical alternative to Parsons's functionalist approach. It rejects the view that power is a societal resource held in trust and directed by those in authority for the benefit of all. Instead, power is seen to be held by a particular group in society at the expense of the rest of society. This is a constant-sum concept of power since a net gain in the power of the dominant group represents a net loss in the power of the rest of society. The dominant group uses power to further its own interests. These interests are in direct conflict with the interests of those subject to its power. This is very different from the picture presented by Parsons in which rulers and ruled pull together for the benefit of society as a whole, undivided by any fundamental conflicts of interest.

From a Marxian perspective, the source of power in society lies in the economic infrastructure. In all stratified societies the forces of production are owned and controlled by a minority, the ruling class. This relationship to the forces of production provides the basis of its dominance. It therefore follows that the only way to return power to the people involves communal ownership of the forces of production. Since everyone will now share the same relationship to the forces of production, power will be shared by all members of society. As previous chapters have indicated, ruling class power is used to exploit and oppress the subject class. Thus in capitalist society, much of the wealth produced by the labour power of the proletariat is appropriated in the form of profit by the bourgeoisie. From a Marxian perspective, the use of power to exploit others is defined as coercion. It is seen as an illegitimate use of power since it forces the subject class to submit to a situation which is against its interests. If ruling class power is accepted as legitimate by the subject class, this is an indication of false class consciousness.

Ruling class power extends beyond specifically economic relationships. In terms of Marxian theory, the relationships of dominance and subordination in the infrastructure will be largely reproduced in the superstructure. For example, in capitalist society the unequal relationship between employers and employees will be reflected and legitimated in the legal system. A range of legal statutes protect the rights of property owners and in particular their right to a disproportionate share of the wealth produced by their employees. The various institutions of society are largely shaped by the infrastructure. Thus a capitalist infrastructure will produce a particular kind of educational system, a particular form of family structure and so on. These institutions will serve to reinforce the power and privilege of the ruling class. This chapter will be mainly concerned with the state in capitalist society. Marxian views on other institutions will be examined in later chapters.

A problem common to all perspectives on the nature and distribution of power in society involves the measurement of power. The American sociologist Robert A. Dahl argues that the measurement of power requires a careful examination of actual decisions. By this method it is possible to determine which individuals and groups realize their objectives and therefore to specify who has power. Dahl argues that, 'I do not see how anyone can suppose that he has established the dominance of a specific group in a community or a nation without basing his analysis on the careful examination of a series of concrete decisions'. However, the problem with this approach is that it ignores the possibility that those with power can prevent many issues from ever reaching the point of 'concrete decisions'. For example, it has often been argued that the principle of capitalism has never been seriously questioned in Western societies and as a result the question of alternatives to a capitalist economy has never reached the point of actual decision. This can be seen as evidence of the power of the capitalist class. Dahl's approach, with its emphasis on decision making, would fail to reveal this aspect of power. As John Urry states, Dahl 'ignores the processes by which certain issues come to be defined as decisions and others do not. The study of decisions is the failure to study who has the power to determine what are decisions'.

Westergaard and Resler provide an alternative to the decision making approach in their study of class in Britain. They argue that power can only be measured by its results. Thus if scarce and valued resources are concentrated in the hands of a minority, that group largely monopolizes power in society. Westergaard and Resler maintain that 'power is visible only through its consequences; they are the first and final proof of the existence of power'. Put simply, the proof of the pudding is in the eating. Whoever reaps the largest rewards at the end of the day holds the largest share of power. Thus Westergaard and Resler claim that the marked inequalities which characterize British society 'reflect, while they also demonstrate, the continuing power of capital'. The concentration of wealth and privilege in the hands of the capitalist class therefore provides visible proof of its power. The absence of any serious challenge to its position is a further indication of the power of capital. Ruling class ideology promotes the view that private property, profit, the mechanisms of a market economy and the inequalities which result are reasonable, legitimate, normal and natural. If this view is accepted then the dominance of capital is ensured since 'no control could be firmer and more extensive than one which embraced the minds and wills of its subjects so successfully that opposition never reared its head'. Westergaard and Resler claim that because of the pervasiveness of ruling class ideology, the capitalist class rarely has to consciously and actively exercise its power. Capitalism and the inequalities it produces are largely taken for granted. A capitalist economy guarantees a disproportionate share of wealth to a minority and generates an ideology which prevents serious questioning of the established order. As a result, issues which might threaten the dominance of capital are usually prevented from reaching the point of actual decision. The capitalist class is therefore able to enjoy advantage and privilege 'merely because of "the way things work", and because those ways are not open to serious challenge'.

In *The State in Capitalist Society*, Ralph Miliband examines various ways in which the subject class is persuaded to accept the status quo. He refers to this as 'the process of legitimation' which he regards as a system of 'massive indoctrination'. Miliband argues that the capitalist class seeks to 'persuade society not only to accept the policies it advocates but also the ethos, the values and the goals which are its own, the economic system of which it is a central part, the "way of life" which is the core of its being'. Miliband illustrates his argument with an analysis of advertising by means of which capitalist enterprises promote both their products and the acceptable face of capitalism. He argues that all advertising is political since it serves to further the power and privilege of the dominant class. Through advertisements, giant, privately owned corporations such as ICI, BICC, Unilever, ITT and the major banks and oil companies promote the view that their major concern is public service and the welfare of the community. Profits are a secondary consideration and portrayed mainly as a means of providing an improved service. The image of the corporation and its products is made even rosier by association in advertisements with 'socially approved values and norms'. Miliband argues that capitalism and its commodities are subtly linked via advertisements to 'integrity, reliability, security, parental love, childlike innocence, neighbourliness, sociability'. With these kinds of associations, the exploitive and oppressive nature of capitalism is effectively disguised. Finally, advertising promotes the view that the way to happiness and fulfilment involves the accumulation of material possessions, in particular the acquisition of the products of capitalism. The individual is encouraged to 'be content to enjoy the blessings which are showered upon him' by the 'benevolent, public-spirited and socially responsible' capitalist enterprise. Miliband argues that advertising provides one example of the ways in which capitalism is legitimated. He regards the process of legitimation as essential for the maintenance of capitalist power. If successful, it prevents serious challenge to the basis of that power, the private ownership of the forces of production. In the following chapters, further aspects of the process of legitimation will be examined in detail.

The capitalist state – a Marxian perspective

Traditionally, the study of politics has focussed on the state. This section examines the role of the state in capitalist society from a Marxian perspective. The state comprises the various institutions of national and local government which include the legislative, executive and administrative branches of government. Thus in Britain it includes Parliament, the various ministries staffed by civil servants, the police, the military and the judiciary. Marx regarded the state as 'but a committee for managing the common affairs of the whole bourgeoisie'. He saw it as 'the form in which the individuals of a ruling class assert their common interests'.

While there is general agreement among modern Marxists that the state in capitalist society represents ruling class interests, there is some disagreement about the exact relationship between the state and the bourgeoisie. Some writers have argued that the various branches of the state are largely staffed by members of the ruling class and, as a result, the interests of capital will be predominant. Thus Aaronovitch has argued that the British Parliament and the main government departments 'are manned and controlled by finance capital. Finance capital is not some "lobby" outside the political system but is built into its foundation'. Aaronovitch bases this claim on the business and financial connections of MPs, top civil servants and members of government advisory bodies. Given these connections, the activities of the state will systematically favour the interests of capital. Aaronovitch maintains that, 'By and large, government in Britain has been concerned with maintaining finance capital and its capitalist basis. It accepts as axiomatic that the Big Five Banks, ICI and the oil companies are vital to Britain and that their interests are basically the interests of the nation'.

While generally agreeing with this summary of state activity, other writers take a rather different view of the relationship between the state and the ruling class. They do not regard the social origins and business connections of state personnel as particularly significant. They argue that the role of the state is ultimately determined by the infrastructure. As a result the state will automatically represent the interests of capital. This position is most strongly advocated by Nicos Poulantzas. He argues that 'the capitalist State best serves the interests of the capitalist class only when members of this class do not participate directly in the State apparatus, that is to say when the *ruling class* is not the *politically governing class*'. Poulantzas argues that the ruling class does not directly govern but rather its interests are served through the medium of the state. As such, the state is 'relatively autonomous' from the ruling class. To some degree it is free from its direct influence, independent from its direct control. However, since the state is shaped by the infrastructure, it is constrained to represent the interests of capital.

Poulantzas argues that the relative autonomy of the state is essential if it is to effectively represent capital. The state requires a certain amount of freedom and independence in order to serve ruling class interests. If it were staffed by members of the bourgeoisie, it may lose this freedom of action. The following reasons have been given for the relative autonomy of the capitalist state. As a group the bourgeoisie is not free from internal divisions and conflicts of interest. To represent its common interests the state must have the freedom to act on behalf of the class as a whole. If the bourgeoisie ruled directly, its power might be weakened by internal wrangling and disagreement. It might fail to present a united front in conflicts with the proletariat. The relative autonomy of the state allows it to rise above sectional interests within the bourgeoisie and to represent that class as a whole. In particular it provides the state with sufficient flexibility to deal with any threats from the subject class to ruling class dominance. To this end the state must have the freedom to make concessions to the subject class which might be opposed by the bourgeoisie. Such concessions serve to defuse radical working-class protest and contain demands within the framework of a capitalist economy. Finally, the relative autonomy of the state enables it to promote the myth that it represents society as a whole. The state presents itself as a representative of 'the people' of 'public interest' and 'national unity'. Thus in its ideological role, the state disguises the fact that essentially it represents ruling class interests.

So far, the discussion of the relationship between the state and the bourgeoisie has remained at a general level. Westergaard and Resler provide the following examples to illustrate the claim that the state represents the interests of capital. In Britain, as in other advanced capitalist societies, the state has implemented a wide range of reforms which appear to directly benefit either the subject class in particular or society as a whole. These include legislation to improve health and safety in the workplace, social security benefits such as old age pensions and unemployment and sickness insurance, a national health service and free education for all. However, these reforms have left the basic structure of inequality unchanged. They have been largely financed from the wages of those they were intended to benefit and have resulted in little redistribution of wealth. They can be seen as concessions which serve to defuse working-class protest and prevent it from developing in more radical directions which might threaten the basis of ruling class dominance. In Westergaard and Resler's words, 'Their effects are to help contain working-class unrest by smoothing off the rougher edges of insecurity'.

In all Western industrial societies, state involvement in economic affairs has steadily grown. Westergaard and Resler argue that state intervention in the economy has aimed at 'establishing conditions of general business prosperity and growth'. To this end the British government has nationalized basic industries such as coal, electricity, gas and the railways. Industry requires a national framework for basic supplies and services in order to ensure its long-term development. By selective nationalization, the state has been able to coordinate the supplies and services required for the growth and development of the private sector. In addition, the state has increasingly stimulated private industry by direct financial contributions. For example, in Britain during the early 1970s, nearly 40% of private industry's expenditure on research and development was met from public funds. On the basis of this type of evidence, Westergaard and Resler claim that state activity in Britain has been geared to 'the maintenance of private property and profit as the mainsprings of the economy'.

From a Marxian perspective power in capitalist society is monopolized by the bourgeoisie. The ultimate source of ruling class power lies in its ownership of the forces of production. The only way to end this monopoly involves communal ownership of the forces of production. In theory power should devolve to the people in communist society but as the previous chapter indicated, many observers claim that in Eastern European communist societies power is concentrated in the hands of a ruling minority. Marx believed that communism would provide 'the conditions for the free development and activity of individuals under their own control'. However, he argued that a 'period of transition' was inevitable before the communist utopia fully emerged. During this period, 'the state can only take the form of a *revolutionary dictatorship of the proletariat*'. Before the proletariat can govern itself, a section of the proletariat must govern on behalf of and in the interests of the proletariat as a whole. During the period of transition, the institutions of capitalism will be dismantled and the framework for individual self-government will be erected. The state will finally 'wither away' and the transition to communism will be complete.

There is little indication of the state withering away in Eastern Europe. There is little evidence that the days of the dictatorship of the proletariat are numbered. The return of power to the people is, as Ralph Miliband admits, 'a programme to which Communist regimes have not so far seriously addressed themselves'. The enduring quality of the dictatorship of the proletariat has led many to argue that the communist utopia represents little more than wishful thinking. This view is most strongly advocated by elite theory which is examined in the following section.

Elite theory

Elite theory was first developed by two Italian sociologists, Vilfredo Pareto (1848–1923) and Gaetano Mosca (1858–1941). Where Marxian theory argues that relationships to the forces of production divide society into dominant and subordinate groups, elite theory claims that the personal qualities of individuals separate rulers from the ruled. The elite owe their position to the superiority of their personal characteristics or attributes. For example, they may possess considerable organizational ability, a talent which Mosca believed to be the basis for leadership. Or they may possess a high degree of cunning and intelligence, qualities which Pareto saw as one of the prerequisites of power. Later versions of elite theory place less emphasis on the personal qualities of the powerful and more on the institutional framework of society. They argue that the hierarchical organization of social institutions allows a minority to monopolize power.

Elite theory developed in part as a reaction to Marxism. It rejected the idea of a communist utopia arguing that an egalitarian society was an illusion. It saw Marxism as ideology rather than an objective analysis of society. Elite theory argues that all societies are divided into two main groups, a ruling minority and the ruled. This situation is inevitable. Should the proletarian revolution occur, it will merely result in the replacement of one ruling elite by another. The economic infrastructure, be it capitalist or communist, will not alter the inevitability of elite rule. Apart from the personal qualities of its members, an elite owes its power to its internal organization. It forms a united and cohesive minority in the face of an unorganized and fragmented mass. In Mosca's words, 'The power of the minority is irresistible as against each single individual in the majority'. Major decisions which affect society are taken by the elite. Even in so-called democratic societies, these decisions will usually reflect the concerns of the elite rather than the wishes of the people. Elite theorists picture the majority as apathetic and unconcerned with the major issues of the day. The mass of the population is largely controlled and manipulated by the elite, passively accepting the propaganda which justifies elite rule.

'Classical' elite theory – Vilfredo Pareto and Gaetano Mosca

Although there are broad similarities between the various elite theorists, there are also important differences. This section briefly examines the work of the early or 'classical' elite theorists, Pareto and Mosca. Pareto places particular emphasis on psychological characteristics as the basis of elite rule. He argues that there are two main types of governing elite, which, following his intellectual ancestor and countryman Machiavelli, he calls 'lions' and 'foxes'. Lions achieve power because of their ability to take direct and incisive action, and, as their name suggests, they tend to rule by force. Military dictatorships provide an example of this type of governing elite. By comparison, foxes rule by cunning and guile, by diplomatic manipulation and wheeling and dealing. Pareto believed that European democracies provided an example of this type of elite. Members of a governing elite owe their positions primarily to their personal qualities, either to their lion-like or fox-like characteristics.

Major change in society occurs when one elite replaces another, a process Pareto calls the 'circulation of elites'. All elites tend to become decadent. They 'decay in quality' and lose their 'vigour'. They may become soft and ineffective with the pleasures of easy living and the privileges of power, or set in their ways and too inflexible to respond to changing circumstances. In addition, each type of elite lacks the qualities of its counterpart, qualities which in the long run are essential to maintain power. An elite of lions lacks the imagination and cunning necessary to maintain its rule and will have to admit foxes from the masses to make up for this deficiency. Gradually foxes infiltrate the entire elite and so transform its character. Foxes however lack the ability to take forceful and decisive action which at various times is essential to retain power. An organized minority of lions committed to the restoration of strong government develops and eventually overthrows the elite of foxes. Whereas history to Marx ultimately leads to and ends with the communist utopia, history to Pareto is a never-ending circulation of elites. Nothing ever really changes and history is, and always will be, 'a graveyard of aristocracies'.

Pareto's view of history is both simple and simplistic. He dismisses the differences between political systems such as Western democracies, communist single party states, fascist dictatorships and feudal monarchies as merely variations on a basic theme. All are essentially examples of elite rule and by comparison with this fact, the differences between them are minor. Pareto fails to provide a method of measuring and distinguishing between the supposedly superior qualities of elites. He simply assumes that the qualities of the elite are superior to those of the mass. His criterion for distinguishing between lions and foxes is merely his own interpretation of the style of elite rule. Nor does Pareto provide a way of measuring the process of elite decadence. He does suggest however that if an elite is closed to recruitment from below it is likely to rapidly lose its vigour and vitality and have a short life. As T. B. Bottomore notes, the Brahmins, the elite stratum in the Indian caste system, were a closed group yet survived for many hundreds of years.

Like Pareto, Gaetano Mosca believed that rule by a minority is an inevitable feature of social life. He bases this belief on the evidence of history claiming that in all societies 'two classes of people appear – a class that rules and a class that is ruled. The first class, always the less numerous, performs all political functions, monopolizes power and enjoys the advantages that power brings, whereas the second, the more numerous class, is directed and controlled by the first'. Like Pareto, Mosca believed that the ruling minority are superior to the mass of the population. He claims that they are 'distinguished from the mass of the governed by qualities that give them a certain material, intellectual or even moral superiority' and he provides a sociological explanation for this superiority seeing it as a product of the social background of the elite. Unlike Pareto, who believed that the qualities required for elite rule were the same for all time, Mosca argued that they varied from society to society. For example, in some societies courage and bravery in battle provide access to the elite, in others the skills and capacities needed to acquire wealth.

Pareto saw modern democracies as merely another form of elite domination. He scornfully dismissed those who saw them as a more progressive and representative system of government. Mosca, however, particularly in his later writings, argued that there were important differences between democracies and other forms of elite rule. By comparison with closed systems such as caste and feudal societies, the ruling elite in democratic societies is open. There is therefore a greater possibility of an elite drawn from a wide range of social backgrounds. As a result, the interests of various social groups may be represented in the decisions taken by the elite. The majority may therefore have some control over the government of society. As he became more favourably disposed towards democracy, Mosca argued that 'the modern representative state has made it possible for almost all political forces, almost all social values, to participate in the management of society'. But he stopped short of a literal acceptance of Abraham Lincoln's famous definition of democracy as 'government of the people, by the people, for the people'. To Mosca, democracy was government of the people, it might even be government for the people but it could never be government by the people. Elite rule remained inevitable. Democracy could be no more than representative government with an elite representing the interests of the people. Despite his leanings towards democracy, Mosca retained his dim view of the masses. They lacked the capacity for self-government and required the leadership and guidance of an elite. Indeed Mosca regretted the extension of the franchise to all members of society believing it should be limited to the middle class. He thus remained 'elitist' to the last. (For a further perspective from early elite theory see the section on Michels, Chapter 7, pp. 288–90.)

Elite theory and the USA – C. Wright Mills and Floyd Hunter

Whereas Pareto and Mosca attempt to provide a general theory to explain the nature and distribution of power in all societies, the American sociologist C. Wright Mills presents a less ambitious and wide-ranging version of elite theory. Mills limits his analysis to American society in the 1950s. Unlike the early elite theorists, he does not believe that elite rule is inevitable. In fact he sees it as a fairly recent development in the USA. Unlike Pareto, who rather cynically accepts the domination of the masses by elites, Mills soundly condemns it.

Mills explains elite rule in institutional rather than psychological terms. He rejects the view that members of the elite have superior qualities or psychological characteristics which distinguish them from the rest of the population. Instead he argues that the structure of institutions is such that those at the top of the institutional hierarchy largely monopolize power. Certain institutions occupy key 'pivotal positions' in society and the elite comprise those who hold 'command posts' in those institutions. Mills identifies three key institutions: the major corporations, the military and the federal government. Those who occupy the command posts in these institutions form three elites. In practice, however, the interests and activities of the elites are sufficiently similar and interconnected to form a single ruling minority which Mills terms 'the power elite'. Thus the power elite involves the 'coincidence of economic, military and political power'. For example, Mills claims that 'American capitalism is now in considerable part military capitalism'. Thus as tanks, guns and missiles pour from the factories, the interests of both the economic and military elites are served. In the same way Mills argues that business and government 'cannot now be seen as two distinct worlds'. He refers to political leaders as 'lieutenants' of the economic elite and claims that their decisions systematically favour the interests of the giant corporations. The net result of the coincidence of economic, military and political power is a power elite which dominates American society and takes all decisions of major national and international importance.

However, things were not always thus. The power elite owes its dominance to a change in the 'institutional landscape'. In the nineteenth century economic power was fragmented among a multitude of small businesses. By the 1950s, it was concentrated in the hands of a few hundred giant corporations 'which together hold the keys to economic decision'. Political power was similarly fragmented and localized and, in particular, state legislatures had considerable independence in the face of a weak central government. The federal government eroded the autonomy of the states and political power became increasingly centralized. The growing threat of international conflict has led to a vast increase in the size and power of the military. The local, state controlled militia have been replaced by a centrally directed military organization. These developments have led to a centralization of decision making power. As a result, power is increasingly concentrated in the hands of those in the command posts of the key institutions.

The cohesiveness and unity of the power elite is strengthened by the similarity of the social background of its members and the interchange and overlapping of personnel between the three elites. Members are drawn largely from the upper strata of society; they are mainly Protestant, native-born Americans, from urban areas in the eastern USA. They share similar educational backgrounds and mix socially in the same high-prestige clubs. As a result they tend to share similar values and sympathies which provide a basis for mutual trust and cooperation. Within the power elite there is frequent interchange of personnel between the three elites. For example, a corporation director may become a politician and vice versa. At any one time, individuals may have footholds in more than one elite. Mills notes that 'on the boards of directors we find a heavy overlapping among the members of these several elites'. Thus a general may sit on the board of a large corporation. Similarity of social origin and the interchange and overlapping of personnel strengthens the unity of the power elite.

Mills argues that American society is dominated by a power elite of 'unprecedented power and unaccountability'. He claims that momentous decisions such as American entry into World War II and the dropping of the atomic bomb on Hiroshima were made by the power elite with little or no reference to the people. Despite the fact that such decisions affect all members of society, the power elite is not accountable for its actions either directly to the public or to any body which represents the public interest. The rise of the power elite has led to 'the decline of politics as a genuine and public debate of alternative decisions'. Mills sees no real differences between the two major political parties, the Democrats and the Republicans, and therefore the public are not provided with a choice of alternative policies. The bulk of the population is pictured as a passive and quiescent mass controlled by the power elite which subjects it to 'instruments of psychic management and manipulation'. Excluded from the command posts of power the 'man in the mass' is told what to think, what to feel, what to do and what to hope for by a mass media directed by the elite. Unconcerned with the major issues of the day, he is preoccupied with his personal world of work, leisure, family and neighbourhood. Free from popular control, the power elite pursues its own concerns – power and self-aggrandizement.

Many critics of Mills have argued that his evidence is circumstantial and suggestive rather than conclusive. One of his severest critics, Robert A. Dahl, has claimed that Mills has simply shown that the power elite has the 'potential for control'. By occupying the command posts of major institutions it would certainly appear that its members have this potential. But, as Dahl argues, the potential for control is not 'equivalent to actual control'. Dahl maintains that actual control can only be shown to exist *'by examination of a series of concrete cases where key decisions are made*: decisions on taxation and expenditures, subsidies, welfare programs, military policy and so on'. If it can then be shown that a minority has the power to decide such issues and to overrule opposition to its policies, then the existence of a power elite will have been established. Dahl claims that by omitting to investigate a range of key decisions, Mills has failed to establish where 'actual control' lies. As a result Dahl argues that the case for a power elite remains unproven.

Mills's conclusions about the nature and distribution of power on the national level are largely echoed in an investigation of power on the local level by Floyd Hunter. *Community Power Structure* is a study of a large southern city in the USA given the pseudonym of 'Regional City' but generally believed to be Atlanta, Georgia. Hunter claims that power rests in a small decision making group which is dominated by 'the businessmen's class'. This primarily economic elite rules by 'persuasion, intimidation, coercion and if necessary force'. Through its finance of local political parties, it directly influences who is elected and largely controls local politicians from the state governor on down. Through its ownership of local newspapers and radio and television stations, or because of the large revenues involved from the advertising it places with them, the economic elite has considerable control over the media and has a major influence on the formation of local opinion. With its power to regulate finance, the economic elite can control the granting of mortgages and loans and the issuing of credit cards. This control provides a powerful lever to influence decisions in its favour. Hunter examines a number of important local policy decisions including urban renewal and a sales tax. He claims that the economic elite formulated policy on these issues which was then translated into legislation by the politicians.

There are two main criticisms of Hunter's research. Firstly, he distinguishes the ruling minority by use of the 'reputational method'. This involves asking local people to make judgments on who holds power in the community. Hunter's critics have argued that this merely provides a picture of what people thought the power structure to be. The reality of power may well be very different. Secondly, although Hunter did study actual decisions, he limited his investigation to those issues in which the economic elite claimed an interest. Had he examined a wide range of decisions, he might well have found that groups other than the economic elite wielded power.

Elite theory and communist societies

As a general theory of power in society, elite theory has been strongly criticized. However, in a more limited application, it has found greater support. In particular a number of researchers have argued that a version of elite theory best describes and explains the nature and distribution of power in communist societies. For example, T. B. Bottomore has argued that 'The political system of Communist countries seems to me to approach the pure type of "power elite", that is, a group which, having come to power with the support or acquiescence of particular classes in the population, maintains itself in power chiefly by virtue of being an organized minority confronting the unorganized majority'. Raymond Aron also maintains that power in communist societies can best be represented in terms of an elite model. He argues that in the USSR political, economic and military power are concentrated in the hands of a 'unified elite' which has 'absolute and unbounded power'. The ruling minority directs the economy, making decisions about investment and wage differentials. It commands the military and controls the media, education and public welfare. It makes all important decisions on national and international issues. Aron claims that the unity of the ruling elite stems from the fact that 'Politicians, trade union leaders, public officials, generals and managers all belong to one party and are part of an authoritarian organization'. In a single party state in which political parties other than the Communist Party are illegal and where all important organizations are under state control, Aron argues that the mass of the population is left 'without any means of defence against the elite'. A number of researchers have also argued that the ruling minority in communist societies employs power primarily for self-enrichment rather than for the benefit of society as a whole. As outlined in the previous chapter this view is adopted by Milovan Djilas.

The view of the USSR as a totalitarian society dominated by a ruling elite with absolute power, concerned primarily with furthering its own interests at the expense of the mass of the population, has been criticized by David Lane. He claims that the principal aim of the Soviet elite has been the industrialization and economic development of the USSR. Centralized state control has been a means to this end 'rather than simply being used to further the interests of the political elites'. Elite rule has not been predominantly exploitive. It has been concerned with mobilizing a largely agrarian peasant population for industrial growth. Compared to pre-revolutionary days, there is greater economic and educational equality in the USSR. Lane rejects the view of a ruling elite with absolute power. For example, he shows how the military, leading scientists and industrial managers influenced the policies and decisions of political rulers during the Khrushchev era. While Lane's arguments do not necessarily lead to a rejection of elite theory as applied to the USSR, they do caution against more extreme versions of the theory.

Pluralism – power and politics in Western democracies

Pluralism is a theory which claims to explain the nature and distribution of power in Western democratic societies. Whereas elite theory and Marxism argue that power is concentrated in the hands of a dominant minority, the pluralist perspective maintains that power is dispersed among a variety of groups in society. Pluralism begins from the observation that industrial society is increasingly differentiated into a variety of social groups and sectional interests. For example, with the increasingly specialized division of labour, the number and diversity of occupational groups steadily grows. Each occupational group develops its own particular needs and concerns. This results in the formation of organizations to represent and articulate these interests. Thus as the range and variety of occupations increases, a growing number of specialized organizations such as trade unions and professional associations develop. Organizations representing particular interests in society are known as interest groups. From a pluralist perspective, politics involves competition between a variety of interest groups, each pressing for its own advantage. Since no one group is seen to be dominant, politics is therefore a business of bargaining and compromise.

Most members of society are not directly involved in the political arena. Instead their interests are represented by a relatively small number of leaders who actively participate in the political struggle. For example, the interests of many wage and salary earners are represented by full-time trade union officials. These leaders are often referred to as elites hence the pluralist perspective is sometimes known as elite pluralism. Power is seen to be dispersed amongst a plurality of elites which actively compete with one another to further particular interests. From a pluralist perspective, there is no inconsistency between democracy and the existence of elites. If democracy is seen as a form of government whereby the various groups in society are able to participate in and influence policy formation and decision making, then there is no necessary contradiction between elites and democratic government. Interest groups headed by elites can be seen as the means whereby various interests are channelled and mobilized for participation in government. In this way the main interests in society are represented and as a result all groups have some say in the running of affairs. From this perspective, democracy is seen as representative government.

Democratic government also involves two or more political parties which compete for the votes of the electorate. Unlike interest groups, political parties must appeal to and represent a wide range of interests in order to gain power and form a government. From a pluralist perspective, the government is pictured as a kind of honest broker, mediating and compromising between the demands of the various elites. It is seen to balance the conflicting interests of a multiplicity of interest groups and in doing so ensures a stable society. In Raymond Aron's words, 'Government becomes a business of compromise'. The bulk of the population is not pictured as a passive and manipulated mass. In particular, it is seen to make its presence felt at local and national elections. Via the ballot box, the public is able to articulate its wishes and influence government policy. Thus Karl Mannheim argues that, 'In a democracy, the governed can always act to remove their leaders or force them to take decisions in the interests of the many'. This view of the democratic process is shared by Talcott Parsons as outlined in an earlier section. From a pluralist perspective, politicians compete for popular support and must be responsive to the wishes of the public in order to gain and retain power. Since they can be removed by the governed, they are therefore accountable to them.

Pluralism and the USA – Robert A. Dahl and Arnold M. Rose

A number of studies have provided support for the pluralist position. One of the most famous, *Who Governs?* by Robert A. Dahl, is an investigation of local politics in New Haven, Connecticut. Dahl uses the 'decision making' method arguing that the only way to discover the distribution of power is to examine actual decisions. He investigated a series of decisions in three main 'issue-areas': urban renewal which involved the redevelopment of the city centre; political nominations with particular emphasis on the post of mayor; and education which concerned questions such as the siting of schools and teachers' salaries. By selecting a range of different issues, Dahl claims that it should be possible to discover whether a single group monopolizes decision making in community affairs.

Dahl found no evidence of a ruling elite in New Haven. He claims that power is dispersed among various interest groups and that this plurality of elites does not form a unified group with common interests. He found that interest groups only became involved in local politics when the issues were seen as directly relevant to their particular concerns. In practice, different groups participated in each issue area and the mayor was the only person involved in all three areas. In addition there was hardly any overlap of personnel between the various elites. This suggests that pluralism rather than elite theory best describes the distribution of power in New Haven. Dahl claims that the evidence shows that local politics is a business of bargaining and compromise with no one group dominating decision making. For example, business interests, trade unions and the local university were involved in the issue of urban renewal. The mayor and his assistants made the major decisions in consultation with the various interest groups and produced a programme which was acceptable to all parties concerned. Dahl rejects the view that economic interests dominate decision making. He concludes that, 'Economic notables, far from being a ruling group, are simply one of many groups out of which individuals sporadically emerge to influence the policies and acts of city officials. Almost anything one might say about the influence of economic notables could be said with equal justice about half a dozen other groups in New Haven'.

Dahl's conclusions about the distribution of power on the local level are echoed in a study of power on the national level by Arnold M. Rose. In *The Power Structure*, Rose rejects the view that the USA is ruled by a unified power elite, arguing instead for a 'multi-influence hypothesis'. This approach 'conceives of society as consisting of many elites, each relatively small numerically and operating in different spheres of life. Among the elites are several that have their power through economic controls, several others that have power through political controls, and still others that have power through military, associational, religious and other controls'. Via this multiplicity of relatively independent elites, the major interests in society are represented.

Rose is particularly concerned to show that the political and economic elites do not work hand in glove and so form a single ruling elite. He examines the policies of the National Association of Manufacturers and the United States Chamber of Commerce, bodies which directly represent the economic elites. His evidence indicates that, 'President and Congress more often go against their programs than support them'. In particular, a range of social welfare legislation has been passed in the face of opposition from economic elites. Rose claims that this shows that national politics are not dominated by economic interests and that politicians respond to the demands of various interest groups in society. Thus, during Lyndon Johnson's administration, large amounts of government money were allocated to improve education and alleviate poverty. In addition, the Civil Rights Act (1964) and the Voting Act (1965) guaranteed equal rights to minorities and can be seen as a response to the demands of Black interest groups. From an analysis of a wide range of decisions taken by the national government, Rose claims that the case for a ruling elite is disproved. Decisions are often a compromise between the demands of various elites and no major interest is either systematically favoured or disregarded. Rose concludes, 'We do not say that the multi-influence hypothesis is entirely the fact, or that the United States is completely democratic; we simply say that such statements are more correct for the United States than for any other society'.

Both Dahl and Rose rely heavily on the decision making approach. As previous sections have indicated, this method largely ignores the possibility that some have the power to decide which issues reach the point of decision. If this is so then only 'safe decisions' will be taken, that is decisions which do not fundamentally alter the existing distribution of power and wealth. The fact that a variety of interest groups are then able to influence these safe decisions does not therefore provide evidence of a wide diffusion of power. In addition, Dahl and Rose fail to consider the more general consequences of the decisions they examine. For example, the monies allocated to fight poverty during the Johnson administration had little effect on the distribution of wealth in society. Such measures can be seen as concessions to defuse radical protest and so protect privilege. Further criticisms of the pluralist approach will be examined shortly (pp. 120–22).

Pluralism – political parties and interest groups

From a pluralist perspective, competition between two or more political parties is an essential feature of representative government. Using F. W. Riggs's definition, a political party is 'any organization which nominates candidates for election to a legislature'. Pluralists claim that competition for office between political parties provides the electorate with an opportunity to select its leaders and a means of influencing government policy. This view forms the basis of Seymour M. Lipset's definition of democracy. According to Lipset, 'Democracy in a complex society may be defined as a political system which supplies regular constitutional opportunities for changing the governing officials, and a social mechanism which permits the largest possible part of the population to influence major decisions by choosing among contenders for political office'. For efficient government, Lipset argues that competition between contenders for office must result in the granting of 'effective authority to one group' and the presence of an 'effective opposition' in the legislature as a check on the power of the governing party.

Pluralists claim that political parties in democratic societies are representative for the following reasons. Firstly, the public directly influences party policy, since, in order to be elected to govern, parties must reflect the wishes and interests of the electorate in their programmes. Secondly, if existing parties do not sufficiently represent sections of society, a new party will usually emerge, such as the Labour Party at the turn of the century in Britain. Thirdly, parties are accountable to the electorate since they will not regain power if they disregard the opinions and interests of the public. Finally, parties cannot simply represent a sectional interest since, to be elected to power, they require the support of various interests in society. However, as Robert McKenzie states, political parties must not be seen 'as the sole "transmission belts" on which political ideas and programmes are conveyed from the citizens to the legislature and the executive'. During their time in office and in opposition, parties 'mould and adapt their principles under innumerable pressures brought to bear by organized groups of citizens which operate for the most part outside the political system'. Such groups are known as interest or pressure groups.

Unlike political parties, interest groups do not aim to take power in the sense of forming a government. Rather they seek to influence political parties and the various departments of state. Nor do interest groups usually claim to represent a wide spectrum of interests. Instead their specified objective is to represent a particular interest in society. Interest groups are often classified in terms of their aims as either 'protective' or 'promotional' groups. Protective groups protect the interests of a particular section of society. Thus trade unions such as the National Union of Mineworkers, professional associations such as the British Medical Association and employers' organizations such as the Confederation of British Industry are classified as protective groups. Promotional groups promote a particular cause rather than guarding the interests of a particular social group. Organizations such as the RSPCA, Friends of the Earth and the Lord's Day Observance Society are classified as promotional groups. Membership of promotional groups is potentially larger and usually more varied than that of protective groups since they require only a commitment to their cause as a qualification for joining. By comparison, membership of protective groups is usually limited to individuals of a particular status, for example miners for membership of the NUM. In practice the distinction between protective and promotional groups is not clear cut since the defence of an interest also involves its promotion.

Interest groups can bring pressure to bear in a number of ways. Firstly, by contributions to the funds of political parties such as trade union contributions to the Labour Party. Secondly, by illegal payments to elected representatives and state officials, in other words bribery. The Lockheed bribery scandal and the Poulson affair, although involving a particular company and individual rather than an interest group as such, provide an indication of how government officials can be corruptly influenced. Thirdly, by appealing to public opinion. An effective campaign by an interest group can mobilize extensive public support especially if it attracts widespread coverage by the mass media. Certain conservation groups have successfully adopted this strategy. Fourthly, by various forms of civil disobedience. This approach has been used by a wide variety of interest groups from rate-payers associations witholding rates to Women's Liberation groups disrupting beauty competitions to Black organizations breaking segregation laws. Fifthly, by the provision of expertise. It has often been argued that in modern industrial society, governments cannot operate without the specialized knowledge of interest groups. By providing this expertise interest groups have an opportunity to directly influence government policy. In Britain, representatives of interest groups now have permanent places on some 500 government advisory committees. Dowse and Hughes argue that 'interest groups constitute a continuous mandate for the government and without them no government could conceivably be regarded as democratic. More to the point, no government could begin to operate without the assistance of interest groups'.

From a pluralist perspective, political parties and interest groups are cornerstones of democracy. They are the means by which representative government is possible in large, complex societies. Via these organizations a multitude of interests are articulated and mobilized to participate in the running of society. Politics is a process of competition and bargaining and government is a process of mediation and compromise. Power is dispersed among a variety of groups and, as a result, all major interests in society are able to have some say in the conduct of affairs. (For views on the role of professional associations in the political process see Chapter 2, pp. 69–74; for trade unions see Chapter 6, pp. 262–7.)

Government in Britain – a pluralist perspective

Support for the pluralist position is provided by a number of studies which investigate the passage of legislation in the British Parliament. In an important study using the decision making approach, Christopher J. Hewitt examined twenty-four policy issues which arose in the British Parliament from 1944 to 1964. The issues covered four main policy areas: foreign policy e.g. the Suez crisis of 1956; economic policy e.g. the nationalization of road haulage; welfare policy e.g. the Rent Act of 1957; and social policy, e.g. the introduction of commercial television. Hewitt compared the decisions reached by Parliament with the views of the interest groups involved and contemporary public opinion. In some cases the decisions favoured certain interest groups to the exclusion of others. In other cases government decisions favoured some groups but 'substantial concessions were made to the opposing interests'. However, Hewitt found that no one interest group consistently got its own way. He states that, 'Neither the business group nor any other appears to be especially favoured by the government'. Poll data on public opinion was available on eleven of the twenty-four issues included in the study. In only one case – the abolition of capital punishment in 1957 – did the decisions of Parliament oppose public opinion. Hewitt's study suggests that both a variety of specialized interests and public opinion in general are represented by the British Parliament. He concludes that the 'picture of national power that is revealed suggests a "pluralist" interpretation since a diversity of conflicting intersts are involved in many issues, without any one interest being consistently successful in realizing its goals'.

A study of the relationship between government and the Confederation of British Industry (CBI) by Wyn Grant and David Marsh reaches similar conclusions. Created in 1965 from an amalgamation of three employers' federations, membership of the CBI includes three-quarters of the top 200 manufacturing companies in Britain. It has direct channels of communication with government ministers and top civil servants, and is concerned with furthering the interests of private industry, particularly the manufacturing sector. In order to assess its influence on government Grant and Marsh examined four pieces of legislation from 1967 to 1972. The CBI fiercely opposed the Iron and Steel Act of 1967 which renationalized the iron and steel industry. Its views were rejected by the Labour government and, according to Grant and Marsh, the CBI 'fought an almost entirely unsuccessful defensive action'. The Clean Air Act of 1968 aimed to reduce air pollution. The two main interest groups involved were the CBI and the National Society for Clean Air. The CBI was successful in obtaining various modifications to the bill and the resulting act was a compromise between the views of the two interest groups. The Deposit of Poisonous Wastes Act of 1972 was concerned with the disposal of solid and semi-solid toxic wastes. The Conservative government was under strong pressure from conservation groups and in particular the Warwickshire Conservation Society which mobilized strong public support. Although the CBI obtained some important concessions, it by no means got all its own way. Grant and Marsh observe that, 'It would seem, then, that a new interest group (The Warwickshire Conservation Society) with hardly any permanent staff can exert as much influence over a specific issue as the CBI'. The Industry Act of 1972 was directed to regional development. The CBI was particularly concerned to prevent the government from having the right to buy shares in private industry. Its members were suspicious of any measures which might give the government more control over private industry. The TUC, on the other hand, favoured direct government investment, particularly in labour intensive service industries, to ease the problem of unemployment. In practice neither interest group appears to have had much influence though the TUC were happier than the CBI with the final act. The government pursued a relatively independent policy which was a response to 'the immediate demands of economic and political situations' rather than to the pressures of either interest group.

Grant and Marsh conclude that 'the CBI has little consistent direct influence over the policies pursued by government'. Despite its powerful membership and its access to the highest levels of government, 'the CBI's ability to influence events is limited by the government's need to retain the support of the electorate and by the activities of other interest groups'.

Pluralism – a critique

A large body of evidence from studies such as those of Dahl and Rose in America, and Hewitt and Grant and Marsh in Britain, appears to support the pluralist position. However, there are a number of serious criticisms of pluralism. Firstly, as noted in the criticisms of Dahl and Rose, pluralists largely ignore 'non-decision making', that is the possibility that some have the power to prevent certain issues from reaching the point of decision. As a result only 'safe-decisions' may be taken: decisions which do not fundamentally alter the structure of inequality. From this point of view, it is in the interests of the powerful to allow a variety of interest groups to influence safe decisions. This provides the illusion of real participation and helps to create the myth of representative government. It disguises the real basis of power and so protects the powerful. Thus evidence drawn from actual decisions does not necessarily prove the pluralists' case. Secondly, pluralists tend to concentrate on the process of decision making rather than the results and consequences of those decisions. As Westergaard and Resler argue, 'power is visible only through its consequences'. Western democracies have done little to change the basic structure of inequality during the past fifty years. Despite a plethora of legislation aimed at improving the lot of the poor, there has been little redistribution of wealth. Studies of actual decisions might give the impression that the interests of the poor are represented in government policy. Studies of the results of that policy may provide a very different picture. Thirdly, there is a tendency for pluralists to assume that the electorate is adequately represented if its opinions are reflected by government. However, from a Marxian perspective, public opinion can be seen as false class consciousness. From this viewpoint, governments which reflect public opinion can hardly be acting in the public interest. Fourthly, pluralists often claim to have disproved the existence of a ruling class by providing evidence of a range of government decisions made in the face of opposition from groups representing the interests of capital. From their study of the CBI, Grant and Marsh conclude that, 'Above all, what has emerged from our study is a reaffirmation of the autonomy of the political sphere from the economic sphere'. But, as Poulantzas has argued, from a Marxian perspective this is to be expected. The state must have 'relative autonomy' in order to effectively represent ruling class interests. In particular, it must have the freedom to make concessions to the subject class in order to prevent radical opposition to the status quo.

Pluralists tend to assume that all major interests in society are represented. This assumption is questionable. The fairly recent emergence in Britain of consumer associations and citizens' advice bureaus can be seen as representing the interests of consumers against big business and of citizens against government bureaucracy. But it cannot be assumed that such interests were absent, unthreatened or adequately represented before the existence of such organizations. Pluralists admit that the power and influence of interest groups varies, but tend to ignore this in their analysis. The existence of an interest group says nothing about its effectiveness in representing its members. The NAACP (National Association for the Advancement of Colored People) is a case in point. Founded in 1910, the NAACP attempted to represent the interests of

Black Americans. Yet it made no important breakthrough until 1954 when NAACP lawyers brought a case to the Supreme Court which resulted in a decision declaring racial segregation in education to be unconstitutional. Pluralists may point to this decision and the civil rights legislation of the 1960s and suggest that Black interests are being represented. However, this ignores the fact that for over forty years, the NAACP could hardly dent the forces of racial prejudice and discrimination, and the fact that the Black masses still form the base of the American stratification system. It is doubtful whether the differences in power between interest groups are consistent with the idea of democracy. Indeed some critics of the pluralist position have denied the whole notion of the compatibility of representative elites in the form of interest groups and democratic government. This view will be examined later in the chapter.

Managers and corporations

Each of the models of the power structure in industrial society emphasizes the importance of the forces of production. In terms of Marxian theory, ownership and control of the forces of production provide the basis of ruling class power. The economic elite of 'corporation chieftains' forms an integral part of Mills's power elite. Industry and finance form major interest groups from a pluralist perspective. A somewhat different version of the relationship of the forces of production and the distribution of power in society is presented by James Burnham in *The Managerial Revolution*, first published in 1941. Burnham argued that the decline of older forms of capitalism and the rise of the joint stock company has led to a separation of ownership and control in industry. The owner-manager is largely a figure of the past and has been replaced by two groups: salaried managers who control the company and shareholders who own it. Effective control has been transferred to the managers since decision making is largely in their hands.

Like Marxists, Burnham argues that power in society is based on control of the forces of production. However, like elite theorists, he maintains that elite rule is inevitable. Major change in society therefore involves the replacement of one elite by another. Burnham believed that such a change was occurring with the replacement of owner-managers by salaried managers. He argued that a skilled and technically qualified managerial elite would become increasingly powerful. Their power would reach its height if and when the state nationalized all industrial enterprises which would end competition between companies. Thus communist societies represent the extreme form of 'managerial societies'.

Burnham was rather pessimistic about the managerial revolution. He pictured a managerial elite with few checks on its power and concerned primarily with its own interests. Later writers have taken a more optimistic view. They foresee a benevolent, socially responsible management which is not simply preoccupied with the pursuit of profit. Instead management is seen to be increasingly concerned with the company as a whole and the service it provides, with growth, productivity and efficiency rather than returns on shareholders' investments. Factors such as the quality of the product and the welfare of the workforce will assume greater priority with profits taking second place.

Burnham's argument and its later development have been strongly criticized by Marxist writers who maintain that the separation of ownership and control is largely illusory. They make the following points. Firstly, many top managers are shareholders in the companies which employ them. As such their interests and those of shareholders in general are broadly similar. Secondly, it is this group of top managers who make the major decisions on vital issues such as investment and mergers. Thirdly, their primary motivation as managers is the maximization of profit. This is due to the fact their salaries depend partly on profit levels and dividends on their shareholdings are solely dependent on profits. In addition, profit is essential for a company to stay in business in a competitive capitalist system. Finally, according to Westergaard and Resler, in a capitalist economy, 'The aim of profit is simply taken for granted'.

The emphasis on managers has stemmed from the concern of many researchers with what they see as the rapidly growing power of giant, privately owned corporations. Conglomerates – companies producing a range of distinct products such as Cadbury/Schweppes – and multinationals – companies with production units in a number of countries such as the Ford Motor Company – are increasingly dominating the economies of advanced capitalist societies. Wealth is more and more concentrated in the hands of a relatively few giant corporations. In 1967, for example, the sales turnover of the General Motors Corporation was larger than the gross national product of Belgium.

While recognizing the growing power of the large corporation, some pluralists have argued that it is restrained by 'countervailing power'. The theory of countervailing power argues that when one interest threatens to dominate others, counterbalancing forces develop either amongst previously unorganized groups or existing groups. Thus consumer organizations develop to balance the power of manufacturers and the retail trade, trade unions to counter employers, and national governments extend their powers to restrain the large corporations. Monopolies commissions, price controls and profit taxes provide examples of the ways in which governments curb the power of the corporation. Some researchers, however, take a rather different view, seeing few restraints on corporation power. Andrew Hacker is particularly concerned about the scope of this power and argues that 'decisions made in the names of these huge companies guide and govern, directly and indirectly, all our lives'.

These decisions include the location of plants and offices and whether to expand or close down particular factories. This affects population movement, employment levels and the growth or decline of towns and cities. Decisions concerning the nature of production – whether or not to automate the production line – and of administration – whether or not to introduce computers into the office – can affect the educational and skill requirements of the labour force and employment levels. The man in the street is unable to participate in these decisions which may well shape his life. Hacker claims that, 'If the contours of the economy and society are being shaped in a hundred or so boardrooms, so far as the average citizen is concerned these decisions are in the lap of the gods'.

Hacker argues that via the mass media, the power of the corporation is felt in every living room in the USA. By means of advertising, companies control 'taste formation', creating a need and therefore a demand for their products. This control of the public through the media goes beyond the content of advertisements. Carl Kaysen argues that by threatening to withdraw their advertising, giant corporations such as General Motors and Standard Oil can directly influence the political content of the media. American television is particularly susceptible to this form of control since corporations often sponsor a series of programmes. If the content offends their views, they can withdraw the advertising revenue on which the television companies depend. Kaysen claims that 'the political tone of the media is far from reflecting even approximately the distribution of attitudes and opinions in society as a whole'.

Pluralists have tended to judge the power of business interests by means of decisions made by local and national government bodies. As Grant and Marsh's study of the CBI shows, the power of business appears to be limited by competing interest groups and the government. However, this is a rather narrow view of politics. It concentrates on the interplay of interest groups and government. As Hacker and Kaysen have indicated, many important decisions are taken outside this particular political arena. The power and influence of giant corporations extend beyond what has traditionally been defined as the political process.

Political recruitment

Top managers and members of the boards of large corporations are largely recruited from a small section of the population. This applies to most other elite groups such as politicians, judges and higher civil servants. As the previous chapter has indicated, there is a considerable degree of elite self-recruitment in Western society. Before considering the possible implications of this process, some of the evidence will be examined.

In an article entitled, *The Social Background and Connections of 'Top Decisions Makers'*, Tom Lupton and Shirley Wilson trace the kinship and marital connections of six categories of 'top decision makers'. These categories are ministers, senior civil servants and directors of the Bank of England, the big five banks, city firms and insurance companies. Lupton and Wilson constructed twenty-four kinship diagrams, usually covering three generations and indicating relationships by birth and marriage. Seventy-three of the top decision makers appear on these diagrams, accounting for 18% of the total number of people included in the twenty-four extended family groupings. Clearly there are close kinship and marital ties between the elites examined and certain families are disproportionately represented in the ranks of top decision makers.

Research on the social background of members of the British Parliament indicates a marked degree of elite self-recruitment. Studies by W. L. Guttsman show that despite its claim to represent the nation, membership of the House of Commons is far from representative in terms of social origin. Table 9 shows the 'social composition' of the House of Commons in 1951 and 1970. The figures refer to the percentage of the total membership which falls into each category.

Table 9

	1951	1970
Elementary school only	13.0	10.0
Public schools	48.7	47.5
Oxbridge (Oxford and Cambridge)	36.2	38.9
All universities	51.9	58.8
Army and navy	5.5	4.0
Lawyers	18.0	19.5
Other professions	13.0	21.0
Commerce and industry	22.0	22.5
Manual workers and clerks	21.0	13.0

(Adapted from Guttsman 'The British Political Elite and the Class Structure' in Stanworth and Giddens (eds) *Elites and Power in British Society*, Cambridge University Press)

The table shows the importance of public school and Oxbridge as a route to the Commons. Nearly 50% of all MPs attended public schools and over 33% went to Oxbridge. During the late 1950s and early 1960s over 50% of the places at Oxbridge went to public school students. Ron Hall's study of the social background of students who attended Eton, the most prestigious British public school, shows that the vast majority are drawn from the families of the aristocracy, landed gentry, the higher professions, high ranking officers in the armed forces and directors and managers in industry and commerce.

A study by Richard Whitley conducted in 1971 of directors of large British companies produced similar findings to those of Lupton and

Wilson and Guttsman. Whitley compiled a list of 261 directors from the top forty industrial firms, the major clearing banks and merchant banks and the leading insurance companies. Sufficient information was available on some 50% of the directors. Again the importance of public schools as a route to elite status is evident. Some 66% of the directors of industrial companies and 80% of the directors of financial companies attended public schools. Oxbridge, the next stage on the road to the top, is again in evidence. Of those directors who went on to higher education, around 66% from industrial companies and 87% from financial firms went to Oxbridge. As in the Lupton and Wilson study, Whitley discovered relationships of kinship and marriage between directors, particularly in the financial firms. Of the twenty-seven financial firms in the study, twenty-six were connected by kinship and marriage when relationships were traced back over three generations.

Elite self-recruitment is particularly apparent when the social background of company chairmen is investigated. From a study of 460 British company chairmen conducted in 1971, Stanworth and Giddens found that only 1% had working-class origins, 10% had middle-class backgrounds and 66% came from the upper class which is defined as 'industrialists, landowners (and) others who possess substantial property and wealth'. There were insufficient data to classify the remaining 23%. Again public schools and Oxbridge figure prominently. 65% of the chairmen attended public schools, 7% were privately educated, 11% went to other forms of secondary school, data on the remaining 17% being unavailable. Despite the expansion of secondary education, there is little evidence of the supposed rise of the 'grammar school executive' from humbler origins. Stanworth and Giddens conclude that 'while this may take place at other levels of management, it is likely to stop short, as in previous generations, at the doors of the boardroom'.

Studies of the social background of elites indicate that their members are drawn largely from a small upper stratum of the population but it cannot simply be assumed that they will automatically represent the interests of that stratum. Nor can it be assumed that if their social origins were representative of the population as a whole, elites would represent the interests of all groups in society. However, some elite theorists and Marxists have argued that inferences which support their respective theories can be drawn from studies of the social background of elites. Thus C. Wright Mills has argued that the cohesion and unity of the power elite owes much to the common origins and education of its members. This provides a basis for trust and understanding and fosters common attitudes, sympathies and loyalties. A consciousness of kind develops which is strengthened by ties of friendship, kinship and marriage. When these factors are combined with the reality of elite power, Mills believes that the unity of the power elite is assured. Westergaard and Resler draw similar inferences with reference to the ruling class in Britain. For example, they suggest that because of the similarity of their backgrounds, top civil servants will tend to be sympathetic to the interests of business-men. John Rex makes a similar point with particular reference to the edu-cational background of elites. He argues that the public schools and Oxbridge serve to socialize future top decision makers into a belief in the legitimacy of the status quo and in particular the rule of the capitalist class. Rex suggests that 'the whole system of "Establishment" education has been used to ensure a common mind on the legitimacy of the existing order of things among those who have to occupy positions of power and decision'.

Taken on their own, studies of the social background of elites are of limited significance. However, a number of plausible inferences can be drawn from the results of such studies, as the preceding discussion has indicated.

Political participation

Many pluralists have argued that representative government does not require the active participation of the mass of the population. This would appear to be the case if democracies operate as they suggest, with elites representing the interests of the majority. In Western societies the bulk of the population is not actively involved in the political process. Lester Milbrath has suggested that members of society can be divided into four categories in terms of their degree of political participation. Firstly, the politically apathetic who are 'unaware literally of the political world around them'. Secondly, those involved in 'spectator activities' which include voting and taking part in discussions about politics. Thirdly, those involved in 'transitional activities' which include attending a politi-cal meeting or making a financial contribution to a political party. Fin-ally, those who enter the political arena and participate in 'gladiatorial activities' such as standing for and holding public and party offices. Mil-brath estimates that in the USA, 30% of the population is politically apa-thetic, 60% reaches the level of spectator activities, from 7 to 9% is involved in transitional activities while only 1 to 3% participates in gladia-torial activities.

These levels of political participation are not uniformly distributed throughout the population. In general the higher an individual's position in the class structure, the greater his degree of participation. Various studies have shown that political participation is directly proportional to income level, occupational status and educational qualifications. It has also been associated with a variety of other factors. For example, men are likely to have higher levels of participation than women, Whites than Blacks, married people than single people, the middle aged than either the young or the old, members of clubs and associations than non-members, long-term residents in a community than short-term residents. The following explanations have been advanced to account for these differences. Firstly, those with low levels of participation often lack the resources and opportunities to become more directly involved in politics. They lack the experience of higher education which brings a greater awareness of the political process and knowledge of the mechanics of participation. They lack the opportunities which high status occupations often bring of contact with officialdom and dealings with the upper levels of hierarchies in various organizations. It can be a relatively short step from this experience to politics in the narrower sense. Secondly, individuals are unlikely to participate in politics if they feel the probability of reward for involvement is low. Those who receive low rewards as part of their daily routine are unlikely to have high levels of political participation since their experience has shown that effort does not bring worthwhile results. This explanation may apply to Blacks, to low paid workers in dead-end jobs and generally to those at the base of the class system. Such groups have little power in society and may well feel that their participation will have little effect. As Robert Dahl argues, an individual is unlikely to become involved in politics if he thinks the probability of his influencing the outcome of events is low. Thirdly, levels of political participation appear to be related to the degree of involvement and integration of the individual in society. Thus an individual is unlikely to become involved in local or national politics if he does not feel a part of either the local community or the wider society. This may explain the low political participation of Blacks who have been segregated from the wider society, of women who are often socially isolated as housewives and mothers, of new residents who have yet to become integrated into the community, of non-members of clubs and associations who may live a privatized life and of the old who have been pensioned off and removed from the mainstream of society. Finally, as Robert Dahl suggests, individuals are unlikely to have high levels of political participation if they believe that the outcome of events will be satisfactory without their involvement. This possibility will be discussed shortly.

The findings referred to above are broad generalizations which permit many exceptions. During the 1970s in the USA, the level of participation of Blacks in politics rose steadily. As the following chapter shows, research has indicated that the poor do not have a uniformly low level of political participation. Involvement in politics varies considerably within the working class. For example, manual workers living in occupational communities, such as miners, have a relatively high level of participation. Miners are strongly unionized and their turnout at national elections is high. Integration in occupational communities may counter other factors which might discourage participation. By comparison, farm labourers who are scattered in relatively small, isolated groups are less likely to be trade union members and have one of the lowest levels of political participation of any occupational group.

Interpretations of the significance of differential political participation vary. Some pluralists have argued that low participation may be an indication that the interests of the politically inactive are adequately represented. Others such as Lipset have argued that, 'The combination of a low vote and a relative lack of organization among the low-status groups means that they will suffer from neglect by politicians who will be receptive to the wishes of the more privileged, participating and organized strata'. The argument that low participation can be equated with adequate representation is difficult to sustain in the case of low-income groups. It can be argued that the interests of the lower strata are those least well served by the political system. Rather than reflecting satisfaction with the status quo, low political participation may indicate a rejection of the political process. This view is taken by Dye and Zeigler who argue that, 'The rejection of politics and politicians is a basic feature of the rejection of democracy itself'. This point can be illustrated by the example of Black riots in American cities during the late 1960s. The rioters rejected the democratic process as a means of representing Black interests. The *Report of the National Advisory Commission on Civil Disorders*, the official inquiry into the riots, states that the 'typical rioter' was 'highly distrustful of the political system'. Many Blacks saw violence as the only effective avenue of political participation open to them. The Commission makes it clear that participation is what they wanted. It states that, 'What the rioters appeared to be seeking was fuller participation in the social order and the material benefits enjoyed by the majority of American citizens'. This example shows clearly that, at least in the case of Black Americans, low political participation does not mean that the politically inactive believe that their interests are adequately represented.

This section has briefly examined some of the research on political participation in Western society. The following section focusses on a specific form of political participation: voting behaviour.

Voting behaviour

It has often been argued that the class struggle, which Marx predicted would end in the proletarian revolution, has been institutionalized in Western society. With the extension of the franchise and the proliferation of interest groups, members of the working class are drawn into the political process. Their interests are represented by political parties and interest groups such as trade unions. They are able to express their discontent within an institutional framework and as a result the more violent expressions of class conflict are unlikely. There is a general consensus in society that the political game should be conducted according to a set of rules within which the class struggle is played out. In view of these factors, the likelihood of class antagonisms leading to revolution is regarded as slim. Seymour M. Lipset, who supports this view, sees national elections as 'the expression of the class struggle' and competition between political parties as the institutionalization of class conflict. He argues that, 'More than anything else the party struggle is a conflict among classes, and the most impressive thing about party support is that in virtually every economically developed country the lower-income groups vote mainly for parties of the left, while higher-income groups vote mainly for parties of the right'.

Parties of the left, such as the British Labour Party, are often seen to represent the interests of the lower strata with their apparent concern with a more equitable distribution of wealth and their commitment to social welfare policies. The division between left and right is rather rough and ready since the left ranges from the American Democratic Party to the British Labour Party to West European Communist Parties. By comparison the right, which includes the American Republican Party and the British Conservative Party, is usually seen as more concerned with maintaining the status quo and with defending the interests of wealth and privilege.

Voting behaviour, however, does not directly reflect these characterizations. It does not strictly follow class lines. For example, in Britain since 1945, about one third of the working class has voted for the Conservative Party. Without this support, the Conservatives could not be returned to power. Many sociologists have tended to assume that working-class support for left-wing parties and middle-class support for parties of the right require little explanation since those parties represent their respective interests. Thus research has concentrated on 'cross-class voting', on those who deviate from the norm of class voting patterns. The working-class Tory, and to a lesser extent the middle-class socialist, have been the focus of considerable research.

Voting behaviour and social class in Britain

One of the earliest explanations of working-class Conservative voting was given in the late nineteenth century by Walter Bagehot. He argued that the British are typically deferential to authority and prone to defer decision making to those 'born to rule' whom they believe 'know better'. Hence the attraction of the Conservative Party which, particularly in the nineteenth century, was largely staffed from the ranks of the landed gentry, the wealthy and the privileged. The Conservatives represented traditional authority and Bagehot argued that party image, rather than specific policies, is the major factor affecting voting behaviour.

In the early 1960s, Robert McKenzie and Alan Silver investigated the relationship between deferential attitudes and working-class support for the Conservative Party. They claim that deference accounts for the voting behaviour of about half the working-class Tories in their sample. Deference was measured by giving respondents a choice between two candidates for Prime Minister. The first candidate had attended Eton, graduated from Oxford and served as an officer in the Guards. He was the son of a Member of Parliament who was a banker by profession. The second candidate was a lorry driver's son. He went to a grammar school, graduated from a provincial university and became an officer in the regular army. Around half the working-class Tories chose the first candidate explaining their choice with statements like, 'Breeding counts every time. I like to be set an example and have someone I can look up to'. By comparison only one fifth of the working-class Labour voters selected this candidate. Deferential Conservative voters tended to be older and to have lower incomes than the overall sample, and were more likely to be female. McKenzie and Silver suggest that deference is part of a more general traditional outlook. This would help to explain the high proportion of older deferential voters. Also many low-income workers have traditional rural backgrounds and women, with their attention centred on the home, have tended to be insulated from change.

Those working-class Tories whose support for the Conservative Party could not be accounted for by deferential attitudes were termed 'secular voters' by McKenzie and Silver. Seculars' attachment to the Conservative Party is based on pragmatic, practical considerations. They evaluate party policy and base their support on the tangible benefits, such as higher living standards, that they hope to gain. They vote Conservative because of a belief in that party's superior executive and administrative ability. McKenzie and Silver suggest that working-class support for the Conservatives has an increasingly secular rather than a deferential basis. They argue that this change helps to explain the increasing volatility of British voting patterns. Seculars are unlikely to vote simply on the basis of party loyalty. Almost all the deferentials but only half the seculars stated that they would definitely vote Conservative in the next election. The seculars were waiting to judge specific policies rather than basing their vote on traditional party loyalties.

Various studies have shown that manual workers who identify themselves as middle class are more likely to vote Conservative than those who see themselves as working class. After the Labour Party lost its third consecutive election in 1959, Butler and Rose suggested that growing numbers of manual workers were identifying with the middle class. They argued that increasing affluence led to the adoption of middle-class attitudes and life styles by many manual workers. From this developed a middle-class identification which led to support for the Conservative Party. This argument is a version of the embourgeoisement thesis discussed in the previous chapter. A study by Eric Nordlinger found no support for this explanation. The Labour voters in Nordlinger's sample earned on average slightly more than the working-class Tories although the factor which appeared to differentiate the two groups was not income as such but the degree of satisfaction with income. Working-class Tories were found to be much more satisfied with their levels of income than their Labour counterparts. Satisfaction would lead to a desire to maintain the status quo, hence support for the Conservative Party with its more traditional image. Dissatisfaction would lead to a desire for change, hence support for Labour, with its image as the party of change.

The argument that working-class affluence leads to Conservative voting was further discredited by Goldthorpe and Lockwood's study of affluent workers in Luton. They found that affluence does not lead to middle-class identification nor to support for the Conservative Party. Of the affluent workers in Luton who voted in the 1955 and 1959 elections, nearly 80% voted Labour which is a significantly higher percentage than for the working class as a whole. Goldthorpe and Lockwood found that the most common reason given for Labour support was 'a general "working-class" identification with Labour' and a feeling that the party more closely represented the interests of the 'working man'. However, there appeared to be little of the deep-seated party loyalty which is supposed to be characteristic of the traditional working class. Like his attitude to work, the Luton worker's support for Labour is largely instrumental. He is primarily concerned with the pay-off for him in terms of higher living standards.

Goldthorpe and Lockwood argue that affluence as such reveals little about working-class political attitudes. They maintain that, 'the understanding of contemporary working-class politics is to be found, first and foremost, in the structure of the worker's group attachments and not, as many have suggested, in the extent of his income and possessions'. The importance of 'group attachments' is borne out by their research. Those affluent workers who voted Conservative usually had white-collar connections. Either their parents, siblings or wives had white-collar jobs or they themselves had previously been employed in a white-collar occupation. These 'bridges' to the middle class appear to be the most important factor accounting for working-class Conservatism in the Luton sample. Attachments with and exposure to members of another class appear to have a strong influence on cross-class voting.

This idea has been developed by Frank Parkin. He argues that through greater exposure to members of the middle class than their Labour counterparts, working-class Tories have internalized the 'dominant value system' which the Conservative Party represents. Bob Jessop finds support for this view from a survey conducted in the early 1970s. He argues that members of the working class vote Conservative 'because they are relatively isolated from the structural conditions favourable to radicalism and Labour voting'. These conditions serve to insulate manual workers from the middle class and from the dominant value system. They are found in their most extreme form in the mining, shipbuilding and dock industries. Traditionally workers in these industries have formed occupational communities in single industry towns. Insulation from members of the middle class both at work and in the community has led to the development of a working-class subculture which provides an alternative to the dominant value system. In this setting strong loyalties to the Labour Party have developed.

Compared to the amount of research on working-class voting behaviour, little attention has been given to the middle class. Around one fifth of middle-class voters regularly support the Labour Party, a smaller proportion of cross-class voting than is found in the working class. In a study of 'middle-class radicals', Frank Parkin found they were likely to have occupations 'in which there is a primary emphasis upon either the notion of service to the community, human betterment or welfare and the like or upon self-expression and creativity'. Such occupations include teaching and social work. Since Labour is seen as the party mainly concerned with social welfare, voting Labour is a means of furthering the ideals which led people to select these occupations. Middle-class Labour voters tend to be outside the mainstream of capitalism. Parkin states that their 'life chances rest primarily upon intellectual attainment and personal qualifications, not upon ownership of property or inherited wealth'. As such they have no vested interest in private industry which the Conservative Party is seen to represent.

Class, party and society

Studies of voting behaviour have shown that social class has an important influence on voting patterns. In Britain some two-thirds of the working class vote Labour and around four-fifths of the middle class vote Conservative. This may lend support to those who claim that the class struggle has been institutionalized by means of elections and competition between political parties. It can be argued that support for parties of either the right or the left is the means by which members of society express their class interests and class based aspirations and antagonisms. As a result class conflict is contained within an institutional framework and social stability is maintained. Yet cross-class voting may be as important to the maintenance of a stable society as voting along class lines. Lipset has argued that the working-class Tory and the white-collar socialist 'are not merely deviants from class patterns, but basic requirements for the maintenance of the political system. A system in which the support of different parties corresponds too closely to basic social divisions cannot continue on a democratic basis, for it reflects a state of conflict so intense and clear cut as to rule out compromise'. Since political parties rely for their support on both working and middle-class voters, they must reflect the interests of both classes in their programmes. This results in the political compromises which Lipset sees as essential for stable democratic government. However, such compromises may reduce the differences between the main political parties to the point where there is little to choose between them. This possibility will now be considered.

Many observers have claimed that there are no important differences between the major political parties in Western democracies. Despite the division into left and right, their basic policies have been seen as essentially similar. Referring to the Labour and Conservative Parties in Britain, Bob Jessop argues that they have 'a common commitment to the managed economy, the welfare state, the parliamentary system and the total social structure. Actual differences in policy and practice are marginal in comparison with this fundamental agreement on the foundations of society'. Dye and Zeigler have made similar observations about the Democratic and Republican Parties in the USA. They claim that, 'American parties do, in fact, subscribe to the same fundamental political ideology'. If these observations are accepted, they can be interpreted from a number of perspectives. From a functionalist viewpoint, the essential similarities between parties are a reflection of value consensus in society. From a pluralist perspective, they can be seen as a result of the compromises that political parties must make if they are to represent the interests of all sections of society. In terms of elite theory, major differences between parties would not be expected since politicians, no matter what their political persuasion, are members of the ruling elite. As such they are concerned primarily with the maintenance of elite power. From a Marxian perspective, political parties in a capitalist system, no matter what their stated policies, will ultimately be forced to act in similar ways by the constraints of the system. In Miliband's words, 'A capitalist economy has its own "rationality" to which any government and state must sooner or later submit, and usually sooner'.

If there is little difference between the major political parties, what is the point of elections? Arguing from the viewpoint of elite theory, Dye and Zeigler make the following points. Elections are a device to divert and pacify the masses. The excitement and razzmatazz which is particularly evident in American elections, serves as a Roman circus to entertain and distract the mass of the population from the true nature of elite rule. Elections create the illusion that power rests with the majority. They foster the myth that the masses are directly participating in the political process. They create the impression that the elite represents the interests of the people. In this way elite rule is justified and legitimated. Dye and Zeigler conclude that, 'Elections are primarily a symbolic exercise that helps tie the masses to the established order'.

The democratic ideal

Abraham Lincoln defined democracy as 'government of the people, by the people, for the people'. Whether or not this definition describes the political process in so-called Western democracies is a matter of opinion. Democracy is an emotive term which to many implies the freedom of the individual to participate in those decisions which affect his life. This suggests that the individual should be directly and regularly involved in the political process. Only then will the ideal of government by the people become a reality. However, from a pluralist perspective, there is no inconsistency between democracy and the exclusion of the majority from active participation in the political process. From this viewpoint, democracy is seen as a system of representative government whereby a plurality of elites represent the range of interests in society. The pluralists suggest that in a complex industrial society this is the only practical form that democracy can take. They imply that direct participation by the majority is not only unnecessary but undesirable. With mass participation, decision making would become so cumbersome and drawn out that the machinery of government would at best be inefficient, at worst grind to a halt. The pluralist perspective therefore implies that representative government is the only way the democratic ideal can be realized in contemporary society.

Pluralists have often been attacked for what many see as their narrow and restricted view of democracy. T. B. Bottomore argues that they tend 'to take representative government as the ideal instead of measuring it against the ideal of direct participation by people in legislation and administration'. Bottomore regards the Western system of government as an 'imperfect realization of democracy in so far as it does permanently exclude many from any experience of government'. He sees this experience as essential for government by the people. He argues that only when the democratic ideal becomes an established feature of everyday life can a democratic system of national government be created. This would involve 'social democracy' whereby people directly participate in the government of their local communities and 'industrial democracy' whereby workers will directly participate in the management of their firms. Only this experience will provide 'the habits of responsible choice and self-government which political democracy calls for'. Bottomore argues that a truly democratic national government will only be possible when all the major institutions of society operate on democratic principles.

Democracy can be seen as a system in which every individual has an equal opportunity to participate in the political process and an equal say in the government of society. From this viewpoint Western societies cannot be considered truly democratic. The presence of widespread social inequality in all Western societies prevents this form of political equality. As Frank Parkin argues, 'A political system which guarantees constitutional rights for groups to organize in defence of their interests is almost bound to favour the privileged at the expense of the disprivileged'. The combination of this kind of freedom and social inequality is very unlikely to result in political equality. Parkin therefore suggests that, 'Only if the main contestants were to enjoy a roughly similar economic and social status could we say that pluralist democracy was a system of genuine political equality'.

One solution to the problem of political equality is to prevent powerful groups from organizing to defend and promote their interests. However this could hardly be called democratic since it denies the right of certain individuals to participate in the political process. A solution along these lines has been attempted in Communist societies although, as Parkin argues, it is unlikely to result in political equality. He states that 'Egalitarianism seems to require a political system in which the state is able continually to hold in check those social and occupational groups which, by virtue of their skills or education or personal attributes, might otherwise attempt to stake claims to a disproportionate share of society's rewards'. In pursuit of political equality, Communist societies have substituted the dictatorship of the proletariat for democracy. While there is little evidence that power is being returned to the people, the dictatorship of the proletariat may yet disappear. At least in theory Marxism offers a means of realizing the democratic ideal since only when all men are equal can political equality become a reality. (The concept of democracy is discussed with reference to bureaucratic organizations in Chapter 7. See particularly pp. 288–95 and 320–21.)

Sociology, ideology and politics and power

As in all areas of sociology, those who adopt a particular perspective on power and politics often claim objectivity and accuse their opponents of ideological bias. As Geraint Parry notes, the early elite theorists such as Pareto and Mosca believed they had established 'a neutral, "objective" political science, free from any ethical consideration'. From this standpoint, they dismissed Marxism as little more than ideology. Marxists have replied in a similar vein accusing elite theorists of merely translating ruling class ideology into sociological jargon. However, it is doubtful whether any perspective has a monopoly on objective truth. It is possible to argue that all views on power and politics owe something to the ideology and values of those who support them.

The ideological basis of Marxism is clearly visible. Marx was not only a sociologist but a political radical committed to the cause of the proletarian revolution. His writings reveal a vehement hatred for what he saw as the oppressive rule of the bourgeoisie. Marxists are committed to the ideal of political equality believing that it can only be realized in an egalitarian society based on communist principles. From this standpoint they condemn the representative democracies of Western capitalist societies. Any reform in the political system which leaves the economic base of capitalism unchanged is seen as merely a concession to the proletariat which serves to maintain the status quo. Given their commitment to communism, it is noticeable that many Marxists writers are far more restrained in their criticisms of political inequality in the USSR than they are in their criticisms of the West. Their writings often reveal the hope, and in many cases the belief, that the dictatorship of the proletariat is simply a transitional stage leading to political equality.

From the point of view of elite theory, Marxism is merely wishful thinking. Given the inevitability of elite rule, the egalitarian society is an illusion. However, the early elite theorists are just as vulnerable to the charge of ideological bias. Parry suggests that Pareto and Mosca began with a formula that was little more than a statement of conviction. They then scoured the history books selecting information which fitted their preconceived ideas. These ideas owed much to Pareto and Mosca's evaluation of the masses. They regarded the majority as generally incompetent and lacking the qualities required for self-government.

Elite theory has often been seen as an expression of conservative ideology. With its assertion of the inevitability of elite rule it can serve to justify the position of ruling minorities. Attempts to radically change the status quo, particularly those aimed at political equality, are dismissed as a waste of time. The removal of one elite will simply lead to its replacement by another. Thus, as Parry observes, early elite theory 'offered a defence, in rationalistic or scientific terminology, of the political interests and status of the middle class'. In fact Mosca went as far as to suggest that members of the working class were unfit to vote. Despite their claims to objectivity and neutrality, the early elite theorists were strongly opposed to socialism. T. B. Bottomore argues that, 'Their original and main antagonist was, in fact, socialism, and especially Marxist socialism'. Thus the debate between Marxists and elite theorists can be seen, at least in part, as a battle between rival ideologies.

Like all members of society, sociologists are products of their time. C. J. Friedrich suggests that the early elite theorists, born in mid-nineteenth-century Europe, were 'offspring of a society containing as yet many feudal remnants'. Elite theory, with its emphasis on rule by superior individuals, echoes feudal beliefs about the natural superiority of those born to rule. Lukács has suggested that elite theory was a product of those European societies in which democratic institutions were least developed. Italy is a case in point and therefore it may be no coincidence that both Pareto and Mosca were Italian.

Pluralism can be seen as an expression of either conservative or liberal ideology depending on the point of view of the observer. By implying that Western democracies are the best form of representative government that can be hoped for in complex industrial societies, pluralists can be seen to advocate the maintenance of the status quo. The inference from their argument is leave well alone. As Bottomore has stated, the pluralist conception of democracy as representative government is limited and restricted compared to the idea of direct participation. A commitment to this idea might well result in a very different analysis of Western political systems. This is evident from Bottomore's own work. He regards the pluralist view of democracy as a poor substitute for the real thing. His belief that direct participation in politics by all members of society is a realistic alternative to representative government may well be influenced by a commitment to this ideal.

Frank Parkin has suggested that 'pluralism is quite plausibly regarded as a philosophy which tends to reflect the perceptions and interests of a privileged class'. Pluralism claims that all major interests in society are represented. However, in an unequal society, the interests of the rich and powerful are likely to be better served than those of the underprivileged. With its emphasis on the representation of all interests, pluralism tends to disguise this situation. It is likely to divert attention from the inequalities which result from the operation of the political process. By doing so it may help to maintain the status quo and provide support for the privileged.

While it has often been seen as a reflection of conservative ideology, pluralism has also been interpreted as a liberal viewpoint. Liberalism is a philosophy which accepts the basic structure of Western society while advocating progressive reforms within that structure. These reforms are directed by a concern for individual liberty and a desire to improve the machinery of democratic government. Many pluralists admit that Western democracies have their faults and are concerned to correct them. Thus Arnold Rose admits that the USA is not 'completely democratic' and looks forward to a number of reforms to make the existing system more representative. But he accepts that the basic framework of American society is sound and therefore does not advocate radical change.

Pluralism has found particularly strong support in the USA and many of the important pluralist writers, such as Dahl and Rose, are American. To some degree their writings can be seen as a reflection of American culture. Since the Declaration of Independence, American society has emphasized the liberty of the individual rather than social equality. In this respect, it is significant that the USA has no major socialist party unlike most of its West European counterparts. This emphasis on liberty rather than equality is reflected in pluralist theory. From a pluralist perspective, democracy is a system of government which provides freedom for members of society to organize in the defence and promotion of their interests. Westergaard and Resler claim that pluralists 'value liberty more than equality' and see the free enterprise capitalist system as 'a bulwark of liberty'. The values of liberty and freedom of the individual are enshrined in the 'American Dream'. As a result, the writings of American pluralists may owe more than a little to the ethos of their society.

4 Poverty

Poverty is a social problem. The first step in the solution of a problem is to identify it and this requires a definition. The second step is to assess the size of the problem which involves the construction of ways to measure it. Once the problem has been identified, defined and measured, the next step is to discover what causes it. Only after answers have been obtained to the questions, 'What is poverty?'; 'What is the extent of poverty?' and 'What are the causes of poverty?' can the question 'What are the solutions to poverty?' be asked. This chapter examines some of the answers that social scientists have given to these four questions.

The definition and measurement of poverty

Absolute poverty

Since the nineteenth century when rigorous studies of poverty began, researchers have tried to establish a fixed yardstick against which to measure poverty. Ideally, such a yardstick would be applicable to all societies and should establish a fixed level, usually known as the poverty line, below which poverty begins and above which it ends. This concept of poverty is known as absolute poverty. It usually involves a judgment of basic human needs and is measured in terms of the resources required to maintain health and physical efficiency. Most measures of absolute poverty are concerned with establishing the quality and amount of food, clothing and shelter deemed necessary for a healthy life. Absolute poverty is often known as subsistence poverty since it is based on assessments of minimum subsistence requirements. It is usually measured by pricing the basic necessities of life, drawing a poverty line in terms of this price, and defining as poor those whose income falls below that figure.

There have been many attempts to define and operationalize – put into a form which can be measured – the concept of absolute poverty. For example Drewnowski and Scott in their 'Level of Living Index', define and operationalize 'basic physical needs' in the following way: nutrition, measured by factors such as intake of calories and protein; shelter, measured by quality of dwelling and degree of overcrowding; and health, measured by factors such as the rate of infant mortality and the quality of available medical facilities.

Some concepts of absolute poverty go beyond the notion of subsistence poverty by introducing the idea of 'basic cultural needs'. This broadens the idea of basic human needs beyond the level of physical survival. Drewnowski and Scott include education, security, leisure and recreation in their category of basic cultural needs. The proportion of children enrolled at school is one indication of the level of educational provision; the number of violent deaths relative to the size of the population is one indication of security; and the amount of leisure relative to work time is one measure of the standard of leisure and recreation.

The concept of absolute poverty has been widely criticized. It is based on the assumption that there are minimum basic needs for all people, in all societies. This is a difficult argument to defend even in regard to subsistence poverty measured in terms of food, clothing and shelter. Such needs vary both between and within societies. Thus Peter Townsend argues, 'It would be difficult to define nutritional needs without taking account of the kinds and demands of occupations and of leisure time pursuits in a society'. For example, the nutritional needs of the nomadic hunters and gatherers of the Kalahari Desert in Africa may well be very different from those of members of Western society. Within the same society, nutritional needs may vary widely, between, for example, the bank clerk sitting at his desk all day and the labourer on a building site. A similar criticism can be made of attempts to define absolute standards of shelter. Jack and Janet Roach give the following illustration: 'City living, for example, requires that "adequate" shelter not only protects one from the elements, but that it does not present a fire hazard to others and that attention be paid to water supplies, sewage, and garbage disposal. These problems are simply met in rural situations'. Thus flush toilets, which may well be considered a necessary part of adequate shelter in the city, could hardly be considered essential fixtures in the dwellings of traditional hunting and gathering and agricultural societies.

The concept of absolute poverty is even more difficult to defend when it is broadened to include the idea of 'basic cultural needs'. Such 'needs' vary from time to time and place to place and any attempt to establish absolute, fixed standards is bound to fail. Drewnowski and Scott's basic cultural need of security is a case in point. Financial security for aged members of the working class in nineteenth-century England involved younger relatives providing for them, whereas today it is largely met by state old age pensions and private insurance schemes. Increasing longevity, reduction in the size of families, and earlier retirement have altered the circumstances of the aged. Definitions of adequate provision for old age have changed since the last century. Thus, in terms of security, both the situation and expectations of the aged in England have changed and are not strictly comparable over time. A similar criticism can be applied to attempts to apply absolute standards to two or more societies. For instance, recreational and leisure provision in the West may be measured in terms of the number of televisions, cinemas, parks and playing fields per head of the population. However, the concept of leisure on which this is based and the items in terms of which it is measured may be largely irrelevant for other societies. For example, the Hopi and Zuñi Indians of the southwestern USA have a rich ceremonial life which forms the central theme of their leisure activities. Recreational needs are therefore largely determined by the culture of the particular society. Any absolute standard of cultural needs is based in part on the values of the researcher which to some degree reflect his particular culture. Peter Townsend notes that when societies are compared in terms of recreational facilities, 'Cinema attendance and ownership of radios take precedence over measures of direct participation in cultural events', such as religious rituals and other ceremonies. This is a clear illustration of Western bias.

Relative poverty

In view of the problems involved, many researchers have abandoned the concept of absolute standards based on notions of physical and/or cultural needs. In their place they have developed the idea of relative standards, that is standards which are relative to the particular time and place. Thus the idea of absolute poverty has been replaced by the idea of relative poverty. Relative poverty is measured in terms of judgments by members of a particular society of what is considered a reasonable and acceptable standard of living and style of life according to the conventions of the day. Just as conventions change from time to time and place to place, so will definitions of poverty. Peter Townsend argues that, 'Individuals, families and groups in the population can be said to be in poverty when they lack the resources to obtain the types of diets, participate in the activities and have the living conditions and amenities which are customary, or at least widely encouraged or approved, in the societies to which they belong. Their resources are so seriously below those commanded by the average individual or family that they are, in effect, excluded from ordinary living patterns, customs and activities'.

In a rapidly changing world, definitions of poverty based on relative standards will be constantly changing. Thus Samuel Mencher writes, 'The argument for relative standards rests on the assumption that for practical purposes standards become so fluid that no definition of need, no matter how broad, satisfies the ever changing expectations of modern life'. The argument is put in a nutshell by I. M. Rubinow, 'Luxuries become comforts, comforts become necessaries'. In Western society, products and services such as hot and cold running water, refrigerators and washing machines, medical and dental care, full-time education and motor cars have or are travelling the road from luxuries, to comforts, to necessaries. Thus in Peter Townsend's words, any definition of poverty must be 'related to the needs and demands of a changing society'.

There are, however, a number of problems with the concept of relative poverty. It cannot be assumed that there are society wide standards of reasonable and acceptable life styles. Within a particular society, ethnicity, class, age, religion, region and a variety of other factors can vary judgments of reasonable living standards. For example, acceptable standards for the lower working class may differ significantly from those of the middle class. Townsend has suggested that it is possible to draw up a list of 'types of customs and social activities practised or approved by the majority of the population'. These may include things like having a refrigerator and taking a summer holiday away from home.

The concept of relative poverty also poses problems for the comparison of the poor in the same society over time, and between societies. For example, an insistence on a purely relative concept of poverty prevents a comparison of the poor in present-day and nineteenth-century England, or of present-day England and Third World countries in Africa, Asia and South America. From the viewpoint of relative poverty, circumstances and expectations differ from time to time and place to place. Comparisons are therefore invalid. Despite this such comparisons are made, for example, between the grinding poverty of the Third World and living standards in Western societies. One solution to the problem of comparison has been suggested by Peter Townsend. He argues that 'two standards of poverty are required, "nation-relational" and "world-relational"'. Nation-relational standards are based on relative poverty according to the conventions of the particular society. World-relational poverty would have to be based on more artificial standards which involves a return to absolute standards of poverty, despite all their drawbacks. In this way it would be possible to compare poverty in different societies.

Subjective poverty

To the concepts of absolute and relative poverty can be added a third, subjective poverty. This refers to whether or not individuals or groups feel they are poor. Subjective poverty is closely related to relative poverty since those who are defined as poor in terms of the standards of the day will probably see and feel themselves to be poor. However, this is not necessarily the case. For example, a formerly wealthy individual reduced by circumstances to a modest lower-middle-class income and life style may feel poor but other members of society may not regard him as such. Conversely, individuals and groups judged in terms of majority standards to be in poverty may not see themselves as poor. Many old age pensioners may fall into this category since their expectations of acceptable living standards may be lower than those of most members of society. The concept of subjective poverty is important since, to some degree, people act in terms of the way they perceive and define themselves. Thus the Black ghetto riots in low-income areas of American cities during the late 1960s, were due more to a growing intensity of subjective poverty than to any change in the circumstances of the poor.

The extent of poverty

In this section attempts to assess the extent of poverty in Britain and the USA will be examined. Clearly, any assessment of the extent of poverty will depend firstly, on which concept of poverty is used, and secondly, on the way the particular concept is operationalized. The following examples provide illustrations of these points.

Seebohm Rowntree

One of the earliest and most famous studies of poverty was conducted by Seebohm Rowntree. Using a concept of subsistence poverty, he conducted a survey in York in 1899. He drew a poverty line in terms of a minimum weekly sum of money which was 'necessary to enable families to secure the necessaries of a healthy life'. The money needed for this subsistence level existence covered fuel and light, rent, food, clothing, household and personal sundries and was adjusted to family size. According to this measure, 33% of the survey population lived in poverty. Rowntree conducted two further studies of York, in 1936 and 1950, based largely on the same methodology. He found that the percentage of his sample population in poverty dropped to 18% in 1936 and 1½% in 1950. He also found that the causes of poverty changed considerably over half a century. For example, inadequate wages, major factors in 1899 and 1936, were relatively insignificant by 1950. Table 10 summarizes the results of Rowntree's surveys.

Table 10   Rowntree's studies of York

Cause of poverty	Percentage of those in poverty		
	1899	1936	1950
Unemployment of chief wage earner	2.31	28.6	Nil
Inadequate wages of earners in regular employment	51.96	42.3	1.0
Old age	5.11	14.7	68.1
Sickness		4.1	21.3
Death of chief wage earner	15.63	7.8	6.4
Miscellaneous (including large family)	24.99	2.5	3.2
Totals	100	100	100
Percentage of survey population in poverty	33	18	1.5

(Adapted from Coates and Silburn, *Poverty: The Forgotten Englishmen,* © Ken Coates and Richard Silburn, 1970, 1973, p. 46, reprinted by permission of Penguin Books Ltd)

By the 1950s it appeared that poverty was a minor problem. Pockets of poverty remained, for example among the aged, but it was believed that increased welfare benefits would soon eradicate this lingering poverty. The conquest of poverty was put down to an expanding economy – the 1950s were the years of the 'affluent society' – to government policies of full employment and to the success of the Welfare State. It was widely believed that the operation of the Welfare State had redistributed wealth from rich to poor and significantly raised working-class living standards.

Throughout the 1950s and 1960s researchers became increasingly dubious about the 'conquest of poverty'. Rowntree's concept of subsistence poverty, and the indicators he used to measure poverty, were strongly criticized. His measurement of adequate nutrition is a case in point. With the help of experts, Rowntree drew up a diet sheet which would provide the minimum adequate nutritional intake, and, in terms of this, decided upon the minimum monies required for food. However it is very unlikely that this minimal budget would meet the needs of the poor. As Martin Rein argues, it is based on 'an unrealistic assumption of a no-waste budget, and extensive knowledge in marketing and cooking. An economical budget must be based on knowledge and skill which is least likely to be present in the low-income groups we are concerned with'. Rowntree's estimates further ignore the fact that the majority of the working class spends a smaller percentage of its income on food than his budget allows. He does not allow for the fact that choice of food is based on the conventions of a person's social class and region, not upon a diet sheet drawn up by experts. Thus Peter Townsend argues that 'in relation to the budgets and customs of life of ordinary people the make-up of the subsistence budget was unbalanced'.

Rowntree's selection of the 'necessaries of a healthy life' was based on the opinions of himself and the experts he consulted. Although he made some alterations in his list of 'necessaries' to account for changing standards and circumstances from 1899 to 1950, his concept of poverty falls far short of a concept of relative poverty. In view of the rise in living standards during the half century covered by his surveys, it is little wonder that his results reveal a drastic reduction in poverty. Studies after 1950 which employed a more relative concept of poverty provide a very different assessment of the extent of poverty.

Abel-Smith and Townsend

A study by Brian Abel-Smith and Peter Townsend entitled *The Poor and the Poorest*, published in 1965, illustrates clearly that the extent of poverty depends upon the concept of poverty adopted and the measuring instruments employed. They defined poverty, or 'low levels of living' as 'less than 140% of the basic national assistance scale plus rent and/or other housing costs'. Families with no means of support received a basic allowance from the National Assistance Board (now the Supplementary Benefits Commission), the size of this allowance being dependent on the circumstances of the family, for example the number of dependent children. To this basic allowance, Abel-Smith and Townsend added 40%, and defined as poor those whose incomes fell below this level. This measure of poverty was less stringent than Rowntree's subsistence level poverty line. It was more sensitive to judgments of reasonable living standards according to the conventions of the day, and, as such, it was closer to a concept of relative poverty.

Abel-Smith and Townsend based their research on a re-analysis of surveys conducted by the Ministry of Labour in 1953/4 and 1960. The 1953/4 survey dealt with household expenditure and the 1960 survey with household income. This poses methodological problems since the data are not strictly comparable. Abel-Smith and Townsend state, 'In general expenditure tends to be overstated and income understated in inquiries of this kind, particularly among low-income households. Thus one would expect to find too few persons recorded as having low levels of living in 1953 and too many in 1960'. From the 1953/4 data, Abel-Smith and Townsend calculated that 7.8% of the survey population was in poverty, from the 1960 data, 14.2%. On the national level, this would suggest that the numbers of the poor increased from nearly 4 million in 1953/4 to nearly 7½ million in 1960. Part of this increase can be explained by the measurements of income and expenditure referred to above and part (a quarter to a third) 'can be explained by the difference in the extent to which the two samples represented the United Kingdom population of the two years'. According to Abel-Smith and Townsend, however, part of the increase is genuine, and is due to a growth in the proportion of the population over sixty-five, in the size of families and numbers of dependent children, and to an increase in the numbers dependent on sickness benefit, particularly men in the age group 55–65, an age group which increased in size relative to the population as a whole.

The most significant finding of the Abel-Smith and Townsend Study was that poverty was not a disappearing problem. A new definition of poverty placed a significant proportion of the population in poverty. It also changed the relative importance of the various causes of poverty. Table 11 compares Rowntree's 1950 survey with Abel-Smith and Townsend's results from the 1960 data.

The table shows that inadequate wages relative to family size are the most important cause of poverty in terms of Abel-Smith and Townsend's definition of poverty whilst in terms of Rowntree's definition, they are of relatively minor consequence. Clearly, this has important implications for government policy in the fight against poverty. Policy based on Rowntree's figures would give priority to the raising of old age pensions. The findings of Abel-Smith and Townsend suggest that the low paid, particularly those with dependent children, may well merit top priority.

Table 11

Percentage of those in poverty Rowntree 1950	Cause of poverty	Percentage of those in poverty Abel-Smith and Townsend 1960
4.2 *	Inadequate wages and/or large families	40
68.1	Old age	33
6.4	Fatherless families	10
21.3	Sickness	10
Nil	Unemployment	7

(* included in this figure is the miscellaneous category which includes items other than a large family)

(Adapted from Coates and Silburn, *Poverty: The Forgotten Englishmen*, 1973, p. 47, reprinted by permission of Penguin Books Ltd)

Official statistics on poverty

Unlike the USA, Britain has no official 'poverty line' but statistics from the Supplementary Benefits Commission, formerly the National Assistance Board, provide some indication of 'official estimates' of the extent of poverty. Table 12 indicates the number of people receiving

Table 12   Persons receiving supplementary benefit

	National assistance				Supplementary benefit					
	1948	1951	1961	1965	1966	1971	1973	1974	1975	1976
Supplementary beneficiaries (thousands): Retirement pensioners and national insurance widows 60 years and over	495	767	1089	1258	1668	1865	1796	1761	1635	1639
Others over pension age	143	202	234	212	203	114	107	106	104	104
Unemployed with national insurance benefit	19	33	48	35	79	134	50	76	138	} 684
Unemployed without national insurance benefit	34	33	94	85	111	273	212	240	418	
Sick and disabled with national insurance benefit	80	121	138	153	161	151	122	98	80	80
Sick and disabled without national insurance benefit	64	98	142	147	151	170	173	175	175	175
Women under 60 with dependent children	32	41	78	110	128	217	233	250	281	310
National insurance widows under 60	81	86	60	58	62	68	56	44	32	30
Others	63	81	18	17	17	22	24	27	27	28
Total persons receiving supplementary benefit	1011	1462	1902	2075	2580	3014	2772	2778	2891	3050

(Source: *Social Trends*, 1973, p. 108; *Social Trends*, 1977, p. 111).

supplementary benefit since 1948 when the National Assistance Board was established. Figures for 1948 and 1951 are for Great Britain only, the remainder are for the United Kingdom.

The figures refer to heads of households receiving supplementary benefits. If their dependents are added, this provides one indication of the numbers in poverty. For example, in 1975, those in receipt of benefits plus their dependents numbered some 4½ million or 8% of the population. To this must be added those eligible for benefits who did not claim them. Government estimates for the first half of the 1970s indicated that from 60 to 70% of those eligible for benefits received them. It is possible to argue that the increase in the numbers receiving supplementary benefit is due, at least in part, to the fact that people are less reluctant to claim, and/or are more aware of, the available benefits. Frank Field, who has conducted considerable research on poverty in Britain, dismisses this view.

Estimates of poverty based on supplementary benefit payments must also take into account the value of those payments in relation to average wages. As Frank Field argues, if their value in relation to average wages decreases, estimates of poverty based on the numbers receiving supplementary benefit will underestimate the extent of poverty. Field provides the following figures. In 1948, the benefit rate for a single person was 17.4% of average weekly earnings, in 1967 it rose to 20.1% but by April

Table 13   Value of earnings of lowest 10% of male and female manual workers: selected years from 1886

	Men as percentage of average	Women as percentage of average
1886	68.6	*
1906	66.5	*
1938	67.7	64.3
1960	70.6	72.0
1963	70.7	68.5
1964	71.6	65.1
1965	69.7	66.5
1966	68.6	66.3
1967	69.8	66.1
1968	67.3	71.1
1970	67.3	69.0
1971	68.2	70.2
1972	67.6	68.9
1973	67.3	69.2
1974	68.7	69.2

(Source: Field, 1975, p. 689, from the Department of Employment Gazettes and New Earnings Survey)

1975 it had fallen to 16.8%. For families, the benefit reached its highest value in 1952. By April 1975, the value of the benefit for a family with two children was 2.7% below that of 1948. Field therefore concludes that if supplementary benefit payments are used to calculate the extent of poverty, they will provide an underestimate because the real value of the payments has declined.

Statistics from the Supplementary Benefits Commission indicate a rise in poverty since 1948. The extent of poverty would be far greater if Abel-Smith and Townsend's definition of poverty were employed. Low wage earners formed the largest group in poverty in Abel-Smith and Townsend's sample. There is no indication that the proportion of low wage earners is decreasing. Table 13 shows the value of the earnings of the lowest paid 10% of male and female manual workers. The value of their earnings is shown as a percentage of average earnings.

The figures show a remarkable consistency. As Frank Field notes, 'From this table it is difficult to tell when governments have initiated policies favouring the low paid, or when incomes policies have been in operation which (according to the government of the time) have positively discriminated in favour of the low paid. Nor can one easily guess which were the periods of free collective bargaining, which unions claim is the most effective way of tackling poverty wages'. Evidence from supplementary benefit payments plus evidence concerning low wages suggests that in terms of Abel-Smith and Townsend's definition of poverty, the numbers of poor have not decreased since 1960 and they may well have increased.

The extent of poverty in the USA

The problems of defining and measuring poverty in Britain are duplicated in the USA. Official statistics on the extent of poverty in America indicate a steady decline in the numbers of the poor. Figures from the Social Security Administration show that the percentage of the population in poverty dropped from 22% in 1959 to 11.6% in 1975. However, as Rowntree's studies show, any measurement which is not based on a strictly relative definition of poverty will automatically indicate a decrease in the numbers of the poor in societies where living standards in general are rising. Some, if not all of the apparent decrease in poverty in the USA is due to the use of a definition of poverty which is closer to an absolute rather than a relative concept.

The 'poverty index' used by the Social Security Administration is based on the minimum cost of an adequate diet multiplied by three since it is estimated that the typical poor family spends one third of its income on food. The poverty line is drawn in terms of the minimum income required to buy a 'subsistence level of goods and services'. The poverty index is stringent and falls well below what would generally be regarded as a relative poverty line. The President's Commission on Income Maintenance Programs, a commission set up in 1968 to investigate poverty in the USA, makes several criticisms of the poverty index. It does not reflect contemporary conventions of reasonable living standards. The minimum income assessed for a family to remain above the poverty line does not allow for many of the goods and services considered necessities by the population as a whole. According to the Commission, such 'necessities' might include, 'a car, an occasional dessert after meals, rugs, a bed for each family member, school supplies, or an occasional movie'. No provision is made in the 'subsistence level goods and services' budget for medical care or insurance or for the purchase of household furnishings. The Commission states that the monies deemed necessary for transportation, 'would not cover even daily transportation for a worker'. The Commission is particularly critical of the monies allocated for food, many of its criticisms echoing those made of Rowntree's food budget. It concludes that 'only about one-fourth of the families who spend that much for food actually have a nutritionally adequate diet'.

Fixed standards of poverty, such as those of the Social Security Administration, will ultimately result in the virtual disappearance of poverty. Although the poverty index is adjusted annually to reflect price changes, it does not reflect changing expectations and living standards. Writing in the mid 1960s, Herman P. Miller, Chief of the Population Division of the US Bureau of the Census stated, 'We have been measuring poverty by an absolute standard based on relationships that existed in 1955. If we continue to use this definition long enough, we will, in time eliminate poverty statistically, but few people will believe it – certainly not those who continue to have housing, education, medical care and other goods and services which are far below standards deemed acceptable for this society'. (Quoted in Miller and Roby, 1970, p. 42.) One indication of the changing extent of poverty is provided by comparing the relative share of national income received over a period of time by low-income groups. This gives a very different picture from the optimistic trend indicated by official statistics. The President's Commission on Income Maintenance Programs states, 'Despite all of our income and welfare programs we have not altered appreciably the structure of this Nation's income distribution'. This means that those at the bottom have not received a larger share of national income. As an indication of relative poverty, no change in income distribution can mean no change in poverty, despite the trend shown by the official statistics.

Towards the concept and measurement of relative poverty

Neither the British nor American governments have measured the extent of poverty in terms of a concept of relative poverty. 'Experts' have assessed the basic requirements for subsistence level existence, costed those requirements and drawn a poverty line in terms of the costings. Although to some degree contemporary standards have influenced their selection of basic requirements, their definitions of poverty fall far short of relative poverty. Researchers such as Rowntree have operated in much the same way. Abel-Smith and Townsend come closer to a concept of relative poverty than most, but their study falls short of the research design outlined by Townsend, which will now be examined.

Peter Townsend argues that studies of poverty have failed in two crucial respects. Firstly, they have failed to accurately measure the value of the resources of individuals or families. Secondly, they have failed to adequately conceptualize relative poverty and to provide ways of measuring it. Most studies of poverty are based on the income levels of individuals and families. Townsend argues that income levels are inadequate measures and that more sensitive and comprehensive indicators are needed to assess resources. He gives the example of two 'identical' fatherless families, each with the same cash income. The first lives in an inner city slum in high-rent, overcrowded accommodation. Local medical and educational facilities are of a low standard. The second family lives in a low-rent, high-quality council house in a new town with modern schools and hospitals nearby. Despite their similarity of income, the 'resources' of the two families are very different. Thus Townsend argues that families should be measured in terms of a range of resources which should not only include actual cash income but 'capital assets' such as savings and household facilities, the 'value of employment benefits' such as employer's pension schemes, the 'value of public social services in kind' such as the quality of local health and educational facilities and 'private income in kind' such as produce from an allotment or services from friends and relatives.

Once this overall picture of 'family resources' has been obtained, it can be related to contemporary judgments of acceptable 'styles of living'. Just as family resources replace income, so style of living replaces narrow definitions of basic subsistence requirements of goods and services. An acceptable style of living would be based on 'types of customs and social activities practiced or approved by the majority of the national population'. Possible examples given by Townsend include a week's holiday away from home in the last year, ownership of a refrigerator and an evening out for entertainment during the past two weeks. Townsend argues that only by relating family resources to acceptable styles of living can a concept of relative poverty be operationalized and effectively measured.

In view of the inadequacy of the concepts and measurements of poverty, theories which claim to explain poverty must be regarded with some caution. These theories will now be examined.

Theories of poverty

Poverty as a positive feedback system

Ken Coates and Richard Silburn who conducted a major study of poverty in Nottingham argue that, 'poverty has many dimensions, each of which must be studied separately, but which in reality constitute a interrelated network of deprivations'. The US Council of Economic Advisors stated in 1964, 'The vicious cycle, in which poverty breeds poverty, occurs through time, and transmits its effects from one generation to another. There is no beginning to the cycle, no end' (quoted in Moynihan, 1968, p. 9). These two statements contain the kernel of the theory that views poverty as a positive feedback system, that is a system in which each part reinforces the others and so maintains the system as a whole. This theory, sometimes known as the 'vicious circle' theory of poverty, argues that the various circumstances of the poor combine to maintain them in poverty. They are trapped in the situation with little chance of escaping. Although the theory has some merit, it will be argued later that it provides only a partial explanation for poverty.

The following data and observations from the President's Commission on Income Maintenance Programs illustrate the view of poverty as a positive feedback system. The majority of Americans officially designated as poor have inadequate diets which can have various consequences. Poor nutrition during pregnancy can hinder foetal brain development and increase the possibility of premature birth. Protein deficiency during early childhood can retard brain development. Inadequate diet can lead to low energy levels which can hinder progress at school and work and which can be interpreted by teachers and employers as evidence of disinterest, lack of motivation and laziness. Since the poor often work in physically demanding jobs, for example as unskilled labourers, low energy levels are particularly significant. Poor nutrition lowers resistance to disease which can lead to longer absences from school and work compared to the non-poor. In America the situation is made worse due to minimal provision of socialized medicine and the high charges of private medicine which are often beyond the means of the poor. Frequent illness and low energy levels can sap the drive and determination needed to escape from poverty.

The majority of the American poor live in accommodation officially classified as 'substandard housing' by the US Department of Housing. Conditions are often overcrowded, insanitary and constitute a health hazard, reinforcing the danger to health caused by inadequate diet. Dilapidated and decaying dwellings can undermine the will to improve the situation and to escape from poverty. As one witness told the Commission, 'The people have an apathy about cleaning a place that is about to fall down on their heads. Believe me, if you lived in a house that had a leaky roof, and the paper's off the wall, with rats and roaches, no matter how you clean'. Public housing (the American equivalent of council housing) could improve the situation but its provision is limited by the state of city finances. Cities are largely financed by rates based on the value of property. The movement of the more wealthy taxpayers and businesses to the suburbs, beyond the city limits, lowers property values and, therefore, the monies available to city governments. Despite grants from central government, many American cities operate on the verge of bankruptcy.

Substandard food and housing are not cheap. This is the paradox of poverty. Poverty is expensive. Rented accommodation in inner city areas is often, in view of its quality, more expensive than housing elsewhere. David Caplovitz has documented the expense of poverty in *The Poor Pay More*. The price of goods and services in poverty areas is often higher than in non-poor areas. According to Caplovitz, this is partly due to exploitation of the poor by local businessmen charging extortionate prices and providing credit at high rates of interest. However this must be related to high rates of defaulted loans and shoplifting in low-income areas. The poor tend to buy smaller quantities of goods, particularly food, than the non-poor because they cannot afford to buy in bulk and often do not have the necessary storage facilities such as refrigerators. This raises the price of goods since small quantities are more expensive to package and handle, and shopkeepers with a relatively small stock and turnover have to pay higher wholesale prices. Thus, in one sense, the poor pay higher prices because they cannot afford lower prices. The same applies to transportation, particularly in the inner city. If the poor can afford cars, they will pay higher insurance because of higher rates of car theft and vandalism in inner city areas. With businesses increasingly moving beyond metropolitan boundaries, the poor often have to travel further to their place of work than the non-poor. The state of city finances often means that public transportation is woefully inadequate. Thus poverty adds to the cost of travel. The Commission on Income Maintenance Programs sums up the situation, 'There are no jobs where the poor live, the poor cannot afford – or are not allowed – to live where the jobs are opening up, and there is no transportation between the two places'.

The above examples illustrating how the various circumstances in the life of the poor combine to maintain poverty can be multiplied. However, despite the abundant evidence to support the view of poverty as a positive feedback system, the theory is inadequate as an explanation of poverty. Instead of answering the question 'Why poverty?' the positive feedback theory directs itself more to the question, 'Once poverty exists, how is it maintained?'

The culture of poverty

Many researchers have noted that the life style of the poor differs in certain respects from that of other members of society. They have also noted that poverty life styles in different societies share common characteristics. The circumstances of poverty are similar, in many respects, in different societies. Similar circumstances and problems tend to produce similar responses, and these responses can develop into a culture, that is the learned, shared, and socially transmitted behaviour of a social group. This line of reasoning has led to the concept of a 'culture of poverty' (or, more correctly, a subculture of poverty), a relatively distinct subculture of the poor with its own norms and values. The idea of a culture of poverty was introduced in the late 1950s by the American anthropologist, Oscar Lewis. He developed the concept from his fieldwork among the urban poor in Mexico and Puerto Rico. Lewis argues that the culture of poverty is a 'design for living' which is transmitted from one generation to the next.

As a design for living which directs behaviour, the culture of poverty has the following elements. In Lewis's words, 'On the level of the individual the major characteristics are a strong feeling of marginality, of helplessness, of dependence and inferiority, a strong present-time orientation with relatively little ability to defer gratification, a sense of resignation and fatalism'. On the family level, life is characterized by 'free union or consensual marriages, a relatively high incidence in the abandonment of mothers and children, a trend towards mother-centred families and a much greater knowledge of maternal relatives'. There are high rates of divorce and desertion by the male family head resulting in matrifocal families headed by women. On the community level, 'The lack of effective participation and integration in the major institutions of the larger society is one of the crucial characteristics of the culture of poverty'. The urban poor in Lewis's research do not usually belong to trade unions or other associations, they are not members of political parties, and 'generally do not participate in the national welfare agencies, and make very little use of banks, hospitals, department stores, museums or art galleries'. For most, the family is the only institution in which they directly participate.

The culture of poverty is seen as a response by the poor to their position in society. According to Lewis it is a 'reaction of the poor to their marginal position in a class-stratified and highly individualistic society'. However, the culture of poverty goes beyond a mere reaction to a situation. It takes on the force of culture since its characteristics are guides to action which are internalized by the poor and passed on from one generation to the next. As such the culture of poverty tends to perpetuate poverty since its characteristics can be seen as mechanisms which maintain poverty: attitudes of fatalism and resignation lead to acceptance of the situation; failure to join trade unions and other organizations weakens the potential power of the poor. Lewis argues that once established, the culture of poverty 'tends to perpetuate itself from generation to generation because of its effect on children. By the time slum children are age six or seven, they have usually absorbed the basic values and attitudes of their subculture and are not psychologically geared to take full advantage of changing conditions or increased opportunities which may occur in their lifetime'.

Lewis argues that the culture of poverty best describes and explains the situation of the poor in colonial societies or in the early stages of capitalism as in many Third World countries. He suggests that it either does not exist or is weakly developed in advanced capitalist societies and socialist societies, although others have argued that the idea of a culture of poverty can be applied to the poor in advanced industrial societies. For example, Michael Harrington in *The Other America* writes of the American poor, 'There is, in short, a language of the poor, a psychology of the poor, a world view of the poor. To be impoverished is to be an internal alien, to grow up in a culture that is radically different from the one that dominates the society'.

The American anthropologist Walter B. Miller has developed his thinking along lines similar to Lewis. Although not directly concerned with poverty, Miller's ideas have been linked to the culture of poverty. Miller argues that the American lower class – the lowest stratum of the working class – has a distinctive subculture with its own set of 'focal concerns'. These include an emphasis on toughness and masculinity, a search for thrills and excitement, present-time orientation, and a commitment to luck and fate rather than achievement and effort as a means of realizing goals. He emphasizes the idea of value to a greater degree than Lewis, arguing that members of the lower class are committed to their focal concerns. Miller's picture is more of a self-contained viable cultural system, without the disorganization and breakdown implied by Lewis. Like Lewis's culture of poverty, Miller's lower class subculture is self-perpetuating, being transmitted from one generation to the next. Miller argues that 'lower class culture is a distinctive tradition, many centuries old with an integrity of its own'. Miller's catalogue of lower class traits, like that of Lewis, offers no handholds to escape from poverty. From one perspective this may be functional. Miller suggests that lower class subculture is functional in providing the necessary adaptation for a 'low-skilled labouring force'. Aspects of this adaptation include 'high boredom tolerance' and the 'capacity to find life gratification outside the world of work'. Faced with boring, low paid jobs and high rates of unemployment, members of the lower class have responded by developing their own focal concerns which provide a measure of satisfaction.

The concepts of the culture of poverty and lower working-class subculture have two important factors in common. Firstly, they see the poor as different from the rest of society, as a group with a distinctive subculture. Secondly, they see this subculture as maintaining the poor in their present circumstances.

Since its introduction, the culture of poverty theory has met with sustained criticism. The actual existence of a culture of poverty has been questioned. Research in low-income areas in Latin American and African countries which are in the early stages of capitalist development and should therefore provide evidence of a thriving culture of poverty, has cast some doubt on Lewis's claims. Kenneth Little's study of West African urbanization reports a proliferation of voluntary associations for mutual aid and recreation organized by poor rural migrants to the cities. William Mangin's research in the *barriadas* of Peru, shanty towns surrounding major cities, reveals a high level of community action and political involvement. Members of the *barriadas* often organize their own schools, clinics and bus cooperatives, have a high level of participation in community politics and show little of the family break-up described by Lewis. Mangin is impressed with 'the capacity for and evidence of popular initiative, self-help and local community organization'. He does concede, however, that some squatter communities and city slums in Latin America can be characterized by the culture of poverty. Audrey J. Schwartz's research in the slum areas or *barrios* of Caracas in Venezuela revealed little evidence of apathy and resignation, present-time orientation or broken families and concludes that the subculture of the *barrios* did not perpetuate and maintain poverty. Evidence from advanced industrial societies casts further doubt on the culture of poverty thesis, and, in particular, its application to Western society. From their research in Blackston (a pseudonym for a low-income Black American community), Charles and Betty Lou Valentine state, 'It is proving difficult to find community patterns that correspond to many of the subcultural traits often associated with poverty in learned writings about the poor'. They found a great deal of participation in local government, constant use of welfare institutions and 'a veritable plethora of organizations' from block associations to an area-wide community council. The Valentines conclude that, 'Apathetic resignation does exist, but it is by no means the dominant theme of the community'. Though casting serious doubts on the culture of poverty, the above evidence does not negate its existence. It may indicate, as S. M. Miller has remarked, that the life of the poor is more variable than had previously been thought.

Situational constraints – an alternative to a culture of poverty

The second and major criticism of the culture of poverty has centred round the notion of culture. Despite the research referred to above, there is evidence from both advanced and developing industrial societies to support Lewis and Miller's characterization of the behaviour of the poor. The use of the term culture implies that the behaviour of the poor is internalized via the socialization process and once internalized is to some degree resistant to change. It also implies, particularly with respect to Miller's 'focal concerns', that aspects of the behaviour of the poor derive from values. Again there is the suggestion of resistance to change. Indeed, Miller argues that members of the lower class have a preference for, and a commitment to their subculture. Thus both Lewis and Miller suggest, with their notion of culture, that despite the fact it was initially caused by circumstances such as unemployment, low income and lack of opportunity, that once established, the subculture of low-income groups has a life of its own. Thus, if the circumstances which produced poverty were to disappear, the culture of poverty may well continue. This is made even more likely by Lewis's and particularly Miller's view that the culture of poverty and lower class subculture respectively are largely self-contained and insulated from the norms and values of the mainstream culture of society. The poor, to a large degree, therefore live in a world of their own.

These arguments have been strongly contested. Rather than seeing the behaviour of the poor as a response to established and internalized cultural patterns, many researchers view it as a reaction to 'situational constraints'. In other words the poor are constrained by the facts of their situation, by low income, unemployment and the like, to act the way they do, rather than being directed by a culture of poverty. The situational constraints argument suggests that the poor would readily change their behaviour in response to a new set of circumstances once the constraints of poverty were removed. Thus Hylan Lewis, an American sociologist who has conducted considerable research on the behaviour of the poor, argues, 'It is probably more fruitful to think of lower class families reacting in various ways to the facts of their position and to relative isolation rather than the imperatives of a lower class culture'. The situational constraints thesis also attacks the view that the poor are largely insulated from mainstream norms and values. It argues that the poor share the values of society as a whole, the only difference being that they are unable to translate many of those values into reality. Again, the situational constraints argument suggests that once the constraints of poverty are removed, the poor will have no difficulty adopting mainstream behaviour patterns and seizing available opportunities.

Tally's Corner by Elliot Liebow is a major piece of research which strongly supports the situational constraints thesis. The study is based on participant observation of Black 'streetcorner men' in a low-income area of Washington DC. The men are either unemployed, underemployed (working part-time) or employed in low paid, unskilled, dead-end jobs as manual labourers, elevator operators, janitors, bus boys and dishwashers. Their view of work is directed by mainstream values. The men want jobs with higher pay and status but they lack the necessary skills, qualifications and work experience. They regard their occupations from the same viewpoint as any other member of society. In Liebow's words, 'Both employee and employer are contemptuous of the job'. When streetcorner men blow a week's wages on a 'weekend drunk' or pack in a job on an apparent whim, the middle-class observer tends to interpret this behaviour as evidence of present-time orientation and inability to defer gratification. However, Liebow argues that it is not the time orientation that differentiates the streetcorner man from members of the middle class, but his future. Whereas the middle-class individual has a reasonable future to look forward to, the streetcorner man has none. His behaviour is directed by the fact that 'he is aware of the future and the hopelessness of it all'. In the same way Liebow argues that it is not inability to defer gratification that differentiates the streetcorner man from members of the middle class, but simply the fact he has no resources to defer. The middle-class individual is able to invest in the future, to save, to commit time and effort to his job and family both because he has the resources to invest and because of the likelihood his investment will pay off in the form of promotion at work and home ownership and home improvement. The streetcorner man lacks the resources or the promise of a payoff if he invests what little he has. With a dead-end job or no job at all, and insufficient income to support his wife and family he is 'obliged to expend all his resources on maintaining himself from moment to moment'. Liebow argues that what appears to be a cultural pattern of immediate gratification and present-time orientation is merely a situational response, a direct and indeed a rational reaction to situational constraints. Rather than being directed by a distinctive subculture, the behaviour of the streetcorner man is more readily understandable as a result of his inability to translate the values of mainstream culture, values which he shares, into reality.

Liebow applies similar reasoning to the streetcorner man's relationship with his wife and family. The men share the values of mainstream culture. They regard a conventional family life as the ideal and strive to play the mainstream roles of father and breadwinner. However their income is insufficient to support a wife and family. Faced daily with a situation of failure men often desert their families. Liebow writes, 'To stay married is to live with your failure, to be confronted with it day in and day out. It is to live in a world whose standards of manliness are forever beyond one's reach'. Increasingly the men turn to the companionship of those in similar circumstances, to life on the streetcorner. Their conversation often revolves around the subject of marriage and its failure which is explained in terms of what Liebow calls the 'theory of manly flaws'. The failure of marriage is attributed to manliness which is characterized by a need for sexual variety and adventure, gambling, drinking, swearing and aggressive behaviour. Men often boast about their 'manly flaws' illustrating their prowess with a variety of anecdotes, many of which have little relation to the truth. The 'theory of manly flaws' cushions failure and in a sense translates it into success, for at least on the streetcorner, 'manly flaws' can bring prestige and respect. In Liebow's words, 'weaknesses are somehow turned upside down and almost magically transformed into strengths'. On closer examination, however, Liebow found little support for the streetcorner man's rationale for marital failure. Marriages failed largely because the men had insufficient income to maintain them. The matrifocal families that resulted were not due to a culture of poverty, but simply to low income. The emphasis on manliness, which coincides with Miller's 'focal concern' of masculinity, was not a valued aspect of lower class culture, but simply a device to veil failure.

Liebow concludes that 'the streetcorner man does not appear as a carrier of an independent cultural tradition. His behaviour appears not so much as a way of realizing the distinctive goals and values of his own subculture, or of conforming to its models, but rather as his way of trying to achieve many of the goals and values of the larger society, of failing to do this, and of concealing his failure from others and himself as best he can'. Liebow therefore rejects the idea of a culture of poverty or lower class subculture and sees the behaviour of the poor as a product of situational constraints, not of distinctive cultural patterns.

A compromise between the extremes of Liebow on the one side and Lewis and Miller on the other is provided by Ulf Hannerz. He sees some virtue in both the situational constraints and cultural arguments. Hannerz, a Swedish anthropologist, conducted research in a Black low-income area of Washington DC. In his book *Soulside*, he argues that if a solution to a problem such as the theory of manly flaws, becomes accepted by a social group, it is learned, shared and socially transmitted and therefore cultural. To some degree it is based on values since the theory of manly flaws provides a male role model to which to aspire. This model is therefore not simply a cushion for failure, a thinly veiled excuse. To some degree it provides an alternative to the mainstream male role model. Like Liebow, Hannerz sees the theory of manly flaws as a response to situational constraints but unlike Liebow, he argues that if these constraints were removed, this 'model of masculinity could constitute a barrier to change'. However, Hannerz concludes that situational constraints are more powerful in directing the behaviour of the poor than cultural patterns. Unlike Miller, he argues that the cultural patterns that distinguish the poor exist alongside and are subsidiary to a widespread commitment to mainstream values. He does not see 'the ghetto variety of the culture of poverty as a lasting obstacle to change'. Since the behaviour of the poor contains a cultural component, it may hinder change once the situational constraints are removed. There may be a 'cultural lag', a hangover from the previous situation, but Hannerz believes that this would only be temporary.

In summary, the criticisms of the culture of poverty are as follows. Firstly, it either does not exist or applies only to particular groups in poverty and therefore poverty life styles are more variable than it suggests. Secondly, the behaviour which characterizes the culture of poverty is due to situational constraints rather than cultural patterns. The poor do not have a distinctive subculture, they are not insulated from mainstream culture and they share the values of society as a whole. Thirdly, if there are cultural aspects to the behaviour of the poor, they are less powerful than situational constraints in directing behaviour and are secondary when compared to the commitment of the poor to mainstream norms and values. Finally, the implication of all these criticisms is that once the situational constraints of poverty are removed, much or all that is distinctive about the behaviour of the poor will disappear. Herbert J. Gans argues that this implication must be tested. He states that, 'the most important method in poverty research is social experimentation which provides people an opportunity to live under improved or more secure conditions, and then measure their response. Only experiments can discover how much the life styles of the poor are persistent cultural patterns, and how much they are *ad hoc* responses to the insecurity, instability, and lack of opportunity that mark the social situations in which they live'. In this way, Gans believes, the debate over situational constraints and cultural patterns will be finally settled.

Poverty and social stratification

The two theories of poverty so far considered have certain similarities. Both focus on the circumstances and behaviour of the poor. Both claim to show how once the situation of poverty is established, it tends to be self-perpetuating. The positive feedback theory shows how the various circumstances of poverty reinforce each other and so maintain the system. The culture of poverty theory claims to show how a distinctive subculture develops within the situation of poverty and so perpetuates the system. However, neither theory satisfactorily answers the question 'Why poverty?' They explain its maintenance rather than its genesis. To explain the basic causes of poverty, sociologists are increasingly focussing their attention on society as a whole and particularly on the stratification system, rather than studying the poor in isolation. As Dorothy Wedderburn asks in her introduction to *Poverty, Inequality and Class Structure*, 'Can poverty be discussed in isolation from the more general question of inequality?' As Peter Townsend states, 'the description, analysis and explanation of poverty in any country must proceed within the context of a general theory of stratification'. From this perspective the poor must be seen in terms of the stratification system as a whole.

Questions about the nature and functioning of stratification systems are directly related to questions about poverty. Theories of stratification should provide theories of poverty since the poor are part of stratification systems – the bottom part.

Poverty – a Marxian perspective

From a Marxian perspective, poverty in capitalist society can only be understood in terms of the system of inequality generated by a capitalist economy. Wealth is concentrated in the hands of a minority: those who own the forces of production. Members of the subject class own only their labour which they must sell in return for wages on the open market. Capitalism requires a highly motivated workforce. Since the motivation to work is based primarily on monetary return, those whose services are not required by the economy, such as the aged and the unemployed, must receive a lower income than wage earners. If this were not the case, there would be little incentive to work. The motivation of the workforce is also maintained by unequal rewards for work. Workers compete as individuals and groups with each other for income in a highly competitive society. In this respect, the low wage sector forms the base of a competitive wage structure. Low wages help to reduce the wage demands of the workforce as a whole, since workers tend to assess their income in terms of the baseline provided by the low paid. J. C. Kincaid argues that, 'standards of pay and conditions of work at the bottom of the heap influence the pattern of wages farther up the scale'. He maintains that low wages are essential to a capitalist economy since, 'from the point of view of capitalism the low-wage sector helps to underpin and stabilize the whole structure of wages and the conditions of employment of the working class. The employers can tolerate no serious threat to the disciplines of the labour market and the competitive values which support the very existence of capitalism'. If the low wage sector were abolished by an increase in the real value of the wages of the low paid, several of the possible consequences would be harmful to the capitalist class. Firstly, the delicate balance of pay differentials would be shattered. Other groups of workers might well demand, and possibly receive, real increases in their wages. This would reduce profit margins. Secondly, wages within the working class might become increasingly similar. This might tend to unite a working class which is now fragmented and divided by groups of workers competing against each other for higher wages. A move towards unity within the working class may well pose a threat to the capitalist class. Thirdly, if the real value of the wages of the low paid was increased, the pool of cheap labour, on which many labour intensive capitalist industries depend for profit, might disappear.

Since, from a Marxian perspective, the state in capitalist society reflects the interests of the ruling class, government measures can be expected to do little except reduce the harsher effects of poverty. Thus Kincaid argues that, 'It is not to be expected that any Government whose main concern is with the efficiency of a capitalist economy is going to take effective steps to abolish the low-wage sector'. Despite claims to the contrary, there is little evidence that the Welfare State has redistributed wealth from the rich to the poor. Westergaard and Resler dismiss the theory that the Welfare State, by using the power of the state to modify the workings of market forces, has created a more equal distribution of wealth. They argue that 'The state's social services are financed largely from the wages of those for whose security they are primarily designed. They make for little redistribution from capital and top salaries . . . they reshuffle resources far more within classes – between earners and dependents, healthy people and the sick, households of different composition, from one point in the individual's life cycle to another – than they do between classes'. Thus the bulk of monies received by members of the working class have been paid or will be paid in the form of taxes by themselves or other members of that class. What the wealthy at first sight appear to lose in the form of social security payments to the poor, they largely regain in the form of tax concessions on private insurance policies, mortgages and the like. Westergaard and Resler argue that the ruling class has responded to the demands of the labour movement by allowing the creation of the Welfare State, but the system operates, 'within a framework of institutions and assumptions that remain capitalist'. In their view, 'the keyword is "containment"'; the demands of the labour movement have been contained within the existing system. Westergaard and Resler argue that poverty exists because of the operation of a capitalist economic system which prevents the poor from obtaining the financial resources to become non-poor.

J. C. Kincaid sees a similar relationship between social security benefits and a capitalist economy. He argues that 'widespread poverty is a direct consequence of the limited effectiveness of social security provision'. Millions in Britain depend on social security but the payments they receive are insufficient to maintain a decent standard of living. In practice, payments function to keep the poor where they are, that is poor and at the bottom of the class structure. The social security system results in little redistribution of wealth from rich to poor. Like Westergaard and Resler, Kincaid sees poverty resulting from the operation of a capitalist economy which produces a particular form of social stratification. Kincaid summarizes the situation in the following way, 'It is not simply that there are rich and poor. It is rather that some are rich *because* some are poor'. Thus poverty can only be understood in terms of the operation of the class system as a whole since the question 'Why poverty?' is basically the same question as 'Why wealth?' Therefore from a Marxian perspective, poverty like wealth, is an inevitable consequence of a capitalist system.

Poverty – a Weberian perspective

The Marxian model of stratification in capitalist society is not particularly sensitive to variations in wealth within the working class. It fails to clearly differentiate the poor from the other wage earners and to provide an explanation for their poverty. Although many of the arguments in this section are provided by researchers committed to Marxian perspectives, their views may be presented within a Weberian framework. Weber argues that an individual's 'class situation' is dependent upon his 'market situation', on the amount of power he has to influence the workings of the market in his favour and on the rewards his skill and expertise can command in a competitive market. From this perspective groups such as the aged, the chronically sick, and single parent families have little power in the market and therefore receive little reward. Indeed, their circumstances largely prevent them from competing in the market. However, not all members of these groups are poor, and this is referable to their market situation prior to their present circumstances. Thus Westergaard and Resler state, 'Subsistence poverty is indeed common among old people, the sick, the handicapped, and so on; but only because the majority of the old, sick and handicapped have previously been dependent on jobs that provided them with few or no other resources to fall back on than meagre benefits from public funds'. The poverty of the old, sick, handicapped and single parent families is largely working-class poverty. Members of other social classes have sufficient income to save, invest in pension schemes, insurance policies and in shareholdings for themselves and their dependents and so guard against the threat of poverty due to the death of the breadwinner, sickness or old age. In this sense, social class rather than personal disability, inadequacy, or misfortune accounts for poverty.

The following explanations have been put forward to account for the market situation of the low paid. In advanced industrial societies, with increasing demand for specialized skills and training, the unemployed and underemployed tend to be unskilled with low educational qualifications. Liebow's streetcorner men, with few skills or qualifications, can command little reward on the labour market. With increasing mechanization and automation, the demand for unskilled labour is steadily contracting. Many, though by no means all, low paid workers are employed either in declining and contracting industries or labour intensive industries such as catering. It has been argued that the narrow profit margins of many such industries maintain low wage levels. It is important to note that pay may be defined as low in relation to the circumstances of the individual. Thus a wage which may provide a family of four with a reasonable living standard may reduce a family of eight to poverty. The circumstances of the poor may therefore be due to family size rather than low wages as such. However, from their study of St Ann's, a low-income district in Nottingham, Coates and Silburn state, 'We found very clear evidence that it was not the legendary fertility of the poor which explained their condition. For most families living on the borderline of poverty, it was the second or third child, rather than the fifth or sixth, who plunged them below it'. The poverty of the low paid is not primarily due to family size, but simply to low pay.

It has been argued that the market situation of the low paid is due not so much to the low profitability of the industries in which they work but rather to their bargaining power. Kincaid argues that, 'A crucial factor determining wage levels is the bargaining power of workers'. Low paid workers are usually older, female, and as a result, traditionally less militant. They often belong to weak trade unions or none at all. In Britain only a quarter of female and just over a half of male employees belong to unions. Low wages are concentrated in the non-unionized sectors of the workforce.

Ralph Miliband examines the bargaining position of the poor in an article entitled *Politics and Poverty*. He argues that in terms of power, the poor are the weakest group competing for the scarce and valued resources in society. Miliband states that, 'The poor are part of the working class but they are largely excluded from the organizations which have developed to defend the interests of the working class'. There are no organizations with the power of trade unions to represent the interests of the unemployed, the aged, the chronically sick or single parent families. Because of their lack of income the poor do not have the resources to form powerful groups and sustain pressure. Even if they were able to finance well organized interest groups, the poor largely lack economic sanctions to bring pressure to bear. Apart from low paid workers, the main groups in poverty cannot take strike action and so threaten the interests of the powerful. Their bargaining position is weakened still further by their inability to mobilize widespread working-class support, since non-poor members of the working class tend not to see their interests and those of the poor as similar. In fact there is a tendency for members of the working class to see certain groups in poverty, such as the unemployed, as 'scroungers' and 'layabouts'. Efforts by the poor to promote their interests and secure public support are weakened by the 'shame of poverty', a stigma which remains alive and well.

Compared to other interests in society which are represented by pressure groups such as employers' federations, trade unions, ratepayers' associations and motoring organizations, the poor are largely unseen and unheard. More often than not they have to rely on others championing their cause, for example, organizations such as Shelter and the Child Poverty Action Group and trade union leaders such as Jack Jones who has campaigned on behalf of the pensioners and low paid. Ralph Miliband concludes that the key to the weak bargaining position of the poor is simply their poverty. He states that 'economic deprivation is a source of political deprivation; and political deprivation in turn helps to maintain and confirm economic deprivation'.

This section has attempted to differentiate the poor from the working class as a whole and explain their poverty. Although this approach has some merit, it also has important drawbacks. As Westergaard and Resler argue, 'it diverts attention from the larger structure of inequality in which poverty is embedded': Thus the poor must be seen in relation to the class system as a whole, not simply as an isolated group. Ralph Miliband makes a similar point. He argues that the position of the poor is not that dissimilar from that of the working class as a whole. The poor are simply the most disadvantaged section of the working class rather than a separate group. To understand poverty, it is therefore necessary to understand the nature of inequality in a class stratified society. Miliband concludes that, 'The basic fact is that the poor are an integral part of the working class – its poorest and most disadvantaged stratum. They need to be seen as such, as part of a continuum, the more so as many workers who are not "deprived" in the official sense live in permanent danger of entering the ranks of the deprived; and that they share in any case many of the disadvantages which afflict the deprived. Poverty is a class thing, closely linked to a *general* situation of class inequality'.

The 'functions' of poverty

In *More Equality*, Herbert J. Gans argues that 'poverty survives in part because it is useful to a number of groups in society'. Poverty benefits the non-poor in general and the rich and powerful in particular. They therefore have a vested interest in maintaining poverty. From this perspective, Gans outlines the following 'functions of poverty' for the non-poor.

Firstly, every economy has a number of temporary, dead-end, dirty, dangerous and menial jobs. The existence of poverty ensures that such work is done. Gans argues that 'poverty functions to provide a low-wage labour pool that is willing – or rather, unable to be unwilling – to perform dirty work at low cost'. Without the low paid, many industries would be unable to continue in their present form. Gans claims that hospitals, the catering trade, large sections of agriculture and parts of the garment industry are dependent on low wage labour. Raising wages would increase costs with 'obvious dysfunctional consequences for more affluent people'. Thus at one and the same time, poverty ensures that 'dirty jobs' are done and, by getting them done cheaply, subsidizes the non-poor sections of the population.

Secondly, poverty directly provides employment and financial security for a fast growing section of the labour force. In Gans's words, 'Poverty creates jobs for a number of occupations and professions that serve the poor, or shield the rest of the population from them'. These include the police, probation officers, social workers, psychiatrists, doctors and the administrators who oversee the 'poverty industry'. In Britain, the social security system employed some 80 000 staff in 1976 and the cost of administration amounted to £649 million. However altruistic their motives, Gans suggests that those employed to deal with the poor have a vested interest in poverty.

Thirdly, Gans argues that the presence of the poor provides reassurance and support for the rest of society. They provide a baseline of failure which reassures the non-poor of their worth. Gans claims that 'poverty helps to guarantee the status of those who are not poor'. It does this by providing 'a reliable and relatively permanent measuring rod for status comparison'. Since they are relatively powerless, the poor also provide an effective scapegoat for the non-poor. Gans maintains that, 'The defenders of the desirability of hard work, thrift, honesty and monogamy need people who can be accused of being lazy, spendthrift, dishonest and promiscuous to justify these norms'. Gans argues that the poor function to reinforce mainstream norms since norms 'are best legitimated by discovering violations'.

From a somewhat different perspective, Gans has reached a similar conclusion to those who argue that poverty must be analysed in terms of class inequality. From both viewpoints poverty exists because it benefits the rich and because the poor are powerless to change their situation. Gans concludes that poverty persists 'because many of the functional alternatives to poverty would be quite dysfunctional for the more affluent members of society'.

Poverty – solutions and ideology

In this section, government measures to deal with poverty and proposals to solve poverty will be considered together with the ideologies which underlie them. First, the ideological aspects of the culture of poverty thesis will be examined, since it formed the basis for government policy in the fight against poverty in the USA.

Like all members of society, sociologists, despite their attempts to be objective, see the world in terms of their own values and political beliefs. This is particularly apparent in the area of poverty research. Herbert J. Gans has suggested that 'perhaps the most significant fact about poverty research is that it is being carried out entirely by middle-class researchers who differ – in class, culture and political power – from the people they are studying'. Some observers argue that the picture of the poor presented by many social scientists is largely a reflection of middle-class value judgments. In particular, the idea of a culture of poverty has been strongly criticized as a product of middle-class prejudice. Charles A.

Valentine in *Culture and Poverty*, a forceful attack on bias in poverty research, states, 'Scarcely a description can be found that does not dwell on the noxiousness, pathology, distortion, disorganization, instability or incompleteness of poverty culture as compared to the life of the middle classes'. From the viewpoint of the culture of poverty, the poor themselves are a major obstacle to the removal of poverty. It therefore follows that at least a part of the solution to poverty is to change the poor, since, by implication, they are partly to blame for their situation. The direction in which the poor are to be changed is also influenced by middle-class values. They must adopt middle-class norms and values and in short, as Valentine puts it, 'the poor must become "middle class"'.

Many observers argue that this line of reasoning formed the basis of USA's government policy towards poverty. In 1964, President Lyndon B. Johnson declared a 'war on poverty' with the passing of the Economic Opportunity Act and the formation of the Office of Economic Opportunity to coordinate measures to fight poverty. The comments of the American anthropologist Thomas Gladwin represent the views of many social scientists on this campaign, 'The whole conception of the War on Poverty rests upon a definition of poverty as a way of life. The intellectual climate in which it was nurtured was created by studies of the culture of poverty, notably those of Oscar Lewis . . . (which) provide the basis for programs at the national level designed very explicitly to correct the social, occupational and psychological deficits of people born and raised to a life of poverty'.

The Office of Economic Opportunity created a series of programmes designed to re-socialize the poor and remove their presumed deficiencies. The Job Corps set up residential camps in wilderness areas for unemployed, inner city youth with the aim of 'building character' and fostering initiative and determination. Many 'work experience' programmes were developed to instil 'work habits'. The Neighbourhood Youth Corps created part-time and holiday jobs for young people. A multitude of job training schemes were started to encourage 'work incentive' and provide the skills required for employment. The aim of many of these schemes was to undo the presumed effect of the culture of poverty by fostering ambition, motivation and initiative. To counter the culture of poverty at an earlier age, government money was pumped into schools in low-income districts with the aim of raising educational standards. Operation Head Start, begun in January 1965, was intended to nip the culture of poverty in the bud. It was an extensive programme of pre-school education for the children of low-income families. According to Charles Valentine, 'Head Start is one of the many current programs designed to inculcate a middle-class "culture" among the poor with the hope that so equipped they may eventually arise from their poverty'. Much of the effort of the Office of Economic Opportunity was directed towards 'community action', the idea of local community self-help. The Office encouraged and financed self-help organizations run by the poor which covered a range of projects from job training and community business ventures to legal services and youth clubs. The idea was for the poor, with help, to pull themselves up by their own bootstraps, to throw aside the culture of poverty and become enterprising and full of initiative like their middle-class mentors. Compared to the above programmes, direct aid in the form of cash payments to the poor received low priority. Edward James in *America Against Poverty*, a study of the 1960s war on poverty, states that direct aid was the 'least popular anti-poverty strategy in America'.

The war on poverty was not designed to eradicate poverty by providing the poor with sufficient income to raise them above the poverty line. Lee Rainwater argues that, 'The goal of the war was not to directly provide resources that would cancel out poverty, but to provide opportunities so that people could achieve their own escape from poverty'. By changing the poor it was hoped to provide them with the opportunity to become upwardly mobile. S. M. Miller and Pamela Roby state, 'The programs aimed at the young, like Head Start, obviously aim for intergenerational social mobility while those designed for older people seek intragenerational mobility'. The war on poverty is a typically American solution reflecting the values of American culture with its emphasis on individual achievement in the land of opportunity. As Walter B. Miller neatly puts it, 'Nothing could be more impeccably American than the concept of opportunity'. The poor must make their own way, they must achieve the status of being non-poor, they must seize the opportunities that are available like every other respectable American. Commenting on the war on poverty, Elinor Graham states, 'Above all, it is "the American way" to approach social-welfare issues, for it places the burden of responsibility upon the individual and not on the socio-economic system. Social services are preferred to income payments in an ideological atmosphere which abhors "handouts"'.

By the late 1960s many social scientists felt that the war on poverty had failed as did the poor if the following comment by a welfare recipient is typical, 'It's great stuff this War on Poverty! Where do I surrender?' (quoted in James, 1970, p. 61). The poor remained stubbornly poor despite the energy and resolve of the Office of Economic Opportunity. Increasingly sociologists argued that solutions to poverty must be developed from stratification theory rather than the culture of poverty theory. From this perspective, Miller and Roby argue that, 'poverty programs be recognized as efforts to engineer changes in the stratification profiles of the United States'. They and others argue that the very concept of poverty and the way in which it spotlights and isolates the poor has disguised the true nature of inequality, and proved to be counter productive in providing solutions. Once poverty is recognized as an aspect of inequality, and not merely a problem of the poor, solutions involve restructuring society as a whole. It can now be argued that the main obstacle to the eradication of poverty is not the behaviour of the poor but the self-interest of the rich. Thus Herbert J. Gans maintains that, 'the prime obstacles to the elimination of poverty lie in an economic system which is dedicated to the maintenance and increase of wealth among the already affluent'.

From the perspective of stratification theory, the solution to poverty involves a change in the stratification system. This war on poverty would be far harder to wage than the previous one since it would require considerable sacrifice by the rich and powerful. The degree of change required is debatable and proposals reflect to some degree the values and political bias of the researchers. The suggestions put forward by Miller and Roby are rather vague. They advocate, 'A re-allocation of American wealth to meet a reasonable set of priorities, a redistribution of goods and power to benefit the bottom half of the population'. However they hasten to add, 'we are not implicitly arguing the case for complete equality'. Lee Rainwater's proposals are more specific. He advocates a redistribution of income so that 'no family has an income that is below the average for all families'. He proposes the money be raised by redistributing only increases in national income rather than reducing the current income of the more wealthy. This he believes 'avoids the problems of direct confrontation involved in the older model of "soaking the rich to give to the poor"'. But neither Rainwater nor Miller and Roby propose an alternative to the capitalist economic system. They assume that the changes they propose can take place within the context of American capitalism.

The war on poverty has its basis in traditional American liberalism. It is American because of its insistence on individual initiative, its emphasis on opportunity and its distaste for direct provision of cash payments to the poor. It is liberal because the reforms it attempted did not seek to alter the basic structure of society. American capitalism was taken for granted and any change in the situation of the poor must take place within its framework. While the solutions to poverty proposed by American sociologists such as Rainwater, Miller and Roby are more radical and would involve modifications to the structure of society, they remain basically liberal. They would take place within the framework of capitalism and would not involve a fundamental change in the structure of society.

The first half of this section has focussed on the USA, on government measures to deal with poverty and proposals for the solution of poverty provided by American sociologists. The remainder of the section examines the British situation and the views of several British sociologists.

With typical British reserve, the UK government has not done anything as dramatic as declaring a war on poverty. It has simply added to the provision of the Welfare State which has gradually developed throughout this century. Benefit provided by the state has taken the form of financial aid to the poor and services given by welfare professionals such as social workers. The British government has been less averse than its American counterpart to providing cash payments to the poor, but in Kincaid's words, these payments are 'pitifully low' and 'leave millions in poverty'. Whatever the differences in policy and style between Britain and America, the results are similar: the poor stay poor. The harsher edges of poverty may have been blunted by the provisions of the Welfare State but poverty remains. Welfare professionals may have cushioned some of the misery produced by poverty, but they have not solved the problem.

Westergaard and Resler argue that many politicians make the fundamental error of assuming that 'the causes of poverty can be read off from the characteristics of the poor'. This has led to the conclusion that poverty is largely the result of old age, family break-up, large families, unemployment, physical or mental handicap or chronic sickness. In this way, 'individual conditions' are regarded as the 'causes' of poverty. It therefore follows that remedies must be directed towards the individual and particular conditions are given particular aid and treatment. For example the unemployed receive financial aid and 'problem families' receive the services of social workers and psychiatrists. This diagnosis of the problem forms the basis of government policy. Westergaard and Resler argue that the diagnosis 'is false precisely because it closes one eye firmly to the total pattern of inequality, only the bottom end of which is visible under the poverty line'. Poverty is not an individual condition, it is a class phenomenon. The poor are working class, not middle class. The mechanisms which generate inequality throughout society are the same mechanisms which generate poverty.

As noted earlier in the chapter, the Welfare State has largely failed to redistribute wealth from rich to poor. It simply shuffles resources within social classes rather than between them. Kincaid argues that the only solution to poverty involves a 'massive redistribution of resources away from the wealthier classes'. This view sees poverty as a social problem rather than as an individual condition. It argues that the problem is society as a whole and therefore society must be changed. Westergaard and Resler adopt a similar position. They argue that government measures to deal with poverty cannot succeed because 'they are not designed to produce wholesale change in the general structure of inequality'.

From a Marxian perspective, the official identification and treatment of poverty can be seen as a means to disguise the true nature of exploitation and oppression. Westergaard and Resler argue that the state, by focussing on one aspect of inequality – the situation of the poor – tends to 'obscure reality' by diverting attention from the larger structure of inequality. The definition of poverty as an individual condition rather than a class phenomenon has the same effect. In this way the privileged position of the wealthy, which rests ultimately on working-class poverty, is protected. In addition, the creation and development of the Welfare State has contained working-class demands for an improvement in their position. Governments have conceded just enough to take the edge off working-class militancy. The role of welfare professionals can also be seen as a means to control the working class and protect the privileged. Kincaid argues that 'most of the individual problems which social workers currently set out to solve are essentially of the sort generated by a society which is not organized on the basis of people's needs'. He argues that many social workers still attribute poverty to a 'defective personality structure, inability to relate to others, and impaired capacity to make realistic judgments of self and others'. This places the blame for poverty squarely on the shoulders of the poor. Some Marxists go even further by seeing welfare professionals as agents of the ruling class. Claiming expert knowledge to diagnose individual deficiencies and provide the correct treatment, welfare professionals, whatever their good intentions, help to maintain ruling class power. They tend to reinforce the myth that poverty is due to personal inadequacy rather than the nature of society.

From a Marxian perspective, the solution to poverty does not involve reforms in the social security system, in the provision of additional payments or services to those defined as poor. Instead it requires a radical change in the structure of society. Thus, Ralph Miliband argues that poverty will only be eradicated with the removal of inequality in general which 'requires the transformation of the economic structures in which it is embedded'. Westergaard and Resler take a similar view maintaining that no substantial redistribution of wealth can occur until capitalism is replaced by a socialist society in which the forces of production are communally owned. As long as the free market system of capitalism determines the allocation of reward, they argue that inequality will remain largely unchanged. Kincaid concludes that since capitalism is based on the maximization of profit rather than the satisfaction of human need, 'Poverty cannot be abolished within capitalist society, but only in a socialist society under workers' control, in which human needs, and not profits, determine the allocation of resources'.

Clearly Marxian views are ideologically based. Sociologists who adopt them are committed to the principles of socialism and equality. They regard capitalism as an exploitive system and condemn the inequality it generates. In their favour, it can be argued that Marxian views may stem less from self-interest than other perspectives on poverty which seek only to modify rather than significantly change the profile of privilege.

5 Education

In advanced industrial societies education is provided by the state as a matter of right for all its citizens. Formal institutions – schools, colleges and universities – are organized for this purpose. They are staffed by full-time professional practitioners – teachers and lecturers. Attendance at schools is compulsory; it is upheld by legal sanctions. Education is provided free of charge, though ultimately it is paid for by the taxpayer. Although free compulsory state education is largely taken for granted today and regarded as a perfectly normal and natural state of affairs, it is important to remember that it is a very recent development in the history of man. In Britain it began in 1870 with the Foster Education Act by which the state assumed responsibility for elementary education and in 1880 school attendance up to the age of ten was made compulsory. Not until 1918 was secondary education clearly defined as the state's responsibility. The Fisher Education Act of 1918 made school attendance compulsory up to the age of fourteen. In 1947, the minimum school leaving age was raised to fifteen, and today it stands at sixteen. These developments were accompanied by a steady expansion of higher education. Education is one of the major growth industries of the last hundred years.

In small-scale, non-literate societies, such as hunting and gathering bands, formal education, as outlined above, was unknown. Young people learned their lessons for life largely by joining in the daily round of the social group. Knowledge and skills were usually learned informally by imitating examples provided by adults. Though adults sometimes instructed the young, they did so as part of their everyday routines. Thus boys accompanied their fathers on hunting trips, girls assisted their mothers to cook and sew. In more complex pre-industrial societies such as those of medieval Europe, specialized educational institutions slowly developed, along with the specialized role of teacher. However, they provided formal education only for a small minority of the population such as future members of the clergy and the sons of the wealthy. Formal education for the masses was only provided after industrialization was well underway.

This chapter is primarily concerned with formal education in advanced Western industrial societies. It considers two main questions: the role of education in society, which is examined in terms of functionalist and Marxian perspectives; and the question of differential educational attainment, the fact that the attainment levels of different social groups vary.

This variation will be explained in terms of a number of theoretical frameworks.

Education – a functionalist perspective

Two related questions have guided functionalist research into education. The first asks, 'What are the functions of education for society as a whole?' Given the functionalist view of the needs of the social system, this question leads, for example, to an assessment of the contribution made by education to the maintenance of value consensus and social solidarity. The second question asks, 'What are the functional relationships between education and other parts of the social system?' This leads, for example, to an examination of the relationship between education and the economic system, and a consideration of how this relationship helps to integrate the society as a whole. As with functionalist analysis in general, the functionalist view of education tends to focus on the positive contributions made by education to the maintenance of the social system.

Emile Durkheim

Writing at the turn of the century, the French sociologist Emile Durkheim saw the major function of education as the transmission of society's norms and values. He maintained that, 'Society can survive only if there exists among its members a sufficient degree of homogeneity; education perpetuates and reinforces this homogeneity by fixing in the child from the beginning the essential similarities which collective life demands'. Without these 'essential similarities', co-operation, social solidarity and therefore social life itself would be impossible. A vital task for all societies is the welding of a mass of individuals into a united whole, in other words the creation of social solidarity. This involves a commitment to society, a sense of belonging and a feeling that the social unit is more important than the individual. Durkheim argues that 'To become attached to society, the child must feel in it something that is real, alive and powerful, which dominates the person and to which he also owes the best part of himself'. Education, and in particular, the teaching of history, provides this link between the individual and society. If the history of his society is brought alive to the child, he will come to see he is a part of something larger than himself, he will develop a sense of commitment to the social group.

Durkheim's views can be illustrated by educational practices in the USA. There a common educational curriculum has helped to instil shared norms and values into a population with diverse backgrounds. It has provided a shared language and a common history for immigrants from every country in Europe. The American student learns about the

Founding Fathers, the Constitution, about Abraham Lincoln who personifies the American values of equality of opportunity and achievement by his journey from the humble origins of a log cabin to the White House. By beginning his schoolday with an oath of allegiance to the Stars and Stripes, the symbol of American society, the student is socialized into a commitment to society as a whole.

Durkheim argues that in complex industrial societies, the school serves a function which cannot be provided either by the family or peer groups. Membership of the family is based on kinship relationships, membership of the peer group on personal choice. Membership of society as a whole is based on neither of these principles. Individuals must learn to cooperate with those who are neither their kin nor their friends. The school provides a context where these skills can be learned. As such, it is society in miniature, a model of the social system. In school, the child must interact with other members of the school community in terms of a fixed set of rules. This experience prepares him for interacting with members of society as a whole in terms of society's rules. Thus Durkheim argues that, 'It is by respecting the school rules that the child learns to respect rules in general, that he develops the habit of self-control and restraint simply because he should control and restrain himself. It is a first initiation into the austerity of duty. Serious life has now begun'.

Finally, Durkheim argues that education teaches the individual specific skills necessary for his future occupation. This function is particularly important in industrial society with its increasingly complex and specialized division of labour. The relatively unspecialized division of labour in pre-industrial society meant that occupational skills could usually be passed on from parents to children without the need for formal education. In industrial society, social solidarity is based largely on the interdependence of specialized skills – for example the manufacture of a single product requires the combination of a variety of specialists. This necessity for combination produces cooperation and social solidarity. Thus schools transmit both general values which provide the 'necessary homogeneity for social survival' and specific skills which provide the 'necessary diversity for social cooperation'. Industrial society is thus united by value consensus and a specialized division of labour whereby specialists combine to produce goods and services.

Durkheim's views are open to a number of criticisms. He assumes that the norms and values transmitted by the educational system are those of society as a whole rather than those of a ruling elite or a ruling class. A consideration of this possibility may well result in a very different view of the role of education in society. Further criticisms of Durkheim's sociology of education will be made later in the chapter.

Talcott Parsons

Drawing on Durkheim's ideas, the American sociologist Talcott Parsons outlined what has become the accepted functionalist view of education. Writing in the late 1950s, Parsons argues that after primary socialization within the family, the school takes over as the 'focal socializing agency'. School acts as a bridge between the family and society as a whole, preparing the child for his adult role. Within the family, the child is judged and treated largely in terms of 'particularistic' standards. Parents treat the child as their particular child rather than judging him in terms of standards or yardsticks which can be applied to every individual. Yet in the wider society the individual is treated and judged in terms of 'universalistic' standards which are applied to all members, regardless of their kinship ties. Within the family the child's status is ascribed, it is fixed by birth. However, in advanced industrial society, status in adult life is largely achieved; for example an individual achieves his occupational status. Thus the child must move from the particularistic standards and ascribed status of the family to the universalistic standards and achieved status of adult society. The school prepares young people for this transition. It establishes universalistic standards in terms of which all pupils achieve their status. Their conduct is assessed against the yardstick of the school rules, their achievement is measured by performance in examinations. The same standards are applied to all students regardless of ascribed characteristics such as sex, race, family background or class of origin. Schools operate on meritocratic principles; status is achieved on the basis of merit. Like Durkheim, Parsons argues that the school represents society in miniature. Modern industrial society is increasingly based on achievement rather than ascription, on universalistic rather than particularistic standards, on meritocratic principles which apply to all its members. By reflecting the operation of society as a whole, the school prepares young people for their adult roles.

As a part of this process, schools socialize young people into the basic values of society. Parsons, like many functionalists, maintains that value consensus is essential for society to operate effectively. In American society, schools instil two major values, the value of achievement and the value of equality of opportunity. By encouraging students to strive for high levels of academic attainment and by rewarding those who do, schools foster the value of achievement itself. By placing individuals in the same situation in the classroom and so allowing them to compete on equal terms in examinations, schools foster the value of equality of opportunity. These values have important functions in society as a whole. Advanced industrial society requires a highly motivated, achievement oriented workforce. This necessitates differential reward for differential achievement, a principle which has been established in schools. Both the winners, the high achievers, and the losers, the low achievers, will see the system as just and fair since status is achieved in a situation where all have an equal chance. Again the principles which operate in the wider society are mirrored by those of the school.

Finally, Parsons sees the educational system as an important mechanism for the selection of individuals for their future role in society. In his words, it 'functions to allocate these human resources within the role-structure of adult society'. Thus schools, by testing and evaluating students, match their talents, skills and capacities to the jobs for which they are best suited. The school is therefore seen as the major mechanism for role allocation.

Like Durkheim, Parsons fails to give adequate consideration to the possibility that the values transmitted by the educational system may be those of a ruling minority rather than of society as a whole. His view that schools operate on meritocratic principles is open to question, a point which will be examined in detail in later sections.

Kingsley Davis and Wilbert E. Moore

Like Parsons, Davis and Moore see education as a means of role allocation, but they link the educational system more directly with the system of social stratification. As outlined in Chapter 2, Davis and Moore see social stratification as a mechanism for ensuring that the most talented and able members of society are allocated to those positions which are functionally most important for society. High rewards which act as incentives are attached to those positions which means, in theory, that all will compete for them and the most talented will win through. The education system is an important part of this process. In Davis's words, it is the 'proving ground for ability and hence the selective agency for placing people in different statuses according to their capacities'. Thus the educational system sifts, sorts and grades individuals in terms of their talents and abilities. It rewards the most talented with high qualifications, which in turn provide entry to those occupations which are functionally most important to society.

General criticisms of Davis and Moore's theory have been examined in Chapter 2. With respect to the relationship between education and social stratification, there are a number of more specific criticisms. Firstly, the relationship between academic credentials and occupational reward is not particularly close. In particular income is only weakly linked to educational attainment. Secondly, there is considerable doubt about the proposition that the educational system grades people in terms of ability. In particular, it has been argued that intelligence has little effect upon educational attainment. Thirdly, there is considerable evidence which suggests that the influence of social stratification largely prevents the educational system from efficiently grading individuals in terms of ability. These points will be considered in detail later.

Education and the economy

Many functionalists have argued that there is a functional relationship between education and the economic system. They point to the fact that mass formal education began in industrial society and is an established part of all industrial societies. They note that the expansion of the economies of industrial societies is accompanied by a corresponding expansion of their educational systems. They explain this correspondence in terms of the needs of industry for skilled and trained manpower, needs which are met by the educational system. Thus the provision of mass elementary education in Britain in 1870 can be seen as a response to the needs of industry for a literate and numerate workforce at a time when industrial processes were becoming more complex and the demand for technical skills was steadily growing.

Advanced industrial society is characterized by a contraction of the primary and secondary sectors of the economy – the extractive and manufacturing industries – and an expansion of the tertiary sector – the service industries. Within the primary and secondary sectors there has been a decline in the demand for unskilled labour, reflecting the increase in mechanization and automation, and a rise in the demand for trained, technically-skilled manual labour. Throughout the twentieth century, the rapid expansion of the tertiary sector has produced an increasing demand for clerical, technical, professional and managerial skills. Education reflects these changes in the economy. Writing in the early 1960s, Halsey and Floud argue that, 'the educational system is bent increasingly to the service of the labour force, acting as a vast apparatus of occupational recruitment and training'. This can be seen from the steady increase in the school leaving age, the increasing specialization of educational provision and the rapid expansion of higher and vocational education, all of which are required to provide the knowledge and training necessary for an increasingly skilled and specialized workforce. Halsey and Floud claim that the economies of advanced industrial societies are 'dependent to an unprecedented extent on the results of scientific research, on the supply of skilled and responsible manpower, and consequently on the efficiency of the educational system'.

Though the above arguments are persuasive, there is considerable doubt about the educational requirements of the labour force in advanced industrial societies. From an examination of studies analysing the relationship between education and the economy, Randall Collins concludes that only a minor part of the expansion of education in advanced industrial societies can be seen as directly serving the demands of industry for skills, training and knowledge. Writing in 1971 about American society, Collins claims that only 'Fifteen per cent of the increase in education of the US labor force during the twentieth century may be attributed to shifts in the occupational structure – a decrease in

177

the proportion of jobs with low skill requirements and an increase in the proportion of jobs with high skill requirements'. However, it could be argued that the *same* jobs have greater skill and knowledge requirements as industrial society develops. For example, plumbers, clerks, doctors and managers today may require greater expertise and technical skills than they did at the turn of the century. Again Collins doubts that the rapid expansion of education is primarily a response to these requirements. He argues, 'It appears that the educational level of the US labor force has changed in excess of that which is necessary to keep up with the skill requirements of jobs'. Collins concludes that the contribution of education to the economic system in advanced industrial societies has been exaggerated.

Collins reaches the following conclusions about the relationship between education and the economy. Studies from various countries suggest that once mass literacy has been achieved, education does not significantly affect economic development. Most occupational skills are learned 'on the job', and where specific training is required, firms provide their own apprenticeship and training schemes. Higher education for particular professions such as medicine, engineering and law may be considered 'vocationally relevant and possibly essential'. However, much higher education, such as schools of business administration, represents an attempt to achieve 'professionalization'. As such, education serves to raise the status of the occupation, rather than to transmit the knowledge and skills necessary for its performance. Collins therefore concludes that the strong and strengthening links between education and the economy, as argued by the functionalists, are not supported by the evidence.

From a functionalist perspective, the functions of education in industrial society may be summarized as follows: the transmission of society's norms and values; the preparation of young people for adult roles; the selection of young people in terms of their talents and abilities for appropriate roles in adult life; the provision of the knowledge, skills and training necessary for effective participation in the labour force.

Education – a liberal perspective

Many of the views on the relationship of education and society to be discussed shortly are highly critical of the functionalist perspective. They are also a reaction to the liberal view of education which, in certain respects, parallels functionalist arguments. The liberal view is not a sociological perspective as such, though it has influenced the thinking of many sociologists. Rather it is the view taken by progressive liberal thinkers and educationalists of the role education does and should play in a modern democratic society. It may be summarized as follows. Education fosters personal development and self-fulfilment. It encourages the individual to develop his mental, physical, emotional and spiritual talents to the full. By providing free schooling for all, education gives everyone an equal opportunity for developing these capacities and talents. Increasingly both the educational system and industrial democracies operate on meritocratic principles. Academic credentials are awarded on merit in a system of fair competition. In the same way, jobs are awarded on merit, and there is a strong relationship between educational qualifications and occupational status. Since schools provide equality of opportunity for all members of society, regardless of their position in the stratification system, a more 'open' society and therefore a higher rate of social mobility will result. The expansion of education will also reduce inequality in society. In particular, as the educational attainment of members of the working class rises, their bargaining position in the market will improve and as a result their income will rise. Though liberals admit that schools have yet to fully realize these ideals, they believe that things are moving in the right direction, that the promise of education is steadily being fulfilled.

Many of the reforms in the educational systems of Western industrial societies have been directed by the liberal ideals outlined above. Such reforms have been based on the belief that education can create a more equal and just society. Thus in the 1960s President Lyndon B. Johnson stated, 'The answer to all our national problems comes down to a single word: education' (quoted in Bowles and Gintis 1976, p. 19). As a result, specially designed programmes of education for the underprivileged became the keynote of Johnson's war on poverty. However, as the chapter on poverty indicates, there is a wide gap between liberal ideals and what actually happens (see pp. 166–9). Over a hundred years of state education have had little effect on economic inequality. In particular, the failure of educational reforms to win the war on poverty has, for many, largely discredited liberal educational philosophy. Many of the arguments presented in the remainder of this chapter are highly critical of liberal views of what education does and can do in society.

Education – a Marxian perspective

As with the functionalist perspective, the Marxian view of the role of education in Western industrial society is guided by several related questions. Given the Marxian view of the nature of society the major question asks, 'How is the educational system shaped by the economic infrastructure?' Questions which derive from this such as 'How does the educational system produce the kind of workforce required by capitalism?' involve an investigation of the links between power, ideology, education and the relations of production in capitalist society. The answers provide a radical alternative to functionalist and liberal views of the role of education in society.

Louis Althusser – the reproduction of labour power

Althusser, a French philosopher, presents a general framework for the analysis of education from a Marxian perspective. As a part of the superstructure, the educational system is ultimately shaped by the infrastructure. It will therefore reflect the relations of production and serve the interests of the capitalist ruling class. For the ruling class to survive and prosper, the 'reproduction of labour power is essential'. Generations of workers must be reproduced to create the profits on which capitalism depends. Althusser argues that the reproduction of labour power involves two processes. First, the reproduction of the skills necessary for an efficient labour force. Second, the reproduction of ruling class ideology and the socialization of workers in terms of it. These processes combine to reproduce a technically efficient and submissive and obedient workforce. The role of education in capitalist society is the reproduction of such a workforce.

Althusser argues that no class can hold power for any length of time simply by the use of force. Ideological control provides a far more effective means of maintaining class rule. If members of the subject class accept their position as normal, natural and inevitable, and fail to realize the true nature of their situation, then they will be unlikely to challenge ruling class dominance. Physical force is an inefficient means of control compared to winning over hearts and minds. The maintenance of class rule largely depends on the reproduction of ruling class ideology. Thus Althusser argues that 'the reproduction of labour power requires not only a reproduction of its skills, but also, at the same time a reproduction of its submission to the ruling ideology'. This submission is reproduced by a number of 'Ideological State Apparatuses' which include the mass media, the law, religion and education. Ideological State Apparatuses transmit ruling class ideology thereby creating false class consciousness which largely maintains the subject class in its subordinate position. In pre-capitalist society, Althusser sees the church as the dominant Ideological State Apparatus. In capitalist society it has largely been replaced by the educational system.

Education not only transmits a general ruling class ideology which justifies and legitimates the capitalist system; it also reproduces the attitudes and behaviour required by the major groups in the division of labour. It teaches workers to accept and submit to their exploitation, it teaches the 'agents of exploitation and repression', the managers, administrators and politicians, how to practise their crafts and rule the workforce as agents of the ruling class. Althusser argues that via the educational system, 'Each mass ejected *en route* is practically provided with the ideology which suits the role it has to fulfil in class society'.

Althusser has produced only a very general Marxian perspective for the analysis of education in capitalist society. His ideas are not supported by evidence, and, as he himself admits, only a preliminary framework has been outlined. A detailed application of this framework is provided in the following section.

Samuel Bowles and Herbert Gintis – *Schooling in Capitalist America*

Like Althusser, the American economists Bowles and Gintis argue that the major role of education in capitalist society is the reproduction of labour power. In particular, they maintain that education contributes to the reproduction of workers with the kinds of personalities, attitudes and outlooks which will fit them for their exploited status. The economic role of education is not so much the reproduction of technical skills needed by the economy, nor the selection and grading of individuals in terms of their talents and abilities for allocation to appropriate jobs. Rather in the words of Bowles and Gintis, 'To capture the economic import of education, we must relate its social structure to the forms of consciousness, interpersonal behavior and personality it fosters and reinforces in students'.

Before examining the relationship between education and social reproduction, it is necessary to outline the type of workforce required if capitalism is to operate efficiently. According to Bowles and Gintis, capitalism is based on the private ownership of the forces of production and the maximization of profit. Wealth is produced by a wage and salary earning workforce and the surplus value – the profit – is appropriated by the capitalists, the owners of the forces of production. The stability of the system depends upon its acceptance as legitimate and just. This involves disguising from the workforce the nature of its exploitation. It also requires the workforce to accept the alienation which the system produces. (For a detailed discussion of the concept of alienation, see Chapter 6, pp. 228–32.) Since alienated workers cannot be motivated by intrinsic rewards, since they cannot find satisfaction and fulfilment in work itself, they must be motivated by extrinsic rewards such as pay and status. Capitalism thus requires a labour force which is motivated by rewards which are external to work. In order to maximize profits, the capitalists must extract as much work as possible from the workers in return for the lowest possible wages. This requires a hardworking and highly motivated workforce. The motivation of the workforce is maintained in part by the threat of unemployment and dismissal. This necessitates a large reserve army of labour and an acceptance by the workers of the employer's right to hire and fire. With unemployment high, wages can be kept low and employers can fire workers in the knowledge that there are plenty more to take their place. High motivation is also maintained by the possibility of promotion for selected members of the workforce to higher status and pay. This requires a workforce which will respond to such incentives. The maximization of profit also requires a weak and fragmented labour force which will not exert strong pressure for higher wages. This fragmentation is accomplished by the stratification of the workforce in terms of pay, status and authority. This tends to prevent, for example, manual and white-collar workers from seeing their interests as common and combining against employers. The fragmentation of the workforce succeeds because of a general acceptance by its members of the justice, or at least the inevitability of differences of pay, status and authority. Most importantly, Bowles and Gintis argue, the success of capitalism depends upon control from the top. This involves an acceptance by the workforce of a hierarchical system of power and control and 'minimal participation in decision making by the majority (the workers)'. The above points lead Bowles and Gintis to conclude that the survival and success of capitalism depends on a submissive, obedient and disciplined workforce.

Having established the workforce requirements of capitalism, Bowles and Gintis go on to examine the US education system, claiming that its major role is to provide 'attitudes and behavior consonant with participation in the labour force'. They analyse the personality characteristics which they claim are fostered and developed by the system. In a study based on a sample of 237 members of the senior year in a New York high school, Bowles, Gintis and Meyer examined the relationship between grades and personality traits. They found that low grades are related to creativity, aggressivity and independence and conclude that such traits are penalized by the school. They found a number of characteristics which they argue indicate 'subordinacy and discipline' associated with high grades and conclude that such characteristics are rewarded by the school. These characteristics include perseverance, consistency, dependability and punctuality. In a survey of similar studies, Bowles and Gintis found that personality traits which can be summarized as 'submission to authority', are strongly related to high grades. Several studies indicated that students with high grades are often below average when measured in terms of creativity, originality and independence of judgment.

From this evidence, Bowles and Gintis conclude that, 'Schools foster types of personal development compatible with the relationships of dominance and subordinacy in the economic sphere'. They argue that, 'The only significant penalized traits are precisely those which are incompatible with conformity to the hierarchical division of labour'. From the majority of its workers capitalism demands obedience and discipline. Large numbers of creative thinkers with initiative and ideas of their own might rock the boat and disrupt the system. Capitalism requires workers who will obey, submit to control from above, take orders rather than question them. By encouraging certain personality characteristics and discouraging others, schools help to produce this kind of worker. Bowles and Gintis therefore reject the liberal view that education promotes self-fulfilment and develops the talents and abilities of the child. Indeed, they suggest that schools actually 'distort personal development'.

Bowles and Gintis next examine the nature of work and social relationships in the educational system and argue that they mirror those of the economic system. In this way young people are prepared for the requirements of the world of work. Schools are organized on a hierarchical principle of authority and control. Teachers give orders, pupils obey. Students have little control over the curriculum, the subjects they learn or the work they do. They are not involved in their work and get little intrinsic satisfaction from it. The actual teaching process tends to prevent the student from finding his own reward in his work since it is still largely based on the 'jug and mug' principle. The teacher possesses knowledge and the authority to dispense it and fills empty mugs – the pupils. This process provides the student with little opportunity for self-fulfilment in his work. Instead he is taught to be content with extrinsic satisfactions, to respond to rewards which are external to the work itself such as examination grades and the approval of teachers. These rewards are given by those in authority and so provide teachers with a powerful instrument of control. Finally, the student, during his school day, moves from one subject to another – from mathematics to history to French to English – seeing little connection between them. Knowledge is fragmented and compartmentalized into academic subjects.

Bowles and Gintis argue that social relationships in schools 'replicate the hierarchical division of labor in the work place'. They suggest that the student's lack of control over work in school mirrors his future situation in the workforce. Lack of personal involvement and fulfilment in school work reflects alienation from work in later life. Responding to external rewards in school corresponds to the reward system in industry where pay, status and authority are awarded by those in power and used to motivate and control the workforce. The fragmentation and compartmentalization of knowledge in schools mirrors the organization of work in the economic system. Bowles and Gintis conclude that pupils are prepared for their work roles 'through a close correspondence between the social relationships which govern personal interaction in the work place and the social relationships of the educational system'.

For capitalism to operate efficiently, the inequalities it produces must be seen as legitimate and just. Bowles and Gintis argue that, 'It is essential that the individual accept, and indeed, come to see as natural, those undemocratic and unequal aspects of the workaday world'. They suggest that a large part of the justification for the inequalities of capitalist society is provided by the educational system. The principle that differential attainment both produces and deserves differential reward is firmly established in schools. Education legitimates inequality by creating the belief that schools provide the opportunity for fair and open competition whereby talents and abilities are developed, graded and certificated. The educational system is thus seen as a meritocracy. Those with the highest qualifications deserve them, they have earned them on merit. The same belief is then applied to the economic system. It is assumed that those students with the highest qualifications receive the highest rewards in the world of work. In this way the educational system justifies and legitimates inequalities in the economic system.

Bowles and Gintis, however, reject the view that rewards in the educational and economic system are based on merit. They argue that educational and occupational attainment are related to family background rather than talent and ability. Thus the children of the wealthy and powerful tend to obtain high qualifications and highly rewarded jobs irrespective of their ability. It is this the educational system disguises with its myth of meritocracy. Thus education provides 'the legitimation of pre-existing economic disparities'.

Bowles and Gintis base their argument on an analysis of the relationships between intelligence (measured in terms of an individual's intelligence quotient or IQ), educational attainment and occupational reward. They argue that IQ accounts for only a small part of educational attainment. At first sight this claim appears incorrect. A large body of statistical evidence indicates a fairly close relationship between IQ and educational attainment. But is IQ the causal factor? Does a high IQ directly cause educational success? If it did, then people with the same IQ should have roughly the same level of educational attainment. Bowles and Gintis examine a sample of individuals with average IQs. Within this sample they find a wide range of variation in educational attainment which leads them to conclude that there is hardly any relationship between IQ and academic qualifications. What then accounts for differences in attainment between people with similar IQs? Bowles and Gintis find a direct relationship between educational attainment and family background. The causal factor is not IQ but the class position of the individual's parents. In general, the higher a person's class of origin, the longer he remains in the educational system and the higher his qualifications. But why do students with high qualifications tend to have higher than average intelligence? Bowles and Gintis argue that this relationship is largely 'a spin-off, a by-product' of continued education. The longer an individual stays in the educational system, the more his IQ develops. Thus IQ is a consequence of length of stay, not the cause of it. The above evidence leads Bowles and Gintis to conclude that, at least in terms of IQ, the educational system does not function as a meritocracy.

They apply a similar argument to the statistical relationship between IQ and occupational reward. In general, individuals in highly paid occupations have above average IQs. However, Bowles and Gintis reject the view that IQ is directly related to occupational success. Within their sample of people with average IQs they find a wide range of income variation. If IQ were directly related to occupational reward, the incomes of those with the same IQ should be similar. Again Bowles and Gintis find that family background is the major factor accounting for differences in income. They conclude that IQ itself has little direct effect on income variation. Thus, at least in terms of IQ, they reject the view that the placement of individuals in the occupational structure is based on meritocratic principles.

Finally, Bowles and Gintis examine the relationship between educational credentials and occupational reward. Again there is a large body of statistical evidence which indicates a close connection between the levels of qualifications and occupational reward. Bowles and Gintis reject the view that this connection is a causal one. They argue, for example, that high qualifications, in and of themselves, do not lead directly to highly paid jobs. They find that the main factors accounting for occupational reward are the individual's class of origin, his race and sex. There is considerable evidence to show that educational qualifications are far more valuable on the job market to the White male than the White female, to the White male than the Black male, to the middle-class male than the working-class male. The apparent connection between occupational reward and educational qualifications is simply due to the fact that in general White middle-class males obtain higher educational qualifications than other social groups and also obtain higher occupational rewards. Their IQ has little effect upon either their educational attainment or their occupational reward; their academic qualifications have little effect upon their future income. Thus Bowles and Gintis conclude that, 'the intellectual abilities developed or certified in school make little *causal* contribution to getting ahead economically. Only a minor portion of the substantial statistical association between schooling and economic success can be accounted for by the school's role in producing or screening cognitive skills'.

If Bowles and Gintis's analysis is correct, then the educational system can be seen as a gigantic myth-making machine which serves to legitimate inequality. It creates and propagates the following myths: educational attainment is based on merit; occupational reward is based on merit; education is the route to success in the world of work. The illusion of meritocracy established in schools leads to the belief that the system of role allocation is fair, just and above board. In particular, the 'emphasis on IQ as the basis for economic success serves to legitimate an authoritarian, hierarchical, stratified and unequal economic system'. Education creates the myth that those at the top deserve their power and privilege, that they have achieved their status on merit and that those at the bottom have only themselves to blame. In this way the educational system reduces the discontent that a hierarchy of wealth, power and prestige tends to produce. Thus Bowles and Gintis conclude that, 'Education reproduces inequality by justifying privilege and attributing poverty to personal failure'. It efficiently disguises the fact that economic success runs in the family, that privilege breeds privilege. Bowles and Gintis therefore reject the functionalist view of the relationship between education and stratification put forward by Talcott Parsons and Davis and Moore. They also reject liberal views which argue that education will create a more 'open' and equal society. Indeed, their analysis suggests that both the functionalist and liberal perspectives are largely shaped by the myths promoted by the educational system.

According to Bowles and Gintis, capitalism requires a surplus of skilled labour. This maintains a high rate of unemployment which provides an effective means of control over the workforce. The threat of dismissal and the possibility of resulting unemployment reduces militancy and keeps wage demands at a relatively low level. The reserve of skilled labour allows workers to be easily replaced. Bowles and Gintis argue that schools produce this surplus of labour. Since the mental and skill requirements of the majority of jobs are fairly low, and since many skills are learned on the job, schools, if anything, over-educate the labour force. Given their schooling, most people could do most jobs. The surplus of skilled labour produced by the schools allows employers to pick and choose their employees and so maintain their control over the labour force.

In *Schooling in Capitalist America*, Bowles and Gintis argue that schooling is organized to meet the requirements of a repressive and exploitive capitalist society. The role of the educational system is social reproduction, the reproduction of a labour force geared to meet the needs of a capitalist economy. Bowles and Gintis are pessimistic about reforms in the educational system having any real chance of success. Since they see the capitalist economic system as the basis of inequality and repression both inside the schools and in society as a whole, they argue that 'the creation of an equal and liberating school system requires a revolutionary transformation of economic life'. In practice this will involve the communal ownership of the forces of production, that is the abolition of capitalism and its replacement by a socialist society.

Bowles and Gintis have been criticized for their insistence that a capitalist economic system is the source of all the evils of American education. Although they recognize that socialism will not automatically produce an 'equal and liberating school system' they place considerable faith in a socialist solution. However, as Jerome Karabel and A. H. Halsey argue, many of the aspects of American schooling condemned by Bowles and Gintis are found in socialist societies. According to Karabel and Halsey, the Cuban educational system places 'heavy reliance on grades and exams as sources of student motivation' and teaching is based on a 'generally authoritarian and teacher-centred method of instruction'.

Richard Dobson's study of educational attainment in Russia shows clearly that the most successful students tend to be the sons and daughters of the privileged. Although this tendency is probably not as marked as in America, it remains significant. Bowles and Gintis's commitment to socialism and condemnation of capitalism tend to divert their attention from these aspects of socialist educational systems.

Ivan Illich – *Deschooling Society*

Although not a Marxist, Ivan Illich has been included in this section for two reasons. Firstly, he is highly critical of both functionalist and liberal views of education. Secondly, his radical critique of the role of education in advanced industrial societies has many parallels with Marxian views. Though not a sociologist by training or profession – he studied theology and philosophy and spent several years as a Roman Catholic priest in New York – Illich's *Deschooling Society*, published in 1971, is an important contribution to the sociology of education.

Illich begins with his views on what education should be. First there is the learning of specific skills such as typing, woodwork and speaking a foreign language. Next there is education as such which is not concerned with the acquisition of particular skills. Education should be a liberating experience in which the individual explores, creates, uses his initiative and judgment and freely develops his faculties and talents to the full. Illich claims that schools are not particularly effective in teaching skills and in practice, diametrically opposed to the educational ideals in which he believes. He argues that the teaching of skills is best left to those who use those skills in daily life. He gives the example of Spanish-speaking teenagers in New York, many of whom were high school dropouts, who were employed to teach Spanish to school teachers, social workers and ministers. Within a week they had been trained to use a teaching manual designed for use by linguists with university qualifications, and within six months they had effectively accomplished their task. However, the employment of such 'skill teachers' is largely prevented by a system which demands professionals, that is officially trained, specialized and certificated teachers.

Illich's main attack is on the failure of schools to match his educational ideals. He regards schools as repressive institutions which indoctrinate pupils, smother creativity and imagination, induce conformity and stupify students into accepting the interests of the powerful. He sees this 'hidden curriculum' operating in the following way. The pupil has little or no control over what he learns or how he learns it. He is simply instructed by an authoritarian teaching regime and, to be successful, must conform to its rules. Real learning, however, is not the result of instruction, but of direct and free involvement by the individual in every part of the learning process. In sum, 'most learning requires no teaching'. The power of the school to enforce conformity to its rules and to coerce its inmates into acceptance of instruction stems from its authority to grant credentials which are believed to bring rewards in the labour market. Those who conform to the rules are selected to go on to higher levels in the educational system. Illich states, 'Schools select for each successive level those who have, at earlier stages of the game, proved themselves good risks for the established order'. Conformity and obedience therefore bring their own rewards. Finally, students emerge from the educational system with a variety of qualifications which they and others believe have provided them with the training, skills and competence for particular occupations. Illich rejects this belief. He argues that, 'The pupil is "schooled" to confuse teaching with learning, grade advancement with education, a diploma with competence'.

Illich sees the educational system as the root of the problems of modern industrial society. Schools are the first, most vital and important stage in the creation of the mindless, conforming and easily manipulated citizen. In schools the individual learns to defer to authority, to accept alienation, to consume and value the services of the institution and to forget how to think for himself. He is taught to see education as a valuable commodity to be consumed in ever increasing quantities. These lessons prepare him for his role as the mindless consumer to whom the passive consumption of the goods and services of industrial society becomes an end in itself. Responding to advertisements and the directives of the powerful he invests time, money and energy in obtaining the products of industry. Deferring to the authority of professionals, he consumes the services of doctors, social workers, lawyers. Trained to accept that those in authority know what's best for him, the individual becomes dependent on the directives of governments, bureaucratic organizations and professional bodies. Illich maintains that modern industrial society cannot provide the framework for human happiness and fulfilment. Despite the fact that goods are pouring from the factories in ever increasing quantities, despite the fact that armies of professionals provide ever more comprehensive programmes to solve social ills, misery, dissatisfaction and social problems are multiplying. The establishment offers a solution which is at once simple and self-defeating – the consumption of even more goods and services. Illich concludes that, 'As long as we are not aware of the ritual through which the school shapes the progressive consumer – the economy's major resource – we cannot break the spell of this economy and shape a new one'.

Illich proposes a simple yet radical solution. As the title of his book, *Deschooling Society* suggests, the answer lies in the abolition of the present system of education. Since schools provide the foundation for all that is to follow, deschooling lies 'at the root of any movement for human liberation'. In place of schools Illich offers two main alternatives. Firstly, 'skill exchanges' in which instructors teach the skills they use in daily life to others. Illich argues that skills can best be learned by 'drills' involving systematic instruction. Secondly, and most importantly, Illich proposes 'learning webs' which consist of individuals with similar interests who 'meet around a problem chosen and defined by their own initiative' and which proceed on a basis of 'creative and exploratory learning'. Illich concludes that deschooling will destroy 'the reproductive organ of a consumer society' and lead to the creation of a society in which man can be truly liberated and fulfilled.

Although in sympathy with much of what Illich says, Marxists such as Bowles and Gintis argue that he has made a fundamental error. Rather than seeing schools as the basis of the problem and their removal as its solution, Bowles and Gintis argue that, 'The social problems to which these reforms are addressed have their roots not primarily in the school system itself, but rather in the normal functioning of the economic system'. From their viewpoint, deschooling would only produce 'occupational misfits' and 'job blues' which are hardly sufficient to transform society as a whole. From a Marxian perspective liberation involves a revolutionary change in the economic infrastructure of society.

This section has examined some of the more important Marxian and radical views of the role of education in society. It is clear that their authors are strongly motivated by their personal values and political beliefs. It can be argued that this prevents them from taking an objective view. However, the same criticism can be made of the functionalists, a point which will be taken up in the final section of the chapter.

Differential educational attainment

Much of the research in the sociology of education has been directed to the question of why members of some social groups reach higher levels of educational attainment than members of others. A large array of statistical evidence shows that, in general, educational attainment rises from the bottom to the top of the class system. Thus, the children of managers and professionals usually obtain higher qualifications than those of manual workers. Statistics also show that the educational attainment of ethnic groups varies. For example, in America, Blacks as a group have a lower attainment level than Whites. This section examines, from a number of different theoretical perspectives, the main explanations for differential educational attainment.

Intelligence and educational attainment

Measured intelligence corresponds fairly closely with educational attainment. In general those with high academic qualifications score highly in intelligence tests. It is tempting to argue that the level of educational attainment is 'caused' by intelligence. It would therefore follow that members of the working class were, on average, less intelligent than members of the middle class; that generally, Whites were more intelligent than Blacks. However, there are many reasons for not jumping to such a simplistic conclusion. As Bowles and Gintis have argued, simply because above average intelligence is associated with high academic qualifications does not necessarily mean that one causes the other. Before reaching any conclusions, it is necessary to examine questions such as 'What is intelligence?', 'How is it measured?', 'Where does it come from?'.

The American psychologist Arthur Jensen defines intelligence as 'abstract reasoning ability' and argues that it is 'a selection of just one portion of the total spectrum of human mental abilities'. It is the ability to discover the rules, patterns and logical principles underlying objects and events and the ability to apply these discoveries to solve problems. Intelligence is measured by intelligence tests which give an individual's intelligence quotient or IQ. Such tests are designed to measure abstract reasoning ability, and so exclude questions such as 'Which is the highest mountain in the world?' which test knowledge and memory rather than the ability to reason. Thus a simple IQ test may ask for the next number in the following sequence: 2, 4, 6, 8. This question requires the individual to discover the pattern underlying the sequence of numbers and to apply his discovery to solve the problem. Despite their widespread use, there is a large body of evidence to suggest that IQ tests are not a valid measure of intelligence, particularly when they are used to compare the intelligence of members of different social groups.

Many researchers argue that IQ tests are biased in favour of the White middle class since they are largely constructed by and standardized upon members of this group. If it is accepted that social classes and ethnic groups have distinctive subcultures and that this affects their performance in IQ tests, then comparisons between such groups in terms of measured intelligence are invalid. This argument is best illustrated by the testing of non-Western populations with Western IQ tests. The Canadian psychologist Otto Klineberg gave a test to Yakima Indian children living in Washington State, USA. The test consisted of placing variously shaped wooden blocks into the appropriate holes in a wooden frame, 'as quickly as possible'. The children had no problem with the test but produced low scores because they failed to finish within the required time. Klineberg argues that this does not indicate low intelligence but simply reflects the children's cultural background. Unlike Western culture the Yakima do not place a high priority on speed. S. D. Porteus provides a similar example when administering IQ tests to Australian aborigines. They were reluctant to perform the tests and found it difficult to understand Porteus's request that they take them as individuals. Aborigine culture states that problems should be solved not by the individual but by the group. Important problems are discussed by the tribal elders until a unanimous decision is reached. These examples suggest that Western IQ tests are inappropriate for non-Western peoples. The same argument has been applied to the use of IQ tests within Western societies which contain different subcultural groups. Thus William Labov suggests that the relatively low scores of Black Americans may in part, be accounted for by their distinctive dialect. Tests which contain words may well be biased against Blacks since the intended meanings of the words will be based on their usage by middle-class Whites. It can therefore be argued that at least a part of the difference in IQ scores between social groups may simply be a reflection of subcultural differences. Many psychologists now argue that it is not possible to construct 'culture-free' or 'culture-fair' tests, that is tests which can provide a valid test of an individual's IQ, no matter what his cultural background. Thus, the British psychologist Philip Vernon states that, 'There is no such thing as a culture-fair test, and never can be'. This suggests that conclusions based on comparisons of the average measured IQ of different social groups must be regarded at best with reservation.

There is general agreement that intelligence is due to both genetic and environmental factors. It stems partly from the genes an individual inherits from his parents and partly from the environment in which he grows up and lives. Environmental influences include everything from diet to social class, from quality of housing to family size. Some psychologists, such as Arthur Jensen in America and Hans Eysenck in Britain, argue that IQ is largely inherited. They maintain that some 80% of intelligence is genetically based. Their estimates are constructed from the following kinds of evidence. Studies of identical twins raised in different environments show that they have different IQ scores. Since the twins are genetically identical, it can be argued that differences in their IQs are caused by environmental factors. But this does not allow an accurate measurement of how much of the IQ score of each twin is due to environmental factors and prevents a reliable estimate of the genetic and environmental component of intelligence. In America, a large body of statistical evidence indicates that on average, Blacks score some ten to fifteen points below Whites in IQ tests. A strong case can be made for environmental factors accounting for this difference – for example Blacks are more likely to live in poverty than Whites. However Jensen and Eysenck point to the fact that a smaller, though significant difference in the IQ scores of Blacks and Whites remains when environments are equalized. When Blacks and Whites with similar income levels and occupational statuses are compared, Blacks, on average, have lower test scores. Whether or not environments can be equalized simply by holding factors such as income and occupation constant is questionable. For example, Bodmer suggests that the effect of over 200 years of prejudice and discrimination against Blacks in America prevents an equalization of environments with Whites.

Despite objections to their views, Eysenck and Jensen maintain that genetically based intelligence accounts for a large part of the differences in educational attainment between social groups. Eysenck claims that, 'What children take out of schools is proportional to what they bring into the schools in terms of IQ'. Jensen is more cautious when he suggests that 'genetic factors may play a part in this picture'. However, he does argue that 'a largely genetic explanation of the evidence on racial and social group differences in educational performance is in a stronger position scientifically than those explanations which postulate the absence of any genetic differences in mental traits and ascribe all the behavioural variation between groups to cultural differences, social discrimination and inequalities of opportunity'.

Those who argue that differences in IQ between social groups are due largely to environmental factors make the following points. It is not possible to estimate the degree to which IQ is determined by genetic and environmental factors. Despite this there is considerable evidence to indicate that environmental factors have an important effect. During the First World War over one million recruits to the US Army were given a series of tests, similar in standard to IQ tests. On average, Blacks from the northern states scored more highly than both Blacks and Whites from the southern states. In the north a number of factors such as schooling, housing and income were superior to those available to many southerners. In addition the repressive discrimination against Blacks in the south was replaced by a milder form in the north. Similar tests given by the US Army in World War II indicate that the IQ of White recruits had risen on average by nine to twelve points. In fact 83% of the recruits had higher test scores than their First World War counterparts. This can be accounted for by a number of environmental factors including higher living standards and longer schooling. Not even the most extreme geneticist would argue that this increase in IQ could be explained by a dramatic improvement in the genes for intelligence within the White population. The above evidence suggests that IQ is not a fixed or finite thing, rather it is something that can be learned and developed like any other skill. In particular it is sensitive to and responds to changes in the environment.

Research has indicated that a wide range of environmental factors can affect performance in IQ tests. Otto Klineberg summarizes some of these factors, 'The successful solution of the problems presented by the tests depends on many factors – the previous experience and education of the person tested, his degree of familiarity with the subject matter of the test, his motivation or desire to obtain a good score, his emotional state, his rapport with the experimenter, his knowledge of the language in which the test is administered and also his physical health and well-being, as well as on the native capacity of the person tested'. Evidence which will be examined in the following sections indicates that the relatively low test scores of certain social groups is due, at least in part, to the factors outlined by Klineberg.

Many researchers now conclude that given the present state of knowledge, it is impossible to estimate the proportions of intelligence due to heredity and environment. Measurement of possible genetically based differences in IQ between social groups would involve the exposure of large numbers of individuals born into those groups to identical environments. Since this is neither morally acceptable nor practically possible, the debate will probably never be resolved. Christopher Jencks, who has conducted a large-scale statistical study into the relationship between IQ, family background and educational attainment in America reached the following conclusion. 'There is no way to resolve such disagreement in the foreseeable future. We cannot expose blacks and whites to the same environments, since skin color itself influences an individual's environment. Nor can we compare the test scores of blacks and whites with identical IQ genotypes, because we do not know which specific genes influence IQ. As a result, everyone will doubtless continue to believe what his prejudices make him want to believe'.

In one sense the whole IQ debate can be seen as a storm in a teacup. It has been regarded as important because of the assumption that IQ directly affects educational attainment and level of income. If Bowles and Gintis are correct, this is not the case. They find that IQ is 'nearly irrelevant' to educational and economic success. Thus differences in IQ between social classes and ethnic groups, whether due mainly to environmental or genetic factors, may well have little real significance.

Class and ethnic subcultures and educational attainment

Various studies have shown that even when IQ is held constant, there are significant differences in educational attainment between members of different social groups. Thus working-class and Black students with the same measured IQ as their middle-class and White counterparts are less successful in the educational system. It has therefore been suggested that class and ethnic stratification are directly related to educational attainment. In particular, it has been argued that the subcultures, the distinctive norms and values of social classes and ethnic groups, influence performance in the educational system.

This position was first spelt out in detail by the American sociologist Herbert H. Hyman in an article entitled, *The Value Systems of Different Classes*. He argues that the value system of the lower classes creates 'a *self-imposed* barrier to an improved position'. Using a wide range of data from opinion polls and surveys conducted by sociologists, Hyman outlines the following differences between working and middle-class value systems. Firstly, members of the working class place a lower value on education. They place less emphasis on formal education as a means to personal advancement, they see less value in continuing at school beyond the minimum leaving age. Secondly, they place a lower value on achieving high occupational status. In evaluating jobs, they emphasize 'stability, security and immediate economic benefits' and tend to reject the risks and investments involved in aiming for high status occupations. Job horizons tend therefore to be limited to a 'good trade'. Thirdly, compared to their middle-class counterparts, members of the working class believe that there is less opportunity for personal advancement. This belief is probably the basis for the lower value placed on education and high occupational status. Hyman argues that although it is based on a realistic assessment of the situation – they do indeed have less opportunity – the belief itself reduces this opportunity still further. The values Hyman outlines do not characterize all members of the working class – a sizeable minority do not share them. This minority includes many manual workers with white-collar parents, a fact which influences their choice of reference group. They identify more with the middle class and as a result tend to have higher aspirations. In general, however, Hyman concludes that, 'the lower-class individual doesn't want as much success, knows he couldn't get it even if he wanted to, and doesn't want what might help him get success'. Thus, the motivation to achieve, whether in school or outside it, will generally be lower for members of the working class.

Barry Sugarman, the British sociologist, relates certain aspects of middle and working-class subcultures more directly to differential educational attainment. He provides an explanation for differences in attitude and outlook between the two classes, arguing that the nature of manual and non-manual occupations largely accounts for these differences. Many middle-class occupations provide an opportunity for continuous advancement in income and status. This encourages planning for the future, for example the investment of time, energy and money in training to meet the requirements of higher status jobs. Many white-collar jobs also provide sufficient income for financial investment in the future in the form of mortgages and insurance policies. By comparison working-class jobs reach full earning capacity relatively quickly, they provide fewer promotion prospects and less income for investment. In addition they are less secure. Manual workers are more likely to be laid off or made redundant than white-collar workers. The absence of a career structure in many working-class jobs means that individual effort has less chance of producing improvements in income, status and working conditions. Collective action in the form of trade union pressure provides a more effective strategy. Sugarman argues that differences in the nature of jobs tend to produce differences in attitude and outlook. Since they have less control over the future, less opportunity to improve their position, and less income to invest, manual workers tend to be fatalistic, present-time oriented and concerned with immediate gratification. Since they are more dependent on joint action to improve wages and working conditions, they tend to emphasize collectivism rather than individualism.

Sugarman argues that these attitudes and orientations are an established part of working-class subculture. Pupils from working-class origins will therefore be socialized in terms of them. This may account at least in part, for their low level of educational attainment. Fatalism involves an acceptance of the situation rather than efforts to improve it. As such it will not encourage high achievement in the classroom. Immediate gratification emphasizes the enjoyment of pleasures of the moment rather than sacrifice for future reward. As such it will tend to discourage sustained effort for the promise of examination success. It will also tend to encourage early leaving for the more immediate rewards of a wage packet, adult status and freedom from the disciplines of school. Present-time orientation may further reduce the motivation for academic achievement. An emphasis on long-term goals and future planning can encourage pupils to remain longer in full-time education by providing a purpose for their stay. Finally collectivism involves loyalty to the group rather than the emphasis on individual achievement which the school system demands. Sugarman therefore concludes that the subculture of pupils from working-class backgrounds places them at a disadvantage in the educational system.

Before continuing the theme of this section, it is important to make a number of criticisms of the concept of social class subculture and the methodology used to establish its existence. Firstly, the content of working-class subculture is sometimes derived from observation. In contrast to the behaviour of many members of the middle class, aspects of working-class behaviour appear to be directed by the attitudes, norms and values outlined above. However, this behaviour may simply be a response in terms of mainstream culture to the circumstances of working-class life. Thus, members of the working class may be realistic rather than fatalistic, they might defer gratification if they had the resources to defer, they might be future oriented if the opportunities for successful future planning were available. From this point of view members of the working class share the same norms and values as any other members of society. Their behaviour is not directed by a distinctive subculture. It is simply their situation which prevents them from expressing society's norms and values in the same way as members of the middle class. (This view is examined in detail in the previous chapter – see pp. 156–60.) Secondly, the content of working-class subculture is sometimes derived from interviews and questionnaires. Hyman's data were largely obtained from these sources. Barry Sugarman gave a questionnaire to 540 fourth year boys in four London secondary schools and his conclusions are largely based on data from this source. However, what people say in response to interviews or questionnaires may not provide an accurate indication of how they behave in other situations. As Robert Colquhoun notes in his criticism of Sugarman, it cannot simply be assumed that 'a response elicited in a questionnaire situation holds in the context of everyday life situations'. Thus social class differences in response to interviews and questionnaires may not indicate subcultural differences which direct behaviour in a wide range of contexts. Finally, in a criticism of American studies R. H. Turner notes that social class differences reported from interviews and questionnaire data are often slight. Sociologists tend to ignore similarities between classes and emphasize the differences. (discussed in Colquhoun, 1976, p. 112).

The warnings contained in the above criticism are applicable to an important longitudinal study (a study of the same group over time) by J. W. B. Douglas and his associates. The study was based partly on questionnaire data and utilized the concept of social class subculture. In *The Home and the School*, Douglas examined the educational career through primary school to the age of eleven of 5362 British children born in the first week of March, 1946. In a second publication. *All Our Future*, he followed the progress of 4720 members of his original sample through secondary school up to the age of sixteen and a half in 1962. Douglas divided the students into groups in terms of their ability which was measured by a battery of tests including IQ tests. He also divided the students into four social class grouping and found significant variations in educational attainment between students of similar ability but from different social classes. Comparing the attainment of 'high ability' students, Douglas found that 77% of upper middle class, 60% of lower middle class, 53% of upper working class and 37% of lower working class students gained good certificates at GCE 'O' level. Comparing students of lower ability, he found even larger attainment differences related to social class. Douglas also found that length of stay in the educational system was related to social class. Within the 'high ability' group, 50% of the students from the lower working class left secondary school in their fifth year compared with 33% from the upper working class, 22% from the lower middle and 10% from the upper middle class. Again social class differences were greater for lower ability students.

Douglas related educational attainment to a variety of factors including the student's health, the size of his family and the quality of the school. The single most important factor appeared to be the degree of parents' interest in their children's education. In general, middle-class parents expressed a greater interest as indicated by more frequent visits to the school to discuss their children's progress. They were more likely to want their children to stay at school beyond the minimum leaving age and to encourage them to do so. Douglas found that parental interest and encouragement became increasingly important as a spur to high attainment as the children grew older. He also attaches importance to the child's early years since, in many cases, performance during the first years of schooling is reflected throughout the secondary school. He suggests that during primary socialization, middle-class children receive greater attention and stimulus from their parents. This forms a basis for high achievement in the educational system. Douglas concludes, 'We attribute many of the major differences in performance to environmental influences acting in the pre-school years'.

Apart from this general observation, Douglas does not examine pre-school socialization in detail. A large amount of research, mainly conducted by psychologists, has explored the relationships between childrearing practices, social class and educational attainment. Although the results of this research are far from conclusive, there is some measure of agreement on the following points. Firstly, behaviour patterns laid down in childhood have important and lasting effects. In particular the child's personality is largely shaped during the years of primary socialization. Secondly, there are social class variations in childrearing practices. Thirdly, these variations have a significant effect upon attainment levels in the educational system. Compared to working-class childrearing practices, those of the middle class have been characterized as follows: there is an emphasis on high achievement; parents expect and demand more from their children; they encourage their children to constantly improve their performance in a wide range of areas from childhood games to talking and table manners; by rewarding success parents instil a pattern of high achievement motivation into their children. By giving their children greater individual attention and setting higher standards for them to attain, parents provide a stimulating environment which fosters intellectual development. In this way, middle-class childrearing practices lay the foundation for high attainment in the educational system.

The above views have been strongly criticized. Even if the variation in childrearing practices between social classes exists, which is far from established, the view that behaviour patterns laid down in childhood have a lasting effect has been challenged. In an important article entitled *Personal Change in Adult Life*, Howard S. Becker shows that behaviour can change radically depending on the situation. He argues that changes in behaviour patterns in adult life show clearly that human action is not simply an expression of fixed patterns established during childhood. If Becker's view is correct educational attainment is a reflection of what happens in the classroom rather than what happens in the cradle.

This section has examined possible subcultural differences between social classes which may account for differential educational attainment. It concludes with a consideration of class differences in speech patterns and their relationship to educational attainment. Since speech is an important medium of communication and learning, attainment levels in schools may be related to differences in speech patterns. Much of the early work in this area was conducted by the English sociologist Basil Bernstein. He distinguishes two forms of speech pattern which he terms the 'elaborated code' and the 'restricted code'. In general, members of the working class are limited to the use of restricted codes whereas members of the middle class use both codes. Restricted codes are a kind of shorthand speech. Those conversing in terms of the code have so much in common that there is no need to make meanings explicit in speech. Married couples often use restricted codes since their shared experience and understandings make it unnecessary to spell out their meanings and intentions in detail. Bernstein states that restricted codes are characterized by 'short, grammatically simple, often unfinished sentences'. There is a limited use of adjectives and adjectival clauses, of adverbs and adverbial clauses. Meaning and intention are conveyed more by gesture, voice intonation and the context in which the communication takes place. Restricted codes tend to operate in terms of 'particularistic meanings' and as such they are tied to specific contexts. Since so much is taken for granted and relatively little is made explicit, restricted codes are largely limited to dealing with objects, events and relationships which are familiar to those communicating. Thus the meanings conveyed by the code are limited to a particular social group, they are bound to a particular social context and are not readily available to outsiders.

In contrast, an elaborated code explicitly verbalizes many of the meanings which are taken for granted in a restricted code. It fills in the detail, spells out the relationships and provides the explanations omitted by restricted codes. As such its meanings tend to be 'universalistic', they are not tied to a particular context. In Bernstein's words, the meanings 'are in principle available to all because the principles and operations have been made explicit and so public'. The listener need not be plugged in to the experience and understandings of the speaker since they are spelled out verbally. To illustrate his points Bernstein gives the example of stories told by two five-year-olds, one with a working-class, the other with a middle-class background. The children were given four pictures on which to base their story. In the first, several boys are playing football. In the second the ball breaks a window. The third shows a woman looking out of the window and a man making a threatening gesture in the boys' direction. The fourth picture shows the boys retreating from the scene. Using an elaborated code to spell out the detail in the pictures, the middle-class child describes and analyses the relationships between the objects, events and participants and his story can be understood by the listener without the aid of the pictures. The working-class child using a restricted code leaves many of his meanings unspoken and the listener would require the pictures to make sense of the story. His story is therefore tied to a particular context whereas the first story is free from context and can be understood with no knowledge of the situation in which it was created.

Bernstein explains the origins of social class speech codes in terms of family relationships and socialization practices and the nature of manual and non-manual occupations. He argues that working-class family life fosters the development of restricted codes. In the working-class family the positions of its members are clear cut and distinct. Status is clearly defined in terms of age, sex and family relationships. This clarity of status therefore requires little discussion or elaboration in verbal communication. Father can simply say 'Shut up' to his offspring because his position of authority is unambiguous. By comparison, members of middle-class families tend to relate more as individuals rather than in terms of their ascribed status as father, son, mother and daughter. Relationships tend to be less rigid and clear cut and based more on negotiation and discussion. As a result meaning has to be made more explicit, intentions spelled out, rules discussed, decisions negotiated. Middle-class family relationships therefore tend to encourage the use of an elaborated code. Bernstein also sees a relationship between the nature of middle and working-class occupations and speech codes. He argues that working-class jobs provide little variety, offer few opportunities to participate in decision making and require manual rather than verbal skills. In a routine occupation in the company of others in a similar situation, the manual worker is discouraged from developing an elaborated code. By comparison, white-collar occupations offer greater variety, involve more discussion and negotiation in reaching decisions and therefore require more elaborated speech patterns.

Bernstein uses class differences in speech codes to account in part for differences in educational attainment. Firstly, formal education is conducted in terms of an elaborated code. Bernstein states that 'the school is necessarily concerned with the transmission and development of universalistic orders of meaning'. This places the working-class child at a disadvantage because he is limited to the restricted code. Secondly, the restricted code, by its very nature, reduces the chances of working-class pupils to successfully acquire some of the skills demanded by the educational system. Bernstein does not dismiss working-class speech patterns as inadequate or substandard: he describes them as having 'warmth and vitality', 'simplicity and directness'. However, particularly in his earlier writings, he does imply that in certain respects, they are inferior to an elaborated code. He suggests that an elaborated code is superior for explicitly differentiating and distinguishing objects and events, for analysing relationships between them, for logically and rationally developing an argument, for making generalizations and handling higher level concepts. Since such skills and operations form an important part of formal education, the limitation of working-class pupils to a restricted code may provide a partial explanation for their relatively low attainment.

This view receives strong support from some educational psychologists. In particular American psychologists such as Martin Deutsch, Carl Bereiter and Siegfried Engelmann argue that the speech patterns of members of low-income groups are central to any explanation of their educational attainment. Where Bernstein is cautious, they state categorically that the speech patterns of low-income Blacks and Whites in America are inferior in practically every respect to those of members of higher income groups. Thus Bereiter states that the speech of many low-income children 'is not merely an underdeveloped version of standard English, but is a basically non-logical mode of expressive behaviour', (quoted in Labov, 1973, p. 25). He argues that it is hopelessly inadequate to meet the requirements of the educational system, particularly with its failure to deal with higher level concepts. Bereiter concludes that the speech patterns of the lower class retard intellectual development, impede progress in school and directly contribute to educational failure.

Both Bernstein's ideas and the more extreme claims of psychologists such as Bereiter have provoked strong criticism. In a detailed critique of Bernstein's views, Harold Rosen attacks his arguments step by step. Firstly, he states that Bernstein's view of social class is vague. At times he talks about the working class in general as having a restricted code, at other times he specifies the lower working class. He lumps together all non-manual workers into a middle class whose members from top to bottom appear equally proficient in handling an elaborated code. Bernstein thus ignores possible variety within these classes. Rosen also criticizes Bernstein's characterizations of working and middle-class family life and work situations, demanding evidence for his assertions. He also notes a further lack of hard evidence for elaborated and restricted codes. Bernstein provides few examples to actually prove their existence. Finally, Rosen accuses Bernstein of creating the myth that the supposed middle-class elaborated code is superior in important respects to working-class speech patterns. Rosen concludes that, 'It cannot be repeated too often that, for all Bernstein's work, we know little about working-class language'.

In a famous article entitled, *The Logic of Nonstandard English*, the American linguist William Labov strongly attacks both Bernstein and educational psychologists such as Bereiter and Engelmann. Labov bases his case on the speech patterns of a small sample of lower class Black children in Harlem, the main Black ghetto in New York City. He argues that Black speech patterns are not inferior to standard English, they are simply different. Labov examines a statement, part of which is quoted below, about the non-existence of heaven by a boy named Larry.

'Cause, you see, doesn' nobody really know that it's a God,
y'know, 'cause I mean I have seen black gods, pink gods,
white gods, all color gods, and don't nobody know it's really
a God. An' when they be sayin' if you good, you goin' t'heaven,
tha's bullshit, 'cause you ain't goin' to no heaven, 'cause
it ain't no heaven for you to go to.'

Labov shows how the statement is perfectly logical by translating it into standard English in the order of the logical sequence of the propositions made.

1 Everyone has a different idea of what God is like.
2 Therefore nobody really knows that God exists.
3 If there is a heaven, it was made by God.
4 If God doesn't exist he couldn't have made heaven.
5 Therefore heaven does not exist.
6 You can't go to somewhere that doesn't exist.

So much for the claim made by Bereiter and others that lower class Black speech patterns cannot deal logically with abstract concepts. You can't get much more abstract than God and heaven!

Labov examines several aspects of Black speech patterns which appear ungrammatical and illogical such as the double negatives used by Larry in the above quotation – for example 'doesn' nobody really know'. Labov argues that Black American speech follows strict rules just like standard English. Its meanings are perfectly clear to the native speaker. It is no more illogical or ungrammatical than many other languages which contain conventions which appear illogical in terms of standard English. Black speech is simply a different form of English with its own rules and conventions. It is just as elaborated as the middle-class elaborated code. It is quite capable of performing all the operations of standard English. Those who condemn it as a substandard form of English are simply showing their ignorance – they don't understand it. Labov maintains that low-income Black children 'receive a great deal of verbal stimulation, hear more well-formed sentences than middle-class children, and participate fully in a highly verbal culture; they have the same basic vocabulary, possess the same capacity for conceptual learning, and use the same logic as anyone else who learns to speak and understand English'.

This section has examined possible subcultural differences between social class and ethnic groups which may account, in part, for the different attainment levels of members of these groups in the educational system. The implications and policies which stem from this view will be examined in the following section.

Cultural deprivation and compensatory education

The picture of working-class subculture is not an attractive one. It is portrayed as a substandard version of mainstream middle-class culture. Its standard deteriorates towards the lower levels of the working class and at rock bottom it becomes the culture of poverty, outlined in the previous chapter. From this portrayal, the theory of cultural deprivation was developed. It states that the subculture of low-income groups is deprived or deficient in certain important respects and this accounts for the low educational attainment of members of these groups. This theory places the blame for educational failure on the child, his family, his neighbourhood and the subculture of his social group. The so-called 'culturally deprived child' is deficient or lacking in important skills, attitudes and values which are essential to high educational attainment. His environment is not only poverty stricken in economic terms but also in cultural terms. The following quotation from Charlotte K. Brooks is typical of the picture of the culturally deprived child which emerged in Britain and the USA in the early 1960s.

> . . . he is essentially the child who has been isolated from those rich experiences that should be his. This isolation may be brought about by poverty, by meagerness of intellectual resources in his home and surroundings, by the incapacity, illiteracy, or indifference of his elders or of the entire community. He may have come to school without ever having had his mother sing him the traditional lullabies, and with no knowledge of nursery rhymes, fairy stories, or the folklore of his country. He may have taken few trips – perhaps the only one the cramped, uncomfortable trip from the lonely shack on the tenant farm to the teeming, filthy slum dwelling – and he probably knows nothing of poetry, music, painting, or even indoor plumbing, (quoted in Friedman, 1976, p. 121).

The catalogue of deficiencies of the culturally deprived child includes linguistic deprivation, experiential, cognitive and personality deficiencies, and a wide range of 'substandard' attitudes, norms and values.

The theory of cultural deprivation poses problems for the liberal ideal of equality of opportunity in education. It had been argued that the provision of similar educational opportunities for all would give every student an equal opportunity to fulfil his talents. In the USA the high school provided a uniform system of secondary education. In Britain supporters of the comprehensive school argued that the replacement of the tripartite system of secondary education – the grammar, technical and secondary modern schools – with the comprehensive system would go a long way towards providing equality of educational opportunity. A single system of secondary schools should provide the same opportunity for all. However it became increasingly apparent that a uniform state educational system would not provide everyone with an equal chance since many would enter and travel through the system with the millstone of cultural deprivation hanging round their necks. This realization slowly changed the notion of equality of educational opportunity. Formerly it had been argued that equality of opportunity existed when access to all areas of education was freely available to all. Now it was argued that equality of opportunity only existed when the attainment levels of all social groups were similar. The emphasis had changed from equality of access to equality of results.

From the viewpoint of cultural deprivation theory, equality of opportunity could only become a reality by compensating for the deprivations and deficiencies of low-income groups. Only then would low-income pupils have an equal chance to seize the opportunities freely provided for all members of society. From this kind of reasoning developed the idea of positive discrimination in favour of culturally deprived children: they must be given a helping hand to compete on equal terms with other children. This took the form of compensatory education – additional educational provision for the culturally deprived. Since, according to many educational psychologists, most of the damage was done during primary socialization when a substandard culture was internalized in an environment largely devoid of 'richness' and stimulation, compensatory education should concentrate on the pre-school years.

This thinking lay behind many of the programmes instituted by the Office of Economic Opportunity during President Johnson's war on poverty. Billions of dollars were poured into 'Operation Head Start', a massive programme of pre-school education beginning in Harlem and extended to low-income areas across America. This and similar programmes aimed to provide 'planned enrichment', a stimulating educational environment to instill achievement motivation and lay the foundation for effective learning in the school system. The results were very disappointing. In a large scale evaluation of Operation Head Start, the Westinghouse Corporation concluded that it produced no long term beneficial results. During the late 1960s and early 1970s the Office of Economic Opportunity tried a system of 'performance contracting'. Experts were contracted to raise the educational standards of low-income pupils on a payment by results basis. Highly structured intensive learning programmes were often used, similar to those developed by Bereiter and Engelmann at the University of Illinois – they devised a programme of pre-school language education which drilled young children in the use of standard English. Again the results were disappointing. Performance contracting sometimes produced short-term improvements but its effects were rarely lasting. From its evaluation of performance contracting, the Office of Economic Opportunity concluded that 'the evidence does not indicate that performance contracting will bring about any great improvement in the educational status of disadvantaged children', (quoted in Jensen, 1973, p. 7).

Despite such gloomy conclusions, there is still support for compensatory education. Some argue that it has failed either because the programmes developed have been inappropriate or because the scale of the operation has been insufficient. Martin Deutsch maintains that only 'long-term enrichment with specially trained teachers, careful planning and supervision and adequate funding can produce positive effects'. B. M. Caldwell argues that programmes have failed to combat the influences of the home environment and suggests that children should be removed from their parents during the day and placed in institutions which provide 'educationally oriented day care for culturally deprived children between six months and three years of age', (quoted in Labov, 1973, p. 56). This she hopes will break the cycle of culturally deprived parents producing culturally deprived children.

In Britain compensatory education began in the late 1960s with the government allocating extra resources for school buildings in low-income areas and supplements to the salaries of teachers working in those areas. Four areas – parts of Liverpool and Birmingham, Conisbrough and Denaby in the then West Riding of Yorkshire and Deptford in southeast London, were designated Educational Priorities Areas (EPAs). Programmes of compensatory education were introduced in the EPAs. They were based mainly on pre-school education and additional measures in primary schools to raise literacy standards. Though it is difficult to evaluate the results, reports from the EPAs are generally disappointing. Eric Midwinter, who headed the Liverpool EPA, argues that compensatory education has concentrated too much on the child in the educational institution. He believes that, 'No matter how much you do *inside* the school, you can make virtually no impact at all without the informed support of the home'. He advocates a community school with strong links between the school and the community as a whole. Parents must be educated to help their children; the community must be educated about education. A. H. Halsey, who directed the EPA projects, argues that positive discrimination in England has yet to be given a fair trial. It has operated on a shoestring compared to American programmes – for example in 1973 only one-fifth of 1% of the total educational budget was spent on compensatory education. Writing in 1977, Halsey states, 'Positive discrimination is about resources. The principle stands and is most urgently in need of application'.

Despite continuing support for compensatory education, criticism of the idea and its theoretical basis has been steadily mounting. The theory of cultural deprivation has been strongly attacked as a smokescreen which disguises the real factors which prevent equality of educational opportunity. By placing the blame for failure on the child and his background it diverts attention from the deficiencies of the educational system. William Labov argues that Operation Head Start is 'designed to repair the child rather than the school; to the extent it is based upon this inverted logic, it is bound to fail'. Basil Bernstein takes a similar view and criticizes the whole concept of compensatory education 'because it distracts attention from the deficiences of the school itself'. Others criticize the concept for diverting attention from inequalities in society. D. C. Morton and D. R. Watson argue that patching up operations such as programmes of compensatory education cannot remove inequality of educational opportunity which is rooted in social inequality in society as a whole. They claim that compensatory education serves as 'a diversion from the pursuit of a genuine egalitarian policy'. In their view equality of educational opportunity can only be possible in a society without social inequality. Compensatory education merely tinkers with a small part of the existing system; what is required is a radical change of the system as a whole.

Class position and educational attainment

In an important publication entitled *Education, Opportunity and Social Inequality*, the French sociologist Raymond Boudon presents a fresh perspective on the relationship between social class and educational attainment. He argues that inequality of educational opportunity is produced by a 'two-component process'. The first component, which he refers to as the 'primary effects of stratification', has been dealt with in the previous section. It involves subcultural differences between social classes which are produced by the stratification system. Although Boudon agrees that differences in values and attitudes between social classes produce inequality of educational opportunity, he argues that the 'secondary effects of stratification' are probably more important. The secondary effects stem simply from a person's actual position in the class structure, hence Boudon uses the term 'positional theory' to describe his explanation. He maintains that even if there were no subcultural differences between classes, the very fact that people start at different positions in the class system will produce inequality of educational opportunity. For example the costs involved and the benefits to be gained for a working-class boy and an upper middle-class boy in choosing the same educational course are very different simply because their starting positions in the class system are different. Thus if the upper middle-class boy chose a vocational course such as catering or building, his choice would probably lead to 'social demotion'. The job he would obtain as a result of the course would be of a lower status than that of his father. However, the situation would be very different for the working-class boy who selected a similar course. It may well lead to 'social promotion' compared to the occupational status of his father. Thus there are greater pressures on the upper middle-class boy to select a higher level educational course, if only to maintain his present social position. These pressures are compounded by the boys' parents. Boudon suggests that parents apply the same cost-benefit analysis as their children to the selection of courses. As a result there will probably be greater pressure from upper middle-class parents for their son to take a course leading to professional status whereas working-class parents would be more likely to settle for a lower level course for their son.

Boudon also relates the costs and benefits of course selection to family and peer group solidarity. If a working-class boy chose to become a barrister and followed the required courses, this would tend to weaken his attachment to his family and peer group. He would move in different circles, live a different life style and continue his education when most or all of his friends had started work. The costs to family and peer group solidarity involved in this choice for the working-class student would result in benefits for the middle-class boy. His friends would probably be following similar courses and aiming for jobs at a similar level. His future occupation would be of a similar status to that of his father. Thus if the upper middle-class boy chose to become a barrister and selected the appropriate educational course, his choice would reinforce family and peer group solidarity. Again position in the class system directly affects the individual's educational career.

Boudon's positional theory argues that people behave rationally. They assess the costs and benefits involved when choosing how long to stay in the educational system and what courses to take. For people in different positions in the stratification system, the costs and benefits involved in choosing the same course are different. As a result, Boudon argues, 'even with other factors being equal, people will make different choices according to their position in the stratification system'. In a complex and sophisticated analysis, Boudon attempts to assess the relative importance of the primary and secondary effects of stratification on educational attainment. He finds that when the influences of primary effects (subcultural differences) are removed, though class differences in educational attainment are 'noticeably reduced', they still remain 'very high'. If Boudon's analysis is correct the secondary effects of stratification are more important in accounting for differential educational attainment. Thus even if all subcultural differences were removed, there would still be considerable differences in educational attainment between social classes and a high level of inequality of educational opportunity.

Boudon's work has important implications for practical solutions to the problem of inequality of educational opportunity. Even if positive discrimination worked and schools were able to compensate for the primary effects of stratification, considerable inequality of educational opportunity would remain. Boudon argues that there are two ways of removing the secondary effects of stratification. The first involves the educational system. If it provided a single compulsory curriculum for all students, the element of choice in the selection of course and duration of stay in the system would be removed. The individual would no longer be influenced by his class position since all students would take exactly the same courses and remain in full-time education for the same period of time. Boudon argues that the more 'branching points' there are in the educational system – points at which the student can leave or choose between alternative courses – the more likely working class students are to leave or choose lower level courses. Thus if there were not a branching point at the age of sixteen in British secondary education, inequality of educational opportunity would be reduced since a greater proportion of working-class students leave at sixteen compared to middle-class students of similar ability. Boudon supports this point with evidence from Europe and the USA. There are fewer branching points in the American educational system compared to those of Europe and statistics suggest that inequality of educational opportunity is lower in the USA. However,

Boudon believes that the possibility of providing a common compulsory curriculum for all is slim. The trend is in the opposite direction – more and more branching points and increasingly specialized and varied curricula. Boudon argues that the gradual raising of the school leaving age in all advanced industrial societies has reduced inequality of educational opportunity but present trends indicate that this reduction will at best proceed at a much slower rate.

Boudon's second solution to the problem of inequality of educational opportunity is the abolition of social stratification. He sees moves in the direction of economic equality as the most effective way of reducing inequality of educational opportunity. As a result, he argues that 'the key to equality of opportunity lies outside rather than inside the schools' but since there is little evidence that economic inequality in Western industrial societies is decreasing, Boudon sees no real evidence to suggest that class differences in educational attainment will decrease significantly in the foreseeable future. He concludes that, 'For inequality of educational opportunity to be eliminated, either a society must be unstratified or its school system must be completely undifferentiated'. Since there is little hope of either occurring in Western society, Boudon is pessimistic about prospects for eliminating inequality of educational opportunity.

Education – an interactionist perspective

The explanations of differential educational attainment that have been presented so far have been based largely on a positivist perspective. They have seen man reacting to stimuli external to himself, to social forces beyond his control. Thus the behaviour of students in the educational system is explained as a reaction to their position in the class structure. Those at the bottom of the stratification system are programmed to fail, those at the top to succeed. They have little say in the matter since their behaviour is largely shaped by forces external to themselves. The positivist approach in sociology is derived from explanations of the behaviour of matter used in the physical sciences. The behaviour of matter can be explained in terms of reactions to external stimuli. For example, particular chemicals under fixed conditions always react in the same way to external stimuli such as heat or pressure. Many sociologists reject positivist explanations of human behaviour arguing that man is fundamentally different from matter and therefore different approaches are needed to explain his actions.

From an interactionist perspective, man actively constructs social reality. His actions are not simply shaped by social forces which act upon him. His behaviour is not merely a reaction to the directives of subcultures or the pressures of stratification systems. Whereas the behaviour of matter is a reaction to external stimuli, the actions of men are directed by meanings. Meanings are constructed by actors in the process of interaction rather than being imposed by an external social system. They are created, developed, modified and changed in a process of negotiation. From an interactionist perspective man becomes the author of his own action rather than passively responding to external constraints. In his interaction with others he interprets and defines situations, develops meanings which direct his action and so constructs his own social world. The importance of this approach and how it differs from those previously considered can be illustrated by William Labov's research in Harlem. (For a general introduction to the issues raised in the preceding paragraphs, see Chapter 1, pp. 15–21).

Cultural deprivation theory provides the standard explanation for the widespread failure of low-income Black American students in the educational system. The students simply react to their position at the bottom of the stratification system and predictably fail. From close observation of interaction situations, Labov provides a very different explanation. He compares three interviews involving an adult and a boy. In the first, a 'friendly' White interviewer presents a Black boy with a toy jet plane. He asks him to describe it and prompts him with various questions. There are long silences followed by short two or three word answers, which hardly provide an adequate description of the plane. This behaviour can easily be explained in terms of cultural deprivation theory. The boy is unable to provide an adequate description because he is linguistically deprived. His behaviour is a predictable reaction to a culturally deprived environment. Labov offers an alternative explanation based on the boy's interpretation of the situation. He defines the situation as hostile and threatening therefore his actions are defensive. His responses are minimal so as little as possible can be held against him. This is clearly no test of the boy's verbal ability, it simply reflects his perception of the situation. Labov examines two further interviews in which the interviewer is Black and raised in Harlem. The first of these is held in a fairly formal setting and Leon, the eight-year-old Black boy interviewed, responds more or less as the boy described above. In the second interview, the context of the interaction is modified. The interviewer sits on the floor, Leon is provided with a supply of potato crisps and his best friend is invited along. The change is dramatic. Leon's conversation is articulate and enthusiastic, and, in linguistic terms, rich and diverse. He now defines the situation as friendly and no longer feels threatened by the interviewer. In the first interview, he is, in Labov's words, a 'monosyllabic, inept, ignorant, bumbling child', in the second he is a direct, confident, articulate, young man. What does this mean? Labov states, 'It means that the social situation is the most powerful determinant of verbal behavior and that an adult must enter into the right social relation with a child if he wants to find out what that child can do. This is just what many teachers cannot do'. More generally, it can be argued from an interactionist perspective that success and failure in schools is a product of interaction situations and the meanings that are created, developed and negotiated in such situations.

Observations such as these lead Labov to claim that, 'It should be immediately apparent that none of the standard tests will come anywhere near measuring Leon's verbal capacity'. A testing situation is an interaction situation and it can therefore be argued that test results may say more about the interaction than the ability of those being tested. The British sociologist Nell Keddie supports this position. She rejects positivist approaches which assume that human behaviour can be objectively measured and quantified by methods similar to those used in the physical sciences. Matter cannot define situations in various ways. Man can. Thus, factors such as ability cannot be measured in the same way as variables such as weight, temperature and pressure. In order to understand and explain educational success and failure, Keddie argues that interaction processes in the classroom must be examined. Sociologists must explore the 'ways in which teachers and students interpret and give meaning to educational situations'.

Given the fact that teachers have the power to award grades and assess students, it is important to discover the meanings which direct this process. An early piece of research which attempted to uncover some of these meanings was conducted by Howard S. Becker. He interviewed sixty teachers from Chicago high schools and found that they tended to classify and evaluate students in terms of a standard of the 'ideal pupil'. This standard included the teachers' views of what constituted ideal work, conduct and appearance. Teachers perceived students from nonmanual backgrounds as closest to this ideal, those from lower working-class origins as farthest from it. They interpreted the behaviour of lower class students as indicating lack of interest and motivation and saw them as unrestrained and difficult to control. Becker argues that simply by perceiving certain students in this way, teachers experience problems in working with them. He concludes that the meanings in terms of which students are assessed and evaluated can have significant effects on interaction in the classroom and attainment levels in general.

In a study entitled, *The Educational Decision Makers*, Aaron V. Cicourel and John I. Kitsuse interviewed counsellors in an American high school in an attempt to uncover the meanings which lay behind their classification of students. The counsellors play an important part in students' educational careers since they largely decide which students should be placed on courses designed for preparation for college entry. Although they claimed to use grades and the results of IQ tests as the basis for classifying students in terms of achievement, Cicourel and Kitsuse found significant discrepancies between these measures and the ways in which students were classified. Like Becker, they found that the student's social class was an important influence on the way he was evaluated. Thus, even when students from different social backgrounds had similar academic records, counsellors were more likely to perceive those from middle and upper middle-class origins as '"natural" college prospects' and place them on higher level courses. Cicourel and Kitsuse find that counsellors' classifications of students' ability and potential are influenced by a whole range of non-academic factors such as the student's appearance, manner and demeanour, assessments of his parents and reports from teachers on his conduct and adjustment. They suggest that a counsellor's evaluation of an individual as a 'serious, personable, well-rounded student with leadership potential' may often have more effect than his grades upon his educational career. Cicourel and Kitsuse conclude that such procedures do not uphold the 'ideal of equal access to educational opportunities for those of equal ability'.

In an article based on the same research, Cicourel and Kitsuse examine the meanings employed by counsellors in the definition of students as 'conduct problems'. Again they found a range of factors which subtly combine to create the counsellors' picture of a conduct problem. These include 'the adolescent's posture, walk, cut of hair, clothes, use of slang, manner of speech'. Again social class is an important basis for classification since the characteristics used to type a conduct problem tend to be found in students from low-income backgrounds.

Studies such as those by Labov, Becker and Cicourel and Kitsuse suggest that teachers' definitions of success and failure cannot be taken for granted, regarded as unproblematic and uncritically used as data by sociologists. From an interactionist perspective, the attainment levels of students are based in large part on interactions in terms of negotiated meanings in the classroom. To understand and explain success and failure it is therefore necessary to discover the meanings directing the interaction which produces these results. In an article entitled *Classroom Knowledge*, Nell Keddie carries this form of analysis a stage further by relating the classification and evaluation of students to the classification and evaluation of knowledge. She argues that sociologists must also examine the meanings which lie behind 'what counts as knowledge to be made available and evaluated in the classroom'. From observation of interaction in a large British comprehensive school, Keddie attempts to discover the criteria used by teachers to categorize and evaluate classroom knowledge. She finds that knowledge defined by teachers as appropriate to the particular course is considered worthwhile, knowledge from the student's experience which does not fit this definition is considered of little consequence. Knowledge presented in an abstract and general form is considered superior to particular pieces of concrete information. The knowledge made available to students depends on the teacher's assessment of their ability to handle it. Thus those students who are defined as bright are given greater access to highly evaluated knowledge.

Like Becker and Cicourel and Kitsuse, Keddie found a relationship between perceived ability and social class. Pupils were streamed into three groups in terms of ability. There was a tendency for pupils from higher status white-collar backgrounds to be placed in the 'A' stream, and for those from semi-skilled and unskilled manual backgrounds to be relegated to the 'C' stream. Keddie observed the introduction of a new humanities course designed for all ability levels. Despite the fact that all streams were supposed to be taught the same material in the same way, Keddie found that teachers modified their methods and the information they transmitted depending on which stream they were teaching. There was a tendency to withold 'higher grade' knowledge from 'C' stream pupils. Some teachers allowed the 'C' stream pupils to make more noise and do less work than those in the 'A' stream. Keddie argues that teachers classified students in terms of a standard of the 'ideal pupil', similar to that described by Becker. The middle-class pupils in the 'A' stream were closest to this ideal and were therefore given greater access to highly evaluated knowledge. This results in 'the differentiation of an undifferentiated curriculum'.

Keddie then examined the students' definition of the situation and accounts for the 'success' of 'A' stream students in the following way. They were more willing to accept on trust the validity of the teacher's knowledge and to work within the framework imposed by the teacher. By comparison, 'C' stream pupils would not suspend their disbelief if the teacher made statements which did not match their own experience. For example, one pupil objected to a teacher's portrayal of the 'British family' because it did not fit his own experience. From the teachers' viewpoint, such objections slowed down the transmission of the 'body of knowledge' they were concerned with getting across. Many of the questions asked by 'C' stream pupils were defined by teachers as irrelevant and inappropriate as were their attempts to relate their personal experience to the course. In general 'C' stream pupils were less willing to work within the guidelines set by teachers. Keddie ironically comments, 'It would seem to be the failure of high-ability pupils to question what they are taught in schools that contributes in large measure to their educational achievements'.

Keddie concludes that classifications and evaluations of both pupils and knowledge are socially constructed in interaction situations. Appropriate knowledge is matched to appropriate pupils. This results in knowledge defined as high grade being made available to students perceived as having high ability. It results in pupils perceived as having low ability, in practice mainly working-class pupils, being actually denied knowledge which is essential for educational success.

Some of the consequences of the classification and evaluation of students in terms of the meanings held by staff have already been examined. They will now be looked at in terms of two closely related theories, the self-fulfilling prophecy theory and labelling theory. Using examples from classroom interaction, the self-fulfilling prophecy theory provides the following explanation. The teacher defines the pupil in a particular way, such as the pupil is 'bright' or 'dull'. Based on this definition, the teacher makes predictions or prophecies about the behaviour of the pupil, for example, he will get high or low grades. The teacher's interaction with the pupil will be influenced by his definition of the pupil. He may, for example, expect higher quality work from and give greater encouragement to the 'bright' pupil. The pupil's self-concept will tend to be shaped by the teacher's definition. He will tend to see himself as 'bright' or 'dull' and act accordingly. His actions will, in part, be a reflection of what the teacher expects from him. In this way the prophecy is fulfilled: the predictions made by the teacher have come to pass. Thus the pupil's attainment level is to some degree a result of interaction between himself and the teacher.

There have been a number of attempts to test the validity of the self-fulfilling prophecy. The most famous was conducted by Robert Rosenthal and Leonora Jacobson in an elementary school in California. They selected a random sample of 20% of the student population and informed the teachers that these children could be expected to show rapid intellectual growth. They tested all pupils for IQ at the beginning of the experiment. After one year the children were re-tested and, in general, the sample population showed greater gains in IQ. In addition, report cards indicated that teachers believed that this group had made greater advances in reading skills. Although Rosenthal and Jacobson did not observe interaction in the classroom, they claim that 'teachers' expectations can significantly affect their pupils' performance'. They suggest that teachers communicated their belief that the chosen 20% had greater potential to those children who responded by improving their performance. They speculate that the teachers' manner, facial expressions, posture, degree of friendliness and encouragement convey this impression which produces a self-fulfilling prophecy.

Rosenthal and Jacobson's study has been strongly criticized for its methodology. In particular it has been suggested that the IQ tests they used were of dubious quality and improperly administered. More sophisticated experiments have since been conducted, some, but not all of which, confirm Rosenthal and Jacobson's findings. Roy Nash, who has made a detailed examination of research in this area, concludes that the self-fulfilling prophecy theory is suggestive rather than conclusive.

Like the self-fulfilling prophecy theory, labelling theory has been used to explain some of the possible effects of teachers' definitions of pupils. Labelling theory is concerned with negative definitions applied to individuals who are seen to deviate from the rules. In terms of classroom interaction, it may be summarized as follows. The pupil is perceived by the teacher as breaking a rule and therefore committing a deviant act. The teacher labels the pupil as deviant. The label defines the pupil as a particular kind of person and from then on there is a tendency to interpret his actions in terms of the label. Thus the pupil may be labelled a 'conduct problem', a 'troublemaker', a 'moron' or a 'clown'. If the label sticks, the pupil may well be selected for special attention. Cicourel and Kitsuse note that pupils labelled as 'conduct problems' may be 'disciplined for behaviour (or even imputed attitudes) that is overlooked or unnoticed among "good" students'. This may lead to further deviance on the part of the pupil in an attempt to resolve the problems of his situation. He may feel he is being discriminated against and may defiantly respond to his alleged deviance by consciously committing deviant acts. Finally, he may seek out others with similar problems, that is those who have been similarly labelled. From their interaction a deviant subculture may develop, a subculture which positively sanctions deviance. Those involved will then tend to see themselves in terms of the deviant label.

David Hargreaves's study of social relations in a British secondary modern school illustrates some of the possible consequences of labelling. Pupils labelled as 'troublemakers' were concentrated in the lower streams. They were defined as failures in a number of ways. Firstly, they had failed to obtain a grammar school place. Secondly, they had been allocated to a low level in the secondary modern, an institution seen as second rate. Thirdly, they had been selected from within this low level and labelled as 'worthless louts'. One way to solve the problem is to accept the label and transform its negative associations into positive ones. Pupils labelled as troublemakers tended to seek out each other's company and within their own group award high status to those who broke the school rules. Thus, disrupting lessons, giving cheek to teachers, failure to hand in homework, cheating and playing truant brought prestige. In this way a delinquent subculture developed which reinforced the effect of the labelling process. (Labelling theory is examined in detail in Chapter 10, pp. 429–38.)

The interactionist approach has added fresh and valuable perspectives to the sociology of education. It has questioned basic concepts such as ability and conduct which previously researchers had tended to take for granted by their acceptance of teachers' definitions of high and low ability students, well and badly behaved students. It has argued that 'bright' and 'dull' students are a product of meanings and definitions which are created in interaction situations. It has claimed that these meanings and definitions are not fixed and unchangeable. Thus students defined as 'dull' in one series of interactions may well be seen as bright in another series based on a different set of negotiated meanings. The interactionist perspective has indicated that pupils do not simply react to their position in the class structure and perform accordingly in the classroom. Rather their level of educational attainment is the result of a complex series of interactions.

The interactionist perspective has important implications for the question of equality of educational opportunity. In particular, it suggests that if teachers did not associate social class characteristics with ability, there would be greater equality of educational opportunity. For example, if American teachers accepted Black speech patterns as equivalent to those of standard English, the attainment of many low-income Black pupils might increase significantly. No longer, as Labov argues, would the Black child 'be labelling himself for the teacher's benefit as "illogical", as a "nonconceptual thinker"' every time he opened his mouth. Nell Keddie sees little real change occurring until 'the categories teachers use to organize what they know about pupils and to determine what counts as knowledge undergo a fundamental change'. She does not see the abolition of streaming and the introduction of an undifferentiated curriculum (teaching the same thing to all pupils) as producing this change, since teachers will still define and evaluate both pupils and knowledge and see particular forms of knowledge as appropriate for particular types of pupils. Keddie argues that teachers should take more account of the knowledge and experiences of their pupils. She states, 'It might be wished that schools should become more flexible in their willingness to recognize and value the life experiences that every child brings to school'. If this were so the contributions of the 'C' stream pupils discussed in Keddie's study would not be so readily dismissed as inconsequential. In *Deviance in Classrooms*, David Hargreaves and his colleagues argue that deviance, with its negative effect on educational attainment, can be reduced in a number of ways. Firstly, if there were fewer rules, there might be less deviance. Hargreaves argues that some rules are necessary, but many, including those concerned with students' dress, hairstyles and appearance in general, could well be abolished. Secondly, Hargreaves suggests that teachers should be more aware of the effects of labelling and in particular should label acts rather than persons. In this way there is less likelihood of the individual being seen as a troublemaker or a clown, instead the emphasis would be upon his particular acts. Hargreaves concludes that much of the deviance created in classroom interactions could be avoided.

Though the interactionist perspective has provided fresh insights, it has important limitations. It is difficult to support its contention that meanings and definitions of the situation are simply constructed in classroom interaction. It is difficult to account for the apparent uniformity of meanings which result from a multitude of interactions. If meanings are negotiated in interaction situations, more variety would be expected. For example, is it simply coincidence that the sixty high school teachers interviewed by Becker all appear to hold the same concept of the 'ideal pupil'? Is it simply a matter of chance that teachers throughout the American educational system tend to evaluate Black speech patterns in similar ways? The relative uniformity of meanings which lie behind what counts as knowledge and ability suggests that such meanings are not simply constructed in the classroom, but rather have a wider and more fundamental basis. As Roger Dale notes, the interactionists fail to adequately answer a number of important questions. Firstly, where do the meanings come from in the first place? Secondly, why these particular meanings and not others? Thirdly, what is the relationship between the nature and distribution of power in society and what goes in the educational system? These questions will be examined in the following section.

Knowledge, power and education

Many sociologists maintain that classroom interaction can only be fully explained by reference to the wider society. In particular, it is argued that the definition and organization of knowledge in the classroom must be seen in terms of the nature and distribution of power in society as a whole. Thus dominant groups in society have the power to define what counts as knowledge in the educational system. If classroom knowledge is based largely upon the knowledge of dominant groups, schooling will automatically favour the children of the powerful and discriminate against those from lower social strata.

Pierre Bourdieu – cultural reproduction and social reproduction

From the mid 1960s onwards, Pierre Bourdieu and his colleagues at the Centre for European Sociology in Paris have produced a series of distinctive books and articles on the sociology of education. Their approach, which is strongly influenced by Marxian perspectives, may be outlined as follows. The major role of the educational system is 'cultural reproduction'. This does not involve the transmission of the culture of society as a whole, as Durkheim argued, but instead, the reproduction of the culture of the 'dominant classes'. These groups have the power to 'impose meanings and to impose them as legitimate'. They are able to define their own culture as 'worthy of being sought and possessed' and to establish it as the basis for knowledge in the educational system. However, this evaluation of dominant culture is 'arbitrary'. There is no objective way of showing that it is any better or worse than other subcultures in society. The high value placed on dominant culture in society as a whole simply stems from the ability of the powerful to impose their definition of reality on others.

Bourdieu refers to the dominant culture as 'cultural capital' because, via the educational system, it can be translated into wealth and power. Cultural capital is not evenly distributed throughout the class structure and this largely accounts for class differences in educational attainment. Students with upper class backgrounds have a built-in advantage because they have been socialized into the dominant culture. Bourdieu claims that, 'The success of all school education depends fundamentally on the education previously accomplished in the earliest years of life'. Education in school merely builds on this basis. It does not start from scratch but assumes prior skills and prior knowledge. Children from the dominant classes have internalized these skills and knowledge during their pre-school years. They therefore possess the key to unlock the messages transmitted in the classroom; in Bourdieu's words, they 'possess the code of the message'. The educational attainment of social groups is therefore directly related to the amount of cultural capital they possess. Thus middle-class students have higher success rates than working-class students because middle-class subculture is closer to the dominant culture.

Bourdieu is somewhat vague when he attempts to pinpoint the skills and knowledge required for educational success. He places particular emphasis on style, on form rather than content, and suggests that the way pupils present their work and themselves counts for more than the actual scholastic content of their work. He argues that in awarding grades, teachers are strongly influenced by 'the intangible nuances of *manners* and *style*'. The closer his style to that of the dominant classes, the more likely the student is to succeed. The emphasis on style discriminates against working-class pupils in two ways. First, because their style departs from that of the dominant culture, their work is penalized. Second, they are unable to grasp the range of meanings which are embedded in the 'grammar, accent, tone, delivery' of the teachers. Since teachers use 'bourgeois parlance' as opposed to 'common parlance', working-class pupils have an inbuilt barrier to learning in schools.

Bourdieu claims that a major role of the educational system is 'the social function of elimination'. This involves the elimination of members of the working class from higher levels of education. It is accomplished in two ways: by examination failure and by self-elimination. Due to their relative lack of dominant culture, working-class pupils are more likely to fail examinations which prevents them from entering higher education. However, their decision to vacate the system of their own volition accounts for a higher proportion of elimination. Bourdieu regards this decision as 'reasonable' and 'realistic'. Working-class students know what's in store for them. They know the dice are loaded against them. Their attitudes towards education are shaped by 'objective conditions' and these attitudes will continue 'as long as real chances of success are slim'.

These arguments lead Bourdieu to conclude that the major role of education in society is the contribution it makes to social reproduction – the reproduction of the relationships of power and privilege between social classes. Social inequality is reproduced in the educational system and as a result it is legitimated. The privileged position of the dominant classes is justified by educational success, the underprivileged position of the lower classes is legitimated by educational failure. The educational system is particularly effective in maintaining the power of the dominant classes since it presents itself as a neutral body based on meritocratic principles providing equal opportunity for all. However, Bourdieu concludes that in practice education is essentially concerned with 'the reproduction of the established order'.

Michael F. D. Young – knowledge and power

In Britain, the work of Michael F. D. Young and his associates has paralleled that of Bourdieu. Young argues that 'those in positions of power will attempt to define what is taken as knowledge'. They will tend to define their own knowledge as superior, to institutionalize it in educational establishments and measure educational attainment in terms of it. This is not because 'some occupations "need" recruits with knowledge defined and assessed in this way'. Rather it is to maintain the established order and to ensure that power and privilege remain within the same social groups. Young has provided a promising framework but, as Karabel and Halsey note, he has yet to apply it to a detailed analysis of the relationship between knowledge and power.

Young and his associates have spent considerable time discussing the philosophical question of the nature of knowledge. They have implied that there is no objective way of evaluating knowledge, of assessing whether or not one form of knowledge is superior to another. If any knowledge is regarded as superior, it is simply because those with power have defined it as such and imposed their definition on others. It therefore follows that *all* knowledge is equally valid. This view is known as cultural relativism. Carried to its extreme, it poses serious problems. As Gerald Bernbaum notes in his criticism of Young, 'It is impossible to say what "being wrong" might constitute'. Thus from the standpoint of cultural relativism, Young's own views are no more valid than any other views.

Dennis Lawton – a common culture curriculum; Jane Torrey – a culturally differentiated curriculum

Research into the relationship between knowledge, power and educational attainment has suggested that changes in the school curriculum are essential if the ideal of equality of educational opportunity is to be realized. Dennis Lawton has proposed a 'common culture curriculum'. He accepts that there are important subcultural differences between social classes, but maintains there are sufficient similarities to form a school curriculum based on a common culture. He claims that, 'A heritage of knowledge and belief which includes mathematics, science, history, literature and, more recently, film and television is shared by all classes'.

Even if such a heritage were shared, which is debatable, Lawton fails to distinguish content from form. As Bourdieu has argued, the important factor is not so much what is known, the content of knowledge, but the manner in which it is presented. To provide equality of educational opportunity, a common culture curriculum would have to select from both aspects of knowledge and elements of style which were common to all social classes.

The culturally differentiated curriculum provides an alternative to the common culture curriculum. In terms of social class, this would result in a number of curricula based on the subcultures of different social classes. Jane Torrey supports this view in her discussion of possible solutions to the low educational attainment of Black American students. She argues that lessons could be conducted in Black speech patterns and standard English taught in much the same way as a foreign language. Thus, just as standard English is accepted as 'knowledge' and skills in its use are tested and assessed, the same would apply to Black speech patterns. However, Torrey argues that the changes she proposes could only be effective if accompanied by changes in society as a whole. In particular, the 'low-status stigma' associated with Black speech patterns must be removed. They must be accepted throughout society as simply a variant of standard English, neither better nor worse. But such changes are unlikely in a country where Blacks form less than 12% of the population and the majority are relegated to the bottom of the stratification system with little influence on the decision making process.

Neither the common culture curriculum nor the culturally differentiated curriculum afford realistic solutions to the problem of inequality of educational opportunity in a stratified society. The very existence of stratification tends to prevent a common culture, since class subcultures largely arise from the position of social groups in stratification systems. A culturally differentiated curriculum could only be successful if the various subcultures were accorded equal prestige. This is improbable in a stratified society. Finally, it is unlikely that the dominant groups will change their definition of what counts as knowledge and allow either proposal to form the basis of the school curriculum. Again it can be argued that equality of educational opportunity is only possible in a society without social stratification. From an orthodox Marxian view, this means the communal ownership of the forces of production. Without stratification, class subcultures will disappear and a common culture will emerge. However, stratification remains in socialist societies and school knowledge still reflects the culture of the powerful. As Karabel and Halsey note, 'And where does cultural capital play a greater role in the transmission of inequality than in those societies that have abolished private ownership of the means of production'. In socialist societies where power and privilege cannot be passed on by the inheritance of property, the inheritance of cultural capital becomes even more important for maintaining the position of dominant social groups.

Education, opportunity and inequality

This section examines a number of questions that have been raised earlier in the chapter but have yet to be discussed in detail. First, what, if any, changes have occurred in the degree of inequality of educational opportunity? Second, what is the relationship between educational attainment and occupational status and income? Third, what effect has the expansion of educational systems had on the degree of social inequality? These questions will be discussed in terms of data from Britain and America.

Inequality of educational opportunity

Many researchers in the field of education, particularly during the 1950s and 1960s, assumed that inequality of educational opportunity was decreasing and would continue to decrease. In Britain the 1944 Education Act provided free secondary education for all. Since that date there has been a rapid expansion of higher education coupled with an increased availability of maintenance grants to provide support for those in need. It was assumed that this would provide greater opportunity of access to all levels of the educational system and as a result the level of attainment of working-class students would increase. A. H. Halsey examines these assumptions using evidence from the Oxford Mobility Study which was based on a sample of the British population in 1972. (See Chapter 2, pp. 86–90 for further details of this study.)

Halsey divided the sample into two age groups: those born between 1913 and 1931 and those born between 1932 and 1947. The first group was educated before the 1944 Act, the second after. He then examined the social class origins of university graduates in the two age groups. The results are shown in table 14.

The results indicate that the numbers of graduates from all social classes have increased. However the proportions of graduates from each social class has changed little over the years. As the table indicates, the percentage of members of class 8 who gained university degrees has risen from 0.9 to 1.8% while the percentage of members of class 1 has risen from 15.0 to 27.0%. Class inequalities are highlighted when Halsey presents his data as follows: an extra 1.5% of working-class children went to university after 1944 compared with an extra 13% from the upper middle class. Halsey concludes that these figures show 'no clear trend towards the elimination of class inequality in educational attainment' and claims that his most significant finding is 'the persistence of influences which flow from class origin to educational attainment'.

Halsey's conclusions for university education are echoed by those of J.

Sociology

Table 14   Social origin and university degree

| | Percentage gaining university degree by class of origin | | | | | | | | |
Born	1	2	3	4	5	6	7	8	Total
1913–31	15.0	7.4	3.8	3.0	1.5	1.3	0.9	0.9	2.6
1932–47	27.0	17.6	5.8	5.1	3.6	2.3	2.4	1.8	6.0

Source: Oxford Mobility Study National Male Sample 1972
Population: Men in England and Wales aged 25–59 in 1972
Sample: 6 700
Social origin: Father's occupational class at respondent's age 14
1   Professional, high managerial and large proprietors
2   Lower professional and managerial
3   White-collar
4   Self-employed (including farmers)
5   Supervisors of manual work
6   Skilled manual workers
7   Semi-skilled and unskilled
8   Agricultural workers (including smallholders without employees)
Relative class chances – percentage from each origin gaining university degree divided by the total percentage gaining a degree in that age cohort
(Source: From *Power and Ideology in Education* by Jerome Karabel and A. H. Halsey. Copyright © 1977 by Oxford University Press, Inc. Reprinted by permission.)

W. B. Douglas for secondary education. His longitudinal study of pupils in primary and secondary education can be seen as a test of the effectiveness of the 1944 Education Act, since it traced the career of a large sample of British schoolchildren to the age of sixteen in 1962. Douglas found that the proportions of pupils with manual and non-manual backgrounds who obtained grammar school places were similar to those before 1944. He concluded that 'the middle-class pupils have retained, almost intact, their historic advantage over the manual working class'.

Raymond Boudon questions the validity of conclusions drawn from studies of higher education, such as Halsey's, and studies covering a short time period, such as that of Douglas. He claims that statistics on secondary education over relatively long time periods indicate a slow but steady

Table 15   Proportions in different classes obtaining education of a grammar school type among children of different generations

| Father's occupation | Percentage obtaining secondary education in grammar and independent schools | | | |
	Born pre-1910	Born 1910–19	Born 1920–29	Born late 1930s
1–3 Professional/managerial	37	47	52	62
4–5 Other non-manual and skilled manual	7	13	16	20
6–7 Semi-skilled and unskilled	1	4	7	10
All children	12	16	18	23

(Source: OCED, Paris)

220

decline of inequality of educational opportunity. Support for his claim is provided by a study based on British data conducted by Westergaard and Little. The results are shown in table 15.

Clearly, as Westergaard and Little note, the expansion of grammar school places has benefitted children from all social classes. However the table indicates a long-term trend towards reduction of inequality of educational opportunity. Comparing children from unskilled and semi-skilled manual backgrounds born before 1910 with those born in the late 1930s, the proportion who obtained a 'grammar school type' of education is ten times greater. Comparing the same two age groups from professional and managerial origins, the proportion is only 1.7 times greater. Thus the rate of increase in the proportion of working-class children attending grammar school is much higher than for those with professional and managerial backgrounds. A somewhat different picture is derived from comparing the proportion *not* receiving a grammar school type of education. Over the time period covered by Westergaard and Little, the proportion of the top social group not receiving a grammar school education was reduced by nearly a half. However, the reduction over the same period for the lowest social group was only one tenth. Thus over thirty to forty years, out of every hundred children, the top social group have been able to send an additional twenty five to grammar school, the bottom group only nine. As Westergaard and Little note, conclusions about changes in inequality of educational opportunity will depend on 'the relative weight one attaches to the proportion achieving, as compared with the portion who fail to achieve, selective secondary schooling'.

It is difficult to reach firm conclusions about changes in inequality of educational opportunity. The statistics can be presented and interpreted in a number of ways. In a survey of data from a number of European countries, Boudon finds similar trends to those indicated by Westergaard and Little's study. He concludes that 'Western societies are characterized by a steady and slow decline of inequality of educational opportunity'. Westergaard and Little reach a more pessimistic conclusion. They argue that even the most favourable interpretation of the evidence leads them to conclude that 'this long-term trend towards a reduction of social differentials in educational opportunity at the secondary stage is moderate and limited'.

Education, occupational status and income

The functionalist view of the relationship between education and occupation argues that educational attainment in advanced industrial societies is increasingly linked to occupational status. There is a steady move from ascribed to achieved status and education plays an important part in this process. Educational qualifications increasingly form the basis for the allocation of individuals to occupational statuses. Thus, there is a 'tightening bond' between education and occupation.

Using data from the Oxford Mobility Study, A. H. Halsey finds some support for this view. He divided the sample into two age groups, those aged from forty to fifty-nine and those aged from twenty-five to thirty-nine in 1972. Comparing the two groups, he found that the direct effect of education on an individual's first job is high and rising (the coefficient of correlation for the first group is 0.468, for the second 0.522), and the direct effect of education on the individual's present job is also rising (from 0.325 to 0.345). Halsey concludes that occupational status is increasingly dependent on educational attainment but he also found that the effect of the father's occupational status upon the son's educational attainment is also rising. He writes, 'The direct effect of the class hierarchy of families on educational opportunity and certification has *risen* since the war'. Thus social background has an increasing effect on educational attainment at the very time when the bonds between education and occupation are tightening. This leads Halsey to conclude that 'education is increasingly the mediator of the transmission of status between generations'. Privilege is passed on more and more from father to son via the educational system. From this viewpoint education can be seen as a mechanism for the maintenance of privilege rather than a means for role allocation based on meritocratic principles.

In the USA, an important publication by Christopher Jencks and his associates entitled *Inequality: A Reassessment of the Effect of Family and Schooling in America*, attempted to assess, among other things, the relationship between educational attainment and occupational status and income. Jencks re-analysed a large body of statistical data collected by sociologists and administrators. He found a fairly close relationship between occupational status and educational attainment claiming that 'education explains about 42% of the variance in status'. However, he argues that to some degree this relationship is inevitable since education is a major determinant of occupational status. He writes 'Americans are impressed by people with a lot of schooling, and they are deferential toward occupations that require extensive schooling'. However, Jencks does find what he regards as 'enormous status differences among people with the same amount of education'.

Jencks found a surprisingly weak relationship between educational attainment and income. He estimates that on average, the completion of high school adds between 10 to 12% to an individual's income, and college education adds a further 4 to 7%. However the rate of return is higher for White middle-class males and less for White working-class males, Blacks and females. Jencks found that none of the expected factors were strongly related to income. He states 'Neither family background, cognitive skill, educational attainment nor occupational status explains much of the variation in men's income. Indeed when we compare men who are identical in all these respects, we find only 12 to 15 percent less inequality than among random individuals'. Jencks therefore concludes that educational attainment has relatively little effect on income.

Jencks's findings have produced a storm of protest, largely because they suggested that as an instrument of social change, education was relatively impotent. In particular, his methodology has been strongly criticized. Several critics have argued that Jencks's disillusionment with education as a means for producing greater equality strongly influenced his methods and the interpretation of his data. For example, James Coleman refers to his 'skillful but highly motivated use of statistics', (quoted in Karabel and Halsey, 1977, p. 23). Thus, though Jencks's findings have not been disproved, they must be regarded with some caution.

Education and equality

If Jencks's findings are correct, they constitute a rejection of the liberal view of the role and promise of education in society. Particularly during the 1960s, many liberals argued that equalizing educational opportunity would reduce economic inequality. In particular, if the educational attainment of the poor and the working class in general improves relative to the rest of society, their bargaining position in the market will show a corresponding improvement. This view was supported by many economists. Lester C. Thurow summarizes their arguments as follows: increased educational attainment will increase an individual's skills, his productivity will therefore rise and with it his income. It will also reduce the supply of low skill workers, increase the demand for their services, which will lead to an increase in their wages. The increased supply of highly skilled workers will tend to reduce their wages. The net result is that productivity rises, more money is made available for wages and wage differentials decrease. Education at one at the same time increases output and reduces economic inequality in society. In America, as Thurow shows clearly in an article entitled *Education and Economic Equality*, this has not happened. The rate of growth of productivity during the 1950s and 1960s was well behind the rate of growth in educational attainment. The rapid expansion of higher education and the flood of college graduates during these years appeared to have had little effect on economic growth. Thurow also rejects the view that a reduction in inequality of educational opportunity will produce a reduction in economic inequality. Measured in terms of years of schooling, there has been a reduction in inequality of educational opportunity in the USA from 1950 to 1970. However from 1949 to 1969 inequality in the distribution of income increased. The statistics supporting Thurow's claim are shown in table 16.

Thurow concludes that 'our reliance on education as the ultimate

Table 16   a   Distribution of education among adult White males
                b   Distribution of income among adult White males

a Percentage share of years of educational attainment			b Percentage shares of total money income		
	1950	1970		1949	1969
Lowest fifth	8.6	10.7	Lowest fifth	3.2	2.6
Second fifth	16.4	16.4	Second fifth	10.9	9.4
Middle fifth	19.0	21.3	Middle fifth	17.5	16.7
Fourth fifth	24.9	22.3	Fourth fifth	23.7	25.0
Highest fifth	31.1	29.3	Highest fifth	44.8	46.3

(Source: Thurow, 1977, p. 327)

public policy for curing all problems, economic and social, is unwarranted at best and in all probability ineffective'.

Jencks's disillusionment with liberal views of the promise of education grew steadily during the 1960s as he observed the failure of the war on poverty which was spearheaded by a drive to improve the educational attainment of the poor. He rejects liberal views on a number of counts. Firstly, he argues that they put the cart before the horse. He echoes many of the views given in this chapter by maintaining that inequality of educational opportunity can only be reduced by first reducing inequality in society as a whole. He states, 'Equalizing opportunity is almost impossible without greatly reducing the absolute level of inequality'. However Jencks's main contribution lies in his claim that educational attainment bears little relationship to income. If this is correct, then a reduction of inequality of educational opportunity will have little effect on income inequality. He argues that, 'the evidence suggests that equalizing educational opportunity would do very little to make adults more equal'. Jencks carries his argument one stage further by suggesting that even if everybody had the same educational qualifications, income inequality would be little changed. He states, 'Giving everyone more credentials cannot provide everyone with access to the best paid occupations. It can only raise earnings if it makes people more productive within various occupations. There is little evidence that it will do this. If this argument is correct, equalizing everyone's educational attainment would have virtually no effect on income inequality'. Put simply, there are well paid jobs and badly paid jobs. If everyone had the same educational qualifications, some would still end up in well paid jobs, others in badly paid jobs.

Jencks thus rejects the view that reforms in the educational system can lead to significant changes in society as a whole. His main concern is inequality of income. He argues that a more equitable distribution of income requires direct government intervention in the economic system rather than 'ingenious manipulations of marginal institutions like the schools'. Direct political action necessitates a commitment to the ideal of equality. He concludes, 'The first step toward redistributing income is not, then, devising ingenious machinery for taking money from the rich and giving it to the poor, but convincing large numbers of people that this is a desirable objective'. Thus Jencks sees changes in values rather than changes in the educational system as the route to the kind of society he wishes to see.

By defining schools as 'marginal institutions' Jencks has relegated them to the sidelines of any radical policy to change society. Karabel and Halsey reject this view arguing that Jencks has ignored what actually goes on inside schools, how they legitimate success and failure, how they justify social stratification, how they legitimate inequality in society as a whole. Karabel and Halsey provide a timely warning in their criticism of Jencks, 'Though it brilliantly demolished the peculiarly American myth that school reform can serve as a substitute for more fundamental social change, "Inequality" may unfortunately have replaced it with another equally destructive myth: that a viable strategy for social equality can afford to ignore the schools'.

Sociology, ideology and education

As members of society, sociologists, like everyone else, are committed to, or at least influenced by political ideologies and values. To some degree, this will affect their choice of theoretical perspective, their methodology, and interpretation of data. Much of the criticism within the sociology of education has been levelled at the ideological assumptions and value judgments which are presumed to underlie the various viewpoints. This criticism will now be briefly examined.

Functionalist perspectives are often criticized for having a conservative bias, a prejudice in favour of maintaining things the way they are. The functions of education outlined by Durkheim, Parsons and Davis and Moore are often similar to the 'official version' presented by government departments. As such they are accused of uncritically accepting the establishment view, and, in doing so, supporting it. Their conservative viewpoint may prevent them from considering many of the possible dysfunctional aspects of education. A more radical political standpoint and less apparent commitment to the dominant values of their society may well produce a very different picture of the role of education in society.

Particularly during the 1950s and 1960s, sociologists were preoccupied with the question of inequality of educational opportunity. They felt it was morally wrong and also their views fitted government policy which was concerned with getting the best return on investment in education. The 'wastage of talent' involved in unequal educational opportunity reduced the efficiency of the educational system in meeting the demands of the economy. It has been argued that a commitment to liberal ideology influenced this type of research, directed the questions asked and the answers provided. Liberalism is concerned with reform within the framework of existing social institutions. It does not advocate radical change. Thus theories such as cultural deprivation and solutions such as compensatory education suggest a reform of existing institutions rather than a revolutionary change in the structure of society. Many sociologists appeared to operate from the viewpoint that education was a good thing and that reforms in the educational system would lead to progressive social change in a society which, while far from perfect, was heading in the right direction. Particularly during the late 1960s and 1970s, sociologists such as Michael Flude argued that reforms such as compensatory education can 'be seen as a part of a persuasive liberal ideology that diverts attention from the exploitive and alienating practices of dominant classes and the need for fundamental social change'. A liberal ideology, with its emphasis on reform rather than radical change tends to prevent a critical examination of the structure of society as a whole.

The ideological basis of liberal reforms has also been attacked by the interactionists. Supporters of compensatory education have been accused of basing their views on a commitment to middle-class values. Thus lower working class subculture is judged to be deficient because it is evaluated in terms of middle-class standards. Nell Keddie suggests that the uncritical acceptance by many sociologists of teachers' definitions of knowledge and ability is based on the fact that both teachers and sociologists share the same middle-class prejudices. She maintains that the middle-class values of many sociologists limit their vision and therefore prevent them from asking important questions. However, the interactionists themselves have been criticized for their value judgments, for their commitment to cultural relativism and what Bill Williamson calls their 'romantic libertarian anarchism'. By this he means that the views of some interactionists seem to be coloured by unrealistic commitment to a vision of society without government in which everybody is free to express themselves in their own way, in which all knowledge and all views are equally valid. Williamson suggests that this view is a romantic dream with little or no chance of translation into practice. As such it diverts attention from a realistic consideration of the nature of power in society.

By comparison with the above viewpoints, the ideological bases of Marxian perspectives are clear cut. They begin from the value judgment that capitalist societies are exploitive, repressive and anti-democratic. This should not, however, detract from their usefulness. They lead to interpretations of the role of education in society which might not be possible if society as a whole were not examined from a critical stance. As Bowles and Gintis state, 'As long as one does not question the structure of the economy itself, the current structure of schools seems eminently reasonable'. Many of the questions that Marxists such as Bowles and Gintis ask derive directly from their commitment to socialism. At worst, their answers provide a fresh and stimulating view of the role of education in capitalist society.

Sociologists, like everyone else, are people of their time. As such their views will tend to reflect those that are current in the wider society. Karabel and Halsey suggest that changing views in the sociology of education are shaped more by changing times than by the logical march of a scientific discipline. They argue this is particularly true of the move from functionalist to Marxian perspectives. Functionalism dominated sociology during the 1950s and early 1960s, a period of relative stability in Europe and America. Karabel and Halsey argue that, 'Reflecting the spirit of the period in which it came to prominence, functionalist theory, particularly as formulated by American scholars, placed undue emphasis on consensus and equilibrium in society'. These concerns are particularly apparent in Talcott Parsons's sociology of education. The rise of Marxian perspectives during the late 1960s and early 1970s emerged from a period of disruption and dissent. Black riots, campus unrest, the New Left, the feminist movement, and protest against the war in Vietnam replaced the relative stability of the 1950s. As products of this age, Bowles and Gintis describe themselves as 'actively involved in campus political movements' during the late 1960s. Karabel and Halsey argue that Marxism with its critical stance and its emphasis on conflict and radical change reflected the the 'dominant mood' of the period more closely than its functionalist predecessor.

6 Work and leisure

Ever since Adam and Eve were expelled from the Garden of Eden, man has had to work for his daily bread. As part of the punishment for original sin, he must earn his living by the sweat of his brow. Any time left over from his daily toil may be spent in leisure, but leisure must first be earned.

A variation on the Christian theme was provided by the Calvinists in seventeenth-century Europe. They saw work as religious calling to be pursued with single-minded determination. Success in work meant that the individual had not lost grace and favour in the sight of the Lord. Leisure, as normally defined by the standards of the day, was attacked as frivolous and timewasting. Drinking, dancing, going to the theatre, recreational sports, gossip and the pleasures of the flesh, were condemned.

In traditional Black American subculture, work is defined at best as an unfortunate necessity. Life, in the title of a song by the O'Jays, is 'Living for the Weekend'. Work begins on 'Blue Monday' when bars in low-income ghetto areas have 'Blue Monday' parties to cheer people up after the worst day of the week.

The three views briefly described above are based on attitudes towards and evaluations of work and leisure. They are not objective views, they are not neutral observations. Many, if not all, of the views of sociologists on work and leisure have a similar basis. They are influenced by the particular sociologist's beliefs about what work and leisure ought to be like. They are coloured by his evaluation of the work and leisure activities he observes. In fact sociologists who are strongly committed to an ideal of work and leisure often produce the most interesting and influential views on the subject. Karl Marx, whose ideas will now be examined, is a case in point.

Work and leisure – a Marxian perspective

Karl Marx – alienated labour

To Marx, work – the production of goods and services – holds the key to human happiness and fulfilment. Work is the most important, the primary human activity. As such it can provide the means either to fulfil man's potential or to distort and pervert his nature and his relationships with others. In his early writings Marx developed the idea of 'alienated labour'. At its simplest alienation means that man is cut off from his work. As such he is unable to find satisfaction and fulfilment in performing his labour or in the products of his labour. Unable to express his true nature in his work, he is estranged from himself, he is a stranger to his real self. Since work is a social activity, alienation from work also involves alienation from others. The individual is cut off from his fellow workers.

Marx believed that work provided the most important and vital means for man to fulfil his basic needs, his individuality and his humanity. By expressing his personality in the creation of a product, the worker can experience a deep satisfaction. In seeing his product used and appreciated by others, he satisfies their needs and thereby expresses his care and humanity for others. In a community in which everyone works to satisfy both their individual needs and the needs of others, work is a completely fulfilling activity. In Marx's words, 'each of us would in his production have doubly affirmed himself and his fellow men'. Apart from possibly the dawn of human history, Marx argued that this ideal has yet to be realized. Throughout history man's relationship to his work has been destructive both to the human spirit and to human relationships.

Marx speculates that the origin of alienation is to be found in an economic system involving the exchange of goods by a method of barter. Within such a system the products of labour become commodities, articles of trade. With the introduction of money as a medium of exchange, they become commodities for buying and selling, articles of commerce. The products of labour are mere 'objects' in the market, no longer a means of fulfilling the needs of the individual and the community. From an end in themselves, they become a means to an end, a means for acquiring the goods and services necessary for survival. Goods are no longer a part of the individual who produces them. In this way 'the worker is related to the *product of his labour* as to an *alien* object'.

Alienation springs initially from the exchange of goods in some form of market system. From this develops the idea and practice of private property, the individual ownership of the forces of production. Marx argues that 'although private property appears to be the basis and the cause of alienated labour, it is rather a consequence of the latter'. Once the products of labour are regarded as commodity objects, it is only a short step to the idea of private ownership. A system of private property then feeds back on to the forces which produced it and heightens the level of alienation. This can be illustrated by capitalist economies in which the ownership of the forces of production is concentrated in the hands of a small minority. Alienation is increased by the fact that workers do not own the goods they produce.

From the idea that the worker is alienated from the product of his labour stems a number of consequences. The worker becomes alienated from the act of production, his actual work. Since work is the primary human activity, he becomes alienated from himself. As a result, 'he does not fulfil himself in his work but denies himself, has a feeling of misery rather than well-being, does not develop freely his mental and physical energies but is physically exhausted and mentally debased. The worker therefore feels himself at home only during his leisure time, whereas at work he feels homeless'. Work ceases to become an end in itself, a satisfaction and fulfilment of human needs. It simply becomes a means for survival. As a means to an end work cannot produce real fulfilment. Alienated from the product of his work, the performance of his labour and from himself, the worker is also alienated from his fellow men. He works to maintain the existence of himself and his family, not for the benefit of the community. Self-interest becomes more important than concern for the social group.

Marx regarded the economic system, the infrastructure, as the foundation of society which ultimately shaped all other aspects of social life. He divided the infrastructure into two parts, the forces of production and the relations of production. The forces of production are the more important since, according to Marx, 'The social relations within which individuals produce, *the social relations of production, are altered, transformed, with the change and development of the material means of production, of the forces of production*'. The forces of production are the means used for producing goods. Thus, under feudalism, an agrarian economy, land is the main force of production. Under capitalism, the raw materials and machinery used to manufacture the products of industry are major aspects of the forces of production. The relations of production are the social relationships associated with the forces of production. In a capitalist economy, the relationship of the two main groups in society to the forces of production is that of ownership and non-ownership. The capitalists own the forces of production, the workers simply own their labour which, as wage earners, they offer for hire to the capitalists.

Marx argued that the nature of work in society can only be understood by examining it in terms of the infrastructure. He believed that a capitalist infrastructure inevitably produced a high level of alienation. In a capitalist economy, a small minority own the forces of production. The worker neither owns nor has any control over the goods he produces. Like his products, the worker is reduced to the level of a commodity. A monetary value is placed on his work and the costs of labour are assessed in the same way as the costs of machinery and raw materials. Like the commodities he manufactures, the worker is at the mercy of market forces, of the law of supply and demand. During an economic recession many workers will find themselves jobless with few means of support. Wage labour is a system of slavery involving the exploitation of workers. Only labour produces wealth yet workers receive, in the form of wages, only a part of the wealth they create. The remainder is appropriated in the form of profits by the capitalists. Thus, the majority of society's members, the proletariat, largely work for and are exploited by a minority, the bourgeoisie. Capitalism is based on self-interest, avarice and greed. It is a system of cutthroat competition concerned with the maximization of profit rather than the satisfaction of real human need. Trapped within this system, both capitalists and workers are alienated from their true selves. Members of both groups are preoccupied with self-interest in a system which sets man against man in a struggle for survival and personal gain.

Marx saw two important characteristics of industrial society – the mechanization of production and a further specialization of the division of labour – as contributing to the alienation of the work-force. However, he stressed that the capitalist economic system, rather than industrialization as such, is the primary source of alienation. Marx argued that the mechanization of production reduces the physical effort involved in work but 'The lightening of the labour even becomes a sort of torture, since the machine does not free the labourer from work, but deprives it of all interest'. Mechanization and associated mass production reduces the need for skill and intelligence and removes from work 'all individual character and consequently all charm for the workman. He becomes an appendage of the machine, and it is only the most simple, most monotonous, and most easily acquired knack, that is required of him'. Industrial society also involves a further extension of the division of labour. Men are trapped in their occupational roles since they must specialize in a particular activity in order to earn their living. In Marx's words 'each man has a particular exclusive sphere of activity, which is forced upon him from which he cannot escape'. Freedom and fulfilment are not possible when man is imprisoned in a specialized occupation since only a limited part of him can be expressed in one job.

Marx's solution to the problem of alienated labour is a communist or socialist society in which the forces of production are communally owned and the specialized division of labour is abolished. He believed that capitalism contained the seeds of its own destruction. The concentration of alienated workers in large-scale industrial enterprises would encourage an awareness of exploitation, of common interest and facilitate organization to overthrow the ruling capitalist class. In a communist society workers would at one and the same time produce goods for themselves and the community and so satisfy both individual and collective needs. This view has been regarded as simplistic and naive by many critics. In his analysis of East European Communism, Milovan Djilas argues that though the forces of production are communally owned, they are controlled by and for the benefit of a ruling elite. He claims that, 'Labour cannot be free in a society where all material goods are monopolized by one group'. However, it can be argued that communist societies have only travelled part of the way to true socialism. The end of the journey will only come when, as Marx argued, the state finally withers away. Marx gives little indication of how the specialized division of labour can be abolished in socialist society. He simply states that 'in a communist society, where nobody has one exclusive sphere of activity but each can become accomplished in any branch he wishes, society regulates the general production and thus makes it possible for me to do one thing today and another thing tomorrow, to hunt in the morning, fish in the afternoon, rear cattle in the evening, criticize after dinner, just as I have a mind, without ever becoming, hunter, fisherman, shepherd or critic'. Marx thus pictures a society in which each member is able to train for those jobs which interest him and move from one task to another as the mood takes him. Many critics have questioned the practical possibility of such a system. Further criticism of Marx's views will be reserved since it will anticipate issues that will be dealt with in detail later in the chapter. (For an examination of the concept of alienation within the general framework of Marxian theory, see Chapter 13, pp. 536–8.)

Samuel Bowles and Herbert Gintis – control in the workplace

The critique of capitalism developed by the American economists Bowles and Gintis is strongly influenced by Marx's views. Like Marx they see capitalism as a repressive and exploitive system concerned with the maximization of profit rather than the satisfaction of human need. Following Marx, they argue that an understanding of the nature of work in capitalist society is only possible by seeing it in relation to the economic and social system in which it is set. Thus, what goes on in the workplace, the social organization of work, can only be explained by reference to the structure of class and power relationships in society as a whole. Bowles and Gintis's major contribution is their rejection of the view that the nature of work in capitalist society is shaped by the demands of efficiency and the requirements of technology. They claim that 'the alienated character of work as a social activity cannot be ascribed to the nature of "modern technology", but is, rather, a product of the class and power relations of economic life'.

Bowles and Gintis examine a number of the characteristics of production under capitalism claiming that they have developed as a means for control and domination of the workforce. First, the fragmentation of tasks is typical not only of factory production but of work in offices and bureaucratic organizations. A task is broken down into small parts and a particular worker specializes in one part. Mass production on assembly lines provides an illustration of this type of work organization. It has been justified on the grounds of efficiency with the claim that job fragmentation will increase the dexterity, skill and speed of the worker who will become a specialist in one particular task. Bowles and Gintis reject this view. They argue that the skill requirements of many jobs can be rapidly learned as shown by the replacement of men with women in factories and offices during wartime. They claim that job fragmentation and specialization have evolved as a means of control based on the principle of 'divide and conquer'. Bowles and Gintis argue that 'if all workers could perform all tasks, their knowledge of the production process would allow them to band together and go into production for themselves'. Next, if workers had this knowledge, it would undermine the legitimacy of the employers' authority to control and coordinate production. By keeping employees in the dark about the overall production process by means of the fragmentation of tasks, employers can fragment the potential power of the workforce and so maintain control. They justify this control with the claim that only they have an overall view of the production process, so only they can plan, coordinate and direct.

The specialized division of labour which typifies industrial society is based on a hierarchical principle of authority and control. For example, in factories, workers on the shop floor are controlled by supervisors and foremen who are responsible to junior management who are subject to the authority of middle and senior management who are answerable to the board of directors. Major decisions travel from the top downwards. Administrative bureaucratic organizations are structured on similar principles. Thus in the British Civil Service an ever more powerful chain of command leads from the lowly clerical assistant through a multitude of intermediaries to the dizzy heights of Whitehall. Again this arrangement is justified on the grounds of efficiency, an argument that will be examined in detail in the following chapter. A hierarchy of authority is said to be necessary in order to coordinate the many specialized tasks in the division of labour. Bowles and Gintis also reject this view. They survey a large number of studies which indicate that efficiency, measured in terms of productivity, is directly related to the degree of workers' control over the production process. The more control workers have, the more they produce. Rather than increasing efficiency, Bowles and Gintis claim that the hierarchical division of labour actually reduces it. They offer the following explanation for this, 'The inefficiency of the hierarchical division of labour is due to its denying workers room for the employment of their creative powers'. Workers are directed and dominated by layer upon layer of authority and provided with little or no opportunity to use their creativity and initiative. As with the fragmentation of tasks, Bowles and Gintis argue that the hierarchical division of labour must be seen primarily as an instrument of control.

If the organization of work can be understood largely in terms of control and domination, why is such control necessary? Primarily because capitalism is based on exploitation. Profits benefit the owners rather than the workforce. Employers are mainly concerned with 'the perpetuation of their class standing' rather than the welfare of their workforce. To maintain such a system, domination and control are essential since the interests of owners and workers are incompatible. As such they are a source of potential or actual conflict. The organization of work in a capitalist society can therefore be seen as a means for maintaining the power of the ruling class. Thus, 'The hierarchical division of labor maximises the control of management, increases the accountability of workers by fragmenting jobs and responsibility, and thwarts the development of stable coalitions among workers'. Bowles and Gintis apply the same argument to Eastern European communist societies where the organization of work often mirrors that of capitalist economies. They argue that this is not surprising since ruling elites use similar methods to maintain power and privilege.

Like Marx, Bowles and Gintis regard work as fundamental for the development of man's potential. They believe that the most important function of work should be, 'the development of the human potentialities of the worker as a social being, as a creator, as a master of nature'. Most workers have little chance of developing these capacities. They are imprisoned in a hierarchical division of labour with little control over their work; they are trapped in the monotony of fragmented tasks with few opportunities to express their creativity and initiative. As long as wage labour is based on the exploitation of the worker, there is little hope of real change. Bowles and Gintis conclude that alienated labour is inevitable as long as ruling classes survive in the West and ruling elites maintain their dominance in the East.

C. Wright Mills – white-collar alienation

In a study of the American middle classes entitled *White Collar*, C. Wright Mills applies Marx's concept of alienation to non-manual workers. Although Mills argues that society is dominated by a 'power elite' rather than a ruling class which owns the forces of production, his analysis of work in capitalist society owes much to Marxian perspectives. Mills states that the expansion of the tertiary sector of the economy in advanced capitalist societies has led to a 'shift from skills with things to skills with persons'. Just as manual workers become like commodities by selling their 'skills with things', a similar process occurs when non-manual workers sell their 'skills with persons' on the open market. Mills refers to this sector of the economy as the 'personality market'. A market value is attached to personality characteristics and as a result people sell pieces of their personality. Therefore managers and executives are employed not simply because of their academic qualifications and experience but for their ability to get on with people. The salesman is given a job for his apparent warmth, friendliness and sincerity. However, because aspects of personality are bought and sold like any other commodity, individuals are alienated from their true selves. Their expression of personality at work is false and insincere. Mills gives the example of a girl working in a department store, smiling, concerned and attentive to the whims of the customer. He states, 'In the course of her work, because her personality becomes the instrument of an alien purpose, the salesgirl becomes self-alienated'. At work she is not herself.

In the salesroom, in the boardroom, in the staffroom, in the conference room, men and women are prostituting their personalities in pursuit of personal gain. Mills regards American society as a 'great salesroom' filled with hypocrisy, deceit and insincerity. Rather than expressing their true personalities and feelings, people assume masks of friendliness, concern and interest in order to manipulate others to earn a living. Mills's pessimistic view of the sale of personality in American capitalist society is summarized in the following quotation:

> The personality market, the most decisive effect and symptom of the great salesroom, underlies the all-pervasive distrust and self-alienation so characteristic of metropolitan people . . . People are required by the salesman ethic and convention to pretend interest in others in order to manipulate them . . . Men are estranged from one another as each secretly tries to make an instrument of the other, and in time a full circle is made – one makes an instrument of himself and is estranged from It also.

In this way man is alienated from himself and from his fellow men.

André Gorz; Herbert Marcuse – alienation from work and leisure

When Marx first outlined his views on alienated labour – in 1844 – workers in industry worked between twelve and sixteen hours a day. Alienated in the factory, the worker had few opportunities for fulfilment in leisure. He had time for little else save what Marx described as 'animal functions' – eating, sleeping and procreating. Existing on subsistence wages, often in appalling living conditions, workers had few means for self-fulfilment in leisure even if they did have the time. Marx regarded non-work time as simply a means for the workforce, the fodder of capitalism, to recover and recuperate from its labour and reproduce itself. Advanced industrial society has seen a significant reduction in working hours – in Western Europe and America industrial employees work on average between forty and forty-six hours a week – and a steady rise in the living standards of the population as a whole. It would appear that the opportunity for self-fulfilment in leisure has greatly increased but many Marxists argue that this opportunity has not been realized.

The French sociologist and journalist André Gorz argues that alienation at work leads the worker to seek self-fulfilment in leisure. However, just as the capitalist system shapes his working day, it also shapes his leisure activities. It creates the passive consumer who finds satisfaction in the consumption of the products of the manufacturing and entertainment industries. Following the directives of the capitalist 'hard sell' is a poor substitute for self-directed and creative leisure. Gorz argues that the directive to consume 'numbs a stunted, mass-produced humanity with satisfactions that leave the basic dissatisfaction untouched, but still distract the mind from it'. Leisure simply provides a 'means of escape and oblivion', a means of living with the problem rather than an active solution to it. Thus in capitalist society, man is alienated from both work and leisure. The two spheres of life reinforce each other. Gorz argues that capitalism has strengthened its hold over the workforce since by 'alienating men in their work it is better equipped to alienate them as consumers; and conversely it alienates them as consumers the better to alienate them in work'.

A similar picture is painted by Herbert Marcuse in *One Dimensional Man*, though his remarks apply to both capitalist and East European communist societies. Marcuse sees the potential for personal development crushed in advanced industrial society. Work is 'exhausting, stupefying, inhuman slavery'. Leisure simply involves 'modes of relaxation which soothe and prolong this stupefaction'. It is based on and directed by 'false needs' which are largely imposed by a mass media controlled by the establishment. Needs are false if they do not result in true self-fulfilment and real satisfaction. If the individual feels gratified by the satisfaction of 'false needs', the result is merely 'euphoria in unhappiness', a feeling of elation on a foundation of misery. Marcuse claims that, 'Most of the prevailing needs to relax, to have fun, to behave and consume in accordance with the advertisements, to love and hate what others love and hate belong to this category of false needs'. Members of society no longer seek fulfilment in themselves and in their relationships with others. Instead, 'The people recognise themselves in their commodities; they find their soul in their automobile, hi-fi set, split-level home, kitchen equipment'. The circle is now complete: industrial man is alienated from every sphere of his life.

Gorz and Marcuse present a very pessimistic view of the nature of leisure in industrial society. They picture a mindless 'happy robot' compulsively chasing 'false needs'. Marcuse suggests that the term 'happy consciousness' which describes the false belief that 'the system delivers the goods' is more appropriate today than Marx's phrase 'false class consciousness'. Relative affluence and the extension of leisure have simply changed chains of iron into chains of gold. Ruling classes and ruling elites have strengthened their hold over the workforce by making its exploitation more bearable. 'False needs' serve to divert attention from the real source of alienation. Their satisfaction simply coats the bitter pill with sugar. At one and the same time 'false needs' provide a highly motivated labour force which works for the money to consume and a ready market for the products of industry.

Marxian perspectives on the nature of work and leisure are open to a number of criticisms. Firstly, they are based partly on a rather vague picture of what man could and ought to be. It can be argued that this view says more about the values of particular sociologists than it does about man's essential being. Secondly, they tend to ignore the meanings held by members of society. If people claim fulfilment in work and/or leisure, there is a tendency to dismiss their views as a product of false class consciousness. Thirdly, Marxian perspectives are very general. As Alasdair Clayre notes, they tend to lump together diverse occupations and leisure activities and create a simple model of 'man in industrial society'. Possible correctives to these shortcomings will be dealt with in later sections.

Emile Durkheim – *The Division of Labour in Society* – a functionalist view

Where Marx was pessimistic about the division of labour in society, Emile Durkheim was cautiously optimistic. Marx saw the specialized division of labour trapping the worker in his occupational role and dividing society into antagonistic social classes. Durkheim saw a number of problems arising from specialization in industrial society but believed the promise of the division of labour outweighed the problems. He outlined his views in *The Division of Labour in Society*, first published in 1893.

Durkheim saw a fundamental difference between pre-industrial and industrial societies. In the former there is relatively little social differentiation, the division of labour is comparatively unspecialized. Social solidarity in pre-industrial societies is based on similarities between individual members. They share the same beliefs and values and, to a large degree, the same roles. This uniformity binds members of society together in a close-knit communal life. Durkheim refers to unity based on resemblance as 'mechanical solidarity'. Durkheim describes the extreme of mechanical solidarity in the following way, 'Solidarity which comes from likeness is at its maximum when the collective conscience completely envelops our whole conscience and coincides with all points in it. But at that moment our individuality is nil. It can be borne only if the community takes a small toll of us'. In a society based on mechanical solidarity, members are, as it were, produced from the same mould.

Solidarity in industrial society is based not on uniformity but on difference. Durkheim referred to this form of unity as 'organic solidarity'. Just as in a physical organism, the various parts are different yet work together to maintain the organism (for example the heart, liver, brain so on in the human body), so in industrial society occupational roles are specialized yet function together to maintain the social unit. Where Marx saw the division of labour as divisive, Durkheim believed it could increase the interdependence of members of society and so reinforce social solidarity. In order to produce goods and services more efficiently, members of industrial society specialize in particular roles. Specialization requires cooperation. For example, a large range of specialists are required to design, manufacture and market a particular product. Members of society are dependent on each other's specialized skills and this interdependence forms the basis of organic solidarity.

However, the interdependence of skills and the exchange of goods and services are, in themselves, insufficient as a basis for social solidarity. The specialized division of labour requires rules and regulations, a set of moral codes which restrain the individual and provide a framework for cooperation. The exchange of goods and services cannot be based solely on self-interest, 'for where interest is the only ruling force each individual finds himself at war with every other'. Durkheim saw the development of contract as a beginning of the moral regulation of exchange. Two parties enter into a legal agreement based on a contract for the exchange of goods and services. Contracts are governed by a general legal framework and grounded in shared beliefs about what is just, reasonable, fair and legitimate but Durkheim saw the growth of contract as only a beginning. It was insufficient as a moral foundation for industrial society.

Durkheim believed that the specialized division of labour and the rapid expansion of industrial society contained threats to social solidarity. They tended to produce a situation of 'anomie' which, literally translated, means normlessness. Anomie is present when social controls are weak, when the moral obligations which constrain individuals and regulate their behaviour are not strong enough to function effectively. Durkheim saw a number of indications of anomie in late-nineteenth-century industrial society, in particular high rates of suicide, marital break-up and industrial conflict. Such behaviour indicates a breakdown of normative control. Industrial society tends to produce anomie for the following reasons. It is characterized by rapid social change which disrupts the norms governing behaviour. In Durkheim's elegant phrasing, 'The scale is upset; but a new scale cannot be immediately improvised. Time is required for the public conscience to reclassify men and things'. In particular Durkheim argued that the customary limits to what people want and expect from life are disrupted in times of rapid change. Only when desires and expectations are limited by general agreement can men be happy, since unlimited desires can never be satisfied. In industrial society men become restless and dissatisfied since the traditional ceiling on their desires has largely disintegrated. Increasing prosperity resulting from economic expansion makes the situation more acute. Durkheim states, 'With increased prosperity desires increase. At the very moment when traditional rules have lost their authority, the richer prize offered these appetites stimulates them and makes them more exigent and impatient of control'. A new moral consensus about what men can reasonably expect from life is required. This will involve the regulation of competition in the exchange of goods and services. Exchange must be governed by norms regulating prices and wages which involves a general agreement on issues such as a fair and reasonable return for services. This agreement will set limits on men's desires and expectations. Not only rapid social change but the specialized division of labour itself tends to produce anomie. It encourages individualism and self-interest since it is based on individual differences rather than similarities. There is a tendency for the individual to direct his own behaviour rather than be guided and disciplined by shared norms. Although Durkheim welcomed this emphasis on individual freedom, he saw it as a threat to social unity. It tends to erode a sense of duty and responsibility towards others, factors which Durkheim saw as essential for social solidarity. He maintains that 'If we follow no rule except that of a clear self-interest in the occupations that take up nearly the whole of our time, how should we acquire a taste for any disinterestedness, or selflessness or sacrifice?'

Whereas Marx's solution to the problem of alienation was radical – the abolition of capitalism and its replacement by socialism – Durkheim believed that the solution to anomie can be provided within the existing framework of industrial society. Self-interest which dominates business and commerce should be replaced by a code of ethics which emphasizes the needs of society as a whole. In Durkheim's words 'economic activity should be permeated by ideas and needs other than individual ideas and needs'. He sees occupational associations as the means to subject economic activity to moral regulation. Various industries should be governed by freely elected administrative bodies on which all occupations in the industry are represented. These bodies would have the power 'to regulate whatever concerns the business: relations of employers and employed – conditions of labour – wages and salaries – relations of competitors one to the other and so on'. Such associations would solve the problem of anomie in two ways. First, they would counter individualism by reintegrating individuals into a social group which would re-establish social controls. Second, by establishing a consensus about the rewards various members of society could reasonably and justifiably expect, normative limits would be placed on individual desire. This consensus would form the basis for rules to regulate economic activity. In particular, Durkheim believed that inheritance as a mechanism for distributing property would gradually die out because of its 'fundamental injustice'. Property would be owned by occupational associations and exchanged by means of contracts. Economic rewards would be based on the contribution of the services of various occupations to the well-being of the community. Then, 'the sole economic inequalities dividing men are those resulting from the inequality of their services'. Durkheim envisaged a delicate balance between the state and occupational associations. In their absence, the state may assume despotic powers and, conversely, without some form of state regulation, each association may assume despotic control over its members. In addition the state would coordinate and regulate economic activity on a national level and enforce a 'common morality', a moral consensus which is essential for social solidarity.

This vision of an efficiently functioning organic solidarity was influenced by Durkheim's view of professional associations – the voluntary associations which administer the practice of professionals such as doctors and lawyers. In professional associations, he saw many of the features that were lacking in industry and commerce. These included a clearly established code of conduct which is binding on all members and a sense of duty, responsibility and obligation to the community as a whole. Durkheim saw professional ethics as the key to a future moral order in industrial society.

The professions – a prototype for a future moral order?

As outlined in Chapter 2, (pp. 70–71), the functionalist view of the professions largely mirrors Durkheim's optimism. The professional association integrates individual members into an occupational group. Through its control of training and education, the association establishes both professional competence and professional ethics. Control of occupational behaviour in terms of these ethics is established by the power of the association to bar particular members from practising if they break the established code of conduct. For example, doctors can be struck off the register and barred from practice for professional misconduct. Professional ethics emphasize altruism, a regard for others rather than a narrow self-interest. The professional is concerned with serving the community in general and his client in particular rather than supporting sectional interests or furthering his own concerns. Thus the lawyer is the guardian of the law in the interests of society as a whole; the doctor, directed by his Hippocratic oath, is concerned first and foremost in his occupation with the health of the community. The relatively high rewards in terms of income and prestige received by professionals reflect their important contribution to the well-being of society. The functionalist view of professionals thus provides a model for Durkheim's future moral order.

Writing in 1970, the British sociologist, Paul Halmos, sees indications that some of Durkheim's hopes are being translated into reality. In a study entitled *The Personal Service Society* he argues that the 'personal service professions' which include psychiatry, social work, nursing, teaching and medicine are having a profound influence on the moral values of Western societies. The ideology of the personal service professions 'advocates concern, sympathy, and even affection for those who are to be helped . . . it admits the central significance of concern and personal involvement'. Halmos believes that this emphasis on concern for others is permeating all areas of social life including the world of business and commerce. Industry is increasingly employing personnel managers and industrial relations experts who have been exposed in their training to the personal service ethic. Although management still put profit first, they are increasingly concerned with the well-being of the workforce and responsibility to the community as a whole. Halmos claims that, 'No matter how hypocritical and mercenary we judge the motives behind these measures and tactics, the new habits of tact and consideration substantially reform the standards of human relationships'. He admits that the personal service ethic is only beginning to filter through into industry, but maintains that 'the ethos of the personal service professional becomes increasingly the ethos of the industrial society in which its constant growth has been made possible'.

This optimism must be tempered with the 'anti-professional' perspectives examined in Chapter 2 (pp. 71–4). One view sees professionalism as a self-interested strategy to improve the market situation of an occupational group. A second sees professionals as servants of ruling classes and ruling elites. From the first view, a profession obtains a monopoly on a particular service which it jealously guards. In the absence of competition it can obtain a high return for its services. By controlling entry into the profession, it can limit the number of practitioners and maintain a high demand and therefore a high reward for its services. It creates a demand for these services by fostering the myth that they are necessary and valuable to the client. The success of this strategy may be seen from the ever increasing demand for medical treatment and legal services. Professional ethics, and in particular the emphasis on altruism, care and community service, are simply a smokescreen which serves to disguise professional self-interest.

The second view sees professionals, in Baritz's phrase, as 'the servants of power'. From a Marxian perspective it involves the proletarianization of the professional which entails the loss of independence by professional groups. Increasingly professionals are directly employed by the state and private industry. Industry employs lawyers specializing in business, commercial and corporation law and accountants dealing with the growing complexity of company finance. Similarly, scientists, civil, mechanical and electrical engineers are salaried employees rather than independent practitioners charging fees for their services. As such, members of these professions can be seen as the servants of the capital. A similar argument applies to the personal service professions. Employed mainly in the service of the state, they serve the interests of ruling classes or ruling elites rather than the community as a whole. Doctors, psychiatrists and social workers clamp down on opposition to capitalist exploitation or elite domination by defining individuals as medical, psychiatric or social problems and treating them as such. In this way attention is diverted from the real cause of 'social problems'. As the previous chapter indicated, the teaching profession can be seen in a similar light. Whatever their professed ideals, teachers maintain establishment power with their role in cultural and social reproduction.

The critical views of the professions outlined above suggest that Durkheim's moral re-integration of a society based on organic solidarity will require more fundamental changes than occupational associations. He sees differences in reward based on a consensus of the occupation's value to the community. He underestimates the possibility that once some are more equal than others, they have the power to define their services as more worthy and valuable than others and so further their own interests.

Technology and work experience

This section returns to issues raised by Marxian approaches to work. It is concerned with the meaning and experience of work but examines these factors largely in terms of specific occupations rather than in terms of society as a whole. In particular it is concerned with the influence of production technology on the organization of work and on the behaviour and attitudes of workers.

Robert Blauner – alienation and technology

In a famous study entitled *Alienation and Freedom*, the American sociologist Robert Blauner examines the behaviour and attitudes of manual workers in the printing, textile, automobile and chemical industries. He sees production technology as the major factor influencing the degree of alienation that workers experience. Blauner defines alienation as 'a general syndrome made up of different objective conditions and subjective feelings and states which emerge from certain relationships between workers and socio-technical settings of employment'. 'Objective conditions' refer mainly to the technology employed in particular industries. Blauner argues that technology largely determines the amount of judgment and initiative required from workers and the degree of control they have over their work. From an analysis of various forms of technology, he assesses the degree of alienation they produce. 'Subjective feelings and states' refer to the attitudes and feelings that workers have towards their work. This information is obtained from questionnaires. Blauner considers workers' attitudes as a valid measure of their level of alienation. Thus if workers express satisfaction with their work, they are not alienated. He thus rejects Marxian views which argue that workers in capitalist society are automatically alienated because of their objective position in the relations of production. From a Marxian perspective, if workers express satisfaction with their jobs, this is an indication of false consciousness.

Blauner claims to account for attitudes towards work in terms of production technology. Thus different forms of technology produce different attitudes towards work and therefore varying degrees of alienation. Blauner divides the concept of alienation into four dimensions: the degree of control workers have over their work; the degree of meaning and sense of purpose they find in work; the degree to which they are socially integrated into their work; and the degree to which they are involved in their work. In terms of these four dimensions, the alienated worker has a sense of powerlessness, meaninglessness, isolation and self-estrangement.

Blauner first examines the printing industry arguing that it typifies pre-industrial craft technology. (His study was conducted at a time when mechanical typesetting was not widespread). Questionnaire data from workers in the four industries shows that printers have the highest level of job satisfaction. For example, only 4% of printing workers found their work dull and monotonous compared to 18% in textiles, 34% in the automobile industry and 11% in the chemical industry. Blauner argues that in terms of his four dimensions of alienation, the printer is a non-alienated worker. He has control over his work and therefore does not experience a sense of powerlessness. Work is done by hand rather than machine. The compositor selects the type, sets it into blocks and arranges the blocks on the page, all by hand. Printing technology demands skill, judgment and initiative. Blauner states that 'because each job is somewhat different from previous jobs, problems continually arise which require a craftsman to make decisions'. The nature of print technology means that the worker is largely free from external supervision. Self-discipline rather than control from supervisors or foremen largely determines the quality of the product, the speed of work and the quantity of output. Work which is based on a craftsman's knowledge, skills and decisions does not lend itself to external supervision. Blauner concludes that the 'printer's freedom and control is largely due to the nature of craft technology'.

Compared to many industries, printing does not involve a highly specialized division of labour or a standardized product. These factors contribute to the relatively high degree of meaning and purpose the printer finds in his job. By working on a large segment of the product, he can see and appreciate his contribution to the finished article – the newspaper, book or magazine. Because each product is in some way different, he can recognize his distinctive contribution. For these reasons, Blauner describes printing as 'work with meaning and purpose'.

Largely because of the nature of print technology, the printer identifies with his craft and other craftsmen. Print technology encourages him to develop his skills and take a pride in his work. He is not tied to a machine and this allows him to move round the shop floor and talk to other craftsmen. In terms of the third dimension of alienation, the degree of social integration, the printer is not socially isolated. He is integrated into an occupational community. He makes friends at work and continues those friendships outside the factory gates. He is active in various craft clubs and associations and has a high level of trade union membership and involvement. (The points raised in this paragraph are developed with reference to print unions in Chapter 7, pp. 291–3.)

Due to his control over his work, the meaning he finds in work and his integration into an occupational community, the printer does not experience self-estrangement from work. Blauner argues that, 'Work for craft printers is a source of involvement and commitment. It is not chiefly a means to life, but an expression of their selfhood and identity'.

If craft industry represents pre-industrial production, the textile industry is typical of the early stages of industrialization. Most textile workers are machine minders. They tend a dozen or so machines, feeding them with yarn and mending breaks in the yarn. The traditional craft skills of weaving are, in Blauner's words 'built into the machine'. In terms of the first dimension of alienation, degree of control, textile workers experience a sense of powerlessness. They are tied to their machines with little freedom of movement. Their tasks are routine and repetitive requiring little judgment or initiative and offering few opportunities to take decisions. The pace and rhythm of their work is largely controlled by machines. The more machines a single worker can tend, the lower production costs. As a result, textile workers are subject to relatively strict supervision by supervisors who are mainly concerned with 'driving workers'. Dominated by machines and policed by supervisory staff, textile workers experience a sense of powerlessness.

Production technology in textiles provides little opportunity for meaning and purpose in work. The product is standardized and the worker performs only a few routine operations. His work involves little skill and variety and his contribution to the finished product is small. These factors largely prevent workers from taking a pride in and deriving a sense of purpose from their work.

Blauner argues that the objectively alienating factors of textile technology should result in subjective alienation in terms of the last two dimensions of alienation. Thus the textile worker should feel isolated and self-estranged. However, this is not the case. Blauner explains this in terms of the community setting of the industry. The workers in his survey lived in small, close-knit communities, united by ties of kinship and religion. The majority of the adults worked in the textile mills. They felt a part of the industry because they were a part of the community. In the USA the industry is set in the 'Deep South'. Small southern towns tend to be traditional in outlook, their inhabitants having lower aspirations and levels of education than the general population. Blauner argues that this accounts for the surprisingly low level of self-estrangement felt by the workers. He states that 'Because of their traditional backgrounds, they do not expect variety in work or inherent interest in millwork and therefore do not define repetitive, non-involving jobs as monotonous'. Thus, some of the alienating tendencies of textile technology are countered by influences from outside the factory.

Blauner argues that alienation is found in its most extreme form in assembly line production in the automobile industry. His data indicate that 34% of manual workers in the industry find their jobs dull and monotonous, but this figure rises to 61% for men working directly on the assembly line. The worker on the line has little control over his work. The line determines the speed of his work and affords him little freedom of movement. His particular job, the tools and techniques he uses are 'predetermined by engineers, time-study technicians and supervisors'. Decisions are taken out of his hands and there is little call for skill, judgment or initiative. Supervision involves policing the workforce since output depends largely on physical effort. Assembly line technology gives the worker little control over his work and as a result he experiences a sense of powerlessness.

Mass production on assembly lines affords little opportunity for experiencing meaning and purpose in work. The product is standardized, the work is routine and repetitious and tasks are highly fragmented – broken down into their simplest components with each worker specializing in a small number of operations. A worker may spend his entire working day attaching wing mirrors or hub caps. As a result he finds it difficult to identify with the product. His particular contribution to and responsibility for the final product is minimal.

Workers on assembly lines are socially isolated. They do not feel a part of the company for which they work nor are they integrated into an occupational community of workmates. They are tied to the line, working as individuals rather than in groups, and have little opportunity to socialize with their fellow workers. Unable to identify with the product or with a particular skill, they do not form occupational communities like the craft printers. The nature of their work does not involve them in close cooperation and consultation with management. As a result there tends to be a clear distinction between management and workers.

Assembly line technology produces a high level of self-estrangement. In fact many workers felt hostility towards their work. The only aspects of the job which those in the survey liked were levels of pay and security of employment. The high degree of alienation produced an 'instrumental' attitude to work – work was simply a means to an end. Hostility towards work and an instrumental approach to work accounts in part for the relatively high level of strikes and unrest in the automobile industry.

Finally, Blauner examines work in the chemical industry which involves the most recent development in production technology. The oil and chemical industries employ automated continuous process technology whereby the raw materials enter the production process, the various stages of manufacture are automatically controlled and conducted by machinery, and the finished product emerges 'untouched by human hand'. Blauner believes that automation reverses the 'historic trend' towards increasing alienation in manufacturing industry. It restores control, meaning, integration and involvement to the worker. Although the product is manufactured automatically, the worker has considerable control over and responsibility for production. Work in chemical plants involves monitoring and checking control dials which measure factors such as temperature and pressure. Readings indicate whether or not adjustments must be made to the process. Blauner states that these decisions require 'considerable discretion and initiative'. Work also involves the maintenance and repair of expensive and complicated machinery. Skilled technicians range freely over the factory floor; there is considerable variety in their work compared to the routine machine minding and assembly line production. In direct contrast to assembly line workers, none of the process workers felt they were controlled or dominated by their technology.

Compared to craft work, Blauner argues that in continuous process technology, 'the dominant job requirement is no longer manual skill but responsibility'. This emphasis on responsibility restores meaning and purpose to work, it is an 'important source of satisfaction and accomplishment'. Process technology halts the increasingly specialized division of labour. It integrates the entire production process and since workers are responsible for the overall process, they can see and appreciate their contribution to the finished product. Their sense of purpose is increased by the fact that process workers operate in teams with collective responsibility for the smooth running of the machinery. Again, this encourages the individual worker to feel a part of the overall production process.

Unlike the assembly line worker, the process worker does not experience social isolation. Maintenance and repair workers are integrated into a team. Movement round the factory floor furthers the integration of the workforce. The line between management and workers tends to become blurred since their relationship is based on consultation rather than coercion. Since physical effort is no longer involved in actual production, management no longer needs to police the workforce to drive it to greater effort. Both management and workforce are concerned with the trouble-free operation of production machinery. To further this shared goal the consultation of workers 'with supervisors, engineers, chemists and other technical specialists becomes a regular, natural part of the job duties'. Blauner argues that the technology of automated production integrates the workforce as a whole. This has important consequences for industrial relations. Blauner claims that the process worker will be 'generally lukewarm to unions and loyal to his employer'. Unlike the craft worker, he does not identify with a craft as such and form strong unions on the basis of this identification. Unlike the assembly line worker, he does not simply work for money and strongly support unions as a means to increase his wage packet.

Because the process worker is non-alienated in terms of the first three dimensions of alienation, he is involved in his work. Blauner claims that process work provides 'an opportunity for growth and development'. He concludes that 'Since work in continuous process industries involves control, meaning and social integration, it tends to be self-actualizing instead of self-estranging'.

Blauner admits that technology does not completely shape the nature of work. He states, 'Whereas technology sets limits on the organization of work, it does not fully determine it, since a number of different organizations of the work process may be possible in the same technological system'. However, he does see technology as the major factor influencing the behaviour and attitudes of workers. It therefore follows that a reduction in levels of alienation, as Blauner defines it, will largely involve changes in production technology. He suggests that variation of work organization within a given technology would go some way to solving the problem. For example, job rotation, 'a policy that permits the worker to move from one subdivided job to another' would have the effect of 'adding variety to his work and expanding his knowledge of the technical process'. Similarly, job enlargement, which reverses the trend towards task fragmentation and increases the worker's area of responsibility, would have some beneficial results. For example, Blauner points to a job enlargement scheme at IBM where machine operators were given the added responsibility of setting up and inspecting their machines. He claims that this 'not only introduced interest, variety and responsibility and increased the importance of the product to the worker, it also improved the quality of the product and reduced costs'. Blauner argues, though, that such variations on existing technology are insufficient to solve the problem of alienation. What is needed is a new technology, designed not only to produce goods at minimum economic cost, but also at minimum personal cost to the worker.

Blauner's study can be criticized on a number of points. Firstly, from a Marxian perspective, he has ignored the basic cause of alienation – the objective position of the worker in the relations of production in a capitalist economic system. From this perspective, the printer and the process worker are just as alienated as the assembly line worker. All are exploited wage labourers. Blauner's solutions to alienation will therefore leave the basic cause untouched. At best they will produce a 'happy robot', who, though he may feel satisfied with his work, will still be alienated from it.

The second major criticism of Blauner's study involves his use of questionnaire data. He relies heavily on this information for measuring the degree of alienation experienced by workers. It is extremely difficult to interpret the results of questionnaires. For example, if a worker states that he likes his job, this may mean he is satisfied with one or more of the following factors – his wages, occupational status, social relationships at work, the amount of interest and involvement his job provides, his present job in comparison with his past jobs and so on. It may be possible to design a sophisticated questionnaire which separates out the various factors involved, but problems still remain. As Blauner admits, the way a question is worded 'may favor one response rather than another' and 'the meaning of the question may not always be the same to the worker as it is to the interviewer'. In addition, there is a tendency for all workers to express satisfaction with their jobs. Since a person's self-image is partly determined by his occupation, an admission of dissatisfaction with work might well undermine his self-respect. Despite all these difficulties, Blauner considers the results of questionnaires are adequate for his purposes. In an article written before the publication of *Alienation and Freedom* he states, 'It is difficult to interpret a finding that 70 per cent of factory workers report satisfaction with their jobs because we do not know how valid and reliable our measuring instrument is. But when 90 per cent of printers and only 40 per cent of automobile workers report satisfaction, the relative difference remains meaningful'.

Goldthorpe and Lockwood – work orientation

From their study of 'affluent workers' in Luton, Goldthorpe and Lockwood question the importance given by Blauner to technology in shaping workers' attitudes and behaviour. They reject Blauner's positivist approach which tends to see workers' behaviour as a predictable reaction to production technology. Instead they adopt a social action perspective which is closer to a phenomenological view of man. This approach emphasizes the 'actors' own definitions of the situations'. Goldthorpe and Lockwood maintain that a large part of the behaviour of the Luton workers cannot be explained as a reaction to production technology. Instead, they maintain that the way workers define and give meaning to their work largely accounts for their attitudes and behaviour.

Goldthorpe and Lockwood studied workers in three firms which employed a range of production technology. Their sample of 250 men included assembly line workers at the Vauxhall car company, machine operators, machine setters and skilled maintenance workers at the Skefko Ball Bearing Company and process workers and skilled maintenance workers at Laporte Chemicals. In terms of intrinsic job satisfaction, that is the satisfaction men derived directly from the performance of their work, the pattern was similar to that described by Blauner. For example, the skilled maintenance workers had a higher level of intrinsic job satisfaction than the machinists and assemblers. However, there was little relationship between technology and 'the range of attitudes and behaviour which they more generally displayed as industrial employees'. Goldthorpe and Lockwood argue that their most significant finding is the similarity in the affluent workers' attitudes and behaviour despite the variation in production technology. In particular, all workers had a strongly 'instrumental orientation' towards their work. They defined work primarily as a means to an end, in particular as a means for obtaining money to raise their living standards. This instrumental orientation cannot be explained in terms of production technology since workers experienced differing technologies. Goldthorpe and Lockwood argue that it can only be explained in terms of 'the wants and expectations which men *bring* to their work'.

An instrumental orientation directs much of the affluent workers' behaviour. All workers were strongly attached to their firms and generally regarded employers in a positive light. This is understandable in terms of their instrumental orientation since the firms paid above average wages for manual work and provided fairly secure employment. If anything, process workers were more likely 'to reveal critical or hostile attitudes towards their firm', a finding in direct contrast to those of Blauner. Again, this can be explained in terms of the affluent workers' instrumental orientation. The wage levels of process workers were below those of the assemblers, machine operators and setters. Since money is the prime consideration, process workers tended to be less satisfied with their employers. In general, the affluent workers formed few close ties with their workmates either on the shop floor or beyond the factory gates. Again, in direct contrast to Blauner's findings, process workers were less likely than other workers to form close relationships with their workmates. Goldthorpe and Lockwood argue that the general lack of close attachments results from the workers' instrumental orientation. They define work simply as a means for making money, not as a place for making friends. This definition also shapes their attitude to trade unions. Four-fifths of all workers believed that trade unions should limit their concerns to obtaining higher wages and better working conditions. Goldthorpe and Lockwood refer to the affluent workers' relationship to their unions as 'instrumental collectivism'. The affluent worker joins a trade union with his fellow workers for instrumental reasons, the union being regarded as a means to personal ends. Most workers do not see union solidarity as a worthwhile end in itself nor do they think trade unions should promote radical change in society as a whole.

Goldthorpe and Lockwood conclude that the attitudes and behaviour of the affluent worker are little influenced by technology. They stem primarily from his instrumental orientation, from the meanings and expectations he brings to work. They find little support for Blauner's comparison of the isolated alienated assembly line worker and the integrated non-alienated process worker. They argue that what happens outside the factory is more important in shaping workers' behaviour and attitudes than what happens inside. In particular, they assign priority to 'ongoing changes in working-class life outside work and most notably in this respect changes *within* the family'. Goldthorpe and Lockwood argue that manual workers are increasingly home and family centred. Largely because of higher living standards, family life is 'more inherently rewarding' which means that workers can satisfy 'their expressive and affective needs through family relationships'. They are therefore less likely to look to work for these satisfactions. The more family life becomes a central life interest, the more the worker will see his work in instrumental terms. It will increasingly become a means to raise family living standards.

Goldthorpe and Lockwood admit that on the surface, the affluent worker appears very similar to Marx's alienated worker. He simply sells his labour to the highest bidder and sees work in instrumental terms. However, unlike Marxists such as André Gorz, they do not see the affluent worker's instrumental orientation and concern with consumption as a reaction to alienation at work. Instead, they argue that, 'Rather than an overriding concern with consumption standards reflecting alienation in work, it could be claimed that precisely such a concern constituted the motivation for these men to take, and to retain, work of a particularly unrewarding and stressful kind which offered high pay in compensation for its inherent deprivations'. Many affluent workers selected highly paid 'alienating' work *because of* their instrumental orientation. Goldthorpe and Lockwood conclude that the emphasis on consumption and instrumentality stems not from alienation at work but from 'whatever social-structural or cultural conditions generate "consumption-mindedness"'.

Goldthorpe and Lockwood also reject the views of Marxists such as Herbert Marcuse who see the emphasis on consumption as the result of false needs imposed by a capitalist mass media. They see no reason why the affluent worker's concern 'for decent, comfortable houses, for labour-saving devices, and even such leisure goods as television sets and cars' should be seen as a reflection of false needs. Goldthorpe and Lockwood conclude that, 'It would be equally possible to consider the amenities and possessions for which the couples in our sample were striving as representing something like the minimum basis on which they and their children might be able to develop a more individuated style of life, with a wider range of choices, than has hitherto been possible for the mass of the manual labour force'.

Before drawing any general conclusions from Goldthorpe and Lockwood's study, it is important to consider their sample. Firstly, the men were married, aged between twenty-one and forty-six and 86% had one or more dependent children. As Goldthorpe and Lockwood admit, men in this situation are more likely than unmarried, younger or older men to see work in instrumental terms. Secondly, the men had moved to Luton from various parts of Britain, specifically for high wages and regular employment. They may well be more instrumentally oriented than manual workers in general. Thirdly, Luton, as 'a town of migrants', would encourage home and family centred life since workers had left many of their relatives and friends in their towns of origin. Finally, the sample contained a higher proportion of downwardly mobile individuals than the national average. Since there is a tendency for downwardly mobile workers to retain a white-collar reference group in terms of which they judge themselves, they may be more likely than manual workers in general to aspire to higher living standards. However, as the following section indicates, an instrumental orientation may well be typical of manual workers in general. (Further aspects of the Luton study are examined in Chapter 2, pp. 57–62, and Chapter 3, p. 132.)

Wedderburn and Crompton – technology and work orientation

From research in northeast England, Dorothy Wedderburn and Rosemary Crompton found some support for the views of both Blauner and Goldthorpe and Lockwood. They studied a large chemical complex which they called 'Seagrass' and concentrated on two works on the same site. The first employed continuous process technology, the second used machines to produce chemically based yarn. In the yarn factory much of the work involved machine minding and the pace of work was largely determined by machines. Wedderburn and Crompton's sample contrasts in several ways with the affluent worker sample. Firstly, only a 'tiny minority' of the workforce had lived outside the area. Secondly, the sample was random – 30% of the sample was made up of workers over forty-six, 10% of unmarried workers. Thirdly, nearly half the men earned wages which were below the national average. Despite these differences, Wedderburn and Crompton found that the men's orientation to work was very similar to that of the Luton workers. In assessing their jobs, the Seagrass workers listed four main considerations – 'the level of pay, the security of the job, the good welfare benefits and good working conditions'. In fact, 'job interest', as a reason for staying in their present employment, was mentioned by fewer members of the Seagrass than the Luton sample. Wedderburn and Crompton conclude that the manual workers at Seagrass were no less instrumental than those of Luton.

Although this general orientation towards work bore no relationship to technology, Wedderburn and Crompton found that, 'different attitudes and behaviour *within the work situation* could be manifested by different groups of workers largely in response to the differences in the prevailing technologies and control systems'. Process workers in the largely automated plant found their jobs interesting, felt they had sufficient freedom to try out their own ideas and adequate discretion in the organization of their work tasks. In contrast workers in the machine shop found their work boring and felt they had little freedom or discretion in the organization of their work. Attitudes produced by technology tended to be transferred to the supervisory system. Workers who found their jobs interesting tended to regard supervisors in a favourable light, those who found work boring tended to resent supervision. In part, these attitudes were shaped by differences in the nature of supervision in the two works, differences which reflected the demands of technology. In the process works, supervisors were 'troubleshooters' who used their technical expertise to assist workers to solve problems. As a result, their relationship with the men tended to be cooperative. In the machine shop, supervisors were more concerned with quality control and tended to police the workforce. Wedderburn and Crompton found that compared to the continuous process plant, workers in the machine shop had a higher rate of absenteeism and a higher strike level. They argue that these factors are strongly influenced by the technologies employed in the two works.

Wedderburn and Crompton's study strikes a balance between those of Blauner and Goldthorpe and Lockwood. They had the benefit of both pieces of research before conducting their study and so were able to frame their questionnaire in terms of both viewpoints. They conclude that the general orientation of the Seagrass workers towards their work cannot be accounted for by technology. However, they maintain that important aspects of work-related attitudes and behaviour are influenced by production technology.

Automation, class and society

As the most recent form of production technology, automation has attracted the interest of a number of sociologists. Several have argued that automation has important consequences which extend well beyond the workplace. In particular, it has been suggested that automation may produce important changes both within the working class and in the relationship of the working class to the rest of society. Three studies which explore the wider implications of automation will now be examined.

Robert Blauner

Blauner saw alienation reaching its height with mass production industry based on mechanized assembly line technology. This posed problems for the integration of industrial society since it tended to produce division rather than unity. The alienation produced by mechanized mass production led to hostility between workers and management, to divisions in the workplace expressed in terms of 'us and them'. The ending of craft production resulted in a shift of power from workers to management. Production was now organized and directed by management and control of the workforce tended to be repressive. The high level of alienation encouraged an instrumental approach to work. The relative weakness of the workforce led to the formation of powerful unions to represent workers' interests. In line with the instrumental orientation of their members, unions exerted strong pressure on employers for higher pay. The result was conflict between employers and managers on the one side and workers and trade unions on the other.

Blauner saw automation as reversing this trend towards instability and division. Automation produced the non-alienated worker, it replaced dissent between workers and management with consensus. Repressive and coercive control was succeeded by consultation and cooperation. Militant trade union activity was transformed into loyalty to the firm. The hostility produced by alienation was dissipated by 'meaningful work in a more cohesive, integrated industrial climate'. These factors combined to transform the worker. His 'social personality' is increasingly like that of 'the new middle class, the white-collar employee in bureaucratic industry'. Blauner concludes that automation has led to a 'decline in the worker's class consciousness and militancy, a development that reflects the growing consensus between employers and employees and the increase in the worker's feeling that he has a stake in industry'. In this way, automation has halted the tendency towards disintegration and division and is increasingly integrating the working class into the structure of capitalist society.

Serge Mallet

The French Marxist sociologist Serge Mallet's view of the promise of automation differs radically from Blauner's interpretation. Where Blauner sees automation reducing the possibility of class conflict, Mallet sees just the opposite. Although he largely agrees with Blauner that automation leads to a greater integration of workers in the factory, Mallet argues that this will not lead to a more general integration of workers into capitalist society. He maintains that automation will highlight the major contradiction of capitalism, the collective nature of production and the private ownership of the forces of production. Since workers in automated industry have greater control over and responsibility for production, they will tend to see themselves as the real controllers of industry. The consultation and cooperation between process workers, technicians and operating managers will tend to unite them and encourage a recognition of common interests. The conflict between their interests and those of the higher level managers and owners of the company will therefore be brought sharply into focus. Workers will increasingly question the basis of ownership and control and demand worker control of the enterprise. This will revitalize the trade union movement which will no longer be represented by centralized, bureaucratic organizations distanced from the shop floor. Instead, union power will be de-centralized and based on syndicalist principles, that is worker control at the level of the company.

Mallet sees workers in automated production forming the vanguard of the class struggle. He believes that they will provide an example which the working class as a whole will tend to follow.

Duncan Gallie

While admiring the boldness and breadth of Blauner and Mallet's interpretations, the British sociologist Duncan Gallie questions the soundness of the data on which they are based. Blauner's data on process workers were taken from a survey conducted in 1947 which included only seventy-eight workers in the chemical industry. To this he added twenty-one interviews with process workers in a Californian company which he conducted in 1961. Apart from the small size of the 1947 sample, it gives no indication of the number of workers directly working with automated technology. This information is necessary since there are other technologies employed in chemical works. From a close examination of Mallet's writings, Gallie states, 'It is difficult to form any impression at all of how he carried out his study'. Gallie concludes his assessment of Blauner and Mallet's methodology with the comment, 'It is difficult to avoid the feeling that the data bases on which these theories rest are perilously frail'.

In a study entitled *In Search of the New Working Class*, Duncan Gallie attempts to test the theories of Blauner and Mallet. If either Blauner or Mallet are correct, automated technology should have important consequences whatever its national or regional setting. Gallie selected four oil refineries for investigation, two in France and two in Britain. By designing his research in this way, he hoped to assess the impact of technology which was independent of the influence of national or regional variations. In Britain, for example, he selected refineries in very different areas. One was in Kent, a prosperous area in southeast England, the other in Grangemouth in Scotland, an area with a history of high unemployment. Gallie's findings provided little support for either Blauner or Mallet. He discovered significant differences between the British and French workers, differences which could only be accounted for by the distinctive histories of the two societies and by the nature of British and French working-class subculture and national culture. Gallie states 'The emergence of new forms of technology occurs, not in some form of social vacuum, but in societies with well-established institutional arrangements, and with distinctive patterns of social conflict'.

Gallie's findings may be summarized as follows. Both British and French workers were paid high wages compared with other manual workers. Blauner and Mallet had argued that pay was no longer a central concern for workers in automated industry. Over 90% of the British workers were satisfied with their pay and living standards, yet over 66% of the French workers were dissatisfied. They expressed their feelings in the form of strikes. From 1963 to 1972, twenty-four strikes brought production to a halt in the two French refineries, pay being the major issue in most of the stoppages. Only one strike closed down production in the British refineries over the same time period. The difference in levels of satisfaction over pay can partly be explained by the methods of establishing wage rates. In France a part of the workers' wages was made up of a 'merit bonus' which was based on length of service and 'good behaviour'. This system produced mistrust and ill-feeling since workers saw it as a means of management coercion and control. French workers also differed from the British in their view of pay differentials between management and workers. Whereas only 2 to 3% of British workers objected to the difference in salaries, the figure for the French workers was around 33%. Gallie maintains that differences in attitudes over pay between the two groups of workers 'can only be understood in terms of the broader context of the workers' perceptions of their societies, and of their reference groups and aspirations'.

Gallie found little support for Blauner's picture of the non-alienated worker who was involved in his work. In both Britain and France, 'The commonest attitude towards work in all our refineries was one of indifference'. Though many of the hardships of mechanized mass production had been removed, others had taken their place. Continuous process industry involves round the clock production which requires shift work. Workers believed that this disrupted their family and social life, and produced ill-health. A second problem in all refineries involved manning levels, since it is difficult to determine adequate levels for automated technology. Such problems threaten the stability and harmony which Blauner sees as typical of automated industry. In general, they were settled peacefully in British refineries whereas in France, they were a source of conflict between workers and management.

Where Blauner saw increasing cooperation and consensus between management and workers, Mallet saw increasing conflict between workers and junior level management on one side and higher level management on the other. Blauner's picture is closest to the situation in British refineries. There, workers largely identified with management objectives such as increasing the efficiency of the firm. They felt that management were concerned with their interests and welfare and not simply with profits for the benefit of shareholders. By comparison, the French workers believed that management were largely concerned with shareholders' interests and cared little for the welfare of workers. Their attitude towards management tended to be antagonistic, based on a view of 'us and them'. Gallie found little evidence to support Mallet's claims about the demand for worker control. Only a very small minority of French workers and an even smaller minority of British actually wanted worker control. However, the French workers did want more participation in decision making than their British counterparts. For example, they were more likely to want a say in high level financial decisions whereas the British defined such issues as management's job. Gallie's data reveal a sharp difference between British and French workers over their view of decision making. In Britain, some 80% of workers believed that decisions about issues such as manning levels and salaries were made by agreement between management and workers. Over 66% of their French counterparts believed that decisions were made either by management alone or by management after consultation with workers. The French workers tended to see the negotiation machinery as a charade whereas the British did not. As a result, Gallie states that for the French workers, 'The predominant feeling was one of powerlessness'.

Gallie argues that a number of factors explains the variation in attitudes between British and French workers. Firstly, working-class subcultures in the two countries differ. In particular, 'French workers were more committed to egalitarian values than their British equivalents'. Secondly, management 'styles' and philosophy differ. French management retains a tighter, more autocratic control over decision making and tends to be paternalistic. (Paternalism refers to a style of authority whereby those in control act like a father, distributing rewards and punishments at their discretion, based on the belief that they know what's best for those subject to their authority.) French management had considerable discretion in deciding the size of the worker's 'merit bonus' which forms an important part of his income. By comparison, British management operated on a 'semi-constitutional' basis. Wages were formally negotiated and there were no discretionary payments by management. Thirdly, there were important differences in the negotiating machinery and trade union representation in the two countries. In France, wages were negotiated at national level, in Britain the important negotiations were at plant level. As a result British workers were more directly involved in the decision making process. Gallie argues that in general, 'The less participative the decision-making system, the less will workers regard it as legitimate. A lower degree of legitimacy will in turn be associated with a higher degree of generalized distrust of management's motives'. Fourthly, the major unions in Britain and France had very different conceptions of their role. Gallie describes the French unions as 'unions of ideological mobilization'. They were committed to the overthrow of capitalism and saw their main role as raising the consciousness of workers. In Britain, unions saw their major role as directly representing the wishes of their members, and as such they were mainly concerned with negotiating for better pay and conditions. Gallie argues that as a result of the above factors, 'The British workers had an image of the firm that was essentially "co-operative" while the French workers had an image that was essentially "exploitive"'.

A number of important conclusions stem from Gallie's study. The British refineries are closer to Blauner's picture, the French closer to that drawn by Mallet. This leads to a rejection of the theories of both authors. Automated production, in and of itself, does not necessarily lead to a closer integration of the workforce into capitalist society, as Blauner suggested, nor does it necessarily herald the emergence of class consciousness and class conflict as Mallet predicted. In fact automated technology itself appears to have little effect on wider social issues. Management style, the nature of decision making, trade union philosophy and organization and working-class subculture appear far more important. Gallie concludes that if the changes predicted by either Blauner or Mallet do occur, it will not be for the reasons that either suggests. He states, 'Rather, it will depend on changing cultural expectations within the working class, on changes in management attitudes, and on changes in trade union objectives. Similarly, it will follow from our argument that if these developments do occur, the automated sector will not be particularly distinctive. Rather, it will be participating in a very much broader movement occuring within industry in the particular society'. The last phrase in this quotation is particularly important. Though both France and Britain share a capitalist mode of production, the response of workers to that fact will be mediated by the factors which Gallie describes, factors which differ considerably between the two countries. This finding has important implications for the study of work. It suggests that studies which concentrate simply on an analysis of work in capitalist systems are inadequate. They require in addition, an analysis of the peculiarities of the particular society in which capitalist economies are set.

Work and leisure

In an earlier section the relationship between work and leisure in capitalist society was examined from a Marxian perspective. Among other things, this approach has been criticized for being too general. It tends to ignore the variation in work and leisure activities. This section examines the relationship between particular occupations and styles of leisure. It also considers the importance of leisure in industrial societies.

Stanley Parker – the influence of work on leisure

Stanley Parker argues that leisure activities are 'conditioned by various factors associated with the way people work'. In particular, he suggests that the amount of autonomy people have at work (the amount of freedom to take decisions and organize their work), the degree of involvement they find in work, and their level of intrinsic job satisfaction are directly related to their leisure activities. Parker bases his findings on a series of interviews he conducted with bank clerks, child care officers and youth employment officers plus published material on a range of occupations studied by sociologists. He sees the relationship between work and leisure falling into three main patterns: the extension pattern, the neutrality pattern and the opposition pattern.

In the extension pattern, work extends into leisure. There is no clear dividing line between the two. Activities in both spheres are similar, and work is a central life interest rather than family and leisure. Time for activities which can be defined exclusively as leisure is short and is used mainly for the 'development of personality', for example reading 'good' literature or going to the theatre. This pattern is associated with occupations providing a high level of autonomy, intrinsic job satisfaction and involvement in work. Jobs which typify this pattern include business, medicine, teaching, social work and some skilled manual trades. For example, outside statutory office hours, businessmen often entertain clients and colleagues at the dinner table or on the golf course, contexts in which business and pleasure are combined. Parker found that the social workers in his survey spent much of their free time in activities connected with their work. Some helped to run youth clubs, others met to discuss clients' problems.

In the neutrality pattern, a fairly clear distinction is made between work and leisure. Activities in the two spheres differ and family life and leisure, rather than work, form the central life interest. This pattern is associated with occupations providing a medium to low degree of autonomy, which require the use of only some of the individual's abilities, and where satisfaction is with pay and conditions rather than work itself. Hours of leisure are long compared to the extension pattern and are used mainly for relaxation. Leisure is often family centred involving activities such as the family outing. Occupations typically associated with the neutrality pattern include clerical workers and semi-skilled manual workers.

In the opposition pattern, work is sharply distinguished from leisure. Activities in the two areas are very different and leisure forms the central life interest. This pattern is associated with jobs providing a low degree of autonomy, which require the use of only a limited range of abilities and which often produce a feeling of hostility towards work. Hours of leisure are long and used mainly to recuperate from and compensate for work. The opposition pattern is typical of unskilled manual work, mining and distant water fishing.

The data for Parker's opposition pattern is drawn mainly from two studies: *Coal is Our Life* by Dennis, Henriques and Slaughter, a study of coal miners in Featherstone, Yorkshire, and *The Fishermen* by Jeremy Tunstall, a study of distant water fishermen in Hull. Both occupations have a high death and injury rate, both involve work in extreme and demanding conditions, all of which produces high levels of stress. The leisure activities of the miners and fishermen revolve around drinking in pubs and workingmen's clubs in the company of their workmates. The authors of both studies see this form of leisure as a means of relief and escape from the demands and dangers of work. Tunstall states 'Fishermen say "Of course fishermen get drunk. Anybody who does what we do has to get drunk to stay sane"'. Dennis, Henriques and Slaughter describe the miners' leisure as 'vigorous' and 'predominantly frivolous' in the sense of 'giving no thought to the morrow'. They argue that the insecurity produced by the high rate of death and injury encourages an attitude of living for the moment which is expressed in having a good time down at the workingmen's club.

Parker admits that 'considerably more research needs to be done to test the validity of these provisional findings' outlined in his research. There is evidence to suggest that the relationship between work and leisure is far more complex than his tidy compartments imply. His opposition pattern may represent a traditional working-class life style, expressed in an extreme form by miners and distant water fishermen, rather than a response to particular occupations. In addition, the fact that miners and fishermen in the studies he refers to lived in long established occupational communities may account as much for their leisure styles as their occupations. Featherstone is a mining town; the fishermen studied by Tunstall were concentrated in traditional dockland areas. Tunstall tends to ignore the fishermen living on new estates, who may well be nearer to the neutrality pattern. In the same way, miners who are less concentrated in occupational communities, such as those in Nottinghamshire, may well be closer to the neutrality pattern. Finally, the research for *Coal is Our Life* was conducted in the early 1950s, the research for *The Fishermen* in the late 1950s. Rising living standards may well have encouraged a more family centred life for the reasons outlined by Goldthorpe and Lockwood.

Research on the leisure activities of managers casts further doubt on Parker's theory. American research indicates that managers fit squarely into the extension pattern. The manager's life is portrayed as all work and no play with a working week of over sixty hours. Even when leisure was used purely for relaxation, nearly three-quarters of the managers in one survey stated that they saw 'leisure time as a refresher to enable you to do better work'. This subordination of leisure to work is not reflected in Britain. A survey by John Child and Brenda Macmillan of 964 British managers revealed that only 2.3% mentioned that leisure time was used 'to improve their careers and performance in their jobs'. Nearly a quarter specifically stated that leisure was a means to escape from and forget about work. British managers come closest to Parker's neutrality pattern. They worked some twenty hours a week less than their American counterparts. They used their relatively long hours of leisure for relaxation and enjoyment. Playing and watching sport, home improvement and hobbies such as photography were major leisure time activities. Child and Macmillan conclude that, 'British managers prefer to compartmentalize their lives so that the job is forgotten during their leisure time'.

The differences between British and American managers suggest that there is no simple, direct relationship between work and leisure. Child and Macmillan argue that a large part of the differences can be explained in terms of the cultures of the two societies. American culture places a greater emphasis on the work ethic, on the importance of individual achievement and self-improvement and upon work as a means to these ends. Child and Macmillan conclude that, 'life-styles are influenced by the different value systems which serve as a point of reference for social behaviour in the two countries'. This point reinforces Gallie's argument: work and leisure can only be understood in terms of their cultural setting.

The retreat from work to leisure

Writing in 1960, the American sociologist Harold Wilensky states, 'Already there are indications that the withdrawal from work as a central life interest, long noted for the working class, is spreading to the vast majority of the population'. As previous sections have indicated, manual workers tend to define their work in instrumental terms. Work is largely a means to an end, a means to provide the income for non-work concerns. Like Parker, Wilensky argues that leisure is influenced by work, but he is concerned with work in general rather than specific occupations. His argument may be summarized as follows. In modern industrial society, elites will increasingly plan and organize the work activities of the labour force. The centralization of planning and innovation will mean that even at the level of middle management, work will become more and more routine and autonomy will diminish. As the following chapter will indicate, the specialized division of labour in large-scale bureaucracies and organizations results in the work situation of the mass of white-collar workers becoming increasingly similar to that of factory workers. As a result, work for the majority of the population offers few opportunities for fulfilment.

In response to this situation, leisure replaces work to a greater extent as a central life interest. Wilensky states, 'Where ties to occupation and work-place become weak, the quest for alternative ties is intensified'. He sees a trend developing whereby the typical wage or salary earner will 'segregate his work from life and retire into the heartwarming circle of kin and friend'. Wilensky believes that this trend holds both promise and danger but he feels the threat of leisure is greater than the promise. The average worker may retreat into a contented apathy, unconcerned about his work or the wider community, snug in the warmth and security of his family and friends. In this situation he is open to manipulation by ruling classes and ruling elites. Marxian views of the dangers of a leisure orientated society have already been examined. The ruling elite version presented by C. Wright Mills, with its picture of a manipulated mass society, is similar.

C. Wright Mills believes that there is a clear division between work and leisure for the mass of the population, a division he calls 'the big split'. Mills argues that the work ethic has been replaced by the leisure ethic. When the two compete, 'leisure wins hands down'. His view of the relationship between work and leisure is summed up in the following pessimistic statement, 'Each day men sell little pieces of themselves in order to try to buy them back each night and weekend with the coin of "fun" '. Yet leisure does not provide the fulfilment which work denies. The techniques of mass production employed in manufacturing industry have been applied to the leisure industry. Organized spectator sport, bingo, movies, radio and television provide mass produced leisure which affords escape rather than fulfilment. Mass leisure activities 'astonish, excite and distract but they do not enlarge reason or feeling, or allow spontaneous dispositions to unfold creatively'. They create a fantasy world into which the masses escape in non-work hours, a world in which 'the amusement of hollow people rests on their own hollowness and does not fill it up'.

Mills's views echo Wilensky's fears about the danger of a leisure oriented society. Wilensky, however, also foresaw the possibility of a positive outcome of the trend towards leisure. It may provide 'new leisure commitments more personally satisfying and socially integrating'. The British sociologist Tom Burns develops this view. Burns argues that leisure provides considerable freedom for the individual to exercise choice and design and to create and find meaning in life. He uses Goffman's idea of 'styling of activities' which refers to the creative process whereby individuals present themselves in particular ways and so portray a desired self-image. The various styles of young people ranging from punks and teddy boys to hippies and Hell's Angels provide obvious examples. 'Styling' occurs throughout society and is expressed in choice of household décor, design of gardens, hair styles, clothes and life styles in general. Burns argues that the styling of activities is not simply shaped by the nature of work as Parker implies. He finds support for his argument from Michael Crozier's study of French office workers. Crozier found a wide range of variation in the form and content of the office workers' leisure activities, a variation which could not be accounted for by the similarity of their work. Burns claims that styling also overrides 'the organized apparatus of leisure and consumption'. The individual does not merely passively consume the products of industry and the provisions of mass entertainment. Instead he actively manipulates and exploits them, accepting some, rejecting some and modifying others. For example, in designing the décor of his house, he selects, modifies and arranges various products to suit his particular style. In this way he actively creates his own identity, he designs a setting which reflects his desired self-image. Burns concludes that styling gives 'meaning and significance' to life.

The priority which the mass of the labour force appears to give to non-work concerns has led some sociologists to suggest that rather than work influencing leisure, the reverse is increasingly the case. The affluent workers studied by Goldthorpe and Lockwood selected and defined their work in terms of non-work concerns. Many gave up jobs which they found more interesting to move to Luton. They defined a relatively high living standard and a family centred life as their main priority. These concerns shaped their choice of occupation, their definition of work, their attitude towards their firms and their view of the role of trade unions.

From his studies in France, Joffre Dumazedier argues that leisure values are increasingly influencing work in a number of ways. He notes that many people, particularly the young, choose jobs with reference to the type of leisure they want. They look at the leisure facilities available in the area when selecting a job. They consider the hours they will have to work in terms of their leisure requirements. Dumazedier argues that industry must adapt to accommodate leisure values by the provision of recreational facilities, flexi-hours and similar amenities and concessions.

Leisure, as a topic in its own right, has not captured the imagination of sociologists in general. Until recently the sociology of leisure has simply been a by-product of the sociology of work. Writing in 1976, Stanley Parker states, 'Until a few years ago the sociology of leisure in Britain (in so far as it existed at all) was treated either as a joke – comparable with the sociology of the bicycle – or as an adjunct of the study of work and industrial society'. This situation is slowly being changed by the increasing importance of leisure values in advanced industrial societies.

Power and conflict in industry

This section considers in detail issues raised in previous chapters. It is concerned with the relative power of employers and employees. It examines the nature of conflict in industry with particular reference to the role of trade unions. It looks at the various forms of industrial conflict with particular emphasis on strikes.

Pluralism, trade unions and the institutionalization of industrial conflict

From the pluralist perspective on the nature and distribution of power in society, power is dispersed among a variety of interest groups. (For an outline of the pluralist position, see Chapter 3, pp. 114–22.) Trade unions form the major groups representing the interests of employees in general and the manual working class in particular. A number of sociologists who support the pluralist position have argued that largely through trade unionism, the working class has been integrated into capitalist society. Conflict between employers and employees has been institutionalized in terms of an agreed upon set of rules and procedures. The net result is increasing stability in industrial society. No longer is the working class seen as a threat to social order as Marx believed; there is less and less chance of the kind of class conflict which Marx predicted.

The German sociologist Ralf Dahrendorf argues that pluralism 'provides an opportunity for success for every interest that is voiced'. He believes that the voice of the working class is growing louder through its formal associations. He sees a trend towards a more equal balance of power between employers and employees and the development of what he terms, 'industrial democracy'. Dahrendorf makes the following case. Democracy in industry begins with the formation of workers' interest groups. In particular, interest groups are necessary to represent workers since employers cannot negotiate with a disorganized collection of employees. For workers' interest groups to be effective, they must be recognized as legitimate by employers and the state. This has been an uphill struggle in capitalist societies. In nineteenth-century Britain employers strongly resisted the formation of trade unions often insisting that their workers sign a document declaring that they were not union members. In America, particularly during the 1930s, organized crime syndicates were sometimes employed by companies to prevent their workforce forming trade unions. However, by the latter half of this century trade unions were generally accepted as legitimate by employers and the state. Dahrendorf regards this as the major step towards industrial democracy and the institutionalization of industrial conflict.

With the formation of workers' interest groups a number of processes occurred which furthered the integration of the working class into the structure of capitalist society. Firstly, negotiating bodies were set up for formal negotiation between representatives of employers and workers. Such negotiations take place within a framework of agreed upon rules and procedures. Conflict is largely contained and resolved within this framework. Secondly, should negotiations break down, a machinery of arbitration has been institutionalized in terms of which outside bodies mediate between the parties in dispute. Thirdly, within each company workers are formally represented, for example by shop stewards, who represent their interests on a day-to-day basis. Finally, there is a tendency 'towards an institutionalization of workers' participation in industrial management'. Dahrendorf gives the example of workers appointed to the board of directors in certain European countries. In the above ways, the voice of labour is heard in capitalist enterprises and there is a trend towards 'joint regulation' of industry by workers and employers.

The American sociologist Seymour M. Lipset has argued that trade unions 'serve to integrate their members in the larger body politic and give them a basis for loyalty to the system'. His views may be illustrated with British examples. From the shop floor to central government, trade unions are actively involved in decision making processes. Trade union officials sit regularly on government advisory committees; cabinets have regular meetings with members of the TUC to discuss important issues of national and international policy. Union officials even find their way to the House of Lords. As V. L. Allen notes, 'A trade union peer or knight or recipient of a lesser award is not a figure of curiosity. Indeed a government honours list which does not include the names of some union officials is itself a curiosity'. Via trade unions, the interests of the working class are represented at the highest level and in this way the working class as a whole is integrated into 'the larger body politic'.

Evidence to support the view of trade unions as a major and effective interest group is provided by the economic benefits and rights they are seen to have won for their members and workers in general. It is argued that unions are responsible for increases in earnings, improvements in working conditions, longer holidays and shorter working weeks. Along with these economic benefits, unions are seen to be largely responsible for establishing and extending the rights of workers. For example, discipline of workers is subject to agreements drawn up between managers and trade unions; management can no longer fire at will. Allan Flanders has argued that 'the most enduring social achievement of trade unionism' is its 'creation of a social order in industry embodied in a code of industrial rights'.

The picture which emerges from this section is one of fully-fledged interest groups – trade unions – effectively representing workers' interests. Industrial conflict has been institutionalized and the working class has been integrated into both the capitalist enterprise and society as a whole. The more disruptive sources of social conflict have been removed resulting in a more stable society.

Trade unions and the power of labour – a Marxian perspective

From a Marxian perspective, the integration of the working class in capitalist society is merely superficial. Beneath the surface, the basic conflict of interest between capitalists and workers remains. In terms of his hopes for the future of the working class, Marx saw both danger and promise in the formation of trade unions. He feared that they might be 'too exclusively bent upon the local and immediate struggles with capitalism'. Trade unions may become preoccupied with furthering the interests of their particular members. In doing so they may lose sight of the overall struggle between capital and labour. In spite of this Marx believed that unions contained the potential to become 'organized agencies for superseding the very system of wage labour and capital rule'. By uniting workers in a struggle against employers, unions could help to create class consciousness. Cooperation between unions against employers on a local level could lead to class solidarity on a national level.

Marx's optimism was shared by few of his successors. For example, Lenin argued that unions were limited to developing 'trade union consciousness', that is a recognition of shared interests by members of a particular union rather than an awareness of the common interests of the working class as a whole. This would tend to limit union demands to improvements in wages, hours and working conditions within specific industries. Lenin feared that trade unions were becoming increasingly self-interested, furthering the interests of their particular members at the expense of other workers. However, he did believe that 'the trade unions were a tremendous step forward for the working class'. He saw them as an important part of the class struggle, but argued that 'trade union consciousness' could only be widened by linking unions to a political party representing the interests of the working class as a whole.

Modern Marxists are generally pessimistic about the role of trade unions in the class struggle. Firstly, they point to the unions lack of real power. Ralph Miliband claims that compared to employers, unions have little power. He states that, 'What a firm produces; whether it exports or does not export; whether it invests, in what and for what, and for what purpose; whether it absorbs or is absorbed by other firms – these and many other decisions are matters over which labour has at best an indirect degree of influence and more generally no influence at all'. Not only do trade unions lack an effective voice in these issues, they show little sign of demanding one. Richard Hyman argues that 'Management still commands; workers are still obliged to obey. Trade unionism permits debate around the terms of workers' obedience; it does not challenge the fact of their subordination'.

The limits of trade union power are apparent from V. L. Allen's analysis of their failure to achieve their basic aim, the economic protection of workers. In pursuit of this aim, unions jealously protect their right to free collective bargaining, the right to bargain freely with individual employers on behalf of their members. Allen argues that they cannot properly represent workers by this procedure. He maintains that workers' economic interests can only be furthered by a significant redistribution of wealth. This would require considerable government interference in the mechanisms of the 'free market economy'. As a result the unions would lose their right to free collective bargaining. As it is, unions operate within the free price mechanism and for this reason are unable to properly represent their members' interests. For example, if they win higher wages, the employer can pass on the increased costs by raising the price of his product. The worker therefore suffers as a consumer; his wage rise is wiped out by rising prices. Free collective bargaining means that trade unions compete in the open market. They compete with each other which means the more powerful unions gain greater rewards than the less powerful. They also compete with employers, but since they have little control over investment, prices and profit and its distribution, the competition is far from equal. As Richard Hyman notes, despite their vigorous efforts, unions have largely failed to improve the economic position of their members. Writing in 1972, Hyman states, 'throughout this century the share of wages and salaries in the national income has barely deviated from the figure of 60 per cent. Trade unions have not succeeded in winning for their members any part of the percentage of production accruing to profits; they have merely held on to the same relative share of a growing economy'.

Given this situation, V. L. Allen argues that trade unions cannot realize even 'their moderate aims of protection satisfactorily without revolutionary change', a change that will involve a massive redistribution of wealth. In practice however, 'Instead of being directly concerned about the redistribution of income and devising a means to achieve this, they show satisfaction with fractional changes in money wage rates. In doing this they accept the expectations which the employers have deemed suitable for them'. By operating within the framework of a capitalist economic system, trade unions accept it and make it legitimate. By negotiating with employers, they recognize and accept the system of employment and wage labour. Allen concludes that, 'Trade unions then, have acquired aims which are legitimate within the context of capitalist society. They are limited aims, concerning wages, hours of work and working conditions, which can be achieved without unduly disturbing the fabric of capitalism'.

From a Marxian perspective, the so-called integration of the working class into capitalist society has blunted its revolutionary potential but it has not removed the basic conflict of interest between capital and labour. Ralph Miliband argues that the incorporation of trade union officials into various branches of government has increased pressure upon them to consider the 'national interest', to act 'reasonably' and 'responsibly'. In practice this 'generally means that they should curb and subdue their members' demands rather than defend and advance them'. In terms of the 'national interest', trade union demands often appear selfish, unrealistic, sectional, inflationary and harmful to the economy. However, Miliband maintains that the 'national interest' is simply a smokescreen which disguises the interests of capital. He concludes that the role of trade unions in government 'has mainly served to saddle them with responsibilities which have further weakened their bargaining position, and which has helped to reduce their effectiveness'.

From a Marxian viewpoint the institutionalization of industrial conflict has merely damped down the more violent expressions of conflict. The essential conflict of interest remains. The supposed integration of the working class into the body politic is merely superficial. Society is still irreconcilably divided into two opposing groups, capital and labour. No amount of 'integration' within the framework of a capitalist economy will remove this division. Capitalism still involves the maximization of profit for the benefit of the owners of the forces of production. It still involves the exploitation of labour. Richard Hyman concludes that, 'Unless and until the basic structure of industry and society is radically recast – with workers controlling the process of production, in the interests of human welfare, rather than being controlled by it, in the interests of profit – the institutionalization of industrial conflict will of necessity remain partial and precarious.'

Trade unionism can be seen as one expression of conflict in industry. Expressions of industrial conflict are, in the words of Clark Kerr, 'as unlimited as the ingenuity of man'. They include strikes, lockouts, sit-ins, working to rule, refusal to work overtime, sabotage, absenteeism and labour turnover. The following sections examine two forms of industrial conflict, sabotage and strikes.

Industrial sabotage

Laurie Taylor and Paul Walton define industrial sabotage as 'that rule-breaking which takes the form of conscious action or inaction directed towards the mutilation or destruction of the work environment (this includes the machinery of production and the commodity itself)'. Drawing on a wide range of data from the writings of journalists, historians and sociologists, Taylor and Walton classify acts of industrial sabotage in terms of the meanings and motives which direct them. They identify three main motives: 'attempts to reduce tension and frustration'; 'attempts at easing the work process'; and 'attempts to assert control'. They argue that each type of sabotage indicates 'the prevalence of distinctive strains or problems within the workplace'.

Taylor and Walton provide the following example to illustrate the first type of sabotage. Two seamen were cleaning out sludge from the tanks of a ship. They had been working for a week and only had two buckets for the purpose. With more buckets the job could have been considerably shortened but the foreman told them he lacked the authority to issue any from the ship's stores. Tired and frustrated, the seamen picked up their buckets and smashed them to smithereens against the bulkhead. This action provided a release for tension and frustration. Saboteurs in similar situations explain their actions in the following way. They have reached the end of their tether, and often an incident occurs which they feel is the last straw. Sabotage makes them feel better, it gets things off their chest. Such actions are usually spontaneous and unplanned. In the above example, the seamen didn't say a word, they just looked at each other and with a single thought, smashed their buckets. Taylor and Walton argue that such forms of sabotage 'are the signs of a powerless individual or group'. They tend to occur in industries where trade unions are absent or ineffective, where there is little or no history of collective industrial action. In this situation there are few opportunities to remove the source of grievances. Sabotage provides a means of temporarily releasing frustration when workers lack the power to remove its source.

The motive directing the second type of sabotage is simply to make work easier. Taylor and Walton give the example of workers in an aircraft factory whose job was to bolt the wing to the fuselage of the plane. When the bolt did not align with the socket some workers used a 'tap' to recut the thread of the socket. This provided the extra thousandth or so of an inch to enable the bolt to be screwed into the socket. The plane was seriously weakened by this procedure, and with sufficient vibration, the bolt could fall out. Despite the fact that 'taps' were officially banned and regular inspections were held to stamp out their use, workers continued to use them. Taylor and Walton argue that this type of sabotage is typical of industries in which the worker has to 'take on the machine', where he works against the clock and his wages are dependent on his output. By cutting corners, workers can increase output and from their point of view, cut through red tape and get on with the job.

The third type of sabotage directly challenges authority and is used by workers in an attempt to gain greater control. Usually it is planned and coordinated. Taylor and Walton give the example of car workers in Turin who smashed production lines and intimidated strike breakers. A series of strikes had failed to bring production to a halt so the strikers turned to vandalism and violence to secure their objectives. Taylor and Walton suggest that this form of sabotage was most common during the early stages of industrialization before trade unions were fully established. For example, machine smashing by groups such as the Luddites in England during the 1820s and 1830s was used as a strategy for raising wages. Taylor and Walton argue that, 'In functional terms we could describe trade-union negotiation as taking over from sabotage and other forms of direct action and institutionalizing conflict through collective bargaining'. However, judging from investigations into a number of industries, sabotage, as an attempt to assert control, still regularly occurs.

In *Working for Ford*, a study of Ford's Halewood plant on Merseyside, Huw Beynon notes a number of examples of sabotage directed by a desire for greater control. During Beynon's research, management refused to accept joint consultation with the unions about the organization of work on the shop floor. Management decided issues such as the speed of particular jobs and manning levels. In their demand for greater control, workers would sometimes pull out the safety wire to stop the assembly line. Action such as this forced management to allow workers some control over the speed of the line. A similar strategy was used by workers in the Paint Shop who sanded down the cars after an early coat of paint. If they believed they were having to work too quickly or there were insufficient men to do the job, they would sand paint off the 'style lines', the angles on the body that give the car its distinctive shape. Usually they won the point and got what they wanted.

Taylor and Walton argue that sabotage directed by a desire to assert control tends to occur in the following situations – where there is a history of militancy, a general recognition of who's to blame for grievances and few opportunities for effective protest through official channels. Motives for sabotage can and often do overlap. The examples from Halewood may be seen as both attempts to reduce frustration and as attempts to assert control. Taylor and Walton expect sabotage motivated by a desire for control to increase in Britain. Writing in 1971, they state, 'There appears to be a systematic government and official trade-union campaign not only to reduce strike activity but at the same time to implement productivity agreements which tend to reduce the workers' area of autonomy within the factory'. If the weapons in the workers's armoury are blunted in this way, his desire for control may be increasingly channelled into industrial sabotage.

Strikes

Strikes are an obvious expression of industrial conflict. Richard Hyman isolates five elements in the definition of a strike. Firstly, it is an actual stoppage of work which distinguishes the strike from activities such as overtime bans and go-slows. Secondly, it is a temporary stoppage of work – employees expect to return to work for the same employer after the strike is over. Thirdly, it is a collective act involving a group of employees and as such it requires a certain amount of worker solidarity and organization. Fourthly it is the action of *employees* which distinguishes the strike from so-called 'rent strikes' and refusals by students to attend lectures. Finally, it is nearly always a 'calculative act', an act which is specifically designed to express grievances, to seek a solution to problems, to apply pressure to enforce demands. Strikes may be 'official' or 'unofficial'. Official strikes have the recognition and backing of the union, unofficial strikes, sometimes known as wildcat strikes, do not.

Striking can be an effective bargaining strategy. Ralph Miliband makes the following observation, 'On innumerable occasions demands which, the unions and workers were told, could not conceivably be granted since they must inevitably mean ruin for a firm or industry or inflict irreparable damage on the national economy, have somehow become acceptable when organized labour has shown in practice that it would not desist'. Strikes bring results. In a study of strikes, Richard Hyman concludes that they 'regularly prove highly effective in speeding negotiations towards an acceptable conclusion'.

Strikes make news. The impression given by the mass media in Britain is that of a strike-prone workforce ready to stop work at the drop of a hat.

However, the Donovan Commission, a government sponsored investigation into industrial relations, reported that in terms of working days lost through strikes, 'the United Kingdom's recent record has been about average compared with other countries' (quoted in Hyman, 1972, p. 31). Statistics on strike activity require careful interpretation. Richard Hyman makes the following observations. Firstly, they are based on reports provided by employers. Some employers may be more conscientious in recording stoppages than others. Some may leave certain disputes unrecorded to give the impression of good industrial relations. Others may include every single stoppage in the hope of providing evidence for legal restrictions on strikes. Secondly, there are a number of ways of measuring the significance of strikes. These include the actual number of stoppages, the number of workers involved in strikes and the number of working days 'lost' through strike action. Table 17 gives statistics for these three measures for Britain from 1900 to 1971.

Table 17   British strike statistics: annual averages from 1900 to 1971

	Number of strikes	Workers involved ('000)	Striker-days ('000)
1900–10	529	240	4 576
1911–13	1 074	1 034	20 908
1914–18	844	632	5 292
1919–21	1 241	2 108	49 053
1922–25	629	503	11 968
1926	323	2 734	162 233
1927–32	379	344	4 740
1933–39	735	295	1 694
1940–44	1 491	499	1 816
1945–54	1 791	545	2 073
1955–64	2 521	1 116	3 889
1965	2 354	868	2 932
1966	1 937	530	2 395
1967	2 116	731	2 783
1968	2 378	2 255	4 719
1969	3 116	1 654	6 925
1970	3 906	1 793	10 908
1971	2 223	1 173	13 558

(Source: Hyman, 1972, p. 27, from the Department of Employment Gazette)

The statistics show no clear trend. There is some indication that since the beginning of the century the actual number of strikes has increased but the number of working days lost through strikes has decreased. In other words there are more strikes but they don't last as long. However, this is only a very rough generalization. Given the fact that the size of the labour force has increased by nearly a half since the turn of the century, the increase in the number of strikes is less significant than the figures suggest.

Most strikes in Britain are unofficial – they do not have official trade union recognition and backing. Unofficial strikes are becoming more and more common. Partly because of this the shop steward has become a central figure in industrial conflict. Beginning as a shop floor representative of the union, collecting union subscriptions and reporting on conditions in the factory, the shop steward increasingly represented workers in negotiations with management. This reflected the growing importance of local agreements on pay and conditions. Employers negotiate with unions on a national level, but, as Richard Hyman states, 'it is the national agreements which are of minor significance, setting a bare minimum standard for wages and conditions; the worker relies primarily on shop floor bargaining to win acceptable terms'. If important decisions are taken at the local level, it is to be expected that workers will often take matters into their own hands rather than channelling their grievances through national union negotiating machinery. In addition, the bureaucratic procedures of national union organizations can be slow and ponderous. A strike can be over and settled before official union recognition is obtained. During this century, the trend in Britain has been away from national strikes, in which all members of a union stop work. Reflecting the increasing importance of local agreements, most strikes are localized and unofficial.

It has been argued that unofficial strikes are harmful to industrial relations in that they prevent the establishment of an ordered and smooth running procedure for settling disputes. However, a number of sociologists see them as an essential means for expressing the grievances of the workforce. Hyman refers to unofficial strikes as a 'safeguard to democracy', arguing that they represent a free and direct expression of workers' feelings. They also serve to counterbalance the conservative tendencies of many national union officials. As Hyman notes, some unofficial strikes are specifically directed against official trade union policy. They can provide workers with an effective means for changing that policy. V. L. Allen sees the growing importance of shop stewards in a similar light. Since they are 'in close and immediate touch with the ordinary members', they are able to 'fulfil an essential democratic need'. The national union organization is distant from the shop floor and cannot deal with the many day-to-day problems which arise. Allen argues that the activities of shop stewards are 'not contrary to those of the unions nor do they usurp the authority of unions, for they are making up for trade union deficiencies'. Thus, the growing importance of shop floor bargaining, the development of the role of the shop steward and the increasing number of unofficial strikes can be seen as a healthy development.

Sociology

Strikes are not spread evenly throughout the labour force. In Britain, from 1966 to 1970, the number of days lost through strikes, relative to the size of the workforce in particular industries, was greatest in the dock industry followed by the car industry, shipbuilding and coalmining. A number of explanations have been put forward to account for why some industries are more 'strike-prone' than others. In a study of strikes in eleven countries Clark Kerr and Abraham Siegel found that miners, dockers and seamen had the highest strike records. They argue that 'community integration' is the key to explaining strike activity in these occupations. Miners, dockers and seamen tend to live in occupational communities which are relatively isolated from the wider society. In such communities, a 'consciousness of kind' develops which involves a strong awareness of shared grievances, a close emotional commitment to trade unionism and a high level of working-class solidarity. Shared grievances and worker solidarity, set in the context of a close-knit community, tend to make strike action, a collective act requiring some degree of solidarity, more likely. Some doubt is thrown on Kerr and Siegel's theory by Stephen Hill's study of London dockers. Hill found little evidence of the 'community integration' which is supposed to be typical of dockland life. The London dockers were remarkably like the affluent workers studied by Goldthorpe and Lockwood. Their life style was largely privatized, their orientation to work and trade unions primarily instrumental. Whatever the merits of Kerr and Siegel's explanation, it is not supported by Hill's particular case study. (For further details of Hill's research see Chapter 2, pp. 61–5.)

A second explanation for variation in strike activity emphasizes the role of technology. This explanation has been used to explain the high frequency of strikes in the car industry. It is based on the type of arguments developed by Robert Blauner. Assembly line technology produces a high level of alienation which leads to hostile relationships between workers and management. Strikes, as an expression of industrial conflict, will therefore be more likely in industries employing this kind of production technology. This explanation is unable, however, to account for variation in strike activity within the same industries in different countries. As Richard Hyman notes, 'Why does the strike record for the British motor industry contrast so markedly with the comparative harmony in Germany or Japan, when the technology of car assembly is internationally uniform'. The weakness of the technological argument has already been seen from Duncan Gallie's account of British and French oil refineries. Despite working with similar technologies the French workers had a far higher strike record than their British counterparts.

A third explanation for variation in strike activity deals with the effectiveness of the negotiating machinery available for settling disputes. A. M. Ross and P. T. Hartman compared strike levels in fifteen countries between 1900 and 1956. They concluded that strikes are least likely to occur when there are well established procedures for consultation and negotiation. If procedures exist whereby grievances can be speedily formulated and efficiently channelled into negotiating machinery, strikes will be unlikely. This view is supported by the Devlin Report, a government sponsored investigation into the dock industry. The Report argued that a major reason for the high level of strikes in the industry was the ineffectiveness of the machinery for resolving disputes. This explanation implies that once the negotiating machinery is perfected, strikes will be a thing of the past. This implication will be challenged later in the chapter.

The above explanations for variations in strike levels between different industries have been criticized by Richard Hyman. He argues that they largely ignore the strikers' definition of the situation. For example, workers in one industry may define strikes as a last resort, those in another may see strikes as a routine and even natural part of industrial life. Hyman argues that workers do not simply react to production technology or negotiating machinery and predictably strike or not strike as the case might be. They define their work situation and the act of striking in a particular way. Hyman does not deny that factors such as production technology can influence behaviour, but maintains that they are translated into action via the meanings men give to them. Thus an explanation of the strike-prone British car industry and the relatively strike-free situation in the same industry in Japan and Germany requires a knowledge of the meanings and definitions that workers give to industrial life.

So far the discussion of strikes has concentrated on the question of why some industries are more strike-prone than others. The remainder of this section considers the reasons for strikes in general. Most strikes centre around wages. The statistics in table 18, produced by the Department of Employment, give some indication of the importance of pay.

Table 18 Industrial disputes

| | United Kingdom | | | | (Millions) | | |
	1966	1970	1971	1972	1973	1974	1975	1976
Working days lost:								
Pay claims and disputes	1.6	9.2	12.3	21.7	5.1	13.1	4.4	1.8
All other causes	0.8	1.7	1.3	2.3	2.0	1.7	1.5	1.7
Total days lost	2.4	10.9	13.6	24.0	7.1	14.8	5.9	3.5

(Source: *Social Trends*, 1977, p. 91).

The emphasis on pay is not surprising in view of the wide-spread instrumental orientation of the labour force. From their analysis of a strike at the Pilkington glass factory in St Helens in 1970, Tony Lane and Kenneth Roberts argue that the promise of a quick financial reward was a major factor accounting for the rapid spread of the strike around the factory.

They claim that, 'This instrumental approach towards work may have several repercussions for industrial relations. Workers with such a disposition may well use whatever tactics appear most effective to maximize their earning power. They may bargain through union officials or shop stewards, they may work-to-rule, go slow, bar overtime or strike'. However, even when a strike is mainly concerned with money, it inevitably involves questions of power. A strike itself is a power struggle and it may well reflect discontent with the nature of authority and control in the day-to-day running of industry. As Lane and Roberts argue, a worker sells more than his labour. He also 'undertakes to abide by a set of rules, he submits to a system of authority'. This involves a sacrifice of certain areas of freedom, a sacrifice which will not be lost on the worker even if he does define work in primarily instrumental terms. Lane and Roberts state that 'If he treats his *labour* as a commodity it does not follow that he expects himself, as a person, to be treated as a commodity'.

It can be argued that, to some degree, discontent about the nature of authority and control in industry underlies all strikes. In some disputes, it is clearly a central issue. From his analysis of the Ford strike of 1969, Huw Beynon states, 'It was, as the Halewood stewards never tired of saying, not a money strike but a strike of principle'. The principle concerned control. Ford had offered the workers a package which, in financial terms, was very acceptable. It involved a wage rise, holiday benefits and lay-off payments. In Beynon's words, 'This would have suited the lads. A pay increase, a holiday bonus and a bit of security. That sounded great'. However, the package also placed important restrictions on the power of the workforce. It included a 'good behaviour clause', which stated that many of the benefits would be cancelled for a six-month period for any 'unconstitutional action' by a group of workers. This covered activities such as unofficial strikes, overtime bans and restriction of output in general. In addition, workers were required to give twenty-one days' notice of an official strike. As one shop steward told Beynon, 'If they get away with this one it will be all up. We'll be back to Victorian times. The ball and chain won't be in it'. In the case of the Ford strike, economic considerations took second place to the principle of control.

A somewhat different approach to the explanation of strikes involves an analysis of events immediately preceding a strike. This approach was used by Alvin Gouldner in his study entitled *Wildcat Strike*. The strike he observed was preceded by a growing sense of grievance and by mounting tension which finally exploded into an outright stoppage of work. New machinery and new management had been introduced into the company and this altered the relationship between management and workers. New rules were enforced and supervision was tightened up. What had been seen as an easy-going relationship with management was now seen by the workers as rigid and coercive. Dissatisfaction with the new regime mounted until it was finally expressed in strike action. Interestingly, the strikers' demands were for higher wages. They did not regard it as legitimate to challenge management's authority to manage. They expressed their discontent in terms of a wage demand which they felt was legitimate according to the rules of the game. In the end the workers accepted a wage rise as compensation for the new authority structure.

The view of the outbreak of a strike as an emotional outburst in response to accumulated grievances and growing tension in the workplace does not explain the origins of all strikes. Lane and Roberts's analysis of the Pilkington strike indicates that it was not preceded by a build up of discontent. Morale was not particularly low, labour turnover not particularly high, there was no change in the number of disputes in the factory, things were 'normal'. Lane and Roberts state, 'This means of course that workers can be drawn into a strike without being conscious of an exceptionally wide range of grievances, and without being subject to unusual stress of the shop floor. A strike, in other words, can gather momentum under "normal" working conditions'. This leads Lane and Roberts to regard strikes as a normal feature of industrial life. The Pilkington workers were dissatisfied with wage levels and relationships with management but these were facts of working life. And it is the facts of working life that Lane and Roberts see as the basis for strikes. They conclude that, ' The nature of work, the terms of the employer–employee relationship, the integration of the trade unions into the power structure, all make strikes inevitable'.

This section concludes with two views of strikes in particular and industrial conflict in general. The first is largely based on the functionalist perspective. If it is assumed that society is based on consensus, that employers and employees ultimately share the same goals and are working for the same ends, then conflict in industry is not inevitable. Summarizing this viewpoint, V. L. Allen states, 'Given the assumption of consensus, of the existence of a common purpose, then it must be possible to envisage a completely strike-free economy as a permanent state'. From this perspective, strikes are a problem which can be solved. Once the machinery of collective bargaining is properly established, disputes between employers and workers can be settled peacefully within the framework of consensus. Since there is no basic conflict of interest between the two sides in industry, conflict represents minor malfunctions of the system. The removal of conflict involves reform of industrial relations rather than a radical change in the structure of industrial society. This reform is proceeding with the institutionalization of industrial conflict and the integration of the workforce into the structure of capitalist society.

The second view of strikes and industrial conflict derives mainly from Marxian perspectives. It sees conflict in industry as inevitable since the interests of employers and employees are irreconcilable. Employers are concerned with maximizing profits, employees with maximizing wages.

The interests of the two groups conflict since one gains at the expense of the other. Conflict in industry is simply one expression of class conflict in capitalist society. Writing from a Marxian perspective, Richard Hyman states, 'The conflicts and contradictions inherent in the capitalist system of industrial society, and the workers' role within it, must be expected to find expression'. Strikes or some other form of industrial conflict are therefore inevitable. No amount of tinkering with negotiation machinery in industry, legally binding agreements between employers and employees, 'cooling off periods' or industrial relations legislation in general will end this conflict. Concluding their study of the Pilkington strike, Lane and Roberts reject the view that strikes are a problem that can be solved within the existing structure of capitalist society. They state, 'But there is another point of view, possibly only apparent to those who take part in strikes, that it is not they who are the problem; rather it is the economic structure, the trade unions, and the nature of work and authority'.

Sociology, ideology and work and leisure

As with every topic in sociology, it is not possible to be objective and neutral about subjects such as work and leisure. Throughout this chapter, it is apparent that the range of views presented owes much to the values and ideology of particular sociologists. At times this is obvious with Marx's passionate condemnation of work in capitalist society, at other times it is less apparent with Blauner's relatively restrained analysis of work in the USA.

As with Marxian perspectives in general, Marxian views of work and leisure are based on a radical utopian ideology. It is radical because it looks forward to a fundamental change in the structure of society. It is utopian because it looks forward to an ideal society. It is ideological because in the last analysis, it is based on a set of values about what man ought to be, about the nature of human fulfilment and how best it can be realized. In evaluating and analysing work and leisure in industrial society, Marxists use their picture of the communist utopia as a point of reference, as a standard of comparison. Since work and leisure in industrial society fall far short of this ideal, Marxian views are openly critical. However, their ideological content should not lead to their outright dismissal. Marx's concept of alienation has been one of the most stimulating and productive ideas in sociology. Ideology can produce important insights. Bowles and Gintis's analysis of the hierarchical system of authority and control in capitalist enterprises owes much to their commitment to Marxist ideology. In seeing it as a mechanism for coercion and control, they provide an interesting alternative to the orthodox view. In the same way, Richard Hyman's interpretation of industrial conflict in capitalist society is strongly influenced by a commitment to an egalitarian society organized on lines similar to those outlined by Marx. It provides an important balance to the more orthodox functionalist view.

It can be argued that ideology intrudes too far into analysis. The picture of leisure presented by Marcuse is clearly based on value judgments. Edward Shils has criticized Marcuse and sociologists who take similar views, claiming that their analysis of society stems from a 'frustrated attachment to an impossible ideal of human perfection and a distaste for one's own society and human beings as they were' (quoted in Swingewood, 1977, p. 18). Marcuse's views can be seen as a reflection of his frustration about the lack of interest shown by the American public in issues he considered vital. Since they apparently enjoyed activities he regarded as superficial, and worse, activities which distracted their attention from important matters, Marcuse saw them as satisfying 'false needs'. It can be argued that Marcuse's *One Dimensional Man* is ideology and little else.

In *Alienation and Freedom*, Robert Blauner states that he studied work 'from the viewpoint of the intellectual observer with his own values and conceptions of freedom and self-realization'. His viewpoint can be seen as an expression of American liberalism. He is largely uncritical of the structure of capitalist society and by implication, accepts it as just and fundamentally sound. His proposals for change are based on liberal ideology in that they involve reform rather than radical change. The changes in production technology which he advocates to improve the quality of work can take place within the existing framework of industrial society. Blauner's liberal views tend to focus his attention on the workplace rather than the wider society.

Whether their views are radical or liberal, many sociologists regard work in industrial society as largely unfulfilling. In particular, they have tended to contrast the independent, creative, presumably fulfilled craftsman of pre-industrial days with the factory worker in industrial society. The 'alienated' factory worker suffers by comparison. Robert Blauner argues that this comparison is based on a romanticized picture of craft work and an idealization of pre-industrial society in general. He notes that less than 10% of the medieval labour force was made up of craftsmen whereas the vast majority of workers were peasants engaged in monotonous drudgery. Blauner argues that an idealized view of the past is partly responsible for the concept of the alienated worker in modern industrial society. Like everybody else, sociologists look at the present in terms of a picture of the past.

7 Organizations and bureaucracy

In the words of the American sociologist Amitai Etzioni, 'Our society is an organizational society'. We are born in hospitals, educated in schools, employed by business firms and government agencies, we join trade unions and professional associations and are laid to rest in churches. In sickness and in health, at work and at play, life in modern industrial society is increasingly conducted in organizational settings. This chapter is concerned with the study of organizations which Etzioni defines as 'social units which are predominantly oriented to the attainment of specific goals'. Organizations therefore differ from social units such as the family, friendship groups and the community because they are designed to realize clearly defined goals. Thus schools are designed to transmit knowledge, hospitals to treat the sick, industrial firms to manufacture goods and so on.

Organizations are not a new invention. Social units have been created to pursue specific goals in many pre-industrial societies. Thus in ancient Egypt, a permanent workforce of several thousand skilled workers was formed to build the pyramids. In addition, a large-scale organization was developed to construct and maintain a complex series of dykes, canals and ditches which served to control the flood waters of the Nile and irrigate the fields. Modern industrial societies, however, are distinguished from their pre-industrial counterparts by the number, size and scope of organizations. In the view of many sociologists, organizations have become the dominant institutions of contemporary society.

The spread of organizations is closely related to the increasingly specialized division of labour in society. In the earliest form of human society, the hunting and gathering band, the division of labour is rudimentary. The men hunt and the women gather nuts, fruit, roots and berries. In order to survive, all adult members of the band must engage in subsistence activities. This largely prevents the development of social units specializing in activities other than the acquisition of food. The invention of agriculture some ten thousand years ago provided the basis for a specialized division of labour and the development of organizations. Agriculture frees a part of the population from subsistence activities and allows some individuals to specialize in particular tasks. Thus in the early farming communities, full-time craftsmen such as potters, weavers and toolmakers emerged.

The growing efficiency of agriculture results in a smaller proportion of

278

the population being able to meet the community's subsistence requirements. This allows more and more members of society to specialize in tasks not directly related to subsistence. As the division of labour becomes more specialized, it requires direction and coordination. For example, in ancient Egypt a range of specialists were employed to construct the pyramids. They included quarrymen, masons, toolmakers, engineers, surveyors, artists, scribes and overseers. Their specialist tasks required direction and coordination if they were to be combined to produce an end product. Similarly, in the modern industrial concern, the organization of a complex series of tasks is essential. For example, the manufacture of motor cars requires the coordination of a range of specialized operations. Some must therefore have the authority to direct and organize the activities of others. For example, if explicit rules did not govern the dimensions of the various components that make up a motor car, they simply would not fit together. Thus a highly specialized division of labour tends to generate a hierarchy of authority and a system of rules. When these factors are combined in the pursuit of a specific goal, an organization is formed.

The work of Max Weber is usually taken as the starting point in the sociology of organizations. Weber believed that a particular form of organization – bureaucracy – is becoming the defining characteristic of modern industrial society. His work is mainly concerned with a comparison of bureaucracy and the forms of organization found in pre-industrial societies.

Max Weber – bureaucracy and rationalization

Max Weber (1864–1920) believed that bureaucratic organizations are the dominant institutions of industrial society. Weber's definition of bureaucracy will be examined in detail shortly. Briefly, he saw it as an organization with a hierarchy of paid, full-time officials who formed a chain of command. A bureaucracy is concerned with the business of administration, with controlling, managing and coordinating a complex series of tasks. Bureaucratic organizations are increasingly dominating the institutional landscape. Departments of state, political parties, business enterprises, the military, education and churches are all organized on bureaucratic lines. To appreciate the nature of modern society, Weber maintained that an understanding of the process of bureaucratization is essential. Marxists see fundamental differences between capitalist and socialist industrial societies. To Weber their differences are minimal compared to the essential similarity of bureaucratic organization. This is the defining characteristic of modern industrial society.

Weber's view of bureaucracy must be seen in the context of his general theory of social action. He argued that all human action is directed by meanings. Thus, in order to understand and explain action, the meanings and motives which lie behind it must be appreciated. Weber identified various types of action which are distinguished by the meanings on which they are based. These include 'affective' or 'emotional action', 'traditional action' and 'rational action'. Affective action stems from an individual's emotional state at a particular time. Loss of temper which results in verbal abuse or physical violence is an example of affective action. Traditional action is based on established custom. An individual acts in a certain way because of ingrained habit, because things have always been done that way. He has no real awareness of why he does something, his actions are simply second nature. By comparison, rational action involves a clear awareness of a goal. It is the action of a manager who wishes to increase productivity, of a builder contracted to erect a block of flats. In both cases the goal is clearly defined. Rational action also involves a systematic assessment of the various means of attaining a goal and the selection of the most appropriate means. Thus if a capitalist in the building trade aimed to maximize profit he would carefully evaluate factors such as alternative sites, raw materials, building techniques, labour costs and the potential market in order to realize his goal. This would entail precise calculation of costs and careful weighing of the advantages and disadvantages of the various factors involved. His action is rational since, in Weber's words, rational action is 'the methodical attainment of a definitely given and practical end by means of an increasingly precise calculation of means'.

Weber believed that rational action had become the dominant mode of action in modern industrial society. He saw it expressed in a wide variety of areas: in state administration, business, education, science and even in Western classical music. He referred to the increasing dominance of rational action as the process of rationalization. Bureaucratization is the prime example of this process. A bureaucratic organization has a clearly defined goal. It involves precise calculation of the means to attain this goal and systematically eliminates those factors which stand in the way of the achievement of its objectives. Bureaucracy is therefore rational action in an institutional form.

Bureaucracy is also a system of control. It is an hierarchical organization in which superiors strictly control and discipline the activities of subordinates. Weber argued that in any large-scale task, some must coordinate and control the activities of others. He states that, 'the imperative coordination of the action of a considerable number of men requires control of a staff of persons'. In order for this control to be effective, it must be regarded as legitimate. There must be a 'minimum of voluntary submission' to higher authority. Legitimacy can be based on various types of meanings. For example it can derive from traditional or rational meanings. Thus legitimacy can take the form of traditional authority or rational authority. The form of the organizational structure derives from the type of legitimacy on which it is based. In Weber's words, 'According to the kind of legitimacy which is claimed, the type of obedience, the kind of administrative staff developed to guarantee it and the mode of exercising authority, will all differ fundamentally'. To understand bureaucracy, it is therefore necessary to appreciate the type of legitimacy on which bureaucratic control is based.

Weber identified three forms of legitimacy which derive from three types of social action. Affective, traditional and rational action each provide a particular motive for obedience, a motive based respectively on emotion, custom and rationality. These types of legitimate control are charismatic authority, traditional authority and rational–legal authority. Each results in a particular form of organizational structure. Weber constructed models to represent each type of authority. They are known as 'ideal types' and represent a 'pure' form which is not expected to exist in historical reality. In practice types of authority only approximate an ideal type, they are closer to one ideal type than to others.

In a system of control based on charismatic authority, obedience derives from the devotion felt by subordinates to what they see as the exceptional qualities of their leader. These qualities are seen as supernatural, superhuman or at least exceptional compared to lesser mortals. Charismatic leaders are able to sway and control their followers by direct emotional appeals which excite devotion and strong loyalties. Historical examples which approximate charismatic authority are provided by Jesus, Mohammed, Alexander the Great, Napoleon and Fidel Castro. Organizational structures which derive from charismatic authority are fluid and ill-defined. Those who occupy positions of authority either share the charisma of the leader or possess a charisma of their own. They are not selected on the basis of family ties to the leader or on the basis of technical qualifications. There is no fixed hierarchy of officials and no legal rules governing the organization of leaders and followers. Jesus's disciples provide an example of leadership positions in a charismatic movement. There is no systematically organized economic support for the movement. Its members typically rely on charity or plunder. Since charismatic authority depends for its control on the person of the leader, it is necessarily shortlived. After his death, the movement must become 'routinized' in terms of either traditional or rational–legal authority if it is to survive. Thus the organizational control of the Christian church is no longer directly based on the charisma of its founder. Instead it has been routinized in terms of both traditional and rational–legal authority.

Traditional authority rests on a belief in the rightness of established customs and traditions. Those in authority command obedience on the basis of their traditional status which is usually inherited. Their subordinates are directed by feelings of loyalty and obligation to long established positions of power. The feudal system of medieval Europe provides an example of traditional authority. Kings and nobles owed their position to inherited status and the personal loyalty of their subjects. The organizational structure which derives from traditional authority takes two main forms. Firstly, a household of personal retainers which include relatives, favourites and servants who are dependent for support on the head of the household. Secondly, a system of vassals such as feudal lords who swear an oath of fealty to the king and hold land on this basis. The duties of household retainers and vassals are defined by custom but may be changed according to the inclination of the particular ruler.

Rational–legal authority differs sharply from its charismatic and traditional counterparts. Legitimacy and control stem neither from the perceived personal qualities of the leader and the devotion they excite nor from a commitment to traditional wisdom and the authority which resides in traditional status. Rational–legal authority is based on the acceptance of a set of impersonal rules. Those who possess authority are able to issue commands and have them obeyed because others accept the legal framework which supports their authority. Thus a judge, a tax inspector or a military commander are obeyed not on the basis of tradition or as a result of their charisma but because of the acceptance of legal statutes and rules which grant them authority and define the limits of that authority. These rules are rational in the sense that they are consciously constructed for the attainment of a particular goal and they specify the means by which that goal is to be attained. As Weber's view of rational action suggests, precise calculation and systematic assessment of the various means of attaining a goal are involved in the construction of rules which form the basis of rational–legal authority.

Like other forms of authority, rational–legal authority produces a particular kind of organizational structure. This is bureaucracy which Weber defines as, 'A hierarchical organization designed rationally to coordinate the work of many individuals in the pursuit of large-scale administrative tasks and organizational goals'. Weber constructed an ideal type of the rational–legal bureaucratic organization. He argued that bureaucracies in modern industrial society are steadily moving towards this 'pure' type. The ideal type bureaucracy contains the following elements:

Firstly, 'the regular activities required for the purposes of the organization are distributed in a fixed way as official duties'. Each administrative official has a clearly defined area of responsibility. Complex tasks are broken down into manageable parts with each official specializing in a particular area. For example, state administration is divided into various departments such as education, defence and the environment. Within each department, every official has a clearly defined sphere of competence and responsibility.

Secondly, 'The organization of offices follows the principle of hierarchy; that is every lower office is under the control and supervision of a higher one'. A chain of command and responsibility is established whereby every official is accountable to his immediate superior both for the conduct of his own official duties and those of everybody below him.

Thirdly, the operations of the bureaucracy are governed by 'a consistent system of abstract rules' and the 'application of these rules to particular cases'. These rules clearly define the limits of the authority held by various officials in the hierarchy. Obedience to superiors derives from a belief in the correctness of the rules. The rules also lay down fixed procedures for the performance of each task. They impose strict discipline and control leaving little room for personal initiative or discretion.

Fourthly, the 'ideal official' performs his duties in 'a spirit of formalistic impersonality . . . without hatred or passion'. The activities of the bureaucrat are governed by the rules, not by personal considerations such as his feelings towards colleagues or clients. His actions are therefore rational rather than affective. Business is conducted 'according to *calculable rules* and "without regard for persons"'.

Fifthly, officials are appointed on the basis of technical knowledge and expertise. Weber states that, 'Bureaucratic administration means fundamentally the exercise of control on the basis of knowledge. This is the feature of it which makes it specifically rational'. Thus officials are selected in terms of the contribution their particular knowledge and skills can make to the realization of organizational goals. Once appointed, the official is a full-time paid employee and his occupation constitutes a career. Promotion is based on seniority or achievement or a combination of both.

Finally, bureaucratic administration involves a strict separation of private and official income. The official does not own any part of the organization for which he works nor can he use his position for private gain. In Weber's words, 'Bureaucracy segregates official activity as something distinct from the sphere of private life'.

The ideal type bureaucracy is only approximated in reality. Several of its characteristics are found in the state administrations of ancient Egypt, China and the later stages of the Roman Empire. The ideal type is most closely approximated in capitalist industrial society where it has become the major form of organizational control. The development of bureaucracy is due to its 'technical superiority' compared to organizations based on charismatic and traditional authority. In Weber's words, 'The decisive reason for the advance of bureaucratic organization has always been its purely technical superiority over any other form of organization'. This superiority stems from the combination of specialist skills subordinated to the goals of the organization. It derives from the exclusion of personal emotions and interests which might detract from the attainment of those goals. It results from a set of rational rules designed explicitly to further the objectives of the organization. Compared to other forms of organization, tasks in a bureaucracy are performed with greater precision and speed, with less friction and lower costs.

Although Weber appreciated the technical advantages of bureaucratic organization, he was also aware of its disadvantages. He saw the strict control of officials restricted to such specialized tasks as a limitation of human freedom. The uniform and rational procedures of bureaucratic practice largely prevent spontaneity, creativity and individual initiative. The impersonality of official conduct tends to produce 'specialists without spirit'. Weber foresaw the possibility of men trapped in their specialized routines with little awareness of the relationship between their jobs and the organization as a whole. He wrote, 'It is horrible to think that the world would one day be filled with little cogs, little men clinging to little jobs and striving towards the bigger ones'. Weber saw the danger of bureaucrats becoming preoccupied with uniformity and order, of losing sight of all else and becoming dependent on the security provided by their highly structured niche in the bureaucratic machine. He believed it is as if 'we were deliberately to become men who need "order" and nothing but order, become nervous and cowardly if for one moment this order wavers, and helpless if they are torn away from their total incorporation in it'. To Weber, the process of rationalization, of which bureaucracy is the prime expression, is basically irrational. It is ultimately aimless since it tends to destroy the traditional values which give meaning and purpose to life. To Weber, the 'great question' is 'what can we oppose to this machinery in order to keep a portion of mankind free from this parceling-out of the soul, from this supreme mastery of the bureaucratic way of life' (quoted in Nisbet, 1967, p. 299).

Despite his forebodings, Weber believed that bureaucracy was essential to the operation of large-scale industrial societies. In particular, he believed that the state and economic enterprises could not function effectively without bureaucratic control. It therefore made little sense to try and dispense with bureaucracies. However, Weber was fearful of the ends to which bureaucratic organizations could be directed. They represented the most complete and effective institutionalization of power so far created. In Weber's eyes, 'bureaucracy has been and is a power instrument of the first order – for the one who controls the bureaucratic apparatus'. Weber was particularly concerned about the control of state bureaucratic administration. He saw two main dangers if this control was left in the hands of bureaucrats themselves. Firstly, particularly in times of crisis, bureaucratic leadership would be ineffective. Bureaucrats are trained to follow orders and conduct routine operations rather than to make policy decisions and take initiatives in response to crises. Secondly, in capitalist society, top bureaucrats may be swayed by the pressure of capitalist interests and tailor their administrative practices to fit the demands of capital. Weber believed that these dangers could only be avoided by strong parliamentary control of the state bureaucracy. In particular, professional politicians must hold the top positions in the various departments of state. This will encourage strong and effective leadership since politicians are trained to take decisions. In addition it will help to open the bureaucracy to public view and reveal any behind the scenes wheeling and dealing between bureaucrats and powerful interests. Politicians are public figures, open to public scrutiny and the criticism of opposition parties. They are therefore accountable for their actions.

Even with politicians at the head of state bureaucracies, problems remain. Weber observes that, 'The political master always finds himself, vis-à-vis the trained official, in the position of a dilettante facing the expert'. The professional politician lacks the technical knowledge controlled by the bureaucracy and may have little awareness of its inner workings and procedures. He is largely dependent on information supplied to him by bureaucrats and upon their advice as to the feasibility of the measures he wishes to take. He may well end up being directed by the bureaucrats. Seymour M. Lipset shows that it is possible for government bureaucracy to exercise considerable control over its 'political masters' in his study of a socialist government in the Canadian province of Saskatchewan. The Cooperative Commonwealth Federation (CCF) came to power in 1944 with a programme of socialist reform. In order to implement this programme the CCF had to operate through the local government bureaucracy. Many top civil servants were opposed to its reforms and succeeded in either modifying or preventing them. They persuaded the new government that parts of its programme 'were not administratively feasible'. At times the bureaucrats actually reversed the directives of the politicians. A cabinet minister decided that government work should be done by government employees rather than by private concerns. Despite this the civil servants continued to give contracts to private industry. The CCF was particularly concerned to grant government aid to less wealthy farmers and provide leases for landless veterans, yet the bureaucrats continued the policy of the previous administration and supported the wealthy farmers. Although they didn't have it all their own way, some top civil servants boasted of ' "running my department completely" and of "stopping harebrained radical schemes" '. Lipset's study illustrates Weber's fears of the power of bureaucrats to act independently from their 'political masters'. Weber believed that only strong parliamentary government could control state bureaucracy. He suggested that state bureaucrats should be made directly and regularly accountable to parliament for their actions. The procedure for doing this is the parliamentary committee which would systematically cross-examine top civil servants. In Weber's view, 'This alone guarantees public supervision and a thorough inquiry'.

Weber's view of bureaucracy is ambivalent. He recognized its 'technical superiority' over all other forms of organization. He believed that it was essential for the effective operation of large-scale industrial society. While he saw it as a threat to responsible government, he believed that this threat could be countered by strong political control. However, he remained pessimistic about the consequences of bureaucracy for human freedom and happiness.

Bureaucracy – a Marxian perspective

To Weber, bureaucracy is a response to the administrative requirements of all industrial societies, whether capitalist or communist. The nature of ownership of the forces of production makes relatively little difference to the need for bureaucratic control but from a Marxian perspective, bureaucracy can only be understood in relation to the forces of production. Thus in capitalist society, where the forces of production are owned by a minority, the ruling class, state bureaucracy will inevitably represent the interests of that class. Many Marxists have seen the bureaucratic state apparatus as a specific creation of capitalist society. Its role and the reasons for its development have been outlined in Chapter 3 (pp. 104–7). Weber believed that responsible government could be achieved by strong parliamentary control of the state bureaucracy. This would prevent the interests of capital from predominating. Lenin, though, maintained that Western parliaments were 'mere talking-shops' while the 'real work of government was conducted behind closed doors by the state bureaucracy'. In his view, 'The state is an organ of class rule, an organ for the oppression of one class by another'.

Since state bureaucracy is ultimately shaped by a capitalist infrastructure, its control can only be eliminated by a radical change in that infrastructure. In terms of Marxian theory, this requires the communal ownership of the forces of production. Since state bureaucracy is basically a repressive means of control, it must be smashed and replaced by new, truly democratic institutions. Lenin believed that after the dictatorship of the proletariat was established in the USSR in 1917, there would be a steady decline in state bureaucracy. He recognized that some form of administration was necessary but looked forward to the proposals outlined by Marx and Engels. Administrators would be directly appointed and subject to recall at any time. Their wages would not exceed those of any worker. Administrative tasks would be simplified to the point where basic literacy and numeracy were sufficient for their performance. In this way, everybody would have the skills necessary to participate in the administrative process. As outlined in the previous chapter, members of a truly communist society would no longer be imprisoned in a specialized occupational role. Lenin looked forward to a future in which 'all may become "bureaucrats" for a time and that, therefore, nobody may be able to become a "bureaucrat"'. He envisaged mass participation in administration which would involve 'control and supervision by all'. In this way the repressive state bureaucracies of the West would be replaced by a truly democratic system.

Lenin offers little more than a vague and general blueprint for the future. He gives few specific details of how the democratization of state bureaucracy is to be accomplished and of how the new institutions will actually work. In practice, the 1917 revolution was not followed by the dismantling of state bureaucracy but by its expansion. Lenin puts this down to the 'immaturity of socialism', but there is no evidence that the increasing maturity of the USSR has reversed the trend of bureaucratization. In fact many observers have seen bureaucracy as the organizing principle of Soviet society. For example, Alfred Meyer argues that, 'The USSR is best understood as a large, complex bureaucracy comparable in its structure and functioning to giant corporations, armies, government agencies and similar institutions in the West'. As outlined in Chapter 2 (pp. 92–3), Milovan Djilas draws a similar picture with particular emphasis on what he sees as the exploitive nature of bureaucratic control. According to Djilas, political bureaucrats in the USSR direct the economy for their own benefit. The mass of the population is seen to have little opportunity to participate in or control the state administration. While admitting that 'bureaucratization does militate against democratic control', David Lane maintains that in the case of the USSR, 'this must not detract from the fact that a centralized administration has been a major instrument in ensuring industrialization and social change'. Lane claims that these changes have benefitted all members of society. He believes that the state bureaucracy is committed to the development of an industrial nation leading eventually to a classless society. As such it will operate in a very different way from state administrations in the West. Whatever the merits of these various viewpoints, one thing remains clear. Communal ownership of the forces of production has not resulted in the dismantling of bureaucratic structures.

Probably the most valiant attempt to remove bureaucratic control was made in China under the leadership of Mao Tse-tung. Ambrose Yeo-chi King gives the following details of the ideals and practice of administration during the 'Cultural Revolution'. While recognizing the need for some form of administrative organization, the Maoists rejected the model of bureaucracy provided by Weber's ideal type. They insisted that organizations must be controlled by and directly serve the 'masses', that is those at the base of the organizational hierarchy and the clientele of the organization. This is to be achieved not simply by the participation of the masses but by placing control of the organization directly in their hands.

The ideal organization is pictured as follows. The rigid hierarchy of officials will be abolished. Hierarchies are seen to block communication, to encourage 'buck passing' and to stifle the creative energies and initiative of the masses. Leaders will remain but they will lead rather than command. The specialized division of labour and the fragmentation of tasks are rejected in favour of a system whereby everyone should 'take care of everything' within the organization. The expert will become a figure of the past since his technical knowledge and expertise will be spread amongst the masses. The full-time professional administrator will disappear. All administrative leaders must spend some of their time involved in actual production in the fields and factories. Finally, the fixed rules and regulations which characterize the typical bureaucracy are seen as instruments to repress the masses. They should therefore be changed as the masses see fit. Yeo-chi King notes that these ideals were put into practice in the following ways. Firstly by means of the 'role-shifting system' whereby leaders moved to the base of the organization. In theory, this would allow them to empathize with the masses and minimize, if not eliminate, status differences. Secondly, by means of 'group-based decision-making systems', where for example, workers directly participate in the various decisions required for running a factory.

While applauding the spirit of these measures, Yeo-chi King has serious doubts about their practicality. At best he believes they have 'a high tendency towards organizational instability'. He sees them offering little hope for the economic modernization of China on which the Maoists placed such emphasis. With China's more recent moves towards the West, it appears that the organizations by which 'the Masses take command' have been put to one side. Yeo-chi King suggests that 'Mao's intervention was a kind of charismatic breakthrough from the bureaucratic routinization'. If Weber is correct and charismatic authority is rapidly routinized into traditional or rational–legal authority structures, then the organizational experiments of the Cultural Revolution were necessarily shortlived.

Robert Michels – bureaucracy and democracy

Marxist hopes for truly democratic organizations are dismissed as mere illusions by the Italian sociologist Robert Michels (1876–1936). *Political Parties*, first published in 1911, is a study of European socialist parties and trade unions with particular emphasis on the German Socialist Party. These organizations were committed to the overthrow of the capitalist state and the creation of a socialist society. They claimed to be organized on democratic principles, directly representing the interests and wishes of their members. Michels claims that these ideals bore little resemblance to what actually happened.

Michels begins his analysis with the observation that, 'Democracy is inconceivable without organization'. In a large complex society, the only way individuals can effectively voice their wishes and press their interests is by joining together and forming an organization. This is particularly true of the relatively powerless working-class masses for whom combination and cooperation are essential. However, organization sounds the death knell of democracy. Direct participation by large numbers of people in the running of an organization is in practice impossible. Apart from the practical difficulties of assembling thousands of people, direct involvement in decision making would be so cumbersome and time consuming that nothing would get done. Since 'direct' democracy is impracticable, it can only be replaced by some form of representative system whereby 'delegates represent the mass and carry out its will'. Yet Michels maintains that even this truncated form of democracy founders in practice.

Once a system of representative democracy is established in trade unions and political parties, it results in the appointment of full-time officials and professional politicians. The administrative tasks involved inevitably lead to the creation of a bureaucracy which by its very nature is undemocratic. The effective operation of the organization requires a specialized division of labour which necessitates control and coordination from the top. The result is a 'rigorously defined and hierarchical bureaucracy'. As the organization grows and administrative duties proliferate, 'it is no longer possible to take them in at a glance'. They become increasingly incomprehensible to those without specialist knowledge and training. Faced with this complexity, rank and file members of trade unions and political parties tend to leave matters to their leaders. Decisions are increasingly taken by executive committees within the bureaucracy rather than by assemblies of the rank and file. Thus the very organization which was created to represent its members ends up by largely excluding them from participation and decision making. In Michels's words, 'The oligarchical structure of the building suffocates the basic democratic principle'. He maintains that organizations inevitably produce oligarchy, that is rule by a small elite. This is the 'iron law of oligarchy'.

Once established, bureaucracy brings with it all the deficiencies which Michels believes are an integral part of such organizations. Dependent on the orders and direction of superiors, the initiative of subordinates is crushed. Individuality is suppressed as bureaucrats slavishly follow official procedures and regulations. There is a 'mania for promotion'. With advancement dependent on the judgment of higher authority, subordinates bow and scrape to their superiors while adopting an arrogant stance to those beneath them in the hierarchy. In Michels's eyes, 'Bureaucracy is the sworn enemy of individual liberty, and of all bold initiative in matters of internal policy'. It is 'petty, narrow, rigid and illiberal'.

Even accepting these deficiencies and the oligarchical nature of bureaucratic structures, may not the interests of the rank and file still find representation? Again Michels is pessimistic. He argues that once the leadership is established at the top of the bureaucratic pyramid, its primary concern is the maintenance of its own power. Leaders wish to retain the privileges and status which their position brings, a concern which takes priority over the stated goals of the organization. This involves a 'displacement of goals' whereby preservation of the organization becomes an end in itself rather than a means to an end. The organization will become increasingly conservative as leaders refrain from taking any action which might endanger their position. This is particularly apparent in the case of the German Socialist Party. Its commitment to the overthrow of the capitalist state was steadily pushed into the background. Its leaders joined the existing ruling elite forming a part of the political power structure. Forceful pursuit of the party's original goals might have resulted in its destruction and with it the leadership's loss of power.

Leaders are able to maintain power for a variety of reasons. They learn the skills of the political game which they play to their own advantage. Such skills include, 'the art of controlling meetings, of applying and interpreting rules, of proposing motions at opportune moments'. Entrenched at the top of a bureaucratic hierarchy, they have the power to control communication to the rank and file. For example, their control over the publications of the party or union enables them to put across their own viewpoint. Leaders have considerable say in the appointment of officials in the organization and can therefore select those who support their policies. Like the early elite theorists, with whom he is usually bracketed, Michels believes that the masses have a psychological need to be led. This is accompanied by a veneration of leaders who often become cult figures. The experience of power tends to make leaders see themselves in a similar light. They come to believe in their own greatness to the point where some take the view that 'Le parti c'est Moi'. Thus leaders see their own interests and the maintenance of the organization as indistinguishable.

The failure of democracy on the organizational level means that it cannot hope to succeed on the societal level. Society is ruled by an elite which consists of the leaders of various organizations and parties. The overriding concern of the ruling elite is the maintenance of its own power. This applies both to capitalist and communist societies. Michels predicted that a proletarian revolution and the establishment of a socialist society would result in 'a dictatorship in the hands of those leaders who have been sufficiently astute and sufficiently powerful to grasp the sceptre of dominion in the name of – socialism'. (Michels belongs within the tradition of classical elite theory. For details of this theory see Chapter 3, pp. 107–9.)

Michels believed that organization was essential to democracy. However, as a matter of 'technical and practical necessity', organizations adopt a bureaucratic structure. This inevitably produces oligarchical control which brings an end to democracy. Michels concludes that, 'It is organization which gives birth to the dominion of the elected over the electors, of the mandatories over the mandators, of the delegates over the delegators. Who says organization, says oligarchy'.

Union Democracy – Lipset, Trow and Coleman

Michels made sweeping generalizations based on an examination of particular cases. He asserted that organizations inevitably result in the exclusion of the majority from participation in decision making and in domination by a self-interested oligarchy. In a famous study entitled *Union Democracy*, Lipset, Trow and Coleman examine the organizational structure of the International Typographical Union (ITU), which they claim provides an exception to the iron law of oligarchy. The ITU, a craft printers' union, is unique among American unions in that it contains two parties. This system provides a constant check on the party in power and serves to generate alternative policies to those of the existing leadership. National and local officials are elected twice a year by the membership. A change in leadership often results in a real change of policy. For example, one administration supported arbitration with employers but was replaced by the more militant opposition which argued that union demands should be enforced by strike action. Frequent elections and a two party system means that the rank and file can actually determine union policy. In addition, many decisions such as basic changes in union regulations and increases in officials' salaries are put to a referendum. More often than not, the proposals of the leadership are defeated. Decisions on whether or not to hold a referendum are not monopolized by the leadership. A method exists whereby referenda can be initiated by the rank and file.

For these reasons, Lipset, Trow and Coleman claim that the ITU is a democratic organization. There is a high degree of participation by the rank and file who have the power to effect real changes in union policy and to control the activities of their leaders. However, the ITU is a unique case. Only a combination of exceptional factors has produced its particular organizational structure. Those factors include the following: printers have a strong identification with their craft which encourages direct participation in union affairs; they tend to form occupational communities and organize a variety of social clubs for members of the craft; from the experience of organizing and running such clubs, many printers learn the political skills necessary for participation in union politics. In addition, social clubs provide union activists with the opportunity to encourage the more apathetic to become involved in union activities. The ITU was formed in 1850 by an amalgamation of local unions. A history of local autonomy led to a resistance to centralized control. Even before the formation of the ITU, something akin to a two party system existed in the local unions. The borderline position of printers between the middle and working class tended to produce moderate and radical factions and therefore a basis for the two party system. Demand for control of union leadership was due partly to the history of secret societies in the printing trade. These societies attempted to control appointments to union offices and foremen's jobs and were distrusted and opposed by non-members. Finally, the income of the rank and file and union leaders was fairly similar and therefore a return to the shop floor did not mean a sharp drop in income for union officials. As a result they would not be motivated to cling to power 'at any cost'.

Lipset, Trow and Coleman argue that the combination of the above factors has led to democracy in the ITU. However, they are pessimistic about the potential for democracy in organizations in general. They argue that large-scale organization requires a bureaucratic structure. This makes democracy unlikely since those at the top have 'control over financial resources and internal communications, a large permanently organized political machine, a claim to legitimacy, and a near monopoly over political skills'. The circumstances which created a strong demand for participation by members of the ITU are exceptional. The average trade union member is not particularly involved in his job and largely preoccupied with home, family and leisure. He will be unlikely to demand participation in union affairs which will tend to produce oligarchical rule. Where leadership positions in organizations carry higher status and income than the rank and file, the leader will be encouraged to 'institutionalize dictatorial mechanisms which will reduce the possibility that he may lose his office'. Given these factors, Lipset, Trow and Coleman admit that the implications of their analysis 'for democratic organizational politics are almost as pessimistic as those postulated by Robert Michels'.

From another viewpoint, an organization can be seen as democratic if it represents the interests of its members. From this perspective it doesn't particularly matter if an oligarchy controls a union as long as the rank and file are effectively represented. It is possible to present a wide range of evidence to support the view that many unions successfully represent their members. Wage rises, improved fringe benefits and working conditions and limitations on the power of employers can be seen as the result of union pressure. However, Lipset, Trow and Coleman have reservations about the effectiveness of representative democracy. They note how top union officials have steadily increased their salaries to the point where they are well above those of the rank and file. They argue that many union leaders adopt policies to further their own political ambitions. For example, they claim that, 'Communist-led unions have on occasion engaged in prolonged strikes which were unjustifiable by any collective-bargaining criteria'. They show how difficult it can be for groups within a union to take action which is disapproved of by the leadership. For example, a minority group within the United Textile Workers attempted to join another union but found it was prevented from transferring its welfare funds. Finally, it is difficult to see how an organization can be representative when 'control over the organizational machinery enables the officialdom of a union to define the choices available to the organization and its members'. Because of this members have little chance of discovering for themselves what courses of action are possible. Lipset, Trow and Coleman conclude that without internal democracy, members of unions and organizations in general are largely forced to put their faith in the leadership. Representative democracy may result but so might a self-interested oligarchy which pursues policies contrary to the interests of the membership. Lipset, Trow and Coleman maintain that members' interests would be more likely to be represented if internal democracy along the lines of the ITU were built into the organizational structure of trade unions.

Philip Selznick – the Tennessee Valley Authority

A somewhat different perspective on the question of democracy and organization is provided by Philip Selznick's famous study of the Tennessee Valley Authority (TVA). Like Michels, he studied an organization which claimed to be democratic and showed how this claim was frustrated in practice. Selznick adopts a functionalist approach arguing that organizations have basic needs, the most fundamental of which is the need for survival. Such needs place severe constraints on the behaviour of members of the organization. In particular, if the goal of democracy threatens the existence of the organization, that goal will be likely to be displaced in order to ensure the organization's survival. In Selznick's words, 'ideals go quickly by the board when the compelling realities of organizational life are permitted to run their natural course'.

The TVA was a government agency created in 1933 to plan and direct the development of the Tennessee River Valley area which covered seven southern states in the USA. It formed part of President Roosevelt's 'New Deal' policy which aimed to combat poverty and lift America out of the Depression. Roosevelt stated that the TVA 'should be charged with the broadest duty of planning for the proper use, conservation, and development of the natural resources of the Tennessee River drainage basin and its adjoining territory for the general social and economic welfare of the nation'. In particular, it was concerned with the construction of dams, flood control, the generation of hydroelectricity, the production and distribution of chemical fertilizer, forestry and improvements in farming and land use in general. The TVA was to develop the region with the aim of directly benefitting all the people living there and ultimately the nation as a whole.

Popular welfare was coupled with the idea of popular participation. The TVA's 'grass roots' policy stated that local people should enter into a partnership with the organization for the development of their region. In pursuit of this end the authority would administer its programme through existing institutions in the area. Local interests would be represented on the policy making bodies of the TVA and in this way people in the

Tennessee Valley would participate in decisions affecting their future. The TVA looked forward to 'a democratic partnership with the people's institutions'.

Selznick argues that the reality of the TVA's administration was very different from its democratic ideals. Most of his research is concerned with the authority's agricultural programme directed by its Agricultural Relations Department. In line with the grass roots policy, the TVA operated through local institutions. It linked up with the land-grant colleges – agricultural colleges established in the previous century by grants of land from the government. Representatives of the colleges were appointed to the Agricultural Relations Department which decided on matters of policy. The agricultural programme was administered through the colleges' extension services run by agents in each of the counties in the states. However, the land-grant colleges were closely tied to the interests of the wealthier farmers. The county agents had little or nothing to do with the impoverished, mainly Black, tenant farmers. The services they offered – advice on new agricultural developments and marketing – were monopolized by the wealthier White farmers. In addition, the land-grant colleges had strong links with the American Farm Bureau Federation, a national association which represented the wealthier farming interests. The county agents recruited members for the Federation and in return, the Federation lobbied at national level in support of the land-grant colleges.

By appointing representatives of the land-grant colleges to its policy making body and administering its agricultural programme through the county agents, the TVA supported the dominant farming interests in the area. This can be seen from the following examples. Part of the agricultural programme was concerned with testing fertilizers and demonstrating their uses to local farmers. The farmers paid the freight charges on the fertilizer and used it as directed. Since freight charges amounted to only a fraction of the fertilizer's value there was no shortage of volunteers for the programme. Participants were selected by the county agents. Following their usual procedures, they chose only the wealthier farmers who thus obtained large supplies of cheap fertilizer and the benefit of TVA expertise regarding its use. As part of its power programme, the TVA built a series of dams along the Tennessee River and its tributaries. This created reservoirs and the authority originally planned to develop the land surrounding them for public recreation. However, the Agricultural Relations Department, 'speaking for the local landowners', strongly opposed this policy. The building of reservoirs enriches the surrounding land and local landowners were therefore anxious to retain control over it. Under pressure from the Agricultural Relations Department, the TVA changed its policy and allowed the land to remain under private ownership. Thus the public, whose funds had paid for the reservoirs, failed to benefit either from the projected recreational areas or the increases in land values.

With these and other examples, Selznick argues that the TVA, far from representing the interests of the public, ended up serving 'the established farm leadership'. By working through the larger and more powerful local interest groups and institutions, it merely reinforced the existing power structure. Selznick argues that the democratic ideals of the TVA failed to materialize for the following reasons. The primary need of any organization is survival. Much of the behaviour of members of an organization can be understood in terms of this requirement. In order to maintain itself, the TVA had to adapt to its environment. In practice, this meant it was forced to compromise its democratic ideals in order to secure the cooperation of the local power structure without which it could not operate. In Selznick's view, the TVA had to adapt itself 'not so much to the people in general as to the actually existing institutions which have the power to smooth or block its way'. By appointing representatives of the dominant farming interests to its policy making body and by delegating the administration of its agricultural programme to those same interests, the TVA averted a major threat to its survival. In doing so, however, it lost all claims to be democratic.

Selznick's research suggests that as long as there are major power differentials within the clientele of an organization – in this case the people of the Tennessee Valley – popular representation and participation in the decisions of the organization will not be possible. Since, in order to survive, an organization must cooperate with powerful interests, it will tend to represent them. While admitting that his conclusions are pessimistic, Selznick does not suggest that the democratic ideal is not worth striving for. He argues that 'it does not follow that we should fail to treasure what is precarious or cease to strive for what is nobly conceived'. Selznick's conclusions are based in part on the priority he gives to an organization's 'need' to survive. Thus despite the fact that the TVA leadership was 'honest', 'morally strong' and committed to the ideals of democracy, its actions were constrained by the organization's survival needs. Selznick's view will be criticized later in the chapter (pp. 309–10).

This section concludes the examination of three of the 'classical' theorists on organizations, Weber, Lenin and Michels, and of aspects of research directly related to the more general questions they raised. The classical theorists were concerned with fundamental issues such as liberty and democracy and set their analysis of organizations in the context of society as a whole and within a broad framework of historical change. Often their analysis lacks precision and their generalizations are sweeping. More recent research on organizations tends to lose sight of the 'big questions' with which they were preoccupied. Many of the issues raised by the classical theorists will be returned to at the close of the chapter.

The debate with Weber

Much of the later research on organizations can be seen as a debate with Weber. Students of organizations have refined, elaborated and criticized his views. In particular they have questioned the proposition that a bureaucracy organized on the lines of Weber's ideal type is the most efficient way of realizing organizational goals. It has often been argued that certain aspects of the ideal type bureaucracy may, in practice, reduce organizational efficiency. Whether such a criticism is justified depends on how Weber's ideal type is interpreted. Weber used the ideal type as a model to compare three forms of authority and the organizational structures which develop from them. Compared to organizations based on traditional and charismatic authority, Weber was clear that the rational–legal bureaucracy is 'technically superior'. But whether or not Weber believed that an organization structured on the lines of his ideal type bureaucracy would, in practice, maximize efficiency is not entirely clear. Certainly he would regard it as the most rational form of organization but does this mean he saw it as the most efficient way of realizing organizational goals?

Many sociologists maintain that Weber argued that rationality equals efficiency. Thus, the more closely an actual organization approximates the ideal type, the more efficient it would be. Peter Blau adopts this interpretation claiming that Weber saw bureaucracy as 'an organization that maximizes efficiency in administration'. However, some sociologists have argued that Weber did not mean that the ideal type bureaucracy, if translated into reality, would be the most efficient form of administration. For example, Martin Albrow argues that Weber saw rational bureaucratic procedures as the most effective means of measuring efficiency, not necessarily of ensuring it. Thus strict bureaucratic procedures allow the amount of money, time and energy expended to realize organizational goals to be calculated. They therefore provide a means of measuring the efficiency of an organization and this is what makes them rational. In and of themselves they do not guarantee efficiency.

Whether or not the criticisms of Weber that follow are justified depend in part on the way his work is interpreted. Certainly there are grounds for arguing that Weber equated rational bureaucratic procedures with efficiency. As Dennis Warwick notes, 'The language which Weber uses in his discussion of bureaucracy fairly glows with notions of the high achievement of this form of administration'.

Robert K. Merton – the dysfunctions of bureaucracy

In an article entitled, *Bureaucratic Structure and Personality*, Robert K. Merton argues that certain aspects of bureaucratic procedure may be dysfunctional to the organization. In particular, they may encourage behaviour which inhibits the realization of organizational goals. Firstly, the bureaucrat is trained to comply strictly with the rules but when situations arise which are not covered by the rules, this training may lead to inflexibility and timidity. The bureaucrat has not been taught to improvise and innovate and in addition, he may well be afraid to do so. His career incentives such as promotion are designed to reward 'disciplined action and conformity to official regulations'. Thus it may not be in his interests to bend the rules even when such action might further the realization of organizational goals. Secondly, the devotion to the rules encouraged in bureaucratic organizations, may lead to a displacement of goals. There is a tendency for conformity to official regulations to become an end in itself rather than a means to an end. The bureaucrat may lose sight of the goals of the organization and therefore reduce its effectiveness. In this way, so-called bureaucratic 'red-tape' may stand in the way of providing an efficient service for the clients of the organization. Thirdly, the emphasis on impersonality in bureaucratic procedures may lead to friction between officials and the public. For example, clients in a job centre or a maternity clinic may expect concern and sympathy for their particular problems. The businesslike and impartial treatment they might receive can lead to bureaucrats being seen as cold, unsympathetic, abrupt and even arrogant. As a result, clients sometimes feel that they have been badly served by bureaucracies.

While agreeing that the various elements of bureaucracy outlined in Weber's ideal type serve to further organizational efficiency, Merton maintains that they inevitably produce dysfunctional consequences. He suggests that 'the very elements which conduce towards efficiency in general produce inefficiency in specific instances'.

Peter Blau – formal and informal structure

Weber has often been criticized for focussing exclusively on the formal structure of bureaucracy, that is the official rules and procedures, the authorized hierarchy of offices and the official duties attached to them. His critics have argued that unofficial practices are an established part of the structure of all organizations. They must therefore be included in an explanation of the functioning of organizations. Peter Blau claims that Weber's approach 'implies that any deviation from the formal structure is detrimental to administrative efficiency'. However, on the basis of the results of his own work and other research, Blau maintains that there is 'considerable evidence that suggests the opposite conclusion'. This view can be illustrated from Blau's study of a federal law enforcement agency.

This study was based on observation of the behaviour of agents working in one of nine district agencies of a federal bureau based in Washington DC. The agents were employed to inspect businesses to determine whether laws dealing with standards of employment had been broken. Roughly half their time was spent 'in the field', auditing company books and interviewing employers and employees. The rest of their time was spent at the agency office processing the various cases. The laws involved were extremely detailed and it was often difficult to determine exactly how they applied to particular cases. The official rules stated that any difficulties which arose must be taken to the supervisor. Agents were not allowed to discuss cases with their colleagues since the records of the firms were strictly confidential but they were often reluctant to consult the supervisor since their promotion prospects were largely dependent on his evaluation of their work. Frequent consultation might well indicate incompetence. Agents therefore sought advice and guidance from each other. They discussed cases with their colleagues in direct violation of the official rules.

Blau claims that this unofficial practice served to increase the agents' efficiency. Information and experience were pooled and problem solving facilitated. Knowledge of the complex regulations was widened and the various ways in which the law could be interpreted were shared. Considerable time was saved since rather than searching through a thousand-page manual of regulations and two shelves of books on court cases, agents simply asked each other about a regulation or a reference. Blau argues that assistance and consultation transformed the agents from a collection of individuals into a cohesive working group. As a result anxiety over decision making, for example whether or not to prosecute a company, was reduced since agents knew they could rely on their colleagues' advice and experience. The case of the federal agents provides an example to illustrate Blau's argument that, 'Paradoxically, unofficial practices that are explicitly prohibited by official regulations sometimes further the achievement of organizational objectives'.

In all organizations, groups of workers form and establish their own norms of work practice. These 'informal groups' and the norms they develop are an integral part of the structure of organizations. One interpretation of Weber's model of bureaucracy argues that the most efficient form of administration involves explicit procedures for the performance of every task. If these procedures are strictly followed and supervised and coordinated by management, then efficiency will be maximized. However, Blau argues that no system of official rules and supervision can anticipate all the problems which may arise in an organization. Efficiency can only be maximized by the development of informal work norms by groups of workers and such norms can also have the effect of reducing organizational efficiency. These points are illustrated by Blau's study of interviewers working in an American employment agency.

The goal of the agency was to place applicants in suitable jobs. The performance of the interviewers was evaluated on the basis of the number of interviews they conducted. After World War II, jobs became increasingly scarce and the interviewers tended to dismiss clients for whom jobs could not be quickly found. In order to increase the efficiency of the agency, a new procedure was introduced. Interviewers were now evaluated in terms of the number of applicants they actually placed in jobs. This change had unanticipated consequences. Interviewers competed for the 'job slips' on which details of job openings were recorded, and even hid them from one another. This tended to result in clients being placed in jobs which were not suited to their training and experience. If interviewers were aware of the full range of available jobs, they would be better able to match jobs and applicants.

Within the employment agency there were two groups of interviewers, Section A and Section B. Interviewers in Section A hoarded job slips and competed with each other. Those in Section B developed cooperative rather than competitive work norms and shared their job slips. Their productivity was higher than that of Section A – they filled a larger proportion of the job openings they received. Blau explains these differences in work practices and productivity in the following way. Most of the interviewers in Section A were appointed on a temporary basis and this produced insecurity. In order to gain a permanent position, they were anxious to impress their superiors. In addition, their supervisor laid great stress on performance records. Those in Section B had permanent appointments and their supervisor did not base his evaluation primarily on productivity. Also members of Section B had shared a similar training programme which emphasized concern for the client and intensive counselling. From this they developed a 'common professional code' in terms of which competition for job slips was rejected on moral grounds. Members of Section A had not shared a similar training programme and this tended to prevent a common code from developing. Because of the above factors, Section B established cooperative norms and a cohesive group developed whereas Section A remained competitive and fragmented. With reference to the goals of the organization, Section B was more efficient.

Blau's study of interviewers in an employment agency indicates that official rules and procedures cannot, in and of themselves, maximize efficiency. No set of rules can anticipate all the problems which arise in a bureaucracy. To some degree such problems will be handled in terms of the informal norms of groups of workers. Variations in these norms will result in differing levels of efficiency. Blau's study of federal agents indicates that, in certain circumstances, contrary to the implications of Weber's argument, breaking official rules can increase organizational efficiency. In general, Blau's research shows the importance of studying the informal structure of organizations. It supports his view that, 'A bureaucracy in operation appears quite different from the abstract portrayal of its formal structure'. Although formal and informal structures can be separated for purposes of analysis, in practice they form a single structure. The subject of informal groups and norms will be returned to later in the chapter.

Alvin W. Gouldner – degrees of bureaucratization

Weber presented an ideal type bureaucracy and argued that organizations in modern industrial society were increasingly moving towards that model. However, he had little to say about why actual organizations varied in terms of their approximation of the ideal type apart from suggesting that bureaucracy was particularly suited to the administration of routine tasks. Alvin W. Gouldner's study of a gypsum plant in the USA seeks to explore this problem. It is concerned to 'clarify some of the social processes leading to different degrees of bureaucratization'.

The plant consisted of two parts, a gypsum mine and a factory making wallboards for which gypsum is a major ingredient. There was a significant difference in the degree of bureaucratization between the mine and the factory. In the mine the hierarchy of authority was less developed, the division of labour and spheres of competence were less explicit, there was less emphasis on official rules and procedures and less impersonality both in relationships between workers and between them and the supervisors. Since, in Gouldner's view, these elements are 'the stuff of which bureaucracy is made', then 'bureaucratic organization was more fully developed on the surface than in the mine'. The following examples illustrate this point. In the mine supervisors usually issued only general instructions leaving it to the miners to decide who was to do the job and how it was to be done. If a miner wanted assistance, he rarely went through the 'proper channels' to obtain orders to direct others to assist him. He simply asked his workmates for help. Official duties were not clearly defined. Miners rotated jobs amongst themselves and often repaired machinery, a job which in the factory was the clear prerogative of the maintenance engineer. Lunch hours were irregular, varying in length and the time at which they were taken. Supervisors accepted and worked within this informal organization. They were 'one of the lads' and placed little emphasis on their officially superior status. One miner summarized the situation as follows, 'Down here we have no rules. We are our own bosses'. By comparison, the factory was considerably more bureaucratic. The hierarchy of authority, the division of labour, official rules and procedures and impersonality were more widespread and developed.

Gouldner gives the following reasons for the difference in degrees of bureaucratization between mine and surface. Work in the mine was less predictable. The miners had no control over the amount of gypsum available and could not predict various dangers such as cave-ins. No amount of official procedures could control such factors. Miners often had to make their own decisions on matters which could not be strictly governed by official rules, for example, strategies for digging out the gypsum and propping up the roof. Since the problems they encountered did not follow a standard pattern, a predetermined set of rules was not suitable for their solution. By comparison, the machine production of wallboard in the factory followed a standard routine and could therefore be 'rationalized' in terms of a bureaucratic system. Fixed rules and a clearly defined division of labour are more suited to predictable operations. The ever present danger in the mine produced strong work group solidarity which in turn encouraged informal organization. Miners depended on their workmates to warn them of loose rocks and to dig them out in the event of a cave-in. In the words of one old miner, 'Friends or no friends, you *got* all to be friends'. A cohesive work group will tend to resist control from above and to institute its own informal work norms.

Part of Gouldner's study is concerned with the arrival of a new manager at the gypsum plant. He came with instructions from head office to cut costs and raise productivity. From the start he attempted to abolish unofficial practices, insisted on the rigorous application of formal rules and instituted a set of new rules which severely limited the workers' autonomy – for example they were not allowed to move round the factory at will. Rule breaking was to be reported to the appropriate authorities, official reports of the details were to be passed up the administrative hierarchy and punishments were to be strictly imposed in accordance with the rules. The new manager thus attempted to increase the degree of bureaucratization in the plant. Gouldner argues that management will tend to do this when it believes that workers are not fulfilling their work roles. The degree to which it achieves this will depend on the 'degree of bureaucratic *striving* on management's part' and the 'degree of resistance to bureaucratic administration among the workers'.

Despite the forceful attempts of the new manager to impose a strongly bureaucratic system, it was effectively opposed by the miners. Gouldner attributes their success to strong work group solidarity. They were able to present a united front to management and frustrate many of its demands. In addition, the miners' immediate supervisors, who worked with them underground, were also opposed to the new system. They believed that the miners should be exempt from certain rules and that this privilege was justified by the dangers of the job.

A number of tentative conclusions may be drawn from Gouldner's study. Firstly, bureaucratic administration is more suited to some tasks than others. In particular, it is not well suited to non-routine, unpredictable operations. Secondly, the advance of bureaucracy is not inevitable as Weber and others have implied. As the case of the gypsum miners indicates, it can be successfully resisted. Thirdly, Gouldner suggests that sociologists who are concerned with a utopian vision which involves the abolition of bureaucracy would be more fruitfully employed in identifying 'those social processes creating variations in the amount and types of bureaucracy. For these variations do make a vital difference in the lives of men'. By directing their research to this area, sociologists may be able to give direction to those who wish to create organizations with greater democracy and freedom.

Tom Burns and G. M. Stalker – mechanistic and organic systems

Gouldner's conclusions are supported by the findings of research by Burns and Stalker. From a study of twenty Scottish and English firms, mainly in the electronics industry, Burns and Stalker argue that bureaucratic organizations are best suited to dealing with predictable, familiar and routine situations. They are not well suited to the rapidly changing technical and commercial situation of many sectors of modern industry such as the electronics industry. Since change is the hallmark of modern society, bureaucratic organizations may well be untypical of the future.

Burns and Stalker construct two ideal types of organization which they term 'mechanistic' and 'organic'. The firms in their research range between these extremes. The mechanistic organization is very similar to Weber's model of bureaucracy. It includes a specialized division of labour with the rights and duties of each employee being precisely defined. Specialized tasks are coordinated by a management hierarchy which directs operations and takes major decisions. Communication is mainly vertical: instructions flow downward through a chain of command, information flows upward and is processed by various levels in the hierarchy before it reaches the top. Each individual in the organization is responsible for discharging his particular responsibility and no more. He 'pursues his task as something distinct from the real tasks of the concern as a whole, as if it were the subject of a sub-contract. "Somebody at the top" is responsible for seeing to its relevance'.

By comparison, areas of responsibility are not clearly defined in organic organizations. The rigid hierarchies and specialized divisions of labour of mechanistic systems tend to disappear. The individual's job is to employ his skills to further the goals of the organization rather than simply carry out a predetermined operation. When a problem arises, all those who have knowledge and expertise to contribute to its solution meet and discuss. Tasks are shaped by the nature of the problem rather than being predefined. Communication consists of consultation rather than command, of 'information and advice rather than instructions and decisions'. Although a hierarchy exists, it tends to become blurred as communication travels in all directions and top management no longer has the sole prerogative over important decisions nor is it seen to monopolize the knowledge necessary to make them.

Burns and Stalker argue that mechanistic systems are best suited to stable conditions, organic systems to changing conditions. In the manufacturing industry, stable conditions exist when demand for a product is relatively constant, when the product is standardized and when there is a low level of innovation in its manufacture and development. In such a situation, tasks are fairly routine and therefore suited to the fixed procedures, specialized division of labour and hierarchical structure of mechanistic systems. Unstable conditions exist when there are rapid changes in the market (for example the loss of old customers and a demand for new and different products); when there are changes in knowledge and technology (for example new scientific discoveries which affect the product and innovations in manufacturing processes); and when the product is not standardized (for example customers demanding an order to fit their specific requirements). Burns and Stalker claim that organic systems are best suited to this type of situation. They are flexible and fluid and can therefore adapt more readily to changing conditions. They allow the pooling of information and knowledge and the formation of various combinations of skills and expertise. As a result, 'the limits of feasible action are set more widely'. When novel and unfamiliar problems arise, an organic system can rapidly mobilize its resources to solve them. In the absence of a clear-cut division of labour and a rigid system of vertical communication, everybody with something to contribute joins in the task at hand. With each individual concerned primarily with furthering organizational goals rather than with a limited area of responsibility, there is an emphasis on cooperating to see the job through. Thus operatives, foremen, draughtsmen, design engineers, product engineers, scientists in the laboratory and works managers discuss policy, share information and technical knowledge and generally contribute to the solution of problems.

Despite the fact that the electronics firms in Burns and Stalker's study were faced with unstable conditions, only some of them had adopted an organic system. Several clung tenaciously to the mechanistic system making only minor changes to meet new and unfamiliar situations. This was in spite of the fact that the existing system was 'clearly inefficient and ineffective' in terms of the stated goals of the organization. However, Burns and Stalker note that the mechanistic system can effectively serve other ends and this, they suggest, is the reason for its retention. They argue that within any organization, individuals and groups have their own goals which are often in conflict with those of others and which may diverge from the stated goals of the organization. From this perspective, Burns and Stalker suggest the following reasons for resistance to an organic system. Firstly, the organic system demands a greater commitment by members of the organization. The individual must become involved in many areas, learn new skills and deal with matters beyond his specialized knowledge. He loses the security of a clearly defined area of competence and responsibility. Burns and Stalker suggest that some individuals resist the change to organic systems because they refuse to make further 'commitments in their occupational existence at the expense of the rest of their lives'. Thus several top managers clung to mechanistic systems because they 'provided protection against the involvements the new order demanded of them'.

Organizations are institutions in which members compete for status and power. They compete for the resources of the organization, for example finance to expand their own departments, for career advancement and for power to control the activities of others. In pursuit of these aims, groups are formed and sectional interests emerge. As a result, policy decisions may serve 'the ends of the political and career systems rather than those of the concern'. In this way the goals of the organization may be displaced in favour of sectional interests and individual ambition. Burns and Stalker suggest that these preoccupations sometimes prevent the emergence of organic systems. Many of the electronics firms in their study had recently created research and development departments employing highly qualified and well paid scientists and technicians. Their high pay and expert knowledge were sometimes seen as a threat to the established order of rank, power and privilege. Many senior managers had little knowledge of the technicalities and possibilities of new developments in electronics. Some felt that close cooperation with the experts in an organic system would reveal their ignorance and show that their experience was now redundant. They feared that they would lose authority and their autonomy in decision making would be reduced. Some reacted by separating the new departments as far as possible physically and administratively from the existing organization. As a result, the research teams were concerned only with the earliest stages of development. Efficiency was impaired since close cooperation between the various departments was essential to further the overall goals of the organization. For example, the research department might develop a product which, for technical reasons, was impossible to manufacture. Cooperation with the production department could well prevent this. In the same way, ongoing communication with the marketing department would be more likely to produce a commodity which would be successful in the market. An organic system would meet these requirements but was often prevented from developing by the internal politics of the organization.

Several important points emerge from Burns and Stalker's research. Firstly, there is no one ideal form of organization which will maximize efficiency in every situation. Mechanistic systems are more suited to stable conditions, organic systems to changing conditions. Secondly, it is difficult to define organizations in terms of their goals since within an organization are individuals and groups pursuing goals which may diverge from those of the organization. In certain instances, the organization may serve individual and group interests rather than its stated goals. Thirdly, organizations do not 'naturally' evolve into forms which can most effectively realize organizational goals. The form they take is also subject to the internal politics of the organization, to private goals and sectional interests.

Professionals and organizations

Burns and Stalker's research reveals some of the problems that can arise with the employment of professional experts in organizations. A number of studies have been directly concerned with this question. They have often taken Weber as their starting point and criticized his view of the relationship between bureaucratic authority and expert knowledge. Weber argued that, 'Bureaucratic administration means fundamentally the exercise of control on the basis of knowledge'. He saw the combination of authority and expertise as the feature of bureaucracies which made them specifically rational. His model implies that there is a match between an individual's position in the hierarchy and his level of technical expertise. Weber saw this aspect of bureaucratic authority as increasingly important arguing that, 'The role of technical qualifications in bureaucratic organizations is continually increasing'. Trends in the employment of professionals lend support to this observation. Growing numbers of professionals – scientists, engineers, accountants, lawyers, doctors – are working in organizational settings.

However, Weber has been criticized for failing to distinguish between bureaucratic and professional authority. Bureaucratic authority is based on tenure of an office in a bureaucratic hierarchy. The official is obeyed, first and foremost, because of the position he holds. Professional authority is based on knowledge and expertise. The professional commands obedience because of this specialist knowledge rather than his position in a bureaucratic hierarchy. There is therefore a basic difference between these two forms of authority. This section is concerned with the conflicts that can arise from this difference when professionals are employed in organizations.

In many organizations the most highly qualified members are found in the middle rather than the highest levels of the hierarchy. As Burns and Stalker's research indicates, the ranking of experts below non-experts can lead to conflict. The increasing pace of technical innovation in electronics means that experts have a growing part to play in the industry. However, this can undermine the legitimacy of senior management whose authority is based ultimately on the position they occupy in the hierarchy rather than technical expertise. Often they lack the specialist knowledge to understand and appreciate the significance of new developments in the industry. Burns and Stalker claim that 'the legitimacy of the hierarchical pyramid of management bureaucracy has been threatened by the sheer volume of novel tasks and problems confronting industrial concerns'. If senior managers recognize the professional authority of their subordinates, their own authority might be called into question. As Burns and Stalker show, managers in some firms were prepared to take this risk and adopt an organic system. This meant that on occasions they deferred to expert knowledge and therefore devolved some of their power to the specialists. This tended to produce insecurity as the chain of command was no longer clearly defined. In other firms senior management clung to the traditional bureaucratic system to ward off the threat of the experts. As noted in the previous section, senior management remained secure but, since they failed to fully harness the expertise of the professionals, the efficiency of the organization suffered. Burns and Stalker's research indicates some of the problems that can develop when both bureaucratic and professional authority are present in the same organization.

A number of researchers have argued that, at least in theory, there is a basic incompatibility between professional and administrative action. Professional action stems from an individual judgment based on specialist knowledge. The professional has the freedom to make decisions on the basis of his expertise. He may consult with colleagues but the final decision is his. Thus Amitai Etzioni argues that 'the ultimate justification for a professional act is that it is, to the best of the professional's knowledge, the right act'. Administrative action has a different basis. In Etzioni's words, 'The ultimate justification for an administrative act is that it is in line with the organization's rules and regulations, and that it has been approved – directly or by implication – by a superior ranking official'. Etzioni argues that professional and administrative action are in principle, fundamentally opposed. The autonomy, self-regulation and individual decision making required by the professional conflicts with the hierarchical control and official rules of bureaucratic administration. As a result, the employment of professionals in organizations may produce role conflict. The professional may experience conflict between his role as an employee and his role as a professional. As an employee, he must follow the rules and obey his superior, as a professional he must follow his professional judgment which might result in his disregarding official regulations and disobeying higher authority.

A number of studies have suggested that this role conflict need not arise. A study by Mary Goss examines supervisory relationships among a group of doctors in an outpatient clinic of a large American teaching hospital. Senior physicians organized the schedule of patients and performed various other administrative tasks. In addition they advised junior doctors about diagnosis and treatment. Potential conflict between an administrative hierarchy and professional autonomy was prevented from materializing for the following reasons. Doctors had the right to accept or reject the advice of their superiors. They made the final decisions and in this way professional autonomy was preserved. The administrative duties of the senior physicians were seen as separate from the professional area of work. As such they did not erode the professional freedom of other doctors since, in Goss's words, 'administrative decisions covered only activities they viewed as non-professional or ancillary to their work'. In this way the individual doctor's authority in terms of patient care remained intact. The professional role requires only that the doctor 'be free to make his own decisions in professional matters as opposed to administrative concerns'. Goss's study therefore shows that an administrative hierarchy and professional authority do not necessarily conflict in practice. However, it deals with the administration of professionals by professionals. It is therefore likely that the senior members of the hierarchy would be particularly sensitive to the requirements of the professional role.

Other research has indicated that in organizations where non-professionals administer the work of professionals, accommodations are made which reduce the possibility of role conflict. In a large-scale study of 154 public personnel agencies and 254 government finance departments in the USA, Peter Blau examines the relationship between the authority structure of the organizations and the qualifications of their employees. He found that the higher the qualifications of the employees, the higher the ratio of management personnel. At first sight this appears strange since the greater the expertise of the staff, the less guidance and supervision they should require. In addition, a highly qualified staff will be likely to have professional status and to demand the autonomy associated with it. On further investigation, however, Blau found that a high ratio of managers was compatible with a low level of supervision and a high degree of autonomy. He discovered that the higher the level of qualifications of the staff, the more authority and decision making was decentralized. When responsibility is delegated, a high ratio of managers is required, not for supervision and direction but for communication and consultation. Since an expert staff can make greater contributions to operating procedures, there is a greater need to ensure that information flows upwards from the lower ranks. Thus a relatively large number of managers is needed to 'facilitate the flow of upward communication' and so take full advantage of the contributions of the experts. Blau argues that, 'What is inappropriate for an organization staffed by experts is a hierarchy in which official authority is centralized in the hands of a few managers'. Blau concludes that authority structures in organizations are modified in relation to the degree of expertise of the staff. The greater the expertise, the more decision making and responsibility is delegated. In this way the requirement of professionals for autonomy and freedom from supervision is at least partially met.

In many organizations it appears that organizational goals are effectively served by granting a relatively high degree of autonomy to professional employees. While those who support individual freedom might welcome this development, others, who fear what they see as the largely unrestricted power of organizations, view it with concern. Blau and Schoenherr regard the methods used to harness professional expertise to the service of organizations as a far more effective means of control than commands issued by an authoritarian hierarchy, than detailed rules and close supervision or the incentives provided by financial reward. They argue that, 'The efforts of men can be controlled still far more efficiently than through wages alone by mobilizing their professional commitments to the work they can do best and like to do most and by putting these highly motivated energies and skills at the disposal of organizations'. Thus men can be controlled by giving them the freedom to exercise their skill and expertise in accordance with the high standards of their profession and by channelling the high motivation associated with the professional role into the service of the organization. This type of control is particularly effective since, because it is compatible with 'our values of human freedom and integrity', it reduces resistance. Yet despite the autonomy given to highly qualified employees, management are still in control because they decide which professionals to recruit and which departments to expand or contract. Blau and Schoenherr claim that in organizations employing a high proportion of professionals, 'That type of power suffices to govern the organization, though there is virtually no domination of individuals within it'. They regard this form of control as 'insidious' because it is deceptive and hidden. It does not involve 'the experience of being oppressed by the arbitrary will of a despot and sometimes not even the need to comply with directives of superiors, but merely the internalized obligation to perform tasks in accordance with standards of workmanship'. Insidious control means that people are far less aware of being controlled.

Blau and Schoenherr argue that the increasing employment of professionals in organizations has two main results. Firstly it increases the control of the organization over its members. Secondly it increases the power of the organization in society since professional skills and expertise are mobilized in the service of organizational goals. Blau and Schoenherr claim that, 'The professionalization of organizations, by which is meant that decisions are made by technical experts both interested and qualified in specialized fields of competence, enhances the internal efficiency and the external power of organizations'. The possible consequences of this development will be considered at the close of the chapter.

Organizations as systems – a functionalist perspective

Commenting on Weber's model of bureaucracy, Peter Blau states, 'Without explicitly stating so, Weber supplies a *functional* analysis of bureaucracy. In this type of analysis, a social structure is explained by showing how each of its elements contributes to its persistence and effective operations'. From a functionalist perspective, organizations are viewed as systems made up of interdependent parts. The presence of the various parts and the relationships between them can be understood in terms of the contribution they make to the maintenance and well-being of the system as a whole. Blau argues that Weber's analysis of bureaucracy is largely based on these assumptions. For example, the presence of a specialized division of labour, the employment of members on the basis of technical expertise and a hierarchy of officials can be understood both in terms of their interrelationship and their contribution to the effective operation of the system. A clearly defined division of labour allows experts to specialize in particular tasks. This requires that the various specialist tasks be coordinated, hence the hierarchy of officials. The combination of specialist expertise and the coordination of the division of labour contributes to the efficiency of the organization. Thus the various parts of Weber's model can be seen as forming a system. From this perspective members of an organization are constrained to act in certain ways by the system. In terms of Blau's interpretation of Weber, 'the combined effect of bureaucracy's characteristics is to create social conditions which constrain each member of the organization to act in ways that, whether they appear rational or otherwise from his individual standpoint, further the rational pursuit of organizational objectives'.

Many of the views of organizations examined in previous sections owe something to functionalist theory. Philip Selznick's analysis of the TVA provides the clearest illustration. He begins from the assumption that organizations are systems and that the primary need of any system is survival. In his words, 'the system is deemed to have basic needs, essentially related to self-maintenance'. Members of an organization are constrained to act in certain ways in order to meet organizational needs. The behaviour of members of the TVA can be therefore understood as a response to the constraints imposed by the organization to ensure its survival.

In order to survive an organization must adapt to its environment. In particular, it must ensure that powerful forces in the environment do not lead to its destruction. Selznick argues that much of the behaviour of members of the TVA can be understood as a response to this need. The TVA was forced to compromise its democratic ideals by the overriding need to maintain the organization. It therefore cooperated with the dominant farming interests in the Tennessee Valley since, without their support, its survival would be threatened. It did little for the Black tenant farmers since any move to improve their status would meet with concerted opposition from the White power structure. An organization also needs stable and effective lines of communication in order to operate. Thus the TVA required an efficient means of reaching the farmers in the Tennessee Valley. This need put pressure on members of the organization to employ the existing system of land-grant colleges with their extension services run by county agents which provided ready access to many of the farmers in the area. This arrangement provided 'the most logical and technically most adequate avenue to the farm population and its problems'. By specifying organizational needs, Selznick claims to be able to explain the behaviour of their members. He argues that 'organizational behaviour may be analysed in terms of organizational response to organizational need'.

The functionalist perspective on organizations has been strongly criticized. In particular, its view of man's actions as a response to organizational needs has been rejected. When Selznick states that 'the *organization* reaches decisions, takes action and makes adjustments', he implies that its members simply respond to constraints imposed by organizational needs and have no part in the direction of their activity. Those who take a phenomenological view of man reject this approach. They argue that action stems from meanings and definitions negotiated in interaction situations. In David Silverman's words, human action 'arises as actors attach meanings to their own actions and the actions of others'. The application of this view to the study of organizations will be considered in a later section.

The managerial tradition

Many of the studies of behaviour in organizations have been influenced by the priorities of management. They have been concerned with how to make organizations more efficient and in particular, how to improve the productivity of workers. Mouzelis has referred to research directed by these concerns as 'the managerial tradition'. Two major schools of thought within this tradition, 'scientific management' and 'human relations', will now be considered.

Scientific management

The theory of scientific management was first spelt out in detail by Frederick W. Taylor whose book, *The Principles of Scientific Management* was published in America in 1911. The turn of the century in the USA was a time of rapid industrial expansion. Compared to today, the organization of work on the shop floor was left much more in the hands of workers and foremen. Men often bought their own tools to suit their individual preferences and decisions about the speed of machines were often left to the particular operator. There were few systematic training programmes to teach workers their jobs and often skills were acquired simply by watching more experienced colleagues. Decisions about the selection of personnel, rest periods and layoffs were frequently left to individual foremen. Taylor argued that such arrangements were haphazard and inefficient. In their place he suggested the following scheme of scientific management which he claimed would maximize productivity.

According to Taylor, there is 'one best way' of performing any work task. It is the job of management to discover this way by applying scientific principles to the design of work procedures. For example, various tools should be tested to find the most efficient for the job, rest periods of differing length and frequency should be tried to discover the relationship between rest and productivity, the various movements involved in the task should be assessed in order to find those that are least time-consuming and produce the lowest level of fatigue. Experimenting with different task designs will result in the discovery of the most efficient way of doing a particular job. With this approach, Taylor laid the foundations for what has come to be known as time and motion studies. Once management has developed 'a science for each element of a man's work', it must then select and train workers in the new methods. Workers and tasks must be closely matched. For example, workers with low intelligence are best suited to simple, repetitive tasks. Once suitable personnel have been selected, they must then be trained to perform tasks according to the directives laid down by management. Instructions are to be followed to the letter. In Taylor's words, 'Each man receives in most cases written instructions, describing in detail the task he is to accomplish, as well as the means to be used in doing the work'. Finally, the cooperation of the workforce is obtained by monetary incentives. Taylor assumed that man's primary motivation for work was financial. Thus in order to maximize productivity and obtain work of the highest quality, the manager must give, 'some *special incentive* to his men beyond that which is given to the average in the trade'. In practice this usually involved a wage incentive scheme based on piece work – payment according to the amount of work done. Taylor believed that the scientific planning of work tasks, the selection and systematic training of suitable workers for the performance of those tasks plus a carrot and stick system of financial incentives would maximize productivity.

Taylor saw scientific management as the solution to many of industry's problems. Firstly, it would increase both the quantity and quality of the product. Secondly, it promised to end conflict between employers and employees. Since the employer is concerned with higher profits and the worker with higher wages, they share an interest in raising productivity. Increased productivity reduces labour costs and results in higher profits which in turn allow for higher wages. A fair day's work and a just system of payment can be established in accordance with the principles of scientific management. This will end conflict between management and labour since nobody can argue about 'scientific facts'.

Taylor's ideas have been strongly criticized despite the fact that many of his critics admit that their application has generally resulted in increased productivity. From a Marxian perspective, Taylor's belief that the interests of capital and labour can be compatible is rejected. His concept of a fair wage is dismissed as a rationalization for exploitation. The American Marxist Harry Braverman has denounced scientific management, seeing it as a means for strengthening the dominance of capital over labour. He claims that in capitalist society, 'its fundamental teachings have become the bedrock of all work design'. It has been adopted as a means of controlling alienated labour and is part of the process whereby the worker is increasingly transformed into an 'instrument of capital'. The detailed planning and design of work tasks by management drastically reduces worker control over the labour process. Work becomes dehumanized as workers, constrained by management directives, simply 'function as cogs and levers'. The reduction of worker control over the labour process is essential for the continuing accumulation of capital. If workers directed their own work, it would not be possible 'to enforce upon them either the methodological efficiency or the working pace desired by capital'. Thus, far from welcoming scientific management, Braverman denounces it as a means for increasing the efficiency of the exploitation of labour in capitalist society.

Two of the assumptions which underlie Taylor's principles have been singled out for particular criticism. Firstly, Taylor assumed that man's primary motivation for work is economic and he will therefore respond positively to financial incentives. This view of motivation, based on a concept of 'economic man', has been rejected as overly simplistic. Secondly, Taylor viewed workers as individuals rather than members of social groups. His plan to increase productivity involved the provision of financial incentives for individual workers. He failed to consider the influence of informal work groups on the behaviour of the individual worker. These points will be examined in the following section.

Human relations

Many of the central ideas of the human relations school grew out of an investigation at the Hawthorne plant of the Western Electric Company in Chicago. From 1927 to 1932, a team headed by Elton Mayo, a professor at the Harvard Business School, conducted a series of experiments designed to investigate the relationship between working conditions and productivity. Mayo began with the assumptions of scientific management believing that the physical conditions of the work environment, the aptitude of the worker and financial incentives were the main determinants of productivity. He therefore examined the relationship between productivity and variables such as levels of lighting and heating, the length and frequency of rest periods and the value of monetary incentives. The results were inconclusive; there appeared to be no consistent relationship between productivity and the various factors examined.

Mayo then changed the direction of his research. Instead of focussing on the factors deemed important by scientific management, he examined workers' attitudes towards their work and their behaviour as members of informal work groups. The two sides of Mayo's research can be seen from the following study. Fourteen men were placed in an observational setting known as the Bank Wiring Observation Room. There were nine wiremen who connected wires to banks of terminals, three soldermen who each soldered the work of three wiremen and two inspectors who tested the completed job. The quality and quantity of the men's output were carefully measured. In addition, the men were given tests to measure their manual dexterity and intelligence. Contrary to expectations, the researchers found no relationship between the results of these tests and the individual worker's output. The men's pay was based in part on a group incentive scheme. The more the group produced above a certain level, the more money each worker received. In theory every worker would maximize his output in terms of his capabilities. In practice this did not happen. Each individual restricted his output so as to maintain a uniform weekly rate of production for the group. The researchers discovered that the workers had established a norm which defined a fair day's work, and that this norm, rather than standards set by management, determined their output. Even so there were marked differences between the output levels of individual wiremen, differences which bore no relationship to dexterity and intelligence. The researchers claimed that these differences could only be explained in terms of the interpersonal relationships within the work group. Most of the workers belonged to one or other of two informal groups. Differences in output were most closely related to informal group membership. One group emphasized that the worker should not produce too much with phrases such as, 'Don't be a ratebuster', the other that he should not produce too little with phrases such as, 'Don't be a chiseler'. Largely as a result of these standards, the output of the wiremen in the two groups differed.

The Hawthorne studies moved the emphasis from the individual worker to the worker as a member of a social group. They saw his behaviour as a response to group norms rather than simply being directed by economic incentives and management designed work schemes. According to Roethlisberger and Dickson, who produced a detailed report on the Hawthorne studies, the behaviour of the wiremen 'could not be understood without considering the informal organization of the group'. They argue that informal work groups develop their own norms and values which are enforced by the application of group sanctions. For example, wiremen who exceeded their group's output norm became the butt of sarcasm and ridicule, they suffered mild forms of physical violence and risked ostracism from the group. Roethlisberger and Dickson argue that the power of such sanctions derives from the dependence of the individual upon the group. He has a basic need to belong, to feel part of a social group. He needs approval, recognition and status, needs which cannot be satisfied if he fails to conform to group norms. Thus when the wiremen stopped work early because they had filled their quota as defined by the group, 'they were yielding to a pressure far stronger than financial incentive', that is the pressure of group norms.

From the Hawthorne studies, and research which they largely stimulated, developed the human relations school. It stated that scientific management provided too narrow a view of man and that financial incentives alone were insufficient to motivate workers and ensure their cooperation. In addition management must attend to a series of needs which are common to all workers. Organizational psychologists have catalogued a range of needs for which workers are assumed to require satisfaction in their employment. These include 'social needs' such as friendship, group support, acceptance, approval, recognition and status and the need for 'self-actualization' which involves the development of the individual's talents, creativity and personality to the full. If these needs are not met, workers suffer psychologically and the efficiency of the organization is impaired. Thus Roethlisberger and Dickson argue that in order to maximize productivity, managers must make sure that the 'personal satisfactions' of workers are met and only then will they be 'willing to cooperate'. Management must accept and cooperate with informal work groups since they provide a context in which many of the workers' needs are satisfied. Through the use of supervisory staff trained in human relations skills, managers must ensure that the norms of informal groups are in line with the goals of the organization. One way of accomplishing this objective is to invite groups of workers to participate in decision making. This is based on the idea that workers will be more committed to their tasks if they have a voice in determining how those tasks are to be performed. By discovering ways of involving informal work groups within the organization, these groups can become a major driving force for the realization of organizational goals.

Research into the application of human relations techniques has produced inconsistent findings which permit no firm conclusions. For example, a study by Coch and French examined methods of introducing changes in production methods and piece rates among women workers in a pyjama factory. Four groups of workers were involved. The first group was simply informed about the changes. The second group met with management who explained the need for changes and discussed them with the group. Representatives of the group later discussed the new piece rate scheme in detail with management and were trained in the new production methods which they then taught to the other members of the group. A third and fourth group participated more directly in the changes. Every member went through the same procedures as the representatives of the second group. Within the first forty days of the changeover, the first group had a 17% rate of labour turnover whereas no member of the other groups resigned, Even when the first group gained experience of the new production methods, its output was consistently lower than that of the other groups. In addition it had a markedly lower level of reported job satisfaction. The third and fourth groups achieved the highest rate of production which suggests that productivity is related to the degree of participation by workers in matters which affect their work. However an attempt to replicate this study in another factory failed to produce similar results (discussed in Tausky, 1970).

Like scientific management, the human relations school sees no inherent conflict of interest between management and workers. It assumes that when conflict arises, it is due largely to the fact that workers' needs have not been satisfied. By reorganizing social relationships within the organization according to human relations principles, discord can be removed and both sides of industry can work together in harmony. Clearly this view finds no support from a Marxian perspective which sees a fundamental conflict of interest between employers and employees. The human relations school concentrates on the individual and group level and tends to ignore the organization as a whole and its place in the wider society. It gives little consideration to the effect on work behaviour of the workers' experience beyond the confines of the organization. From their study of affluent workers in Luton, Goldthorpe and Lockwood make the following criticisms of the human relations school. Firstly, the work behaviour of the affluent worker cannot be understood from an examination of social relationships within the factory. It is largely directed by the meanings he gives to work which are generated by factors outside the work situation. Secondly, it makes little sense to talk about basic needs common to all workers. If such needs exist, they are conditioned by the culture of society and the individual's place in the social structure. In this respect they will not be common to all workers. Thus the affluent worker's wants and expectations with regard to work are shaped partly by his class subculture and partly by the culture of the wider society. He shows little desire to satisfy many of the needs outlined by the human relations theorists. For example, there is no indication that he wants to belong to a solidary work group or experience the satisfactions that membership of such a group is supposed to bring. Nor is there any indication that either the workers or the organization suffered as a result. (For a discussion of Goldthorpe and Lockwood's research see Chapters 2, pp.57–62 and 6, pp.248–51.) The affluent worker study and similar research suggests that the human relations school has serious limitations which result in part from its failure to look beyond the factory gates.

Organizations – an interactionist perspective

In an earlier section organizations were viewed as systems and the behaviour of their members as a response to the system's needs. Thus Selznick argued that members of the TVA acted as they did in response to the needs of the system, in particular its need to survive in a potentially hostile environment. From this perspective, members of an organization are constrained to act in particular ways and have little say in the direction of their activity. This is an essentially positivist view since it sees human behaviour as a reaction to external stimuli, to the constraints imposed by the needs of the system. The organization rather than its members is seen to control organizational behaviour. From an interactionist perspective action is not determined by external forces. Instead it is directed by the meanings which actors give to objects, events and the activities of themselves and others. In David Silverman's words, 'Action arises out of meanings which define social reality'. For example, a range of meanings may be attached to an order issued by a member of a bureaucracy. It may be defined by a subordinate as reasonable or unreasonable, he may regard obedience as demeaning or involving no loss of self-respect. As a result of the meaning given to the order it may be obeyed willingly or unwillingly, it may be ignored or flatly refused. In order to understand the action of the subordinate, it is therefore necessary to discover the meanings which direct it. From an interactionist perspective, meanings are not determined by forces external to the actor. They are created, modified and changed by actors in interaction situations. Thus in order to understand action, the sociologist must examine the process of interaction and interpret the meanings which develop within it and which guide and direct it.

The first major study of an organization from an interactionist perspective was conducted by Erving Goffman in the late 1950s. He spent a year observing interaction in a mental hospital in Washington DC with the aim of understanding the social world of the inmate 'as this world is subjectively experienced by him'. In particular, he was concerned with how the patient's self-concept, his view of self, was modified or changed by his experience within the institution. Goffman claims that this can only be understood by interpreting the meanings given to that experience by the patient. The study was widened to include organizations which share certain characteristics with mental hospitals. They include prisons, concentration camps, orphanages, monasteries and army barracks, organizations Goffman refers to as 'total insitutions'. A total institution is defined as 'a place of residence and work where a large number of like-situated individuals, cut off from the wider society for an appreciable period of time, together lead an enforced, formally administered round of life'. Goffman draws on a range of published material – novels, autobiographies and social science research – to suggest that there are basic similarities between many of the social processes which occur in such institutions.

Goffman claims that total institutions are 'the forcing houses for changing persons; each is a natural experiment on what can be done to the self'. In order to understand this process, it is necessary to examine the interactions which take place from the viewpoint of the inmates. Within a total institution they are largely cut off from the outside world and from longstanding relationships with family, friends and work groups. In such social contexts an individual's self-concept is sustained. His picture of himself as a father, breadwinner, friend and workmate is mirrored and reflected in his interaction with others who respond to him in terms of these identities. These reflections of self are largely absent in total institutions. An individual's self-concept is also embedded in his name, his appearance, his clothes and personal possessions. Admission procedures to total institutions involve the removal of many items from this identity kit. A person may lose his name, being referred to by a number as in some military and penal institutions or adopt a new name as in the French Foreign Legion and some religious orders. His clothes may be replaced by those issued by the institution such as army and prison uniforms and monks' habits. His appearance may be changed, for example by prison and military haircuts and shaven heads in certain religious orders. Some or all of his personal possessions may be removed as in prisons, mental hospitals and many religious institutions. Since a part of the individual's self-concept is invested in his name, appearance and possessions, Goffman argues that changes in these aspects are 'saying' something to the new inmate. Specifically they state that he is no longer the person he was.

Many of the admission procedures and future interactions within total institutions not only tend to change but also to mortify the self. In Goffman's words, the inmate 'begins a series of abasements, degradations, humiliations, and profanations of self. His self is systematically, if often unintentionally, mortified'. He may be searched, undressed, bathed, disinfected and fingerprinted. He may be forced to humble himself before superiors. Thus in a monastery the novice may have to prostrate himself before the abbot; in the army the raw recruit may have to snap to attention in the presence of an officer and accept a string of abuse from noncommissioned officers. In some total institutions, the inmate requires permission to perform even the most basic of human functions and in certain cases his humiliation is increased by an absence of privacy.

Such experiences tend to break down the inmates' former self-concept. The self is then slowly rebuilt, partly by means of rewards and punishments administered by those in authority. Especially in prisons and mental hospitals, 'a small number of clearly defined rewards or privileges are held out in exchange for obedience to staff in action and spirit'. Thus a cigarette ration, an additional cup of coffee or an extra hour's recreation are awarded to those whose behaviour is deemed appropriate by the staff. Failure to humble the self and act in accordance with official directives results in punishments which continue the mortification process. Many such punishments are known 'in the inmate's home world as something applied to children or animals'. They may include solitary confinement, a diet of bread and water and the withdrawal of privileges such as cigarettes and recreation. Goffman argues that many of the actions of inmates can only be understood with reference to the strict supervision and mortification of self that occurs in many total institutions. Smuggling food from the kitchen, fiddling the cigarette ration, and conning the staff in various ways may assume great importance to the inmate. According to Goffman such actions tell him that 'he is still his own man, with some control over the environment'. Were he to completely submit to those in authority he would lose all sense of self-determination and personal efficacy.

Not all inmates respond in the same way to life in total institutions. Goffman identifies five modes of adaptation which an inmate may employ at different stages in his career in the institution or alternate between during one point in that career. The first is 'situational withdrawal'. The inmate withdraws attention from everything except events immediately surrounding his body and minimizes his interaction with others. In mental hospitals this is known as 'regression', in penal institutions as 'prison psychosis'. A second response is the 'intransigent line'. The inmate flatly refuses to cooperate with the staff and exhibits sustained hostility towards the institution. The staff often makes strident efforts to break this line of resistance. In military barracks the inmate may be locked in the stockade, in prisons he may be placed in solitary confinement, in mental hospitals he may be isolated from other patients, given electric shock treatment or even a lobotomy. The strong reprisals against the intransigent line often mean that it is a shortlived adaptation. A third response is 'colonization'. The inmate becomes 'institutionalized', he finds a home from home and defines life in the institution as more desirable than life on the outside. Such inmates often make concerted efforts to remain inside as their day of release approaches. A fourth response is 'conversion'. Here the individual adopts the staff's definition of the model inmate and acts out the part. This adaptation reaches it most extreme form in Chinese prisoner of war camps where some Americans enthusiastically embraced communist doctrine. Finally, in most total institutions, the majority of inmates adopt a strategy which some of them call 'playing it cool'. The aim is to stay out of trouble and involves alternating between the other modes of adaptation depending on the situation. By playing it cool, the inmate will have 'a maximum chance, in the particular circumstances, of eventually getting out physically and psychologically undamaged'.

Despite the sustained assault on the self in total institutions, Goffman claims that for most inmates a radical and permanent change of self does not occur. This is partly because they are able to defend themselves from the mortification process by playing it cool. Goffman is scornful of the official goals of organizations such as prisons and mental hospitals which present themselves as institutions which treat, cure and rehabilitate their clients. He concludes that, 'Many total institutions, most of the time, seem to function merely as storage dumps for inmates'.

Goffman's analysis of total institutions differs from previous approaches to organizations because of its emphasis on understanding action in terms of meanings. From an interactionist perspective, an answer to the question, 'What happens in organizations?' involves an investigation and interpretation of the meanings which actors assign to objects, events and activities. Goffman argues that an individual's name, his clothes and possessions are symbols, they are impregnated with meaning. By interpreting this meaning he is able to assess the significance of the removal of these symbols. Clearly this form of analysis relies heavily on the sensitivity and interpretive skills of the observer. Since it is not possible to enter the consciousness of others, there is no certainty that the meanings identified by the observer are those employed by the actors.

The interactionist perspective has often been criticized for what many see as its narrow focus. It tends to concentrate on small-scale interaction contexts and ignore the wider society. Thus Goffman gives little consideration to the inmates' experiences in the outside world before they entered total institutions. The possible significance of this omission can be seen from John Irwin's study of prison life in California. Irwin argues that an understanding of particular inmates' responses to imprisonment requires a knowledge of their pre-prison experience. He distinguishes a number of 'criminal identities' which inmates bring with them to prison. These include 'the thief' and 'the dope fiend'. Thieves see themselves as professional criminals and are committed to this identity and its associated life style. They regard society in general as corrupt and see nothing immoral about their criminal activities. Dope fiends are or have been addicted to an opiate – morphine or more usually heroine. They see themselves as junkies and view their addiction as a way of escaping from a dull, routine and monotonous world. However, their commitment to a criminal identity is less strong than that of the thief. Irwin identifies a number of adaptations to prison life. The first is 'doing time' which involves maximizing the comforts of prison life, avoiding trouble and getting out as soon as possible. This strategy is typically selected by thieves who maintain their commitment to a criminal career and are anxious to resume it. A second adaptation, 'gleaning', is chosen by the individual who, 'sets out to "better himself" or "improve himself" and takes advantage of the resources that exist in prison to do this'. Thus the 'gleaner' often enrols for educational courses and is frequently found in the prison library. Thieves rarely adopt this strategy whereas dope fiends, who are less strongly committed to a criminal identity, are more likely to turn to gleaning. Despite the fact that gleaning involves a desire to change one's identity, the dope fiend is still influenced by his former view of life. In line with his previous concern to escape dullness and routine, he tends to 'avoid practical fields and choose styles which promise glamor, excitement or color'. He sometimes finds what he's looking for in creative arts, social sciences or philosophy. Irwin's study suggests that pre-institutional experience may have important influences on modes of adaptation within total institutions. Analysis which is limited to the confines of the institution may therefore prove inadequate for an understanding of organizational behaviour.

The interactionist approach concentrates on meanings in the context of interaction situations. As such it has been criticized for failing to consider the possibility that these meanings may be generated by the wider society. For example, definitions of criminality and psychological disorder may have their origins in the structure of society. In particular, they may be related to the nature and distribution of power in society. Thus the powerholders may define activities which threaten their interests as criminal or as a product of mental illness. Their definitions of criminality and psychological disorder may provide guides to action for staff in prisons and mental hospitals. Therefore many of the meanings that direct action in total institutions may be a product of the structure of society. This view will be considered in detail in Chapter 10 (pp.437–45).

The problem of organizations

Organizations in modern society have been pictured as threatening individual liberty and undermining democracy. Yet paradoxically, they have also been seen as essential requirements for a democratic society and as a means for the protection of individual freedoms. This ambivalent view of organizations is contained in the writings of Peter Blau. He claims that, 'Democratic objectives would be impossible to attain in modern society without bureaucratic organizations to implement them'. Thus 'equal justice under the law', a basic democratic principle, requires a bureaucratic organization for its implementation. Those who enforce the law must be subject to uniform standards and strict rules in order to ensure its equity and fairness and to prevent personal considerations from influencing their conduct. In Blau's words, 'This is another way of saying that bureaucratically organized enforcement agencies are necessary for all members of society to be equal under the law'.

Yet Blau, like many other writers, fears that organizations are moving beyond popular control and undermining democracy. He sees this process as the major problem of Western industrial society. Power and resources are increasingly concentrated in organizational settings. They are employed in the first instance for the benefit of the organization rather than for society as a whole. Thus when a corporation decides to invest in a particular area, its major concern is not the welfare of the local people but its priorities as a corporation. (For further views on the power of organizations see Chapter 3, pp.122–4.) In addition, the vast majority of the population is excluded from any participation in its decisions. Blau claims that, 'The concentration of organizational power in the hands of a few men shielded from public surveillance and control poses a serious threat to democracy'. The life of modern man is shaped more and more by organizations over which he has little or no control. Blau argues that 'what is required is a readjustment of our democratic institutions to make them capable of controlling the power of organizations'. But having diagnosed the problem, Blau gives no specific suggestions for its solution.

In a study of state bureaucracy, B. Guy Peters examines the question of popular control. He sees the major problem not so much in terms of the mechanisms which exist to control and influence bureaucracies – parliamentary committees, the judiciary and interest groups – but in terms of the motivation of the public to utilize these mechanisms. Peters argues that, 'In practice, most methods of accountability depend upon individual or group actions to press demands before the mechanisms go into operation'. He regards public apathy as the greatest danger to bureaucratic accountability and a democratic state. However, Peters is cautiously optimistic for the following reasons. Firstly, the development of public education and the mass media serves to increase information about bureaucratic activity. Secondly, in some Western democracies, there are signs that state bureaucracy is becoming more open. In the USA, Watergate was followed by President Carter's policy of 'open government' and the so-called 'sunshine laws' which allow public access to the meetings and records of many administrative bodies. In Sweden state bureaucrats make written records of both their decisions and the reasons for them. This information is available to citizens on request. Peters argues that such measures are a necessary first step towards popular control of bureaucracy. Without information, members of the public will have great difficulty contesting bureaucratic decisions. In the light of these trends, Peters concludes that, 'We may expect greater public concern and involvement in public affairs. How effective this will be will ultimately depend upon the willingness of the population to persist in pressing their demands and using the mechanisms available to them'. The cautious optimism of this conclusion must, however, be tempered with the more pessimistic views discussed in earlier sections and the various perspectives on power and politics outlined in Chapter 3.

Sociology, ideology and organizations

Alvin Gouldner has written that, 'A commitment to a theory may be made because the theory is congruent with the mood or deep-lying sentiments of its adherents, rather than merely because it has been cerebrally inspected and found valid'. Thus support for a particular theory may owe more to the ideology of the sociologist than the explanatory power of the theory. Gouldner goes on to suggest that a part of organization theory is to some degree a product of the sentiments of either unrealistic dreamers or dyed in the wool pessimists. Gouldner's ideas may be illustrated by a comparison of Marxian theory and the views of elite theorists such as Michels.

Marxian predictions of the disappearance of bureaucracy in a classless society owe much to a commitment to a utopian vision. Even when faced with the proliferation of bureaucracy in East European communist societies, many Marxists argue that this situation merely represents a stage of transition to an egalitarian society. They hope and even believe that the days of the dictatorship of the proletariat are numbered. This can be seen as a product of wishful thinking rather than a scientific prediction. According to Nicos Mouzelis, 'This kind of optimism, as well as the conception of history as a succession of well-defined stages leading towards freedom and human happiness, is a part of the eighteenth and nineteenth-century humanist faith in the future of man and in the idea of progress'.

This faith and the radical changes it advocates finds no support in the conservative views of Michels. His dictum that organization equals oligarchy suggests that Marxists should stop dreaming the impossible dream, that they should accept the inevitable and learn to live with it. Like the early elite theorists such as Pareto and Mosca, with whom he is often bracketed, Michels was Italian and his ideas may well owe something to his cultural background. As C. J. Friedrich observes, the elite theorists were 'offspring of a society containing as yet many feudal remnants'. The authoritarian nature of feudalism contained in these survivals may well have encouraged a belief in the inevitability of rule by a minority. In addition, as Lukács suggests, elite theory found its strongest support in European societies such as Italy in which democratic institutions were least well-developed. Contrary to these observations, Michels was committed to socialist principles in his younger days. However he later transferred his allegiance to the fascist dictator Benito Mussolini who personified the 'iron law of oligarchy'. Mouzelis sees the pessimism and conservative bias of elite theory as a reaction to the over-optimistic predictions which preceded it. He claims that 'The increasing stress on the pessimistic side reflects a general disillusionment and loss of faith which partly came as a reaction to the earlier overconfidence in the human reason and the inevitable march of history towards progress'.

Gouldner chides both those he considers unrealistic optimists and those he sees as confirmed pessimists, a description he applies to both Michels and Selznick. He claims that the former look forward to 'a utopian and hence unattainable vision of democracy' whereas the latter picture 'an attainable but bureaucratically undermined, hence imperfect democracy'. Gouldner argues that the choice does not lie with one or other of these alternatives, with either perfection or flawed reality. Limiting choice to these alternatives closes other options. Gouldner suggests a cautiously optimistic and in his view a more realistic approach which would explore ways in which organizations could be made more democratic. The results of such research might well fall far short of the utopian ideals of many Marxists, but they may give direction to those who wish to develop more democratic organizations. And, in Gouldner's view, such developments might well make 'a vital difference to the lives of man'.

It is difficult, if not impossible, for sociologists to avoid being influenced by the attitudes which they bring with them to their research. These attitudes influence both their choice of topic for research and the way they select and interpret their data. From his work on total institutions and other studies, it is clear that Erving Goffman's sympathies lie with the underdog. He admits that in his study of psychiatric patients, he adopted a 'partisan view', a bias which is strengthened by his admission that he came to the mental hospital 'with no great respect for the discipline of psychiatry'. In addition, Goffman suggests that his former experience may have led him to overemphasize the effect of the degradations suffered by the inmates. He states, 'I want to warn that my view is probably too much that of a middle-class male; perhaps I suffered vicariously about conditions that lower class patients handled with little pain'.

This chapter has focussed on the sociology of organizations. As such it has dealt only briefly with a large body of research which derives from the managerial tradition. This tradition, which includes scientific management and the human relations school, has been strongly attacked for what many see as its pro-management bias. Its critics have argued that its priorities are those of management, that the problems it seeks to solve are those for which managers require solutions. Thus the managerial tradition has been concerned with increasing organizational efficiency and raising productivity. Its critics have argued that when workers' needs have been considered, it has been in terms of these priorities. They claim that the concern for workers' needs is based on the assumption that fulfilled workers produce more. In *Labor and Monopoly Capitalism*, the American Marxist Harry Braverman launches a blistering attack on Frederick Taylor. Braverman claims that scientific management, 'starts, despite occasional protestations to the contrary, not from the human point of view but from the capitalist point of view, from the point of view of the management of a refractory work force in a setting of antagonistic social relations. It does not attempt to discover and confront the cause of this condition, but accepts it as an inexorable given, a "natural" condition. It investigates not labor in general, but the adaptation of labor to the needs of capital. It enters the workplace not as the representative of science, but as the representative of management masquerading in the trappings of science'. Thus Braverman argues that Taylor begins from an acceptance of the capitalist system and therefore fails to see the exploitive nature of capitalist relations of production. Braverman sees scientific management as simply a further weapon in the armoury of oppression.

Similar charges have been levelled at the human relations school. However, as Mouzelis argues, 'the fact that human relations findings might help the employer to manipulate his employees in a more effective way, does not destroy their scientific validity'. Many sociologists may be too ready to dismiss the findings of their colleagues because they disagree with the ideological assumptions which they see underlying those findings.

8 The family

Many sociologists have regarded the family as the cornerstone of society. It forms the basic unit of social organization and it is difficult to imagine how human society could function without it. Although the composition of the family varies, for example in many societies two or more wives are regarded as the ideal arrangement, such differences can be seen as minor variations on a basic theme. In general, therefore, the family has been seen as a universal social institution, as an inevitable part of human society. On balance, it has been regarded as a good thing, both for the individual and society as a whole. This view has tended to divert attention from interesting and important questions. For example, it has discouraged serious and detailed consideration of alternatives to the family. Recently, new perspectives on the family have questioned many of the assumptions of the more traditional view. These approaches have not assumed that the family is inevitable. Often, they have been openly critical of the institution of the family. During the late 1960s the Women's Liberation Movement began shaking the foundations of the family by attacking the role of women within it. This attack was developed by some feminist writers into a condemnation of the family as an institution. This chapter begins by examining the assumption of the universality of the family.

Is the family universal?

George Peter Murdock: the family – a universal social institution

In a study entitled *Social Structure*, George Peter Murdock examined the institution of the family in a wide range of societies. Murdock took a sample of 250 societies ranging from small hunting and gathering bands to large-scale industrial societies. He claimed that some form of family existed in every society and concluded, on the evidence of his sample, that the family is universal. Murdock defines the family as follows, 'The family is a social group characterized by common residence, economic co-operation and reproduction. It includes adults of both sexes, at least two of whom maintain a socially approved sexual relationship, and one or more children, own or adopted, of the sexually co-habiting adults'. Thus the family lives together, pools its resources and works together and produces offspring. At least two of the adult members conduct a sexual relationship according to the norms of their particular society. Such norms vary from society to society. For example, among the Banaro of New Guinea, the husband does not have sexual relations with his wife until she has borne a child by a friend of his father. The parent–child relationship is not necessarily a biological one. Its importance is primarily social, children being recognized as members of a particular family whether or not the adult spouses have biologically produced them.

The structure of the family varies from society to society. The smallest family unit is known as the nuclear family and consists of a husband and wife and their immature offspring. Units larger than the nuclear family are usually known as extended families. Such families can be seen as extensions of the basic nuclear unit, either vertical extensions – for example the addition of members of a third generation such as the spouses' parents – and/or horizontal extensions – for example the addition of members of the same generation as the spouses such as the husband's brother or an additional wife. Thus Bell and Vogel define the extended family as 'any grouping broader than the nuclear family which is related by descent, marriage or adoption'.

Either on its own or as the basic unit within an extended family, Murdock found that the nuclear family was present in every society in his sample. This led him to conclude that, 'The nuclear family is a universal human social grouping. Either as the sole prevailing form of the family or as the basic unit from which more complex forms are compounded, it exists as a distinct and strongly functional group in every known society'. However, as the following sections will indicate, Murdock's conclusions might not be well founded.

The New World Black family – an exception to the rule?

Murdock's definition of the family includes at least one adult of each sex. A significant proportion of Black families in the islands of the West Indies, parts of Central America such as Guyana and the USA do not include adult males. The 'family unit' often consists of a woman and her dependent children, sometimes with the addition of her mother. This may indicate that the family is not universal as Murdock suggests, or that it is necessary to redefine the family and state that the minimal family unit consists of a woman and her dependent children, own or adopted, and that all other family types are additions to this unit. Female-headed families are sometimes known as matriarchal families, sometimes as matrifocal families, though both these terms have been used in a number of senses. The term matrifocal family will be used here to refer to female-headed families.

Matrifocal families are common in low-income Black communities in the New World. In the USA in 1971, 29% of all Black families were headed by women. The percentage is often higher in other New World societies. For example, Nancie González in her study of Livingston, Honduras in 1956, found that 45% of Black Carib families had female heads. The high level of matrifocal families has been seen as a result of one or more of the following factors. Melville J. Herskovits argues that the West African origin of New World Blacks influenced their family structure. In traditional West Africa, a system of polygyny (a form of extended family with one husband and two or more wives) and considerable female economic independence meant that the husband played a relatively marginal role in family life. Herskovits maintains that this pattern continues to influence Black family life. A second argument sees the system of plantation slavery as a major factor accounting for matrifocal families. M. G. Smith, one of the main supporters of this view, notes that under slavery, mother and children formed the basic family unit. Families were often split with the sale of one or more of their members, but mothers and dependent children were usually kept together. The authority of the male as head of the family was eroded because he was subject to the authority of the plantation owner who, with his White employees, had the right of sexual access to all female slaves. Formed under slavery, the model of the matrifocal family is seen to have persisted. A third argument sees the economic position of Blacks in the New World as the basic cause of the matrifocal family. Elliot Liebow, whose views are outlined in Chapter 4 (pp. 157–9), sees female-headed families resulting from desertion by the husband because he has insufficient funds to play the role of father and breadwinner. A final argument accepts that poverty is the basic cause of matrifocal families but states also that matrifocality has become a part of the subculture of the poor. This view is contained in Oscar Lewis's concept of the culture of poverty. From his research in a low-income Black area of Washington DC, Ulf Hannerz argues that female-headed families are so common that to some degree they have become an expected and accepted alternative to the standard nuclear family. From this argument matrifocal families are not simply a product of poverty but also of culture. (See Chapter 4, pp. 154–60, for a general discussion of the relationship between poverty, culture and family structure.)

Can the matrifocal family be regarded as an exception to Murdock's claim that the family is universal, or, if it is accepted as a family, to his claim that the nuclear family is a universal social group? First, the arguments which support Murdock will be examined. Statistically, the female-headed family is not the norm either within Black communities or in the societies in which they are set. Secondly, the matrifocal family is often a nuclear family that has been broken. Particularly in the USA, it is usually a product of separation or divorce. It did not begin life as a matrifocal family. Thirdly, the mainstream model of the nuclear family is valued by Blacks and regarded as the ideal. Finally, many sociologists view the female-headed family as a family 'gone wrong', as a product of social disorganization and not, therefore, a viable alternative to the nuclear family. It has been accused of producing maladjusted children, juvenile delinquents and high school dropouts. Since it does not appear to perform the functions of a 'proper family', it is regarded as a broken family and not as a viable unit in its own right.

The following arguments support the view that the matrifocal family should be recognized as an alternative to the nuclear family. First, simply because in statistical terms it is not the norm, does not mean it cannot be recognized as an alternative family structure. In many societies which practise polygyny, polygynous marriages are in the minority yet sociologists accept them as a form of extended family. Secondly, as Hannerz argues, in low-income Black communities matrifocal families are to some extent expected and accepted. Thirdly, members of matrifocal families regard the unit as a family. Fourthly, the matrifocal family should not be seen simply as a broken nuclear family. From West Indian data, González argues that the female-headed family is a well organized social group which represents a positive adaptation to the circumstances of poverty. By not tying herself to a husband, the mother is able to maintain casual relationships with a number of men who can provide her with financial support. She retains strong links with her relatives who give her both economic and emotional support. González states, 'By dispersing her loyalties and by clinging especially to the unbreakable sibling ties with her brothers, a woman increases her chances of maintaining her children and household'. In a situation of poverty, 'the chances that any one man may fail are high'. Finally, the supposed harmful effects of the matrifocal family on the children are far from proven. From an analysis of data from the USA, Herbert J. Gans states that 'the matriarchal family structure and the absence of a father has not yet proven pathological, even for the boys who grow up in it'.

The above arguments suggest that the matrifocal family can be regarded as a form of family structure in its own right. If these arguments are accepted, it is possible to see the matrifocal family as the basic, minimum family unit and all other family structures as additions to this unit.

The kibbutz – the abolition of the family?

The family in the Israeli kibbutz presents another possible exception to Murdock's claim for the universality of the nuclear family. About 4% of Israel's population live in some 240 kibbutzim settlements. Capital and property are collectively owned by kibbutzim members and the main economy is agriculture plus some light industry. The 'family' in the kibbutz has been shaped by a number of ideological and economic factors. Particularly during the early days, all able-bodied adults were needed to get the settlements off the ground which left little time for intimate relationships between mothers and children. Kibbutzim ideology emphasized sexual equality and rejected the Western pattern of parental roles, especially the mother role. In particular there was a reaction against the traditional 'Jewish mamma', the supposedly overprotective Jewish mother, a well-known figure in American folklore and humour.

Although there are differences between kibbutzim, the general pattern of family life can be described as follows. Marriage is monogamous (one spouse of each sex), the married couple sharing a single bedroom cum living room. Common residence does not extend to their children who live in communal dormitories where they are raised by child 'caretakers' or 'educators'. They eat and sleep in the dormitories spending most of the day and all of the night away from their parents. They usually see their parents for an hour or two each day, often visiting them in their apartment. These visits are viewed as 'fun time' rather than occasions for socialization and child training. Bruno Bettelheim, who studied childrearing practices in a kibbutz, states that 'parents have transferred their power to the community. All children are viewed and cared for as "children of the kibbutz"'. Parents told Bettelheim that collective childrearing protected their children from 'bad mothering'. Stanley Diamond, who has written extensively about the kibbutzim system, states that, 'The collective method of childrearing represents a rejection of the family, with particular reference to parental roles'.

Economic cooperation between the married couple as such hardly exists. Neither works for the family but rather for the kibbutz as a whole. They receive the goods and services they require from the kibbutz as do their children. They eat in the communal dining room, food is cooked in the communal kitchen and services such as laundering are provided for the entire kibbutz rather than being the responsibility of the family. Economic cooperation is on a community rather than a family level, each spouse working for the kibbutz as a whole and receiving his or her share of the goods and services produced.

In terms of Murdock's definition, the family does not exist in the kibbutz on two counts. Firstly, family members do not share a common residence. Secondly, their relationship is not characterized by economic cooperation. The anthropologist Melford E. Spiro examined the kibbutz family in terms of Murdock's definition and reached the following conclusion, 'It can only be concluded in the absence of the economic and educational functions of the typical family, as well as of its characteristic of common residence, that the family does not exist in the kibbutz'. However, Spiro argues that from a functional and psychological viewpoint it is possible to see the kibbutz as 'a large extended family'. As a unit the kibbutz performs all the functions of a nuclear family. In psychological terms, members of the kibbutz act as if they were members of a large family. Adults, with or without children, refer to all children in the kibbutz as 'our children'. Those born and raised in the kibbutz usually practise group exogamy, that is they marry outside the kibbutz just as members of a family marry outside the family. Members of the same generation view their peers as brothers and sisters. In this way the kibbutz can be seen as a large extended family.

Some four years after reaching these conclusions, Spiro reconsidered his position. He claimed that Murdock's definition of the family is 'unduly specific' and that it is possible to argue that families exist in the kibbutz for the following reasons. Permanent unions are formed between spouses, ideally there is an exclusive sexual relationship between them which leads to the production of children. The relationship between parents and children is a unique relationship in the kibbutz. Parents refer to their children as 'son' or 'daughter', children to their parents as 'mother' or 'father'. Parents provide a special kind of 'love and security' for their children and there are powerful emotional ties between them. Spiro concludes that it is possible to see this 'unique relationship' in the kibbutz as a family.

In terms of Murdock's definition, it can be argued that the family is not universal. The case of the New World Black family does not satisfy Murdock's criterion of at least one spouse of each sex. The kibbutz case does not satisfy the criteria of common residence and economic cooperation. However, as Spiro argues, Murdock's definition can be regarded as 'unduly specific'. From a phenomenological perspective which looks to the perception of reality held by members of society, the family may well be universal. Members of matrifocal families certainly perceive their social group as a family. Members of the 'nuclear family' in the kibbutz see that social group as a form of family distinguished by relationships which are different from all others in the kibbutz.

The family – a functionalist perspective

The analysis of the family from a functionalist perspective involves three main questions. Firstly, 'What are the functions of the family?' Answers to this question deal with the contributions made by the family to the maintenance of the social system. It is assumed that society has certain functional prerequisites or basic needs that must be met if it is to survive and operate efficiently. The family is examined in terms of the degree to which it meets these functional prerequisites. A second and related question asks, 'What are the functional relationships between the family and other parts of the social system?' It is assumed that there must be a certain degree of fit, integration and harmony between the parts of the social system if society is going to function efficiently. For example, the family must be integrated to some extent with the economic system. This question will be examined in detail in a later section when the relationships between the family and industrialization will be considered. The third question is concerned with the functions performed by an institution or a part of society for the individual. In the case of the family, this question considers the functions of the family for its individual members.

George Peter Murdock – the universal functions of the family

From his analysis of 250 societies, Murdock argues that the family performs four basic functions in all societies. These universal functions he terms the sexual, reproductive, economic and educational. They are essential for social life since without the sexual and reproductive functions there would be no members of society, without the economic function, for example the provision and preparation of food, life would cease, and without education, a term Murdock uses for socialization, there would be no culture. Human society without culture could not function. Clearly, the family does not perform these functions exclusively. However, it makes important contributions to them all and no other institution has yet been devised to match its efficiency in this respect. Once this is realized, Murdock claims, 'The immense utility of the nuclear family and the basic reason for its universality thus begin to emerge in strong relief'.

The family's functions for society are inseparable from its functions for its individual members. It serves both at one and the same time and in much the same way. The sexual function provides an example. Husband and wife have the right of sexual access to each other and in most societies there are rules forbidding or limiting sexual activity outside marriage. This provides sexual gratification for the spouses. It also strengthens the family since the powerful and often binding emotions which accompany sexual activities unite husband and wife. The sexual function also helps to stabilize society. The rules which largely contain sexual activity within the family prevent the probable disruptive effects on social order that would result if the sex drive were allowed 'free play'. The family thus provides both 'control and expression' of sexual drives and in doing so performs important functions both for its individual members, for the family as an institution and for society as a whole. Murdock applies a similar logic to the economic function. He argues that like sex, it is 'most readily and satisfactorily achieved by persons living together'. He refers in glowing terms to the division of labour within the family whereby the husband specializes in certain activities, the wife in others. For example in hunting societies men kill game animals which provide the meat for their wives to cook and skins for them to make into clothing. This economic cooperation within the family not only goes a long way to fulfilling the economic function for society as a whole but provides 'rewarding experiences' for the spouses working together which 'cement their union'.

Murdock argues that his analysis provides a 'conception of the family's many-sided utility and thus of its inevitability'. He concludes that, 'No society has succeeded in finding an adequate substitute for the nuclear family, to which it might transfer these functions. It is highly doubtful whether any society will ever succeed in such an attempt'.

Murdock's picture of the family is rather like the multi-faceted, indispensable boy scout knife. The family is seen as a multi-functional institution which is indispensable to society. Its 'many-sided utility' accounts for its universality and its inevitability. In his enthusiasm for the family, however, Murdock does not seriously consider whether its functions could be performed by other social institutions. He does not examine alternatives to the family. As D. H. J. Morgan notes in his criticism, Murdock does not answer 'to what extent these basic functions are inevitably linked with the institution of the nuclear family'. In addition, Murdock's description of the family is almost too good to be true. As Morgan states, 'Murdock's nuclear family is a remarkably harmonious institution. Husband and wife have an integrated division of labour and have a good time in bed'. As later sections will indicate, Murdock's emphasis on harmony and integration is not shared by some researchers.

Talcott Parsons – the 'basic and irreducible' functions of the family

Parsons concentrates his analysis on the family in modern American society. However his ideas have a more general application since he argues that the American family retains two 'basic and irreducible functions' which are common to the family in all societies. These are the 'primary socialization of children' and the 'stabilization of the adult personalities of the population of the society'.

Primary socialization refers to socialization during the early years of childhood which takes place mainly within the family. Secondary socialization occurs during the later years when the family is less involved and other agencies such as the peer group and the school exert increasing influence. There are two basic processes involved in primary socialization: the internalization of society's culture and the structuring of the personality. Unless culture is internalized, society would cease to exist since without shared norms and values, social life would not be possible. However, culture is not simply learned, it is 'internalized as part of the personality structure'. The child's personality is moulded in terms of the central values of the culture to the point where they become a part of him. In the case of American society, his personality is shaped in terms of independence and achievement motivation which are two of the central values of

American culture. Parsons argues that families 'are "factories" which produce human personalities'. He believes they are essential for this purpose since primary socialization requires a context which provides warmth, security and mutual support. He can conceive of no institution other than the family which could provide this context.

Once produced, the personality must be kept stable. This is the second basic function of the family, the 'stabilization of adult personalities'. The emphasis here is on the marriage relationship and the emotional security the couple provide for each other. This acts as a counterweight to the stresses and strains of everyday life which tend to make the personality unstable. This function is particularly important in Western industrial society since the nuclear family is largely isolated from kin. It does not have the security once provided by the close-knit extended family. Thus the married couple increasingly look to each other for emotional support. Adult personalities are also stabilized by the parents' role in the socialization process. This allows them to act out ' "childish" elements of their own personalities which they have retained from childhood but which cannot be indulged in adult society. For example, father is 'kept on the rails' by playing with his son's train set. The family therefore provides a context in which husband and wife can express their childish whims, give and receive emotional support, recharge their batteries and so stabilize their personalities.

This brief summary of Parsons's views on the family is far from complete. Other aspects will be considered later in this chapter (pp. 344–6) and in the following chapter (pp. 371–2). As with Murdock, Parsons has been accused of idealizing the family with his picture of well-adjusted children and sympathetic spouses caring for each other's every need. Secondly, his picture is based largely on the American middle-class family which he treats as representative of American families in general. As D. H. J. Morgan states, 'there are no classes, no regions, no religious, ethnic or status groups, no communities' in Parsons's analysis of the family. For example, he fails to explore possible differences between middle and working-class families. Thirdly, like Murdock, Parsons largely fails to explore functional alternatives to the family. He does recognize that some functions are not necessarily tied to the family. For example he notes that the family's economic function has largely been taken over by other agencies in modern industrial society. However, his belief that its remaining functions are 'basic and irreducible' prevents him from examining alternatives to the family. Finally, Parsons's view of the socialization process may be criticized. He sees it as a one-way process with the child being pumped full of culture and its personality moulded by powerful parents. He tends to ignore the two-way interaction process between parents and children. There is no place in his scheme for the child who twists its parents round its little finger.

Ezra F. Vogel and Norman W. Bell – functions and dysfunctions of the family

In an article entitled, *The Emotionally Disturbed Child as the Family Scapegoat*, Vogel and Bell present a functional analysis of certain families which avoids the tendency of many functionalists to concentrate solely on the positive aspects of the family. When examining the functional significance of the family, they ask functional 'for whom?' and 'for what?' Vogel and Bell base their findings on an intensive study of a small number of American families containing an 'emotionally disturbed child'. They argue that the tension and hostility of unresolved conflicts between the parents are projected on to the child. The child is thus used as an emotional scapegoat by the parents to relieve their tension. For example, in one case a son was criticized by his mother for all the characteristics she disliked in her husband. Clearly, the process of scapegoating is dysfunctional for the child. He becomes 'emotionally disturbed'. He is unable to adjust to life at school and in the neighbourhood. However, what is dysfunctional for the child can be seen as functional for the parents, for the family unit and for society as a whole. The parents release their tension and so control the conflict between them. As a result the family as a whole is stabilized and strengthened. Vogel and Bell argue that the cost to the child is 'low relative to the functional gains of the whole family'. Scapegoating the child serves as a 'personality-stabilizing process' for the parents which allows them to effectively perform their roles in the wider society as 'steady workers and relatively respectable community members'.

Whether the costs to the child are indeed low, compared to the gains of family solidarity and effective role performance by the adults outside the family, is a matter of opinion. To some extent this judgment reflects the functionalist view of the vital importance of the family to society. However, Vogel and Bell's analysis does have the merit of dealing with dysfunctional aspects of the family within a functionalist framework.

Critical views of the family

Even Vogel and Bell's analysis suggests that, all things considered, the family is functional both for its members and society as a whole. Increasingly, this picture of the family is coming under strong criticism. Some observers are suggesting that, on balance, the family may well be dysfunctional both for society and its individual members. This criticism has mainly been directed at the family in Western industrial society.

Edmund Leach – *A Runaway World?*

In a study entitled, *A Runaway World?* Edmund Leach presents a pessimistic view of the family in industrial society. Leach, an anthropologist, has spent many years studying small-scale pre-industrial societies. In such societies the family often forms a part of a wider kinship unit. An extensive network of social relationships between a large number of kin provides practical and psychological support for the individual. This support is reinforced by the closely-knit texture of relationships in the small-scale community as a whole. By comparison, in modern industrial society, the nuclear family is largely isolated from kin and the wider community. Leach summarizes this situation and its consequences as follows, 'In the past kinsfolk and neighbours gave the individual continuous moral support throughout his life. Today the domestic household is isolated. The family looks inward upon itself; there is an intensification of emotional stress between husband and wife and parents and children. The strain is greater than most of us can bear'. Thrown back almost entirely on its own resources, the nuclear family becomes like an overloaded electrical circuit. The demands made upon it are too great and fuses blow. In their isolation, family members expect and demand too much from each other. The result is conflict. In Leach's words, 'The parents and children huddled together in their loneliness take too much out of each other. The parents fight; the children rebel'.

Problems are not confined to the family. The tension and hostility produced within the family find expression throughout society. Leach argues that the 'isolation and the close-knit nature of contemporary family life incubates hate which finds expression in conflict in the wider community'. The families in which people huddle together create barriers between them and the wider society. The privatized family breeds suspicion and fear of the outside world. Leach argues that, 'Privacy is the source of fear and violence. The violence in the world comes about because we human beings are forever creating barriers between men who are like us and men who are not like us'. Only when individuals can break out of the prison of the nuclear family, rejoin their fellows, and give and receive support will the ills of society begin to diminish. Leach's conclusion is diametrically opposed to the functionalist view of the family. He states, 'Far from being the basis of the good society, the family, with its narrow privacy and tawdry secrets is the source of all our discontents'.

R. D. Laing – *The Politics of the Family*

In *The Politics of the Family* and a number of other publications, R. D. Laing presents a radical alternative to the functionalist picture of the 'happy family'. Laing is a phenomenological psychiatrist. He is concerned with interaction within the family and the meanings which develop in that context. His work is largely based on the study of families in which one member has been defined as schizophrenic. Laing argues that the behaviour of so-called schizophrenics can only be understood in terms of relationships within the family. Far from viewing schizophrenia as madness, he argues that it makes sense in terms of the meanings and interactions which develop within the family. As such it can be seen as reasonable behaviour. Laing maintains that the difference between so-called 'normal' and 'abnormal' families is small. It therefore follows that a lot can be learned about families in general by studying those labelled as abnormal.

Laing views the family in terms of sets of interactions. Individuals form alliances, adopt various strategies and play one or more individuals off against others in a complex tactical game. Laing is preoccupied with interaction situations which he regards as harmful and destructive. Throughout his work he concentrates on exploitive aspects of family relationships. The following example illustrates his approach. Jane is defined as schizophrenic. She is in a perpetual reverie, her own little dream world, which consists of a game of tennis. It is a mixed doubles; she is the ball. Jane sits motionless and silent and eats only when fed. The adults in the family are in a state of conflict, her father and his mother being ranged against her mother and her mother's father. The two halves of the family communicate only through Jane; she is the go-between. The strain eventually becomes too much for her and she escapes into her dream world. However, as her 'dream' shows, even in this world she cannot escape from the clutches of the family. The game of tennis symbolizes the interaction patterns in her family. With examples such as this, Laing shows how the family can be a destructive and exploitive institution.

Laing refers to the family group as a 'nexus'. He argues that 'the highest concern of the nexus is reciprocal concern. Each partner is concerned about what the other thinks, feels, does'. Within the nexus there is a constant, unremitting demand for mutual concern and attention. As a result there is considerable potential for harm; family members are in an extremely vulnerable position. Thus if a father is ashamed of his son, given the nature of the nexus, his son is deeply affected. As he is emotionally locked into the nexus, he is concerned about his father's opinion and cannot brush it off lightly. In self-defence he may run to his mother who offers protection. In this way Laing argues that, 'A family can act as gangsters, offering each other mutual protection against each other's violence'.

From interaction within the nexus, 'reciprocal interiorization' develops. Family members become a part of each other and the family as a whole. They interiorize or internalize the family. Laing argues that, 'To be in the same family is to feel the same "family" inside'. The example of

Jane illustrates this process – her little world is an interiorization of family interaction patterns. Laing regards the process of interiorization as psychologically damaging since it restricts the development of the self. The individual carries the blueprint of his family with him for the rest of his life. This prevents any real autonomy or freedom of self, it prevents the development of the individual in his own right. Self-awareness is smothered under the blanket of the family. As a result of family interiorization, Laing states, 'I consider most adults (including myself) are or have been more or less, in a hypnotic trance induced in early infancy'.

Like Leach, Laing argues that problems in the family create problems in society. Due to the nature of the nexus and the process of interiorization, a boundary or even a defensive barrier is drawn between the family and the world outside. This can reach the point where, 'Some families live in perpetual anxiety of what, to them, is an external persecuting world. The members of the family live in a family ghetto as it were'. Laing argues that this is one reason for so-called maternal overprotection. However, 'It is not "over" protection from the mother's point of view, nor indeed, often from the point of view of other members of the family'. This perception of the external threat of a menacing society tends to unite and strengthen the nexus. The barrier erected between the family and the world outside may have important consequences. According to Laing it leads family members, particularly children, to see the world in terms of 'us and them'. From this basic division stem the harmful and dangerous distinctions between Gentile and Jew, Black and White and the separation of others into 'people like us' and 'people like them'.

Within the family children learn to obey their parents. Laing regards this as the primary link in a dangerous chain. Patterns of obedience laid down in early childhood form the basis for obedience to authority in later life. They lead to soldiers and officials blindly and unquestioningly following orders. Laing implies that without family obedience training, people would question orders, follow their own judgment and make their own decisions. If this were so, American soldiers might not have marched off to fight what Laing regards as a senseless war in Vietnam. We might no longer live in a society which Laing believes is largely insane.

Despite Laing's preoccupation with the dark side of family life, he stated in an interview in 1977, 'I enjoy living in a family. I think the family is still the best thing that still exists biologically as a natural thing. My attack on the family is aimed at the way I felt many children are subjected to gross forms of violence and violation of their rights, to humiliation at the hands of adults who don't know what they're doing'.

David Cooper – *The Death of the Family*

David Cooper is a phenomenological psychiatrist who has worked closely with Laing. His book, *The Death of the Family* is an outright condemnation of the family as an institution. Like Laing, he sees the family as a stultifying institution which stunts the self and largely denies people the freedom to develop their own individuality. To develop an autonomous self, the child must be free to be alone, free from the constant demands made upon him in the family, free from the 'imprisoning and ambiguous love' which engulfs him. Like Laing, Cooper argues that individuals interiorize the family. Because of this the self can never be free since it is made up of other family members. In the process of interiorization, 'one glues bits of other people onto oneself' and for most people, this results in 'the chronic murder of their selves'.

Cooper develops his ideas along Marxian lines. He argues that the family operates 'as an ideological conditioning device in an exploitive society – slave society, feudal society, capitalist society'. The behaviour patterns and controls laid down within the family produce the 'well-conditioned, endlessly obedient citizen' who is easily manipulated by ruling classes. As a result of the social controls implanted into the child by family socialization, 'The child is in fact primarily taught not how to survive in society but how to submit to it'. Each child has the potential to be an artist, a visionary and a revolutionary but this potential is crushed in the family. Artists, visionaries and revolutionaries tend to think for themselves and to see through ruling class ideologies. However the opportunity to develop in this way is stifled by the submission of the self to the demands of the family. Social controls implanted by the family are particularly effective because of the 'elaborate system of taboos' which saturate family life. For example, after they have reached a certain age boys are not supposed to kiss their fathers and breaking this taboo can produce strong guilt feelings. The association of guilt with the breaking of family taboos provides the basis for conformity and submission to the laws and requirements of the powerful.

Cooper argues that 'the family specializes in the formation of roles for its members rather than laying down conditions for the free assumption of identity'. Thus children are taught to play the roles of son and daughter, male and female. Such roles are constricting. They confine behaviour within narrow limits and restrict the development of self. They lay the groundwork for 'indoctrination' into roles at school, work and in society generally. The family prepares the individual for his induction into the role he is to play in an exploitive society, the role of 'the endlessly obedient citizen'. Cooper's view of the relationship between the family and society is summarized in the following quotation, 'So the family goes on and is externally reflected in all our relationships'. An exploitive family produces an exploitive society.

Leach, Laing and Cooper in their different ways have presented a radical alternative to the functionalist perspective on the family. Their work is open to a number of criticisms. None have conducted detailed fieldwork on the family in contemporary industrial society. Laing and

Cooper's research is limited to investigations of families in which one member has been defined as schizophrenic. All talk about 'the family' with little reference to its position in the social structure. For example, there is no reference to social class in either Laing or Cooper's work and therefore no indication of the relationship between class and family life. Leach examines the family over time, but apart from vague references to capitalism and previous eras in Cooper's writings, the work of both Cooper and Laing lacks any historical perspective. All three authors examine the Western family from their particular specialized knowledge, Leach from his work on family and kinship in small-scale non-Western societies, Laing and Cooper from their studies of schizophrenia and family life. This inevitably colours their views. In itself, this is not a criticism, but it is important to be aware of the source of their perspectives. To some degree Leach, Laing and Cooper begin with a picture of a society out of control or even gone mad. Leach in *A Runaway World?* implies that society has got out of hand, Laing and Cooper go even further by suggesting that many aspects of contemporary society are insane. Such views of society will produce what many consider to be an extreme and unbalanced picture of the family. However, it is possible to accuse the functionalists of the opposite bias. For example, Parsons gives the impression of an immensely reasonable society ticking over like clockwork. In this context a well-adjusted, contented family is to be expected.

Leach, Laing and Cooper have provided a balance to the functionalist view which has dominated sociological thinking on the family for many years. Laing in particular, has given important insights into interaction patterns within the family. In doing so he may, as D. H. J. Morgan suggests, have come 'closer to family life as it is actually experienced than do many of the more orthodox presentations'.

The family – a Marxian perspective

Marxian sociologists have tended to bypass the family in their preoccupation with social class. Apart from Friedrich Engels, who wrote an important work on the origin and evolution of the family entitled *The Origin of the Family, Private Property and the State*, (first published in 1884), until the late 1960s few writers attempted to apply Marxian theory to the family.

Like many nineteenth-century scholars, Engels took an evolutionary view of the family, attempting to trace its origin and evolution through time. He combined an evolutionary approach with Marxian theory arguing that as the mode of production changed, so did the family. During the early stages of human evolution, Engels believed that the forces of production were communally owned and the family as such did not exist. This era of 'primitive communism' was characterized by promiscuity.

There were no rules limiting sexual relationships and society was, in effect, the family. Although Engels has been criticized for this type of speculation, the anthropologist Kathleen Gough argues that his picture may not be that far from the truth. She notes that man's nearest relatives, the chimpanzees, live in 'promiscuous hordes' and this may have been the pattern for early man.

Engels argued that throughout man's history, more and more restrictions were placed on sexual relationships and the production of children. He speculated that from the promiscuous horde, marriage and the family evolved through a series of stages which included polygyny to its present stage, the monogamous nuclear family. Each successive stage placed greater restrictions on the number of mates available to the individual. The monogamous nuclear family developed with the emergence of private property, in particular the private ownership of the forces of production, and the advent of the state. The state instituted laws to protect the system of private property and to enforce the rules of monogamous marriage. This form of marriage and the family developed to solve the problem of the inheritance of private property. Property was owned by males and in order for them to pass it on to their heirs, they must be certain of the legitimacy of those heirs. They therefore needed greater control over women so there would be no doubt about the paternity of their offspring. The monogamous family provided the most efficient device for this purpose. In Engels's words, 'It is based on the supremacy of the man, the express purpose being to produce children of undisputed paternity; such paternity is demanded because these children are later to come into their father's property as his natural heirs'.

Engels's scheme of the evolution of the family is much more elaborate than the brief outline described above. It was largely based on *Ancient Society*, an erroneous interpretation of the evolution of the family by the nineteenth-century American anthropologist, Lewis Henry Morgan. Modern research has suggested that many of its details are incorrect. For example monogamous marriage and the nuclear family are often found in hunting and gathering bands. Since man has lived in hunting and gathering bands for 99.9% of his existence, the various forms of group marriage postulated by Engels, such as the promiscuous horde, may well be figments of his imagination. However, Kathleen Gough argues that 'the general trend of Engels's argument still appears sound'. Although nuclear families and monogamous marriage exist in small-scale societies, they form a part of a larger kinship group. When individuals marry they take on a series of duties and obligations to their spouse's kin. Communities are united by kinship ties and the result is like a large extended family. Gough argues that, 'It is true that although it is not a group marriage in Engels's sense, marriage has a group character in many hunting bands and in most of the more complex tribal societies that have developed with the domestication of plants and animals. With the development of privately owned, heritable property, and especially with the rise of the state, this group character gradually disappears'. (Further aspects of Engels's views on the family are examined in the following chapter, pp. 390–91.)

Marxian analysis of the family in capitalist society developed mainly in the late 1960s and 1970s, when several feminist writers employed Marxian concepts in their criticism of the family. From this perspective, the family is seen as a unit which produces one of the basic commodities of capitalism, labour. It produces it cheaply from the point of view of the capitalists, since they do not have to pay for the production of children or their upkeep. In particular, the wife is not paid for producing and rearing children. Margaret Benston states that 'the amount of unpaid labor performed by women is very large and very profitable to those who own the means of production. To pay women for their work, even at minimum wage scales, would involve a massive redistribution of wealth. At present, the support of the family is a hidden tax on the wage earner – his wage buys the labor power of two people'. The fact that the husband must pay for the production and upkeep of future labour acts as a strong discipline on his behaviour at work. He cannot easily withdraw his labour with a wife and children to support. These responsibilities weaken his bargaining power and commit him to wage labour. Benston argues that, 'As an economic unit, the nuclear family is a valuable stabilizing force in capitalist society. Since the production which is done in the home is paid for by the husband–father's earnings, his ability to withhold labour from the market is much reduced'.

Not only does the family produce and rear cheap labour, it also maintains it in good order at no cost to the employer. In her role as housewife, the woman attends to her husband's needs thus keeping him in good running order to perform his role as a wage labourer. Fran Ansley translates Parsons's view, that the family functions to stabilize adult personalities, into a Marxian framework. She sees the emotional support provided by the wife as a safety-valve for the frustration produced in the husband by working in a capitalist system. Rather than being turned against the system which produced it, this frustration is absorbed by the comforting wife. In this way the system is not threatened. In Ansley's words, 'When wives play their traditional role as takers of shit, they often absorb their husbands' legitimate anger and frustration at their own powerlessness and oppression. With every worker provided with a sponge to soak up his possibly revolutionary ire, the bosses rest more secure' (quoted in Bernard, 1976, p. 233). Kathy McAfee and Myrna Wood make a similar point in their discussion of male dominance in the family. They claim that, 'The petty dictatorship which most men exercise over their wives and families enables them to vent their anger and frustration in a way which poses no challenge to the system' (quoted in Rowbotham, 1973, p. 58).

The social reproduction of labour power does not simply involve producing children and maintaining them in good health. It also involves the reproduction of the attitudes essential for an efficient workforce under capitalism. Thus David Cooper argues that the family is 'an ideological conditioning device in an exploitive society'. Within the family children learn to conform, to submit to authority. The foundation is therefore laid for the obedient and submissive workforce required by capitalism. A similar point is made by Diane Feeley who argues that the structure of family relationships socializes the young to accept their place in a class stratified society. She sees the family as an authoritarian unit dominated by the husband in particular and adults in general. Feeley claims that the family with its 'authoritarian ideology is designed to teach passivity, not rebellion'. Thus children learn to submit to parental authority and emerge from the family pre-conditioned to accept their place in the hierarchy of power and control in capitalist society. (Marxian views on the role of the family in capitalist society mirror Marxian analysis of the role of education; see Chapter 5, pp. 179–87.)

Some of the criticisms of previous views of the family also apply to Marxian approaches. There is a tendency to talk about 'the family' in capitalist society without regard to possible variations in family life between social classes and over time. As D. H. J. Morgan notes in his criticism of both functionalist and Marxian approaches, both 'presuppose a traditional model of the nuclear family where there is a married couple with children, where the husband is the breadwinner and where the wife stays at home to deal with the housework'. Although there is some justice to this criticism, Marxian views of the family have developed to include families in which the wife is also a wage earner. These views will be examined in detail in the following chapter (pp. 390–97).

The family and industrialization

A major theme in sociological studies of the family is the relationship between the structure of the family and the process of industrialization. Industrialization refers to the mass production of goods in a factory system which involves some degree of mechanized production technology. There are a number of problems which arise from relating the family to industrialization. Firstly, the process of industrialization does not follow the same course in every society. Secondly, industrialization is not a fixed thing but a developing process. Thus the industrial system in nineteenth-century Britain is different in important respects to that of today. Further difficulties arise from the fact that there is not one form of pre-industrial family but many. Much of the research on the family and industrialization has led to considerable confusion because it is not always clear what the family in industrial society is being compared to. In addition, within industrial society there are variations in family structure. As a starting point, it is necessary to examine the family in pre-industrial societies in order to establish a standard for comparison.

In many small-scale, non-literate societies, the family and kinship relationships in general are the basic organizing principles of social life. Societies are often divided into a number of kinship groups such as lineages which are groups descended from a common ancestor. The family is embedded in a web of kinship relationships. Kinship groups are responsible for the production of important goods and services. For example, a lineage may own agricultural land which is worked, and its produce shared, by members of the lineage. Members of kinship groups are united by a network of mutual rights and obligations. In some cases, if an individual is insulted or injured by someone from outside the group, he has the right to call on the support of members of his group to seek reparation or revenge. Many areas of an individual's behaviour are shaped by his status as a kinsman. For example, as an uncle he may have binding obligations to be involved with aspects of his nephew's socialization and be responsible for the welfare of his nieces and nephews should their father die. Something of the importance of family and kinship relationships in many small-scale societies is illustrated by the following statement by a Pomo Indian of northern California, 'What is a man? A man is nothing. Without his family he is of less importance than that bug crossing the trail. In the white ways of doing things the family is not so important. The police and soldiers take care of protecting you, the courts give you justice, the post office carries messages for you, the school teaches you. Everything is taken care of, even your children, if you die; but with us the family must do all of that' (from *A Pomo's Soliloquy*, Aginsky, 1968). This brief description of the family in small-scale, pre-industrial society has glossed over the wide variation in family and kinship patterns which are found in such societies. However, it serves to highlight some of the more important differences between the family in kinship based society and the family in industrial society.

A second form of pre-industrial family, sometimes known as the 'classic' extended family, is found in some traditional peasant societies. This family type has been made famous by C. M. Arensberg and S. T. Kimball's study of Irish farmers entitled, *Family and Community in Ireland*. As in kinship based societies, kinship ties dominate life. But in this case, the basic unit is the extended family rather than the wider kinship grouping. The traditional Irish farming family is a patriarchal extended family, so-called because of the considerable authority of the male head and the fact that property is passed down the male line. Within the family, social and economic roles are welded together, status being ascribed by family membership. On the farm the father–son relationship is also that of owner–employee. The father–owner makes all important decisions, for example whether to sell cattle, and directs the activities of all other members of the extended family. He is head of the family and director of the firm. Typically, the classic extended family consists of the male head, his wife and children, his aging parents from whom he has inherited the farm and any unmarried brothers and sisters. Together they work as a 'production unit', producing the goods necessary for the family's survival.

There is general agreement that as industrialization proceeds, kinship based society and the classic extended family tend to break up and the nuclear family or some form of modified extended family emerge as the predominant family form.

Talcott Parsons – the 'isolated nuclear family'

Talcott Parsons argues that the 'isolated nuclear family' is the typical family form in modern industrial society. It is 'structurally isolated' because it does not form an integral part of a wider system of kinship relationships. Obviously there are social relationships between members of nuclear families and their kin but these relationships are more a matter of choice than binding obligations. Parsons sees the emergence of the isolated nuclear family in terms of his theory of social evolution. (This theory is outlined in Chapter 13, pp. 529–30.) The evolution of society involves a process of 'structural differentiation'. This means that institutions evolve which specialize in fewer functions. In this sense, no longer do the family and kinship groups perform a wide range of functions. Instead specialist institutions such as business firms, schools, hospitals, police forces and churches take over many of their functions. This process of differentiation and specialization involves the 'transfer of a variety of functions from the nuclear family to other structures of the society'. Thus in industrial society, with the transfer of the production of goods to factories, specialized economic institutions became differentiated from the family. The family ceases to be an economic unit of production.

Functionalist analysis emphasizes the importance of integration and harmony between the parts of society. An efficient social system requires the parts to fit smoothly rather than abrade. The parts of society are functionally related when they contribute to the integration and harmony of the social system. Parsons argues that there is a functional relationship between the isolated nuclear family and the economic system in industrial society. In particular the isolated nuclear family is shaped to meet the requirements of the economic system. A modern industrial system with a specialized division of labour demands considerable geographical mobility from its labour force. Individuals with specialized skills are required to move to places where those skills are in demand. The isolated nuclear family is suited to the need for geographical mobility. It is not tied down by binding obligations to a wide range of kin, and compared to the pre-industrial families described above, it is a small, streamlined unit.

Status in industrial society is achieved rather than ascribed. An individual's occupational status is not automatically fixed by his ascribed status in the family or kinship group. Parsons argues that the isolated nuclear family is the best form of family structure for a society based on achieved status. In industrial society, individuals are judged in terms of the status they achieve. Such judgments are based on what Parsons terms 'universalistic values', that is values that are universally applied to all members of society. However, within the family, status is ascribed and, as such, based on 'particularistic values', that is values that are applied only to particular individuals. Thus a son's relationship with his father is conducted primarily in terms of their ascribed statuses of father and son. The father's achieved status as a bricklayer, schoolteacher or lawyer has relatively little influence on their relationship since his son does not judge him primarily in terms of universalistic values. Parsons argues that in a society based on achieved status conflict would tend to arise in a family unit larger than the isolated nuclear family. In a three generation extended family in which the children remained as part of the family unit, the following situation could produce conflict. If the son became a doctor and the father was a labourer, the particularistic values of family life would give the father a higher status than his son. Yet the universalistic values of society as a whole would award his son higher social status. Conflict may result from this situation which could undermine the authority of the father and threaten the solidarity of the family. The same conflict of values may occur if the nuclear family were extended horizontally. Relationships between a man and his brother may be problematic if they held jobs of widely differing prestige.

The isolated nuclear family largely prevents these problems from arising. There is one main breadwinner, the husband–father. His wife is mainly responsible for raising the children and the latter have yet to achieve their status in the world of work. No member of the family is in a position to threaten the ascribed authority structure by achieving a status outside the family which is higher than the achieved status of the family head. These problems do not occur in pre-industrial society. There, occupational status is largely ascribed since an individual's position in the family and kinship group usually determines his job. Parsons concludes that given the universalistic, achievement oriented values of industrial society, the isolated nuclear family is the most suitable family structure. Any extension of this basic unit may well create conflict which would threaten the solidarity of the family.

As a consequence of the structural isolation of the nuclear family, the conjugal bond – the relationship between husband and wife – is strengthened. Without the support of kin beyond the nuclear family, spouses are increasingly dependent on each other, particularly for emotional support. As outlined in a previous section, Parsons argues that the stabilization of adult personalities is a major function of the family in industrial society. This is largely accomplished in terms of the husband–wife relationship.

William J. Goode

In *World Revolution and the Family* William J. Goode surveys the relationship between family structure and industrialization in various parts of the world. Like Parsons, he argues that industrialization tends to undermine the extended family and larger kinship groupings. Goode offers the following explanations for this process. The high rate of geographical mobility in industrial society decreases 'the frequency and intimacy of contact among members of the kin network'. The relatively high level of social mobility also tends to weaken kinship ties. For example, if a member of a working-class family becomes upwardly mobile, he may adopt the life style, attitudes and values of his new social class. This would tend to cut him off from his working-class kin. Many of the functions once performed by the family have been taken over by outside agencies such as schools, business and welfare organizations. This reduces the dependency of the individual on his family and kin. The importance of achieved status in industrial society means that the family and kinship group have less to offer their members. The family cannot guarantee its members a job or directly provide the necessary education and training to obtain one. The highly specialized division of labour in industrial society makes it even more difficult for an individual to obtain a job for a relative. As Goode states, 'He may not be in a suitable sector of the occupational sphere, or at a level where his influence is useful'.

However, Goode does not regard the pressures of industrialization as the only reason for the breakdown of extended family ties. He argues that the move to nuclear families has been 'far more rapid than could be supposed or predicted from the degree of industrialization alone'. Goode believes that the ideology of the nuclear family has encouraged its growth, particularly in non-Western societies. This is due partly to the prestige of Western ideas and life styles. Since the nuclear family is found 'in many areas where the rate of industrialization is slight' Goode recognizes 'the independent power of *ideological* variables'. He also argues that the spread of the nuclear family is due in part to the freedom it affords its members. Kenneth Little supports this point in his study of migration from rural kinship based societies to urban industrial centres in West Africa. Many migrants welcomed the freedom from obligations to their kinsmen which they experienced in the towns.

Goode applies the concept of role bargaining to his study of the family. This means that the individual attempts to obtain the best possible 'bargain' in his relationships with others. He will attempt to maximize his gains. In terms of family relationships, this means he will maintain relationships with kin and submit to their control if he feels he is getting a good return on his investment of time, energy and emotion. With respect to the extended family and industrialization, Goode argues that, 'It is not so much that the new system is incompatible, as it offers an alternative pattern of payments'. In other words, extended family patterns can operate in industrial society. Although it costs time and money, the rapid transport system in modern society means that 'the individual can maintain an extended kin network if he *wishes* to do so'. However, the 'alternative pattern of payments' offered by industrial society provides a better bargain for many people. They gain more by rejecting close and frequent contacts with kin beyond the nuclear family than by retaining them.

Goode uses the concept of role bargaining to explain social class differences in family structure. From his world survey, Goode finds that extended family patterns are most likely to occur in the upper classes. Since members of ruling classes and elites have an important influence on appointments to top jobs, the retention of family ties makes economic sense. In Goode's terms it is an effective role bargain. Lupton and Wilson's study of the kinship connections of 'top decision makers' gives some indication of the importance of family connections in the British upper class. (See Chapter 3, pp. 124–7, for details of this study and related research.) By comparison, members of the lower strata 'have little to offer the younger generation to counteract their normal tendency to independence'. Goode concludes that extended kinship ties are retained if individuals feel they have more to gain than to lose by maintaining them.

Peter Laslett – the family in pre-industrial England

The family in kinship based society and the classic extended family represent only two possible forms of family structure in pre-industrial society. Historical research in Britain and America suggests that neither was typical of those countries in the pre-industrial era. Peter Laslett, a Cambridge historian, has studied family size and composition in pre-industrial England. From 1564 to 1821 he found that only about 10% of households contained kin beyond the nuclear family. This percentage is the same as for England in 1966. Evidence from America presents a similar picture. This surprisingly low figure may be due in part to the fact that people in pre-industrial England and America married relatively late in life and life expectancy was short. On average, there were only a few years between the marriage of a couple and the death of their parents. However, Laslett found no evidence to support the formerly accepted view that the classic extended family was widespread in pre-industrial England. He states that, 'There is no sign of the large, extended coresidential family group of the traditional peasant world giving way to the small, nuclear conjugal household of modern industrial society'.

It is now possible to suggest that it was not industrialization that produced the nuclear family but rather the reverse. The nuclear family may have been one of the factors encouraging the development of the industrial revolution in England. As the predominant form of family structure, it was pre-adapted to the requirements of industrial society.

Michael Anderson – *Household Structure and the Industrial Revolution*

Further historical evidence suggests that far from encouraging the formation of nuclear families, the early stages of industrialization in England may well have strengthened kinship ties beyond the nuclear family. Using data from the 1851 census of Preston, Michael Anderson found that some 23% of households contained kin other than the nuclear family, a large increase over Laslett's figures and those for today. The bulk of this 'co-residence' occurred among the poor. Anderson argues that co-residence occurs when the parties involved receive net gains from the arrangement. He states that, 'If we are to understand variations and changes in patterns of kinship relationships, the only worthwhile approach is consciously and explicitly to investigate the manifold advantages and disadvantages that any actor can obtain from maintaining one relational pattern rather than another'.

Preston in 1851 was largely dependent on the cotton industry. Life for many working-class families was characterized by severe hardship resulting from low wages, periods of high unemployment, large families, a high death rate and overcrowded housing. In these circumstances, the maintenance of a large kinship network could be advantageous to all concerned. In the absence of a welfare state, individuals were largely dependent on kin in times of hardship and need. Aging parents often lived with their married children, a situation which benefitted both parties. It provided support for the aged and allowed the mother to work in the factory since grandparents could care for the dependent children. The high death rate led to a large number of orphans, many of whom found a home with relatives. Again the situation benefitted both parties. It provided support for the children who would soon, in a age of child labour, make an important contribution to household income. A high rate of sickness and unemployment encouraged a wide network of kin as a means of mutual support. In the absence of sickness and unemployment benefits, individuals were forced to rely on their kin in times of hardship. Co-residence also provided direct economic advantages to those concerned. Additional members of the household would lower the share of the rent paid by each individual. Finally, the practice of recruiting for jobs through kin encouraged the establishment of a wide kinship network. Anderson notes that the system of '"Asking for" a job for kin was normal in the factory towns, and the employers used the kinship system to recruit labour from the country'.

Anderson's study of Preston indicates that in the mid nineteenth century, the working-class family functioned as a mutual aid organization. It provided an insurance policy against hardship and crisis. This function encouraged the extension of kinship bonds beyond the nuclear family. Such links would be retained as long as they provided net gains to those involved. Anderson concludes that the early stages of industrialization increased rather than decreased the extension of the working-class family.

Michael Young and Peter Willmott – four stages of family life

Michael Young and Peter Willmott have been conducting studies of family life in London for over twenty years. In their latest book, *The Symmetrical Family*, they attempt to trace the development of the family from pre-industrial England to the present day. Using a combination of historical research and social surveys – large-scale surveys based on random samples within a particular area – they suggest that the family is moving through four main stages. This section will concentrate on their analysis of the working-class family.

Stage 1 is represented by the pre-industrial family. The family is a unit of production, the husband, wife and unmarried children working as a team, typically in agriculture or textiles. This type of family was gradually supplanted by the industrial revolution. However, it continued well into the nineteenth century and is still represented in a small minority of families today. The Stage 2 family began with the industrial revolution, developed throughout the nineteenth century and reached its peak in the early years of the twentieth. The family ceased to be a unit of production since individual members were employed as wage earners. Throughout the nineteenth century working-class poverty was widespread, wages were low and unemployment high. Like Anderson, Young and Willmott argue that the family responded to this situation by extending its network to include relatives beyond the nuclear family. This provided an insurance policy against the insecurity and hardship of poverty. The extension of the nuclear family was largely conducted by women who 'eventually built up an organization in their own defence and in defence of their children'. The basic tie was between a mother and her married daughter and in comparison, the conjugal bond – the husband–wife relationship – was weak. Women created an 'informal trade union' which largely excluded men. Young and Willmott claim that, 'Husbands were often squeezed out of the warmth of the female circle and took to the pub as their defence'. Compared to later stages, the Stage 2 family was often headed by a female. Unlike the situation of New World Black families, however, this resulted more from the high male death rate than from desertion by the husband.

The Stage 2 family began to decline in the early years of the twentieth century but it is still found in many low-income, long established working-class areas. Its survival is documented in Young and Willmott's famous study entitled *Family and Kinship in East London*. The study was conducted in the mid 1950s in Bethnal Green, a low-income borough in London's East End. Bethnal Green is a long settled, traditional working-class area. Children usually remain in the same locality on marriage. At the time of the research, two out of three married people had parents living within two to three miles of their residence. There was a close tie between female relatives. Over 50% of the married women in the sample had seen their mothers during the previous day, over 80% within the previous week. There was a constant exchange of services such as washing, shopping and babysitting, between female relatives. Young and Willmott argue that in many families, the households of mother and married daughter are 'to some extent merged'. As such they can be termed extended families which Young and Willmott define as 'a combination of families who to some degree form one domestic unit'. Although many aspects of the Stage 2 family were present in Bethnal Green, there were also indications of a transition to Stage 3. For example, fathers were increasingly involved in the rearing of their children.

In the early 1970s, Young and Willmott conducted a large-scale social survey in which 1 928 people were interviewed in Greater London and the outer Metropolitan area. The results formed the basis of their book, *The Symmetrical Family*. Young and Willmott argue that the Stage 2 family has largely disappeared. For all social classes, but particularly the working class, the Stage 3 family predominates. This family is characterized by 'the separation of the immediate, or nuclear family from the extended family'. The trade union of women is disbanded and the husband returns to the family circle. Life for the Stage 3 nuclear family is largely home-centred, particularly when the children are young. Free time is spent doing chores and odd jobs around the house and leisure is mainly 'home-based', for example watching television. The conjugal bond is strong and relationships between husband and wife are increasingly 'companionate'. In the home, 'They shared their work; they shared their time'. The nuclear family has become a largely self-contained, self-reliant unit. The Stage 3 family is very similar to the privatized home-centred affluent worker family described by Goldthorpe and Lockwood (see Chapter 2, pp. 59–60) and the isolated nuclear family which Talcott Parsons sees as typical of modern industrial society.

Young and Willmott use the term 'symmetrical family' to describe the nuclear family of Stage 3. Symmetry refers to an arrangement in which the opposite parts are similar in shape and size. With respect to the symmetrical family, conjugal roles, although not the same – wives still have the main responsibility for raising the children through husbands help –

are similar in terms of the contribution made by each spouse to the running of the household. They share many of the chores, they share decisions, they work together, yet there is still men's work and women's work. Conjugal roles are not interchangeable but they are symmetrical in important respects.

Young and Willmott give the following reasons for the transition from Stage 2 to Stage 3 families. A number of factors have reduced the need for kinship based mutual aid groups. They include an increase in the real wages of the male breadwinner, a decrease in unemployment and the male mortality rate and increased employment opportunities for women. Various provisions of the welfare state such as family allowances, sickness and unemployment benefits and old age pensions have reduced the need for dependence on the kinship network. Increasing geographical mobility has tended to sever kinship ties. In their study of Bethnal Green, Young and Willmott show how the extended kinship network largely ceased to operate when young couples with children moved some twenty miles away to a new council housing estate. The reduction in the number of children from an average of five or six per family in the nineteenth century to just over two in 1970 has had a number of consequences. Coupled with the fact that women live longer, it provides a greater opportunity for wives to work. This in turn leads to greater symmetry within the family since both spouses are more likely to be wage earners and to share financial responsibility for the household. Reduction in the number of children per family also reduced the financial burden on parents. As living standards rose, the husband was drawn more closely into the family circle since the home was a more attractive place. Better housing, less overcrowding, gas, electricity, improved plumbing facilities, fitted carpets and three-piece suites, household technology such as vacuum cleaners and washing machines, all produced a more comfortable environment. Home entertainment in the form of radio, television and record players provided further attractions for the former 'absentee husband'. To the above points can be added Goldthorpe and Lockwood's conclusions from the affluent worker study. They argue that the privatized nuclear family stems largely from the values placed by the affluent worker on home-centredness and materialism. The major concern of the affluent worker was to raise the living standards of himself and his immediate family, a concern that largely shapes his family structure and domestic life. (See Chapter 2, pp. 57–60.)

Young and Willmott found that the home-centred symmetrical family was more typical of the working class than the middle class. They argue that members of the working class are 'more fully home-centred because they are less fully work-centred'. Partly as compensation for boring and uninvolving work, and partly because relatively little interest and energy are expended at work, manual workers tend to focus their attention on family life. Young and Willmott argue that, 'The home-centred sort of

Stage 3 family was predominant in 1970 because the great majority of people (in the sample) were manual workers or in equally routine non-manual jobs. They had no alternative object of allegiance as compelling. If that changes and the majority of people no longer have such emotionally and intellectually unrewarding work, the predominant kind of family will change also'. Young and Willmott therefore see the nature of work as a major influence on family life.

In *The Symmetrical Family*, Young and Willmott devise a general theory which they term the 'Principle of Stratified Diffusion'. They claim that this theory explains much of the change in family life in industrial society. Put simply, the theory states that what the top of the stratification system does today, the bottom will do tomorrow. Life styles, patterns of consumption, attitudes and expectations will diffuse from the top of the stratification system downwards. They argue that industrialization is the 'source of momentum', it provides the opportunities for higher living standards and so on. However, industrialization alone cannot account for the changes in family life. For example it cannot fully explain why the mass of the population has chosen to adopt the life style of Stage 3 families. To complete the explanation, Young and Willmott maintain that the Principle of Stratified Diffusion is required. Industrialization provides the opportunity for a certain degree of choice for the mass of the population. This choice will be largely determined by the behaviour of those at the top of the stratification system. Values, attitudes and expectations permeate down the class system; those at the bottom copy those at the top. There are a number of problems with this theory. In particular, it largely ignores the possibility that working-class subculture can direct behaviour. In the Luton study, Goldthorpe and Lockwood argue that behaviour of the affluent worker can be understood in terms of the adaptation of working-class norms and values to a new situation. They reject the view that the affluent worker simply absorbs the norms and values of higher social strata and acts accordingly.

Applying the Principle of Stratified Diffusion to the future, Young and Willmott postulate a possible Stage 4 family. They examine in detail the family life of managing directors, which in terms of their theory, should diffuse downwards in years to come. Managing directors are work-centred rather than home-centred, 'my business is my life' being a typical quote from those in the sample. Their leisure activities are less home-centred and less likely to involve their wives than those of Stage 3 families. Sport was an important area of recreation, particularly swimming and golf. The wife's role was to look after the children and the home. As such the managing director's family was more asymmetrical than the Stage 3 family. Young and Willmott suggest that changes in production technology may provide the opportunity for the Stage 4 family to diffuse throughout the stratification system. As technology reduces routine work, larger numbers of people may have more interesting and involving jobs and become increasingly work-centred. Young and Willmott admit that, 'We cannot claim that our 190 managing directors were representative of managing directors generally'. However, given the evidence available, they predict that the asymmetrical Stage 4 family represents the next major development. Evidence examined in Chapter 6 provides little support for their prediction. Several studies indicate that changes in production technology have done little, if anything, to increase work involvement for manual workers. For example, Duncan Gallie's study of workers in automated industry, which employs the most advanced form of production technology, shows that the typical attitude towards work was one of indifference. (For details of this research see Chapter 6, pp. 254–7.)

The middle-class family

Many of the arguments examined in preceding sections suggest that the middle-class family should be less attached to kin beyond the nuclear unit that its working-class counterpart. Given the nature of the middle-class job market, it is more geographically mobile. It is also more financially secure. There is therefore less opportunity and less need to maintain a wide kinship network. However, a number of studies have shown that middle-class families maintain close contacts with kin beyond the family. Research conducted in the late 1950s by Willmott and Young in Woodford, a largely middle-class London suburb, shows that, despite the fact that kin were more geographically dispersed compared to Bethnal Green, fairly regular contacts were maintained. In Bethnal Green, 43% of husbands and wives had seen their mothers in the previous twenty-four hours, compared to 30% in Woodford. Although in Woodford there was less frequent contact with parents while the latter were employed, the frequency of contact was much the same as Bethnal Green when parents retired. On retirement, middle-class parents often moved to Woodford to live near their married children. In their study of Swansea, conducted in the early 1960s, Rosser and Harris found that levels of contact between parents and married children were similar to those in Bethnal Green. This applied both to middle and working-class families. Despite the wider dispersal of kin in Swansea, improved transportation facilities, particularly the family car, made frequent contact possible. Rosser and Harris state that, 'The picture that emerges, then, is of a vigorous kinship grouping wider than the elementary (nuclear) family, similar to that described in the Bethnal Green studies'. As in Bethnal Green, the Swansea families exchanged services with kin beyond the nuclear family and provided each other with support in times of need. Rosser and Harris conclude that, 'In Swansea, a high level of industrialization, social mobility and a wider dispersal of the family has not prevented the maintainance of high levels of contact and the interchange of services between related households'.

A major problem in studies of the family is the difficulty of measuring the importance of kin beyond the nuclear family. In a study of middle-class family life in Swansea, Colin Bell questions whether the frequency of actual face to face contacts between kin provides an accurate assessment. Bell points to the importance of contact by telephone and mail. He also distinguishes between the quantity and quality of contacts. For example, bumping into mum on a street corner in Bethnal Green may have far less significance than a formal visit to mother by her middle-class daughter. Bell found a lower level of direct face to face contact with kin beyond the nuclear family than in either the Woodford sample or Rosser and Harris's middle class sample. Despite this relatively low level of contact, he argues that compared with the working class, 'Middle-class kin networks may have fewer day-to-day demands but I think that there is little evidence to suggest that they necessarily show any different affective quality'. Thus direct contact may be less frequent but the emotional bonds are the same. Bell makes a similar point about the provision of services for kin beyond the nuclear family. They may not be as numerous as those provided in the working class, but they may be just as significant. He found that aid from parents, especially the son's father, was particularly important during the early years of marriage. It often took the form of loans or gifts to help with the deposit on a house or the expenses of the first baby. Bell concludes that kin beyond the nuclear family still play an important part in the lives of many middle-class families.

Evidence from America provides a similar picture. Studies from a number of cities in the USA show that for both middle and working classes, the degree of contact and the exchange of services with kin beyond the nuclear family is similar to the British pattern.

The isolated nuclear family?

The evidence so far presented under the heading of 'The family and industrialization' provides a somewhat confusing picture. On the one hand there is Talcott Parsons's isolated nuclear family, on the other a large body of evidence suggesting that kin beyond the nuclear family play an important part in family life. To make matters more confusing, Young and Willmott do not provide sufficient data to allow an assessment of the importance of kin to the Stage 3 family. In America a number of researchers have rejected Parsons's concept of the isolated nuclear family. For example, Sussman and Burchinal argue that the weight of evidence from a large body of research indicates that the modern American family is far from isolated. They maintain that the family can only be properly understood 'by rejection of the isolated nuclear family concept'.

Parsons replied to his critics in an article entitled *The Normal American Family*. He argues that close relationships with kin outside the nuclear family are in no way inconsistent with the concept of the isolated nuclear family. Parsons states that 'the very psychological importance for the individual of the nuclear family in which he was born and brought up would make any such conception impossible'. However, he maintains that the nuclear family is structurally isolated. It is isolated from other parts of the social structure such as the economic system. For example, it does not form an integral part of the economic system as in the case of the peasant farming family in traditional Ireland. In addition, the so-called 'extended families' of modern industrial society 'do not form firmly structured units of the social system'. Relationships with kin beyond the nuclear family are not obligatory, they are a matter of individual choice. In this sense, 'extended kin constitute a resource which may be selectively taken advantage of within considerable limits'. Thus extended families do not form 'firmly structured units' as in the case of the classic extended family or the family in kinship based societies. Evidence from Rosser and Harris's Swansea research supports Parsons's arguments. Rosser and Harris maintain that the nuclear family is 'a basic structural unit of the society' and though kinship relationships beyond the nuclear family are important to individuals, in terms of the social structure as a whole they are 'not of major and critical importance'. The Swansea study revealed a 'vast variation' in kinship relationships. Members of some families were in daily contact with kin beyond the nuclear family, members of other families rarely saw their relatives. This is the expected finding in view of Parsons's emphasis upon individual choice. It supports his claim that extended families are not 'firmly structured units of the social system'.

In order to clear up the confusion surrounding the term 'isolated nuclear family', Eugene Litwak argues that a new term, the 'modified extended family' should be introduced to describe the typical family in modern industrial society. Litwak defines the modified extended family as 'a coalition of nuclear families in a state of partial dependence. Such partial dependence means that nuclear family members exchange significant services with each other, thus differing from the isolated nuclear family, as well as retain considerable autonomy (that is not bound economically or geographically) therefore differing from the classical extended family' (quoted in Morgan, 1975, p. 65).

The functions of the family in modern industrial society

Many sociologists argue that the family has lost a number of its functions in modern industrial society. Institutions such as businesses, political parties, schools, and welfare organizations now specialize in functions formerly performed by the family. Talcott Parsons argues that the family has become 'on the "macroscopic" levels, almost completely function-less. It does not itself, except here and there, engage in much economic production; it is not a significant unit in the political power system; it is not a major direct agency of integration of the larger society. Its indivi-dual members participate in all these functions, but they do so as "indivi-duals", not in their roles as family members'. However, this does not mean that the family is declining in importance. It has simply become more specialized. Parsons maintains that its role is still vital. By structur-ing the personalities of the young and stabilizing the personalities of adults, the family provides its members with the psychological training and support necessary to meet the requirements of the social system. Par-sons concludes that, 'the family is more specialized than before, but not in any general sense less important, because society is dependent *more* ex-clusively on it for the performance of *certain* of its vital functions'. Thus the loss of certain functions by the family has made its remaining func-tions more important.

This view is supported by N. Dennis who argues that impersonal bureaucratic agencies have taken over many of the family's functions. As a result the warmth and close supportive relationships which existed when the family performed a large range of functions have largely disap-peared. Dennis argues that in the impersonal setting of modern industrial society, the family provides the only opportunity 'to participate in a rela-tionship where people are perceived and valued as whole persons'. Out-side the family, individual's must often interact with strangers in terms of a number of roles. Adopting roles such as employee, customer, teacher and student, they are unable to express many aspects of themselves or de-velop deep and supportive relationships. Dennis argues that 'marriage has become the only institution in which the individual can expect esteem and love. Adults have no one on whom they have the right to lean for this sort of support at all comparable to their right to lean on their spouse'. Young and Willmott make a similar point arguing that the emotional sup-port provided by family relationships grows in importance as the family loses many of its functions. They claim that the family 'can provide some sense of wholeness and permanence to set against the more restricted and transitory roles imposed by the specialized institutions which have flou-rished outside the home. The upshot is that, as the disadvantages of the new industrial and impersonal society have become more pronounced, so the family has become more prized for its power to counteract them'.

Not all sociologists argue that the family has lost many of its functions in modern industrial society. Ronald Fletcher, a British sociologist and a staunch supporter of the family, maintains that just the opposite has hap-pened. In *The Family and Marriage in Britain* Fletcher argues that not only has the family retained its functions but those functions have 'increased in detail and importance'. Specialized institutions such as schools and hospitals have added to and improved the family's functions rather than superseded them. Fletcher maintains that the family's responsibility for socializing the young is as important as it ever was. State education has added to rather than removed this responsibility since 'Parents are expected to do their best to guide, encourage and support their children in their educational and occupational choices and careers'. In the same way, the state has not removed the family's responsibility for the physical welfare of its members. Fletcher argues that, 'The family is still centrally concerned with maintaining the health of its members, but it is now aided by wider provisions which have been *added* to the family's situation since pre-industrial times'. Rather than removing this function from the family, state provision of health services has served to expand and improve it. Compared to the past, parents are preoccupied with their children's health. State health and welfare provision has provided additional support for the family and made its members more aware of the importance of health and hygiene in the home.

Even though he admits that the family has largely lost its function as a unit of production, Fletcher argues that it still maintains a vital economic function as a unit of consumption. Particularly in the case of the modern home-centred family, money is spent on and in the name of the family rather than the individual. Thus the modern family demands fitted carpets, three-piece suites, washing machines, television sets and 'family' cars. Young and Willmott make a similar point with respect to their symmetrical Stage 3 family. They argue that, 'In its capacity as a consumer the family has also made a crucial alliance with technology'. Industry needs both a market for its goods and a motivated workforce. The symmetrical family provides both. Workers are motivated to work by their desire for consumer durables. This desire stems from the high value they place on the family and a privatized life style in the family home. This provides a ready market for the products of industry. In this way the family performs an important economic function and is functionally related to the economic system. In Young and Willmott words, 'The family and technology have achieved a mutual adaptation'.

As previous chapters have indicated, this economic function looks rather different from a Marxian perspective. Writers such as Marcuse and Gorz argue that alienation at work leads to a search for fulfilment outside work. However, the capitalist controlled mass media, with its advertisements that proclaim the virtues of family life and associate the products of industry with those virtues, simply creates 'false needs'. With pictures of the 'Persil mum' and the happy family in the midst of its consumer durables, the myth that material possessions bring happiness and fulfilment is promoted. This myth produces the obedient, motivated worker and the receptive consumer that capitalism requires. The family man is therefore ideal material for exploitation. (For details of Marcuse and Gorz's views see Chapter 6, pp. 235–7.)

In summary, most sociologists who adopt a functionalist perspective, argue that the family has lost several of its functions in modern industrial society but they maintain that the importance of the family has not declined. Rather, the family has adapted and is adapting to a developing industrial society. It remains a vital and basic institution in society.

Conjugal roles

A major characteristic of Young and Willmott's symmetrical family is the degree to which the spouses share domestic work and leisure activities. Relationships of this type are known as joint conjugal roles as opposed to segregated conjugal roles. In the Stage 2 family, conjugal roles, the marital roles of husband and wife, were largely segregated. There was a clear-cut division of labour between the spouses in the household, and the husband was relatively uninvolved with domestic chores and raising the children. This segregation of conjugal roles extended to leisure. The wife associated mainly with her female kin and neighbours, the husband with his male workmates, kin and neighbours. This pattern was typical of the traditional working-class community of Bethnal Green. In the Stage 3 symmetrical family, conjugal roles became more joint. Although the wife still has primary responsibility for housework and childrearing, husbands become more involved, often washing clothes, ironing and sharing other domestic duties. Husband and wife increasingly share responsibility for decisions which affect the family. They discuss matters such as household finances and their children's education to a greater degree than the Stage 2 family. Young and Willmott argue that the change from segregated to joint conjugal roles results mainly from the withdrawal of the wife from her relationships with female kin and the drawing of the husband into the family circle. The reasons they give for this have been discussed in a previous section (pp. 350–51).

In a famous study entitled, *Family and Social Network*, Elizabeth Bott presents an interesting and original interpretation of the nature of conjugal roles. She based her study on in-depth interviews with twenty families in Greater London. She found a relationship between conjugal roles and social class. The most extreme segregation occurred in working-class families. However, since joint conjugal roles were also found in working-class families, class alone could not explain the nature of husband–wife relationships. Bott claims that the explanation for variation in conjugal roles lies in social relationships which the husband and wife bring with them to the marriage. Each spouse before marriage has a social network – a number of people with whom he or she interacts with on a fairly regular basis. If most or all of the members of a social network know each other and meet regularly, Bott terms the network 'close-knit'. It has a high degree of 'connectedness'. If, on the other hand, members of the network are linked only or mainly through one individual, that is they are either strangers or meet infrequently, Bott terms the network 'loose-knit'. It has a low degree of 'connectedness'. Bott found that close-knit networks are associated with segregated conjugal roles, loose-knit networks with joint conjugal roles. In her words, 'The degree of segregation in the role-relationship of husband and wife varies directly with the connectedness of the family's social network. The more connected the network, the greater the degree of segregation between the roles of husband and wife. The less connected the network, the smaller the degree of segregation between the roles of husband and wife'.

Bott explains the relationship between social network and conjugal roles in the following way. If husband and wife each bring a close-knit network with them to the marriage, they will be less dependent on each other for companionship and emotional support. Each will have a close-knit group of friends and relatives to fall back on. Also, with most or all members of the network knowing each other, there will tend to be more pressure on the member who gets married to keep in touch and maintain his or her obligations to the group. By comparison, there is likely to be less emotional support from a loose-knit network and less pressure on a married member to retain contact. Spouses who bring loose-knit networks to their marriage will tend to be thrown together. They will be more dependent on each other for companionship and support, they will be more likely to join together in domestic work and leisure activities.

Bott's study has been criticized for its methodology. Her sample consists of only twenty couples. Her measurements of network connectedness and degree of conjugal role segregation have been criticized as imprecise. However, her work remains influential and has stimulated considerable research.

Rosser and Harris examined Bott's arguments in their study of family life in Swansea. They accept her point that there is a relationship between conjugal roles and social networks but they place greater emphasis on what happens during married life rather than the social relationships which precede it. In particular, they argue that the 'critical factor' is the 'degree of *domesticity* of the women involved'. If the wife, as in the past, is tied to the house with frequent pregnancies and has to spend a large part of her life involved in childrearing, she will tend to build up a close-knit network of female kin and neighbours who are similarly involved with domestic matters. Associated with this pattern of family life are traditional attitudes concerning the domesticity of women contained in such phrases as 'a woman's place is in the home'. With an increasing number of women in paid employment and a change in attitudes towards the female role, women are losing their former 'compulsive domesticity'. Now they have less time to retain or build up a separate network of female relatives and friends. They also have less in common with them. As a result their social networks are becoming increasingly loose-knit, their conjugal roles increasingly joint.

Bott's ideas have also been used to explain the high degree of conjugal role segregation often found in kinship based societies and in the classic extended family. In many small-scale societies and peasant communities, spouses bring a close-knit social network to the marriage and retain it during their married life. The anthropologist Max Gluckman argues that spouses 'were compelled to maintain attachments to the larger groups or groupings of kin who constituted the economically and politically functional groups of the society'. As a result, conjugal roles are segregated and there is a clear distinction between the roles of husband and wife. Gluckman notes that this distinction often became so institutionalized that it was reflected in 'ceremonial and even ritual practices and occult beliefs'. Arensberg's study of Irish peasant farmers illustrates how beliefs about conjugal role segregation are rooted in traditional folklore. He observes that, 'The plough, the harrow, the mower, the scythe, the spade and the turf-cutting *slan* are regarded as masculine instruments. The attitudes of the countryside forbid women's using them. In the same way, they heap ridicule upon the thought of a man's interesting himself in the feminine sphere, in poultry or in churning. Immemorial folklore bolsters this division. The woman is unlucky to masculine enterprises, for instance: it is dangerous to see a woman on the road to the fair. Likewise man is dangerous to woman's work. If he so much as takes his lighted pipe out of the house while she is churning, he may "take the butter" through fairy magic'.

As Rosser and Harris and Young and Willmott have indicated, there is an increasing trend in industrial society towards joint conjugal roles. However, something of the attitudes and behaviour described by Arensburg, still exists though in a much diluted form. The possibility of their disappearance will be discussed in detail in the following chapter.

Marital breakdown

Much of this chapter has been concerned with why families are formed in the first place, and why they remain together. This section will consider the other side of the coin, why families, or more specifically marriages, break down. Before examining this question, a definition of marital breakdown and a critical examination of the relevant statistics is necessary.

Marital breakdown can be divided into three main categories: divorce, which refers to the legal termination of a marriage; separation, which refers to the physical separation of the spouses: they no longer share the same dwelling; and so-called 'empty-shell' marriages, where the spouses live together, remain legally married, but their marriage exists in name only. These three forms must be considered in any assessment of the rate of marital breakdown.

Despite minor fluctuations, there has been a steady rise in divorce rates in industrial societies throughout this century. In 1911, 859 petitions for divorce were filed in England and Wales of which some three-quarters were granted a decree absolute. Table 19 presents statistics on divorce for England and Wales from 1951 to 1975.

Table 19   Divorce in England and Wales

	(Thousands and percentages)						
	1951	1961	1971	1972	1973	1974	1975
Petitions filed (thousands)	38.4	31.9	110.9	110.7	115.5	131.7	140.1
Decrees nisi granted (thousands)	30.5	26.9	89.3	110.7	107.3	117.9	123.2
Decrees absolute granted (thousands)	28.8	25.4	74.4	119.0	106.0	113.5	120.5
Rate per thousand married population	2.6	2.1	6.0	9.5	8.4	9.0	9.6

(Source: Social Trends, 1977, p. 59)

The dramatic increase in petitions in 1971 was due in part to new divorce legislation. This increase does not simply represent a backlog of couples waiting to legally end an unsatisfactory marriage, since the number of petitions continued to rise during the following years. Some indication of the significance of the above figures is provided by the following comparisons. A comparison of the number of marriages with the number of divorces in the mid 1970s gives an approximate three to one ratio, that is for every three marriages per year, there is one divorce. A comparison of the number granted a divorce in any one year compared to the number who remain married gives a somewhat different perspective. The rate for 1951 was 2.6 per 1 000 of the married population, for 1975, 9.6. These comparisons are somewhat misleading without an indication of the number of remarriages. For example, 13.1% of all marriages in 1951 were remarriages for one or both partners, 29.5% in 1975. Whichever way the figures are presented, the increase in divorce is dramatic. International comparisons provide a similar picture. Though there is some variation between industrial societies in the divorce rate – for example compared to England and Wales the divorce rate per 1 000 of the population was higher in the USA and Denmark in 1970, lower in Belgium and Japan – the divorce rate in all industrial societies is rising steadily.

Reliable figures for separation are unobtainable. In Britain, some indication is provided by applications to a magistrates' court for a legal separation order but many spouses separate without recourse to the courts, and for these there are no figures available. Robert Chester estimates that the number of recorded separations increased during the 1960s by about 65%. However, this does not necessarily mean an actual increase in separations. Chester suggests that, 'It might be expected that modern couples would be more ready than others in the past to regularize unsatisfactory marital situations, and that the number of unrecorded breakdowns has been falling'. This statement may well apply to empty-shell marriages, though estimates of the extent of such marriages can only be based on guesswork. Even where data exist, the concept is difficult to operationalize, that is put into a measurable form. For example, if a couple express a high level of dissatisfaction with their relationship, should this be termed an empty-shell marriage? Historical evidence gives the impression that empty-shell marriages are more likely to end in separation and divorce today than in the past. William J. Goode argues that in nineteenth-century America, 'People took for granted that spouses who no longer loved one another and who found life together distasteful should at least live together in public amity for the sake of their children and of their standing in the community'. Even though an increasing number of empty-shell marriages may end in separation and divorce today, this does not necessarily mean that the proportion of such marriages, in relation to the total number of marriages, is decreasing. In view of the problems involved in measuring marital breakdown, Robert Chester reaches the following conclusion, 'Contemporary marriages certainly have higher *recorded* breakdown rates, and they very probably have higher total breakdown rates, although the latter conclusion should be regarded as tentative'.

In *When Marriage Ends*, Nicky Hart argues that any explanation of marital breakdown must consider the following factors: those which affect the value attached to marriage; those which affect the degree of conflict between the spouses; and those which affect the opportunities for individuals to escape from marriage. These factors will first be considered from a functionalist perspective. From this viewpoint, behaviour is largely a response to shared norms and values. It therefore follows that a change in the rate of marital breakdown is to some degree a reflection of changing norms and values in general, and, in particular, those associated with marriage and divorce. Functionalists such as Talcott Parsons and Ronald Fletcher argue that the rise in marital breakdown stems largely from the fact that marriage is increasingly valued. People expect and demand more from marriage and consequently are more likely to end a relationship which may have been acceptable in the past. Thus Ronald Fletcher argues that, 'a relatively high divorce rate may be indicative not of *lower* but of *higher* standards of marriage in society'. This view finds some support from the increasing priority given to marriage and the family by the spouses in Young and Willmott's 'symmetrical family' and Goldthorpe and Lockwood's 'privatized family'. The high rate of remarriage also lends support to Parsons and Fletcher's arguments. Thus, paradoxically, the higher value placed on marriage may result in increased marital breakdown.

Nicky Hart argues that the second set of factors which must be considered in an explanation of marital breakdown are those which affect the degree of conflict between the spouses. From a functionalist perspective it can be argued that the adaptation of the family to the requirements of the economic system has placed a strain on the marital relationship. It has led to the relative isolation of the nuclear family from the wider kinship network. William J. Goode argues that as a result, the family 'carries a heavier emotional burden when it exists independently than when it is a small unit within a larger kin fabric. As a consequence, this unit is relatively fragile'. Edmund Leach makes a similar point. He suggests that the nuclear family suffers from an emotional overload which increases the level of conflict between its members.

In industrial society, the family specializes in fewer functions. It can be argued that, as a result, there are fewer bonds to unite its members. For example, the economic bond is considerably weakened when the family ceases to be a unit of production. N. Dennis suggests that the specialization of function which characterizes the modern family will lead to increased marital breakdown. Dennis argues that, 'In so far as companionship, a close, durable, intimate and unique relationship with one member of the opposite sex becomes the prime necessity in marriage, a failure in this respect becomes sufficient to lead to its abandonment'. Put simply, when love goes, there's nothing much left to hold the couple together.

From a functionalist perspective it can be argued that what is functional for one part of the social system can be dysfunctional for another part. In the same way, what is on balance functional for society as a whole, may have dysfunctional consequences for parts of society. Thus the functional relationship between the family and the economic system, which involves the relative isolation of the nuclear family from extended kin, may have dysfunctional consequences for the family. The structural differentiation of society, which involves the establishment of institutions specializing in particular functions, may increase the efficiency of the social system but at the same time produce dysfunctional effects on the family. Thus a high rate of marital breakdown may be the price the family has to pay for the greater good of the social system.

So far factors which affect the value attached to marriage and those which affect the degree of conflict between the spouses have been considered. The third set of factors which Nicky Hart considers essential to an explanation of marital breakdown are those which affect the opportunities for individuals to escape from marriage. If, as the functionalists argue, behaviour is directed by norms and values, a change in the norms and values associated with divorce would be expected. It is generally agreed that the stigma attached to divorce has been considerably reduced. This, in itself, will make divorce easier. Goode argues that the change in attitudes towards divorce is part of the more general process of secularization in Western societies. Secularization refers to the declining influence of the church and of religious belief in general (for a detailed discussion of secularization, see Chapter 11, pp. 473–88). During the nineteenth century, the church strongly denounced divorce, insisting that the phrase 'till death do us part' be taken literally. During this century, despite a strong rearguard action, the church has had to accommodate the rising divorce rate by taking a less rigid view. However, the official church position is probably less important than the declining influence of religious beliefs and values in general in industrial society. Many sociologists argue that secular, that is non-religious, beliefs and values increasingly direct behaviour. In terms of divorce, Goode argues this means that, 'Instead of asking, "Is this moral?" the individual is more likely to ask, "Is this a more useful or better procedure for my needs?"'.

The changing attitudes towards divorce have been institutionalized by various changes in the law which have made it much easier to obtain. In Britain, before 1857, a private act of parliament was required to obtain a divorce. This was an expensive procedure beyond the means of all but the most wealthy. Since 1857, the costs of obtaining a divorce have been reduced and the grounds for divorce have been widened. Divorce legislation was influenced by the idea of 'matrimonial offence', the notion that one or both spouses had wronged the other. This was the idea behind the Matrimonial Causes Act of 1857 which largely limited grounds for divorce to adultery. Though divorce legislation in 1950 widened the grounds to include cruelty and desertion, it was still based on the same principle. The Divorce Reform Act, which came into force in 1971, no longer emphasized the idea of matrimonial offence and so avoided the need for 'guilty parties'. It defined the grounds for divorce as 'the irretrievable breakdown of the marriage'. This made divorce considerably easier and accounts in part for the dramatic rise in the number of divorces in 1971.

Despite a reduction in costs, divorce was still an expensive process during the first half of this century. It was beyond the means of many of the less wealthy. This was partly changed by the Legal Aid and Advice Act of 1949 which provided free legal advice and paid solicitors' fees for those who could not afford them. The economics of divorce were further eased by the extension of welfare provisions, particularly for single parents with dependent children. Although many consider these provisions far from generous, they do provide single parent families with the means to exist without the support of the second parent.

So far, the analysis of marital breakdown has proceeded mainly from a functionalist perspective. Nicky Hart presents a Marxian alternative though it does not form the theoretical basis of her work. She argues that the increasing divorce rate can be seen as a 'product of conflict between the changing economic system and its social and ideological superstructure (notably the family)'. In advanced capitalist industrial societies, there is an increasing demand for cheap female wage labour. Wives are encouraged to take up paid employment not only because of the demand for their services, but also because the capitalist controlled media has raised 'material aspirations' – the demand for goods that families desire.

These material aspirations can only be satisfied by both spouses working as wage earners. However, conflict results from the contradiction between female wage labour and the normative expectations which surround married life. 'Working wives' are still expected to be primarily responsible for housework and raising children. In addition, they are still expected, to some degree, to play a subservient role to the male head of the household. These normative expectations contradict the wife's role as a wage earner since she is now sharing the economic burden with her husband. Conflict between the spouses can result from this contradiction, and conflict can lead to marital breakdown.

This section concludes with an examination of the variation in divorce rates between various social groups within society. Marital breakdown is not spread evenly across the population. The changes which have influenced the rate of marital breakdown do not affect all members of society in the same way. They are mediated by the social structure. For example, changes in society are filtered through the class system and to some degree affect members of different classes in different ways. As a result there are class differences in rates of marital breakdown. In the USA, there is an inverse relationship between income and marital breakdown; the lower family income, the higher the rate of separation and divorce. Low income places a strain on the marital relationship, particularly upon the husband who has largely failed in his role as breadwinner. It has been argued that in poverty areas, expectations of marital success are lower as is the stigma attached to marital breakdown. It has been suggested that marital breakdown has become self-perpetuating in many low-income groups, especially Blacks in the New World but as outlined earlier in the chapter, there are special circumstances surrounding their position. A fuller discussion of the relationship between poverty and marital breakdown is presented in Chapter 4 (pp. 158–9).

In Britain, the situation is somewhat different. The highest divorce rates are found in the lower middle class and the lower working class. This suggests that the class system in Britain is more highly structured than in America. Individuals will therefore be more likely to judge themselves in terms of class norms and expectations rather than by society-wide standards. Thus in Britain, the highest divorce rates occur in those groups which are at the bottom of their respective social classes. In terms of middle-class norms and expectations, the lower middle class is badly off; relative to working-class norms and expectations, the lower working class is poor. Thus, the strain of being unable to live up to material expectations will affect relationships between spouses in both groups.

Apart from social class, a number of other factors are associated with variation in divorce rates. There is an inverse relationship between age at marriage and divorce; the lower the age at marriage, the higher the rate of divorce. In Britain, from 1960 to 1970, the divorce rate for teenage marriages was roughly double the overall rate. A number of reasons have been given for this. There may be greater economic pressure on the marriage since the spouses are only beginning their working lives and their wages are likely to be low. Compared to all marriages, a higher proportion of teenage marriages are undertaken to legitimize a pregnancy. In addition, teenagers are more likely to change their outlook and so 'grow apart'. They are less likely to have the experience to select a compatible partner and less likely to be aware of the responsibilities that marriage entails. The fact that the average age at marriage is declining may account in part for the overall rise in marital breakdown.

There is an association between an individual's likelihood to get divorced and the marital status of his parents. If one or both spouses have parents who are or have been divorced, there is a greater likelihood that their marriage will end in divorce. The usual explanation is that marital conflict produces psychological instability in the children who express this instability in their own marriage. However, Nicky Hart argues that the experience of having divorced parents may reduce the individual's aversion to divorce. In addition, his parents may be more likely if not to encourage his divorce, at least not to oppose it as strongly as nondivorced parents.

Statistics indicate that the chances of marital breakdown are increased if the spouses have different social backgrounds, for example if they come from different class or ethnic groups. Conflict may result from partners having different marital role expectations which stem from the subculture of their particular social group. When spouses share similar backgrounds, there is a greater likelihood that their friends will be similar and this will tend to reinforce the marriage. In Goode's words, it is probable 'that those who are alike in many respects will share a similar and approving circle'. In advanced industrial society, the increasing rate of social and geographical mobility results in greater opportunities for marriage between individuals of differing social backgrounds and therefore a greater potential for marital conflict.

Finally, various studies have indicated a relationship between particular occupations and high rates of divorce. Nicky Hart finds that long-distance lorry drivers, sales representatives and some engineers and technicians, whose jobs require frequent separation from their spouses, have higher than average divorce rates. Apart from the possibility of lessening the dependence of the spouses upon each other, such jobs provide the husband in particular with a greater opportunity to meet members of the opposite sex away from the company of his spouse. T. Noble finds a similar relationship between particular occupations and high rates of divorce. Actors, authors, artists, company directors and hotel-keepers have high divorce rates which Noble argues result from their high degree of involvement in their work and a correspondingly low involvement in their marriage.

Only some of the many factors associated with variation in divorce rates have been examined. The researcher is faced with a multitude of factors and it is difficult to establish which are more important than others. With reference to the particularly rapid rise in the overall rate of marital breakdown in recent years, Nicky Hart assigns priority to the changing role of women in society. This will be examined in detail in the following chapter.

Sociology, ideology and the family

Writing about the values which surround the American family, Sussman and Burchinal state that, 'Most Americans reject the notion that receiving aid from their kin is a good thing. The proper ideological stance is that the individual and his family should fend for themselves. The family in this instance is nuclear in structure and consists of husband and wife and children'. Like those they write about, sociologists are members of society and members of families. They too have been exposed to family ideology. Their views of the family are unlikely to be free from their beliefs about what the family ought to be. In fact Talcott Parsons's picture of the isolated nuclear family is essentially no different from Sussman and Burchinal's description of family ideology in American society. It can be argued that the concept of the isolated nuclear family owes more than a little to ideology.

As in all areas of sociology, functionalist perspectives on the family have been accused of having a conservative bias. With their emphasis on the universality and inevitability of the family, they justify its existence. With their preoccupation with the positive aspects of the family they provide it with legitimation. As Barrington Moore argues, these views may say more about the hopes and ideals of sociologists than the reality of their subject matter. He states that, 'Among social scientists today it is almost axiomatic that the family is a universally necessary social institution and will remain such through any foreseeable future . . . I have the uncomfortable feeling that the authors, despite all their elaborate theories and technical research devices, are doing little more than projecting certain middle-class hopes and ideals onto a refractory reality' (quoted in Morgan, 1975, p. 3). In other words, the view that the family is here to stay through time immemorial may be primarily a reflection of middle-class values. D. H. J. Morgan argues that functionalist perspectives on the family 'give emphasis to the limits of human activity rather than the potentialities'. In doing so they adopt a conservative stance. By emphasizing the universal necessity for the family and the vital functions it performs for the social system, they imply that individuals must accept the inevitable. Members of society must form families and act accordingly within the limits set by the requirements of the social system. This view diverts attention from a consideration of alternatives to the family.

It gives little regard to the possibility that the human potential for creativity will find expression.

It is difficult to avoid the feeling that many functionalists are committed to the institution of the family. Indeed their descriptions are often little short of an idealization of family life. The families portrayed by Murdock, Parsons and Fletcher are examples to us all. Even when things begin to go wrong and the divorce rate rises, the happy families split up so they can re-form as even happier families. However, despite what is probably a strong ideological bias, functionalist analysis should not be dismissed out of hand. It can be argued that it is no more ideologically based than other approaches. Rather, in recent years, it has simply gone out of fashion.

Like the functionalists, Laing and Cooper begin with a picture and an evaluation of society. Whereas the functionalists picture a rather reasonable society, operating smoothly with perhaps the odd stress and strain in the social system, Laing and Cooper start with a picture of a society which is largely insane, a society gone mad. This initial value judgment colours their views from then on. Whereas the functionalists emphasize the needs of the social system, Laing and Cooper are committed to the needs of the individual. They are preoccupied with individuality, with self-awareness, self-actualization and individual autonomy and freedom. As a result the close bonds of family life appear suffocating, constricting and restraining. It is clear where Cooper's sympathies lie with his exhortation of the artist, the visionary and the revolutionary. Cooper advocates a radical change in the social order when he preaches a version of the hippy message of love and peaceful revolution, a philosophy which seems rather outdated in today's world.

The revival of Marxian approaches to the family in the late 1960s and 1970s owed much to the Women's Liberation Movement. Many feminist writers found that the Marxian emphasis on exploitation, oppression and revolutionary change harmonized with their own situation and commitments. They begin with two value judgments. First, capitalism is an evil and exploitive system. Second, women are oppressed and exploited, particularly within the family. They put these two value judgments together and from then on their analysis of the family follows a predictable pattern. Everything they dislike about the family is blamed on capitalism. Everything that is bad about the family is seen to support the capitalist system. Although this does not apply to all feminist writers who operate within a Marxian framework, it does apply to some of the more committed socialists within their ranks. It can lead to a rather narrow view of the family. A broader perspective would show that many of the aspects of family life which are seen as exploitive are not limited to capitalist society.

9 Women and society

Original sin in the Garden of Eden was woman's. She tasted the forbidden fruit, tempted Adam and has been paying for it ever since. In Genesis, the Lord said, 'I will greatly multiply thy sorrow and thy conception; in sorrow thou shalt bring forth children; and thy desire shall be to thy husband, and he shall rule over thee'. Sociologists would regard the above quotation as a mythological justification for the position of women in society. Many women might see the summary it contains of their relationship with their spouses as a fair description of their status through the ages.

Women produce children; women are mothers and wives; women do the cooking, mending, sewing and washing; they take care of men and are subordinate to male authority; they are largely excluded from high status occupations and from positions of power. These generalizations apply, to some degree, to practically every known human society. The most basic division of labour appears to be founded on sex or gender. There are men's jobs and women's jobs in the simplest hunting and gathering bands and the most complex industrial societies. In terms of the rewards of prestige, wealth and power attached to gender roles, women almost invariably come off worst. In recent years, particularly with the rise of the Women's Liberation Movement, the reasons for a sexually based division of labour and for the inequality between male and female roles have been hotly debated. Two main positions have emerged from the debate. The first maintains that the sexual division of labour and inequality between the sexes is determined to some degree by biologically or genetically based differences between men and women. This position is opposed by those who argue that gender roles are culturally determined and inequality between the sexes results from socially constructed power relationships.

The role of women – genes and biology

Clearly women are biologically different from men. Though there is disagreement about the exact nature and consequences of this difference, some sociologists, anthropologists and psychologists argue that it is sufficient to explain the basic sexual division of labour in all societies. This view will now be considered.

369

Lionel Tiger and Robin Fox – the human biogrammar

Anthropologists Lionel Tiger and Robin Fox argue that social scientists who assume that human beings behave simply in terms of the culture of their society are ignoring what they call the human 'biogrammar'. The biogrammar is a genetically based programme which predisposes mankind to behave in certain ways. These predispositions are not the same as instincts since they can be considerably modified by culture but they remain basic influences on human behaviour. In part they are inherited from man's primate ancestors, in part they have developed during man's existence in hunting and gathering bands. Since 99.9% of man's existence has been spent as a hunter and gatherer, Tiger and Fox argue that it is reasonable to assume that, to some degree, he is genetically adapted to this way of life. Although the biogrammars of men and women are similar in many respects, there are important differences between them.

Tiger and Fox argue that compared to women, men are more aggressive and dominant. These characteristics are genetically based; in particular they result from differences between male and female hormones. These differences are due partly to genetic inheritance from man's primate ancestors, partly to a genetic adaptation to a hunting way of life. Males hunt which is an aggressive activity. They are responsible for the protection of the band and for alliances or wars with other bands. Thus men monopolize positions of power. Since Tiger and Fox see dominance as a 'sex-linked characteristic', it comes as no surprise that politics is the province of men from the male elders in Australian Aborigine hunting and gathering bands to the House of Commons and House of Lords in present-day Britain.

By comparison, women are programmed by their biogrammars to reproduce and care for children. Tiger and Fox argue that the basic family unit consists of mother and child. In their words, 'Nature intended mother and child to be together'. It does not particularly matter how this basic unit is supported and protected. It can be by the addition of a single male, as in the case of the nuclear family, or by the impersonal services of a welfare state. The close emotional bond between mother and child is a genetically based predisposition for both parties and it is particularly important for the welfare of the child. Tiger and Fox maintain that, 'The mother is totally essential to the well-being of the child'. Unless this close emotional bond obtains, the child will be unable to establish successful relationships in later life.

In short, Tiger and Fox argue that male and female biogrammars are adapted to a sexual division of labour in a hunting society. As they put it, 'We are wired for hunting'. Compared to cultural change, genetic change is slow. Thus the male and female biogrammars of a hunting existence continue in modern industrial society. From this it follows that attempts to abolish gender roles and replace them with unisex roles, however desirable this may be, will 'go against nature'.

George Peter Murdock – biology and practicality

Though an anthropologist like Tiger and Fox, George Peter Murdock operates from very different assumptions. He sees biological differences between men and women as the basis of the sexual division of labour in society. However, he does not suggest that men and women are directed by genetically based predispositions or characteristics to adopt their particular roles. Instead, he simply suggests that biological differences, such as the greater physical strength of men and the fact that women bear children, lead to gender roles out of sheer practicality. Given the biological differences between men and women, a sexual division of labour is the most efficient way of organizing society.

In a cross-cultural survey of 224 societies ranging from hunting and gathering bands to modern nation states, Murdock examines the activities assigned to men and women. He finds tasks such as hunting, lumbering and mining to be predominantly male roles, cooking, gathering wild vegetable products, water carrying and making and repairing clothes to be largely female roles. He states that, 'Man with his superior physical strength can better undertake the more strenuous tasks, such as lumbering, mining, quarrying, land clearance and housebuilding. Not handicapped, as is woman by the physiological burdens of pregnancy and nursing, he can range farther afield to hunt, to fish, to herd and to trade. Woman is at no disadvantage, however, in lighter tasks which can be performed in or near the home, e.g. the gathering of vegetable products, the fetching of water, the preparation of food, and the manufacture of clothing and utensils'. Thus, because of her biological function of childbearing and nursing, woman is tied to the home base; because of her physique she is limited to less strenuous tasks. Murdock finds that the sexual division of labour is present in all of the societies in his sample and concludes that, 'The advantages inherent in a division of labour by sex presumably account for its universality'.

Talcott Parsons – biology and the 'expressive' female

Similar arguments are advanced to account for the role of women in industrial society. As noted in the previous chapter (pp. 332–3), Talcott Parsons sees the isolated nuclear family in modern industrial society specializing in two basic functions: the socialization of the young and the stabilization of adult personalities. For socialization to be effective, a close, warm and supportive group is essential. The family meets this requirement. Parsons implies that the family, or something very much like it, is essential for this purpose. Within the family, the woman is primarily responsible for socializing the young. Parsons turns to biology for his explanation of this fact. He states that, 'In our opinion the fundamental explanation of the allocation of roles between the biological sexes lies in the fact that the bearing and early nursing of children establish a strong presumptive primacy of the relation of mother to the small child'. Thus, because mothers bear and nurse children, they have a closer and stronger relationship with them. This is particularly so in modern industrial society since the isolation of the nuclear family 'focuses the responsibility of the mother role more sharply on one adult woman. Furthermore the absence of the husband–father from the home premises so much of the time means that she has to take the primary responsibility for the children'.

Parsons characterizes the woman's role in the family as 'expressive' which means she provides warmth, security and emotional support. This is essential for effective socialization of the young. It is only a short step from applying these expressive qualities to her children to applying them also to her husband. This is her major contribution to the second function of the isolated nuclear family, the stabilization of adult personalities. The male breadwinner spends his working day competing in an achievement oriented society. This 'instrumental' role leads to stress and anxiety. The expressive female relieves this tension by providing the weary breadwinner with love, consideration and understanding. Parsons argues that for the family to operate efficiently as a social system, there must be a clear-cut sexual division of labour. In this sense, the instrumental and expressive roles complement each other. Like a button and a buttonhole, they lock together to promote family solidarity.

Although Parsons moves a long way from biology, it forms his starting point. Biological differences between the sexes provide the foundation on which the sexual division of labour is based.

John Bowlby – the mother–child bond

John Bowlby examines the role of women, and in particular, their role as mothers, from a psychological perspective. Like Parsons, he argues that a mother's place is in the home, caring for her children especially during their early years. Bowlby conducted a number of studies of juvenile delinquents and found that the most psychologically disturbed had experienced separation from their mothers at an early age. Many had been raised in orphanages and as a result had been deprived of maternal love. They appeared unable to give or receive love and seemed compelled to adopt a career of destructive and anti-social relationships. Bowlby concludes that it is essential for mental health that 'the infant and young child should experience a warm, intimate and continuous relationship with his mother'. Bowlby's arguments imply that there is a genetically based psychological need for a close and intimate mother–child relationship. Thus the mother role is firmly attached to the female. (For further details of Bowlby's views and related research, see Chapter 10, pp. 409–10.)

This section has examined some of the arguments which base the sexual division of labour on biological differences between the sexes. Although all the arguments allow some variation in the way gender roles are played, none holds out much hope for those who seek to abolish them. Apart from peripheral areas such as teenage clothes, they suggest that the day of unisex will never dawn.

The role of women – culture and society

Many sociologists begin from the assumption that human behaviour is largely directed and determined by culture, that is the learned recipes for behaviour shared by members of a society. Thus norms, values and roles are culturally determined and socially transmitted. From this perspective, gender roles are a product of culture rather than biology. Individuals learn their respective male and female roles. The sexual division of labour is supported and justified by a belief and value system which states that gender roles are normal, natural, right and proper.

Ann Oakley – the cultural division of labour

Ann Oakley, a British sociologist and a supporter of the Women's Liberation Movement, comes down strongly on the side of culture as the determinant of gender roles. Her position is summarized in the following quotation, 'Not only is the division of labour by sex *not* universal, but there is no reason why it should be. Human cultures are diverse and endlessly variable. They owe their creation to human inventiveness rather than invincible biological forces'. Oakley first takes George Peter Murdock to task arguing that the sexual division of labour is not universal nor are certain tasks always performed by men, others by women. She maintains that Murdock's interpretation of his data is biased because he looks at other cultures through both Western and male eyes. In particular, she claims that he pre-judges the role of women in terms of the Western housewife–mother role.

Oakley finds plenty of evidence from Murdock's own data to attack the assumption that biology largely determines the sexual division of labour. There are fourteen societies in Murdock's sample in which lumbering is done either exclusively by women or shared by both sexes, thirty-six societies in which women are solely responsible for land clearance and thirty-eight in which cooking is a shared activity. Oakley examines a number of societies in which biology appears to have little or no influence on women's roles. The Mbuti Pygmies, a hunting and gathering society who live in the Congo rain forests, have no specific rules for the division of labour by sex. Men and women hunt together. The roles of father and mother are not sharply differentiated, both sexes sharing responsibility for the care of children. Amongst the Australian Aborigines of Tasmania, women were responsible for seal hunting, fishing and catching opossums (tree-dwelling mammals). Turning to present-day societies, Oakley notes that women form an important part of many armed forces, particularly those of China, Russia, Cuba and Israel. In India, some 12% of labourers on building sites are women and in some Asian and Latin American countries, a quarter of the labour force in mines is female. Oakley claims that the above examples show clearly that there are no exclusively female roles and that biological characteristics do not bar women from particular jobs. She regards as a myth the supposed 'biologically based incapacity of women to carry out heavy and demanding work'.

Oakley also attacks the arguments of Parsons and Bowlby by pointing to the kibbutz to show that systems other than the family and the female mother role can effectively socialize the young. The kibbutz system of childrearing will be examined in detail in the following section. Using the example of Alor, an island in Indonesia, Oakley shows how in this and other small-scale horticultural societies, women are not tied to their offspring, and this does not appear to have any harmful effects on the children. In traditional Alorese society, women were largely responsible for the cultivation and collection of vegetable produce. This involved them spending considerable time away from the village. Within a fortnight of the birth of their child, women returned to the fields leaving the infant in the care of a sibling, the father or a grandparent. Turning to Western society, Oakley dismisses Bowlby's claim that an 'intimate and continuous' relationship between mother and child is essential for the child's well-being. She notes that a large body of research shows that the employment of the mother has no detrimental effects on the child's development. Some studies indicate that the children of working mothers are less likely to be delinquent than those of mothers who stay at home. In fact Oakley claims that, 'Working mothers enjoy their children more and are less irritable with them than full-time mothers'.

Oakley is particularly scathing in her attack on Parsons's view of the family and the role of the 'expressive' female within it. She accuses him of basing his analysis on the beliefs and values of his own culture and in particular on the myths of male superiority and of the sanctity of marriage and the family. Oakley argues that the expressive housewife–mother role is not necessary for the functioning of the family unit. It merely exists for the convenience of men. She claims that Parsons's explanation of gender roles is simply a validating myth for the 'domestic oppression of women'.

Oakley draws the following conclusions. Gender roles are culturally rather than biologically determined. Evidence from a number of different societies shows that there are no tasks (apart from childbearing) which are performed exclusively by females. Biological characteristics do not bar women from particular occupations. The mother role is a cultural construction. Evidence from several societies indicates that children do not require a close, intimate and continuous relationship with a female mother figure.

Bruno Bettelheim – collective childrearing

Bruno Bettelheim is a psychiatrist specializing in child development. His study of collective childrearing in a kibbutz, discussed in the previous chapter (p. 328–30), indicated that a close, continuous mother–child relationship is not essential for effective socialization. Bettelheim found there was little mental illness among kibbutz children and little evidence of jealousy, rivalry or bullying. The children appeared hardworking and responsible, there was no delinquency and no equivalent of the high school 'dropout'. Compared to Western society, there is a strong pressure to conform to group norms and as a result, Bettelheim found that children tend to be less individualistic. He argues that they develop a 'collective' rather than a personal sense of self. By Western standards, the children appear 'emotionally flat', they 'shun any show of emotion' and seem unable to establish 'really deep, intimate and loving relationships'. Bettelheim claims that parents raised in the kibbutz 'expect little intimacy with their children, do not hope for or wish for a unique one-to-one relationship with them. Hence their relations with their children are more comfortably relaxed – neither intimate nor intense'.

Any assessment of the results of collective childrearing involves value judgments. From a Western viewpoint the system has advantages and disadvantages for the children. They appear more stable and less prone to anxiety and neuroses than children in the West. However, this advantage may be paid for by a sacrifice of individuality and warmth and intimacy in personal relationships. Bettelheim draws the following conclusion from his study. 'The kibbutz experience clearly demonstrates to me that children raised by educators in group homes can and do fare a lot better than many children raised by their mothers in poverty-striken homes, and better than quite a few raised at home by their middle-class parents'.

Ernestine Friedl – male dominance and the sexual division of labour

The data and arguments provided by Oakley and Bettelheim suggest that gender roles are not inevitable, that particular tasks are not universally assigned exclusively to one sex or the other. However they do not contain an adequate explanation for the existence of a clear-cut sexual division of labour in practically all known human societies. Nor do they explain why the tasks of women are similar in most societies, why those tasks are usually given less prestige than those of men, and why men generally have power and authority over women.

In *Women and Men: An Anthropological View*, Ernestine Friedl provides an explanation for the sexual division of labour and male dominance. Like Oakley, she supports a cultural explanation, noting the great variation in gender roles between societies. For example, she observes that in some societies, activities such as weaving, pottery making and tailoring are thought to be 'naturally' men's tasks, in others, women's. However, it is significant that in societies where such tasks are defined as male roles, they generally carry higher prestige than in societies where they are assigned to women. Friedl sees this as a reflection of male dominance which she maintains exists to some degree in all societies. She defines male dominance as 'a situation in which men have highly preferential access, although not always exclusive rights, to those activities to which society accords the greatest value and the exercise of which permits a measure of control over others'. She argues that the degree of male dominance is 'a consequence of the frequency with which men have greater rights than women to distribute goods outside the domestic group'. Thus men are dominant because they control the exchange of valued goods beyond the family group. This activity brings prestige and power. The greater their control over the exchange of valued goods outside the family, the greater their dominance.

Friedl tests this hypothesis by examining hunting and gathering bands and small-scale horticultural societies. In hunting and gathering bands, men hunt and women gather vegetable produce, nuts and berries. To explain this sexual division of labour, Friedl turns to biological arguments. Childbearing, nursing and carrying are not compatible with the demands of hunting, whilst they do not seriously inconvenience gathering. Yet this does not explain why hunting carries greater prestige than gathering. The explanation lies in the fact that meat is a scarce resource and as such it is more highly valued than vegetable produce. The latter is usually readily available, can be gathered with ease and is therefore not exchanged. The successful outcome of a hunt cannot be guaranteed. Some men return empty-handed. For the whole band to enjoy a regular protein diet, which meat provides, it is necessary for the successful hunters to distribute their kill to other members of the band. Friedl argues that the 'distribution of scarce or irregularly available resources is a source of power'. Those who distribute such resources gain prestige, those who receive them are indebted and obligated. Since hunting is largely a male monopoly, men, by exchanging meat, are thus plugged in to a major power source.

Friedl then tests her hypothesis on horticultural societies, small-scale societies which practise shifting cultivation. These societies are usually found in savannah regions or tropical forests. The technique of slash-and-burn cultivation is often practised. Trees and undergrowth are cut down and burned, crops planted, and after a few years when the nutrients in the soil have been exhausted, a new site is prepared. Clearing the land is primarily a male responsibility as is the defence of the cultivated area. Warfare is common among horticultural societies since shifting cultivation brings groups into competition for land. Friedl argues that the control by men of land allocation and its defence involves them in political and economic alliances with other groups. Men exchange, barter, distribute, negotiate and fight for land and agricultural produce with men in other groups. They therefore control the distribution of goods beyond the domestic group which brings prestige and power. In particular they control land which is the basic resource of a horticultural society.

Again Friedl returns to biological arguments to explain the sexual division of labour. Women are primarily responsible for cultivation, men for clearing and defending the land and exchanging goods with other groups. Friedl argues that these tasks are allocated to men because of the dangers involved. She maintains that 'a population can survive the loss of men more easily than that of women'. The loss of women will reduce the potential size of the population, the loss of men will not necessarily do so, since one man can impregnate many women.

Friedl's ideas are novel and interesting and reveal a fascinating interplay between biology and culture. Although she claims that her work shows that male dominance and gender roles are culturally determined, she fails to completely dismiss biological arguments. The fact that women bear children forms an important part of her explanation for the sexual division of labour, and, though less directly, for her explanation of male dominance. However, her arguments reveal the importance of culture and avoid the simplistic claims of the biological arguments outlined at the beginning of the chapter.

Sherry B. Ortner – the devaluation of women

A somewhat different, though equally interesting, explanation for the subordinate status of women is presented by Sherry B. Ortner. She attempts to provide a general explanation for the 'universal devaluation of women'. Ortner claims that it is not biology as such that ascribes women to their status in society but the way in which every culture defines and evaluates female biology. Thus, if this universal evaluation changed, then the basis for female subordination would be removed.

Ortner argues that in every society, a higher value is placed on culture than on nature. Culture is the means by which man controls and regulates nature. By inventing weapons and hunting techniques, man can capture and kill animals. By inventing religion and rituals, man can call upon supernatural forces to produce a successful hunt or a bountiful harvest. By the use of culture, man does not have to passively submit to nature, he can regulate and control it. Thus man's ideas and technology, that is his culture, have power over nature and are therefore seen as superior to nature.

The universal evaluation of culture as superior to nature is the basic reason for the devaluation of women. Women are seen as closer to nature than men and therefore as inferior to men. Ortner argues that women are universally defined as closer to nature because their bodies and physiological functions are more concerned with 'the natural processes surrounding the reproduction of the species'. These natural processes include menstruation, pregnancy, childbirth and lactation, processes for which the female body is 'naturally' equipped. Women's social role as mothers is also seen as closer to nature. They are primarily responsible for the socialization of the young. Infants and young children are seen as 'barely human', as one step away from nature because their cultural repertoire is small compared to adults. Women's close relationships with young children further associate them with nature. Since the mother role is linked to the family, the family itself is regarded as closer to nature compared to activities and institutions outside the family. Thus activities such as politics, warfare and religion are seen as more removed from nature, as superior to domestic tasks and therefore as the province of men. Finally, Ortner argues that 'woman's psyche', her psychological make-up, is defined as closer to nature. Because women are concerned with child care and primary socialization, they develop more personal, intimate and particular relationships with others, especially their children. By comparison, men, by engaging in politics, warfare and religion have a wider range of contacts and less personal and particular relationships. Thus men are seen as being more objective and less emotional. Their thought processes are defined as more abstract and general and less personal and particular. Ortner argues that culture is, in one sense, 'the transcendence, by means of systems of thought and technology, of the natural givens of existence'. Thus men are seen as closer to culture since their thought processes are defined as more abstract and objective than those of women. Since culture is seen as superior to nature, 'woman's psyche' is devalued and once again, men come out on top. Ortner concludes that in terms of her biology, physiological processes, social roles and psychology, woman 'appears as something intermediate between culture and nature'.

Ortner fails to show conclusively that in all societies culture is evaluated more highly than nature. Although many societies have rituals which attempt to control nature, it is not clear that nature is necessarily devalued in comparison to culture. Indeed it could be argued that the very existence of such rituals points to the superior power of nature. However, Ortner's argument does have one important virtue. It provides a universal explanation for a universal phenomenon, the second-class status of women. If Ortner's view is correct, the subordination of women owes nothing to biology as such, but rather to the cultural evaluation of their biological make-up. A change in this evaluation will remove the basis for female subordination.

The first part of this chapter has been concerned with explanations for the sexual division of labour and the status of gender roles which can be applied to all societies. The changing status of women in industrial societies will now be examined. This will provide both data and ideas to refine and develop the general arguments presented so far.

Women and industrial society

No blanket statement can be made about the position of women in industrial society. Industrialization is a developing process, the early stages of the industrial revolution being very different from modern industrial society. Nor are industrial societies which are at similar stages of economic development similar in all other respects. Thus the position of women in industrial society must be examined in relation to the particular society at a particular stage in its development. In a later section, the position of women in communist industrial societies will be analysed. First, the changing status of women in Western industrial societies will be examined, with particular emphasis on Britain and the USA.

Women and industrialization – an historical perspective

Ann Oakley has traced the changing status of women in British society from the eve of the industrial revolution to the 1970s. She claims that, 'The most important and enduring consequence of industrialization for women has been the emergence of the modern role of housewife as "the dominant mature feminine role"'. Oakley's view of the emergence of the housewife role is summarized in this section.

In pre-industrial Britain, the family was the basic unit of production. Marriage and the family were essential to individuals for economic reasons since all members of the family were involved in production. Agriculture and textiles were the main industries and women were indispensable to both. In the production of cloth, the husband did the weaving while his wife spun and dyed the yarn. On the farm women were in charge of dairy produce. Most of the housework – cooking, cleaning, washing, mending and child care – was performed by unmarried children. The housewife role, which involved the domesticity of women and their economic dependence on men, had yet to arrive.

During the early stages of industrialization, which Oakley dates from 1750 to 1841, the factory steadily replaced the family as the unit of production. Women were employed in factories where they often continued their traditional work in textiles. The first major change which affected their status as wage earners was a series of factory acts, beginning in 1819, which gradually restricted child labour. Children became increasingly dependent upon their parents and this necessitated care and supervision, a role which fell to women. Oakley argues that, 'The increased differentiation of child and adult roles, with the child's growing dependence, heralded the dependence of women in marriage and their restriction to the home'.

From 1841 to the advent of the First World War in 1914, a combination of pressure from male workers and philanthropic reformers restricted female employment in industry. Women were seen by many male factory workers as a threat to their employment. As early as 1841, committees of male factory workers called for the 'gradual withdrawal of all female labour from the factory'. In 1842 the Mines Act banned the employment of women as miners. In 1851, one in four married women were employed, by 1911 this figure was reduced to one in ten. Helen Hacker states that with the employment of women as wage earners, 'Men were quick to perceive them as a rival group and make use of economic, legal and ideological weapons to eliminate or reduce their competition. They excluded women from the trade unions, made contracts with employers to prevent their hiring women, passed laws restricting the employment of married women, caricatured the working woman, and carried on ceaseless propaganda to return women to the home and keep them there'.

Victorian ideology, particularly the versions of the upper and middle classes, stated that a woman's place was in the home. No less a figure than Queen Victoria announced, 'Let woman be what God intended, a helpmate for man, but with totally different duties and vocations' (quoted in Hudson, 1970, p. 46). The following quotations from articles in the Saturday Review illustrate the ideal of womanhood in mid-Victorian times. In 1859, 'Married life is a woman's profession, and to this life her training – that of dependence – is modelled'. And in 1865, 'No woman can or ought to know very much of the mass of meanness and wickedness and misery that is loose in the wide world. She could not learn it without losing the bloom and freshness which it is her mission in life to preserve' (quoted in Hudson, 1970, pp. 53–54). Oakley claims that during the second half of the nineteenth century these attitudes began to filter down to the working class. Thus a combination of factors which included ideology, the banning of child labour and restrictions on the employment of women, locked the majority of married women into the mother–housewife role.

Oakley states that from 1914 to 1950, there was a 'tendency towards the growing employment of women coupled with a retention of housewifery as the *primary* role expected of all women'. During these years women received many legal and political rights, for example the vote in 1928, but these had little effect on the central fact of their lives, the mother–housewife role. Oakley concludes that industrialization has had the following effects on the role of women. First, the 'separation of men from the daily routines of domestic life'. Second, the 'economic dependence of women and children on men'. Third, the 'isolation of housework and child care from other work'. In twentieth-century British society, the housewife–mother role has become institutionalized as 'the primary role for all women'.

Women and the labour market

Despite the primacy of the mother–housewife role, women are entering the labour market in ever increasing numbers. In Britain from 1951 to 1976, the number of employed females rose by some three million compared to a rise in the number of employed males of around three hundred thousand. In 1951, women made up 31.0% of the labour force, by 1976 they accounted for 38.7%. In Britain today around a half of all married women are employed compared to one in five in 1951. Despite their increasing share of the labour market, women are not employed evenly throughout the occupational structure. They are concentrated in low paid, low status jobs. They are less likely than men to have interesting work or opportunities for promotion, more likely to work in poor conditions and to become redundant. Women are employed mainly in unskilled and semi-skilled manual jobs and in intermediate and low grade white-collar occupations. In Britain, in 1976, 87% of the female labour force was employed in those areas compared to 38% of the male labour force. Wage differentials between the sexes are wide. Taking an average of gross hourly earnings for men and women in full-time employment, Barron and Norris calculate that in 1972, only 7.8% of men in manual jobs and 2.8% of men in non-manual jobs were paid less than two-thirds of this average. This stands in stark contrast to the figures for women. In 1972, 70.3% of women in manual work and 38.6% of women in non-manual work were paid less than two-thirds of the average wage. Barron and Norris estimate that women outnumber men by a ratio of five to one in the low paid sector.

As in the family, there is a sexual division of labour in the job market. Women are concentrated in particular types of jobs which are typically seen as female occupations. They include nursing, primary school teaching, factory work involving packing and producing domestic products, secretarial and lower level clerical jobs, lower grade catering work and retail sales occupations such as cashiers and shop assistants. Oakley argues that the position of women in the family is reflected in the employment sector. Women's jobs are often extensions of their domestic role which involves caring for, waiting on, serving, clearing and tidying up after others. This point is made forcefully by Mary K. Benet in *Secretary: An Enquiry into the Female Ghetto*. She maintains that the secretary 'also acts as wife, mother, mistress and maid'. Benet argues that office work is 'the business equivalent of housekeeping' since 'both jobs are custodial, concerned with tidying up, putting away, and restoring order rather than producing anything'. She compares filing with washing the dishes arguing that both tasks produce the same sense of frustration. The analogy between housework and paid employment can even be extended to professions such as schoolteaching. In Britain although just over half of all schoolteachers are women, three-quarters of them are concentrated in the primary school sector. In many respects, this mirrors their domestic child care role. The fact that women tend to be employed in 'women's jobs' means that measures such as equal pay will not significantly affect their market situation. Equality with men in the labour market requires either an abolition of the sexual division of labour or an upgrading of 'women's jobs'. The first alternative would involve men and women being represented at all grades in all occupations in proportion to their numbers in the labour force. For example, if men make up over 60% of the labour force, over 60% of nurses should be male. The second alternative would involve raising the pay and status of 'women's jobs' to a level where they fell within the same range of pay and status differentials as men's jobs.

Ann Oakley argues that a major reason for the subordination of women in the labour market is the institutionalization of the mother–housewife role as 'the primary role for all women'. This emphasis makes paid employment a secondary consideration. In addition, a strong commitment to and involvement in work is largely incompatible with the successful performance of the mother–housewife role. In a study conducted in the late 1950s and early 1960s entitled, *Britain's Married Women Workers*, Viola Klein stated that, 'The outstanding impression gained from this survey is that women's lives, today as much as ever, are dominated by their role as wives and mothers'. She found that the primary reason for wives taking up paid employment was to supplement family income. The decision to work outside the home was based on domestic priorities. The primacy of the mother–housewife role is seen from a 1968 survey which revealed that 34% of employed women in Britain were in part-time work, and that four out of five gave the following reasons as to why they had not taken up full-time employment – 'responsibility for husband'; 'responsibility for children'; 'other domestic duties' (discussed in Oakley, 1974, p. 78). Some indication of the incompatibility of the mother–housewife role and a career is provided by the relatively small numbers of female managers and professionals. In Britain, in 1976, only 5% of the female labour force compared to 20% of the male labour force was classified as 'professional, employers and managers'. Though the requirements of the woman's domestic role are not the only reasons for this imbalance, they are probably important. Oakley notes that female professional workers are three to four times more likely to be unmarried than their male counterparts.

Until recently, few sociologists have given serious and detailed consideration to the position of women on the labour market. One of the few who has, the American sociologist Theodore Caplow, gives the following reasons for the relegation of women to the bottom of the occupational structure. Firstly, he points to the primary status of women as mothers and housewives. As such, their careers are discontinuous due to the fact that they move out of the labour market to produce and rear children. Secondly, women are 'secondary breadwinners' compared to the male family head. This encourages the attitude that it is right and proper that women should be paid less than men. Thirdly, due to the mother–housewife role, which ties wives to their husbands, women are less geographically mobile than men. The family is much more likely to move house to follow the husband's career than that of the wife. This helps to explain the link between women and low status jobs, since a successful career often requires residential mobility. Fourthly, there is a large reserve of employable women, which usually means that the demand for work will exceed its supply. As a result, employers will not have to attract female labour with high wages, career opportunities and improved working conditions. Finally, there is a vast array of rules and statutes dealing with the employment of women. These regulations limit their hours of work and bar them from many occupations, particularly the more strenuous. According to Caplow, some of these statutes are 'designed for their protection, some intended to reduce their effectiveness as competitors, and some adroitly contrived to both purposes at once'.

Caplow argues that the market situation of women is further influenced by two 'themes' of American culture. The first states that except in family relationships, males should not be directly subordinate to females. The second states that except in family or sexual relationships, 'intimate groups' should be composed of either sex but never both. These themes are expressed in the occupational sphere in the following way. Men generally occupy positions of authority and work groups are usually single sexed. From single sexed work groups, it is only a short step to the sexual division of labour and the idea of 'men's work' and 'women's work' in the job market.

In view of the disadvantages that women bring with them to the labour market, Caplow argues that the range of jobs open to them is limited. In particular, he suggests that because of the discontinuous nature of their working life, 'a woman's occupation must be one in which employment is typically by short term, in which the gain in skill achieved by continuous experience is slight, in which interchangeability is very high, and in which the loss of skill during long periods of inactivity is relatively small'. This means that an employer will tend to place women in temporary jobs, he will not normally invest in expensive training programmes for female workers, he will make sure his female employees are easily replaceable. All of this means placing women in low skill jobs. Caplow concludes that the net result of the various factors he has analysed is that women in general occupy low skill, low status, low paid jobs. Although Caplow's work was published in 1954, which means that some of his observations are somewhat dated, his main arguments remain relevant.

Education and work orientation

The position of women in the labour market is partly mirrored by their performance in the educational system. The *Robbins Report*, published in Britain in 1963, showed that three times as many girls as boys left school at fifteen, only a third of 'A' level students were girls and only a quarter of university students. However, as table 20 indicates, the performance of girls in secondary education has improved significantly relative to boys.

Table 20   The academic attainment of school leavers

| | Percentages for England and Wales | | | | | | | |
| | 1965/66 | | 1973/74 | | 1974/75 | | 1975/76 | |
	Boys	Girls	Boys	Girls	Boys	Girls	Boys	Girls
3 or more 'A' level passes	8.9	4.8	9.2	6.6	9.3	6.8	9.9	7.0
2 'A' level passes	4.0	3.8	4.1	4.4	4.0	4.2	4.1	4.5
1 'A' level pass	2.8	2.8	3.1	3.5	2.8	3.6	2.9	3.3
5 or more higher grade 'O' level GCE or CSE	7.1	9.6	7.7	10.0	7.4	9.7	5.4	7.4
1–4 higher grades GCE or CSE	15.2	16.4	23.1	25.8	24.0	26.9	24.6	28.3
1 or more other grades GCE or CSE	62.0	62.5	30.7	29.7	31.9	30.4	34.2	32.5
No GCE or CSE qualifications			22.1	20.0	20.6	18.4	18.9	17.0
All leavers (thousands)	320.81	302.39	349.64	331.81	353.68	338.11	363.88	343.56

(Source: *Social Trends*, 1977, p. 74)

In higher education, however, there is still a marked difference between the sexes. Statistics for school leavers for 1974/5 indicate that girls accounted for only 36% of university entrants and 33% of polytechnic entrants. The importance of academic qualifications must not be over-emphasized. As Chapter 5 (pp. 185 and 221–3) has indicated, the link between educational credentials and occupational reward is not particularly strong. The constraints of women's market situation are not likely to be significantly changed by equality between the sexes in educational attainment. In fact Kelsall, Poole and Kuhn, from their study entitled, *Graduates: the Sociology of an Elite* find that married women graduates 'were much less likely than women as a whole to be in employment'. There are indications that the more highly qualified a woman, the less likely she is to find a job which matches her qualifications.

Some of the reasons for differences in educational attainment between the sexes are suggested by studies of the attitudes and expectations of girls towards work, marriage and the future in general. A large-scale survey of school leavers in two southern counties in England by T. Veness was published in 1962. Nearly half of the 600 girls in the survey saw marriage as their probable 'job' by the age of twenty-five. Compared to a comparable sample of boys, girls in general were considerably less ambitious, they had lower expectations of promotion at work and they tended not to see 'success' in terms of jobs or careers. A study by J. Maizels, published in 1970, of workers under the age of eighteen who where employed in London, produced similar results. Maizels states that like the Veness inquiry, 'references to marriage and children dominated the replies of girls to the question of what they hoped to be doing by the age of twenty-five'.

Research conducted by Sue Sharpe in the early 1970s indicates little change. Her sample was made up of mainly working-class girls in secondary schools in the London Borough of Ealing. The girls' priorities were 'love, marriage, husbands, children, jobs and careers, more or less in that order'. Sharpe notes that the secondary school curriculum is still partly gender based, though less so than in the past. Girls were steered towards arts subjects and directed particularly to cookery, needlework, housecraft, typing and commerce. By comparison, boys were encouraged to take scientific and technical subjects. Significantly, the 'girls' subjects' were awarded a lower status than those of the boys. Sharpe argues that girls 'are still schooled with the marriage market in mind, although this might not be acknowledged consciously'. The girls' attitudes to work reflected their school experience and the general cultural definitions of women's roles. Office work was the most popular job choice, followed by a group of occupations which included teachers, nurses, bank clerks and shop assistants. Sharpe observes that, 'All the chosen occupations were safely within the realm of "women's work"'. The girls rejected many jobs such as mechanics, electricians, driving instructors and engineers either because they defined them as 'men's work' or because they felt employers and society at large classified them as such. They believed they would find it difficult if not impossible to be accepted for employment in these areas. Sue Sharpe concludes that the girls in her study 'lack the confidence, the opportunities and the desire to challenge the strict divisions of work. Attitudes, popular ideology and the economic and occupational structure all contribute to girls' inhibitions'.

An important American study illustrates a crucial point in the transition from school to work. In the USA, high school and college students discuss their career prospects and plans with counsellors. Pietrofesa and Schlossberg studied interviews between students and counsellors who were undergoing training. Despite the fact that the counsellors denied any gender bias, their interviews with female students revealed considerable bias. As a general rule, counsellors made forceful attempts to dissuade their female clients from entering 'masculine occupations'.

Sue Sharpe makes the following observations about women's journey from the cradle to the job market, 'Their upbringing in the family prepares them for "femininity", their education reinforces the sex divisions through school organization, and the curriculum teaches them "skills" suitable for "women's work" in which they encounter some measure of discrimination throughout all parts of the occupational structure'. The attitudes and expectations revealed in the surveys examined in this section mirror the constraints of the market situation and the reality which awaits the majority of women. However, they also serve to reinforce that reality and to reduce the chances of changing it. Many girls are preconditioned to their adult roles.

Women, men and marriage

The girls in the surveys referred to in the previous section were looking forward to happiness and fulfilment in marriage. Judging from the picture painted by Young and Willmott of the 'symmetrical family' (see Chapter 8, pp. 350–51), their chances of finding happiness have increased in recent years. Conjugal roles are becoming increasingly joint, decisions are based on consultation, and power is increasingly balanced between husband and wife. But the symmetrical family represents one view of marriage and the family derived from responses to questions framed and interpreted by male sociologists. A very different picture is presented by some female sociologists. The give and take, equal shares and reciprocity suggested by Young and Willmott find little support in *The Future of the Family* by the American sociologist Jessie Bernard.

Bernard argues that any analysis of marriage must contain two parts: an examination of the husband's marriage and the wife's marriage. She maintains that the benefits each draws from the marriage are radically different. Bernard examines a wide range of evidence dealing with the situation of married and unmarried men. It points overwhelmingly to the the beneficial effects of marriage for men. Compared to single men, married men are more likely to have successful careers, high income and high status occupations; their mental and physical health is significantly better and they are likely to live longer and happier lives. The evidence indicates that marriage itself produces these effects rather than suggesting that healthier, happier and successful men are more likely to get married.

Bernard sums up the husband's marriage by claiming that, 'there is no greater guarantor of long life, health and happiness for men than a wife well socialized to perform the "duties of a wife", willing to devote her life to taking care of him, providing, even enforcing, the regularity and security of a well-ordered home'.

The wife's marriage presents a very different picture. Survey after survey has shown that more wives than husbands express marital frustration and dissatisfaction, consider their marriages unhappy, and initiate divorce proceedings. Compared to their husbands, wives suffer considerably more stress, anxiety and depression. A comparison of married women with unmarried women gives some indication of the gains and losses of the marriage transaction. Compared to single women, wives are more likely to suffer from depression, a range of neuroses and various other psychological problems. In terms of physical health, single women are significantly healthier than their married counterparts. The most striking comparison is between unmarried men and unmarried women. A number of surveys reveal that compared to single women, single men are beset by various psychological maladies, and their level of earnings and job status are well below those of their female counterparts. Part, but not all of this difference is due to the 'marriage gradient' which refers to the fact that men tend to marry below their status. Thus never-married women tend to be, in Bernard's words, 'the cream of the crop', never married men, 'the bottom of the barrel'. Finally, Bernard compares married men with unmarried women and finds few differences between them apart from the fact that 'women are spectacularly better off so far as psychological distress symptoms are concerned, suggesting that women start out with an initial advantage which marriage reverses'.

In terms of the gains and losses of marriage, it is difficult not to see the husband as the winner and the wife as the loser. Paradoxically, many if not most wives state that they are satisfied with and find fulfilment in marriage. Bernard argues that this is simply due to the fact that women have been socialized to believe that they ought to feel this way. She singles out two main factors to account for the relative distress of the wife. They are the 'Pygmalion effect' and the housewife role. The 'Pygmalion effect' is a phrase adopted from George Bernard Shaw's play *Pygmalion* (retitled as *My Fair Lady* for the film version), which deals with the re-socializing of a working-class cockney girl into an upper class lady. In terms of marriage, the 'Pygmalion effect' refers to the wife's 'redefinition of the self and an active reshaping of the personality to conform to the wishes or needs of husbands'. Various studies have shown that, in marriage, the wife rather than the husband makes the adjustments, conforms to his wishes and increasingly comes to resemble him. To some degree she becomes his reflection and as such relatively passive, subordinate and helpless. Her self-image deteriorates as she accommodates to her husband rather than fulfilling herself as a person in her own right. The second major source of distress, the housewife role, will be dealt with in the following section.

The housewife role

Jessie Bernard writes, 'In truth, being a housewife makes women sick'. She intends this statement to be taken literally. In *Housewife*, Ann Oakley states that the housewife role in modern industrial society has the following characteristics: it is exclusively allocated to women; it is economically dependent on men; it has the status of 'non-work' compared to 'real' or economically productive work; and it takes precedence over all other roles as *the* role for women. Housework is unpaid, privatized and isolated. The housewife works long hours – an average of seventy-seven hours a week according to Oakley – and her work is accorded little prestige as reflected in the oft-heard statement, 'I'm only a housewife'. Housewives have little bargaining power compared to wage earners, for example they have no trade unions to represent their interests. They also lack many of the benefits available to wage earners. Glazer-Malbin and Waehrer state, 'For while workers in the labour force receive such benefits as health insurance, pensions and paid holidays and have access to retraining programs, the housewife receives benefits to a substantially lesser extent, if at all'. Housework is dull, tedious and unfulfilling. From a survey of forty housewives, Oakley concludes that they suffer from more monotony, social isolation and pressure of time than even assembly line workers, who are often seen as the most alienated workers in the labour force. The role of housewife is a dead-end job with no chance of promotion and little or no opportunity for job enrichment or personal development.

Some indication of the effects of the housewife role is provided by a comparison of full-time housewives with wives employed outside the home. A number of studies have suggested that in terms of mental health, 'working wives' fare far better than their housebound counterparts. Jessie Bernard argues that it is 'being relegated to the role of housewife rather than marriage itself which contributes to the poor mental and emotional health of married women'. She suggests that the debilitating effects of the housewife role are so great that, 'In terms of the number of people involved, the housewife syndrome might well be viewed as Public Health Problem Number One'.

Women and social stratification

The previous sections have documented the position of women in contemporary Western industrial society, with particular reference to Britain and America. However, they have not set this information within a theoretical framework. They have not provided a general theory to account for the subordination of women. Class theory provides a possible explanatory framework. Could women, for example, be regarded as a social class? Frank Parkin dismisses this idea, maintaining that the family and not the individual is the basic unit of analysis in the class system. He argues that the social and economic rewards of women are largely determined by their marital and family relationships and, in particular, by the status of the male breadwinner. Parkin states that 'If the wives and daughters of unskilled labourers have some things in common with the wives and daughters of wealthy landowners, there can be no doubt that the *differences* in their overall situation are far more striking and significant'. In other words, the inequalities of sexual status are insignificant compared to the inequalities of class status. Clearly this is partly a matter of judgment and some feminist writers, whose views will be examined shortly, would disagree with Parkin.

If Parkin's views are accepted, the classification of women as a minority group provides an alternative. This approach is taken by Helen Mayer Hacker. She adopts Louis Wirth's definition of a minority group which reads, 'A minority group is any group of people who because of their physical or cultural characteristics, are singled out from others in the society in which they live for differential and unequal treatment, and who therefore regard themselves as objects of collective discrimination'. By comparing the situations of American Blacks and women, Hacker indicates some of the advantages of classifying women as a minority group. Firstly both groups have 'high social visibility', Blacks in terms of their 'racial' characteristics and to some extent their styles of dress, women in terms of their sexual characteristics and feminine clothes. Secondly, both groups have similar 'ascribed attributes', that is attributes which are assigned to them by the majority group simply on the grounds of their minority group membership. Blacks have been characterized as emotional, 'primitive' and childlike, women as irresponsible, inconsistent and emotionally unstable. Both groups, to some degree, have been or are regarded as having low intelligence. Compared to Whites, Blacks have been labelled 'inferior', compared to men, women have been labelled as 'weaker'. Thirdly, the status of both Blacks and women is rationalized in similar ways by the majority group. Their position is seen as a reflection of their ascribed characteristics. Blacks are all right in their place and contented with their lot. The same applies to women. Their place is in the home and they find happiness and fulfilment in their roles as wife and mother. Fourthly, both groups adopt accommodating behaviour in adapting to their situation. Both are deferential and flattering to the majority group. Relative powerlessness forces both to adopt devious methods in their dealings with members of the majority group. Blacks have various strategies for outwitting Whites, women use so-called 'feminine wiles' for getting their own way. Finally, both groups suffer from similar discriminatory practices. Their education is limited to fit

389

them for their ascribed status. Barriers are erected to prevent them from entering the political arena. In the labour market, Blacks are largely confined to 'Black jobs', women to 'women's jobs'. These jobs have certain factors in common – low skill, low status and low pay.

Hacker's comparison of Blacks and women indicates the explanatory value of classifying women as a minority group. The interrelationship of high social visibility, ascribed characteristics, rationalization of status, accommodative behaviour and discrimination adds to an understanding of many aspects of the position of women in society. Yet despite valuable insights, minority group theory provides only partial explanations. In particular, it does not offer an adequate explanation for the relative powerlessness of women's position in society. One such explanation is provided by Marxian theory which will be examined in the following section.

Women – a Marxian perspective

As outlined in the previous chapter (pp. 339–41), Engels saw female subordination as a result of the emergence of private property, in particular the private ownership of the forces of production. Monogamous marriage developed to protect the institution of private property. Engels states that, 'Monogamy arose out of the concentration of considerable wealth in the hands of one person – that of a man – and out of the desire to bequeath this wealth to this man's children and to no one else's'. Men needed control over women to ensure the 'undisputed paternity' of their offspring and heirs. Male dominated monogamous marriage which involved the economic dependence of the wife upon her husband, provided this control. Engels states that, 'The predominance of the man in marriage is simply a consequence of his economic predominance and will vanish with it automatically'.

Both Marx and Engels believed they were witnessing the beginnings of women's liberation in nineteenth-century capitalist society. They argued that the demand for female wage labour would raise the status and power of proletarian women within the family. Marx believed that despite its many evils, capitalist industry 'creates a new economic foundation for a higher form of the family and of relations between the sexes'. Female employment would largely free women from economic dependence upon their husbands and so from male dominance within the family. Engels took a similar view maintaining that with female wage labour, 'the last remnants of male domination in the proletarian home have lost all foundation – except, perhaps, for some of the brutality towards women which became firmly rooted with the establishment of monogamy'. However, the bourgeois wife in capitalist society was still required to produce heirs and so forced to submit to male control.

Marx and Engels believed that true equality between the sexes could only be achieved in a socialist society in which the forces of production were communally owned. In this context, the bourgeois wife would not be mere property for the production of heirs, since there would be no privately owned wealth for them to inherit. The onerous duties of housework and motherhood would no longer be performed by individual women since all work was the responsibility of the community. In Engels words, 'Private housekeeping is transformed into a social industry. The care and education of the children becomes a public matter'. In the communist utopia of the future, men and women would unite in truly egalitarian unions based on 'mutual affection'. Such unions would represent 'true monogamy' since Engels, possibly rather naively, believed that 'sex love is by its very nature exclusive'.

Marxism, women and capitalist society

In this section Marx and Engels's ideas will be examined in the context of capitalist societies. Despite the increasing entry of women into the labour force, the evidence presented earlier in the chapter suggests that this development has not had the beneficial effects which Marx and Engels predicted. A number of studies have compared the situations of 'working wives' and full-time housewives. In a study published in 1958, Blood and Hamblin found that the employment of the wife outside the home did not appreciably alter power relationships within the family. They assessed the power of each spouse in terms of who made 'important' family decisions. They found that working wives had only marginally more power than full-time housewives. Blood and Hamblin reject what they call 'theories of economic determination' which argue that a wife's power and status will increase in direct relationship to the financial contribution she makes to the family.

In her study of married women workers in Britain, Viola Klein notes some beneficial results from employment outside the home. She claims it 'helped to restore to women their sense of usefulness' and 'renewed their self-confidence'. Yet Klein found that the mother-housewife role remained primary. She observes that, 'Home and family are the focal point of their interests and are regarded by themselves as well as by others as their main responsibility'. Klein found no evidence to suggest that paid employment produced demands for freedom from traditional female roles. She states, 'There is no trace of feminist egalitarianism – militant or otherwise – in any of the women's answers to our questionnaires'.

However, the findings of Blood and Hamblin and Klein that married women's entry into the labour market has little effect on their traditional roles does not mean that this will always be the case. Sheila Rowbotham argues that female wage labour in capitalist society involves a basic contradiction between the roles of mother–housewife and wage labourer. She believes that from this contradiction will emerge the demand for women's liberation. Rowbotham argues that, 'Traditionally, the interior, private world of the home is feminine and thus the integration of women into the public world of work and industry is only partial. The contradiction which appears clearly in capitalism between family and industry, private and public, personal and impersonal, is the fissure of women's consciousness through which revolt erupts. The clash between the mass scale of commodity production and the micro-unit of the family and intimate sexual fantasy is the moment of women's liberation'. Thus the contradiction between the warm, intimate and caring world of the family, and the cold, impersonal and uncaring world of capitalism will eventually become apparent to women as they move further into the labour market. This contradiction will focus women's attention on their position, highlight their inequality and lead to demands for liberation.

Even accepting Rowbotham's ideas, it can be argued that Marx and Engels overestimated the significance of women's entry into the labour market. They failed to foresee that women would enter a specifically female labour market. Blackburn and Stewart have reversed their argument with the suggestion that, 'The fact that more women are going to work has not in itself aided sexual equality, but has served to reinforce their inferior status'. In their view, sexual inequality in the labour market simply reinforces sexual inequality in other areas.

Rather than seeing female wage labour in capitalist society as a step towards women's liberation, some Marxist writers argue that it simply strengthens the capitalist system. Margaret Benston argues that capitalism benefits from a large reserve labour force of women 'to keep wages down and profits up'. In their roles as secondary breadwinners, married women provide a source of cheap and easily exploitable labour. Because women have been socialized to comply and submit, they form a docile labour force that can be readily manipulated and easily fired when not required. Compared to male workers, women are less likely to join trade unions, less likely to go on strike or take other forms of militant action against employers. Even when women join trade unions, they often find themselves in male dominated organizations where, according to Barron and Norris, men 'often do not share the interests or outlook of their fellow female unionists'. To some degree sexist ideology splits the working class and in doing so serves the interests of capital. It divides workers along sex lines and thereby makes them easier to control.

Marxism, women and socialist society

Engels predicted that the communal ownership of the forces of production would be accompanied by the socialization of housework and child care. Sexual inequality would end. Gender roles would disappear. His views will now be examined in the light of evidence from socialist societies.

The Soviet Union

From his study of the USSR, David Lane states, 'The position of women *in society* is more equal to that of men than in capitalist states, but within the family much of women's traditional underprivilege remains'. Lane presents the following evidence to support this conclusion. Women in Soviet Russia have steadily increased their share of the labour market. In 1922 they made up 22% of the labour force, by 1973, 51%. Though there are 'no serious structural limitations on their employment', women are not equally represented in all industries. They make up over half the employees in communications, in housing and domestic service, in health, physical culture and social insurance and in education and culture. They make up less than a quarter of the employees in transport and forestry. In general their wages are lower than those of men. Wages in the industries in which women are largely employed are usually below the national average.

Women in the Soviet labour force are unequally represented in positions of responsibility and authority. Figures published in 1969 show that although 30% of engineers are women, they make up only 6% of factory directors, 16% of chief engineers and 20% of foremen. In politics, their representation on governing bodies decreases with the power and importance of those bodies. In 1973, women made up 47% of the membership of the local soviets, which carry out Communist Party policy and are responsible for many of the duties of British local authorities such as education, municipal services and public health and welfare. In 1971, women accounted for 35% of the elected members of the supreme soviets of the Union republics, the governing bodies of the various republics which make up the Soviet Union. However the number of women on the powerful central governing bodies is small. In 1974 they made up only 1% of the Council of Ministers of the USSR. A similar picture emerges from the power structure of the Communist Party. Although about a quarter of Party members were women in 1974, they were sparsely represented on its central governing bodies. Only 4% of the members of the Central Committee were female and there were no women in the Politbureau, the main policy making body.

From a survey of a number of studies of family life in the Soviet Union, David Lane states, 'Within the family, women have a particularly hard task'. Despite the fact that over half the labour force is female, women are still primarily responsible for housework and child care. Many women find it difficult to combine their domestic and occupational roles. Traditional attitudes about a women's place still linger, particularly in rural areas. A study conducted in a rural area near Moscow revealed that

30% of the sample 'thought it better for the wife to devote herself exclus-ively to the home and children'.

A survey of published material on the Soviet family by Mark G. Field, presents a similar picture. Field argues that the entry of women into the labour force has done little to change their domestic roles. He states that husbands, 'jealous of their masculinity', give their wives little assistance around the home. There is some evidence that state provision of nursery schools and other insitutions for child care is increasing in Russia, but places are available for only a small minority of the infant population. Field concludes that, 'As long as it is not possible for the state to under-take the complete care of a child for every woman who wishes it to do so, the blueprint outlined by Engels for the complete emancipation of women will have to remain just that'.

Although David Lane concedes that there is 'considerable male domination' in the Soviet Union, he believes that communism has made considerable advances toward sexual equality. However, communism alone, though a necessary step, is not sufficient to abolish sexual inequa-lity. In Lane's words, collective ownership of the forces of production is 'a necessary but not a sufficient condition for female liberation'. He argues that cultural attitudes, though influenced by economic changes, are not simply shaped by them. To some degree culture has an 'indepen-dent effect' on behaviour. Lane concludes that, 'Thousands of years of history of the subjection of women influence attitudes which men learn, and while communist governments may significantly alter the insti-tutional arrangements of society, it is much more difficult to change atti-tudes to get women accepted in authority roles on the same basis as men'.

Czechoslovakia and Eastern Europe

Available evidence from East European communist societies suggests that despite official ideology endorsing sexual equality, women are lag-ging behind their counterparts in the USSR. Hilda Scott, who lived in Czechoslovakia from 1948 to 1973, surveys the evidence on the position of women there and in Eastern Europe in general. Scott states that a labour shortage during the 1940s and 1950s resulted in women increas-ingly moving into areas traditionally defined as male employment. How-ever, the sexual division within the labour market was largely re-established with the ending of the labour shortage. Although there is less sexual inequality compared to the West, the evidence Scott presents is familiar. For example, in Czechoslovakia in 1968, the average wage of female workers was 27.9% less than the average for men. Half the employees in the Czech food industry are female, yet in 1973, only 5 out of the 579 plant directors were women. As in the West, there is a clearly defined sector of the job market labelled 'women's work'. Women's domestic responsibilities in Eastern Europe are similar to those in the USSR. A Czech survey conducted in 1966/7 of 500 female managers revealed that half of them did all the housework themselves.

Scott argues that socialism alone will not produce sexual equality. It will only come, she believes, with changes in two major areas. First, the state must take over the housewife–mother role and remove domestic tasks from the exclusive province of the wife. However, she is none too optimistic about this development, believing that, 'The removal of barbarously unproductive, petty, nerve-racking drudgery from the home, and its transfer to the public sector, has been postponed in all socialist countries until it has become a barely visible pinpoint on the horizon marked "communism"'. Secondly, Scott argues that equality will not be realized until the last vestiges of prejudice against women have disappeared. She sees few signs of this happening in the foreseeable future. However, she does admit that the position of women in Russia is better than in Eastern Europe because the Soviet Union has had thirty more years of communism which has helped to overcome prejudice. Scott concludes that, 'The early proponents of Marxism evidently did not realize that a lag in consciousness is involved which is more difficult to overcome than it is to win recognition for the rights of labor or the rights of Blacks or other minorities or oppressed nations, because belief in women's inferiority is older and more deeply ingrained, and involves the total population, since woman sees herself in the mirror man holds up'.

Israeli kibbutzim

The organization and culture of the socialist Israeli kibbutzim go a long way towards meeting Scott's two preconditions for sexual equality. The mother–housewife role has largely been taken over by the community. Sexual equality is reflected both in official kibbutzim ideology and in the beliefs of their members but several studies of kibbutzim have shown that there is an important difference between what people say and what they do.

In the early days of the kibbutzim during the 1920s, 1930s and 1940s, it appears that official ideology, which emphasized sexual equality and advocated the abolition of gender roles, was translated into action. Women worked alongside men, building roads and working in the fields. Men shared the traditional female tasks of cooking and laundering. However, despite official ideology, a sexual division of labour has gradually developed. From a large-scale study of kibbutzim, Lionel Tiger and Joseph Shepher found that by the 1970s, 'The sexual division of labour is highly polarized in the kibbutz'. Yonina Talmon, who has made several studies of kibbutz society, produces similar findings. Men are employed primarily in agriculture, construction and in traditional male roles as carpenters, mechanics, plumbers and electricians. Women predominate in service occupations such as nursing, kindergarten and infant teaching, cooking, catering and laundering. Men now dominate political life. In the kibbutzim studied by Tiger and Shepher and Talmon, between 85 and

95% of the major public offices were held by men. Tiger and Shepher state that, 'Generally, the higher the level of authority of office or committee, the lower the percentage of women in its personnel'. Even family life is moving closer to models in the outside world. The 'hour of love', the time allocated for children to be with their parents, was institutionalized in most kibbutzim by the mid 1960s. Mothers in particular spend more time with their children and have more contact with their nurses and teachers. The spouses' quarters have increased in size and now often include a kitchenette. A sexual division of labour has emerged, the wife doing the cooking, ironing and some washing, the husband being responsible for household repairs and heavier jobs such as taking and picking up the laundry. However, housework remains a minor concern – wives spend some eight hours a week, husbands between three and four hours on household chores. Many domestic tasks are still performed collectively. Despite changes in the kibbutzim, relationships between spouses remain egalitarian, decisions are made jointly and authority is largely shared.

Women in the kibbutzim have probably come nearer to sexual equality than women in other socialist societies yet their position still falls short of both official ideology and their role during the early years of the kibbutzim. Yonina Talmon suggests the following reasons for this situation. Firstly, the kibbutzim do not exist in isolation, they form a part of Israeli society and are therefore exposed to external norms and values. Secondly, during the early days of the kibbutzim, the birth rate was low and the demand for productive labour, particularly in agriculture, was high. As the standard of living rose, there was less demand for productive labour and there was a corresponding rise in the birth rate. Increasing emphasis was placed on services and child care, which now account for half the labour force. More and more women entered the service sector of the kibbutz economy. Talmon argues that the 'primary determinant of the shift in the division of labour is the woman's sex-linked childbearing role which accentuates biological differentiation'. Pregnancy and nursing tended to reduce woman's ability to perform the more physically demanding agricultural jobs. Since childbirth, childrearing and household duties were often considered part and parcel of the same thing, they increasingly became the province of women. With this emphasis on domestic matters, women tended to avoid the more demanding executive and administrative positions, which, Talmon argues, 'do not leave them enough time and energy for their familial roles'. Talmon concludes that, 'When practical consideration of efficiency gain precedence over ideological considerations, sex differentiated job allocation comes to be regarded as inevitable'. These arguments are familiar since they echo those of George Peter Murdock, outlined earlier in the chapter. If Talmon is correct, biology, even in the socialist kibbutz, is slowly directing women to their traditional place.

Tiger and Shepher return to a different version of the biological argument to account for changes in the role of women in the kibbutz. They present evidence which indicates that it is women themselves who are primarily responsible for these changes. Despite the fact that official ideology and the majority of men oppose traditional gender roles, women are increasingly demanding their return. Tiger and Shepher argue that this is due to the female biogrammar which contains 'genetically programmed behavioural propensities'. Changes in the role of women are therefore due to genetically based predispositions in the female, the most important of which is the need to have a close relationship with their offspring.

Despite the evidence which can be marshalled from socialist societies to support biological theories of gender roles, it does not lead to a dismissal of Marxian views. Although socialization of the forces of production does not eliminate sexual inequality, it does appear to reduce it significantly. It can be argued that changes in the infrastructure take time to effect changes in the superstructure. In Hilda Scott's words, there may be a 'lag in consciousness'. It may take time for culture to catch up with economic change. Evidence giving some support to this view is provided by the comparison of the position of women in the USSR and East European communist societies. Sexual inequality is less marked in the USSR where socialism is some thirty years older than in Eastern Europe. Evidence from the kibbutzim, however, suggests changes in the opposite direction with the sexual division of labour becoming more pronounced over time. But, as Talmon argues, the kibbutzim are a part of Israeli capitalist society and are, therefore, influenced by the norms and values of the wider society.

The origins of oppression – Shulasmith Firestone

Many feminist writers are dissatisfied with Marxian theory. They argue that it fails to provide an adequate explanation for sexual inequality. They are disillusioned with the promise that socialism will liberate women. The theories outlined in the first part of the chapter provide alternatives to Marxian approaches but they largely fail to combine a general theory of social stratification with an explanation of sexual inequality. Shulasmith Firestone in *The Dialectic of Sex* attempts to do just this.

Firestone argues that the sexual division of labour and the 'sexual class system' pre-dates and is more basic than the specialized division of labour which differentiates all members of society and the economic class system which divides both males and females. She claims that sexual inequality is rooted in biological differences. She argues that, 'Unlike economic class, sex class sprang directly from a biological reality; men and women were created different and not equally privileged'. Because women bore children they were dependent on men for their survival. Dependence on men produced unequal power relationships and 'power psychology' which formed the basis for all future stratification systems. Men derived pleasure from their power over women which led to 'power psychology', the desire to dominate others. Thus stratification is based ultimately on biology rather than economics. It began not with private property, but with the reproductive functions of men and women.

From the sexual class system, it is a relatively short step to the economic class system. 'Power psychology' provided the motivation and the impetus. Domination of men over women was extended to domination of some men over other men. The sexual class system provided the blueprint and the prototype for the economic class system. The economic class system provided the means by which some men came to dominate other men. Since, in Firestone's view, all domination is bad, both the sexual class system and the economic class system must go. Both women and men must be liberated. Since the sexual class system is the primary form of stratification, it is the main target for attack. In Firestone's words, 'The sexual class system is the model for all other exploitive systems and thus the tapeworm that must be eliminated first by any true revolution'.

The sexual class system can only end when women cease to be slaves to their biology. Reliable birth control techniques have begun to free women but true freedom will only be realized by means of artificial reproduction. Only when babies can be conceived and developed outside the womb will women be freed from their reproductive role. This step, though the most important, only provides the foundation for freedom. The economic class structure and the cultural superstructure, which have been built on the basis of the sexual class system, must also be destroyed.

This brief outline hardly does justice to Firestone's elegant and comprehensive theory. Whatever its shortcomings, her theory does contain an explanation for all forms of social stratification. As it stands, however, it contains a number of deficiencies. In particular, it fails to explain the variation in the status of women over time and in different societies. Despite its inadequacies, Marxian theory does help to explain historical changes in the position of women in society.

Women's liberation – proposals and prospects

From the late 1960s onwards, a vast literature in support of women's liberation has poured from the presses. Many of the famous feminist writers are socialists. However, they go beyond a simple socialist solution, maintaining that the abolition of private property will not automatically result in women's liberation. They propose a 'socialist feminism' which involves not only an attack on the economic class structure, but also a direct attack, led by women, on all forms of male domination. The feminist part of 'socialist feminism' will now be examined. First, it is important to analyse the various options open to women as a social group in their relationship to society as a whole.

Women and society – three alternatives

Alice Rossi applies three models, derived from minority group theory, to the possible future place of women in society. The first model, 'pluralism', argues that minority groups should maintain and develop many of their distinctive characteristics while removing those circumstances which result in their inequality. This model would foresee a future in which men and women retain their differences. These differences would be welcomed and respected by both sexes in a context of equality of situation and status between them. Put simply men and women would be different but equal. Rossi rejects the pluralist model on the grounds that much that is distinctive about women results from their oppression and exploitation. The idea of separate but equal development has been applied to Blacks in the USA and is still being applied in South Africa. In practice separate and equal has resulted in separate and unequal. It has served as an ideology to justify inequality.

The second model, 'assimilation', argues that minority groups should join the mainstream of society. This would involve them losing their distinguishing characteristics and so their minority group status. In terms of women, this would mean a unisex society, in which women became like men. Rossi argues that assimilation is impossible since men's life style is based on the housewife in the background, ministering to their needs. For women to successfully adopt male roles they would have to find a functional equivalent for the housewife.

The third alternative, which Rossi terms the 'hybrid' model, rejects both pluralism and assimilation. It rejects the idea that men and women are basically different and also the idea that women should adopt traditional male roles. Instead it proposes a society in which the roles of men and women are similar. This will involve a change in the traditional roles of both sexes. Many of the proposals to remove sexual inequality can be classified in terms of Rossi's hybrid model. Although they concentrate on changes in women's roles, they imply that men's roles should also change.

The abolition of gender roles

Many feminist writers advocate the abolition of gender roles with the mother-housewife role being selected as the prime target. Ann Oakley argues that the following steps must be taken to liberate women. First, the housewife role must be abolished. Oakley rejects less radical solutions such as payment for housework, which, she argues, will simply reinforce the woman equals housewife equation. Second, the family as it now stands, must be abolished. This proposal follows from the first since

399

the housewife and mother roles are part and parcel of the same thing. Abolishing the family will also serve to break the circle of daughter learning her role from mother, son learning his role from father. Third, the sexual division of labour must be eradicated in all areas of social life. Oakley argues that, 'We need an ideological revolution, a revolution in the ideology of gender roles current in our culture, a revolution in concepts of gender identity'. Thus, men and women must be seen as people, not as gender. Kate Millett, a radical feminist writer, argues that in a society without culturally defined gender roles, each individual will be free to 'develop an entire – rather than a partial, limited, and conformist – personality'. Thus females may develop so-called male traits, and vice versa. This would involve complete tolerance of homosexual and lesbian relationships, 'so that the sex act ceases to be arbitrarily polarized into male and female'. Thus, those who are biologically male and female may develop their personality and behaviour along lines best suited to themselves, rather than being cramped and confined by the culturally defined labels, male and female.

Modifications and alternatives to the family

The continuing debate on the role of women in society has produced a whole spectrum of modifications and alternatives to the housewife–mother role and the family. They range from Oakley's radical demands to abolish both, to more moderate suggestions which, in many cases, largely maintain the status quo with proposals to lighten the burdens of housework and motherhood. Ideas which fall into the latter category include payment for housework, the provision of crèches by employers, a free system of child care provided as of right by the state for every mother who requires it, and maternity leave plus maternity benefits paid by employers or government, with the mother's job being held open should she wish to return to work. Many radical feminists argue that such measures will not necessarily alter the position of women in the home. There, despite the fact that her burdens might be eased, she may still be relegated to the role of housewife and mother.

One of the simplest solutions to this problem has been put forward by Susan Brownmiller. She suggests that husband and wife should split their traditional roles down the middle. Each should work for half a day and spend the rest of the time taking care of the children. Jessie Bernard supports this idea, arguing that, 'With one stroke, it alleviates one of the major responsibilities of men (sole responsibility for the provider role) and of women (exclusive responsibility for housework and child care)'. A variation of this shared role pattern was examined by R. and R. Rapaport in *Dual-Career Families*. They made a detailed study of five families in which each spouse followed his or her career. As things stand, this is not a viable alternative for most people because of the expense involved. The families studied by the Rapaports were fairly wealthy and all employed domestic help to perform many of the duties of the mother–housewife role.

Systems of collective childrearing provide an alternative to role sharing within the nuclear family. Suggestions range from re-creations of classic extended family networks to kibbutz type collectives with specialized provision for childrearing. The Hungarian Marxist writers Vajda and Heller propose a commune or 'collective family' which functions only as a family. All adults are responsible for the care of children within the commune. Relationships between adults can range from monogamy to promiscuity since 'the commune does not have value preferences concerning sexual relationships'. The 'family commune' differs from the kibbutz since it deals only with domestic and child care relationships and does not form a unit of production which involves the organization of occupational roles. However, the evidence of history shows that communes, especially those involving promiscuity, tend to be shortlived.

A novel alternative to the present-day family is suggested by Alvin Toffler in *Future Shock*. He proposes a system of professional parents. These 'pro-parents' would simulate family groups and adopt the roles of 'father', 'mother', 'uncle', 'aunt' and 'grandparent'. They would specialize in childrearing as a paid occupation. This would end the amateur status of childrearing and free many biological parents from their family roles. They would simply hand over their offspring to the professionals.

Many writers foresee a range of alternatives for the family's future. Juliet Mitchell advocates various experiments in communal living to suit the personalities and circumstances of the individuals involved. She supports a 'range of institutions which match the free invention and variety of men and women'. Jessie Bernard takes a similar view. She looks forward to 'a future of marital options' hoping that 'people will be able to tailor their relationships to their circumstances and preferences'. Two main themes dominate much of the writing on the future of the role of women in relation to the family. The first demands equality between the sexes, the second advocates freedom of choice with tolerance by all of the range of 'family life' that will emerge as a result.

Women and the labour market

Proposals to end discrimination against women in the labour market involve many of the suggested changes outlined above. Women must be freed from domestic burdens or share them equally with men if they are to compete for jobs on equal terms. An end to discrimination in the labour market would also involve the abolition of the sexual division of labour, the removal of distinctions between 'men's jobs' and 'women's jobs'. The failure of women's entry into the labour market to end the sexual division of labour there has led some writers to suggest that women as a group must gain control over a significant part of the forces of production in order to remove discrimination. Juliet Mitchell argues on these lines when she states that, 'Clearly then, their entry into the labour force is not enough: they must enter in their own right with their own independent economic interest'. Women's capitalism has made tentative beginnings in America with the founding of several women's banks. However, at least one has already gone out of business and women's capitalism remains a blueprint which has scarcely got off the drawing board.

Many feminist writers reject women's capitalism as a goal in itself. They argue that it will simply result in equality of exploitation; most men and most women will be equally exploited. However, it could provide, as Juliet Mitchell suggests, a power base from which to move towards socialism and equality for all people.

Raising consciousness and creating solidarity

D. H. J. Morgan has applied the Marxian concepts of ideology, class consciousness and class solidarity to the position of women in society. Just as the class system is justified and legitimated by ruling class ideology, so the position of women is justified and legitimated by what may be termed male ideology. This ideology defines a woman's place, how she should act, think and feel as a woman, and so maintains her subordination and justifies her exploitation. Just as ruling class ideology creates false class consciousness, so male ideology produces what can be seen as false gender consciousness. From a Marxian perspective, class consciousness and class solidarity are essential before the subject class can overthrow its oppressors. In terms of the Marxian analogy, gender consciousness and female solidarity are necessary for women's liberation.

Many feminist writers consider that both 'raising consciousness', that is making women aware of the reality of their situation, and female solidarity are essential pre-conditions for women's liberation. These are among the stated objectives of many Women's Liberation groups but Juliet Mitchell warns of the dangers of 'consciousness raising sessions', particularly in the context of middle-class ladies' coffee mornings. They may become an excuse for avoiding more radical and direct action. Put simply, they may become all show and no go. Female solidarity involves problems which are peculiar to women. Many women are socially isolated and loyal to and dependent on particular men. These factors limit their ability to unite as a group in opposition to a common enemy.

The Women's Liberation Movement

From the evidence presented in this chapter, the underlying causes of the Women's Liberation Movement are clear. This section will consider the particular causes which triggered the formation and growth of the movement.

The Women's Liberation movement emerged during the late 1960s, primarily in America. For most of this century militant feminists have been fighting for civil rights, that is equality for all adults as citizens, regardless of sex. The battle for the legal emancipation of women has largely been won, at least on paper. For example in Britain, the Equal Pay Act was passed in 1970, the Sex Discrimination Act in 1975. At first sight it appears strange that the Women's Liberation Movement should emerge at the very time when women's legal freedoms have been largely achieved. Emancipation, however, is not the same as liberation. Legal emancipation has highlighted the fact that women are far from free. There is a parallel between the Women's Liberation Movement and the Black Power Movement in the USA. The Black Power Movement began in the late 1960s *after* the civil rights legislation which gave Blacks equal rights under the law. The full realization of inequality only came when Blacks were told they were equal and free whereas in reality, they were far from so. In the same way, the Women's Liberation Movement can be seen as a response to the fact that civil rights did not automatically bring women's liberation. Rather they highlighted their subjugation.

Juliet Mitchell argues that the Women's Liberation Movement was partly triggered by the radical movements of the middle and late 1960s. She points to the various civil rights organizations which campaigned for the rights of ethnic minority groups, the Black Power Movement which spearheaded the demands of more militant Blacks, the Youth Movement represented by organizations such as Students for a Democratic Society and the Peace Movement which coordinated protest against the war in Vietnam and later in Cambodia. These movements preceded and paralleled the Women's Liberation Movement in the USA. They emphasized freedom, questioned established truths and attacked what they saw as oppression and exploitation. Mitchell argues that they provided part of the impetus and philosophy for the Women's Liberation Movement. Women increasingly realized that they needed a movement of their own, since even as members of other radical movements, they were often treated in terms of their traditional stereotypes. For example when Stokely Carmichael, then leader of SNCC (Student Nonviolent Coordinating Committee), a Black civil rights organization of the mid 1960s, was asked about the role of women in the organization, he replied, 'The only position for women in SNCC is prone'. Barbara Deckard summarizes the results of women's participation in civil rights movements during the early and mid 1960s. She states that, 'Here many young women learned both the rhetoric and the organization of protest. Not surprisingly, as they became more sensitive to the Blacks' second-class status, they became more aware of their own'. The result was the Women's Liberation Movement.

Sociology, ideology and women

Defining a situation as a problem involves a value judgment. It means that things are not as they ought to be. A large body of research in sociology has been directed by value judgments which state that particular social arrangements and circumstances are morally wrong. For example, alienating work, poverty and ruling elites are immoral. Such judgments draw attention to a subject, define it as worthy of study, commit the sociologist to his research topic and give him the feeling that the questions he asks are of vital importance to the well-being of mankind. Traditionally, men have defined problems in sociology. They have defined them in terms of male concerns and on the basis of male prejudice. As a result, sociology has, in many respects, been the sociology of men. For example, standard textbooks on the sociology of work have scarcely mentioned women. They could, with some justification, be retitled as 'the sociology of men's work'. Theodore Caplow's *The Sociology of Work* is an exception – it contains one chapter on women in the labour force.

No sociologist wants to study something he considers insignificant. Given the prevailing definition of women in Western society and the fact that most sociologists are men, there have been few serious studies of women. It took a woman, Ann Oakley, to produce the first detailed study of housework. In terms of cultural definitions of housework as relatively unimportant work, as somehow not 'real work', it is not surprising that male sociologists avoided this area of research. In practice, the sociology of women has been largely an adjunct to the sociology of the family. Again this is not surprising given the traditional view that a woman's place is in the home. Sociologists study what they consider important. From the viewpoint of a male dominated culture, women are not very important.

Two factors have been primarily responsible for the development of the sociology of women. First, the definition of women's position in society as a social problem. Second, the reassessment of women as people who are just as important as men. In many areas of sociology, a subject and its treatment is influenced more by what happens in society than by developments within the discipline itself. In the case of women, changes in society and in particular, the Women's Liberation Movement, have led to the emergence of the sociology of women as a subject area in its own right. It has largely been developed by women, by radical feminists such as Shulasmith Firestone and Juliet Mitchell, by a new generation of female sociologists committed to feminist ideals such as Ann Oakley and by established female sociologists such as Jessie Bernard who responded to current ideas and turned their attention to the study of women. They and others like them were largely responsible for resurrecting Engels's writings on women. They have produced the most original and stimulating ideas in the area.

Beginning with different values, priorities and concerns, women often ask different questions than men. For example, when male sociologists talk about marriage and the family, they do so from a male viewpoint. The limitations of this approach are clearly revealed by Jessie Bernard's study of the 'wife's marriage'. But it is not simply a case of asking different questions. Male and female researchers often produce very different answers to the same questions. Many feminist writers argue that the views of male sociologists on the position of women in society are largely rationalizations and justifications for male dominance. The feminist critique of a sociology based on male ideology can be summarized as follows. Operating from a commitment to male dominance, male sociologists assume that the subordinate position of women is beneficial for society. However, the phrase 'beneficial for society' should read 'beneficial for men'. Male sociologists start from the value judgment that what's good for men is good for society.

Ann Oakley gives a number of examples of the intrusion of male ideology into scientific analysis. Particularly in America, the 'mighty-hunter myth' is a part of the mythology of male dominance. This has simply been translated by Tiger and Fox into the jargon of the male biogrammar. Thus a 'scientific myth' has been created to justify male dominance. George Peter Murdock, a Western male, looks at the role of women in non-Western societies in terms of the values of a male dominated culture. He selects and interprets the evidence in terms of his prejudices and finds that the sexual division of labour is universal. His conclusions suggest that changes in the traditional roles of women would be dysfunctional for society. Talcott Parsons, a product of American culture, argues that the 'expressive' female role is essential for the performance of the two 'irreducible functions' of the family. In Oakley's view this is simply a justification for the status quo. It relegates women to domestic roles and legitimizes male dominance.

Although it can be argued that feminist writers are just as biased as their male counterparts, they have at least redressed the balance. More than this, they have been largely responsible for the development of an important substantive area in sociology, the sociology of women.

10 Deviance

In everyday language to deviate means to stray from an accepted path. Many sociological definitions of deviance simply elaborate upon this idea. Thus deviance consists of those acts which do not follow the norms and expectations of a particular social group. Deviance may be positively sanctioned (rewarded), negatively sanctioned (punished), or simply accepted without reward or punishment. In terms of the above definition of deviance, the soldier on the battlefield who risks his life above and beyond the normal call of duty may be termed deviant, as may the physicist who breaks the rules of his discipline and develops a new theory. Their deviance may be posititively sanctioned: the soldier might be rewarded with a medal, the physicist with a Nobel prize. In one sense, though, neither is deviant since both conform to the values of society, the soldier to the value of courage, the physicist to the value of academic progress. By comparison, a murderer not only deviates from society's norms and expectations but also from its values, in particular the value placed on human life. His deviance generally results in widespread disapproval and punishment. A third form of deviance consists of acts which depart from the norms and expectations of a particular society but are generally tolerated and accepted. The little old lady with a house full of cats or the old gentleman with an obsession for collecting clocks would fall into this category. Usually their eccentricities are neither rewarded nor punished by others. They are simply defined as a 'bit odd' but harmless, and therefore tolerated.

In practice, the field of study covered by the sociology of deviance is usually limited to deviance which results in negative sanctions. In fact the American sociologist Marshall B. Clinard has suggested that the term deviance should be reserved for 'those situations in which behavior is in a disapproved direction, and of a sufficient degree to exceed the tolerance limit of the community'. Though not all sociologists would accept this definition, it does describe the area usually covered by studies of deviance. In terms of Clinard's definition, crime and delinquency are the most obvious forms of deviance. Crime refers to those activities which break the law of the land and are subject to official punishment; delinquency refers to the criminal activities of young people. However, many disapproved deviant acts are not defined as criminal. For example, alcoholism and attempted suicide are not illegal in Britain today. In practice sociologists have tended to focus their attention on the following types of deviance which generally fall within Clinard's definition: crime and delinquency, illegal drug use, prostitution, mental illness, suicide, alcoholism and homosexuality.

Deviance is relative. This means that there is no absolute way of defining a deviant act. Deviance can only be defined in relation to a particular standard and no standards are fixed or absolute. As such deviance varies from time to time and place to place. In a particular society an act which is considered deviant today may be defined as normal in the future. An act defined as deviant in one society may be seen as perfectly normal in another. Put another way, deviance is culturally determined and cultures change over time and vary from society to society. The following examples will serve to illustrate the above points. At certain times in Western society it has been considered deviant for women to smoke, use make-up and consume alcoholic drinks in public. Today this is no longer the case. In the same way definitions of crime change over time. Homosexuality was formerly a criminal offence in Britain. Since 1969, however, homosexual acts conducted between consenting adults in private are no longer illegal. A comparison of modern Western culture with the traditional culture of the Teton Sioux Indians of the USA illustrates how deviance varies from society to society. As part of their religious rituals during the annual Sun Dance ceremony, Sioux warriors mutilated their bodies. Leather thongs were inserted through strips of flesh on the chest and attached to a central pole. Warriors had to break free by tearing their flesh and in return were granted favours by the supernatural powers. Similar actions by members of Western society may well be viewed as masochism or madness. In the same way behaviour accepted as normal in Western society may be defined as deviant within Sioux society. In the West the private ownership of property is an established norm, members of society strive to accumulate wealth and substantial property holding brings power and prestige. Such behaviour would have incurred strong disapproval amongst the Sioux and those who acted in terms of the above norms would be regarded as deviant. Generosity was a major value of Sioux culture and the distribution rather than the accumulation of wealth was the route to power and prestige. Chiefs were expected to distribute gifts of horses, beadwork and weapons to their followers. The norms of Sioux culture prevented the accumulation of wealth. The Sioux had no conception of the individual ownership of land; the produce of the hunt was automatically shared by all members of the group.

So far, the concept of deviance suggested is fairly simple. Deviance refers to those activities which do not conform to the norms and expectations of members of a particular society. As studied by sociologists it usually refers to those activities which bring general disapproval from members of society. Deviance is a relative concept. Actions are only deviant in relation to the standards of a particular society at a particular time in its history. This view of deviance will become more complex as the chapter develops. First, however, some early research on deviance will be considered. The main concern of earlier research was to explain why certain individuals engage in deviant behaviour. It asked straightforward questions such as, 'Why do some people commit suicide?' and 'Why do some individuals steal?' Often the answers were similarly straightforward being based on the following line of reasoning. Deviant behaviour is different from normal behaviour. Therefore deviants are different from normal people. Deviant behaviour is a social problem since it has a disruptive effect on social life. Therefore deviants are a social problem. Since they are both different and a problem there must be something wrong with deviants. They must have some kind of pathology, some form of 'sickness'. The answer to the question 'Why deviance?' therefore lies in diagnosing the illness from which the deviant is presumed to be suffering. Much of this reasoning had strong moral overtones since it was assumed that any normal person would have no desire to stray from the straight and narrow. The two main diagnoses of the deviant were physiological and psychological. The first argued that deviants had some organic defect or pathology which they were born with and which influenced or caused their behaviour. The second argued that deviants were psychologically unbalanced due to some emotional disturbance in their past. This imbalance influenced or caused their deviant behaviour.

Physiological and psychological theories of deviance

Physiological or biological explanations of deviance argue that particular individuals are more prone to deviance than others because of their genetic make-up. Genetically inherited characteristics either directly cause or predispose them towards deviance. Such theories are similar to 'common-sense' notions contained in phrases such as 'the born criminal' and 'he can't help it because he's made that way'. An early version of physiological theories is given by Cesare Lombroso, an Italian army doctor, in his book *L'Uomo Delinquente*, published in 1876. Lombroso argued that criminals were throwbacks to an earlier and more primitive form of man. He claimed to have identified a number of genetically determined characteristics which were often found in criminals. These included large jaws, high cheek bones, large ears, extra nipples, toes and fingers and an insensitivity to pain. These were some of the outward signs of an inborn criminal nature. Later research found no support for Lombroso's picture of the criminal as a primitive biological freak.

Despite these crude beginnings, there is still support for physiological theories of deviance. Sheldon and Eleanor Glueck claim to have found a causal relationship between physical build and delinquent activity. They argue that stocky, rounded individuals, a body type known as meso-morph, tend to be more active and aggressive than those with other builds. Their research has shown that delinquent behaviour is associated with mesomorphs. The British psychologist Hans Eysenck argues that there is a link between genetically based personality characteristics and deviant behaviour. He maintains that there is a connection between personality traits such as extraversion and criminal behaviour (the extravert 'craves excitement, takes chances, often sticks his neck out, acts on the spur of the moment, and is generally an impulsive individual'). The modern supporters of genetic theories of deviance are more cautious than their predecessors. They do not suggest that an individual is a total prisoner of his genes. Instead they argue that genetically based characteristics predispose an individual to deviant behaviour. Thus Eysenck states that 'heredity is a very strong predisposing factor as far as committing crimes is concerned'.

Sociologists tend to dismiss biological theories of deviance, arguing that any association between physical and personality characteristics and deviant behaviour can be explained in other ways. For example, Taylor, Walton and Young provide an alternative explanation for the link between mesomorphism and delinquency. They suggest that, 'It may well be that lower working-class children, who are more likely to be found in the criminal statistics, are also by virtue of diet, continual manual labour, physical fitness and strength, more likely to be mesomorphic'. Similarly, an alternative explanation may be provided for Eysenck's association of extravert personality traits with criminal behaviour. Eysenck's description of extravert characteristics is very similar to the 'subterranean values' which, according to Matza and Sykes, direct delinquent behaviour. Values are learned rather than being genetically determined. (Matza and Sykes's views will be discussed in pp. 422–5.) Finally, a major difficulty with all biological theories is the problem of showing that particular behaviour is genetically based. It is not yet possible to isolate a gene or a combination of genes and to show conclusively that they influence particular actions.

Psychological theories of deviance share certain similarities with biological theories. First, they see the deviant as different from the population as a whole. Second, he is abnormal in a normal population. Third, his abnormality predisposes him to deviance. However, psychological theories differ in their claim that the deviant's abnormality is learned rather than genetically determined. They see abnormal experience rather than abnormal genes as the basis for deviance. This experience produces 'character defects' and 'maladjusted personalities' which in turn produce deviance. Often psychological theories argue that something has gone wrong in the socialization process, usually in the mother–child relationship. This 'defective socialization' involves emotional disturbance which leads to the formation of maladjusted personality traits. Early childhood experience, it is claimed, can have a lasting effect upon adolescent and adult behaviour.

John Bowlby's *Forty-four Juvenile Thieves* is a pioneering work in the psychology of deviance. He argued that a child has certain basic needs, the most important being emotional security, which can be provided most effectively by a close, intimate relationship with its mother. If the child is deprived of maternal love, particularly during its early years, a psychopathic personality can develop. Psychopaths tend to act impulsively with little regard for the consequences of their actions. They rarely feel guilt and show little response to punishment or treatment. Bowlby claimed that those delinquents who were 'chronic recidivists', that is they constantly broke the law with little regard for the possible consequences, had suffered from 'maternal deprivation' during their early years. They revealed psychopathic traits, had often been raised in institutions such as orphanages, and so been deprived of an intimate relationship with a mother figure. (For further details and criticisms of Bowlby's views, see Chapter 9, pp. 372–3 and 374.) Other studies have argued that a boy's relationship with his father, particularly during the early years of his adolescence, can have important effects upon his behaviour. Robert G. Andry claimed that boys who had hostile and unsatisfactory relationships with their fathers projected this hostility and acted it out in their relationships with other boys and authority figures. Such unsatisfactory relationships between boys and their fathers produced a 'chip on the shoulder' mentality rather than the more severe psychological disturbances described by Bowlby. Andry claims that the 'character defects' which resulted were an important factor in accounting for delinquency.

As with biological theories, sociologists tend to dismiss psychological explanations of deviance. Firstly, they argue that such theories tend to ignore social and cultural factors in the explanation of deviance. Such factors form the basis of the sociological theories which will be examined shortly. Secondly, they argue that the methodology of the studies is suspect. There is little agreement among psychologists about what constitutes mental health and on how to measure personality characteristics. Thirdly, many sociologists reject the priority given to childhood experience. They dismiss the view that the individual is a prisoner of his early experience which he simply acts out in later life. This approach ignores the influence of a vast number of social factors which influence behaviour during an individual's life. Marshall B. Clinard rather scornfully likens psychological theories of deviance to the older notion of possession by devils. The devil has been replaced by the character defect, exorcism by the priest has been replaced with treatment by the psychiatrist.

Despite their rejection by many sociologists, biological and particularly psychological theories are still widespread and often accepted as valid by the various agents of social control. Both theories have serious implications for the treatment of deviance. Put simply, if deviants are 'sick', they must be treated and cured. This view has resulted in treatment ranging from the use of drugs, electric shock treatment, various forms of psychotherapy, to lobotomy – the removal of a portion of the frontal region of the brain. Carried to its extreme, the implications of such treatment are frightening, particularly in the hands of a powerful ruling elite. Soviet 'dissidents' have been defined as mentally ill, confined to institutions and plied with a variety of dangerous drugs in order to 'cure' their 'sickness'. Aldous Huxley's *Brave New World* would no longer be a work of fiction if one New York psychiatrist had his way. In 1970 he proposed that psychological tests be given to the nation's six-year olds to uncover any criminal tendencies. He advocated psychiatric treatment for those who revealed such tendencies. Apparently this scheme was seriously considered by the American government, but not put into practice, (discussed in Cohen, 1971, pp. 11–12).

The remainder of the chapter examines sociological theories of deviance. The criticisms of the above theories from a sociological perspective will become clearer as the chapter develops.

Deviance – a functionalist perspective

The functions of deviance

Rather than starting with the individual, a functionalist analysis of deviance begins with society as a whole. It looks for the source of deviance in the nature of society rather than in the biological or psychological nature of the individual. At first sight it seems strange that some functionalists should argue that deviance is a necessary part of all societies, that it performs positive functions for social systems. Deviance breaks social norms and values. With the functionalist emphasis on the importance of shared norms and values as the basis for social order, it would appear that deviance is a threat to order and should therefore be seen as dysfunctional for society. All functionalists agree that social control mechanisms are necessary to keep deviance in check and so protect social order. However, many argue that a certain amount of deviance has positive functions, that it contributes to the maintenance and well-being of society.

Emile Durkheim develops this argument with his discussion of crime in *The Rules of Sociological Method*. He argues that crime is an inevitable and normal aspect of social life, it is 'an integral part of all healthy societies'. It is inevitable because not every member of society can be equally committed to the 'collective sentiments', the shared values and moral beliefs of society. Since individuals are exposed to different influences and circumstances, it is 'impossible for all to be alike'. Therefore not everybody shares the same restraints about breaking the law.

Crime is not only inevitable, it can also be functional. Durkheim argues that it only becomes dysfunctional when 'its rate is unusually high'. He argues that all social change begins with some form of deviance. In order for change to occur, yesterday's deviance must become today's normality. Since a certain amount of change is healthy for society, so it can progress rather than stagnate, so is deviance. For change to occur, the collective sentiments must not be too strong, too hostile to change; they must have only 'moderate energy'. If they were too strong they would crush all originality, both the originality of the criminal and the originality of the genius. In Durkheim's words, 'to make progress, individual originality must be able to express itself. In order that the originality of the idealist whose dreams transcend this century may find expression, it is necessary that the originality of the criminal, who is below the level of his time, shall also be possible. One does not occur without the other'. Thus the collective sentiments must not be sufficiently powerful to block the expression of people like Jesus, William Wilberforce, Martin Luther King and Mother Theresa. Durkheim regarded some crime as 'an anticipation of the morality of the future'. Thus heretics who were denounced by both the state and the established church may represent the collective sentiments of the future. In the same way terrorists or freedom fighters may represent a future established order.

If crime is inevitable, what is the function of punishment? Durkheim argues that its function is not to remove crime in society. Rather it is to maintain the collective sentiments at their necessary level of strength. In Durkheim's words, punishment 'serves to heal the wounds done to the collective sentiments'. Without punishment the collective sentiments would lose their force to control behaviour and the crime rate would reach the point where it became dysfunctional. Thus in Durkheim's view, a healthy society requires both crime and punishment; both are inevitable, both are functional.

Durkheim's views of the positive functions of deviance have been developed by a number of sociologists. Albert K. Cohen analyses several possible functions of deviance. Firstly, deviance can function as a safety valve, providing a relatively harmless expression of discontent. In this way social order is protected. For example, Cohen suggests that 'prostitution performs such a safety valve function without threatening the institution of the family'. It can provide a release from the stress and pressure of family life without undermining family stability, since the relationship between a prostitute and her client usually avoids strong emotional attachment. Secondly, Cohen suggests that certain deviant acts may provide a useful warning device to indicate that an aspect of society is malfunctioning. They may draw attention to the problem and lead to measures to solve it. Thus truants from school, deserters from the army or runaways from Borstal institutions may 'reveal unsuspected causes of discontent, and lead to changes that enhance efficiency and morale'.

Durkheim and Cohen have moved away from the picture of the deviant as psychologically or biologically abnormal. Durkheim suggests that society itself generates deviance for its own well-being. Cohen argues that certain forms of deviance are a normal and natural response to particular circumstances. Yet apart from his work on suicide – examined in Chapter 12, pp. 495–7 – Durkheim does not explain why particular individuals or groups appear to be more prone to deviance than others. Nor does he explain why certain forms of deviance appear to be associated with particular groups in the population. It was not until Robert K. Merton's famous work in the 1930s that answers to these questions were provided within a functionalist framework.

Robert K. Merton – *Social Structure and Anomie*

Merton argues that deviance results not from 'pathological personalities' but from the culture and structure of society itself. He begins from the standard functionalist position of value consensus, that is all members of society share the same values. However, since members of society are placed in different positions in the social structure, for example they differ in terms of class position, they do not have the same opportunity of realizing the shared values. This situation can generate deviance. In Merton's words, 'the social and cultural structure generates pressure for socially deviant behaviour upon people variously located in that structure'.

Using the USA as an example, Merton outlines his theory as follows. Members of American society share the major values of American culture. In particular they share the goal of success, for which they all strive and which is largely measured in terms of wealth and material possessions. The 'American Dream' states that all members of society have an equal opportunity of achieving success, of owning a Cadillac, a Beverley Hills mansion and a substantial bank balance. In all societies there are institutionalized means of reaching culturally defined goals. In America, the accepted ways of achieving success are through educational qualifications, talent, hard work, drive, determination and ambition. In a balanced society an equal emphasis is placed upon both cultural goals and institutionalized means, and members are satisfied with both. But in America great importance is attached to success and relatively less importance is given to the accepted ways of achieving success. As such, American society is unstable, unbalanced. There is a tendency to reject the 'rules of the game' and to strive for success by any available means. The situation becomes like a game of cards in which winning becomes so important that the rules are abandoned by some of the players. When rules cease to operate a situation of normlessness or 'anomie' results. In a situation of 'anything goes', norms no longer direct behaviour and deviance is encouraged. However, individuals will respond to a situation of anomie in different ways. In particular, their reaction will be shaped by their position in the social structure.

Merton outlines five possible ways in which members of American society can respond to success goals. The first and most common response is 'conformity'. Members of society conform both to success goals and the normative means of reaching them. They strive for success by means of accepted channels. A second response is 'innovation'. This response rejects normative means of achieving success and turns to deviant means, in particular, crime. Merton argues that members of the lower social strata are most likely to select this route to success. They are least likely to succeed via conventional channels, thus there is greater pressure upon them to deviate. Their educational qualifications are usually low, their jobs provide little opportunity for advancement. In Merton's words, they have 'little access to conventional and legitimate means for becoming successful'. Since their way is blocked, they innovate, turning to crime which promises greater rewards than legitimate means. Merton stresses that membership of the lower strata is not, in itself, sufficient to produce deviance. In some more traditional European societies those at the bottom of the social structure are more likely to accept their position since they have not internalized mainstream success goals. Instead they have developed distinctive subcultures which define success in terms which differ from those of the wider society. (See Chapter 2, pp. 54–6, Chapter 4, pp. 154–6, Chapter 5, pp. 193–7, for discussions of traditional working-class subculture and the 'culture of poverty'.) Only in societies such as the USA, where all members share the same success goals, does the pressure to innovate operate forcefully on the lower classes. Finally Merton argues that those who innovate have been 'imperfectly socialized so that they abandon institutional means while retaining success-aspirations'.

Merton uses the term 'ritualism' to describe the third possible response. Those who select this alternative are deviant because they have largely abandoned the commonly held success goals. The pressure to adopt this alternative is greatest for members of the lower middle class. Their occupations provide less opportunity for success than those of other members of the middle class. (See Chapter 2, pp. 66–9, for an analysis of the market situation of the lower middle class.) However, compared to members of the working class, they have been strongly socialized to conform to social norms. This prevents them from turning to crime. Unable to innovate and with jobs that offer little opportunity for advancement, their only solution is to scale down or abandon their success goals. Merton paints the following picture of a typical lower middle-class ritualist. He is a low grade bureaucrat, ultra-respectable but stuck in a rut. He is a stickler for the rules, follows the book to the letter, clings to red tape, conforms to all the outward standards of middle-class respectability, but has given up striving for success. The ritualist is deviant because he has rejected the success goals held by most members of society.

Merton terms the fourth, and least common response, 'retreatism'. It applies to 'psychotics, autists, pariahs, outcasts, vagrants, vagabonds, tramps, chronic drunkards and drug addicts'. They have strongly internalized both the cultural goals and the institutionalized means yet are unable to achieve success. They resolve the conflict of their situation by abandoning both the goals and the means of reaching them. They are unable to cope and 'drop out' of society, defeated and resigned to their failure. They are deviant in two ways; they have rejected both the cultural goals and the institutionalized means. Merton does not relate retreatism to social class position.

'Rebellion' forms the fifth and final response. It is a rejection of both the success goals and the instutionalized means and their replacement by different goals and means. Those who adopt this alternative wish to create a new society. Thus urban guerillas in Western European capitalist societies adopt deviant means – terrorism – to reach deviant goals such as a communist society. Merton argues that 'it is typically members of a rising class rather than the most depressed strata who organize the resentful and rebellious into a revolutionary group'.

To summarize, Merton claims that his analysis shows how the culture and structure of society generates deviance. The overemphasis upon cultural goals in American society at the expense of institutionalized means creates a tendency towards anomie. This tendency exerts pressure for deviance, a pressure which varies depending on a person's position in the class structure. The way a person responds to this pressure will also depend upon his position in the class structure. Merton thus presents a sociological theory of deviance. He explains deviance in terms of the nature of society rather than the nature of the individual. Since its publication, Merton's theory has been frequently modified and criticized. This response will be examined as the chapter develops.

Structural and subcultural theories of deviance

Structural theories of deviance are similar to Merton's theory. They explain the origins of deviance in terms of the position of individuals or groups in the social structure. Subcultural theories explain deviance in terms of the subculture of a social group. They argue that certain groups develop distinctive norms and values which deviate from the mainstream culture of society. Often structural and subcultural explanations are combined as in Albert Cohen's analysis of delinquency.

Albert K. Cohen

Cohen's work is a modification and development of Merton's position. From his studies of delinquency, he makes two major criticisms of Merton's views on working-class deviance. Firstly, he argues that delinquency is a collective rather than an individual response. Whereas Merton sees the individual responding to his position in the class structure, Cohen sees individuals joining together in a collective response. Secondly, Cohen argues that Merton fails to account for 'non-utilitarian crime' such as vandalism and joy-riding which do not produce monetary reward. Cohen questions whether such forms of delinquency are directly motivated by the success goals of the mainstream culture. He agrees however that Merton's theory is 'highly plausible as an explanation for adult professional crime and for the property delinquency of some older and semi-professional thieves'.

Cohen begins in a similar vein to Merton. Lower working-class boys hold the success goals of the mainstream culture, but due largely to educational failure and the dead-end jobs which result from this, they have little opportunity to attain them. This failure can be explained by their position in the social structure. Cohen supports the view that 'cultural deprivation' accounts for the lack of educational success of members of the lower working class. (See Chapter 5, pp. 201–2, for an outline of cultural deprivation theory.) Stuck at the bottom of the stratification system with avenues to success blocked, many lower working-class boys suffer from 'status frustration'. They are frustrated and dissatisfied with their low status in society. They resolve their frustration not by turning to criminal paths to success, as Merton suggested, but by rejecting the success goals of the mainstream culture. They replace them with an alternative set of norms and values in terms of which they can achieve success and gain prestige. The result is a delinquent subculture. It can be seen as a collective solution to the common problems of lower working-class adolescents.

The delinquent subculture not only rejects the mainstream culture, it reverses it. In Cohen's words, 'the delinquent subculture takes its norms from the larger culture but turns them upside down'. Thus a high value is placed on activities such as stealing, vandalism and truancy which are condemned in the wider society. Cohen describes the delinquent subculture in the following way, 'Throughout there is a kind of *malice* apparent, an enjoyment of the discomfiture of others, a delight in the defiance of taboos'. He illustrates this theme with the example of defecating on the teacher's desk. But the delinquent subculture is more than an act of defiance, a negative reaction to a society which has denied opportunity to some of its members. It offers positive rewards. Those who perform successfully in terms of the values of the subculture gain recognition and prestige in the eyes of their peers. Thus stealing becomes, according to

Cohen, not so much a means of achieving success in terms of mainstream goals, but 'a valued activity to which attaches glory, prowess and profound satisfaction'. Cohen argues that in this way lower working-class boys solve the problem of 'status frustration'. They reject mainstream values which offer them little chance of success and substitute deviant values in terms of which they can be successful. Cohen thus provides an explanation for delinquent acts which do not appear to be motivated by monetary reward.

Like Merton, Cohen begins from a structural perspective. Because there is unequal access to opportunity, there is greater pressure on certain groups within the social structure to deviate. However, he parts company from Merton when he sees some delinquency as being a collective response directed by subcultural values. In this way he shows how pressure from the social structure to deviate is reinforced by pressure from the deviant subculture.

Cohen has been criticized for his selective use of the idea of lower class subculture. David Bordua argues that he uses it to explain the educational failure of lower working-class boys, with the notion of 'cultural deprivation', but he does not use it to explain delinquency. Thus whereas 'cultural deprivation' is passed on from one generation to the next, this does not seem to happen with the delinquent subculture. It appears to be created anew by each generation of boys reacting to their position in the social structure.

Walter B. Miller

Miller parts company from both Merton and Cohen in his explanation of lower class delinquency. Firstly, he rejects Merton's view that it represents an alternative means of achieving mainstream goals. Secondly, he rejects Cohen's argument that it results from a delinquent subculture which is a reaction to failure to attain mainstream goals. Instead he sees lower class delinquency as simply resulting from lower class subculture. Miller argues that, 'Following cultural practices, which comprise essential elements of the total life pattern of lower class culture, automatically violates certain legal norms'. Miller develops his argument in the following way.

There is a 'distinctive cultural system' which may be termed 'lower class'. It includes a number of 'focal concerns', that is major areas of interest and involvement. Included in these focal concerns are 'toughness', 'smartness' and 'excitement'. Toughness involves a concern for masculinity and finds expression in courage in the face of physical threat and a rejection of timidity and weakness. In practice this can lead to assault and battery in order to maintain a reputation for toughness. Smartness involves the 'capacity to outsmart, outfox, outwit, dupe, "take", "con" another'. It is expressed in the repertoire of the hustler, the con man, the card sharp, the pimp, the pickpocket and the petty thief. Excitement involves the search for thrills, for emotional stimulus. In practice it is sought in gambling, sexual adventures and alcohol, all of which can be combined in a night out on the town. This 'heady mixture' can result in damage to limb, life and property.

Two factors tend to emphasize and exaggerate the focal concerns of lower class subculture in the lives of adolescents: firstly, their tendency to belong to a peer group which demands close conformity to group norms; secondly, the concern of young people with status which is largely achieved in terms of peer group norms. Thus the status of a lower working-class youth can depend on his reputation for toughness and smartness in the eyes of his friends.

Miller concludes that delinquency is simply the acting out, albeit in a somewhat exaggerated manner, of the focal concerns of lower class subculture. It results from socialization into a subculture with 'a distinctive tradition, many centuries old with an integrity of its own'. Although this subculture has a life of its own, Miller does give reasons for its origin and maintenance. It stems from and is partly sustained by the necessity for a pool of low-skilled labour. Low-skilled workers require the ability to endure routine, repetitive and boring activity and to tolerate recurrent unemployment. Lower class subculture provides the means to live with this situation. Its focal concerns provide satisfactions outside of work and help to deal with the dissatisfaction produced by work: the emphasis on excitement compensates for the boredom of work.

Miller presents a picture of members of the lower class living in a world of their own, totally insulated from the rest of society. They appear to pursue their focal concerns with no reference to the mainstream culture. Many sociologists would disagree with this view. Thus David Bordua, in his criticism of Miller states, 'Miller seems to be saying that the involvements in lower class culture are so deep and exclusive that contacts with agents of middle-class dominated institutions, especially the schools, have no impact'. (For detailed criticisms of the concept of lower class subculture, see Chapter 4, pp. 156–60 and Chapter 5, pp. 195–6.) Unlike Miller, most sociologists who use the concept of subculture to explain deviance, see it as secondary to a structural explanation. The final part of the section returns to this position.

Richard A. Cloward and Lloyd E. Ohlin

In *Delinquency and Opportunity* the American sociologists Cloward and Ohlin combine and develop many of the insights of Merton and Cohen. While largely accepting Merton's view of working-class criminal deviance, they argue that he has failed to explain the different forms that deviance takes. For example why do some delinquent gangs concentrate on theft while others appear preoccupied with vandalism and violence?

Cloward and Ohlin argue that Merton has only dealt with half the picture. He has explained deviance in terms of the 'legitimate opportunity structure' but failed to consider the 'illegitimate opportunity structure'. Thus, just as opportunity to be successful by legitimate means varies, so does opportunity for success by illegitimate means. For example in one area there may be a thriving adult criminal subculture which may provide access for adolescents, in another area this subculture may not exist. Thus, in the first area, the adolescent has more opportunity to become a successful criminal. By examining access and opportunity for entry into illegitimate opportunity structures, Cloward and Ohlin provide an explanation for different forms of deviance.

They begin their explanation of working-class delinquency from the same point as Merton. There is greater pressure on members of the working class to deviate because they have less opportunity to succeed by legitimate means. Cloward and Ohlin then distinguish three possible responses to this situation, the 'criminal subculture', the 'conflict subculture' and the 'retreatist subculture'. The development of one or other of these responses by young people depends upon their access to and performance in terms of the illegitimate opportunity structure.

Criminal subcultures tend to emerge in areas where there is an established pattern of organized adult crime. In such areas a 'learning environment' is provided for the young; they are exposed to criminal skills, deviant values and presented with criminal role models. Those who perform successfully in terms of these deviant values have the opportunity to rise in the professional criminal hierarchy. They have access to the illegitimate opportunity structure. Criminal subcultures are mainly concerned with 'utilitarian crime' which produces financial reward. Conflict subcultures tend to develop in areas where adolescents have little opportunity for access to illegitimate opportunity structures. There is little organized adult crime to provide an apprenticeship for the young criminal and an opportunity for him to climb the illegitimate ladder to success. Such areas usually have a high turnover of population and a lack of unity and cohesiveness. This situation tends to prevent a stable criminal subculture from developing. Thus access to both legitimate and illegitimate opportunity structures is blocked. The response to this situation is often gang violence. This serves as a release for anger and frustration and a means of obtaining prestige in terms of the values of the subculture. Finally Cloward and Ohlin analyse Merton's retreatist response in terms of legitimate and illegitimate opportunity structures. They suggest that some lower class adolescents form retreatist subcultures organized mainly around illegal drug use because they have failed to succeed in both the legitimate and illegitimate structures. In this sense they are double failures. They have failed to become successful by legitimate means, they have failed in terms of either criminal or conflict subcultures. As failed criminals or failed gang members they retreat, tails between their legs, into retreatist subcultures.

Cloward and Ohlin present one of the most sophisticated analyses of lower class delinquency from a structural and subcultural viewpoint. They provide an explanation for various forms of delinquency by adding the notion of the illegitimate opportunity structure to Merton's scheme and by placing Cohen's views in a wider context. However, despite the virtues of the various structural and subcultural approaches, they are open to damaging criticism. This will be considered in later sections.

The ecology of deviance – 'the Chicago school'

During the 1920s, a group of sociologists based in Chicago, who later became known as the 'Chicago school', developed an ecological approach to the study of social life. Ecology refers to the relationship between organisms and their environment. Members of the Chicago school applied this concept to the growth of cities and argued that behaviour could be explained in terms of the urban environment. In particular, they argued that the growth of cities produced distinctive neighbourhoods, each with its own characteristic style of life. Clifford Shaw and Henry McKay applied this perspective to the study of deviance.

Shaw and McKay divided the city of Chicago into five zones, drawn at two-mile intervals, and radiating outwards in concentric circles from the central business district. They examined the rate of crime for each of these zones. Using statistics on male delinquency from the Juvenile Court they discovered that the delinquency rate steadily decreased from zone I, the area surrounding the central business district, to zone V on the outskirts of the city. The delinquency rates shown on the map indicate the proportion of delinquents as a percentage of the total male population aged from ten to sixteen living in each zone. Thus, for the five-year period 1927 to 1933, 9.8% of boys in zone I were charged with criminal offences. Shaw and McKay found that similar patterns applied in Chicago from 1900 to 1906 and from 1917 to 1923. Their method was applied to a number of American cities and produced similar results.

Shaw and McKay explain their results in the following way. Zone I is a 'zone of transition'; it has a relatively high rate of population turnover. There are two main reasons for this. Firstly, rural migrants to the city usually begin their urban life in zone I. They often have little money and zone I provides the cheapest accommodation; it is the typical inner city slum. In Chicago it houses mainly low-income White and Black migrants from the southern states. Many migrants move out to higher income areas once they have become established, so making room for new arrivals. The expansion of the central business district into the zone of transition provides the second reason for high population turnover. This produces population movement as the business district 'invades' former

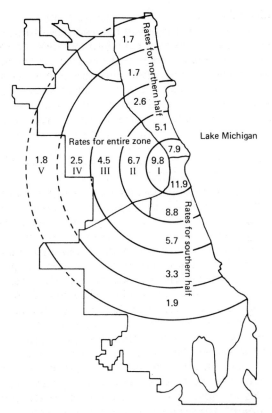

Map of Chicago showing zone rates of male juvenile delinquents from 1927 to 1933

(Source: Reprinted from p. 74 of *Juvenile Delinquency and Urban Areas* by Shaw and McKay, 1942, by permission of The University of Chicago Press)

residential areas. Shaw and McKay argue that these processes of city growth explain the high concentration of crime and delinquency in the zone of transition.

A high rate of population turnover prevents the formation of a stable community and results in 'social disorganization'. Indications of social disorganization include delinquency, prostitution, gambling, illegal drug use, a high consumption of alcohol, violence and broken families, behaviour which is characteristic of the zone of transition. Such behaviour can flourish because, in an area of shifting population, social controls are weak. Controls such as gossip, public opinion, public surveillance and parental control are not sufficiently strong to prevent the development of deviant norms and values. Bernard Lander applied the methods of the Chicago school in his study of Baltimore. He obtained somewhat different results but confirmed the conclusions of Shaw and McKay. Within

421

zone I he found areas of stable population. Despite the fact that they were low-income areas, the rate of criminal deviance was low. However, in adjacent areas with shifting populations, social disorganization was widespread and the rate of crime and delinquency was high. Lander argues that social disorganization provides the key to explaining criminal deviance. He concludes that in an unstable community, 'the breakdown of social cohesion frees the individual from the pressure of public opinion and the informal social controls which, in more solidary groups, operate to secure conformity to the norms of conventional behaviour'.

The perspective of the Chicago school has the virtue of linking structural and subcultural theories with theories of community. Shaw and McKay note that the rate of delinquency corresponds closely to economic factors. Income rises steadily from zone I to zone V. Delinquency rates decline steadily from the inner city slums to the tree-lined suburbs. A part of their explanation echoes Merton's views. Shaw and McKay argue that crime in low-income areas 'may be regarded as one of the means employed by people to acquire, or attempt to acquire, the economic and social values generally idealized in our culture, which persons in other circumstances acquire by conventional means'. Their views also echo those of the subcultural theorists. Referring to delinquency, Shaw and McKay state that, 'year after year, decade after decade, the same areas have been characterized by these concentrations'. This is due in part to the development of deviant norms and values which are transmitted from one generation to the next but structural and subcultural theories fail to provide sufficient explanation of criminal deviance. Before crime can flourish, the community must be sufficiently disorganized to provide the freedom for deviant norms and values to develop. This freedom is greatest in the zone of transition.

Several criticisms have been made of the Chicago school. Firstly, the emphasis on social disorganization tends to underplay the degree of organization of criminal and delinquent subcultures. Secondly, there is a tendency for the theory to be tautological, that is saying the same thing twice over in different words. Since crime and delinquency are evidence of social disorganization, social disorganization cannot be used to explain them. Thirdly, the theory tends to see man simply reacting to forces outside him and beyond his control. The 'natural' growth of cities shapes his behaviour and he has little say in the matter. Many sociologists reject this positivist approach which tends to see man simply reacting to external stimuli. They see man playing a more active role in shaping his situation rather than being simply shaped by it.

David Matza – a cautionary note on delinquency

Three sociological theories, the structural, the subcultural and the ecological, which claim to explain the origins of deviance in general and delinquency in particular, have been examined. All tend to see the deviant produced and directed by forces beyond his control. He is pressured by his position in the social structure, by his membership of a deviant subculture or his presence in an area of social disorganization to stray from the path of convention. In a series of writings during the 1960s, the American sociologist David Matza provides a timely warning about the implications of the above theories. Firstly, he suggests that they make the deviant appear more distinctive than he really is. Secondly, he argues that they present an over-deterministic view of the origins of deviance. Determinism is the doctrine that man has little or no freedom to direct his actions since they are controlled by external forces. Thus trapped by circumstances, the individual is automatically propelled down the path of deviance. Matza argues that this view ignores the choices and alternatives which are always available for human action.

In a paper written with Gresham Sykes entitled, *Techniques of Neutralization: A Theory of Delinquency*, Matza emphasizes the similarities between delinquents and other young people. He rejects Albert Cohen's notion that delinquency is directed by a delinquent subculture which reverses the norms and values of mainstream society. He does not see delinquents as being committed to deviant values. Matza argues that since many delinquents express 'guilt and shame' about their criminal activities, they must be 'at least partially committed to the dominant social order'. Deviant behaviour is possible, not because of an outright rejection of mainstream norms and values, but by the employment of a set of excuses, justifications and rationalizations for deviance, which Matza terms 'techniques of neutralization'. The use of such techniques makes deviance acceptable by neutralizing much of the blame and disapproval associated with deviant activities. Techniques of neutralization include denial of responsibility for a deviant act – the delinquent may remove responsibility from himself by blaming his parents or the area in which he lives; denial of injury resulting from the act – for example the delinquent may argue that joyriding does not harm anyone, it is just a bit of mischief and that he was borrowing rather than stealing the car; denial that the act was basically wrong – for example an assault on a homosexual or a robbery from an extortionate store owner can be presented as a form of 'rough justice'; condemnation of those who enforce the rules – for example the police may be seen as corrupt, teachers as unjust and hypocritical; 'appeal to higher loyalties' – the delinquent may argue that he broke the law not out of self-interest but to help his family or friends.

Matza argues that the use of techniques of neutralization throws serious doubt on the idea of deviant subcultures. Firstly, they are evidence of guilt and shame which indicates at least a partial acceptance of mainstream norms and values. If there really were a delinquent subculture, there would be no need to resort to techniques of neutralization, since there would be no guilt to neutralize. Secondly, techniques of neutralization often employ one set of mainstream norms to justify breaking others. Thus assaulting homosexuals is justified as support for mainstream norms of sexual behaviour. Again, this shows some degree of commitment to mainstream culture.

In a later paper entitled, *Juvenile Delinquency and Subterranean Values*, Matza and Sykes again emphasize the similarity between delinquents and young people in general. Again they reject the notion of a fully fledged delinquent subculture. They argue that so-called delinquent values 'are closely akin to those embodied in the leisure activities of the dominant society'. Thus the search for excitement and adventure and the emphasis on verbal and physical aggression as a means of demonstrating toughness and masculinity are found in leisure pursuits throughout society. In mainstream society, however, these values are expressed only in particular situations, such as the bar, the bowling alley and the football field. Matza and Sykes refer to them as 'subterranean values', they exist side by side with other values, but are expressed only in limited contexts. They argue that subterranean values often direct and motivate delinquent activity. If this view is correct, then at least some delinquency is not a product of a deviant subculture.

Matza and Sykes argue that the main difference between delinquents and the population as a whole is simply the degree of emphasis placed on subterranean values. Young people attach greater importance to subterranean values simply because they have the freedom to become more involved in leisure, a freedom which allows such values to flourish. Matza and Sykes argue that 'All adolescents at all class levels are to some extent members of a leisure class, for they move in a limbo between earlier parental domination and future integration with the social structure through the bonds of work and marriage'. If subterranean values do direct delinquent behaviour, Matza and Sykes's theory is able to explain middle-class delinquency. The structural and subcultural theories are limited to an explanation of working-class delinquency.

Again Matza and Sykes cast doubt on theories which attribute distinctive norms and values to deviant behaviour. Firstly, they see little difference between delinquents and young people in general. Secondly, the subterranean values of young people are found throughout society. The only difference is one of emphasis.

In *Delinquency and Drift*, David Matza develops some of the themes outlined above. He rejects the deterministic perspectives of structural and subcultural theories and emphasizes the choices and alternatives available for human action. He suggests that many young people simply 'drift' into delinquent activities. They have no real commitment to delinquency and simply 'flirt' with deviant behaviour. Their delinquency is not a full-time 'career', but rather a sporadic and episodic activity, an occasional alternative to conventional behaviour. This view helps to explain why many delinquents find their deviant activities fairly easy to give up. The idea of a delinquent subculture makes it difficult to explain the ease with which many abandon delinquency, since it suggests a commitment to deviant norms and values. Thus Matza argues that many delinquents casually adopt the occasional deviant alternative rather than being impelled upon a deviant career by powerful social forces. Again the picture of the deviant draws closer to the non-deviant member of society.

The theories of deviance so far presented have moved steadily away from the view of the deviant as distinct from the non-deviant. Physiological theories locate the origin of deviance in the genetic make-up of the individual. He is born abnormal in a normal population. Psychological theories place the origin of deviance in early childhood experience. They begin with a normal individual who early in life is shunted off the straight and narrow. Abnormal personality characteristics develop which find expression in deviant behaviour and distinguish the individual from the non-deviant population. Structural, subcultural and ecological theories of deviance all begin with a normal individual or group. They locate deviance in the social structure and in processes of community development. They see deviance as the response of normal people to their social situation, not as an expression of a genetic peculiarity or an abnormal personality trait. However, in responding to their position in society, deviants tend to become distinct from the non-deviant population. They may, for example, develop a deviant subculture. Finally, Matza presents a picture of the deviant which differs only in superficial respects from the population as a whole. This developing theme of the deviant as 'normal' will be continued in later sections.

Deviance and official statistics

Many theories of deviance are based in part on official statistics provided by the police, the courts, and various government departments. Such statistics provide evidence of the extent of deviance and information about the social characteristics of the deviant, for example his class position. But official statistics cannot be taken at face value and therefore nor can theories which are based on their use. This section examines the reasons why official statistics must be handled with caution.

There is increasing evidence to suggest that there is a systematic bias in favour of the powerful in the application of the law. As a general rule, if an individual has committed a criminal act, the higher he is in the stratification system the less likely he is to be arrested, if arrested to be prosecuted, if prosecuted to be found guilty, and if found guilty, to be imprisoned. For example, various studies have shown that middle-class delinquents are less likely to be arrested and prosecuted than their working-class counterparts. If this is so, then the assumption that many forms of criminal deviance are largely working-class phenomena may be incorrect and theories which attempt to explain deviance as a response of individuals or groups to their position in the stratification system may also be incorrect.

Even if the bias referred to above were removed, official statistics would still not provide sociologists with reliable evidence about the extent of deviance. As a result they would not provide reliable information on the social characteristics of deviants, for example their social class, ethnicity, age, sex, occupation and place of residence. Statistics on crime and delinquency illustrate these points. They are based on 'crimes known to the police'. Such figures may bear little resemblance to the actual number of crimes committed. The United States President's Commission on Law Enforcement and the Administration of Justice found that many victims of criminal acts did not report this fact to the police. The rate of non-reporting was over 50% for certain crimes. Studies of the extent of non-reporting, have led many sociologists to conclude that recorded crime cannot be used as an indication of the extent of actual crime. Thus Paul Wiles argues that, 'there is a dark figure of crime sufficiently large to render reported and recorded offences highly suspect as a basis upon which to make inferences upon criminal behaviour in general'.

The problem is made worse by the fact that only a proportion of crime known to the police results in arrests. For example, in the USA only 27% of robberies and 19% of burglaries and larcenies were cleared by arrest in 1971. For this reason the supposed social characteristics of criminals are based on those who have been caught, which hardly provides a representative sample. Not surprisingly the President's Commission on Law Enforcement and Criminal Justice found that many individuals admitted criminal acts for which they had not been apprehended. The Commission found that 91% of adult Americans 'admitted that they had committed acts for which they might have received jail or prison sentences'. Given the fact that a large proportion of crime is not known to the police and that a large proportion of known crime remains undetected, plus the possibility of systematic bias in the arrest and prosecution of individuals, theories of crime and delinquency must be regarded with suspicion. Marshall B. Clinard, a leading writer on the sociology of deviance, concludes that, 'official statistics of deviant behaviour are not accurate measures of the number and characteristics of deviants, regardless of whether statistics deal with delinquency, crime, mental hospitals, or arrests for drunkenness or drug use'.

The possibility of systematic bias in the application of laws to individuals of different social status who have committed similar offences has already been noted. There is evidence of even greater bias in the application of laws which apply directly to the activities of individuals in the upper levels of the stratification system. Edwin H. Sutherland was the first sociologist to systematically study what has come to be known as 'white-collar crime'. Sutherland defines white-collar crime as 'crimes committed by persons of respectability and high social status in the course of their occupations'. Such crimes include bribery and corruption in business and politics, misconduct by professionals such as doctors and lawyers, the breaking of trade regulations, food and drug laws and safety regulations in factories, the misuse of patents and trademarks, and misrepresentation in advertising. There is evidence to suggest that such offences are not only widespread, but are often accepted practice in business and political life. The Lockheed bribery scandal and the British Leyland 'slush fund', both of which involved bribes to foreign officials for preferential treatment of the companies' products, may only represent the tip of a large iceberg. They were defended by both companies on the grounds that such payments were standard practice. The 'Poulson Affair', which revealed widespread corruption in British local government was similarly defended on the grounds that 'everybody's doing it'. The 'Watergate Affair', though probably an extreme example of political malpractice, is evidence of what many regard as widespread corruption in local and national government in the USA. Less colourful evidence of white-collar crime is provided by W. G. Carson's study of the enforcement of factory legislation. Based on a sample of 200 firms in southeast England, Carson's research revealed that every firm committed at least some violations during a four and a half year period from 1961 to 1966. In a study of seventy large American corporations, Edwin Sutherland found that 'many types of violations are industry-wide in the sense that practically all firms in the industry violate the law. This has been documented by many of the investigations of the Commissioner of Corporations, the Federal Trade Commission and various Congressional committees'.

A number of factors combine to reduce the apparent extent and seriousness of white-collar crime. It is difficult to detect. Many white-collar crimes are 'crimes without victims'. In cases of bribery and corruption, both parties involved may see themselves as gaining from the arrangement, both are liable to prosecution, therefore neither is likely to report the offence. In cases where the victim is the public at large, such as misrepresentation in advertising, few members of the public have the expertise to realize that they are being misled or a knowledge of the legal procedure to redress the wrong. In such cases detection and prosecution is often left to a government agency. Such agencies rarely have the manpower or finance to do other than bring a few cases to court in the hope of deterring the practice.

Many white-collar crimes if detected, are rarely prosecuted. Carson's study of violations of factory legislation revealed that in nearly 75% of the cases where the Inspectorate made an 'enforcement decision', they simply notified the firm that a particular matter 'required attention'. Only 1.5% of the violations resulted in prosecution. Often white-collar crimes are dealt with administratively by the various boards, commissions and inspectorates appointed to deal with them. 'Official warnings' rather than prosecutions are frequently the rule. In the case of professionals, their own associations usually deal with misconduct. Again prosecution is rare. In extreme cases doctors and lawyers may lose their licence to practice, but more often their professional associations simply hand down a reprimand.

The sociological study of white-collar crime provides some support for the view that there is one law for the rich and another for the poor. Edwin Sutherland argues that there is a consistent bias 'involved in the administration of criminal justice under laws which apply to business and the professions and which therefore involve only the upper socio-economic group'. The matter is neatly summarized by Willy Sutton, a professional bank robber, who stated, 'Others accused of defrauding the government of hundreds of thousands of dollars merely get a letter from a committee in Washington asking them to come in and talk it over. Maybe it's justice but its puzzling to a guy like me' (quoted in Clinard, 1974, p. 266).

Official statistics probably underestimate the extent of white-collar crime to a far greater degree than they underestimate the extent of crime in general. As a result official statistics portray crime as predominantly working-class behaviour. Many sociological theories of crime and delinquency have tended to accept this portrayal. As a result they have seen social class as the key to explaining criminal deviance. This conclusion may not be justified in view of the nature of official statistics.

This section has examined some of the problems associated with the use of official statistics on deviance. It has shown that such statistics cannot be assumed to represent either the extent of deviance or the social characteristics of the deviant. Many theories of deviance are based on an examination of 'officially classified deviants', on the selection of those characteristics which appear to distinguish them from the non-deviant population and on the assumption that such distinguishing characteristics are the cause of deviant behaviour. Thus deviants have particular biological characteristics, distinctive childhood experiences, a particular place in the social structure and so on. Given the nature of official statistics it can be argued that explanations of the causes of deviance cannot be approached until a representative sample of deviants has been obtained. However, many sociologists argue that more important problems than this arise from a consideration of the nature of official statistics. These problems cannot be solved by obtaining more reliable data, by better statistics based upon better samples. They demand new ways of looking at deviance, new questions about deviance and perspectives which differ radically from those so far considered.

Deviance – an interactionist perspective

The interactionist perspective differs from previous approaches in two ways. Firstly, it views deviance from a different theoretical perspective. Secondly, it examines aspects of deviance which have been largely ignored by previous approaches. It directs attention away from the deviant as such and the motivations, pressures and social forces which are supposed to direct his behaviour. Instead it focusses upon the interaction between the deviant and those who define him as deviant. The interactionist perspective examines how and why particular individuals and groups are defined as deviant and the effects of such a definition upon their future actions. For example, the interaction between the deviant and various agents of social control such as parents, teachers, doctors, police, judges and probation officers may be analysed. The effects upon the individual of being defined as a criminal or delinquent, as mentally ill, as an alcoholic, prostitute or homosexual may be examined. The interactionist approach emphasizes the importance of the meanings the various actors bring to and develop within the interaction situation. Thus it may examine the picture of the 'typical delinquent' held by the police and note how this results in a tendency to define lower class rather than middle-class lawbreakers as delinquents. Meanings are not, however, fixed and clear cut. They are modified and developed in the interaction process. Thus, from an interactionist perspective, the definition of deviance is negotiated in the interaction situation by the actors involved. For example, whether or not a person is defined as mentally ill will depend on a series of negotiations between him and a psychiatrist. With this emphasis on negotiated meaning, the interactionist perspective comes closer to a phenomenological view of man. The approaches so far considered, with their emphasis on the deviant simply reacting to forces which are external to himself and largely beyond his control, are closer to a positivist position.

Howard S. Becker – labelling theory

One of the most influential statements on deviance is contained in the following quotation from Howard S. Becker, one of the early exponents of the interactionist approach. Becker argues that '*social groups create deviance by making the rules whose infraction constitutes deviance*, and by applying those rules to particular people and labelling them as outsiders. From this point of view, deviance is *not* a quality of the act the person commits, but rather a consequence of the application by others of the rules and sanctions to an "offender". The deviant is one to whom the label has successfully been applied; deviant behavior is behavior that people so label'. Becker is suggesting that in one sense there is no such thing as a deviant act. An act only becomes deviant when others perceive and define it as such. The act of nudity in Western society provides an illustration. Nudity in the bedroom, where the actors involved are husband and wife, is generally interpreted as normal behaviour. Should a stranger enter, however, nudity in his presence would usually be considered deviant. Yet, in particular contexts, such as nudist camps or certain holiday beaches, nudity in the presence of strangers would be seen as perfectly normal by the participants. A spectator at a cricket match who 'streaked' across the pitch may be viewed as 'a bit of a lad' but if he stood and exposed himself to the crowd, he might be regarded as 'some kind of pervert'. Thus there is nothing intrinsically normal or deviant about the act of nudity. It only becomes deviant when others label it as such. Whether or not the label is applied will depend on how the act is interpreted by the audience. This in turn will depend on who commits the act, when and where it is committed, who observes the act, and the negotiations between the various actors involved in the interaction situation.

Becker illustrates his views with the example of brawl involving young people. In a low-income neighbourhood, it may be defined by the police as evidence of delinquency, in a wealthy neighbourhood as evidence of youthful high spirits. The acts are the same but the meanings given to them by the audience differ. In the same way those who commit the act may view it in one way, those who observe it may define it in another. The brawl in the low-income area may involve a gang fighting to defend its "turf" (territory). In Becker's words, they are only doing what they consider 'necessary and right, but teachers, social workers and police see it differently'. If the agents of social control define the boys as delinquents and they are convicted for breaking the law, those boys then become deviant. They have been labelled as such by those who have the power to make the labels stick. Thus Becker argues, 'Deviance is not a quality that lies in behavior itself, but in the interaction between the person who commits an act and those who respond to it'. From this point of view deviance is produced by a process of interaction between the potential deviant and the agents of social control.

Becker then examines the possible effects upon an individual of being publicly labelled as deviant. A label defines an individual as a particular kind of person. A label is not neutral, it contains an evolution of the person to whom it is applied. It is a 'master status' in the sense that it colours all the other statuses possessed by an individual. If a person is labelled as criminal, mentally ill or homosexual, such labels largely override his status as father, worker, neighbour and friend. Others see him and respond to him in terms of the label and tend to assume he has the negative characteristics normally associated with such labels. Since an individual's self-concept is largely derived from the responses of others, he tends to see himself in terms of the label. This may produce a self-fulfilling prophecy whereby 'the deviant identification becomes the controlling one'. Becker outlines a number of possible stages in this process. (For further details on the self-fulfilling prophecy, see Chapter 5, pp. 211–13.)

Initially the individual is publicly labelled as deviant. This may lead to his rejection from many social groups. Regarded as a 'junkie', a 'queer', a 'nutter', a 'wino' or a 'tearaway', he may be rejected by family and friends, lose his job and be forced out of the neighbourhood. This may encourage further deviance. For example, the drug addict may turn to crime to support his habit since 'respectable employers' refuse to give him a job. The official treatment of deviance may have similar effects. The ex-convict may have difficulty finding employment and be forced to return to crime for his livelihood. Becker argues that, 'the treatment of deviants denies them the ordinary means of carrying on the routines of everyday life open to most people. Because of this denial, the deviant must of necessity develop illegitimate routines'. The 'deviant career' is completed when the individual joins 'an organized deviant group'. In this context he confirms and accepts his deviant identity. He is surrounded by others in a similar situation who provide him with support and understanding. Within the group a deviant subculture develops. The subculture often includes beliefs and values which rationalize, justify and support deviant identities and activities. For example, Becker states that organized homosexual groups provide the individual with a rationale for his deviance, 'explaining to him why he is the way he is, that other people have also been that way, and why it is all right for him to be that way'. The subculture also provides ways of avoiding trouble with conventional society. Thus the young thief, socialized into a criminal subculture, can learn various ways of avoiding arrest from older and more experienced members of the group. Becker argues that once an individual joins an organized deviant group, he is more likely than before to see himself as a deviant and to act in terms of this self-concept. In this context the deviant identification tends to become 'the controlling one'.

Becker argues that the process described above is by no means inevitable. Ex-convicts do get jobs and go 'straight', drug addicts do give up their habit and re-enter conventional society. However, once labelled, 'societal reaction' to the deviant places pressure upon him to follow the route which leads to the organized deviant group. Becker's analysis of deviance begins where previous approaches tend to stop. It locates the origin of deviance within the interaction process between the potential deviant and the agents of social control. It sees the development and reinforcement of deviance resulting from the reaction of members of society to the individual who has been labelled as deviant.

The value of Becker's approach can be seen from its application by Jock Young in his study of 'hippie' marihuana users in Notting Hill in London. Young examines the meanings which colour the police view of the hippies, how their reaction to the hippies is directed by these meanings, and the effects upon the hippies of this reaction. The police tend to see hippies as dirty, scruffy, idle, scrounging, promiscuous, depraved, unstable, immature, good-for-nothing drug addicts. Young argues that police reaction to the hippies in terms of these meanings can 'fundamentally alter and transform the social world of the marihuana smoker'. In particular, drug taking which begins as 'essentially a peripheral activity of hippie groups' becomes a central concern.

Police action against marihuana users tends to unite them and make them feel different. As such, they rationalize and accept their difference. In self-defence they retreat into a small, closed group. They exclude 'straights' not only for reasons of security – secrecy about marihuana use is important to avoid arrest – but also because they develop a deviant self-concept which makes it more difficult to include members of conventional society. In this context deviant norms and values develop. Having been defined and treated as outsiders, the hippies tend to express and accentuate this difference. Hair is grown longer, clothes become more and more unconventional. Drug use becomes transformed from a peripheral to a central activity, especially as police react more strongly against the deviance they have helped to create. Young argues that because of increased police activity, 'drug taking in itself becomes of greater value to the group as a symbol of their difference, and of their defiance of perceived social injustices'. In this situation a deviant subculture evolves and deviant self-concepts are reinforced, all of which makes it increasingly difficult for the hippies to re-enter conventional society.

Edwin M. Lemert – societal reaction – the 'cause' of deviance

Like Becker, Edwin M. Lemert emphasizes the importance of societal reaction – the reaction of others to the deviant – in the explanation of deviance. Lemert distinguishes between 'primary' and 'secondary' deviation'. Primary deviation consists of deviant acts before they are publicly labelled. There are probably any number of causes of primary deviation and it is largely a fruitless exercise to inquire into them for the following reasons. Firstly, samples of deviants are based upon those who have been labelled and are therefore unrepresentative. For example, it makes little sense to delve into the background of convicted criminals to find the cause of their deviance without examining criminals who have not been caught. Secondly, many so-called deviant acts may be so widespread as to be normal in statistical terms. Thus most males may at some time commit a homosexual act, engage in delinquent activities and so on. In fact, Lemert suggests that the only thing 'known' deviants probably have in common is the fact that they have been publicly labelled as such. Not only is the search for the causes of primary deviation largely fruitless, primary deviation itself is relatively unimportant. Lemert argues that it 'has only marginal implications for the status and the psychic structure of the person concerned'. Thus Lemert suggests that the odd deviant act has little effect on the individual's self-concept, on his status in the community, and does not prevent him from continuing a normal and conventional life.

The important factor in 'producing' deviance is societal reaction, the public identification of the deviant and the consequences of this for the individual concerned. Secondary deviation is the response of the individual or the group to societal reaction. Lemert argues that studies of deviance should focus on secondary deviation which has major consequences for the individual's self-concept, his status in the community and his future actions. In comparison, primary deviation has little significance. Lemert argues that, 'In effect the original "causes" of the deviation recede and give way to the central importance of the disapproving, degradational, and isolating reactions of society'. Thus, Lemert claims that societal reaction can be seen as the major 'cause' of deviance. This view, he argues, 'gives a proper place to social control as a dynamic factor or "cause" of deviance'. In this way Lemert neatly reverses traditional views of deviance. The blame for deviance lies with the agents of social control rather than with the deviant.

Lemert is particularly convincing in his paper entitled, *Stuttering among the North Pacific Coastal Indians* which examines the relationship between societal reaction and deviance. Previous research had indicated a virtual absence of stuttering among North American Indians. Indeed most tribes did not even have a word for this speech irregularity. However, Lemert's investigation of deviance in various tribes living in the North Pacific coastal area of British Columbia revealed evidence of stuttering both before and after contact with Whites. In addition the languages of these tribes contained clearly defined concepts of stutterers and stuttering. It is particularly significant that their inland neighbours, the Bannock and Shoshone, had no words for stuttering and research, using a large-scale sample of members of these tribes, found no evidence of actual stuttering.

The North Pacific coastal Indians have a rich ceremonial life, involving singing, dancing and speechmaking. Their legends and stories are filled with references to famous orators and outstanding speeches. From an early age, children are initiated into ceremonial life, and parents stress the importance of a faultless performance. There are rigorous and exacting standards to be met; rituals must be performed exactly as they should be. If they do not meet these standards, children shame their parents and suffer the ridicule of their peers. In particular there is a highly developed sensitivity to any speech defect. Children and parents alike are anxious about any speech irregularity and respond to it with guilt and shame. Lemert concludes that stuttering is actually produced by societal reaction. The concern about and the reaction to speech irregularities actually creates them. He argues that the culture, both past and present, 'seems favorable to the development of stuttering, that stutterers were and still are socially penalized, that parents tended to be specifically concerned or anxious about the speech development of their children, that children were anxious about ritual performances involving solo verbal behavior'. In other American Indian societies, where such concerns were largely absent, stuttering was unknown. Thus Lemert argues that societal reaction, prompted by a concern about particular forms of deviance, can actually produce those forms of deviance.

Aaron V. Cicourel – the negotiation of justice

So far, the interactionist studies of deviance have been largely concerned with societal reaction to the deviant once he has been labelled. Aaron V. Cicourel's important study entitled *The Social Organization of Juvenile Justice* looks at the actual process of defining deviance. It examines the interaction between the potential deviant and the agents of social control to discover exactly how and why the label deviant is applied to particular individuals. Cicourel's research is based on an investigation of the treatment of delinquency in two Californian cities.

The process of defining a young person as a delinquent is not simple, clear cut and unproblematic. It is complex, involving a series of interactions, based on sets of meanings held by the participants, meanings which can be modified during the interaction, so that each stage in the process is negotiable. The first stage is the decision by the police to stop and interrogate an individual. This decision is based on meanings held by the police of what is 'suspicious', 'strange', 'unusual' and 'wrong'. Such meanings are related to particular geographical areas. Inner city, low-income areas are seen as 'bad areas' with a high crime rate, consequently behaviour in such areas is more likely to be viewed as suspicious. Interrogation need not lead to arrest. The process is negotiable but depends largely on the picture held by the police of the 'typical delinquent'. If the appearance, language and demeanour of the young person fits this picture, he is more likely to be arrested.

Once arrested, the young person is handed over to a juvenile officer (probation officer). Like the police, he too has a picture of the 'typical delinquent'. If the boy's background corresponds to this picture, he is more likely to be charged with an offence. Factors assumed to be associated with delinquency include, 'coming from broken homes, exhibiting "bad attitudes" toward authority, poor school performance, ethnic group membership, low-income families and the like'. It is not therefore surprising that Cicourel found a close relationship between social class and delinquency. Most young people convicted of offences had fathers who were manual workers. On a seven-class occupational scale, Cicourel found that one third come from class 7. He explains the preponderance of working-class delinquents by reference to the meanings held by the police and juvenile officers and the interactions between them and the juveniles. When a middle-class juvenile was arrested, there was less likelihood of his being charged with an offence. His background did not fit the standard picture of the delinquent. His parents were better able to negotiate successfully on his behalf. Middle-class parents can present themselves as respectable and reasonable people from a nice neighbourhood, who look forward to a rosy future for their child. They promise cooperation with the juvenile officer, assuring him that their offspring is suitably remorseful. As a result, the middle-class juvenile is often defined as ill rather than criminal, as accidentally straying from the path of righteousness rather than committed to wrongdoing, as cooperative rather than recalcitrant, as having a real chance of reforming rather than being a 'born loser'. He is typically 'counselled, warned and released'. Thus in Cicourel's words, 'what ends up being called justice is negotiable'.

Cicourel based his research on two Californian cities, each with a population of around 100 000. The socio-economic characteristics of the two populations were similar. In terms of structural theories, the numbers of delinquents produced by the pressures of the social structure should be similar in each city. However, Cicourel found a significant difference in the numbers of delinquents arrested and charged. He argues that this difference can only be accounted for by the size, organization, policies and practices of the juvenile and police bureaus. For example, the city with the highest rate of delinquency employed more juvenile officers and kept more detailed records on offenders. In the second city, the delinquency rate fluctuated sharply. Cicourel argues that in this city the response of the police to delinquency 'tends to be quite variable depending on publicity given to the case by the local paper, or the pressure generated by the mayor or chief or Captain of Detectives'. Thus societal reaction can be seen to directly affect the rate of delinquency.

Cicourel argues that delinquents are produced by the agencies of social control. Certain individuals are selected, processed and labelled as deviant. Justice is the result of negotiation in the interaction process. The production of delinquents is also dependent on the ways in which police and juvenile bureaus are organized, their policies, and the pressures from local media and politicians that are brought to bear on them. In view of these observations Cicourel questions structural and subcultural theories of deviance which see deviance as a product of pressure from the social structure. He concludes, 'The study challenges the conventional view which assumes "delinquents" are "natural" social types distributed in some ordered fashion and produced by a set of abstract "pressures" from the "social structures"'.

Erving Goffman – deviance and the institution

In general, interactionists view the various institutions for the treatment of deviance – the prisons, mental hospitals and reform schools – as a further set of links in a long chain of interactions which confirm the label of deviance both for the individual so labelled and for society as a whole. In a series of trend setting essays, Erving Goffman examined the treatment of mental patients in institutions. He argues that although the stated aim of such institutions is to cure and rehabilitate, a close examination of interaction patterns within the institution reveals a very different picture.

Goffman is particularly concerned with how, via a series of interactions, pressure is placed upon the inmate to accept the institution's definition of himself. Upon entry, 'he begins a series of abasements, degradations, humiliations, and profanities of self. His self is systematically, if often unintentionally, mortified'. This 'mortification process' strips the inmate of the various supports which helped to maintain his former self-concept. Often his clothes, an important symbol of identity are removed. His possessions, a further symbol of identity, may be taken away and stored for the duration of his stay. He may be washed, disinfected and his hair cut. He may then be issued with a new 'identity kit' such as regulation clothes and toilet articles. Such standardized items tend to remove individuality and define the inmate simply as a member of a uniform mass.

Once the entry phase is over, the inmate settles down to an endless round of 'mortifying experiences'. Each day is strictly timetabled into a set of compulsory activities controlled by the staff. The patient is allowed little freedom of movement, few opportunities to show initiative or take decisions. Throughout his stay, his actions are scrutinized and assessed by the staff in terms of the rules and standards which they have set. Many of these regulations can be degrading. For example, in some mental hospitals, a spoon is the only utensil provided for the patients to eat with. Goffman summarizes what mental hospitals in particular and treatment institutions in general 'say' to the inmate about himself, 'In the mental hospital, the setting and the house rules press home to the patient that he is, after all, a mental case who has suffered from some kind of social collapse on the outside, having failed in some over-all way, and that here he is of little social weight, being hardly capable of acting like a fully-fledged person at all'.

Not surprisingly, inmates in treatment institutions become anxious as their day of release approaches. At best they have not been prepared for life on the outside, at worst they have accepted the institution's definition of themselves as hopeless, hapless deviants. A small minority become 'institutionalized' – they believe themselves unable to function in the outside world, cling to the security of the institution and go to great lengths to remain inside. Despite this Goffman argues that the effects of the institution upon the majority of inmates are not usually lasting. There is a period of temporary 'disculturation', which means that the former inmate must re-learn some of the basic recipes for living in the outside world. However, the most lasting and important consequence is the label 'ex-mental patient' or 'ex-convict'. This, rather than the experience of being inside, makes re-entry into conventional society difficult.

Goffman reaches the rather pessimistic conclusion that many treatment institutions, 'seem to function merely as storage dumps for inmates'. Like societal reaction in general, treatment institutions serve to reinforce rather than reduce deviance. (For further details of Goffman's research, see Chapter 7, pp. 316–20.)

Deviance and the interactionist perspective – criticisms

The interactionist view of deviance has provoked strong criticism. Firstly, its critics argue that interactionism fails to explain the origin of deviant acts. In starting with the label, it provides no way of explaining the actions of the individual before he was labelled deviant. Even accepting that labelling and societal reaction are important factors in an explanation of deviance, critics argue that deviant activity is not simply created by the label. Why, for example, do certain individuals smoke marihuana in the first place, and others do not? Using Lemert's example, why do particular members of Indian tribes in British Columbia stutter and why are the vast majority free from this speech irregularity? From an interactionist perspective there seems to be no pressure on particular individuals to deviate; there is no indication of the motivation for their deviance. Thus David Bordua states, 'The process of developing deviance seems all societal response and no deviant stimulus'.

The interactionist approach tends to picture the deviant as having no awareness that his actions could be seen as deviant until he is stopped in his tracks by a label. Thus Ronald Akers states, 'One sometimes gets the impression from reading the literature that people go about minding their own business, and then – "wham" – bad society comes along and stops them with a stigmatized label', (quoted in Gibbons and Jones, 1975, p. 131). But many deviants are aware that their behaviour is regarded by others as deviant. As Taylor, Walton and Young argue, 'whilst marihuana smokers might regard their smoking as acceptable, normal behaviour in the company they move in, they are fully aware that this behaviour is regarded as deviant by the wider society'. Thus they actively make decisions to break the law. They are not passive, blinkered creatures, suddenly woken from blissful ignorance as a label is slapped upon them. Indeed, many individuals are not only aware of their deviance, they are proud of it and cultivate it. Thus urban guerillas have labelled themselves as deviant long before the agents of social control ever get their hands on them. As Alvin W. Gouldner notes in a lengthy critique of Becker, the interactionists tend to portray the deviant as a passive 'man-on-his-back' rather than as an active 'man-fighting-back'.

The interactionists tend to give the impression that members of society do not see behaviour as deviant until it is officially labelled as such. Jack Gibbs argues that if this view were carried to its logical conclusion, it would result in 'a police officer saying or thinking: "This individual has committed a criminal act because I arrested him"'. Gibbs argues that the interactionists tend to lose sight of the fact that there are social norms, that deviance is behaviour that breaks them and that members of society perceive reality in terms of such norms. Thus an individual who breaks social norms will be defined as deviant whether or not he has been officially labelled as such.

Finally, it is argued that the interactionists fail to fully explain societal reaction to deviance. Why, for example, do the police and juvenile officers in Cicourel's study have particular meanings and definitions of deviance which lead them to label some individuals and not others? Why are some activities regarded as deviant in a particular society and not others? Why, for example, is marihuana smoking against the law? To answer such questions it is important to know who makes the rules and for what purpose. This involves an analysis of the distribution of power and the nature of decision making in society. Such questions form the major focus of the next section.

Though the above criticisms have some merit, they should not detract from the important contributions made by interactionist theory to the study of deviance. In an article entitled, *Labelling Theory Reconsidered*, Howard Becker assesses these contributions. Firstly, the interactionists have shown that the definition of deviance is not a simple process. For example, the legal authorities do not simply arrest, try and punish deviants. In Becker's words, 'If we look long enough and close enough, we discover that they do this sometimes, but not all the time; to some people but not to others; in some places but not others'. Secondly, the interactionists have drawn attention to the important consequences which stem from the labelling process. Becker argues that critics have overstated their case when they suggest that the interactionists claim that an individual automatically acts in terms of the label placed upon him. He states, 'To suggest that defining someone as deviant may under certain circumstances dispose him to a particular line of action is not the same as saying that mental hospitals drive people crazy or that jails turn people into habitual criminals'. Thirdly, the interactionists have drawn attention to the fact that deviance results from interaction situations in which differences in power between the participants can have an important effect upon the outcome. In Becker's words, 'We see that social rules, far from being fixed and immutable, are continually constructed anew in every situation, to suit the convenience, will and power of various participants'.

The question of power will now be considered.

Deviance and power

This section examines the following questions: Who makes the rules? For whose benefit are they made? How are the rules enforced? These questions involve a consideration of the nature and distribution of power in society, and link the study of deviance directly to the study of power and politics. The section is mainly concerned with Marxian perspectives on deviance and power, but will first consider functionalist and interactionist approaches.

Deviance and power – a functionalist perspective

Functionalists begin their analysis of the relationship between deviance and power by assuming that there is a value consensus in society. This consensus represents an agreement by members of society on deeply held values. From a functionalist perspective deviance consists of those acts which depart from shared values. Thus Durkheim defines crime as acts which 'offend strong and definite states of the collective conscience'. The law is therefore a reflection of society's value consensus, a translation of shared values into legal statutes. Those who execute the law, the police and the judges, are therefore translating shared values into action. Their power is therefore seen as legitimate authority, as just, right and proper because it is based on the value consensus of members of society. The operation of the law benefits society as a whole since deviance must be kept in check and shared values must be maintained. As noted in a previous section, Durkheim argues that punishment under the law 'serves to heal the wounds done to the collective sentiments'. It restores shared values to their required strength, and therefore contributes to the maintenance and well-being of society.

Many functionalists adopt a version of the pluralist view of the nature and distribution of power in advanced capitalist society. (See Chapter 3, pp. 99–101 and 114–22 for details and criticisms of functionalist and pluralist perspectives on power.) Interest groups and political parties are seen to represent the interests of various groups in society. Political decisions and legal statutes take account of and compromise between these interests. The state does not consistently favour particular groups but represents society as a whole. William Chambliss summarizes the pluralist view of the relationship of power and the law as follows, 'The law represents the interests of society at large by mediating between competing interest groups'.

The above views have provoked strong criticism, especially from a Marxian perspective. Critics have argued that the functionalists have ignored laws which clearly serve the interests of the powerful, that they have disregarded the systematic bias in favour of the powerful in the execution of the law. Laurie Taylor makes these points nicely in his criticism of Merton. He writes, 'It is as though individuals in society are playing a gigantic fruit machine, but the machine is rigged and only some players are consistently rewarded. The deprived ones either resort to using foreign coins or magnets to increase their chances of winning (innovation), or play on mindlessly (ritualism), give up the game (retreatism), or propose a new game altogether (rebellion). But in the analysis nobody appeared to ask who put the game there in the first place and who takes the profits'. Thus Taylor criticizes Merton for not carrying his analysis far enough, for failing to consider who makes the laws and who benefits from the laws. To continue Taylor's analogy, the whole game may have been rigged by the powerful with rules which guarantee their success. These rules may be the laws of society. Such a possibility will result in very different explanations of deviance from those put forward by the functionalists.

Deviance and power – an interactionist perspective

The interactionists have made two important contributions to an understanding of the relationship between deviance and power. Firstly, they have questioned the functionalist view of value consensus by suggesting that there is no general agreement about what constitutes deviance. Secondly, they have shown that definitions of deviance are related to the power of the actors involved in the interaction situation. However, their concentration on the interaction process itself largely prevents an analysis of the nature and distribution of power in society as a whole. In fact when they consider the general relationship between power and deviance, writers such as Becker and Lemert move away from an interactionist perspective.

In his criticism of Merton, Edwin Lemert rejects the idea of value consensus. He describes various situations in which definitions of deviance do not reflect the consensus of society as a whole but rather the views of the powerful. This is particularly obvious in colonial situations where a ruling elite applies its own laws to a conquered majority. Such laws often contradict the norms and values of the native population, which can result in individuals being defined as criminal simply by following their traditional norms. Lemert makes a similar point about multi-cultural societies, such as the USA, which contain a large number of ethnic groups each with its own subculture. Simply by acting in terms of the norms and values of their particular subculture, members of ethnic groups can be defined as criminals in terms of American law. Lemert gives the example of American Indians who are prosecuted for breaking fish and game laws, yet their behaviour is neither deviant not criminal in terms of their traditional culture. The same applies to Mexican migrants to the USA who often see common law marriage, statutory rape (sexual intercourse with a female under sixteen years), the use of marihuana and carrying concealed weapons as normal and acceptable behaviour. Lemert concludes that, 'criminal deviation in the ethnic minorities can be explained in the same way as conformity among members of the dominant population segment, *i.e.*, by reference to traditionally patterned values and norms'. Thus Lemert rejects the idea of value consensus in multi-cultural societies such as the USA and suggests that definitions of crime and deviance will reflect the views of the powerful.

Like Lemert, Becker questions the idea of value consensus. He claims that, 'people are in fact always *forcing* their rules on others, applying them more or less against the will and without the consent of those others'. In particular, he suggests that in the West the old make rules for the young, men for women, Whites for Blacks, Anglo-Saxon Protestants for ethnic minorities, the middle class for the working class. In place of value consensus, Becker argues that rules reflect power. He states that, 'Those groups whose social position gives them weapons and power are best able to enforce their rules'. Such groups have the power to impose their definitions of crime and deviance on the less powerful.

The interactionists raise the question of the relationship between power and deviance but do not really answer it. They provide interesting suggestions, but stop short of a detailed analysis of the nature of power and deviance in society as a whole. In practice they have concentrated on the actual 'drama of interaction'. They have tended to deal with particular agencies of social control such as the courts, the police and the juvenile bureau and examined the creation of deviance in these contexts. But as Jock Young argues, 'it is not the criminal nor even the administration of crime but, in the final analysis, the system itself that must be investigated'. Thus the relationship between deviance and power must be examined in the context of the social system as a whole.

Deviance and power – a Marxian perspective

Sociologists such as William Chambliss, Milton Mankoff, Frank Pearce and Jock Young argue that only Marxian perspectives can deal adequately with the relationship between power and deviance in society. From this viewpoint, power is held by those who own and control the forces of production. The superstructure reflects the relationship between the powerful and the relatively powerless, the ruling and subject classes. As part of the superstructure, the state, the agencies of social control, the law and definitions of deviance in general, reflect and serve ruling class interests. As an instrument of the ruling class, the state passes laws which support ruling class interests, maintain its power and coerce and control the subject class. (Marxian views on the role of the state are examined in Chapter 3, pp. 104–7.) Laws are not an expression of value consensus but a reflection of ruling class ideology. They serve to legitimize the use of ruling class power. Thus, a general commitment to laws by members of society as a whole is an aspect of false class consciousness since, in practice, laws benefit only the ruling minority. These views and their implications will now be examined in detail.

Who makes the law? Who benefits?

From a Marxian perspective laws are made by the state which represents the interests of the ruling class. Perhaps the strongest evidence in support of this view is provided by William Chambliss's analysis of the imposition of English law in East African colonies. Chambliss argues that, 'the entire history of colonial law legislation is that of a dominant social class defining as criminal those acts which it served their economic interests to so define'. In East Africa the British established large tea, coffee and sisal plantations to raise cash crops for export. The plantations needed a plentiful supply of cheap labour to operate profitably. To force the native Africans to work, the colonial rulers instituted a tax which could only be paid by working for wages on the plantations. Non-payment of the tax was a criminal offence, punishable by fines, corporal punishment and imprisonment. Wages were maintained at a low level since higher wages would enable the Africans to pay the tax and return to their villages without working throughout the growing season. Thus, by a legal device, the plantation owners obtained a plentiful supply of cheap wage labour.

Chambliss argues that the vagrancy laws of medieval England served a similar purpose. The first vagrancy statute, enacted in 1349, made it illegal to provide assistance in the form of money, food or shelter, to beggars. The statute also stated that any unemployed person should be required to work if an employer so wished. If he refused to work he would be liable to imprisonment. Chambliss argues that vagrancy statutes were introduced as a response to the Black Death, a plague which reduced the labour force by half. Feudal landowners resorted to the law in an attempt to make good this deficit. Once instituted, vagrancy laws remained on the statute books because they proved an efficient means of controlling labour and provided a steady and cheap supply of workers.

Many sociologists have noted the large number of laws dealing with property in capitalist society. For example, Hermann Mannheim writes, 'the history of criminal legislation in England and many other countries, shows that excessive prominence was given by the law to the protection of property'. According to William Chambliss such laws were largely unnecessary in feudal society where land, unmovable property, was the main source of wealth and landowners were 'the undisputed masters of the economic resources of the country'. However, the increasing importance of trade and commerce, which involves movable property, and the eventual replacement of feudalism by capitalism, resulted in a vast number of laws protecting the property interests of the emerging capitalist class. Chambliss argues that, 'The heart of a capitalist economic system is the protection of private property, which is, by definition, the cornerstone upon which capitalist economies function. It is not surprising, then, to find that criminal laws reflect this basic concern'.

At first sight it appears difficult to apply the view that laws serve ruling class interests to legislation designed to protect the consumer against private enterprise. In all advanced capitalist societies there are laws, apparently framed in the national interest, which provide the state with powers to control industry and commerce. Yet it can be argued that many such laws not only serve ruling class interests, but are often shaped and promoted by the very groups whose power they are supposed to curb. Gabriel Kolko's studies of the development of laws regulating the meat packing and railroad industries in the USA illustrate these points. At the turn of the century, hygiene standards in the meat packing industry were appalling. This resulted in illness to the consumer and the loss of European export markets. With the support of the major companies, sanitation laws were introduced to control meat processing and packing. Kolko argues that this support was motivated by self-interest rather than a concern for the health of the consumer. Profits of the larger companies had been declining due to fierce competition from smaller companies which undercut their prices. The new legislation increased the cost of meat processing which resulted in many smaller companies going out of business. Because of the volume of their output, the increased production costs to the larger companies were relatively small. Thus a neat legal device largely eliminated competition from smaller firms, regained export markets and increased profit margins. Kolko applies a similar argument to state intervention in the railroad industry. During the last half of the nineteenth century profits in the railroad industry were declining rapidly and many firms went bankrupt. Competition was intense and firms were undercutting each other in desperate bids for larger shares of the market. The major railroad companies approached the state requesting legislation to govern the industry. Laws were passed fixing standard prices which guaranteed profits to the industry. The official justification for this legislation was that it would prevent monopolies. In practice it did just the opposite. It favoured the larger companies by preventing smaller firms from undercutting their prices and so reduced competition.

A more recent example of ruling class control of legislation is provided by James Graham's study of the Drug Abuse Prevention and Control Act passed by the Nixon adminstration in 1970. Attempts were made to place greater controls on the manufacture and supply of amphetemine, known in illegal drug circles as 'speed'. Amphetemine is a stimulant which if taken in large quantities can do considerable harm. Over 90% of amphetemine on the illicit market was legally manufactured by the large drug corporations. Graham claims that due to pressure placed on politicians by the drug corporations, attempts to place stricter controls on amphetemine manufacture and distribution failed. Graham concludes that, 'The end result is a national policy which declares an all out war on drugs which are not a source of corporate income'. His conclusion is echoed by Senator Eagleton who maintains that public welfare takes second place to corporation profits. Eagleton states, 'When the chips were down, the power of the drug companies was simply more compelling', (quoted in Graham, 1976, p. 121).

This section has argued that the law is an instrument of the ruling class, used to maximize its profits, control its workforce, and further its interests in general. Can all laws be seen in this light? Jock Young argues that although laws are strongly biased in favour of capitalist interests, they do 'contain within them gains and concessions wrested from the bourgeoisie by the labour movement'. Thus it can be argued that laws guaranteeing the existence of trade unions and their right to strike and legislation protecting the health and safety of people at work represent gains by the subject class. However, Frank Pearce argues that many such laws benefit both ruling and subject classes. Factory legislation protecting the health and safety of workers provides an example. Pearce writes, 'The majority of laws in Britain and America work in favour of the capitalists, yet many laws do also benefit the other social classes, not only because the system needs a healthy, safe population of producers and consumers but also because it needs their loyalty'.

This section has also given the impression that laws are directly instituted and promoted by the ruling class. There is, though, considerable evidence against this view. Government bureaucracies and interest groups are important sources of law but from a Marxian perspective, the law will generally support ruling class interests no matter what its source. As Poulantzas has argued, the state can most effectively represent the ruling class when members of that class do not directly govern (see Chapter 3, pp. 104–5). From this viewpoint government bureaucracies can be expected to act independently from direct ruling class control and to take initiatives. Marihuana legislation in the USA provides an example. The Federal Narcotics Bureau was largely responsible for the Marihuana Tax Act of 1937 and since that date has initiated much of the legislation prohibiting the use and sale of marihuana. This action can be interpreted as supporting the interests of the ruling class. Jock Young argues that marihuana use is associated with groups such as hippies which can be seen as a threat to capitalism. Hippies reject the work ethic, achievement motivation, and materialism, all of which can be seen as essential to capitalism. They regard the 'American Dream' as a nightmare, a view which can threaten to unveil false class consciousness. Marihuana laws can be seen as a useful device for discrediting them and therefore their views.

Similar arguments can be applied to legislation promoted by interest groups. The Southern Christian Leadership Conference led by Martin Luther King can be seen as partly responsible for the civil rights laws of the mid 1960s. This legislation guaranteed Black Americans equal rights under the law in areas such as voting, education and employment. However, Michael Haralambos argues that such laws can also be seen as serving ruling class interests. In the Deep South mechanical cotton pickers and chemical weed killers had removed the need for Black fieldhands. Racial prejudice and discrimination were no longer needed to provide a large, passive, low-paid workforce. Movements such as the Southern Christian Leadership Conference which mobilized hundreds of thousands of Blacks in the southern states, may well have threatened capitalist interests. In the late 1960s some Black Power groups in the urban ghettoes were openly anti-capitalist. Concessions such as the civil rights legislation effectively defused the massive, organized Black protest movements in the South.

Just as important as laws that are passed are laws that are not passed. Non-decision making is as important as decision making. In Chapter 3 (pp. 102–3) it was argued that the ruling class had the power to ensure that only 'safe decisions' were taken and to prevent many issues from ever reaching the point of decision. William Chambliss applies this argument to the law. He suggests that 'much of what takes place in the creation of rules is "non-decision making"'. He gives examples of situations which may well be legally defined as criminal if the ruling class did not control beliefs about what should and should not be. Thus a movie magnate hires a nightclub and spends $20 000 on a lavish birthday party for his daughter, while people are starving a few blocks away. The wife of the US Attorney General has 200 pairs of shoes while in the Appalachian Mountains, parents cannot afford to buy their children a single pair. Such behaviour is justified by ruling class ideology with statements such as, 'They've earned their money; they have a right to spend it as they see fit'. Few break through the barriers of false class consciousness. Angela Davis, a former leader of the Black Panthers, a militant Black American organization, is the exception rather than the rule when she claims, 'The real criminals in this society are not all the people who populate the prisons across the state, but those people who have stolen the wealth of the world from the people', (quoted in Taylor, Walton and Young, 1973, p. 27). In her eyes the real criminals are members of the capitalist class. Ruling class control of the superstructure prevents such views from becoming widespread, from developing into major issues and from being translated into law.

Who breaks the law? Who gets caught?

Marxists such as William Chambliss argue that crime is widespread in every social stratum in capitalist society. The impression given by official statistics that crime is largely a working-class phenomenon is simply due to the selective application of the law. In *Crimes of the Powerful*, Frank Pearce examines the illegal activities of large American business corporations. Measured in monetary terms, Pearce claims that the criminal activities of the working class are a drop in the ocean compared with the huge sums illegally pocketed by private enterprise. For example, the US Federal Trade Commission estimated that in 1968, robbery accounted for some fifty-five million dollars compared to *detectable* business frauds amounting to one billion dollars. Ramsay Clarke claims that, 'One corporate price-fixing conspiracy criminally converted more money each year it continued than all of the hundreds of thousands of burglaries, larcenies or thefts in the entire nation during those same years', (quoted in Pearce, 1976). In monetary terms, crime in the USA is a ruling class 'problem'.

Pearce examines the operation of the American anti-trust laws which have as their stated purpose the maintenance of prices at their lowest possible level. The anti-trust laws are supposed to maintain competition by preventing monopolies and prohibiting price-fixing arrangements between companies. Pearce claims that the anti-trust laws rarely achieve their stated aims. Price-fixing cartels are widespread and 'free' competition between large companies is virtually non-existent. The US Federal Trade Commission has estimated that if anti-trust laws were rigorously applied, prices would fall by 25% or more. This would involve breaking the stranglehold of a few giant companies on major industries and creating a really competitive market. Pearce refers to the few cases that have been successfully prosecuted under the anti-trust laws to indicate the large sums involved. In 'The Heavy Electrical Equipment Cases' in 1961, General Electric made at least fifty million dollars illegal excess profit. Pearce claims that, 'Such "business activity" is typical not only of General Electric but of large corporations in America generally. The corporations provide the most efficient and largest examples of organized crime in America'.

Despite the apparent widespread nature of corporation crime, companies are rarely prosecuted under the anti-trust laws. For example, in 1962, only ninety-two cases were brought to court. Pearce argues that if violations are widespread, yet the numbers of prosecutions are small, then prosecutions must serve a purpose other than the regulation of business. This purpose, he claims, is to maintain the myth that the law applies equally to rich and poor, that the state is a neutral body, above sectional interests, guarding the welfare of society as a whole. A second reason for the small number of prosecutions is to create the impression that corporate crime is minimal. Revelation of the widespread nature of corporation crime may well threaten capitalist power.

Pearce then turns to the relationship between the ruling class and organized crime in America. He argues that organized crime 'has been encouraged, ignored or repressed in direct relationship to its utility to the American ruling class'. Pearce claims that particularly during the 1920s and 1930s, gangsters were often employed by large companies for a variety of purposes. They were used to break strikes by intimidating workers, to infiltrate and control trade unions, and to put competitors out of business. During the 1930s, the Detroit automobile companies fought a long battle against attempts by their workers to form trade unions. Fords and General Motors hired gangsters in an effort to terrorize workers into submission. They lost the battle but continued the war, using gangsters to intimidate militant left-wing trade union leaders. During the 1950s these leaders were replaced by more moderate men, the need for gangsters was over and they were dropped from the payroll. In Pearce's words, 'they are a poor substitute for compliant right-wing trade unionists'. Using examples such as this, Pearce sees organized crime as the servant of the ruling class, to be used when and where it suits its purposes.

In an important study of crime in Seattle, Washington, William Chambliss argues that organized crime is not merely the servant of the ruling class but rather an integral part of it. His research covered nearly ten years, from 1962 to 1972, and was based on interviews with a variety of informants including police officers, government officials, professional thieves, racketeers and prostitutes. Chambliss argues that crime occurs throughout all social strata. The major differences between strata are the types of crimes committed and the nature of law enforcement. Chambliss claims that power in the form of money and influence is the key factor which determines who gets arrested and who does not. During the time of his study, over 70% of the arrests in Seattle were for public drunkenness. Skid row rather than upper class suburbia preoccupied the police. The courts and the jails were filled with the poor and the powerless.

Chambliss claims that the major crime syndicate in Seattle was made up of leading businessmen, political leaders and law enforcement officers. The syndicate organized illegal gambling, bookmaking, prostitution, pornography and the sale and distribution of drugs. Its tentacles spread throughout the ruling class. The vice president of a local bank helped the syndicate to conceal its large tax-free profits and sat on the board of a syndicate-owned 'shark' loan company. Those who threatened to 'blow the whistle' on the syndicate's activities were murdered. Drowning was a favourite method since it could be conveniently glossed as suicide by the coroner, a brother-in-law of a member of the syndicate. Payoffs and bribes to local politicians and government officials were standard practice with the result that local government bureaucracy turned a blind eye to the syndicate's activities. Complaints from residents in low-income areas about the presence of brothels and gambling casinos in their neighbourhoods were ignored by the powers that be. From this type of evidence, Chambliss reaches the following conclusions. Firstly, those who operate organized crime in American cities are not members of some 'criminal class', they belong to the economic and political elite. Secondly, it is not only the small minority of active syndicate members within the ruling class who profit from crime. The class as a whole benefits, since monies gained from illegal activities are used to finance legal business operations. Thirdly, corruption of local political and law enforcement agencies is essential for organized crime to flourish. Fourthly, criminal acts which favour ruling class interests will not be penalized, those that do not will be subject to legal sanctions.

Why break the law? Why enforce the law?

Many Marxists see crime as a natural outgrowth of capitalist society. They argue that a capitalist economic system generates crime for the following reasons. The economic infrastructure is the major influence upon social relationships, beliefs and values. The capitalist mode of production emphasizes the maximization of profits and the accumulation of wealth. Economic self-interest rather than public duty motivates behaviour. Capitalism is based on the private ownership of property. Personal gain rather than collective well-being is encouraged. Capitalism is a competitive system. Mutual aid and cooperation for the betterment of all are discouraged in favour of individual achievement at the expense of others. Competition breeds aggression, hostility, and particularly for the losers, frustration.

William Chambliss argues that the greed, self-interest and hostility generated by the capitalist system motivates many crimes on all levels of society. Members of each stratum use whatever means and opportunities their class position provides to commit crime. Thus in low-income areas the mugger, the petty thief, the pusher, the pimp and the prostitute use what they've got to get what they can. In higher income brackets, businessmen, lawyers and politicians have more effective means at their disposal to grab a larger share of the cake.

Given the nature of capitalist society, and particularly American society, David Gordon argues that crime is rational, it makes sense. In a 'dog eat dog' society where competition is the order of the day, individuals must fend for themselves in order to survive. This is particularly true for the American poor, since the USA has minimal welfare services compared to other advanced industrial societies. Gordon concludes that, 'Most crimes in this country share a single important similarity – they represent rational responses to the competitiveness and inequality of life in capitalist societies'.

From a Marxian viewpoint, the selective enforcement of the law has a number of important consequences. As noted above, the occasional prosecution of ruling class crime provides the fiction that the law operates for the benefit of society as a whole, that the state represents the public interest and that the extent of ruling class crime is small. Conversely, frequent prosecution of members of the subject class has equally important consequences. David Gordon argues that the practice of law enforcement in the USA supports the capitalist system in three ways. Firstly, by selecting members of the subject class and punishing them as individuals it protects the system which is primarily responsible for their criminal deviance. Individuals are defined as 'social failures' and as such they are responsible for their criminal activities. In this way blame and condemnation are directed at the individual rather than the institutions of capitalism. Gordon argues that the practice of law enforcement serves to 'reinforce a prevalent ideology in this society that individuals, rather than institutions are to blame for social problems'. Secondly, the imprisonment of selected members of the subject class 'legitimately' neutralizes opposition to the system. This view can be applied to police practices in Black American ghetto areas which house the most potentially revolutionary section of the American population. Despite the fact they form only 12% of the population, 61% of those arrested for robbery in 1968 were Black as were nearly 50% of those arrested for aggravated assault. A New York Chief of Police neatly summarized the situation when he compared the role of the police in Harlem, (the main Black ghetto in New York City), to that of an army of occupation. Few have the insight of one Black ex-convict who sums up Gordon's view of imprisonment when he states, 'It didn't take me any time to decide I wasn't going back to commit crimes. Because it's stupid, it's a trap, it only makes it easier for them to neutralize you', (quoted in Gordon, 1976, p. 208). Thirdly, Gordon argues that defining criminals as 'animals and misfits, as enemies of the state', provides a justification for incarcerating them in prisons. This keeps them hidden from view. In this way the most embarrassing extremes produced by the capitalist system are neatly swept under the carpet. If something were really done to help those who broke the law, if their problems were made public, the whole system might be questioned. But, Gordon concludes, 'By keeping its victims so thoroughly hidden and rendering them so apparently inhuman, our system of crime and punishment allows us to forget how sweeping a "transformation" of our social ideology we would require in order to begin solving the problem of crime'.

Gordon argues that the selective enforcement of the law serves to maintain ruling class power, to reinforce ruling class ideology. Further arguments in support of this view can be added to those he outlines. The selective application of the law gives the impression that criminals are mainly located in the working class. This serves to divert attention from ruling class crime. It can also serve to divert the attention of members of the subject class from their exploitation and oppression. It directs a part of the frustration and hostility produced by this situation onto the criminals within their own class. The muggers, murderers and thieves can provide a scapegoat for the frustrations of the alienated masses. This provides a safety valve, releasing aggression which might otherwise be directed against the ruling class. It also serves to divide the subject class, particularly in low-income areas, where there is a tendency for people to see their enemies as criminals within their own class.

Finally, what effect does selective law enforcement have upon crime itself? From his study of Seattle, William Chambliss reaches the following conclusion: law enforcement agencies are '*not* organized to *reduce crime* or to enforce public morality. They are organized rather to *manage* crime by cooperating with the most criminal groups and enforcing laws against those whose crimes are minimal. By cooperating with criminal groups law enforcement essentially produces more crime'.

A society without crime?

From a Marxian perspective the basis of crime is the private ownership of the forces of production and all that that entails. Thus a socialist society, in which the forces of production are communally owned, should result in a large reduction of many forms of crime. In theory, individual gain and self-interest should be largely replaced by collective responsibility and concern. There is some evidence to suggest that societies which have moved further along the road to socialism than the USA, have a lower crime rate. Though the evidence is shaky and the arguments speculative, Milton Mankoff makes the following case.

The crime rate in Western Europe is lower than that of the USA. For example, there are more murders in a few months in New York City than in England during a whole year. 'Street crime' is largely an American phenomenon despite the apparent rise in muggings in European cities. The difference in the crime rate is due in part to the following factors. Firstly, the welfare benefits provided for the poor in Western Europe are considerably more extensive than those available in America. Mankoff argues that as a result the European poor 'do not reach the level of dehumanization possible in the United States. With a greater sense of dignity there is less likelihood of striking out violently against innocent fellow citizens to vent one's grievances'. Thus the hostility and frustration produced by capitalism, particularly for those at the bottom of the stratification system, are reduced by the more humane welfare provisions of Western Europe. Secondly, compared to the USA, there is a higher working-class involvement in trade unions in Europe. Working-class interests are also represented by socialist political parties in practically every advanced capitalist industrial society with the exception of the USA. Such organizations provide means for constructively channelling working-class protest. In America, crime provides one of the few means of expression for such protest. Thus Mankoff suggests that in the USA working-class crime 'represents a primitive pre-political form of protest against powerlessness, alienation, and class society'. If Mankoff's arguments are correct, the solution to crime lies on the road to socialism.

The application of Marxian theory to the study of deviance became increasingly popular during the 1970s. It promised to provide a more comprehensive explanation than previous approaches. Thus it offered explanations not only for the origins of crime and deviance but also for the nature of law and law enforcement and definitions of non-criminal deviance. In particular, Marxism provided an explanation of the relationship between deviance and the nature and distribution of power in society. However, its claim that all forms of deviance can be ultimately accounted for in terms of the economic infrastructure is questionable. Even if Marxian theory proved sufficiently flexible and Marxists sufficiently ingenious to explain all forms of deviance in Western society in terms of the capitalist system, problems would still remain. There is ample evidence of crime and deviance in communist society ranging from petty theft to political and religious dissidence. To suggest that such activities are hangovers from a previous era and will disappear once the dictatorship of the proletariat has established a truly socialist society is stretching credulity. Marxian theory fails to provide an adequate explanation for deviance in societies where the forces of production are communally owned.

Sociology, ideology and deviance

It is clear from this chapter that the sympathies of many sociologists tend to lie with the deviant. This will inevitably influence their research. In a paper entitled, *Who's Side are We On*, Howard Becker argues that it is impossible to conduct research 'uncontaminated by personal and political sympathies'. Like many sociologists he believes that a value-free sociology is not possible. Becker claims that his sympathies are with the 'underdog', the deviant who is labelled by the agencies of social control. These sympathies tend to colour the views of the entire interactionist school. The villains of the piece are the agents of social control, the police, the judges, the probation and prison officers, the doctors and the psychiatrists, those who process the deviants and slap on the labels. In terms of their critical view of control agencies, Becker claims that politically, 'interactionist theories look (and are) rather Left'.

Alvin Gouldner takes a rather different view. He accuses the interactionists of adopting a 'bland liberal position' which advocates cosmetic reform rather than radical change. In criticizing the agencies of social control they fail to attack the real causes of deviance which lie in society itself. Gouldner argues that this failure is due to the interactionists' ideological stance. Their liberal views lead them to regard the basic foundations of society as sound. More radical commitments would demand fundamental changes in the structure of society rather than the less repressive measures of social control which the interactionists advocate.

Gouldner claims that many members of the interactionist school have a romantic identification with the more colourful and exotic deviants. He suggests that they 'get their kicks' from a 'titillated attraction to the underdog's exotic difference'. He claims that 'theirs is a school of thought that finds itself at home in the world of hip, drug addicts, jazz musicians, cab drivers, prostitutes, night people, drifters, grifters and skidders: "the cool world"'. Gouldner argues that this identification by largely middle-class sociologists with the 'cool underworld' colours their choice of research subjects, their perspectives and conclusions. It leads at best to rather bland sympathies with the underdog and a relatively mild reproach to the agencies of social control to lay off and leave the deviants alone. Gouldner regards this as a poor substitute for a radical critique of society as a whole.

Functionalists such as Merton have also been accused of 'bland liberalism' by their more radical critics. Merton's view of society is critical but the changes indicated by his conclusions suggest reform rather than radical change. He sees inequality of opportunity as the major cause of crime and delinquency and implies that measures to increase equal opportunity will solve many of society's problems. With a basic commitment to US society in the first place and a belief that its foundations are fundamentally sound, Merton is directed towards criticism and reform rather than condemnation and radical change. This may well have prevented him from questioning the system itself, and, as Laurie Taylor suggested, asking basic questions such as, 'Who made the rules in the first place?'.

If the interactionists and functionalists can be accused of liberal bias, the same can hardly be said of the Marxists. Commitment to radical change reverberates through their writings. Starting from the value judgment that private property is theft, Marxist sociologists reject the basic structure of class society. Their political views result in a condemnation of ruling class crime and a sympathetic treatment of the crimes of the subject class. When Marxists such as Frank Pearce refer to the 'naked barbarity' of capitalism it is clear that commitments other than scientific objectivity direct and influence their choice of subject matter, their methods of analysis and their conclusions.

11 Religion

'In the beginning was the Word, and the Word was with God, and the Word was God'. The God of Christianity is a supreme being, his word is the ultimate truth, his power is omnipotent. His followers worship him and praise him and live by his commandments.

The Dugum Dani live in the Highlands of New Guinea. They have no god, but their world is inhabited by a host of supernatural beings known as mogat. The mogat are the ghosts of the dead. They cause illness and death and control the wind and the rain. The Dugum Dani are not pious, they do not pray. Their rituals are not to honour or worship the mogat but to placate and appease them.

The Teton Sioux lived on the northern prairies of the USA. The world of nature, on which they were dependent, is controlled by the Wakan powers. The powers are stronger and more mysterious than man. They cause the seasons to change, the rains to fall, the plants to grow and the animals to multiply. In this way they care for the Sioux. The Wakan powers were not worshipped, rather their aid was invoked: they were appealed to for assistance or protection.

Supernatural beliefs are present in every known society. Their variety seems endless. Any definition of religion must encompass this variety. At its simplest, religion is the belief in the supernatural. This definition, however, fails to incorporate the idea that supernatural forces have some influence or control upon the world, a notion that always accompanies belief in the supernatural. Thus Roland Robertson states that religion, 'refers to the existence of supernatural beings which have a governing effect on life'. Melford E. Spiro adopts a similar definition when he states that religion is based on 'beliefs in superhuman beings and in their power to assist or harm man'. All definitions emphasize certain aspects of religion and exclude others. Those of Robertson and Spiro focus on the nature of religious belief. Definitions which place greater emphasis on other aspects of religion, for example religious practice, will be examined throughout the chapter.

The origin and evolution of religion

In the nineteenth century the sociology of religion was concerned with two main questions, 'How did religion begin?' and 'How did religion evolve?' This evolutionary approach was influenced by Darwin's *On the Origin of Species*, published in 1859. Just as Darwin attempted to explain the origin and evolution of species, so sociologists tried to explain the origin and evolution of social institutions and society. In terms of religion, two main theories, animism and naturism, were advanced to account for its origin.

Animism means the belief in spirits. Edward B. Tylor believes this to be the earliest form of religion. He argues that animism derives from man's attempts to answer two questions, 'What is it that makes the difference between a living body and a dead one?' and, 'What are those human shapes which appear in dreams and visions?' To make sense of these events, early philosophers invented the idea of the soul. The soul is a spirit being which leaves the body temporarily during dreams and visions, and permanently at death. Once invented, the idea of spirits was applied not simply to man, but also to many aspects of the natural and social environment. Thus animals were invested with a spirit, as were man-made objects such as the bullroarer of the Australian aborigines. Tylor argues that religion, in the form of animism, originated to satisfy man's intellectual nature, to meet his need to make sense of death, dreams and visions.

Naturism means the belief that the forces of nature have supernatural power. F. Max Müller believes this to be the earliest form of religion. He argues that naturism arose from man's experience of nature, in particular the effect of nature upon man's emotions. Nature contains surprise, terror, marvels and miracles, such as volcanoes, thunder and lightning. Awed by the power and wonder of nature, early man transformed abstract forces into personal agents. Man personified nature. The force of the wind became the spirit of the wind, the power of the sun became the spirit of the sun. Where animism seeks the origin of religion in man's intellectual needs, naturism seeks it in his emotional needs. Naturism is man's response to the effect of the power and wonder of nature upon his emotions.

From the origin of religion, nineteenth-century sociologists turned to its evolution. Several schemes were developed, Tylor's being one example. Tylor believed that human society evolved through five major stages, beginning with the simple hunting and gathering band, and ending with the complex nation state. In the same way, religion evolved through five stages, corresponding to the evolution of society. Animism, the belief in a multitude of spirits, formed the religion of the simplest societies, monotheism, the belief in one supreme god, formed the religion of the most complex. Tylor believed that each stage in the evolution of religion arose from preceding ones and that the religion of modern man, 'is in great measure only explicable as a developed product of an older and ruder system'.

There are many criticisms of the evolutionary approach. The origin of religion is lost in the past. The first indication of a possible belief in the supernatural dates from about 60 000 years ago. Archaeological evidence reveals that Neanderthal man in the Near East buried his dead with flowers, stone tools and jewelry. However, theories about the origin of religion can only be based on speculation and intelligent guesswork. Evolutionists such as Tylor and Müller came up with plausible reasons for why certain beliefs were held by members of particular societies but this does not necessarily explain why those beliefs originated in the first place. Nor can it be argued that all religions necessarily originated in the same way. In addition, the neat, precise stages for the evolution of religion do not fit the facts. As Andrew Lang points out, many of the simplest societies have religions based on monotheism, which Tylor claimed was limited to modern societies.

Religion – a functionalist perspective

Evolutionists such as Tylor and Müller attempted to explain religion in terms of human needs. Tylor saw it as a response to man's intellectual needs, Müller saw it as a means for satisfying man's emotional needs. The functionalist perspective changes the emphasis from human needs to society's needs. Functionalist analysis is primarily concerned with the contribution religion makes to meeting the functional prerequisites or basic needs of society. From this perspective, society requires a certain degree of social solidarity, value consensus, and harmony and integration between its parts. The function of religion is the contribution it makes to meeting such functional prerequisites, for example, its contribution to social solidarity.

Emile Durkheim

In *The Elementary Forms of the Religious Life*, first published in 1912, Emile Durkheim presented what is probably the most influential interpretation of religion from a functionalist perspective. Durkheim argues that all societies divide the world into two categories, 'the sacred' and 'the profane', or more simply, the sacred and the non-sacred. Religion is based upon this division. It is 'a unified system of beliefs and practices related to sacred things, that is to say things set apart and forbidden'. It is important to realize that, 'By sacred things one must not understand simply those personal things which are called gods or spirits; a rock, a tree, a spring, a pebble, a piece of wood, a house, in a word anything can be sacred'. There is nothing about the particular qualities of a pebble or a tree which makes them sacred. Therefore sacred things must be symbols, they must represent something. To understand the role of religion in society, the relationship between sacred symbols and that which they represent must be established.

Durkheim uses the religion of various groups of Australian aborigines to develop his argument. He sees their religion, which he calls totemism, as the simplest and most basic form of religion. Aborigine society is divided into several clans. A clan is like a large extended family with its members sharing certain duties and obligations. For example, clans have a rule of exogamy – members may not marry within the clan. Clan members have a duty to aid and assist each other; they join together to mourn the death of one of their number and to revenge a member who has been wronged by someone from another clan. Each clan has a totem, usually an animal or a plant. The totem is a symbol. It is the emblem of the clan, 'It is its flag; it is the sign by which each clan distinguishes itself from all others'. However, the totem is more than this, it is a sacred symbol. It is carved on the bullroarer, the most sacred object in aborigine ritual. The totem is 'The outward and visible form of the totemic principle or god'. Durkheim argues that if the totem, 'Is at once the symbol of god and of the society, is that not because the god and the society are only one?' Thus he suggests that in worshipping god, men are in fact worshipping society. Society is the real object of religious veneration.

How does man come to worship society? Sacred things are 'considered superior in dignity and power to profane things and particularly to man'. In relation to the sacred, man's position is inferior and dependent. This relationship between man and sacred things is exactly the relationship between man and society. Society is more important and powerful than the individual. Durkheim argues that, 'Primitive man comes to view society as something sacred because he is utterly dependent on it'. But why does man not simply worship society itself? Why does he invent a sacred symbol like a totem? Because, Durkheim argues, 'it is easier for him to visualize and direct his feelings of awe toward a symbol than towards so complex a thing as a clan'.

Durkheim argues that social life is impossible without the shared values and moral beliefs which form the 'collective conscience'. In their absence, there would be no social order, social control, social solidarity or cooperation. In short, there would be no society. Religion reinforces the collective conscience. The worship of society strengthens the values and moral beliefs which form the basis of social life. By defining them as sacred, religion provides them with greater power to direct human action. The attitude of respect towards the sacred is the same attitude applied to social duties and obligations. In worshipping society, men are, in effect, recognizing the importance of the social group and their dependence upon it. In this way religion strengthens the unity of the group, it promotes social solidarity. Durkheim emphasizes the importance of collective worship. The social group comes together in religious rituals infused with drama and reverence. Together, its members express their faith in common values and beliefs. In this highly charged atmosphere of collective worship, the integration of society is strengthened. Members of society express, communicate and comprehend the moral bonds which unite them.

Durkheim's ideas remain influential, though they are not without criticism. Some anthropologists have argued that he is not justified in seeing totemism as a religion. Most sociologists believe that Durkheim has overstated his case. Whilst agreeing that religion is important for promoting social solidarity and reinforcing social values, they would not support the view that religion is the worship of society. Durkheim's views on religion are more relevant to small, non-literate societies, where there is a close integration of culture and social institutions, where work, leisure, education and family life tend to merge, and where members share a common belief and value system. They are less relevant to modern societies, which have many subcultures, social and ethnic groups, specialized organisations and a range of religious beliefs, practices and institutions.

Bronislaw Malinowski

Like Durkheim, Malinowski uses data from small-scale non-literate societies to develop his thesis on religion. Many of his examples are drawn from his field work in the Trobriand Islands off the coast of New Guinea. Like Durkheim, Malinowski sees religion as reinforcing social norms and values and promoting social solidarity. Unlike Durkheim, however, he does not see religion reflecting society as a whole, nor does he see religious ritual as the worship of society itself. Malinowski identifies specific areas of social life with which religion is concerned, to which it is addressed. These are situations of emotional stress which threaten social solidarity.

Anxiety and tension tend to disrupt social life. Situations which produce these emotions include 'crises of life' such as birth, puberty, marriage and death. Malinowski notes that in all societies these life crises are surrounded with religious ritual. He sees death as the most disruptive of these events and argues that, 'The existence of strong personal attachments and the fact of death, which of all human events is the most upsetting and disorganizing to man's calculations, are perhaps the main sources of religious beliefs'. Religion deals with the problem of death in the following manner. A funeral ceremony expresses the belief in immortality, which denies the fact of death, and so comforts the bereaved. Other mourners support the bereaved by their presence at the ceremony. This comfort and support checks the emotions which death produces, and controls the stress and anxiety which might disrupt society. Death is 'socially destructive' since it removes a member from society. At a funeral ceremony the social group unites to support the bereaved. This expression of social solidarity re-integrates society.

A second category of events, undertakings which cannot be fully controlled or predicted by practical means, also produces tension and anxiety. From his observations in the Trobriand Islands, Malinowski noted that such events were surrounded by ritual. Fishing is an important subsistence practice in the Trobriands. Malinowski observed that in the calm waters of the lagoon, 'fishing is done in an easy and absolutely reliable manner by the method of poisoning, yielding abundant results without danger and uncertainty'. However, beyond the barrier reef in the open sea there is danger and uncertainty. A storm may result in loss of life. The catch is dependent on the presence of a shoal of fish which cannot be predicted. In the lagoon, 'where man can rely completely on his knowledge and skill', there are no rituals associated with fishing whereas fishing in the open sea is preceded by rituals to ensure a good catch and protect the fishermen. Although Malinowski refers to these rituals as magic, others argue it is reasonable to regard them as religious practices. Again we see ritual addressed to specific situations which produce anxiety. Rituals reduce anxiety by providing confidence and a feeling of control. As with funeral ceremonies, fishing rituals are social events. The group unites to deal with situations of stress, and so the unity of the group is strengthened.

Malinowski's distinctive contribution to the sociology of religion is his argument that religion promotes social solidarity by dealing with situations of emotional stress which threaten the stability of society.

Talcott Parsons

Talcott Parsons argues that human action is directed and controlled by norms provided by the social system. The cultural system provides more general guidelines for action in the form of beliefs, values and systems of meaning. The norms which direct action are not merely isolated standards for behaviour, they are integrated and patterned by the values and beliefs provided by the cultural system. For example, many norms in Western society are expressions of the value of materialism. Religion is part of the cultural system. As such, religious beliefs provide guidelines for human action and standards against which man's conduct can be evaluated. In a Christian society the Ten Commandments operate in this way. Many of the norms of the social system are integrated by religious beliefs. For example, the commandment, 'Thou shalt not kill', integrates such diverse norms as the ways to drive a car, to settle an argument and to deal with the suffering of the aged. The norms which direct these areas of behaviour prohibit manslaughter, murder and euthanasia. They are all based on the same religious commandment. In this way religion provides general guidelines for conduct which are expressed in a variety of norms. By establishing general principles and moral beliefs, religion helps to provide the consensus which Parsons believes is necessary for order and stability in society.

Parsons, like Malinowski, sees religion addressed to particular problems which occur in all societies. He argues that in everyday life, people 'go about their business without particular strain'. If life were always like this, 'religion would certainly not have the significance that it does'. However, life does not always follow this smooth pattern. The problems which disrupt it fall into two categories. The first 'consists in the fact that men are "hit" by events which they cannot foresee and prepare for, or control, or both'. Such an event is death, particularly premature death. Like Malinowski, and for similar reasons, Parsons sees religion as a mechanism for adjustment to such events and as a means for restoring the normal pattern of life. The second problem area is that of 'uncertainty'. This refers to endeavours in which a great deal of effort and skill have been invested, but where unknown or uncontrollable factors can threaten a successful outcome. An example is man's inability to predict or control the effect of weather upon agriculture. Again, following Malinowski, Parsons argues that religion provides a means of adjusting and coming to terms with such situations through rituals which act as 'a tonic to self-confidence'. In this way religion maintains social stability by allaying the tension and frustration which could disrupt social order.

As a part of the cultural system, religious beliefs give meaning to life, they answer 'man's questions about himself and the world he lives in'. This function of religion is particularly important in relation to the frustrations referred to above, which threaten to shatter beliefs about the meaning of life and so make human existence meaningless. Why should a premature death occur? It is not something man expects to happen or feels ought to happen. Social life is full of contradictions which threaten the meaning man places on life. Parsons argues that one of the major functions of religion is to 'make sense' of all experiences, no matter how meaningless or contradictory they appear. An example is the question of suffering, 'Why must men endure deprivation and pain and so unequally and haphazardly, if indeed at all?' Religion provides a range of answers: suffering is imposed by God to test a person's faith; it is a punishment for sins; suffering with fortitude will bring its reward in Heaven. Suffering thus becomes meaningful. The problem of evil is common to all societies. It is particularly disconcerting when people profit through evil actions. Religion solves this contradiction by stating that evil will receive its just deserts in the afterlife. Parsons therefore sees a major function of religion as the provision of meaning to events that man does not expect or feels ought not to happen, events that are frustrating and contradictory. Religion 'makes sense' of these events in terms of an integrated and consistent pattern of meaning. This allows intellectual and emotional adjustment. On a more general level, this adjustment promotes order and stability in society.

The functionalist perspective emphasizes the positive contributions of religion to society and tends to ignore its dysfunctional aspects. With its preoccupation with harmony, integration and solidarity, functionalism neglects the many instances where religion can be seen as a divisive and disruptive force. It bypasses the frequent examples of internal divisions within a community over questions of religious dogma and worship, divisions which can lead to open conflict. It gives little consideration to hostility between different religious groups within the same society, such as Catholics and Protestants in Northern Ireland. In such cases religion can be seen as a direct threat to social order. As Charles Glock and Rodney Stark state in their criticism of functionalist views on religion, 'We find it difficult to reconcile the general theory with considerable evidence of religious conflict. On every side it would seem that religion threatens social integration as readily as it contributes to it. The history of Christianity, with its many schisms, manifests the great power of religion not merely to bind but to divide'.

Religion – a Marxian perspective

In Marx's vision of the ideal society, exploitation and alienation are things of the past. The forces of production are communally owned which results in the disappearance of social classes. Members of society are fulfilled as human beings: they control their own destinies and work together for the common good. Religion does not exist in this communist utopia because the social conditions which produce it have disappeared. To Marx, religion is an illusion which eases the pain produced by exploitation and oppression. It is a series of myths which justify and legitimate the subordination of the subject class and the domination and privilege of the ruling class. It is a distortion of reality which provides many of the deceptions which form the basis of ruling class ideology and false class consciousness.

In Marx's words, 'Religion is the sigh of the oppressed creature, the sentiment of a heartless world and the soul of soulless conditions. It is the opium of the people'. Religion acts as an opiate to dull the pain produced by oppression. It does nothing to solve the problem, it is simply a misguided attempt to make life more bearable. As such, religion merely stupefies its adherents rather than bringing them true happiness and fulfilment. In Lenin's words, 'Religion is a kind of spiritual gin in which the slaves of capital drown their human shape and their claims to any decent life'. From a Marxian perspective, most religious movements originate in oppressed classes. Their social conditions provide the most fertile ground for the growth of new religions. Thus Engels argues that, 'Christianity was originally a movement of oppressed people; it first appeared as the religion of slaves and emancipated slaves, of poor people deprived of all rights, or peoples subjugated or dispersed by Rome'.

Religion can dull the pain of oppression in the following ways. Firstly, it promises a paradise of eternal bliss in life after death. Engels argues that the appeal of Christianity to oppressed classes lies in its promise of 'salvation from bondage and misery' in the afterlife. The Christian vision of heaven can make life on earth more bearable by giving people something to look forward to. Secondly, some religions make a virtue of the suffering produced by oppression. In particular, those who bear the deprivations of poverty with dignity and humility will be rewarded for their virtue. This view is contained in the well-known biblical quotation, 'It is easier for a camel to pass through the eye of a needle, than for a rich man to enter the Kingdom of Heaven'. Religion thus makes poverty more tolerable by offering a reward for suffering and promising redress for injustice in the afterlife. Thirdly, religion can offer the hope of supernatural intervention to solve the problems on earth. Members of religious groups such as the Jehovah's Witnesses live in anticipation of the day when the supernatural powers will descend from on high and create heaven on earth. Anticipation of this future can make the present more acceptable. Fourthly, religion often justifies the social order and a person's position within it. God can be seen as creating and ordaining the social structure as in the following verse from the Victorian hymn, 'All Things Bright and Beautiful'.

> The rich man in his castle,
> The poor man at his gate,
> God made them high and lowly,
> And ordered their estate.

In this way, social arrangements appear inevitable. This can help those at the bottom of the stratification system to accept and come to terms with their situation. In the same way, poverty and misfortune in general have often been seen as divinely ordained as a punishment for sin. Again the situation is defined as immutable and unchangeable. This can make life more bearable by encouraging people to accept their situation philosophically.

From a Marxian viewpoint, religion does not simply cushion the effects of oppression, it is also an instrument of that oppression. It acts as a mechanism of social control, maintaining the existing system of exploitation and reinforcing class relationships. Put simply, it keeps people in their place. By making unsatisfactory lives bearable, religion tends to discourage people from attempting to change their situation. By justifying the existing social structure, it dissuades ideas to alter it. By offering an illusion of hope in a hopeless situation, it prevents thoughts of overthrowing the system. By providing explanations and justifications for social situations, religion distorts reality. It helps to produce a false class consciousness which blinds members of the subject class to their true situation and their real interests. In this way it diverts attention from the real source of their oppression and so helps to maintain ruling class power.

Religion is not, however, solely the province of oppressed groups. From a Marxian perspective, ruling classes adopt religious beliefs to justify their position both to themselves and to others. The lines, 'God made them high and lowly and ordered their estate', show clearly how religion can be used to justify social inequality not simply to the poor, but also to the rich. Religion is often directly supported by ruling classes to further their interests. In the words of Marx and Engels, 'the parson has ever gone hand in hand with the landlord'. In feudal England the lord of the manor's power was often legitimated by pronouncements from the pulpit. In return for this support landlords would often richly endow the established church.

There is considerable evidence to support the Marxian view of the role of religion in society. There is also plenty of evidence which contradicts it. For example, many Black American Christian groups have tradition-ally placed great emphasis on the joys of the afterlife as a release from oppression on earth. Radical members of the Black Power Movement have denounced ministers for preaching 'pie in the sky' and so diverting their congregations from their real interests, but it was the Southern Christian Leadership Council, an organization of churches headed by the Reverend Martin Luther King, which directed mass protest during the early years of the Black civil rights campaign. Yet it is important to note that many church leaders condemned the more militant and violent Black protest that was to follow in the late 1960s. In the shanty towns around large Brazilian cities, Pentecostalism is growing rapidly in popularity. Ministers tell their poverty-striken followers that their poverty results from their sins. Some Roman Catholic priests, however, have directed the blame for poverty onto the government rather than the poor. The Brazilian government condones Pentecostalism, it has gaoled some of the more outspoken Catholic priests. Religion has often buttressed and legitimated power and privilege. The caste system of traditional India is justified by Hindu religious beliefs. In Medieval Europe, kings ruled by divine right. The Egyptian pharoahs went one step further by combining both god and king in the same person. But fascist leaders such as Hitler and Mussolini owed little to the support of the church. Slave owners in the southern states of America often supported the conversion of slaves to Christianity, believing it to be a controlling and gentling influence. Susan Budd notes that in the early days of the industrial revolution in England, employers 'explicitly supported religion as a means of subjugat-ing the masses and keeping them sober and working'. Whether or not re-ligion had the desired effect is difficult to say. The above evidence suggests that a case can be made to support Marxian propositions about the role of religion in society. However, conflicting evidence suggests that Marxian views must be limited to the operation of religion at certain times and in certain places. Religion does not always legitimate power. It is not simply an expression of alienation or a justification of privilege.

Marx stated that, 'Religion is only the illusory sun which revolves round man as long as he does not revolve round himself'. In a truly socialist society man revolves round himself and religion, along with all other illusions and distortions of reality, disappears. Whatever the merits of this prophecy, it certainly does not reflect the situation in the socialist Israeli kibbutzim. Many kibbutzim are fervently religious and their members appear to experience no contradiction between religion and socialism. The situation in the USSR is difficult to assess. From his detailed study of Soviet society, David Lane states that although religion probably has 'little hold over the population' there is evidence that 'religion has shown a certain resilience to communism'. Certainly organized Christianity has declined in Russia but how much of this is due to the policy of the ruling elite and how much to communism in general is difficult to say. For example, the attack by the Khrushchev regime on the Russian Orthodox Church resulted in the closure of nearly half of its 20 000 churches between 1960 and 1965. Lane argues that lack of evidence makes it impossible to estimate the extent of religious belief in Russia. However one estimate places the number of baptized Orthodox Christians in the period 1947–57 at ninety million which is roughly the same as in 1914. Religion in Russia is not simply a hangover from pre-communist days. Despite official disapproval a number of small religious movements such as the Baptists and Evangelical Christians continue to spring up.

It is doubtful whether Marx would regard either kibbutzim, set in the context of a capitalist Israel, or the USSR with its marked inequality, as truly socialist societies. Even so, these examples suggest that there is more to religion than a set of beliefs and practices which develop in societies based on the private ownership of the forces of production. (See Chapter 13, pp. 536–7, for an analysis of religion within the general framework of Marxian theory.)

Religion and the sociology of knowledge

The work of Peter Berger and Thomas Luckmann is an important development in the sociology of religion. They see the sociology of religion as part of a larger field, the sociology of knowledge, which is concerned with the meanings and definitions of reality held by members of a society. Every society has its own body of knowledge. For example, traditional Eskimo society has a shared knowledge of life and the world which differs from other societies. This 'universe of meaning', as Berger and Luckmann term it, is socially derived; it is a product of society and in turn feeds back and helps produce society. A universe of meaning includes not only high level philosophical ideas about the meaning of life, but also everyday knowledge which is taken for granted. A universe of meaning requires constant 'legitimation'. It needs repeated reinforcement and justification. Members of society must be told and re-told that their universe of meaning is real, true, correct, 'legitimate'. Without this support, a universe of meaning would tend to crumble, life would become meaningless, and the stability of society would be threatened.

Religion helps to build, maintain and legitimate universes of meaning. Berger and Luckmann write, 'Throughout human history religion has played a decisive part in the construction and maintenance of universes'. Religion performs this function in the following way. Berger states, 'Religion is the audacious attempt to conceive the entire universe as being humanly significant'. In this way man constructs knowledge and meaning about the whole universe and his place within it. An example, is the Christian view of the creation of the world and mankind given in the Book of Genesis. Berger continues, 'Religion legitimates so effectively because it relates the precarious reality of empirical societies with ultimate reality'. In this way knowledge learned from observation and experience is supported and 'made real'. Religion provides ultimate answers which cannot be questioned by those who believe. For example, men observe that the sun rises every morning and, in some societies, this is confirmed and explained by the idea that the sun is controlled by supernatural powers. Religion also legitimates social institutions. It does this 'by locating them within a sacred and cosmic frame of reference'. In this sense law is located in religion when a legal offence becomes a sin against God; authority is located in religion when kings speak for gods or become gods as in the case of the pharoahs of ancient Egypt. In this way religion legitimates, and so supports, social institutions.

Each universe of meaning is grounded in a social base. This social base – the social structure of society – is called its 'plausibility structure'. If this plausibility structure is destroyed, so is the universe of meaning. Neither can exist without the other. For example, when the Inca Empire was destroyed by the Spaniards, the social base of Inca religion was shattered. Without its plausibility structure, Inca religion died.

Berger and Luckmann argued that all certainty is basically uncertain; it has a very precarious foundation. Things are real because people believe they are real. Life is meaningful because of the meaning men give to it. Things make sense because they are defined in terms of common sense. However, this reality, these meanings, this sense are arbitrary. There is no universal standard or yardstick against which they can be measured and shown to be true. The universe of meaning is a social construction of reality. One society's reality is another's pretence; things defined as meaningful in one society are meaningless in another; common sense in one society is nonsense in another. Because of the arbitrary nature of the universe of meaning, it is precarious, insecure, easily shattered. It therefore requires constant legitimation. Berger and Luckmann argue that religion is probably the most effective mechanism for the legitimation of universes of meaning. Unlike other sources of legitimation, only religion links meaning with ultimate reality.

Religion and social change – Max Weber

From a Marxian perspective, religion, as a part of the superstructure of society, is shaped ultimately by the infrastructure. Thus, changes in the forces of production will be mirrored by changes in religious belief and practice. Max Weber rejects the view that religion is always shaped by economic factors. He does not deny that at certain times and in certain places, religious behaviour may be largely shaped by economic forces, but he maintains that this is not always the case. Under certain conditions the reverse can occur, that is religious beliefs can be a major influence on economic behaviour.

Weber's social action theory argues that human action is directed by meanings. (See Chapter 7, pp. 279–82, for a discussion of Weber's general theory.) From this perspective, action can only be understood by appreciating the world view, the image or picture of the world held by members of society. From their world view, individuals derive meanings, purposes and motives which direct their actions. Religion is often an important component of a world view. In certain places and times, religious meaning and purposes can direct action in a wide range of contexts. In particular, religious beliefs can direct economic action.

In his most famous work, *The Protestant Ethic and the Spirit of Capitalism*, Weber examines the relationship between the rise of certain forms of Protestantism and the development of Western industrial capitalism. He argues that the essence of capitalism is 'the pursuit of profit and forever renewed profit'. Capitalist enterprises are organized on rational bureaucratic lines. Business transactions are conducted in a systematic and rational manner with costs and projected profits being carefully assessed. (Weber's views on 'rational action' are examined in detail in Chapter 7, pp. 280–84, and in this chapter, pp. 484–6.) Underlying the practice of capitalism is the 'spirit of capitalism', a set of ideas, ethics and values. Weber illustrates the spirit of capitalism with quotes from two books by Benjamin Franklin, *Necessary Hints to Those that would be Rich* (1736) and *Advice to a Young Tradesman* (1748). Franklin writes, 'Remember that time is money'. Time wasting, idleness and diversion lose money. 'Remember that credit is money'. A reputation for 'prudence and honesty' will bring credit as will paying debts on time. A businessman should behave with 'industry and frugality', and 'punctuality and justice' in all his dealings. Weber argues that this 'spirit of capitalism' is not simply a way of making money, but a way of life which has ethics, duties and obligations. Weber's concern is to 'discover to what extent religious forces have taken part in the formation and expansion of that spirit over the world'.

Weber now turns to examine the rise of 'ascetic Protestantism' which, he maintains, preceded the development of Western capitalism. (Ascetic means abstinent, austere, practising rigorous self-discipline.) He looks at a number of Protestant religions, particularly Calvinism, which developed in seventeenth-century Western Europe. Weber is concerned with the guidelines and directives for conduct laid down by ascetic Protestantism. He sees them as follows. A man must have a calling in life, a well-defined career which he pursues in a determined, single-minded manner. God has commanded the individual to work for His glory. Success in one's calling means the individual has not lost grace in God's sight. Making money is a concrete indication of success in one's calling. John Wesley, a leader of the great Methodist revival which preceded the expansion of English industry at the close of the eighteenth century, writes, 'For religion must necessarily produce industry and frugality, and these cannot but produce riches. We must exhort all Christians to gain what they can and to save all they can; that is, in effect to grow rich' (quoted in Weber, 1958, p. 175). These riches must not be spent on luxuries, fine clothes, lavish houses, frivolous entertainment, but in the glory of God. In effect this meant being more successful in terms of one's calling, which in practice meant reinvesting profits in the business. The Protestants attacked time wasting, laziness, idle gossip and more sleep than was necessary – six to eight hours a day at the most. They frowned on sexual pleasures – sexual intercourse should remain within marriage and then only for the procreation of children (a vegetable diet and cold baths were sometimes recommended to remove temptation). Sport and recreation were accepted only for improving fitness and health, and condemned if pursued for entertainment. The impulsive fun and enjoyment of the pub, dancehall, theatre and gaming house were prohibited to ascetic Protestants. In fact anything which might divert or distract a man from his calling was condemned. Living life in terms of these guidelines was an indication that the individual had not lost grace and favour in the sight of God.

Weber claims that ascetic Protestantism was a vital influence in the creation and development of the spirit and practice of capitalism. A methodical and single-minded pursuit of a calling encourages rational capitalism. Weber writes, 'restless, continuous, systematic work in a worldly calling must have been the most powerful conceivable lever for the expansion of the spirit of capitalism'. Making money became both a religious and business ethic. The Protestant 'interpretation of profit-making justified the activities of the businessman'. Weber argues that two major features of capitalist industry, standardization of production and the specialized division of labour, were encouraged by Protestantism. The Protestant 'uniformity of life immensely aids the capitalist in the standardization of production'. The emphasis on the 'importance of a fixed calling provided an ethical justification for this modern specialized division of labour'. Finally, Weber notes the importance of the creation of wealth and the restrictions on spending it, which encouraged saving and reinvestment, 'When the limitation of consumption is combined with this release of acquisitive activity, the inevitable result is obvious: accumulation of capital through an ascetic compulsion to save. The restraints which were imposed on the consumption of wealth naturally served to increase it, by making possible the productive investment of capital'.

Weber argues that ascetic Protestantism preceded the growth of Western capitalism. He maintains that the Protestant ethic, a religiously based moral orientation towards the world, was an important factor in the development of the spirit of capitalism. In turn, the spirit of capitalism directed the practice of capitalism. Weber does not claim that ascetic Protestantism 'caused' capitalism. He argues that many other factors were involved. However, Weber does maintain that ascetic Protestantism had an important influence on the origin and development of capitalism in Western Europe.

Weber's views on the relationship between religion and capitalism have generated a large body of research. Historians such as Tawney and Trevor-Roper have produced modifications of and alternatives to Weber's thesis. Sociologists such as Kautsky have defended the Marxian view of the relationship between religion and social change. Kautsky argues that early capitalism preceded and largely determined Protestantism. He sees Calvinism developing in cities where commerce and early forms of industrialization were already established. In his view Protestantism becomes the ideology of capitalists to legitimate their position. Space precludes a summary of research on the relationship between the rise of Protestantism and the emergence of capitalism. Summaries may be found in Eisenstadt (1967), Robertson (1970) and Towler (1974).

Religion, stratification, and change

In *The Protestant Ethic and the Spirit of Capitalism*, Weber shows the close relationship between a particular social group – the emerging capitalist class – and a particular form of religion – ascetic Protestantism. The question of the relationship between religion, social stratification and social change, particularly with reference to the development of new forms of religion, has led to considerable research. Before examining some of this research, it is necessary to define types of religious organizations.

Church and denomination

The term church refers to a large, formal organization with a hierarchy of officials. In theory it ministers to all members of a society. It recruits from all social strata, but in practice, higher status groups are usually over-represented in its congregations. A church identifies with the state and is integrated with the social and economic structure of society. For example, the Roman Catholic Church in the Middle Ages had important social, political and educational functions. A church generally accepts the norms and values of society and frequently regards itself as the guardian of the established social order. It often jealously guards its monopoly on religious truth. For example, the Roman Catholic Church used the Inquisition to stamp out 'heresy'.

The membership of a denomination forms a minority in society. For example, in 1975 the Methodists in Great Britain had 542 000 members. Unlike a church, a denomination does not identify with the state and approves of the separation of church and state. It is content to both co-exist with other denominations and churches and to cooperate with them. Membership of denominations is drawn from all levels of society though the lower working class is usually least likely to be represented. Denominations generally accept the norms and values of society, though they may impose some minor restrictions upon their members. For example, Methodists are against the consumption of alcohol but drinking in moderation does not result in exclusion from the denomination. Like a church, a denomination has a hierarchy of paid officials and a bureaucratic structure, though there is a tendency for more lay preaching. Denominations typify religious organizations in the USA, where there is no established church. In terms of the above definitions, some sociologists argue that the Church of England today more closely resembles a denomination than a church.

Sects

A sect is a relatively small religious group. Its members are usually, though by no means always, drawn from the lower classes and the poor. Sects often reject many of the norms and values of the wider society and replace them with beliefs and practices which sometimes appear strange to the non-believer. As a result, sects are, in Peter Berger's words, 'in tension with the larger society and closed against it'. Sects are insular groups which are largely closed to those who have not gone through the initiation procedures for membership. They institute a strict pattern of behaviour for members to follow and make strong claims on their loyalty. Belonging to a sect is often the dominant factor in a member's life. The organization of sects tends to be in terms of small face to face groups, without a hierarchy of paid officials and a bureaucratic structure. Often worship is characterized by an intensity and open commitment which is lacking in many churches and denominations. The Black Muslim sect illustrates many of the above points. It also shows the relationship between the circumstances of its members and the beliefs and practices of the sect.

Founded in Detroit in the early 1930s, the Black Muslims, or more correctly, the Nation of Islam, had some fifty Temples in 1959 in low-income Black ghetto areas. The sect rose to prominence in the early 1960s when the Black American movement for self-determination developed. Members are largely drawn from those in poverty; the stated objective of the sect is to recruit 'the Negro in the mud'. The Black Muslims believe that Blacks are 'by nature divine' and that Whites are inferior and evil by nature. They prophesy that Whites and their religion will be destroyed in the year 2000 and that Blacks will then rule forever 'under Allah's guidance in a 'New World'. On initiation into the sect, members replace their 'slavename' with a Muslim name. They are told, 'You are not a Negro from this day on. You are now a Muslim. You are now free'. Accompanying this identity transformation is a rejection by members of their former life style, of their non-Muslim friends and of lower class Black society which is referred to as 'the dead world'. In most large cities the Muslims operate small businesses – barber's shops, clothing stores and restaurants. Their *Economic Blueprint for the Blackman* advocates economic independence from White America. The Muslims are encouraged to work hard, save and abstain from luxuries. A strict moral code, similar to ascetic Protestantism, which forbids the use of alcohol, tobacco and narcotics, sexual intercourse outside of marriage, dancing, dating and many forms of sport, is imposed on all members. In particular, the responsibilities of the man as husband, father and breadwinner are emphasized. Life revolves around the Temple. Members are either attending services or courses on self-improvement, looking after the welfare of fellow members or recruiting new members.

The early 1960s was a period which promised change and improvement in the position of Blacks in America. For many Blacks in the areas of greatest poverty, the Black Muslim sect offered a means to translate this promise into reality. It provided possible solutions to the problems of poverty, unemployment, broken families and the negative self-concept produced by the stigmas of blackness and poverty. Statements by members indicate that sect membership gave them purpose, direction, pride, self-respect and hope for the future.

Max Weber argues that sects are most likely to arise within groups which are marginal in society. Members of groups outside the mainstream of social life often feel they are not receiving either the prestige and/or the economic rewards they deserve. One solution to this problem is a sect based on what Weber calls a 'theodicy of disprivilege' (a theodicy is a religious explanation and justification). Such sects contain an explanation for the disprivilege of their members and promise them a 'sense of honour' either in the afterlife or in a future 'new world' on earth.

An explanation for the development of sects must account for the variety of social background represented in their membership. Sects are not confined to the lower strata of society. For example, the Christian

Science sect has a largely middle-class membership. The concept of relative deprivation can be applied to members of all social classes. Relative deprivation refers to subjectively perceived deprivation, that which people actually feel. In objective terms the poor are more deprived than the middle class. However, in subjective terms certain members of the middle class may feel more deprivation than the poor. Relative deprivation applies to the middle-class hippy in California who rejects values of materialism and achievement and seeks fulfilment in Transcendental Meditation. It applies equally to the unemployed Black American who joins the Black Muslims. Both experience deprivation in terms of their own particular viewpoints. Sects can therefore be seen as one possible response to relative deprivation.

Sects tend to arise during a period of rapid social change. In this situation traditional norms are disrupted, social relationships tend to lack consistent and coherent meaning and the traditional 'universe of meaning' is undermined. Thus Bryan Wilson sees the rise of Methodism as a response by the new urban working class to the 'chaos and uncertainty of life in the newly settled industrial areas'. He argues that, 'newly emergent social groups are, at least in the context of a society in which the religious view of the world dominates, likely to need and to evolve new patterns of religious belief to accommodate themselves to their new situation'. In a situation of change and uncertainty, the sect offers the support of a close-knit community organization, well defined and strongly sanctioned norms and values and a promise of salvation. It provides a new and stable 'universe of meaning' which is legitimated by its religious beliefs.

Sects and denominations

H. Richard Niebuhr argues that sects are necessarily shortlived for the following reasons: the fervour and commitment of members cannot be sustained past the first generation; the social marginality and isolation of the group, which was a major factor in the formation of the sect, may disappear. Sects with an ascetic creed tend to accumulate wealth which affords them entry into the mainstream of society. The sect then either ceases to exist or develops into a denomination. Its extreme teachings and rejection of the wider society no longer fit the social situation of its membership. If it changes into a denomination, its beliefs are modified to fit in with those of the mainstream of society; it develops a bureaucratic organization with a hierarchy of paid officials. This is the path taken by some sects. As the Methodists rose in status during the nineteenth century, the strict disciplines of the sect and its opposition to the wider society were dropped, and it became a denomination. But death or denominationalism are not the only alternatives open to a sect. Some sects, such as Jehovah's Witnesses and Seventh Day Adventists, continue as sects. In the process they lose some of their 'sectarian characteristics' – they adopt a bureaucratic structure – but they maintain their original principles and beliefs.

Bryan Wilson offers the following explanation for why some sects develop into denominations whilst others do not. The crucial factor is the way the sect answers the question, 'What shall we do to be saved?' Sects can be classified in terms of how they answer this question. Only one type, the 'conversionist sect', is likely to develop into a denomination. This is the evangelical sect, typical of America, whose aim is to convert as many people as possible by means of revivalist preaching. Becoming a denomination does not necessarily compromise its position. It can still save souls. However, the other types of sect cannot maintain their basic position in a denominational form. 'Adventist sects' such as the Seventh Day Adventists and Jehovah's Witnesses provide an example. 'Adventist sects' await the second coming of Christ, who will judge mankind and establish a new world order. Only sect membership will guarantee a place in the new order. The rich and powerful and those who follow conventional religions will be excluded from Christ's kingdom on earth. 'Adventist sects' are founded on the principle of separation from the world in the expectation of the second coming. To become a denomination they would have to change this basic premise. Separation from the world and denominationalism are not compatible. Thus Wilson concludes that a sect's prescription for salvation is a major factor in determining whether or not it becomes a denomination.

Millenarian movements

Like sects, millenarian movements reveal a close relationship between social situations and religious activity (they can be classified as a type of sect). Millenarian movements are religious movements which promise that the world will be transformed suddenly and soon. Peter Worsley defines them as movements, 'in which the imminence of a radical and supernatural change in the social order is prophesied or expected, so as to lead to organization and activity, carried out in preparation for this event, on the part of the movement's adherents'. Millenarian movements prophesy a merger of the world of the supernatural and the world of man in a new order, free from pain, death, sin and all human imperfections. The Ghost Dance religion of the Teton Sioux illustrates the development of a millenarian movement.

From 1860 to 1877 the Teton fought numerous battles with White settlers and the US army to protect their territory and maintain their way of life. After their final defeat in 1877, they lost most of their land and were confined to relatively small reservations. With the virtual extermination of the buffalo herds, the economic base of Teton society was destroyed, and with it their traditional way of life. Reservation authorities instructed

471

the Teton to take up farming. This largely failed because the land was unsuitable, and the few crops that did grow were often destroyed by drought or plagues of grasshoppers. By 1890 the Teton were largely dependent on government beef rations. From 1889 to 1890 the hardship of the Teton became acute. Crop failures and disease among their cattle were coupled with a drastic reduction in government beef rations and outbreaks of measles, influenza and whooping cough to which the Teton had a low natural resistance. On one reservation, the death rate rose to forty-five a month in a population of five and a half thousand. Apathy and despair were widespread.

From these circumstances the Ghost Dance religion developed. It prophesied that the world would be renewed, the Whites would be buried under a new layer of earth and the buffalo would be restored in abundance. Dead Indians would return to earth and the Teton would live according to their traditional culture, forever free from death, disease and misery. To fulfil this prophecy, the Teton had merely to believe and perform the Ghost Dance. Excitement and anticipation swept through the reservations. Fearing trouble reservation authorities called in the army. An encampment of dancers at Wounded Knee was surrounded by troops and a chance shot led to a massacre of three hundred Teton. Many were wearing 'ghost shirts' which were supposed to make them invulnerable to bullets. The failure of the 'ghost shirts' ended the Ghost Dance religion.

Millenarian movements have occurred in many areas of the world and in all levels of society. However, they are found primarily in deprived groups: oppressed peasants, the urban poor, and peoples under colonial rule. They are often a response to disasters such as plague, famine and drought and to severe economic depression although they can occur without acute economic and physical deprivation, as in the case of the 'cargo cults' of the Melanesian Islands of the South Pacific. The concept of relative deprivation can be applied to this situation. The islanders feel deprived when they compare their position with that of their European rulers. The cargo cults promise a new world in which the islanders will enjoy the wealth of the Europeans. Millenarian movements are usually found in situations of rapid social change, involving the disruption of traditional social norms. They are often a response by native peoples to the impact of Western culture. In a study of millenarian movements in Europe between the eleventh and sixteenth centuries, Cohn finds that they tended to develop in expanding urban areas where traditional norms have been undermined. Millenarian movements are usually preceded by a crisis which brings discontent to a head and a feeling that the normal ways of solving problems are inadequate. In David Aberle's words, 'A sense of blockage, of the insufficiency of ordinary action is the source of the more supernaturally based millenarian movements'. Millenarian movements do not inevitably occur in response to the above conditions;

they are only one possible response to them. The history of the Teton Sioux shows a number of alternative responses: armed aggression; a new way of life – farming; a religion based on passive acceptance and resignation – the Ghost Dance was followed by the Peyote Way, an inward-looking religion based on an Indian version of Christianity and mystical experiences produced by the drug peyote; political agitation – the rise of 'Red Power' in the late 1960s and early 1970s.

The Marxian view of religion as a response to exploitation and oppression helps to explain many millenarian movements. Engels argues that millenarian movements are an awakening of 'proletarian self-consciousness'. He sees them as an attempt by oppressed groups to change the world and remove their oppression here and now, rather than in the afterlife. Peter Worsley takes a similar view in his study of cargo cults. He sees them as a forerunner of political awareness and organization. Some millenarian movements, particularly in Africa and Melanesia, do develop into political movements. However, this is generally not the case in Medieval Europe and North America.

Secularization

In *Family And Neighbourhood*, a study conducted in Oxford in the early 1950s, J. M. Mogey found the prevailing attitude to religion in general, and churchgoing in particular, to be one of indifference. Most people regarded the church as a place for the young and the old, but not for themselves. Many would argue that such findings indicate a decline in the influence of religion in society. This view will now be examined.

Many sociologists maintain that Western societies are undergoing a process of secularization. This means that the influence of religion in all areas of social life is steadily diminishing. Bryan Wilson, who supports this view, defines secularization as 'the process whereby religious thinking, practice and institutions lose social significance'. Like all key concepts in sociology, the concept of secularization has been used in a variety of ways. From his review of studies on secularization, Larry Shiner states that, 'the lack of agreement on what secularization is and how to measure it stands out above everything else'. Any research on secularization must begin with a definition of religion. Immediately problems arise because of the absence of a generally accepted definition. Differing views of religion will result in differing views of secularization. Glock and Stark argue that, 'Perhaps the most important attribute of those who perceive secularization to be going on is their commitment to a particular view of what religion means'. Thus one researcher might see the essential characteristic of religion as worship in a religious institution. As a result he may see a decline in church attendance as evidence of secularization. Another might emphasize religious belief which he might see as having nothing necessarily to do with attending a religious institution. In an attempt to clarify the issue, studies of secularization will be classified in terms of some of the many ways in which the process has been conceptualized and measured.

Institutional religion – participation

Some researchers have seen religious institutions and activity associated with them as the key element in religious behaviour. From this viewpoint they have measured the importance of religion in society in terms of factors such as church attendance and marriages performed in church. From such measures they argue that secularization is occurring in most Western societies. Statistics on church attendance in England and Wales indicate a steady decline over the past century. The 1851 'Census of Religion' showed that just under 40% of the adult population attended church each week. By the turn of the century, this figure had dropped to 35%, by 1950 to 20% and by 1970 only 10 to 12% of the population of England and Wales attended church on an average Sunday. There has also been a steady, though less sharp, decrease in the number of baptisms, confirmations, church marriages and Sunday school attendances. For example, in 1929, 56% of all marriages in England and Wales were conducted in the Church of England compared with only 37% in 1973. During these years the percentage of registry office marriages rose from 25.7 to 47%. The decline in church oriented religious activity has been paralleled by a decrease in the numbers of clergy. Bryan Wilson gives the following figures. In 1861, there was one Anglican clergyman for every 960 people in England and Wales, a century later there was fewer than one for every 4 000 people. Certainly, on the basis of counting heads, there has been a marked decline in institutional religion in England and Wales. This trend applies not only to the Church of England but to all the important denominations. Evidence from most West European countries provides a similar picture. Evidence from the USA will be discussed later.

Statistics on religious activity must be regarded with caution. Methods of data collection, particularly in the nineteenth century, do not meet today's standards of reliability. In addition, information about smaller religious groups is often unavailable. Even with these qualifications, the weight of evidence strongly suggests a decline in participation in institutional religion. What does this mean? It may mean what the statistics say and no more. However researchers such as Bryan Wilson, who rely heavily on this type of information, go further. Wilson argues that, 'The decline in organized religious participation indicates a way in which the Churches are losing direct influence over the ideas and activities of man'. Researchers who see a decline in institutional religion as an indication of a more general decline of religion in society are influenced by the traditional view that a religious person goes to church. Peter Glasner argues that, 'These studies have in common the identification òf religion with "church-oriented" religion and the utilization of conventional definitions of religious institutions'.

The decline in participation in institutional religion can be interpreted in a number of ways. From a phenomenological perspective, it is essential to discover the meanings associated with participation. David Martin argues that in Victorian times, church attendance was more strongly motivated by non-religious factors such as middle-class respectability. Today, church attendance is no longer an indication of respectability for many members of the middle class. Thus, their absence from church may have nothing to do with a change in their religious beliefs. National opinion polls over the past twenty years reveal that a high proportion of those who regard themselves as Christians, do not see regular church attendance as a necessary part of being a Christian. Robert N. Bellah argues that the decline in institutional religion cannot be taken as an indication of a decline in religious belief and commitment. Religion today may simply be expressed in a different way. Bellah argues that there has been a move from collective worship to privatized worship and from clerical to individual interpretation of doctrine. He claims that, 'The assumption in most of the major Protestant denominations is that the Church member can be considered responsible for himself'. While there is little dispute that participation in instutional religion has declined over the past century in most European countries, there is considerable disagreement over the interpretation of this process.

Institutional religion – disengagement and differentiation

Some researchers, as noted above, have seen the truly religious society in terms of full churches. They have therefore seen empty churches as evidence of secularization. Others have seen the truly religious society as one in which the church as an institution, is directly involved in every important area of social life. In terms of this emphasis, a disengagement of the church from the wider society is seen as secularization. David Martin states that this view is concerned with 'the ecclesiastical institution, and specifically with any decline in its power, wealth, influence, range of control and prestige'.

Compared to its role in Medieval Europe, the church in contemporary Western society has undergone a process of disengagement. In the Middle Ages, there was a union of church and state. Today, apart from the right of bishops to sit in the British House of Lords, the church is hardly represented in government. Ecclesiastical control of education and social welfare has been superseded by secular organizations under state control. Church patronage of the arts was reflected by the fact that most art in the Middle Ages was based on religious themes. Today secular themes predominate. Bryan Wilson argues that the Church of England today provides little more than traditional ritual to dramatize important turning points in the life cycle, namely, birth, marriage and death. He sees its disengagement from the wider society as evidence of secularization. However, the power of the church in the Middle Ages need not necessarily be seen as a golden age of religion. As David Martin suggests, 'the height of ecclesiastical power can be seen either as the triumph of the religious or its more blasphemous secularization'. Thus today, the church's specialization in specifically religious matters may indicate a purer form of religion, untainted by involvement with secular concerns such as politics.

An alternative to the view that disengagement equals secularization is provided by Talcott Parsons. Parsons agrees that the church as an institution has lost many of its former functions. He argues that the evolution of society involves a process of structural differentiation. Various parts of the social system become more specialized and so perform fewer functions. (This idea forms part of Parsons's theory of social evolution, outlined in Chapter 13, pp. 529–30.) However, the differentiation of the units of the social system does not necessarily lessen their importance. As outlined in a previous section, Parsons argues that religious beliefs still give meaning and significance to life. Churches are still the fount of religious ethics and values. As religious institutions become increasingly specialized, Parsons maintains that their ethics and values become increasingly generalized. In American society they have become the basis for more general social values. Thus many of the values of American society are at once Christian and American. This has resulted in the 'endowment of secular life with a new order of religious legitimation'. From this perspective disengagement, or in Parsons's terminology, structural differentiation, does not equal secularization. To some degree this interpretation rests on Parsons's belief that Christian values direct behaviour in American society. Many critics of the American way of life would disagree with this view.

Institutional religion – religious pluralism

Some researchers imply that the truly religious society has one faith and one church. This picture is influenced by the situation in some small-scale, non-literate societies, such as the Australian aborigines, where the community is a religious community. Members share a common faith and at certain times of the year, the entire community gathers to express this faith in religious rituals. In terms of Durkheim's view of religion, the community is the church. Medieval European societies provide a similar picture. There the established church ministered to the whole society. In contemporary Western societies, one church has been replaced by many.

A multiplicity of denominations and sects have replaced the common faith and the established church. In terms of the model of a truly religious society provided by small-scale societies and Medieval Christendom, today's religious pluralism has been interpreted as evidence of secularization. In particular, it has been argued that a range of competing religious institutions has reduced the power of religion in society. Only when a single religion has a monopoly on the Truth can it effectively reinforce social norms and values and integrate society.

Bryan Wilson argues that if there are a number of denominations in society, each with its own version of the Truth, they can at best only reflect and legitimate the beliefs of a section of the population. In this way, 'religious values cease now to be community values'. Religion no longer expresses and reinforces the values of society as a whole and so ceases to perform its traditional function of promoting social solidarity. Berger and Luckmann make a similar point. Instead of one religious institution with a single, unchallenged view of the supernatural, there are now many with divergent views. Berger and Luckmann argue that the emergence of denominations weakens the influence of religion. No longer is a single 'universe of meaning' provided for all members of society.

During the past thirty years, there has been a movement towards the unity of Christian churches and denominations known as the ecumenical movement. This may reverse the trend towards religious pluralism. Wilson however, interprets the ecumenical movement as further evidence of secularization. He argues that 'Organizations amalgamate when they are weak rather than when they are strong, since alliance means compromise and amendments of commitment'. He believes that ecumenism represents a declining Christianity grasping at straws. Though it has caught the imagination of some churchmen, Wilson argues that the ecumenical movement has aroused little general interest and produced few positive results.

The continuing proliferation of sects has been interpreted by some researchers in much the same way as the spread of denominations. It has been seen as a further fragmentation of institutional religion and therefore as evidence of the weakening hold of religion over society. Accurate measurements of the numbers of sects and the size of their memberships are not available. However, impressionistic assessments, particularly of the USA, indicate a steady growth of new religious movements. These include the Christian World Liberation Front, the Happy-Healthy-Holy Organization usually called 3HO, the Krishna Consciousness movement more commonly known as Hare Krishna, and quasi-religious movements such as Transcendental Meditation. Although it is difficult to classify such movements – they often fall outside the accepted definition of a sect – they have certain characteristics in common with sects. They are small religious groups and their beliefs and practices are regarded as unconventional by mainstream society and contain an implicit and more often an explicit criticism of mainstream culture. Apart from the possible growth of new religious movements, there is some evidence that longer established sects are increasing their membership. For example, in Britain from 1970 to 1975, the Church of Jesus Christ of Latter-Day Saints (the Mormons) claims to have increased its membership from 88 000 to 100 000; the Jehovah's Witnesses claim an increase from 62 000 to 79 000 members.

Peter Berger sees the continuing vitality of sects as evidence of a secular society. He argues that belief in the supernatural can only survive in a sectarian form in a secular society. In order to maintain a strong religious belief and commitment, individuals must cut themselves off from the secularizing influences of the wider society, and seek out the support of others of like mind. The sect, with its close-knit community organization, provides a context where this is possible. From this viewpoint, the sect is the last refuge of the supernatural in a secular society. Sects are therefore evidence of secularization. Bryan Wilson takes a similar view maintaining that sects are 'a feature of societies experiencing secularization, and they may be seen as a response to a situation in which religious values have lost social pre-eminence'. Sects are therefore the last outpost of religion in societies where religious beliefs and values have little consequence.

Bryan Wilson is particularly scathing in his dismissal of the religious movements of the young in the West, such as Krishna Consciousness, which emerged during the 1960s in the USA. He regards them as 'almost irrelevant' to society as a whole claiming that, 'They add nothing to any prospective reintegration of society, and contribute nothing towards the culture by which a society might live'. By comparison, Methodism, in its early days as a sect, provided standards and values for the new urban working class, which helped to integrate its members within the wider society. In addition, its beliefs 'steadily diffused through a much wider body of the population'. The new religious movements show no such promise. Their members live in their own enclosed, encapsulated little worlds. There they emphasize 'hedonism, the validity of present pleasure, the abandonment of restraint and the ethic of "do your own thing"'. Wilson is scornful of their 'exotic novelty' which he believes offers little more than self-indulgence, titillation and shortlived thrills. He believes that movements which seek for truth in Asian religions and emphasize the exploration of the inner self, for example Krishna Consciousness, can give little to Western society. They simply 'offer another way of life for the self-selected few rather than an alternative culture for mankind'. Rather than contributing to a new moral reintegration of society, they simply provide a religious setting for 'dropouts'. They do not halt the continuing process of secularization and are 'likely to be no more than transient and volatile gestures of defiance' in the face of a secular society.

Wilson judges the significance of new religious movements in terms of their potential contribution to the wider society. Since he believes that in the West, they have little or nothing to offer, he regards them as insignificant. However, from another perspective, such movements can be seen as the least secularized of religious institutions and therefore as the most religious. Their members have not compromised their religious beliefs to fit in with the wider society like members of denominations. Their lives often revolve around their religion which has a vitality and commitment not often found in denominations. In this sense true religion lives on in the sects and the new religious movements. It has not been tainted or diluted by the secular influences of the wider society. From this perspective, Pfautz has defined secularization as 'the tendency of sectarian religious movements to become both part of and like "the world"'. Something of this viewpoint is found in the work of Will Herberg which is examined in the following section.

Institutional religion – the secularization of religious institutions

To return to a quotation from Charles Glock and Rodney Stark noted earlier, 'Perhaps the most important attribute of those who perceive secularization to be going on is their commitment to a particular view of what religion means'. The relevance of this remark will already be apparent. It is particularly true of Will Herberg, a longtime observer of religion in the USA. To Herberg, 'authentic religion' means an emphasis on the supernatural, a deep inner conviction of the reality of supernatural power, a serious commitment to religious teachings, a strong element of theological doctrine and a refusal to compromise religious beliefs and values with those of the wider society. This is just what Herberg does not find in the established denominations in America. He claims that, 'Denominational pluralism, on the American plan means thorough-going secularization'. The major denominations have increasingly emphasized this world as opposed to the other world, they have moved away from traditional doctrine and concern with the supernatural, they have compromised their religious beliefs to fit in with the wider society. Because of this, they have become more like the secular society in which they are set.

Compared to Western Europe, membership and attendance of religious institutions in the USA is high. The *Yearbook of American Churches* states that from 1940 to 1957, their membership rose from 49% of the population to 61%, while average weekly attendance rose from 37% to 40%. Though there was a slight decline in attendance during the 1960s and early 1970s, average weekly attendance still involves around 40% of the population. Despite this relatively high level of participation in religious institutions, Herberg argues that it is directed by secular rather than religious concerns. In *Protestant – Catholic – Jew: An Essay in American Religious Sociology*, he presents the following arguments.

Firstly, Herberg sees a need for Americans to identify with a social group. This is particularly apparent with the third generation of the major wave of immigrants to America. Rather than identifying with their ethnic groups, members of this generation now 'identify and locate themselves socially in terms of one of the three great subcommunities – Protestant, Catholic, Jewish – defined in religious terms'. This generation regards itself as American first and foremost (rather than Irish, Polish, German, Swedish etc.) and church membership and attendance is a symbol and expression of this identification. It is a way of announcing that a person is a complete American. In Herberg's words, 'Not to be – that is not to identify oneself and be identified as – either a Protestant, a Catholic, or a Jew is somehow not to be an American'.

Secondly, Herberg believes that American society is becoming increasingly 'other-directed'. The 'other-directed' man is concerned with 'fitting in', conforming, being popular and sociable, whereas the 'inner-directed' man is concerned with achievement and is less influenced and directed by the opinions that others may have of him. The 'other-directed' man wants, above all, to be accepted by, and feel he belongs to, a social group. Herberg sees church membership as a means to this sense of belonging. He writes, 'Being religious and joining a church is, under contemporary American conditions, a fundamental way of "adjusting" and "belonging"'. The church provides the sociable, secure and conforming environment that 'other-directedness' requires. Religion has become 'a way of sociability or "belonging" rather than a way of reorienting life to God. It is thus frequently a religiousness without serious commitment, without real inner conviction'.

Thirdly, Herberg argues that religion in America is subordinated to the 'American Way of Life', to the central values and beliefs of American culture. The American Way of Life 'embraces such seemingly incongruous elements as sanitary plumbing and freedom of opportunity, Coca Cola and an intense faith in education'. It includes a commitment to democracy and free-enterprise. Christianity and Judaism have been shaped by the American Way of Life, they have become 'Americanized'. The late President Eisenhower once said 'Our government makes no sense unless it is founded on a deeply held religious faith – and I don't care what it is'. The particular denomination is not important because they all support and sanctify the American Way of Life. There is relatively little emphasis on theology and doctrine, rather 'ethical behaviour and a good life' are stressed. The 'good life' is based on the central values of American society rather than the word of God. Sermons in American churches often echo the vast American literature on success and motivation, which reflects the high value placed on achievement in American society. Thus the Rev. Irving E. Howard writes in the magazine *Christian*

Economics, 'Jesus recommends faith as a technique for getting results'.

Herberg claims that the major denominations in America have undergone a process of secularization. They increasingly reflect the American Way of Life rather than the word of God. For the typical churchgoer, religion is 'something that reassures him about the essential rightness of everything American, his nature, his culture and himself'. But from Herberg's viewpoint, this has little to do with the real meaning of religion.

Berger and Luckmann are in general agreement with Herberg's thesis. Luckmann argues that denominations were forced to undergo a 'process of internal secularization' in order to survive and prosper in a secular society. If they retained their traditional teachings, their beliefs would no longer have a 'plausibility structure' in a changed society. They would appear irrational, irrelevant or contradictory in a new social setting. Denominations have adapted to society and their teachings have, therefore, remained 'plausible'. However, this has required a sacrifice of considerable religious content. Peter Berger likens American religious institutions to commodities sold in the market place. A successful sales campaign means that 'the "supernatural" elements are pushed into the background, while the institution is "sold" under the label of values congenial to secularized consciousness'. Denominations have succeeded in attracting full houses 'by modifying their product in accordance with consumer demands', that is the demands of a secular society. This accounts for the differences in participation in organized religion between Europe and America. In Europe, religious institutions have remained largely unchanged in the context of changing societies. The result is empty churches. In the USA, religious institutions have adapted to a changing society and the result is full churches.

Herberg's views on American religion have been criticized by Seymour M. Lipset. Lipset argues that there is some evidence to suggest that evangelical Christianity is growing at a faster rate than the traditional denominations. Evangelical movements are much closer to Herberg's view of 'real religion'. They are more closely based on biblical teachings. There is a strong supernatural element and a direct and emotional commitment from their members. In addition, Lipset suggests that, 'the secularized religion which observers see as distinctly modern may have been characteristic of American believers in the past'. In support of this argument, he refers to the observations of foreign visitors to the USA in the nineteenth century. They often commented on the lack of depth and specifically religious content in American religion. The debate on the secularization of religious institutions rests ultimately on the observer's judgment of 'authentic religion'. Herberg's view may reveal as much if not more about his own beliefs and values than it does about the nature of religion in the USA.

Religion and society – generalization

The previous sections have examined approaches to secularization largely in terms of institutional religion. The focus now changes to a more general view of the role of religion in Western society. It is concerned with the influence of religious beliefs and values on social norms and values, social action and consciousness. As in previous sections, assessments of the importance of religion depend largely on the observer's interpretation of what constitutes a 'religious society' and religiously motivated action. Four main views of the changing role of religion in Western industrial society will be examined. They can be classified under the headings of generalization, individuation, transformation and desacrilization.

As noted in a previous section, Talcott Parsons argues that as religious institutions become more specialized, religious values become increasingly generalized. He begins from the judgment that American society is a highly moral society and this morality is based ultimately on Christian values. Although social values are no longer recognized as distinctly religious values, they are grounded on Christian principles. Religious beliefs no longer specifically direct particular actions. However, since they are incorporated within society's value system, they provide general guidelines for conduct. In this sense, they have become generalized. The practice of medicine provides an example. The curing of illness is no longer surrounded by religious ritual. In many small-scale, non-literate societies religion and medicine went hand in hand in the person of the *shaman*. As both a religious leader and a curer, the *shaman* combined 'practical' medicine with religious ritual to cure the sick. Today, hospitals are secular institutions. Yet the practice of medicine is based on the Christian value that the community has a duty to care for and cure the sick. This general directive has replaced the specific religious rituals which surrounded the cure of illness. In this way Parsons argues that religious beliefs and values have become generalized. They form the basis of social values and so provide general guidelines for action.

David Martin applies a similar argument to British society. He maintains that Christian values are an integral part of social values. For example, they provide 'a check in terms of divine limits set to any form of power whatsoever; they are absolutely fundamental in British society in a manner scarcely paralleled elsewhere'. Unfortunately, Martin does not develop this statement and his analysis remains at a rather vague and abstract level.

As with Martin's statement, the main problem with the generalization thesis is its vagueness. Neither Parsons nor Martin provide much evidence to support their views. Beginning with the assumption that the USA and Britain are basically Christian societies, it is possible to see

Christian values directing many aspects of social life. However, it is just as possible to argue that social values have a secular foundation.

Religion and society – individuation

Robert N. Bellah states that, 'The analysis of modern man as secular, materialistic, dehumanized and in the deepest sense areligious seems to me fundamentally misguided'. Bellah argues that sociologists who judge the significance of religion in terms of religious institutions are mistaken. He maintains that, 'Now less than ever can man's search for meaning be confined to the church'. Religion is increasingly an individual quest for meaning rather than a collective act of worship. In this way religion has undergone a process of individuation whereby the individual works out his own salvation and follows his own path to ultimate meaning. The importance of religion has not declined, rather its form of expression has changed. Bellah claims that in contemporary Western society, there is an 'increasing acceptance of the notion that the individual must work out his own ultimate solutions and that the most the church can do is provide him with a favourable environment for doing so, without imposing on him a prefabricated set of answers'. No longer is religious doctrine imposed. Modern man has a greater freedom than ever before to search for and construct his own ultimate meaning.

Bellah's arguments are based in part on his view of religion which he defines as 'a set of symbolic forms and acts which relate man to the ultimate conditions of his existence'. This definition contains no mention of the supernatural. It simply suggests that any search for ultimate meaning, for answers to questions concerning the meaning and purpose of life, is basically a religious quest. Many researchers would argue that Bellah has stretched the concept of religion too far. In addition, Bellah fails to provide detailed evidence to show that the search for ultimate meaning is widespread in contemporary Western society.

Religion and society – transformation

Rather than seeing religious beliefs as either generalized or individuated, a number of sociologists argue that they have become transformed into secular guides to action in Western society. Though many of society's values have religious origins, their connection with religion has been severed. The most famous statement of this position is made by Max Weber. He sees the origin of the spirit of capitalism in ascetic Protestantism. However, even by the eighteenth century, particularly in the USA, the 'pursuit of wealth' has been 'stripped of its religious and ethical meaning'.

Weber believed that ascetic Protestantism contained the seeds of its own destruction. It encouraged involvement and success in this world. Its strict disciplines provided a rational outlook on life. Once its teachings were incorporated into a rational capitalist system, religious direction and validation were rapidly eroded. Two factors were instrumental in transforming ascetic Protestantism into secular guides to action. The first is the 'secularizing influence of wealth'. Wealth provides its own rewards and satisfactions. Gradually they alone provided sufficient motivation for the continued accumulation of wealth. As a result, Weber believed that 'material goods have gained an increasing and finally an inexorable power over the lives of men as at no previous period of history'. The second factor involves the mechanization of production in industrial society. Religious motivation provided the initial drive to work hard and accumulate wealth. Mechanized production technology rather than man provides the basic driving force of industrial society and technology does not require religious motivation. The 'spirit of religious asceticism' is no longer necessary because 'victorious capitalism, since it rests on mechanical foundations, needs its support no longer'. Industrial society has developed its own driving force, its own impetus.

As outlined earlier in the chapter, there is considerable controversy over Weber's interpretation of the relationshhip between ascetic Protestantism and capitalism. It is debatable whether or not the guides to action in modern society had their origin in religious beliefs. Even if Weber's interpretation is accepted, it is still not clear whether the beliefs of ascetic Protestantism have been transformed or generalized. It could be argued that the Protestant ethic which sees hard work as a virtue and a moral duty still survives as a general guide to action. Although evidence presented in Chapter 6 suggests that this is not the case, it does not disprove the possibility of generalization. (See pp. 248–51 for evidence which suggests that work in Western society is increasingly seen in instrumental terms and pp. 260–62 for evidence which suggests that leisure values are replacing the work ethic.)

Religion and society – desacrilization

A number of sociologists have argued that the sacred has little or no place in contemporary Western society, that society has undergone a process of desacrilization. This means that supernatural forces are no longer seen as controlling the world. Action is no longer directed by religious belief. Man's consciousness has become secularized.

Max Weber's interpretation of industrial society provides one of the earliest statements of the desacrilization thesis. He claimed that industrial society is 'characterized by rationalization and intellectualization and, above all, by the "disenchantment of the world"'. The world is no longer charged with mystery and magic; the supernatural has been banished from society. The meanings and motives which direct action are now rational. Weber's concept of rational action and his view that industrial society is undergoing a process of rationalization have been examined in detail in Chapter 7 (pp. 279–86). Briefly, rational action involves a deliberate and precise calculation of the importance of alternative goals and the effectiveness of the various means for attaining chosen goals. For example, if an individual's goal is to make money, he will coldly and carefully calculate the necessary initial investment and the costs involved in producing and marketing a commodity in the most economical way possible. His measurements will be objective, they will be based on factors which can be quantified and accurately measured. He will reject means to reach his goal which cannot be proven to be effective. Rational action rejects the guidelines provided by emotion, by tradition or by religion. It is based on the cold, deliberate reason of the intellect which demands that the rationale for action can only be based on the proven results.

A number of sociologists have accepted Weber's interpretation of the basis for action in industrial society. In *Religion in a Secular Society*, Bryan Wilson states that, 'Religious *thinking* is perhaps the area which evidences most conspicuous change. Men act less and less in response to religious motivation: they assess the world in empirical and rational terms'. Wilson argues that the following factors encouraged the development of rational thinking and a rational world view. Firstly, ascetic Protestantism, which 'created an ethic which was pragmatic, rational, controlled and anti-emotional'. Secondly, the rational organization of society which results in men's 'sustained involvement in rational organizations – firms, public service, educational institutions, government, the state – which impose rational behaviour upon them'. Thirdly, a greater knowledge of the social and physical world which results from the development of the physical, biological and social sciences. Wilson maintains that this knowledge is based on reason rather than faith. He claims that, 'Science not only explained many facets of life and the material environment in a way more satisfactory (than religion), but it also provided confirmation of its explanation in practical results'. Fourthly, the development of rational ideologies and organizations to solve social problems. Ideologies such as communism and organizations such as trade unions offer practical solutions to problems. By comparison, religious solutions such as the promise of justice and reward in the afterlife, do not produce practical and observable results.

Wilson argues that a rational world view is the enemy of religion. It is based on the testing of arguments and beliefs by rational procedures, on assessing truth by means of factors which can be quantified and objectively measured. Religion is based on faith and as such is non-rational. Its claim to truth cannot be tested by rational procedures.

Peter Berger develops some of Weber's and Wilson's ideas within the framework of the sociology of knowledge. He maintains that people in Western society increasingly 'look upon the world and their own lives without the benefit of religious interpretations'. As a result there is a 'secularization of consciousness'. Berger argues that the 'decisive variable for secularization' is 'the process of rationalization that is the prerequisite for any industrial society of the modern type'. A rational world view rejects faith which is the basis of religion. It removes the 'mystery, magic and authority' of religion.

In *The Homeless Mind*, Peter Berger, Brigitte Berger and Hansfried Kellner present a novel interpretation of the reasons for the secularization of consciousness. Compared to industrial society, they argue that pre-industrial societies were more closely knit, more integrated. As a result people had a single 'life world', a single set of meanings, a single reality. Family life, work, education and politics were closely integrated, They formed part of the same pattern. This pattern could be comprehended and made sense of in terms of a single universe of meaning. Typically religious beliefs formed the foundation of this universe of meaning. Modern industrial society is highly differentiated and segmented, and, as a result, members have a 'plurality of life worlds', several sets of meanings, several realities. There is the world of private life, the world of technological production, the world of bureaucracy, the world of education, the many worlds presented by the mass media. The individual participates in all these worlds, each of which has, to some extent, different meanings and values, a different reality. The individual has a plurality of life worlds. Pluralization of life worlds has a 'secularizing effect' for the following reasons. Firstly, since the various life worlds have different and even contradictory meanings, for example the worlds of business and family life, it is difficult for religion to integrate this plurality of social life in one overarching and comprehensive universe of meaning. Second, plurality of life worlds produces a 'general uncertainty'. With different sets of meanings, the individual is not certain about anything, including religion and the meanings it provides. Thus, 'the plausibility of religious definitions of reality is threatened from within, that is within the subjective consciousness of the individual'. Religion provides a single, comprehensive universe of meaning. In a fragmented world this universe tends to shatter.

This section has examined the desacrilization thesis, that is the view that religion and the sacred have largely been removed from the meanings which guide action and interpret the world and from the consciousness of man. This view is difficult to evaluate since it is largely based on the impressions of particular researchers rather than 'hard' data. In addition, it compares industrial society with often unspecified pre-industrial societies in which, presumably, religion provided a guide to action and a basis for meaning. The problems involved with this approach will be dealt with in the following section.

Secularization – conclusion

As the previous sections have indicated, the term secularization has been used in many different ways. This has led to considerable confusion since writers discussing the process of secularization are often arguing about different things. David Martin states that the concept of secularization includes 'a large number of discrete, separate elements loosely put together in an intellectual hold-all'. He maintains that there is no necessary connection between the various processes lumped together under the same heading. Because the range of meaning attached to the term secularization has become so wide, Martin advocates its removal from the sociological vocabulary.

Many of the arguments in support of secularization are based on the assumption of the existence of 'truly religious societies' in pre-industrial times. As Larry Shiner notes, those who argue that the social significance of religion has declined have 'the problem of determing when and where we are to find the supposedly "religious" age from which decline has commenced'. The anthropologist Mary Douglas argues that the use of supposedly 'religious', small-scale non-literate societies as a basis for comparison with modern 'secular' societies is unjustified. She states that, 'The contrast of secular with religious has nothing whatever to do with the contrast of modern with traditional or primitive . . . The truth is that all varieties of scepticism, materialism and spiritual fervour are to be found in the range of tribal societies'. It is simply an illusion concocted by Western man that 'all primitives are pious, credulous and subject to the teaching of priests or magicians'. In the same way, the search for the golden age of religion in the European past may provide an equally shaky standard for comparison. From his study of religion in sixteenth and seventeenth-century England, K. V. Thomas states, 'We do not know enough about the religious beliefs and practices of our remote ancestors to be certain of the extent to which religious faith and practice have actually declined (quoted in Glasner, 1977, p. 71). W. M. William's study of Gosforth, a village in Cumbria, indicates one of the traps into which some sociologists may have fallen. The parish records indicated a low level of church attendance for some 400 years, but each new Anglican vicar believed this to be a recent trend.

The problem of measurement has dogged the secularization debate. Bryan Wilson, although he is convinced that secularization in its various forms is occurring in Western society, admits that there is 'no adequate way of testing the strength of religious commitment'. Public opinion polls over the last twenty years indicate that from 80 to 90% of the British population and between 90 and 95% of the population of the USA believe in God. However, such data give no indication of the strength of religious belief, the extent to which it guides and directs action, or the importance of a belief in God is to those who claim one.

Charles Glock argues that researchers have been unable to measure the significance of religion because 'they have not given adequate attention to conceptualizing religion or religiousness in a comprehensive way'. Until they have clearly thought out and stated exactly what they mean by religion and religiousness, Glock maintains that the secularization thesis cannot be adequately tested. In an attempt to solve this problem, Glock and Stark define five 'core dimensions of religiousness'. First, the belief dimension – the degree to which people hold religious beliefs. Second, religious practice – the degree to which people engage in acts of worship and devotion. Third, the experience dimension – the degree to which people feel and experience contact and communication with the supernatural. Fourth, the knowledge dimension – the amount of knowledge people have of their religion. Fifth, the consequences dimension – the degree to which the previous dimensions affect people's day-to-day lives. Glock and Stark argue that a clearly defined system in which to classify people in religious terms is necessary before any scientifically valid statement about religiousness can be made. Only with such a system can the extent of religiousness be measured. Only when different researchers use the same conceptualization of religion can their results be compared with any degree of validity.

Even though Glock and Stark's scheme may represent an improvement on previous research designs, it does not solve a basic problem of research methodology. It is unlikely that any research technique will be developed to accurately measure subjective factors such as the strength of religious commitment or to uncover, with any degree of certainty, the meanings and motives which lie behind social action.

The new religious consciousness

There has been a tendency for sociologists to consider the emergence of new religious movements in the context of the secularization debate. This rather narrow concern can prevent a consideration of many interesting questions. During the early 1970s, a team of sociologists led by Robert Bellah and Charles Glock investigated several new religious movements in the San Francisco Bay area. This section examines Robert Bellah's interpretation of their findings.

Bellah describes the traditional guidelines for action in American culture as 'utilitarian individualism'. This philosophy states that the individual should make his own way and maximize his own self-interest. In a system of free enterprise, all have the freedom to fulfil their talents and reap their just reward for achievement. In practice this led to the accumulation of wealth as an end in itself. Everything else was a secondary consideration. Bellah illustrates the idea of utilitarian individualism with the story of an American farmer who was asked why he worked so hard. 'To raise more corn, was his reply. But why do you want to do that? To make more money. What for? To buy more land. Why? To raise more corn?' These answers show the poverty of spiritual values in utilitarian individualism. The only reason for making money is to make more money.

Bellah believes that the disruption which swept American society in the 1960s was, above all, a rejection of utilitarian individualism. When Martin Luther King talked about freedom, he did not mean the freedom of the individual to pursue his own selfish ends. Rather, he meant the freedom of all Americans to share the benefits of society. When young people demand the freedom to love one another, they rejected the freedom of utilitarian individualism which allows some to exploit others. Bellah believes that during the 1960s, there was a 'massive erosion of the legitimacy of American institutions–business, government, education, the churches, the family'. To large sections of American society, the continuous expansion of wealth and power did not seem 'so self-evidently good'. Young people, women and Blacks questioned established truths and conventions. Many young people demanded the freedom to express those sides of the self which had been mutilated and stunted by the single-minded pursuit of wealth and power. They explored the inner self emphasizing the immediacy of experience, the importance of feeling and self-awareness. They experimented in new life styles which rejected individual achievement and competition and replaced them with love and mutual concern in a communal setting. Bellah states, 'I would interpret the crisis of the sixties above all as a crisis of meaning, a religious crisis'.

By the 1970s, the ferment of the previous decade had died down. However, many new religious movements which began in the 1960s as a response to the 'crisis of meaning' lived on. Some like Krishna Consciousness and 3HO took their inspiration from Asian religions. Bellah summarizes their essential quality in the following way, 'To external achievement it posed inner experience; to the exploitation of nature, harmony with nature; to impersonal organization, an intense relation to the guru'. Other movements such as the Christian World Liberation Front, an offshoot of the Jesus movement, drew inspiration from the bible. They insisted on direct experience of the love of Jesus who changes man and sets him free. Many of the movements share the following factors. Their members have largely withdrawn from the wider society. They believe that the USA is corrupt, sunk in materialism and heading for disaster. To some degree they all believe in the essential oneness of all men and nature. In Bellah's words, it therefore follows that, 'If man and nature, men and women, white and black, rich and poor are really one, then there is no basis for the exploitation of the latter by the former'.

Bellah believes that the new religious movements offer an alternative future to America. The acceptance of this alternative is improbable but possible. This future would involve 'a firm commitment to the quest for ultimate reality'. In addition, 'Priorities would shift away from endless accumulation of wealth and power to a greater concern for harmony with nature and between human beings'. Bellah hopes this possible future will become a reality. He concludes, 'It may be, however, that only the implementation of a utopian vision, a holistic reason that unites subjectivity and objectivity, will make human life in the twenty-first century worth living'.

Sociology, ideology and religion

Throughout this chapter it is evident that the ideological commitments of particular researchers have influenced their definition of religion and their view of its role in society. In terms of their value judgments, they have considered some aspects of religion as worthy of study and dismissed others as irrelevant. The influence of ideology in the study of religion is clearly evident in Marxian perspectives. Marx believed that man's salvation lay in himself. He would find salvation when he fulfilled his true nature. Fulfillment could only be found in a truly socialist society, a society created by man. Marx's utopian vision left no room for religion. Since religion had no place in the ideal socialist society, it must be a response to the flaws of non-socialist societies. From this set of beliefs and values, Marxian analysis of religion follows a predictable course. Religion represents either a salve to the pain of exploitation or a justification for oppression. In either case, it is a distortion of reality which man can well do without.

The conservative tendencies of functionalism with its preoccupation with social order, provide a similarly predictable analysis. The concern of the functionalist approach with discovering the basis of stability and order in society leads to an emphasis on particular aspects of religion. From this perspective religion is seen as reinforcing social norms and values and promoting social solidarity, all of which are required for a stable and smooth running social system. By its very nature, functionalist theory tends to discount the divisive and disruptive effects of religion and ignore the role of religion as an agency of social change.

The intrusion of value judgments into research is clear in the secularization debate. Many of the arguments are based on particular researchers' judgments of the 'truly religious society' in terms of which they evaluate what they see in contemporary society. Thus Will Herberg sees the religion of American denominations as a poor substitute for true religion. Max Weber observes industrial society in the early twentieth century and pictures a rather pathetic and disenchanted populace without the support of the deep spirituality which religion provides. By contrast Talcott Parsons rather smugly observes American society in the middle years of the twentieth century, notes its high moral standards and assumes they must be based ultimately on Christian values. Such divergent interpretations say as much about the observers as the reality of their sub-ject matter. This is particularly apparent from Bryan Wilson's and Robert Bellah's assessments of the new religious movements. Wilson clearly does not like them. His condemnation is scathing and scornful. By contrast Robert Bellah evinces a deep sympathy with many of their ideals. From these value judgments stem different interpretations of the significance of the new religious movements. Wilson thinks they have little or nothing to offer society. Bellah believes their potential value is enormous. Compared to the self-interested materialism which he sees as rampant in American society, they offer a depth of inner experience and a promise of harmony of man with nature and with his fellow man. Bellah hopes that the reservoir of love and compassion he sees contained in these small groups will spill over into American society to make human life worth living.

12 Methodology

A sociologist intending to study religious behaviour might construct a questionnaire to gather information for his research. It may contain questions about church attendance, individual acts of worship, commitment to religious beliefs and so on. He will ask members of the public to fill in the questionnaire and in this way obtain information for his study. Alternatively, he may wish to gather data by first-hand observation of religious behaviour. Thus he may join congregations in places of worship and directly observe religious services. He may decide, however, that informal interviews will provide the best method for obtaining the information he requires. He will therefore arrange a series of interviews with members of the public to discuss aspects of their religious beliefs and practices. Questionnaires, observation and interviews are three of the main research methods employed by sociologists for gathering data. Methodology is concerned with the study of research methods, with the nature and quality of the data produced by various methods and the logic and rationale behind the use to which those data are put in sociological research.

Apart from generating their own data, sociologists also make use of existing sources of information. These range from official statistics produced by government bodies, such as statistics on crime and suicide, to historical documents such as parish records and contemporary material such as newspapers, magazines, films and novels. Methodology is concerned with analysing the nature of these types of data and examining the ways in which they can be used in sociological research. For example, consideration is given to the problems involved in using official statistics on crime as an indication of the extent of criminal behaviour in society.

Research methods and data form only part of the complex process of sociological research. They cannot be separated from this process. Sociological investigation is based ultimately upon the researcher's assumptions about the nature of man and society. These assumptions guide his entire research operation from the selection of a problem for investigation to the analysis of the data and the interpretation of the results. They influence the research methods he employs and the type of data he obtains. Methodology is therefore concerned with the entire process of sociological research and the logic and assumptions on which it is based.

The many varieties of sociological research may be pictured as lying between two extremes. These extremes represent diametrically opposed research methodologies which derive from very different assumptions about the nature of man and society. The first part of this chapter is concerned specifically with these two approaches to the study of human behaviour.

Positivism and sociology

Many sociologists have argued that the logic, methods and procedures of the natural sciences are applicable to the study of man. A science of human behaviour is therefore possible and sociology has as much claim to scientific status as physics, chemistry and biology. Such claims were often made by the founding fathers of sociology. For example, Auguste Comte (1798–1857) argued that the application of natural science methodology to the study of man would produce a 'positive science of society'. It would reveal that the evolution of society followed 'invariable laws'. It would show that behaviour in the social world is governed by laws in the same way as behaviour in the natural world. Contemporary sociologists are more cautious about claims for the scientific status of their discipline. Indeed many reject the view that natural science methodology is appropriate for the study of human behaviour. Despite these reservations a considerable body of sociological research has been and still is directed by research methodology drawn from the natural sciences. This approach to the study of man is often known as positivism.

Before examining positivist methodology in sociology it is necessary to look at the logic and method of scientific inquiry. The account that follows is overly simple and represents only one view of natural science methodology. However, it does contain many of the ideas which have guided sociologists who assume that such methodology is appropriate to the study of human behaviour.

The natural scientist is concerned with investigating and explaining the behaviour of matter in the natural world. He assumes that this behaviour is subject to unalterable laws. Since the behaviour of matter is governed by laws, it is therefore determined: every event in the material universe has a cause. By systematic observation and experimentation, the natural scientist seeks to reveal the causes of behaviour and so discover the laws by which it is governed. He assumes that matter always reacts in a predictable way to external stimuli. This can be shown experimentally. In laboratory experiments scientists are able to show that under fixed conditions, matter will always behave in exactly the same way in response to a particular stimulus. To take a simple example, water always boils at the same temperature. Matter is compelled to react in this way because it has no consciousness. It has no intentions, purposes or motives which direct its behaviour. Matter does not define an external stimulus in terms of a range of meanings and therefore vary its response to that stimulus.

493

As a result the natural scientist is not required to explore and take account of the internal consciousness of matter in order to explain its behaviour. He can simply observe its activity 'from the outside'. He is able to explain its behaviour merely as a reaction to an external stimulus.

The natural scientist systematically observes and measures the behaviour of matter. The results of these observations are regarded as objective facts, as data which are not distorted by the value judgments and ideology of the particular scientist. This is due to the availability of objective systems of classification and measurement, for example measuring systems for temperature, volume and pressure. The results of observations using such objective criteria can be confirmed by other scientists. Their accuracy can be checked by replication, that is by the repetition of a series of observations or an experiment under the same conditions. For example, it can be shown that a given amount of heat applied to a fixed volume of a particular liquid will always produce the same amount of gas. By such controlled experiments it is possible to establish causal relationships between the factors or variables involved. From this kind of observation the natural scientist constructs theories to explain the behaviour of matter. If behaviour is observed which differs from that predicted by a theory, then the theory is either modified or changed. Thus by constant reference to observable and measurable data, the natural scientist is able to develop and refine theories which predict and explain the behaviour of matter.

If it is assumed that behaviour in the social and natural worlds is governed by the same principles, then natural science methodology is appropriate for the study of human society. Positivist sociology is largely based on this assumption. It argues that both man and matter are a part of the natural universe and that the behaviour of both is governed by natural laws. Just as matter reacts to external stimuli, so man reacts to forces external to his being. Social and natural behaviour is therefore determined and can be explained in terms of cause and effect relationships. The data of the natural sciences are drawn from direct observation of the behaviour of matter, behaviour which can be quantified according to objective criteria. The same procedures are possible in the observation of human behaviour. Only factors which can be directly observed and objectively measured form acceptable data. Thus the motives, feelings and mental states of individuals, factors which can not be directly observed, are inadmissible. In fact it is unnecessary to probe the consciousness of the individual since his behaviour is caused by external forces rather than internal feeling states. It is these forces which must be examined in order to explain human behaviour. Just as natural science involves the construction of theories based on observable data, so sociology can develop theories based on direct observation of human behaviour. Given these assumptions, natural science methodology is applicable to the study of man.

Durkheim and positivism

The positivist approach in sociology is most clearly evident in the work of Emile Durkheim. In *The Rules of Sociological Method*, Durkheim outlined his view of the logic and method of sociological inquiry. He argued that, 'The first and most fundamental rule is: *Consider social facts as things*'. Thus the belief systems, customs and institutions of society, the facts of the social world, should be considered as things in the same way as the objects and events of the natural world. As such they can be directly observed and objectively measured. Although social facts enter the consciousness of individuals, for example the belief systems of society form a part of the outlook of its members, social facts are external to individuals. They are impressed upon them by society, they exist outside the individual, and can therefore be studied 'objectively as external things'. In Durkheim's view, society is not simply a collection of individuals, each acting independently in terms of his or her particular psychology or mental state. Instead members of society are directed by collective beliefs, values and laws, by social facts which have an existence of their own. In Durkheim's words, 'collective ways of acting or thinking have a reality outside the individuals'. Social facts therefore constrain individuals to behave in particular ways. The explanation of human behaviour thus involves an examination of how that behaviour is shaped by social facts. Just as the behaviour of matter can be regarded as a reaction to external stimuli, so the behaviour of man can be seen as a response to the external constraints of social facts. Given this view of the nature of man and society, social facts are amenable to analysis in terms of natural science methodology.

In 1897, Durkheim's now famous work, *Suicide: A Study in Sociology*, was published. Durkheim believed that this study provided the evidence to support his views on methodology outlined two years earlier in *The Rules of Sociological Method*. He argued that his research on suicide demonstrated that 'real laws are discoverable', that social phenomena obey laws in the same way as natural phenomena. It showed that suicide was not simply an individual act but a product of social forces external to the individual. Its causes are to be found in society. It is the product of social facts, of 'real, living, active forces which, because of the way they determine the individual, prove their independence of him'.

Certain aspects of *Suicide* will now be examined to illustrate positivist methodology. Durkheim identified various types of suicide which are distinguished by the factors which are seen to cause them. One type, 'egoistic suicide', will be briefly examined. Durkheim began his study with a detailed analysis of official statistics on suicide from a number of European societies. He discovered that in each society the suicide rate was fairly constant over a period of years, that there were significant differences in the suicide rate between societies and between social groups

495

within each society. From these observations, Durkheim argued that suicide rates should be regarded as social facts. Since the rates varied systematically between societies, it may be assumed that they are socially determined. Thus Durkheim claimed that, 'Each society is predisposed to contribute a definite quota of voluntary deaths'. An explanation of differing rates of suicide therefore lies in an examination of society rather than an exploration of the consciousness of individuals.

From an analysis of the relationships between suicide rates and a range of social facts, Durkheim argued that the greater the integration of individuals within social groups, the less likely they were to commit suicide. Social integration is measured by the number and strength of a person's social relationships with others. Durkheim established various statistical correlations between suicide rates and the social situations of individuals. He found, for example, that Protestants had a higher rate of suicide than Catholics, city dwellers than rural dwellers, the unmarried than the married and older adults than younger adults. In each instance he claimed that the former have a lower level of social integration than the latter.

In the case of 'domestic society' which refers to family relationships, Durkheim argued that the more family ties binding the individual to the domestic group, the greater his social integration and the less likely he is to commit suicide. His research indicates that the unmarried person has the highest rate of suicide, followed by married people without children and the greater the number of children in the family, the less likely the parents are to commit suicide. In the case of 'religious society', Durkheim employed similar arguments. His research indicates that Protestant countries have a higher rate of suicide than Catholic countries and within the same society, Protestant communities have higher suicide rates than their Catholic counterparts. Durkheim argued that the Catholic religion integrates its members more strongly into a religious community. The long-established beliefs and traditional rituals of the Catholic church provide a uniform system of religious belief and practice into which the lives of its members are closely intertwined. The Catholic faith is rarely questioned and the church has strong controls over the conscience and behaviour of its members. The result is a homogeneous religious community, unified and integrated by uniform belief and standardized ritual. By comparison, the Protestant church encourages its members to develop their own interpretation of religion. Protestantism advocates 'free inquiry' rather than the imposition of traditional religious dogma. In Durkheim's view, 'The Protestant is far more the author of his faith'. As a result, Protestants are less likely to belong to a community which is unified by a commitment to common religious beliefs and practices. Durkheim concluded that the higher rate of suicide associated with Protestantism 'results from its being a less strongly integrated church than the Catholic church'.

Durkheim developed the following theory to explain the relationship between suicide rates and levels of social integration. Firstly, suicide is morally condemned in all European societies but the degree to which this moral imperative controls the behaviour of individuals is dependent on the level of social integration. In a highly integrated social group, control over the behaviour of individuals is strong. Thus there will be considerable moral pressure against suicide. However, where the level of social integration is low, the pressures preventing the individual from taking his own life will be relatively weak. Secondly, and more importantly, man is above all else a social being. His goals and values have been given to him by society. His sense of purpose and reason for being are found in society. According to Durkheim, 'Social man necessarily pre-supposes a society which he expresses and serves'. The greater his social isolation, the less the individual participates as a social being. As a result his life lacks purpose and meaning. Socialized to become a member of society, 'The individual alone is not a sufficient end for his activity. He is too little'. In this situation, 'The individual yields to the slightest shock of circumstance because the state of society has made him ready prey to suicide'.

Durkheim claimed that the study of suicide showed that behaviour was a product of social facts rather than individual motives. Since each society had a particular suicide rate which remained relatively constant over time, the cause of that rate was to be found in the nature of society, not in the nature of the individual. Thus Durkheim maintained that, 'There is, therefore, for each people (society) a collective force of a definite amount of energy, impelling men to self-destruction'. Although suicide appears to be a uniquely personal and private act, its causes lie in the nature of social groups. It is therefore a product of social forces which are external to and act upon the individual. By showing that 'suicide varies inversely with the degree of integration of the social groups of which the individual forms a part', Durkheim claimed to have demonstrated that 'real laws are discoverable' from the observation of human behaviour.

Durkheim's study of suicide has often been taken as a model for research methodology in sociology. A large body of research has been based on similar assumptions and conducted on similar lines. It has been judged successful because its findings are seen to be based on data which can be directly observed and measured. Its assumptions about the nature of man and society are seen to be justified because its findings appear to indicate that man's behaviour is shaped by forces external to his being. In Durkheim's terminology, human behaviour is determined by social facts.

Phenomenology and sociology

Phenomenological perspectives in sociology offer a radical alternative to positivist methodology. Following the usage adopted in the main part of the book, the term phenomenology will be applied to a number of related theoretical viewpoints. These will be distinguished in the final chapter. From a phenomenological perspective, there is a fundamental difference between the subject matter of the natural and social sciences. The natural sciences deal with matter. Since matter has no consciousness, its behaviour can be explained simply as a reaction to external stimuli. It is compelled to react in this way because its behaviour is essentially meaningless. Unlike matter, man has consciousness. He sees, interprets and experiences the world in terms of meanings; he actively constructs his own social reality. Meanings do not have an independent existence, a reality of their own which is somehow separate from social actors. They are not imposed by an external society which constrains members to act in certain ways. Instead they are constructed and reconstructed by actors in the course of social interaction.

To treat social reality as anything other than a construction of meanings is to distort it. This has serious implications for much of the work done in sociology. For example, to see official statistics on crime and suicide as referring to activities which have an objective reality of their own is to misunderstand their nature. Such statistics are simply the meanings given by social actors to events which they have perceived and interpreted as crime and suicide. Those events have no existence outside of the meanings and interpretive procedures which created them. The implications of this view for the study of suicide will now be considered.

In a series of writings on suicide, the British sociologist J. Maxwell Atkinson rejects the logic and procedures of positivist methodology. He maintains that the social world is a construction of actors' perceptions and subjective interpretations. As such it has no reality beyond the meanings given to it by social actors. Thus an act of suicide is simply that which is defined as suicide by social actors. Certain events come to be defined as suicide by coroners, medical practitioners, newspaper reporters, the family and friends of the deceased and so on. Definitions of suicide depend on their interpretations of the event. Sociologists who adopt a positivist approach assume that it is possible to determine objectively whether or not an act is suicide. From this it follows that the 'real' suicide rate, or at least an approximation of that rate, is discoverable. Atkinson rejects this assumption arguing that suicide is not an objective fact that can somehow be separated from the perceptions of social actors. It therefore makes no sense for sociologists to treat suicides as facts and seek to explain their cause. Instead Atkinson suggests that the appropriate question for sociologists to ask is, 'How do deaths get categorized as suicide?' An answer to this question involves an investigation of the meanings employed by those concerned with interpreting the cause of what is seen as unnatural death. Such an approach is least likely to distort the social world since it seeks to explore and understand the procedures used by its members to construct their social reality.

Before examining Atkinson's findings, the problems involved in using official statistics for research purposes will be considered from a positivist perspective. In theory a real, finite and absolute suicide rate for a given population exists. Official statistics, however, do not provide an accurate record of this rate. As such they do not represent the actual extent of suicide. Durkheim has often been criticized for failing to recognize the possibility of serious inaccuracies in the statistics he employed in his research. There was no systematic medical examination of the dead in Europe until the last half of the nineteenth century and even then, examinations in rural areas were less frequent and thorough than in urban areas. Since Durkheim's statistics were drawn from the 1840s to the 1870s they may well be subject to considerable error. Researchers have long recognized that the family and friends of the deceased may go to great lengths to disguise an apparent suicide. There is evidence to suggest that religious censure of suicide is stronger among Catholics than Protestants. As a result, Catholics may go to greater lengths to disguise a suicide. This may account in part for the differences Durkheim discovered between the suicide rates of Catholic and Protestant populations. A further source of error in official statistics results from the actions of those intending to commit suicide. Some individuals skillfully contrive their deaths in order to make them appear accidental. Research indicates that the procedures for investigating and recording unnatural death vary from society to society. Compared to other European societies, Sweden and Denmark have particularly high rates of suicide, but this may be due to the particular procedures used to investigate and classify unnatural death in those countries. Various studies conducted in America and Europe suggest that the official rate of suicide significantly underestimates the actual rate. For example, a study of suicide in Dublin by McCarthy and Walsh reached the conclusion that the actual rate was twice the official rate (discussed in Atkinson, 1978, pp. 50–52). Despite the recognized 'inaccuracies' and 'errors' of official statistics, many researchers have argued that by systematic investigation and improvements in research techniques it will be possible to establish, or at least closely approximate, the 'true rate' of suicide. Once the 'real facts' have been uncovered, it will then be possible to explain their cause.

Atkinson rejects this view. He does not accept that a 'real' rate of suicide exists as an objective reality waiting to be discovered. Sociologists who proceed with this assumption will end up producing 'facts' on suicide which have nothing to do with the social reality they seek to understand. By constructing a set of criteria to categorize and measure suicide – in scientific language by operationalizing the concept of suicide – they will merely be imposing their reality on the social world. This will inevitably distort that world. As Michael Phillipson observes, the positivist methodology employed by Durkheim and other researchers 'rides roughshod over the very social reality they are trying to comprehend'. Suicide is a construct of social actors, an aspect of social reality. Official statistics on suicide are not therefore 'wrong', 'mistaken', 'inaccurate' or 'in error'. They are a part of the social world. They are the interpretations made by officials of what is seen to be unnatural death. Since the object of sociology is to comprehend the social world, that world can only be understood in terms of the categories, perceptions and interpretations of its members. Thus, with reference to suicide, the appropriate question for sociologists to ask is, in Atkinson's words, 'How do deaths get categorized as suicide?'.

Atkinson's research focusses on the methods employed by coroners and their officers to categorize death. His data are drawn from discussions with coroners, attendance at inquests in three different towns, observation of a coroner's officer at work and a part of the records of one particular coroner. Atkinson argues that coroners have a 'common-sense theory' of suicide. If information about the deceased fits the theory they are likely to categorize his or her death as suicide. In terms of this theory, coroners consider the following types of evidence relevant for reaching a verdict. Firstly, whether or not suicide notes were left or threats of suicide preceded death. Secondly, particular modes of dying are judged to be more or less likely to indicate suicide. Road deaths are rarely interpreted as an indicator for suicide whereas drowning, hanging, gassing and drug overdose are more likely to be seen as such. Thirdly, the location and circumstances of death are judged to be relevant. For example, death by gunshot is more likely to be defined as suicide if it occurred in a deserted lay-by than if it took place in the countryside during an organized shoot. In cases of gassing, a suicide verdict is more likely if windows, doors and ventilators have been blocked to prevent the escape of gas. Fourthly, coroners consider the biography of the deceased with particular reference to his or her mental state and social situation. A history of mental illness, a disturbed childhood and evidence of acute depression are often seen as reasons for suicide. A recent divorce, the death of a close relative, a lack of friends, problems at work or serious financial difficulties are regarded as possible causes for suicide. Referring to the case of an individual found gassed in his car, a coroner told Atkinson, 'There's a classic pattern for you – broken home, escape to the services, nervous breakdown, unsettled at work, no family ties – what could be clearer'. Thus coroners' views about why people commit suicide appear to influence their categorization of death.

Coroners' common-sense theories of suicide contain explanations of the causes of suicide. If information about the deceased's background fits these explanations, then a verdict of suicide is likely. Atkinson provides the following summary of the procedures used to categorize unnatural death. Coroners 'are engaged in analysing features of the deaths and of the biographies of the deceased according to a variety of taken-for-granted assumptions about what constitutes a "typical suicide", "a typical suicide biography", and so on'. Suicide can therefore be seen as an interpretation placed on an event, an interpretation which stems from a set of taken-for-granted assumptions. This view has serious implications for research which treats official statistics on suicide as 'facts' and seeks to explain their cause. Researchers who look for explanations of suicide in the social background or mental state of the deceased may simply be uncovering and making explicit the taken-for-granted assumptions of coroners. Atkinson found that coroners' theories of suicide were remarkably similar to those of sociologists and psychologists. Since coroners use their theories of the cause of suicide as a means for categorizing suicide, this similarity might be expected. Thus social scientists who look for the causes of suicide in the social situation or mental condition of those officially classified as suicides may simply be revealing the common-sense theories of coroners.

Atkinson's conclusions are echoed by Aaron V. Cicourel in his study of juvenile justice outlined in Chapter 10 (pp. 434–5). The categories of crime and criminal cannot be treated as objective facts with causes which can be explained. Instead they are constructions of meaning placed on certain individuals and actions which are seen to be of a certain kind. Researchers who treat official statistics on crime as facts and then attempt to explain their cause may simply reveal the assumptions used by police and probation officers to categorize what they see as crime. Thus sociologists who explain crime as a response to broken homes, low income, inner city poverty and the like may merely be uncovering the common-sense theories of crime employed by the agents of social control. As Atkinson suggested for suicide, the appropriate question for sociologists who study crime is, 'How do actions come to be categorized as criminal?'.

From a phenomenological perspective, the social world is a world of meaning. There is no objective reality which lies behind that meaning. Thus the social world is not made up of entities which are external to the subjective experience of its members. To treat its aspects as 'social facts', as 'things', is to distort and misrepresent social reality. Thus sociologists who treat crime and suicide as anything other than constructions of meaning are imposing their own reality on the social world and so distorting the very reality they seek to understand.

Clearly positivist and phenomenological perspectives employ very different research methodologies. They proceed from diametrically opposed assumptions about the nature of social reality. This leads on the one hand to an acceptance of the logic and methods of the natural sciences as appropriate for the study of man and, on the other, to an outright rejection of this research strategy. The result is conflicting views on the nature of evidence and explanation. In particular there is a basic disagreement about the essential qualities and characteristics of the data of sociological research. This leads to very different explanations and understandings of human action.

Research methods

In practice, the distinctions between positivist and phenomenological research methodologies are not as clear cut as the previous sections have implied. They have been placed at opposite ends of the spectrum for purposes of emphasis and illustration. A large body of sociological research falls somewhere between the two extremes. In the same way, the methods of data collection discussed in the following sections cannot be neatly categorized as aspects of positivist or phenomenological methodologies. However, certain methods are regarded as more appropriate by supporters of one or other of these perspectives.

Participant observation

Apart from using one way observation screens or observing from a distance, all observation is to some degree participant observation – the observer takes part to some extent in the activities of those he observes. As a means for gathering data, participant observation has a long history in sociology. It has been used by researchers with widely differing theoretical perspectives. As such it is a research technique which has been adapted to meet the requirements of sociologists with various views on the nature of social reality.

The participant observer joins the everyday routines of those he wishes to study. He attempts to observe action in its 'normal', 'natural' context. Thus he may join a group of workers in a factory or a teenage gang on the streetcorner, he may accompany policemen on the beat or spend time with patients in a mental hospital. As a means of directly observing action in everyday social contexts, participant observation has a particular appeal to those who adopt phenomenological perspectives. The reasons for this may be illustrated by the logic and methods employed by Aaron V. Cicourel in his study of juvenile justice. Cicourel assumes that juvenile delinquency is generated by the 'everyday activities' of police, probation officers and court officials in their interaction with juveniles. He also assumes that juveniles are categorized in terms of the taken-for-granted assumptions held by officials. These taken-for-granted assumptions are not made explicit, they are an unconsidered part of everyday activity. To uncover them therefore requires direct observation of routine interactions between officials and juveniles. Requesting officials to fill out a questionnaire or answer questions in an interview situation would be unlikely to reveal the ways in which they categorized juveniles simply because those ways are taken-for-granted. Officials are therefore largely unaware of the interpretive procedures they employ. Since these procedures are triggered and developed in routine interaction, direct observation of everyday activity is necessary in order to uncover them. Thus Cicourel argues that in order to understand 'the actor's conception of objects and events', the sociologist must examine the 'routine, practical activities of everyday life'.

Cicourel spent over four years observing interaction in juvenile courts, police and probation departments. Part of this time was spent as an unpaid probation officer. He was concerned with discovering the interpretive procedures used by officials to categorize juveniles. He paid particular attention to the meanings they gave to the appearance, speech and manner of juveniles. From examining the subtle cues and nuances of interaction, Cicourel makes observations such as, 'a juvenile's tone of voice is often the basis for a police officer or probation officer or judge calling the juvenile's behaviour "in defiance of authority" or an indication of a "bad attitude"'. Cicourel observed how officials selected particular items, such as evidence of a poor school performance and previous trouble with the police, from records on the juvenile's background. On the basis of this kind of information, officials made inferences about the juvenile's character and motives which led to assessments such as 'poor risk for probation' and 'born loser'. From these and similar observations, Cicourel claims to show that interaction in juvenile courts, police and probation departments proceeds on the basis of a set of taken-for-granted assumptions in terms of which juveniles are categorized.

Cicourel's study relies heavily on his observational and interpretive skills. This immediately raises the problem of the 'validity' of his findings. How is he able to verify that the taken-for-granted assumptions which he identifies are in fact those employed by the actors concerned? Simply by asking them to verify his findings will not solve the problem since actors are largely unaware of the assumptions they employ. Cicourel admits that 'the complications are enormous' when it comes to the unequivocal identification of the meanings which actors assign to a tone of voice, a gesture, a phrase or a mode of dress. He presents lengthy extracts from conversations between probation officers and juveniles coupled with detailed descriptions of the interaction to allow the reader to judge for himself. While this may convince the reader of Cicourel's findings, it does not solve the problem of validity. It merely places the reader in a similar position to the author and asks him to make his own interpretations. At the end of the day, many would argue that the problem of validity is insoluble. Others must simply rely on the interpretive skills of the observer and make a judgment on the evidence he presents. Despite this problem, however, supporters of participant observation have claimed that it provides the best available means of discovering social reality. Compared to other research techniques, it brings the sociologist closer to the social world which he seeks to understand.

The authors of many of the classic studies in sociology have used participant observation as a means for gathering their data. Two such studies will now be examined to illustrate the procedures involved and the possible advantages and disadvantages of this research technique. *Street Corner Society: The Social Structure of an Italian Slum* by William Foote Whyte is a study of an Italian American streetcorner gang in a low-income district of south Boston. Whyte spent three and a half years living in the area as a participant observer. *Tally's Corner: A Study of Negro Streetcorner Men* by Elliot Liebow is a study of Black American men who hung out on the streetcorner in a low-income inner city district of Washington DC (parts of this research are discussed in Chapter 4, pp. 157–9). Liebow spent a year conducting participant observation in the area.

Supporters of participant observation have argued that, compared to other research techniques, it is least likely to lead to the sociologist imposing his reality on the social world he seeks to understand. It therefore provides the best means of obtaining a valid picture of social reality. With a structured interview – a predetermined set of questions which the interviewee is requested to answer – or a questionnaire – a set of printed questions to which the respondent is asked to provide written answers – the sociologist has already decided what is important. With preset questions he imposes his framework and priorities on those he wishes to study. By assuming the questions are relevant to his respondents he has already made many assumptions about their social world. Although the participant observer begins his work with some preconceived ideas, for example he will usually have studied the existing literature on the topic he is to investigate, he at least has the opportunity to directly observe the social world. The value of this opportunity is clear from Whyte's observation, 'As I sat and listened, I learned the answers to questions I would not have had the sense to ask if I had been getting my information solely on an interviewing basis'. Intensive observation over a period of years provided Whyte with a picture of what was important in the lives of the Italian Americans he studied. Without this exposure to their daily routine he would have remained ignorant of many of their priorities. Had he relied solely on interviews, this ignorance would have prevented him from asking important and relevant questions.

Liebow was particularly concerned about the danger of distorting the reality he wished to observe. He states that from the outset of his research, 'there were by design, no firm presumptions of what or was not relevant'. He did his best to simply look and listen and to avoid any preconceptions of what was or was not important. Liebow chose participant observation because he believed that method would provide a 'clear, firsthand picture' of the 'life of ordinary people, on their grounds and on their terms'. By observing what was said and done, where, when and by whom, he hoped to discover how a group of Black streetcorner men saw and organized their lives. Liebow claims that, 'Taking this inside view makes it easier to avoid structuring the material in ways that might be alien to the material itself'.

The success of participant observation depends initially upon the acceptance of the observer by the group he wishes to study. The presence of a stranger requires some form of explanation. Whyte told members of the gang that he intended to write a book about the area. However, he found that 'acceptance in the district depended on the personal relationships I developed far more than any explanations I might give'. Whyte gained the friendship of key individuals in the group. In particular, Doc, the gang leader, became his sponsor and the rest of the group followed Doc's lead. Liebow's experience was similar. He gained the trust and friendship of Tally, the dominant personality on the streetcorner, and this led to his acceptance by the rest of the group.

Once accepted, a major problem for the participant observer is that his presence will to some degree influence the actions of those he observes. In this way he may modify or change the social world he wishes to investigate. Whyte was well aware of this problem. He writes, 'I tried to avoid influencing the group, because I wanted to study the situation as unaffected by my presence as possible'. To this end he tried not to make decisions for the group and avoided 'accepting office or leadership positions'. He refrained from passing moral judgments on sensitive issues and tried, whenever possible, to blend into the background and watch and listen but to some degree, his presence must have influenced the actions of others. As Doc once told him, 'You've slowed me down plenty since you've been here. Now, when I do something, I have to think what Bill Whyte would want to know about it and how I can explain it. Before I used to do things by instinct'. As a middle-class White Jew, Liebow's presence in a group of lower class Blacks might be expected to significantly change their everyday routines. However, he found that, 'The disadvantage of being white was offset by the fact that, as an outsider, I was not a competitor. I had no "vested interests"'. Liebow adapted his speech and dress to fit in with the streetcorner men without trying to ape or mimic them. He still remained fairly conspicuous but by making these changes he claims that, 'I probably made myself more accessible to others and certainly more acceptable to myself'.

Once accepted by the group, both Whyte and Liebow believed that their presence produced few if any significant changes in its normal round of everyday activities. They joined those activities rather than changed them. Whyte went bowling, dancing, hung round on the streetcorner and visited cafés and bars with members of the gang. Liebow participated in similar activities. Whyte writes, 'I began as a non-participating observer. As I became accepted into the community, I found myself becoming almost a non-observing participant'. There is a danger that by becoming too involved, the observer may lose his detachment, take too much for granted and dull the sharpness of his observation. Yet such involvement means that the observer has been accepted by the group. It is therefore reasonable to assume that those he observes will act normally and naturally in his presence. Both Whyte and Liebow argue that rather than changing the activities of those they observed, they blended into and became a part of those activities.

To be successful, the participant observer must gain the trust of those he observes. Only when Liebow gained Tally's trust did Tally admit that he had lied to him at the start of their acquaintance. The close and relatively long lasting relationships established through participant observation provide greater opportunities for developing trust than are provided by other research techniques. Interviews and questionnaire surveys usually involve one-off, shortlived encounters. Particularly with groups such as low-income Blacks and teenage gangs, a relationship of trust is necessary to secure cooperation. As Lewis Yablonsky notes from his research on teenage gangs, 'Their characteristic response to questionnaires investigating the gang's organization or personal activities is one of suspicion and distrust. To the gang boy every researcher could be a "cop"'. In this type of situation participant observation might well provide more valid data than other research techniques.

Those who argue that research methods in sociology should be drawn from the natural sciences are often highly critical of participant observation. In particular they argue that the data obtained from participant observation lack 'reliability'. In the natural sciences data are seen to be reliable, if other researchers using the same methods of investigation on the same material produce the same results. By replicating an experiment it is possible to check for errors in observation and measurement. Once reliable data have been obtained, generalizations can then be made about the behaviour observed. No sociologist would claim that the social sciences can attain the standards of reliability employed in the natural sciences. Many would argue, however, that sociological data can attain a certain standard of reliability. They criticize participant observation for its failure to approach this standard. The data obtained by participant observation are seen to be unreliable because, as a method, its procedures are not made explicit, its observations are unsystematic and its results are rarely quantified. Thus there is no way of replicating a study and checking the reliability of its findings. As Whyte admits, 'To some extent my approach must be unique to myself, to the particular situation, and to the state of knowledge existing when I began research'. Since participant observation relies heavily on the sensitivity, interpretive skills and personality of the observer, precise replication of studies using this method are difficult if not impossible. As a result it is not possible to generalize from such studies. Their value is seen to lie in providing useful insights which can then be tested on larger samples using more rigorous and systematic methods. Only then will it be possible to make generalizations about the behaviour of groups such as Italian American gangs and Black streetcorner men.

The above criticisms derive mainly from those who adopt a strongly positivist approach. Others would argue that what the findings of participant observation lack in reliability, they often more than make up for in validity. By coming face to face with social reality, the participant observer at least has the opportunity to make valid observations. Many would argue that the systematic questionnaire surveys favoured by many positivists have little or no chance of tapping the real social world.

Interviews

Interviews are one of the most widely used methods of gathering data in sociology. They consist of the researcher asking the interviewee or respondent a series of questions. Interviews can be classified as 'structured' or 'unstructured' though many fall somewhere between these two extremes. In a structured interview, the wording of the questions and the order in which they are asked remains the same in every case. The result is a fairly formal question and answer session. Unstructured interviews are more like an informal conversation. The interviewer usually has particular topics in mind to cover but few if any preset questions. He has the freedom to phrase questions as he likes, ask the respondent to develop his answers and probe responses which might be unclear and ambiguous. This freedom is often extended to the respondent who may be allowed to direct the interview into areas which interest him.

Data from structured interviews are generally regarded as more reliable. Since the order and wording of questions are the same for all respondents, it is more likely that they will be responding to the same stimuli. Thus different answers to the same set of questions will indicate real differences between the respondents. Different answers will not therefore simply reflect differences in the way questions are phrased. Thus the more structured or standardized an interview, the more easily its results can be tested by researchers investigating other groups. By comparison data from unstructured interviews are seen as less reliable. Questions are phrased in a variety of ways and the relationship between interviewer and respondent is likely to be more intimate. It is unclear to what degree answers are influenced by these factors. Differences between respondents may simply reflect differences in the nature of the interviews. It is therefore more difficult to replicate an unstructured interview but the greater flexibility of unstructured interviews may strengthen the validity of the data. They provide more opportunity to discover what the respondent 'really means'. Ambiguities in questions and answers can be clarified and the interviewer can probe for shades of meaning.

In general, structured interviews are regarded as appropriate for obtaining answers to questions of 'fact' such as the age, sex and job of the respondent. Unstructured interviews are seen as more appropriate for eliciting attitudes and opinions. As the chapter on religion indicated, it is very difficult to obtain valid data on religious commitment from a structured interview. If a respondent replied, 'Yes', to the question, 'Do you believe in God?', this says very little about the nature and strength of his religious belief. Though further questions might amplify his views, a clearer picture is likely to emerge from the more conversational setting of the unstructured interview.

Interview data are often taken as indications of respondents' attitudes and behaviour in everyday life although what a person says in an interview may have little to do with his normal routines. Even if the respondent does his best to provide honest answers, he may be unaware, as Cicourel's study suggests, of the taken-for-granted assumptions which he employs in everyday life. William F. Whyte's research shows that, contrary to accepted views, slum life in south Boston could not be characterized as 'socially disorganized'. The streetcorner gang had a 'complex and well-established organization of its own'. This was not explicitly recognized by its members; their behaviour was largely 'unreflective'. Participant observation therefore provides opportunities to gather data which might not be forthcoming in interviews. However interviews do have certain advantages. They are less costly and time-consuming and can cover much larger samples. The participant observer is limited to small numbers. For example Liebow's study involved only two dozen streetcorner men. In addition the participant observer is limited by the fact he can only be in one place at one time. Interviews can fill in the picture by providing data on the respondent's past and his activities in a range of contexts.

Various studies have suggested, though, that interviews pose serious problems of reliability and validity. This is partly due to the fact that interviews are interaction situations. Thus the results of an interview will depend in part on the way the participants define the situation, their perceptions of each other and so on. As Labov's observations of Black schoolchildren, discussed in Chapter 5 (pp. 208–9) indicate, variations in context and interviewer can result in important changes in the information volunteered. Most studies have been concerned about the effects of interviewers on respondents. The significance of what has come to be known as 'interviewer bias' can be seen from research conducted by J. Allan Williams Jr. He suggests that the greater the status differences between interviewer and respondent, the less likely the respondent will be to express his true feelings. To test this proposition, Williams organized a series of interviews with 840 Blacks in North Carolina during the early 1960s. All the interviewers were female, thirteen were Black and nine White. Important differences were revealed between the results obtained by Black and White interviewers. For example, a significantly higher proportion of those interviewed by Blacks said they approved of civil rights demonstrations and school desegregation. In addition more respondents refused to give any answers to these questions when faced with a White interviewer. Williams argues that Blacks often tended to give the answers they felt that White interviewers wanted to hear. He sees this as due to the nature of the power structure in the American South at the time of the research. Williams's findings suggest that when status differences are wide, as is often the case with middle-class sociologists interviewing members of the lower working class, interview data should be regarded with caution.

Interviewers, like everybody else, have values, attitudes and expectations. However much the interviewer tries to disguise his views they may well be communicated to the respondent. This is particularly likely in the more informal situation of the unstructured interview. As a result the interviewer may 'lead' the respondent whose answers will then reflect something of the interviewer's attitudes and expectations. This can be seen from a study conducted by Stuart A. Rice in 1914 (discussed in Deming, 1971, p. 347). Two thousand destitute men were asked, among other things, to explain their situation. There was a strong tendency for those interviewed by a supporter of prohibition to blame their demise on alcohol but those interviewed by a committed socialist were much more likely to explain their plight in terms of the industrial situation. The interviewers apparently had their own views on the reasons for destitution which they communicated to the respondents. It appears that the down and outs were only too glad to please anyone who showed an interest in them.

To counter this problem, interviewers are often advised to be 'nondirective', to refrain from offering opinions, to avoid expressions of approval and disapproval. It is suggested they establish 'rapport' with their respondents, that is a warm, friendly relationship which implies sympathy and understanding, while at the same time guard against communicating their own attitudes and expectations. Yet Howard Becker suggests that interviewers may be inhibited by adopting this relatively passive approach and a 'bland, polite style of conversation'. He suggests that on certain occasions, a more active and aggressive approach can provide much fuller data. This involves the interviewer taking 'positions on some issues' and using 'more aggressive conversational tactics'. Becker adopted these tactics in his interviews with Chicago schoolteachers (discussed in Chapter 5, p. 209). He claims that American schoolteachers believe they have a lot to hide from what they regard as a 'prying, misunderstanding, and potentially dangerous public'. They are therefore unlikely to volunteer certain information. By adopting an aggressive stance, being skeptical and at times even playing dumb, Becker managed to prize out much of this information. In particular he claimed to have uncovered the ways in which teachers categorized and evaluated students in terms of their class and ethnic backgrounds, information they would prefer to keep hidden for fear of being accused of prejudice and discrimination. Becker states, 'I coerced many interviewees into being considerably more frank than they had originally intended'. He suggests that this approach is particularly useful for one-off interviews. Similar information can be picked up more subtly over a series of interviews without running the risk of antagonizing respondents. The apparent success of Becker's rather unorthodox tactics suggests that there is no one best way of interviewing.

Interviews involve words and phrases; interviewers are usually middle class and White. Since the meanings of words and phrases vary from one social group to another, interview questions can mean different things to members of different social groups. To take an obvious example, the word 'uptight' in low-income Black American areas usually refers to a close relationship between friends. However when it entered the vocabulary of mainstream America, it changed its meaning to anxious and tense. Even common words and phrases carry different associations for different groups. As Irwin Deutscher observes, 'Within a society, as well as between societies, the sociologist seeks information from and about people who operate verbally with different vocabularies, different grammars and different kinds of sounds'. Thus a structured interview, which provides little opportunity to qualify meaning, might not provide comparable data when administered to members of different social groups. This problem will be examined in greater detail in the following section.

Members of different social groups may also attach different meanings to the content of questions. For example, certain activities may be regarded as more 'socially desirable' by members of one group than by members of another. As a result there may be differences between social groups in terms of their members' willingness to admit to particular activities. The importance of this can be seen from a study conducted by Bruce Dohrenwend in New York to investigate the relationship between mental health and ethnicity (discussed in Phillips, 1971, pp. 41–44). Respondents were asked whether or not they had experienced a list of symptoms associated with mental illness. Compared with Jews, Irish and Blacks, Puerto Ricans reported experiencing more of the symptoms and therefore appeared to have a higher rate of mental illness. Yet Dohrenwend found that the symptoms were regarded as less undesirable by Puerto Ricans than by members of the other ethnic groups. As a result they were more ready to admit to them. A study by Derek Phillips and Kevin Clancy produced similar findings with reference to social class. It indicated that members of the lower class were more willing to report a range of symptoms associated with mental illness than members of other social classes. This reflects class differences in judgments of the social desirability of the items in question. Such findings cast serious doubt on the validity of interview data and therefore on the use to which that data is put. Thus there may be few, if any, grounds for arguing, on the basis of such data, that mental illness is a lower class 'problem' resulting from the assumed strains and stresses of lower class life. As Derek Phillips suggests, the frequently discovered relationship between social class and mental health may well be due 'to a greater willingness of lower class persons to *admit to* or *report* certain behaviours and experiences which middle and upper class persons regard as highly undesirable'.

In view of the many problems associated with interviews, it might seem reasonable to abandon them. However, this is probably too drastic a step. Sociologists are aware of the problems involved and are increasingly refining interviewing techniques. On the positive side, some of the most interesting and original insights in sociology have emerged from interview data. Elizabeth Bott's research on conjugal roles, reported in Chapter 8 (pp. 358–60), provides an example. Bott conducted an average of thirteen unstructured interviews with husbands and wives in twenty London families. She began with a few vague ideas and gradually focussed on the relationship between the spouses' social networks and their conjugal roles. From ideas which developed in the course of her interviews, Bott produced one of the most original insights in the sociology of the family.

Questionnaires

A questionnaire consists of a list of preset questions to which respondents are asked to supply answers. Questionnaires may be administered by an interviewer in which case they take the form of structured interviews. Researchers who use questionnaires regard them as a comparatively cheap, fast and efficient method for obtaining large amounts of quantifiable data on relatively large numbers of people.

Examples of the types of questions used will now be examined. They are drawn from the questionnaire used in the affluent worker study by Goldthorpe and Lockwood (see Chapters 2, pp. 57–61 and 6, pp. 248–51)

Questions usually fall into the following categories. Firstly, questions may be 'open-ended'. For example, 'This firm has an exceptionally good industrial relations record. Why do you think this is?' Open-ended questions allow the respondent to compose his own answer rather than choosing between a number of given answers. This may provide more valid data since he can say what he means in his own words. However, this kind of response may be difficult to classify and quantify. Answers must be carefully interpreted before the researcher is able to say that a certain percentage of respondents attribute good industrial relations to effective management, an efficient trade union, high pay or whatever.

A second type of question, sometimes known as a 'closed' or 'fixed-choice' question, requires a choice between a number of given answers. For example, 'How about the idea of becoming a foreman? Would you like this very much, quite a lot, not much or not at all?' Sometimes the respondent is asked to choose between two stated alternatives. For example, 'Which would you prefer: a job where someone tells you exactly how to do the work or one where you are left to decide for yourself how to go about it?' A similar type of question requires the respondent to agree or disagree with a particular statement. For example, 'Some people say that trade unions have too much power in the country: would you agree or disagree, on the whole?' Compared to the open-ended type, fixed-choice questions provide responses which can be more easily classified and quantified. It requires relatively little time, effort and ingenuity to arrive at statements such as, 46% of affluent workers would very much like the idea of becoming a foreman and, of those who are members of trade unions, 41% agree that unions have too much power. However, fixed-choice questions do not allow the respondent to qualify and develop his answer. It is therefore difficult for the researcher to know exactly what he is measuring. Thus when a respondent agrees with the statement that trade unions have too much power does he mean too much power over their members, over management, over the Labour Party or over the government? Other questions can be included to obtain further information -- in fact Goldthorpe and Lockwood include a number of questions about workers' attitudes to trade unions. Yet many would argue that an unstructured interview would be required to examine as complex an area as trade union power.

Questionnaires may be administered in a number of ways. Often they are given to individuals by interviewers, in which case they take the form of structured interviews. This method was used by Goldthorpe and Lockwood in the affluent worker study and by Young and Willmott in their survey of family life in London conducted in 1970. (See Chapter 8, pp. 350–53.) It has the advantage of having a trained interviewer on hand to make sure the questionnaire is completed according to instructions and to clarify any ambiguous questions. But questionnaires administered by interviewers involve the problem of 'interviewer bias' discussed in the previous section. In addition this method is expensive compared to the following alternatives. The postal questionnaire, as its name suggests, is mailed to respondents with a stamped addressed envelope for return to the researcher. It provides an inexpensive way of gathering data, especially if respondents are dispersed over a wide geographical area. The return rate, though, does not often exceed 50% of the sample population and is sometimes below 25%. This may seriously bias the results since there may be systematic differences between those who return questionnaires and those who do not. For example, the main response to a postal questionnaire on marital relationships might come from those experiencing marital problems and wishing to air their grievances. If most non-respondents were happily married, the researcher would be unjustified in making generalizations about married life on the basis of his returns. A far higher return rate is usually obtained when questionnaires are administered to a group such as a class of students or workers at a trade union meeting. This method is less expensive than dealing with individual respondents while maintaining the advantages of the presence of an interviewer. However, the interviewer must ensure that respondents do not discuss questions within the group since this might affect their answers.

Once a survey has begun, the questionnaire cannot be changed since the object of the exercise is to present all respondents with the same stimuli and so obtain comparable data. Great care is therefore needed in the design of a questionnaire. Sometimes the main survey is preceded by a 'pilot study' which involves giving the questionnaire to a group similar to the population to be surveyed. This helps to clear up any ambiguity in the wording of questions and to ensure their relevance to future respondents. For example, there would be little point in asking affluent workers a series of questions about their experience of unemployment if the vast majority has never been out of work. Ideally the questions should mean the same thing to all respondents. As the previous section has indicated, this is extremely difficult to ensure, particularly if respondents are drawn from different social classes and ethnic groups. In addition, the researcher must be aware of the meaning respondents give to the question. He cannot simply assume that they will share his interpretation. The danger of making this assumption can be seen from the following example. A Gallup poll survey in 1939 found that 88% of a sample of the US population described themselves as middle class, a result which surprised the researchers. Respondents were offered a choice of three alternatives, 'upper', 'middle' and 'lower' class. The survey was repeated shortly afterwards and the term 'lower' class was replaced by 'working' class. Now 51% of the sample classified itself as working class. There was no indication of a radical shift in class identification in America. Instead, the results suggest that different meanings were attached to the terms lower and working class, (discussed in Worsley, 1977, p. 428). Researchers must be aware of such meanings if they are to make any sense of their data.

Questionnaires provide data which can be easily quantified. They are largely designed for this purpose. Studies which employ questionnaires abound with statements such as 87% of affluent workers are members of trade unions (Goldthorpe and Lockwood, 1969) and 61% of assembly line workers find their jobs dull and monotonous (Blauner, 1964). Those who adopt a positivist approach insist that this kind of measurement is essential if sociology is to progress. They argue that only when the social world is expressed in numerical terms can precise relationships be established between its parts. Only when data are quantified by means of reliable measuring instruments can the results of different studies be directly compared. Without quantification sociology will remain on the level of impressionistic guesswork and unsupported insight. It will therefore be impossible to replicate studies, establish causal relationships and support

Sociology

generalizations. The questionnaire is one of the main tools of measurement in positivist sociology. Questionnaire design will now be considered from this perspective.

In the construction of a questionnaire concepts are operationalized. This means they are put into a form which can be measured. Sociologists classify the social world in terms of a variety of concepts. For example, social class, power, family, religion, alienation and anomie are concepts used to identify and categorize social relationships, beliefs, attitudes and experiences which are seen to have certain characteristics in common. In order to transpose these rather vague concepts into measuring instruments, a number of steps are taken. Firstly, an operational definition is established. This involves breaking the concept down into various 'components' or 'dimensions' in order to specify exactly what is to be measured. Thus when Robert Blauner attempted to operationalize the concept of alienation, he divided it into four components – powerlessness, meaninglessness, isolation and self-estrangement. (See Chapter 6, pp. 242–3.) Similarly when Stark and Glock operationalized the concept of religion, they constructed five 'core dimensions of religiousness'. (See Chapter 11, p. 488.) Once the concept has been operationally defined in terms of a number of components, the next step involves the selection of 'indicators' for each component. Thus an indicator of Blauner's component of powerlessness might be an absence of opportunities for workers to make decisions about the organization of work tasks. Indicators of 're-ligious practice', one of Stark and Glock's 'dimensions of religiousness', might include attendance at a place of worship and acts of prayer. Finally, indicators of each dimension are put into the form of a series of questions which will provide quantifiable data for measuring each dimension. Thus indicators of 'religious practice' may be transposed into the following questions: 'How often do you attend church?' and 'How often do you pray?' Once questions have been constructed, the concept is then operationalized.

Whether such procedures succeed in producing valid measurements of human behaviour is open to question. Those who adopt phenomenological perspectives often reject the entire procedure of operational definitions, selecting indicators, constructing questionnaires and quantifying the results. They argue that rather than providing a valid picture of the social world, such operations merely serve to distort it. Since the social world is constructed by its members, the job of the sociologist is to investigate members' constructs. Positivist research procedures merely impose sociological constructs, categories and logic on that world. Thus when Blauner seeks to measure alienation, he is employing a concept which may have no reality in the social world he hopes to understand. As a result workers' responses to a questionnaire may have little or nothing to do with what the researcher is trying to measure. Indeed Blauner admits that, 'It is difficult to interpret a finding that 70% of factory workers report satisfaction with their jobs because we do not know how valid or reliable our measuring instrument is'. From a phenomenological view, the appropriate procedure is not to measure degrees of job satisfaction. Instead the sociologist should discover whether workers categorize jobs in terms of satisfaction and if so, investigate the procedures they employ to arrive at this categorization. This involves an exploration of the ways in which actors construct social reality rather than imposing sociological categories and measuring instruments on the social world. Stark and Glock's operational definition of religion is open to similar criticism. They admit that 'the term religiousness is used in a number of different ways and is subject to a great deal of ambiguity in conventional usage'. Rather than accepting this variety and ambiguity as an aspect of social reality and therefore as worthy of study, they impose their own definition of religion on the social world. In doing so they impose an order and system which might have no place in that world. As Michael Phillipson observes, 'the instruments of the observer create the very order they are supposedly designed to reveal'. Thus Stark and Glock's operational definition of religion may have little correspondence with the social reality they seek to understand. From a phenomenological perspective, an understanding of religion can only be approached by investigating how members themselves construct the category of religion. This critique suggests that positivist sociologists end up by constructing their own version of social reality which may have little correspondence with the actual social world they are trying to describe and explain.

Social surveys

Questionnaires and structured interviews are the usual methods employed to gather data for a research design known as the 'social survey'. A social survey involves the collection of standardized information from a sample selected as being representative of a particular group or population. The group from which the sample is drawn may be the population as a whole, a particular class, ethnic, gender or age group, or individuals with certain characteristics in common such as married or divorced persons, manual workers or professionals. The group selected for study will, of course, depend on what the researcher wishes to investigate. Standardized information is obtained by asking the same set of questions to all members of the sample.

Social surveys may be roughly divided into two categories, 'descriptive' and 'analytical'. A descriptive survey, as its name suggests, is concerned with description rather than explanation. It aims to provide an accurate measurement of the distribution of certain characteristics in a given population. Rowntree's surveys of York, discussed in Chapter 4 (pp. 144–5), are examples of a descriptive survey. They aimed to measure the extent of poverty in a given population rather than to explain the causes of poverty. Analytic surveys are concerned with explanation.

They are designed to test hypotheses about the relationships between a number of factors or variables. Thus an analytic survey may seek to discover possible relationships between social class and religious behaviour, ethnicity and mental health, family size and educational attainment or age and voting behaviour. Analytic surveys are not simply concerned with discovering relationships but also with explaining them, a point which will be examined shortly.

Since it is usually impracticable to administer a questionnaire to all members of the group concerned, a sample is selected to represent the group as a whole. If generalizations are to be made from the findings of a social survey, it is essential that the sample is representative. This means it must share the characteristics of the group from which it is drawn. This is often accomplished by means of a 'random sample'. A number is given to each individual in the group under investigation and a set of random numbers is then used to select the members of the sample. In this way each individual has a known probability of being selected. By means of random sampling the researcher can predict with some assurance that the sample is representative of the group as a whole. The importance of representative sampling can be seen from the famous case of the *Literary Digest* poll in 1936. The magazine polled its readership with the aim of predicting the results of the US presidential election. The poll forecast a Republican president whereas in fact a Democrat was elected to the White House. In addition the number of votes predicted for each candidate was substantially different from the election results. The failure of the poll can be largely accounted for by the fact that the readership of *Literary Digest* was primarily middle class. As such it was not representative of the US electorate. A random sample of the voting population would have been far more likely to provide an accurate prediction (discussed in Franklin and Osborne, 1971, p. 162).

Random sampling can be refined by a technique known as 'stratified sampling'. This reduces the risk of a random selection producing an unrepresentative sample. The population from which the sample is to be drawn is divided into 'strata' in terms of particular characteristics. Thus strata may consist of members of the same social class, gender, age or ethnic group. Individuals are then randomly selected from each strata in proportion to their presence in the population under investigation. For example, if women make up 60% of that population, then 60% of the female stratum will be selected to form the sample. Thus stratified sampling is more likely to ensure that the sample is representative of the population from which it is drawn than a simple random selection. Once the researcher is satisfied that he has obtained a representative sample, he can begin the survey proper and feel some justification in generalizing from its findings.

Analytic surveys are usually designed to test the effects of a number of variables or factors on some other variable. The researcher often begins with a hypothesis which postulates a relationship between variables and the direction of cause and effect. For example, he may suggest that social class differences in some way cause or determine variations in mental health. There may be other factors affecting mental health, however, and these must also be considered if the influence of social class is to be accurately assessed. For example, variables such as age, ethnicity and gender may account for some variation in mental health. As a result researchers usually gather data on a range of factors which might influence the variable in question.

The method used to analyse relationships between variables is known as 'multivariate' or 'variable analysis'. With the aid of various statistical techniques, the analyst attempts to measure the effects of a number of variables upon another. This method was pioneered in sociology by Durkheim in his study of suicide. Official statistics revealed significant variations in suicide rates between European societies. Durkheim's research indicated that predominantly Protestant societies had a higher rate of suicide than societies in which Catholicism was the majority faith. But before a causal relationship could be claimed between religion and suicide rates, it was necessary to eliminate other possibilities. For example, could variations in suicide rates be the result of differences in national cultures? To test this possibility, Durkheim held the variable of national culture constant by examining differences in suicide rates between Catholics and Protestants within the same society. The relationship still held. Within the same society Protestants had higher suicide rates than Catholics. Durkheim then went a step further and examined the possibility that regional differences rather than religion might account for variations in suicide rates. He found, for example, that Bavaria had the lowest suicide rate of all the states in Germany and it also had the highest proportion of Catholics. Yet might the suicide rate be due to the peculiarities of Bavaria as a region rather than its predominantly Catholic population? To test this possibility Durkheim compared the suicide rates and the religious composition of the various provinces within Bavaria. He found that the higher the proportion of Protestants in each province, the higher the suicide rate. Again the relationship between religion and rates of suicide was confirmed. By eliminating variables such as national culture and region, Durkheim was able to strengthen the relationship between religion and suicide rates and provide increasing support for his claim that the relationship is a causal one.

The success of any survey is, however, ultimately dependent on the quality of its data. As previous sections have indicated, the validity of Durkheim's data on suicide is highly questionable. However sophisticated the techniques of analysis may be, they remain a secondary consideration. At the end of the day a social survey stands or falls on the validity of its data.

The problem of methodology

From a detailed study of methodology, Derek L. Phillips states, 'In my view, sociologists spend a disproportionate amount of time and energy trying to account for what may be nonexistent "facts" and nonexistent relationships'. Phillips believes that far too little attention has been given to the problems involved in obtaining valid data. He claims that many sociologists have tended to brush the problem of validity under the carpet and spent their time accumulating more and more data, devising ever more sophisticated means of analysing that data and spinning ingenious theories to account for the relationships which their analysis reveals. Phillips is scathing in his assessment of this process. He states, 'Given the demonstrably faulty quality of sociological data, these efforts are a monstrous waste of time and effort'.

If Phillips's observations are correct, then finding ways of improving the quality of data is of paramount importance to sociology. A possible solution involves more 'research on research'. From this point of view studies on research procedures and methods of data collection are needed to reveal sources of error, bias and invalidity. There are very few studies of the type conducted by Williams on differing responses to Black and White interviewers and by Dohrenwend on the social desirability of items in a questionnaire. Little systematic research has been directed to the effects of the language in which questionnaires are phrased and interviews conducted. Such studies will produce greater knowledge of the research process and may help to control or even eliminate sources of bias and invalidity.

While research on research may well provide sociologists with a greater awareness of how the data they collect are shaped by their research methods, it will not necessarily solve the problem of validity. Williams's study of Black respondents in North Carolina indicates the difficulties involved. Are the responses of some Blacks to White interviewers on the questions of school desegregation and civil rights demonstrations invalid? Had they been interviewed by Blacks, would 'interviewer bias' disappear and valid data result? Certainly on the basis of Williams's study it is reasonable to infer that different data would result. But all data are influenced by the context of the interview, the interaction of the participants, their definition of the situation and so on. In this sense all interview data are biased. There is no such thing as the respondent's 'real', 'true' attitudes because in an interview, as in the 'real world', his responses are a product of the particular context of interaction. Thus Phillips argues that sociologists should recognize the 'impossibility of bias-free research in situations where human beings collect data from active, thinking people like themselves'. From this point of view, investigations into research procedures might provide insights into the meanings which govern the actions of respondents. However, they will not solve the problem of validity. Data which result from human interaction are inevitably biased in one way or another simply because of the nature of interaction.

To many sociologists, an objective science of society remains the goal of sociology. Their view of objectivity is summarized by Robert Bierstedt who states, '*Objectivity* means that the conclusions arrived at as the result of inquiry and investigation are independent of the race, color, creed, occupation, nationality, religion, moral preference, and political predispositions of the investigator. If his research is truly objective, it is independent of any subjective elements, any personal desires, that he may have'. An increasing number of sociologists now argue that the pursuit of an objective, value-free sociology is the pursuit of an illusion. The view that sociological inquiry is inevitably ideologically based has been examined in the closing sections of the preceding chapters. It argues that the sociologist cannot shed his taken-for-granted assumptions, prejudices and commitments. He cannot escape from his past experiences which will colour everything he sees. With respect to methodology, this means that the entire research process will be influenced by these factors. They will shape the sociologist's assumptions about the nature of social reality, his methods of data collection, the type of data considered appropriate for his study, the way he analyses that data and his interpretation of the results. Thus Derek Phillips argues that, 'An investigator's values influence not only the problems he selects for study but also his methods for studying them and the sources of data he uses'.

The implications of this view are serious. They suggest that there are no fixed or absolute standards against which the validity of data can be judged. If this is the case then the only lesson to be learned from sociology may well be the impossibility of knowing anything. Sociological knowledge thus becomes the constructions of reality created by a group of people called sociologists. These constructions have no more claim to 'the truth' than those of any other members of society.

To some degree these arguments have been used by phenomenological sociologists to criticize what they see as the failings of mainstream sociology. They have argued that many sociologists simply impose their own views of reality on the social world. As a result they distort and misrepresent the very reality they seek to understand. Research techniques such as interviews, questionnaires and social surveys are a part of this process of distortion. They come between the sociologist and the social world and so remove any opportunity he might have of discovering social reality. From a phenomenological perspective, direct observation of everyday activity provides the most likely if not the only means of obtaining valid knowledge of the social world. This at least allows the researcher to come face to face with the reality he seeks to understand. Since the social world is seen to be a construction of its members, that world can only be understood in terms of members' categories and constructs. Thus Jack Douglas argues that sociologists must 'study the phenomena of everyday life on their own terms', they must 'preserve the integrity of that phenomena'. While phenomenologists might be looking in the right direction, the problem of validity remains unsolved. Though face to face with social reality, the observer can only see the social world through his own eyes. Given the nature of man, no two sociologists will see that world in exactly the same way. Douglas recognizes the difficulties involved when he writes, 'Given the early stage of the work, it seems inevitable that we shall have great problems in making our work objective and shall, consequently, have to make use of our own partially unexplicated common-sense understandings of everyday life'. However, he believes that the 'fundamental aspects of everyday life' can be grasped intuitively and the creative insights that result 'may someday be made objective knowledge'.

13 Sociological theory

A theory is a set of ideas which provides an explanation for something. A sociological theory is a set of ideas which provides an explanation for human society. Critics of sociology sometimes object to the emphasis which sociologists place on theory and suggest it might be better to let 'the facts' speak for themselves. But there are no facts without theory. For example, in Western society, the generally accepted facts that the world is round and orbits the sun are inseparable from theories which explain the nature and movement of heavenly bodies. However, in some non-Western societies whose members employ different theories, the view that the world is flat and the solar system revolves around it is accepted as a statement of fact. Clearly the facts do not speak for themselves.

Like all theory, sociological theory is selective. No amount of theory can hope to explain everything, account for the infinite amount of data that exist or encompass the endless ways of viewing reality. Theories are therefore selective in terms of their priorities and perspectives and the data they define as significant. As a result they provide a particular and partial view of reality. As previous chapters have indicated, there are various sociological theories. Each presents a distinctive explanation of the social world. There is no firm agreement as to the actual number of theories in sociology. This chapter examines four which are generally considered to be among the more important.

Functionalism

Functionalist analysis has a long history in sociology. It is prominent in the work of Auguste Comte (1798–1857) and Herbert Spencer (1820–1903), two of the founding fathers of the discipline. It was developed by Emile Durkheim (1858–1917) and refined by Talcott Parsons (1902–79). During the 1940s and 1950s functionalism was the dominant social theory in American sociology. Since that time it has steadily dropped from favour, partly because of damaging criticism, partly because other approaches are seen to answer certain questions more successfully and partly because it simply went out of fashion.

Functionalism views society as a system, that is as a set of interconnected parts which together form a whole. The basic unit of analysis is society and its various parts are understood primarily in terms of their relationship to the whole. Thus social institutions such as the family and religion are analysed as a part of the social system rather than as isolated units. In particular, they are understood with reference to the contribution they make to the system as a whole. The early functionalists often drew an analogy between society and an organism such as the human body. They argued that an understanding of any organ in the body, such as the heart or lungs, involves an understanding of its relationship to other organs and in particular, of its contribution towards the maintenance of the organism. In the same way, an understanding of any part of society requires an analysis of its relationship to other parts and most importantly, of its contribution to the maintenance of society. Continuing this analogy, they argued that just as an organism has certain basic needs which must be satisfied if it is to survive, so society has basic needs which must be met if it is to continue to exist.

These basic needs or necessary conditions of existence are sometimes known as functional prerequisites of society. Various approaches have been used to identify functional prerequisites. Some sociologists have examined a range of societies in an attempt to discover what factors they have in common. For example, Davis and Moore claim that all societies have some form of social stratification and George Peter Murdock maintains that the family exists in every known human society. From these observations it is assumed that institutional arrangements such as social stratification and the family meet needs which are common to all societies. Thus from the universal presence of social stratification it is argued that all societies require some mechanism to ensure that social positions are adequately filled by motivated persons. From the universality of the family it is assumed that some mechanism for the reproduction and socialization of new members is a functional prerequisite of society. However, the problem with this approach is its assumption that the presence of the same institution in every society indicates that it meets the same need. Simply because a form of stratification exists in all societies does not necessarily mean it reflects 'the universal necessity which calls forth stratification in any social system', as Davis and Moore claim. Put another way, it cannot be assumed that stratification systems perform the same function in all societies. (Davis and Moore's theory of stratification is outlined in Chapter 2, pp. 32–4.)

An alternative approach to the identification of functional prerequisites involves an analysis of those factors which would lead to the breakdown or termination of society. Thus Marion J. Levy argues that a society would cease to exist if its members became extinct, if they became totally apathetic, if they were involved in a war of all against all or if they were absorbed into another society. Therefore in order for a society to survive it must have some means of preventing these events from occurring. These means are the functional prerequisites of society. For example, to ensure that members of society do not become extinct, a system for reproducing new members and maintaining the health of existing members is essential. This involves role differentiation and role assignment. Individuals must be assigned to produce food and to reproduce and care for new members of society. In order for these essential services to be maintained, individuals must be sufficiently motivated to perform their roles. If they were totally apathetic, the social system would collapse through lack of effort. A system of goals and rewards is necessary to motivate members of society to want to do what they have to do in order to maintain the system. By specifying the factors which would lead to the termination of society, Levy claims to have identified the basic requirements which must be met if society is to survive. The problem with this approach to the specification of functional prerequisites is its reliance on common sense and ingenuity. In the case of a biological organism it is possible to identify basic needs since it can be shown that if these needs are not met, the organism dies. However, societies change rather than die. As a result it is not possible to identify unequivocally those aspects of a social system which are indispensable to its existence. Functionalists using Levy's approach have drawn up lists of functional prerequisites which are often similar in content but never quite the same.

A related approach involves the deduction of functional prerequisites from an abstract model of the social system. For example, if society is viewed as a system, certain survival needs can be deduced from an abstract model of a system. Any system is made up of interconnected parts. If a system is to survive, there must be a minimum amount of integration between its parts. There must be some degree of fit which requires an element of mutual compatibility of the parts. From this type of analysis, the functional prerequisites of society may be inferred. Thus any social system requires a minimum amount of integration between its parts. From this assumption, functional analysis turns to an examination of the parts of society to investigate how they contribute to the integration of the social system. In this respect religion has often been seen as a powerful mechanism for social integration. Religion is seen to reinforce the basic values of society. Social norms which derive from these values structure and direct behaviour in the various institutions of society. The parts of the social system are integrated in that they are largely infused with the same basic values. Were the various institutions founded on conflicting values, the system would tend to disintegrate. Since religion promotes and reinforces social values, it can be seen as an integrating mechanism. But the problem of deducing functional prerequisites such as integration from an abstract model of the social system is that they are inferred rather than unequivocally identified.

The concept of function in functionalist analysis refers to the contribution of the part to the whole. More specifically, the function of any part of society is the contribution it makes to meeting the functional prerequisities of the social system. Parts of society are functional in so far as they maintain the system and contribute to its survival. Thus a function of the family is to ensure the continuity of society by reproducing and socializing new members. A function of religion is to integrate the social system by reinforcing common values. Functionalists also employ the concept of dysfunction to refer to the effects of any social institution which detract from the maintenance of society. However, in practice they have been primarily concerned with the search for functions and relatively little use has been made of the concept of dysfunction.

Functionalist analysis has focussed on the question of how social systems are maintained. This focus has tended to result in a positive evaluation of the parts of society. With their concern for investigating how functional prerequisites are met, functionalists have concentrated on functions rather than dysfunctions. This emphasis has resulted in many institutions being seen as beneficial and useful to society. Indeed some institutions, such as the family, religion and social stratification, have been seen as not only beneficial but indispensable. This view has led critics to argue that functionalism has a built in conservative bias which supports the status quo. The argument that certain social arrangements are beneficial or indispensable provides support for their retention and rejects proposals for radical change. Response to this criticism will be examined in a later section, (see page 531). (For various views on the ideological basis of functionalism, see the concluding sections of Chapter 1–11.)

This section has presented a brief outline of some of the main features of functionalist analysis. The following sections will consider the views of some of the major functionalist theorists.

Emile Durkheim

Critics of functionalism have often argued that it pictures the individual as having little or no control over his own actions. Rather than constructing their own social world, members of society appear to be directed by the system. For example, they are organized into families and systems of stratification because society requires these social arrangements in order to survive. Many have questioned the logic of treating society as if it were something separate from its members, as if it shaped their actions rather than being constructed by them. Durkheim rejects this criticism. He argues that society has a reality of its own over and above the individuals who comprise it. Members of society are constrained by 'social facts', by 'ways of acting, thinking, and feeling, external to the individual, and endowed with a power of coercion, by reason of which they control him'. Beliefs and moral codes are passed on from one generation to the next and shared by the individuals who make up a society. From this point of view it is not the consciousness of the individual which directs his behaviour but common beliefs and sentiments which transcend the individual and shape his consciousness. Having established to his own satisfaction that social facts can, at least for purposes of analysis, be treated separately from social actors, Durkheim is free to treat society as a system which obeys its own laws. He is now in a position to 'seek the explanation of social life in the nature of society itself'.

Durkheim argues that there are two ways of explaining social facts. In both cases the explanation lies in society. The first method involves determining the cause of a social fact, of seeking to explain its origin. In Durkheim's view, 'The determining cause of a social fact should be sought among the social facts preceding it and not among the states of individual consciousness'. As the previous chapter indicated (pp. 495–7), the causes of variations in suicide rates are to be found in social facts, in society rather than the individual. However, the explanation of a social fact also involves an analysis of its function in society, of its contribution to 'the general needs of the social organism', of its 'function in the establishment of social order'. Durkheim assumes that the explanation for the continuing existence of a social fact lies in its function, that is in its usefulness for society. He is at pains to point out the distinction between cause and function. Thus the cause of the Christian religion lies in the specific circumstances of its origin amongst a group of Jews under Roman rule. Yet its functions, the reasons for its retention over a period of nearly 2 000 years, require a different form of explanation. Durkheim argues that 'if the usefulness of a fact is not the cause of its existence, it is generally necessary that it be useful in order that it might maintain itself'. Social facts therefore continue in existence because they contribute in some way to the maintenance of society, because they serve 'some social end'.

Much of Durkheim's work is concerned with functional analysis, with seeking to understand the functions of social facts. He assumes that society has certain functional prerequisites, the most important of which is the need for 'social order'. Durkheim begins with the question of how a collection of individuals can be integrated to form an ordered society. He sees the answer in consensus, in a 'collective conscience' consisting of common beliefs and sentiments. Without this consensus or agreement on fundamental moral issues, social solidarity would be impossible and individuals could not be bound together to form an integrated social unit. Without social obligations backed by moral force, the cooperation and reciprocity which social life requires would be absent. If narrow self-interest rather than mutual obligation was the guiding force, conflict and disorder would result. In Durkheim's words, 'For where interest is the only ruling force each individual finds himself in a state of war with every other'. The collective conscience constrains individuals to act in terms of the requirements of society. Since the collective conscience is a social fact and therefore external to the individual, it is essential that it be impressed upon him. Thus Durkheim argues that, 'society has to be present in the individual'.

Durkheim's functionalism is set in the framework of the above argument. It may be illustrated by his analysis of the functions of religion. Social order requires that individuals experience society within themselves, realize their dependence upon it and recognize their obligations which are fundamentally social. By symbolizing society and so making it sacred religion meets these requirements. It makes social life possible by expressing, maintaining and reinforcing the sentiments or values which form the collective conscience. Social obligations are represented in sacred terms and so transformed into religious duties. Thus Peter Berger, commenting on Durkheim's views notes, 'To marry becomes a sacrament, to work becomes a duty pleasing to the gods, and to die in war, perhaps, becomes a passport to a happier afterlife'. In symbolizing society, religion awakens in the individual an appreciation of his reliance on society. By recognizing his dependence on supernatural power, the individual recognizes his dependence on society. Religion integrates the social group since those who share religious beliefs 'feel themselves united to each other by the simple fact that they have a common faith'. The highly charged atmosphere of religious rituals serves to dramatize this unity and so promotes social solidarity. In this way religion functions to meet the essential requirements of social life. It ensures that society is 'present within the individual'. (See Chapter 11, pp. 455–7, for other aspects of Durkheim's analysis of religion. Durkheim's views on education, Chapter 5, pp. 173–4, provide further illustration of the ideas outlined in this section.)

Talcott Parsons

Today the name of Talcott Parsons is synonymous with functionalism. Over a period of some fifty years, Parsons published numerous articles and books and during the 1940s and 1950s he became the dominant theorist in American sociology. This section will briefly examine aspects of his work. Like Durkheim, Parsons begins with the question of how social order is possible. He observes that social life is characterized by 'mutual advantage and peaceful cooperation rather than mutual hostility and destruction'. A large part of Parsons's sociology is concerned with explaining how this state of affairs is accomplished. He starts with a consideration of the views of the seventeenth-century English philosopher Thomas Hobbes who claimed to have discovered the basis of social order. According to Hobbes, man is directed by passion and reason. His passions are the primary driving force, reason being employed to devise ways and means of providing for their satisfaction. If man's passions were allowed free reign, he would use any means at his disposal, including force and fraud, to satisfy them. The net result would be 'the war of all against all'. However, fear of this outcome is generated by the most basic of man's passions, that of self-preservation. Guided by the desire for self-preservation man agrees to restrain his passions, give up his liberty and enter into a social contract with his fellows. He submits to the authority of a ruler or governing body in return for protection against the aggression, force and fraud of others. Only because of this sovereign power is the war of all against all prevented and security and order established in society.

Hobbes presents a picture of man as rational, self-interested and calculating. He forms an ordered society with his fellows through fear of the consequences if he does not. This is very different from Durkheim's view of man acting in response to moral commitments and obeying social rules because he believes them to be right. Parsons shares Durkheim's views. He argues that Hobbes's picture of man pursuing personal ends and restrained only by sovereign power fails to provide an adequate explanation for social order. Parsons believes that only a commitment to common values provides a basis for order in society.

Parsons illustrates this point by reference to social relationships which at first sight would appear to exemplify Hobbes's view of man as self-interested and calculating. He examines transactions in the market place. In a business transaction, the parties concerned form a contract. In order for the conduct of business to be orderly, it is essential that contracts be bound by a 'system of regulatory, normative rules'. In Parsons's view fear of the consequences is insufficient to motivate men to obey the rules. A moral commitment is essential. Thus rules governing business transactions must ultimately derive from shared values which state what is just, right and proper. Order in the economic system is therefore based on a general agreement concerning business morality. From this agreement stem rules which define a contract as valid or invalid. For example, a contract obtained by force or fraud is not binding. Parson argues that the world of business, like any other part of society, is, by necessity, a moral world.

Value consensus forms the fundamental integrating principle in society. If members of society are committed to the same values, they will tend to share a common identity which provides a basis for unity and cooperation. From shared values derive common goals. Values provide a general conception of what is desirable and worthwhile. Goals provide direction in specific situations. For example, in Western society, members of a particular workforce will share the goal of efficient production in their factory, a goal which stems from the general value of economic productivity. A common goal provides an incentive for cooperation. Roles provide the means whereby values and goals are translated into action. A social institution consists of a combination of roles. For instance a business firm is made up of a number of specialized roles which combine to further the goals of the organization. The content of roles is structured in terms of norms which define the rights and obligations applicable to each particular role. Norms can be seen as specific expressions of values. Thus the norms which structure the roles of manager, accountant, engineer and shop-floor worker owe their content partly to the value of economic productivity. Norms tend to ensure that role behaviour is standardized, predictable and therefore orderly. This means that from the most general level, the central value system, to the most specific, normative conduct, the social system is infused with common values. This provides the basis for social order.

The importance Parsons places on value consensus has led him to state that the main task of sociology is to analyse the 'institutionalization of patterns of value orientation in the social system'. When values are institutionalized and behaviour structured in terms of them, the result is a stable system. A state of 'social equilibrium' is attained, the various parts of the system being in a state of balance. There are two main ways in which social equilibrium is maintained. The first involves socialization by means of which society's values are transmitted from one generation to the next and internalized to form an integral part of individual personalities. In Western society, the family and the education system are the major institutions concerned with this function. (See Chapter 5, pp. 175–6, for Parsons's views on the functions of education; Chapter 8, pp. 344–6, for his views on the functions of the family.) Social equilibrium is also maintained by the various mechanisms of social control which discourage deviance and so maintain order in the system. The processes of socialization and social control are fundamental to the equilibrium of the social system and therefore to order in society.

Parsons views society as a system. He argues that any social system has four basic functional prerequisites – adaptation, goal attainment, integration and pattern maintenance. These can be seen as problems which society must solve if it is to survive. The function of any part of the social system is understood as its contribution to meeting the functional prerequisites. Solutions to the four survival problems must be institutionalized if society is to continue in existence. In other words, solutions must be organized in the form of ordered, stable social institutions which persist through time.

The first functional prerequisite, adaptation, refers to the relationship between the system and its environment. In order to survive, social systems must have some degree of control over their environment. At a minimum, food and shelter must be provided to meet the physical needs of their members. The economy is the institution primarily concerned with this function. Goal attainment refers to the need for all societies to set goals towards which social activity is directed. Procedures for establishing goals and deciding on priorities between goals are institutionalized in the form of political systems. Governments not only set goals but allocate resources to achieve them. Even in a so-called free enterprise system, the economy is regulated and directed by laws passed by governments. Integration refers primarily to the 'adjustment of conflict'. It is concerned with the coordination and mutual adjustment of the parts of the social system. The law is the main institution which meets this need. Legal norms define and standardize relations between individuals and between institutions and so reduce the potential for conflict. When conflict does arise it is settled by the judicial system and does not therefore lead to the disintegration of the social system. Pattern maintenance refers to 'the maintenance of the basic pattern of values, institutionalized in the society'. Institutions which perform this function include the family, the educational system and religion. In Parsons's view, 'the values of society are rooted in religion'. Religious beliefs provide the ultimate justification for the values of the social system. (See Chapter 11, pp. 458–9, 482–3, for Parsons's analysis of the functions of religion.) Parsons maintains that any social system can be analysed in terms of the functional prerequisites he identifies. Thus all parts of society can be understood with reference to the functions they perform in the adaptation, goal attainment, integration and pattern maintenance systems.

Functionalism has often been criticized for failing to provide an adequate explanation for social change. If the system is in equilibrium with its various parts contributing towards order and stability, it is difficult to see how it changes. Parsons approaches this problem in the following way. In practice no social system is in a perfect state of equilibrium although a certain degree of equilibrium is essential for the survival of societies. The process of social change can therefore be pictured as a 'moving equilibrium'. This may be illustrated in the following way. The adaptation, goal attainment, integration and pattern maintenance systems are interrelated. A change in one will therefore produce responses in the others. For example, a change in the adaptation system will result in a disturbance in the social system as a whole. The other parts of the system will operate to return it to a state of equilibrium. In Parsons's words, 'Once a disturbance has been introduced into an equilibriated system there will tend to be a reaction to this disturbance, which tends to restore the system to equilibrium'. This reaction will lead to some degree of change, however small, in the system as a whole. Though social systems never attain complete equilibrium, they tend towards this state. Social change can therefore be seen as a 'moving equilibrium'.

Parsons views social change as a process of 'social evolution' from simple to more complex forms of society. He regards changes in adaptation as a major driving force of social evolution. The history of human society from the simple hunting and gathering band to the complex nation-state represents an increase in the 'general adaptive capacity' of society. As societies evolve into more complex forms, control over the environment increases. Whilst economic changes might provide an initial stimulus, Parsons believes that in the long run, cultural changes, that is changes in values, determine the '*broadest* patterns of change'. For example, he argues that the structure of modern societies owes much to values inherited from ancient Israel and classical Greece. Social evolution involves a process of social differentiation. The institutions and roles which form the social system become increasingly differentiated and specialized in terms of their function. Thus religious institutions become separated from the state, the family and the economy become increasingly differentiated, each specializing in fewer functions. This produces a problem of integration. As the parts of society become more and more specialized and distinct, it becomes increasingly difficult to integrate them in terms of common values. This problem is solved by the generalizing of values, a process discussed in Chapter 11 (pp. 482–3), with reference to religion. Values become more general and diffuse, less specific and particular. In Western society, for example, the highly generalized values of universalism and achievement can be applied to all members of society despite the wide variation in their roles. Universal standards of achievement are generally accepted and provide the basis for differential reward and role allocation. Thus despite increasing social differentiation, social integration and order are maintained by the generalizing of values. Parsons admits that his views on social evolution represent little more than a beginning. However, they do offer a possible solution to the problem of explaining social change from a functionalist perspective.

Robert K. Merton

In a closely reasoned essay, originally published in 1949, the American sociologist Robert K. Merton attempts to refine and develop functionalist analysis. He singles out three related assumptions which have been employed by many functionalists and questions their utility. The first he terms the 'postulate of the functional unity of society'. This assumption states that any part of the social system is functional for the *entire* system. All parts of society are seen to work together for the maintenance and integration of society as a whole. Merton argues that particularly in complex, highly differentiated societies, this 'functional unity' is doubtful. He provides the example of religious pluralism to illustrate this point. In a society with a variety of faiths, religion may tend to divide rather than unite. Merton argues that functional unity is a matter of degree. Its extent must be determined by investigation rather than simply beginning with the assumption that it exists. The idea of functional unity implies that a change in one part of the system will automatically result in a change in other parts. Again Merton argues that this is a matter for investigation. It should not simply be assumed at the outset. He suggests that in highly differentiated societies, institutions may well have a high degree of 'functional autonomy'. Thus a change in a particular institution may have little or no effect on others.

Merton refers to the second assumption as the 'postulate of universal functionalism'. This assumption states that 'all standardized social or cultural forms have positive functions'. Merton argues that the assumption that every aspect of the social system performs a positive function is not only premature, it may well be incorrect. He suggests that functionalist analysis should proceed from the assumption that any part of society may be functional, dysfunctional or non-functional. In addition, the units for which a particular part is functional, dysfunctional or non-functional must be clearly specified. These units may be individuals, groups or society as a whole. Thus poverty may be seen as dysfunctional for the poor but functional for the non-poor and for society as a whole. (This view forms the basis of Herbert Gans's analysis of poverty outlined in Chapter 4, pp. 165–6.) Merton suggests that the postulate of universal functionalism should be replaced by 'the provisional assumption that persisting cultural forms have a *net balance of functional consequences* either for the society considered as a unit or for subgroups sufficiently powerful to retain these forms intact, by means of direct coercion or indirect persuasion'.

Merton's third criticism is directed towards the 'postulate of indispensability'. This assumption states that certain institutions or social arrangement are indispensable to society. Functionalists have often seen religion in this light. For example Davis and Moore claim that religion 'plays a unique and indispensable part in society'. Merton questions the assumption of indispensability arguing that the same functional prerequisites may be met by a range of alternative institutions. Thus there is no justification for assuming that institutions such as the family, religion and social stratification are a necessary part of all human societies. To replace the idea of indispensability, Merton suggests the concept of 'functional equivalents' or 'functional alternatives'. From this point of view, a political ideology such as communism can provide a functional alternative to religion. It can meet the same functional prerequisites as religion. However, Merton is still left with the problem of actually identifying functional prerequisites.

Merton argues that the postulates of the functional unity of society, universal functionalism and indispensability are little more than articles of faith. They are matters for investigation and should not form prior assumptions. Merton claims that his framework for functionalist analysis removes the charge that functionalism is ideologically based. He argues that the parts of society should be analysed in terms of their 'effects' or 'consequences' on society as a whole and on individuals and groups within society. Since these effects can be functional, dysfunctional or non-functional, Merton claims that the value judgment present in the assumption that all parts of the system are functional is therefore removed.

Functionalism – a critique

Functionalism has been subjected to considerable criticism. Part of this criticism is directed to the logic of functionalist inquiry. In particular, it is argued that the type of explanation employed is teleological. A teleological explanation states that the parts of a system exist because of their beneficial consequences for the system as a whole. The main objection to this type of reasoning is that it treats an effect as a cause. Thus Davis and Moore's theory of stratification outlines the positive effects or functions of social stratification and then proceeds to argue that these effects explain its origin. But an effect cannot explain a cause since causes must always precede effects. Therefore the effects of stratification cannot occur until a system of social stratification has already been established. It may be argued that members of society unconsciously respond to social needs and so create the institutions necessary for the maintenance of society. However, there is no evidence of the existence of such unconscious motivations.

Functionalism is on stronger logical ground when it argues that the continued existence of an institution may be explained in terms of its effects. Thus once an institution has originated, it continues to exist if it has, on balance, beneficial effects on the system. But there are problems with this type of explanation. It is extremely difficult to establish that the net effect of any institution is beneficial to society. A knowledge of all its effects would be required in order to weigh the balance of functions and dysfunctions. As the debate on the functional merits and demerits of stratification indicates, there is little evidence that such knowledge is forthcoming. (See Chapter 2, pp. 30–38.) The problems involved in assessing the effects of a social institution may be illustrated in terms of the analogy between society and a physical organism. Biologists are able to show that certain parts of an organism make positive contributions to its maintenance since if those parts stopped functioning life would cease. Since societies change rather than die, sociologists are unable to apply similar criteria. In addition standards exist in biology for assessing the health of an organism. In terms of these standards, the contribution of the various parts can be judged. There are no comparable standards for assessing the 'health' of a society. For these reasons there are problems with the argument that a social institution continues to exist because, on balance, its effects are beneficial to society.

Functionalists such as Parsons who see the solution to the problem of social order in terms of value consensus have been strongly criticized. Firstly, their critics argue that consensus is assumed rather than shown to exist. Research has failed to unequivocally reveal a widespread commitment to the various sets of values which are seen to characterize Western society. Secondly, the stability of society may owe more to the absence rather than the presence of value consensus. For example a lack of commitment to the value of achievement by those at the bottom of stratification systems may serve to stabilize society. Thus Michael Mann argues that in a society where members compete for unequal rewards, 'cohesion results precisely because there is no common commitment to core values' (quoted in Mennell, 1974, p. 126). If all members of society were strongly committed to the value of achievement, the failure in terms of this value of those at the base of the stratification system may well produce disorder. Thirdly, consensus in and of itself will not necessarily result in social order. In fact it may produce the opposite result. As Pierre van den Berghe notes, 'consensus on norms such as extreme competition and individualistic *laissez-faire*, or suspicion and treachery . . . , or malevolence and resort to witchcraft is hardly conducive to social solidarity and integration' (quoted in Mennell, 1974, p. 127). Therefore the content of values rather than value consensus as such can be seen as the crucial factor with respect to social order.

Functionalism has been criticized for what many see as its deterministic view of human action. Its critics have argued that in terms of functionalist theory, human behaviour is portrayed as determined by the system. In particular, the social system has needs and the behaviour of its members is shaped to meet these needs. Rather than creating the social world in which he lives, man is seen as a creation of the system. Thus David Walsh argues that Parsons treats human action 'as determined by the characteristics of the system *per se*'. By means of socialization man is programmed in terms of the norms and values of the social system. He is kept on the straight and narrow by mechanisms of social control which exist to fulfil the requirements of the system. His actions are structured in terms of social roles which are designed to meet the functional prerequisites of society. Man is pictured as an automaton, programmed, directed and controlled by the system. Walsh rejects this view of man. Arguing from a phenomenological perspective, he claims that man actively constructs his own social world rather than being shaped by a social system which is somehow external to his being. Walsh maintains that the concept of a social system represents a 'reification' of the social world. Functionalists have converted social reality into a natural system external to social actors. In doing so they have translated the social world into something that it is not. They have tended to portray the social system as the active agent whereas, in reality, only human beings act.

Critics of functionalism have argued that it tends to ignore coercion and conflict. For example, Alvin Gouldner states, 'While stressing the importance of the ends and values that men pursue, Parsons never asks *whose* ends and values these are. Are they pursuing their own ends or those imposed upon them by others?' Few functionalists give serious consideration to the possibility that some groups in society, acting in terms of their own particular interests, dominate others. From this point of view social order is imposed by the powerful and value consensus is merely a legitimation of the position of the dominant group. In his criticism of one of Parsons's major works – *The Social System* – David Lockwood argues that Parsons's approach is 'highly selective in its focus on the role of the normative order in the stabilization of social systems'. In focussing on the contribution of norms and values to social order, Parsons largely fails to recognize the conflicts of interest which tend to produce instability and disorder. Lockwood argues that since all social systems involve competition for scarce resources, conflicts of interest are built into society. Conflict is not simply a minor strain in the system which is contained by value consensus. Instead it is a central and integral part of the system itself. Lockwood's view of society is strongly influenced by Marxian theory which forms the subject of the following section.

Marxism

This section will focus on certain major themes in the work of Karl Marx (1818–83). Marx's views on various aspects of society have been examined in the main part of the book. This section will seek to combine them in an overall perspective. The volume of Marx's writings over a period of forty-odd years was enormous. Many of his major projects remained unfinished and part of the material published after his death is drawn from rough notes outlining future projects. Marx's writings contain inconsistencies, ambiguities and changes in emphasis. For these reasons there are many and varied interpretations of his work. This section therefore represents a particular interpretation of Marx's ideas.

Marx regards man as both the producer and the product of society. Man makes society and himself by his own actions. History is therefore the process of man's self-creation. Yet man is also a product of society. He is shaped by the social relationships and systems of thought which he creates. An understanding of society therefore involves an historical perspective which examines the process whereby man both produces and is produced by social reality. A society forms a totality and can only be understood as such. The various parts of society are interconnected and influence each other. Thus economic, political, legal and religious institutions can only be understood in terms of their mutual effect. Economic factors, however, exert the primary influence and largely shape other aspects of society. The history of human society is a process of tension and conflict. Social change is not a smooth, orderly progression which gradually unfolds in harmonious evolution. Instead it proceeds from contradictions built into society which are a source of tension and ultimately the source of open conflict and radical change.

It is often argued that Marx's view of history is based on the idea of the dialectic. From this viewpoint any process of change involves tension between incompatible forces. Dialectical movement therefore represents a struggle of opposites, a conflict of contradictions. Conflict provides the dynamic principle, the source of change. The struggle between incompatible forces grows in intensity until there is a final collision. The result is a sudden leap forward which creates a new set of forces on a higher level of development. The dialectical process then begins again as the contradictions between this new set of forces interact and conflict, and propel change. The idea of dialectical change was developed by the German philosopher Hegel. He applied it to the history of human society and in particular to the realm of ideas. Hegel saw historical change as a dialectical movement of men's ideas and thoughts. He believed that society is essentially an expression of these thoughts. Thus in terms of the dialectic, conflict between incompatible ideas produces new concepts which provide the basis for social change. Marx rejects the priority Hegel gives to thoughts and ideas. He argues that the source of change lies in contradictions in the economic system in particular and in society in general. As a result of the priority he gives to economic factors, to 'material life', Marx's view of history is often referred to as 'dialectical materialism'. Since men's ideas are primarily a reflection of the social relationships of economic production, they do not provide the main source of change. It is in contradictions and conflict in the economic system that the major dynamic for social change lies. Since all parts of society are interconnected, however, it is only through a process of interplay between these parts that change occurs.

History begins when men actually produce their means of subsistence, when they begin to control nature. At a minimum this involves the production of food and shelter. Marx argues that, 'The first historical act is, therefore, the production of material life'. Production is a social enterprise since it requires cooperation. Men must work together to produce the goods and services necessary for life. From the social relationships involved in production develops a 'mode of life' which can be seen as an expression of these relationships. This mode of life shapes man's nature. In Marx's words, 'As individuals express their life so they are. What they are, therefore, coincides with their production, with *what* they produce and *how* they produce it'. Thus the nature of man and the nature of society as a whole derive primarily from the production of material life.

The major contradictions which propel change are found in the economic infrastructure of society. At the dawn of human history, when man supposedly lived in a state of primitive communism, those contradictions did not exist. The forces of production and the products of labour were communally owned. Since each member of society produced both for himself and for society as a whole, there were no conflicts of interest between individuals and groups. However, with the emergence of private property, and in particular, private ownership of the forces of production, the fundamental contradiction of human society was created. Through its ownership of the forces of production, a minority is able to control, command and enjoy the fruits of the labour of the majority. Since one group gains at the expense of the other, a conflict of interest exists between the minority who own the forces of production and the majority who perform productive labour. The tension and conflict generated by this contradiction is the major dynamic of social change.

For long periods of history, men are largely unaware of the contradictions which beset their societies. This is because man's consciousness, his view of reality, is largely shaped by the social relationships involved in the process of production. Marx maintains that, 'It is not the consciousness of men that determines their being, but, on the contrary, their social being determines their consciousness'. The primary aspect of man's social being is the social relationships he enters into for the production of material life. Since these relationships are largely reproduced in terms of ideas, concepts, laws and religious beliefs, they are seen as normal and natural. Thus when the law legitimizes the rights of private property, when religious beliefs justify economic arrangements and the dominant concepts of the age define them as natural and inevitable, men will be largely unaware of the contradictions they contain. In this way the contradictions within the economic infrastructure are compounded by the contradiction between man's consciousness and objective reality. This consciousness is false. It presents a distorted picture of reality since it fails to reveal the basic conflicts of interest which exist in the world which man has created. For long periods of time man is at most vaguely aware of these contradictions, yet even a vague awareness produces tension. This tension will ultimately find full expression and be resolved in the process of dialectical change.

The course of human history involves a progressive development of the forces of production, a steady increase in man's control over nature. This is parallelled by a corresponding increase in man's alienation, an increase which reaches its height in capitalist society. Alienation is a situation in which the creations of man appear to him as alien objects. They are seen as independent from their creator and invested with the power to control him. Man creates his own society but will remain alienated until he recognizes himself within his creation. Until that time he will assign an independent existence to objects, ideas and institutions and be controlled by them. In the process he loses himself, he becomes a stranger in the world he has created, he becomes alienated. Religion provides an example of man's alienation. In Marx's view, 'Man makes religion, religion does not make man'. However, members of society fail to recognize that religion is of their own making. They assign to the gods an independent power, a power to direct their actions and shape their destiny. The more man invests in religion, the more he loses himself. In Marx's words, 'The more man puts into God, the less he retains of himself'. In assigning his own powers to supernatural beings, man becomes alienated from himself. Religion appears as an external force controlling man's destiny whereas, in reality, it is man-made. Religion, though, is a reflection of a more fundamental source of alienation. It is essentially a projection of the social relationships involved in the process of production. If man is to find himself and abolish the illusions of religion, he must 'abandon a condition which requires illusions'. He must therefore eradicate the source of alienation in the economic infrastructure. (Marxian views on religion are examined in Chapter 11, pp. 460–63.)

In Marx's view, productive labour is the primary, most vital human activity. In the production of objects man 'objectifies' himself, he expresses and externalizes his being. If the objects of man's creation come to control his being, then man loses himself in the object. The act of production then results in man's alienation. This occurs when man regards the products of his labour as commodities, as articles for sale in the market place. The objects of his creation are then seen to control his existence. They are seen to be subject to impersonal forces, such as the law of supply and demand, over which man has little or no control. In Marx's words, 'the object that labour produces, its product, confronts it as an alien being, as a power independent of the producer'. In this way man is estranged from the object he produces, he becomes alienated from the most vital human activity, productive labour.

Alienation reaches its height in capitalist society where labour is dominated by the requirements of capital, the most important of which is the demand for profit. These requirements determine levels of employment and wages, the nature and quantity of goods produced and their method of manufacture. The worker sees himself as a prisoner of market forces over which he has no control. He is subject to the impersonal mechanisms of the law of supply and demand. He is at the mercy of the periodic booms and slumps which characterize capitalist economies. The worker therefore loses control over the objects he produces and becomes alienated from his product and the act of production. His work becomes a means to an end, a means of obtaining money to buy the goods and services necessary for his existence. Unable to fulfil his being in the products of his labour, the worker becomes alienated from himself in the act of production. Therefore the more the worker produces, the more he loses himself. In Marx's words, 'the greater this product the less he is himself'. (Alienation and labour in capitalist society are examined in Chapter 6, pp. 228–32.)

In Marx's view, the market forces which are seen to control production are not impersonal mechanisms beyond the control of man, they are man-made. Alienation is therefore the result of human activity rather than external forces with an existence independent of man. If the products of labour are alien to the worker, they must therefore belong to somebody. Thus Marx argues that, 'The alien being to whom the labour and the product of the labour belongs, whom the labour serves and who enjoys its product, can only be man himself. If the product of labour does not belong to the worker but stands over against him as an alien power, this is only possible in that it belongs to another man apart from the worker'. This man is the capitalist who owns and controls the forces of production and the products of labour, who appropriates for himself the wealth that labour produces. Alienation therefore springs not from impersonal market forces but from relationships between men. An end to alienation thus involves a radical change in the pattern of these relationships. This will come when the contradiction between man's consciousness and objective reality is resolved. Then man will realize that the situation in which he finds himself is man-made and therefore subject to change by human action.

Given the priority Marx assigns to economic factors, an end to alienation involves a radical change in the economic infrastructure. In particular, it requires the abolition of private property and its replacement by communal ownership of the forces of production, that is the replacement of capitalism by communism. Marx saw communism as 'the positive abolition of private property and thus of human self-alienation and therefore the real reappropriation of the human essence by and for man. This is communism as the complete and conscious return of man himself as a social, that is human being'. In communist society conflicts of interest will disappear and antagonistic groups such as capitalists and workers will be a thing of the past. The products of labour will no longer be appropriated by some at the expense of others. With divisions in society eradicated, man will be at one with his fellows, a truly social being. As such he will not lose himself in the products of his labour. He will produce both for himself and others at one and the same time. In this situation 'each of us would have doubly affirmed himself and his fellow man'. Since he is at one with his fellows, the products of man's labour in which he objectifies himself will not result in the loss of self. In productive labour each member of society contributes to the well-being of all and so expresses both his individual and social being. The objects which he produces are owned and controlled at once by himself and his fellow man.

In Marx's view man is essentially a social being. He writes that, 'society does not consist of individuals, but expresses the sum of inter-relations, the relations within which these individuals stand'. An understanding of human history therefore involves an examination of these relationships, the most important of which are the relations of production. Apart from the communities based on primitive communism at the dawn of history, all societies are divided into social groups known as classes. The relationship between classes is one of antagonism and conflict. Throughout history opposing classes have stood in 'constant opposition to one another, carried on an uninterrupted, now hidden, now open fight that each time ended either in a revolutionary reconstruction of society at large, or in the common ruin of contending classes'. Class conflict forms the basis of the dialectic of social change. In Marx's view, 'The history of all hitherto existing society is the history of the class struggle'.

Class divisions result from the differing relationships of members of society to the forces of production. The structure of all societies may be represented in terms of a simplified two class model consisting of a ruling and subject class. The ruling class owes its dominance and power to its ownership and control of the forces of production. The subjection and relative powerlessness of the subject class is due to its lack of ownership and therefore lack of control of the forces of production. The conflict of interest between the two classes stems from the fact that productive labour is performed by the subject class yet a large part of the wealth so produced is appropriated by the ruling class. Since one class gains at the expense of another, the interests of their members are incompatible. The classes stand opposed as exploiter and exploited, oppressor and oppressed.

The labour of the subject class takes on the character of 'forced labour'. Since its members lack the necessary means to produce for themselves they are forced to work for others. Thus during the feudal era, landless serfs were forced to work for the landowning nobility in order to gain a livelihood. In the capitalist era, the means necessary to produce goods – tools, machinery, raw materials and so on – are owned by the capitalist class. In order to exist, members of the proletariat are forced to sell their labour power in return for wages. Ownership of the forces of production therefore provides the basis for ruling class dominance and control of labour.

Members of both social classes are largely unaware of the true nature of their situation, of the reality of the relationship between ruling and subject classes. Members of the ruling class assume that their particular interests are those of society as a whole, members of the subject class accept this view of reality and regard their situation as part of the natural order of things. This false consciousness is due to the fact that the relationships of dominance and subordination in the economic infrastructure are largely reproduced in the superstructure of society. In Marx's words, the relations of production constitute 'the real foundation on which rise legal and political superstructures and to which correspond definite forms of social consciousness. The mode of production in material life determines the general character of the social, political and spiritual processes of life'. Ruling class dominance is confirmed and legitimated in legal statutes, religious proscriptions and political legislation. The consciousness of all members of society is infused with ruling class ideology which proclaims the essential rightness, normality and inevitability of the status quo.

While the superstructure may stabilize society and contain its contradictions over long periods of time, this situation cannot be permanent. The fundamental contradictions of class societies will eventually find expression and will finally be resolved by the dialectic of historical change. A radical change in the structure of society occurs when a class is transformed from a 'class in itself' to a 'class for itself'. A class in itself refers to members of society who share the same objective relationships to the forces of production. Thus, as wage labourers, members of the proletariat form a class in itself. However, a class only becomes a class for itself when its members are fully conscious of the true nature of their situation, when they are fully aware of their common interests and common enemy, when they realize that only by concerted action can they overthrow their oppressors, and when they unite and take positive, practical steps to do so. When a class becomes a class for itself, the contradiction between the consciousness of its members and the reality of their situation is ended.

A class becomes a class for itself when the forces of production have developed to the point where they cannot be contained within the existing relations of production. In Marx's words, 'For an oppressed class to be able to emancipate itself, it is essential that the existing forces of production and the existing social relations should be incapable of standing side by side'. Revolutionary change requires that the forces of production on which the new order will be based have developed in the old society. Therefore the 'new higher relations of production never appear before the material conditions of their existence have matured in the womb of the old society'. This process may be illustrated by the transition from feudal to capitalist society. Industrial capitalism gradually developed within the framework of feudal society. In order to develop fully, it required, 'the free wage labourer who sells his labour-power to capital'. This provides a mobile labour force which can be hired and fired at will and so efficiently utilized as a commodity in the service of capital. However, the feudal relations of production, which involved 'landed property with serf labour chained to it', tended to prevent the development of wage labourers. Eventually the forces of production of capitalism gained sufficient strength and impetus to lead to the destruction of the feudal system. At this point the rising class, the bourgeoisie, became a class for itself and its members united to overthrow the feudal relations of production. When they succeeded the contradiction between the new forces of production and the old relations of production was resolved.

Once a new economic order is established, the superstructure of the previous era is rapidly transformed. The contradiction between the new infrastructure and the old superstructure is now ended. Thus the political dominance of the feudal aristocracy was replaced by the power of the newly enfranchised bourgeoisie. The dominant concepts of feudalism such as loyalty and honour were replaced by the new concepts of freedom and equality. In terms of the new ideology the wage labourer of capitalist society is free to sell his labour power to the highest bidder. The relationship between employer and employee is defined as a relationship between equals, the exchange of labour for wages as an exchange of equivalents. But the resolution of old contradictions does not necessarily mean an end to contradictions in society. As in previous eras, the transition from feudalism to capitalism merely results in the replacement of an old set of contradictions by a new.

The predicted rise of the proletariat is not strictly analogous with the rise of the bourgeoisie. The bourgeoisie formed a privileged minority of industrialists, merchants and financiers who forged new forces of production within feudal society. The proletariat forms an unprivileged majority which does not create new forces of production within capitalist society. Marx believed, however, that the contradictions of capitalism were sufficient to transform the proletariat into a class for itself and bring about the downfall of the bourgeoisie. He saw the magnitude of these contradictions and the intensity of class conflict steadily increasing as capitalism developed. Thus there is a steady polarization of the two major classes as the intermediate strata are submerged into the proletariat. As capital accumulates, it is concentrated more and more into fewer hands, a process accompanied by the relative pauperization of the proletariat. Production assumes an increasingly social and cooperative character as larger and larger groups of workers are concentrated in factories. At the same time the wealth produced by labour is appropriated by fewer and fewer individuals as greater competition drives all but the larger companies out of business. Such processes magnify and illuminate the contradictions of capitalism and increase the intensity of conflict. It is only a matter of time before members of the proletariat recognize that the reality of their situation is the alienation of labour. This awareness will lead the proletariat to 'a revolt to which it is forced by the contradiction between its *humanity* and its situation, which is an open, clear and absolute negation of its humanity'. (Marxian views on class and class conflict are outlined in Chapter 2, pp. 38–44, and 76–82.)

The communist society which Marx predicted would arise from the ruins of capitalism will begin with a transitional phase, 'the dictatorship of the proletariat'. Once the communist system has been fully established, the reason for being of the dictatorship and therefore its existence will end. Bourgeois society represents 'the closing chapter of the prehistoric stage of human society'. The communist society of the new era is without classes, without contradictions. The dialectical principle now ceases to operate. The contradictions of human history have now been negated in a final harmonious synthesis.

Judging from the constant reinterpretations, impassioned defences and vehement criticisms of Marx's work, his ideas are as alive and relevant today as they ever were. Specific criticisms of Marx's views on society have been examined in previous chapters and will not therefore be covered in detail in this section. Many of his critics have argued that history has failed to substantiate Marx's views on the direction of social change. Thus they claim that class conflict, far from growing in intensity, has become institutionalized in advanced capitalist society. They see little indication of the proletariat becoming a class for itself. Rather than a polarization of classes, they argue that the class structure of capitalist society has become increasingly complex and differentiated. In particular, a steadily growing middle class has emerged between the proletariat and bourgeoisie. Turning to communist society, critics have argued that history has not borne out the promise of communism contained in Marx's writings. Significant social inequalities are present in communist regimes and there are few, if any, signs of a movement towards equality. The dictatorship of the proletariat clings stubbornly to power and there is little indication of its eventual disappearance. Particular criticism has been directed towards the priority that Marx assigns to economic factors in his explanation of social structure and social change. Max Weber's study of ascetic Protestantism argued that religious beliefs provided the ethics, attitudes and motivations for the development of capitalism. Since ascetic Protestantism preceded the advent of capitalism, Weber maintained that at certain times and places aspects of the superstructure can play a primary role in directing change. (See Chapter 11, pp. 465–7.) The priority given to economic factors has also been criticized by elite theorists who have argued that control of the machinery of government rather than ownership of the forces of production provides the basis for power. They point to the example of communist societies where, despite the fact that the forces of production are communally owned, power is largely monopolized by a political and bureaucratic elite. (See Chapter 3, pp. 107–13.) However, as previous chapters have indicated, Marxism is sufficiently flexible to counter these criticisms, and to provide explanations for historical changes which have occurred since Marx's death.

This section closes with a brief examination of what many see as the central issue of Marxism, the question of 'economic determinism'. Critics have often rejected Marxism on this basis though they admit that the charge of economic determination is more applicable to certain of Marx's followers than to Marx himself. It is possible to select numerous quotations from Marx's writings which support the views of his critics. In terms of these quotations, history can be presented as a mechanical process directed by economic forces which follow 'iron laws'. Man is compelled to act in terms of the constraints imposed by the economy and passively responds to impersonal forces rather than actively constructing his own history. Thus the proletariat is 'compelled' by its economic situation to overthrow the bourgeoisie. The contradictions in the capitalist infrastructure will inevitably result in its destruction. The superstructure is 'determined' by the infrastructure and man's consciousness is shaped by economic forces independent of his will and beyond his control. In this way Marx can be presented as a crude positivist who sees causation solely in terms of economic forces.

On closer examination, however, Marx's writings prove more subtle and less dogmatic than many of his critics have suggested. Marx rejects a simplistic, one-directional view of causation. Although he gives priority to economic factors, they form only one aspect of the dialectic of history.

From this perspective the economy is the primary but not the sole determinant of social change. The idea of the dialectic involves an interplay between the various parts of society. It rejects the view of unidirectional causation proceeding solely from economic factors. Instead it argues that the various parts of society are interrelated in terms of their mutual effect. Marx described the economic infrastructure as the 'ultimately determinant element in history'. Yet he added that, 'if somebody twists this into saying that the economic element is the *only* determining one, he transforms that proposition into a meaningless, abstract and senseless phrase. The economic situation is the basis, but the various elements of the superstructure . . . also exert their influence upon the course of the historical struggle and in many cases preponderate in determining their *form*'. Thus the various aspects of the superstructure have a certain degree of autonomy and a part to play in influencing the course of history. They are not automatically and mechanically determined by the infrastructure.

Marx consistently argued that 'man makes his own history'. The history of human society is not the product of impersonal forces, it is the result of man's purposive activity. In Marx's view, 'It is not "history" which uses men as a means of achieving – as if it were an individual person – *its* own ends. History is *nothing* but the activity of men in pursuit of their ends'. Since men make society only men can change society. Radical change results from a combination of consciousness of reality and direct action. Thus members of the proletariat must be fully aware of their situation and take active steps in order to change it. Although a successful revolution depends ultimately on the economic situation, it requires human initiative. Men must make their own utopia.

Symbolic interactionism

Symbolic interactionism, usually referred to as interactionism in the main part of the text, is a distinctly American branch of sociology. It developed from the work of a group of American philosophers who included John Dewey, William I. Thomas and George Herbert Mead. It is sometimes described as a phenomenological perspective because of its emphasis on the actor's views and interpretations of social reality. Thus Manis and Meltzer state that symbolic interactionism is concerned with 'the "inner", or phenomenological aspects of human behaviour'. However, it developed separately from the phenomenological tradition in European philosophy and differs in certain respects from sociological perspectives which are more closely linked to that tradition. Of the various philosophers who contributed to the growth of symbolic interactionism, George Herbert Mead (1863–1931) is usually regarded as the major figure.

George Herbert Mead

In Mead's view, human thought, experience and conduct are essentially social. They owe their nature to the fact that human beings interact in terms of symbols, the most important of which are contained in language. A symbol does not simply stand for an object or event: it defines them in a particular way and indicates a response to them. Thus the symbol 'chair' not only represents a class of objects and defines them as similar, it also indicates a line of action, that is the action of sitting. Symbols impose particular meanings on objects and events and in doing so largely exclude other possible meanings. For example, chairs may be made out of metal, cane or wood and on this basis be defined as very different objects. However such differences are rendered insignificant by the fact that they are all categorized in terms of the symbol 'chair'. Similarly, chairs can be stood on, used as a source of fuel or as a means for assaulting another but the range of possible activities that could be associated with chairs is largely excluded by the course of action indicated by the symbol 'chair'. Symbols provide the means whereby man can interact meaningfully with his natural and social environment. They are man-made and refer not to the intrinsic nature of objects and events but to the ways in which men perceive them.

Without symbols there would be no human interaction and no human society. Symbolic interaction is necessary since man has no instincts to direct his behaviour. He is not genetically programmed to react automatically to particular stimuli. In order to survive he must therefore construct and live within a world of meaning. For example he must classify the natural environment into categories of food and non-food in order to meet basic nutritional requirements. In this way men both define stimuli and their response to them. Thus when hunters on the African savannah categorize antelope as a source of food, they define what is significant in the natural environment and their response to it. Via symbols, meaning is imposed on the world of nature and human interaction with that world is thereby made possible.

Social life can only proceed if the meanings of symbols are largely shared by members of society. If this were not the case meaningful communication would be impossible. However, common symbols provide only the means by which human interaction can be accomplished. In order for interaction to proceed each person involved must interpret the meanings and intentions of others. This is made possible by the existence of common symbols, but actually accomplished by means of a process which Mead terms 'role-taking'. The process of role-taking involves the individual taking on the role of another by imaginatively placing himself in the position of the person with whom he is interacting. For example, if he observes another smiling, crying, waving his hand or shaking his fist, he will put himself in that person's position in order to interpret his intention and meaning. On the basis of this interpretation he will make his response to the action of the other. Thus if he observes someone shaking his fist, he may interpret this gesture as an indication of aggression but his interpretation will not automatically lead to a particular response. He may ignore the gesture, respond in kind, attempt to defuse the situation with a joke and so on. The person with whom he is interacting will then take his role, interpret his response and either continue or close the interaction on the basis of this interpretation. In this respect human interaction can be seen as a continuous process of interpretation with each taking the role of the other.

Mead argues that through the process of role-taking the individual develops a concept of 'self'. By placing himself in the position of others he is able to look back upon himself. Mead claims that the idea of a self can only develop if the individual can 'get outside himself (experientially) in such a way as to become an object to himself'. To do this he must observe himself from the standpoint of others. Therefore the origin and development of a concept of self lies in the ability to take the role of another. The notion of self is not inborn, it is learned during childhood. Mead sees two main stages in its development. The first, known as the 'play stage', involves the child playing roles which are not his own. For example the child may play at being mother or father, a doctor or a nurse. In doing so he becomes aware that there is a difference between himself and the role that he is playing. Thus the idea of a self is developed as the child takes the role of a make-believe other. The second stage in the development of self is known as the 'game stage'. In playing a game, the child comes to see himself from the perspective of the various participants. In order to play a game such as football or cricket, the child must become aware of his relationship to the other players. He must place himself in their roles in order to appreciate his particular role in the game. In doing so he sees himself in terms of the collective viewpoint of the other players. In Mead's terminology he sees himself from the perspective of 'the generalized other'.

In Mead's view, the development of a consciousness of self is an essential part of the process of becoming a human being. It provides the basis for thought and action and the foundation for human society. Without an awareness of self, the individual could not direct action or respond to the actions of others. Only by acquiring a concept of self can the individual take the role of self. In this way thought is possible since in Mead's view, the process of thinking is simply an 'inner conversation'. Thus unless the individual is aware of a self, he would be unable to converse with himself and thought would be impossible. By becoming 'self-conscious', he can direct his own action by thought and deliberation. He can set goals for himself, plan future action and consider the consequences of alternative courses of action. With an awareness of self, the individual is able to see himself as others see him. When he takes the role of others, he observes

himse..
that othe
The individua.
to modify his actions
tudes of the community and juuge
generalized other. From this perspective thoug
versation going on between this generalized other and the individual'.
Thus a person is constantly asking what will people think and expect
when he reflects upon himself. In this way conduct is regulated in terms of
the expectations and attitudes of others. Mead argues that, 'It is in the
form of the generalized other that the social process influences the behaviour of the individuals involved in it . . . that the community exercises
control over the conduct of its individual members'.

Mead's view of human interaction sees man as both actively creating
the social environment and being shaped by it. The individual initiates
and directs his own action while at the same time being influenced by the
attitudes and expectations of others in the form of the generalized other.
The individual and society are regarded as inseparable for the individual
can only become a human being in a social context. In this context he
develops a sense of self which is a prerequisite for thought. He learns to
take the roles of others which is essential both for the development of self
and for cooperative action. Without communication in terms of symbols
whose meanings are shared, these processes would not be possible. Man
therefore lives in a world of symbols which give meaning and significance
to life and provide the basis for human interaction.

Herbert Blumer

Blumer, a student of George Herbert Mead, has systematically developed the ideas of his mentor. In Blumer's view, symbolic interactionism
rests on three basic premises. Firstly, human beings act on the basis of
meanings which they give to objects and events rather than simply reacting either to external stimuli such as social forces or internal stimuli such
as organic drives. Symbolic interactionism therefore rejects both societal
and biological determinism. Secondly, meanings arise from the process
of interaction rather than simply being present at the outset and shaping
future action. To some degree meanings are created, modified, developed and changed within interaction situations rather than being fixed
and preformed. In the process of interaction actors do not slavishly
follow preset norms or mechanically act out established roles. Thirdly,
meanings are the result of interpretive procedures employed by actors
within interaction contexts. By taking the role of the other, actors interpret the meanings and intentions of others. By means of 'the mechanism
of self-interaction', individuals modify or change their definition of the
situation, rehearse alternative courses of action and consider their

possible consequ~~~
context of interaction via ~ ~

Blumer argues that the intera~ ~ ~ply
with the view of social action presen~ ~ogy. He
maintains that society must be seen as an c~ of interaction
involving actors who are constantly adjusting ~ ~her and contin-
uously interpreting the situation. By contrast, ma~ ~am sociology and
functionalism in particular have tended to portray ac~ion as a mechanical
response to the constraints of social systems. This view fails to see 'the
social actions of individuals in human society as being constructed by
them through a process of interpretation. Instead action is treated as a
product of factors which play on and through individuals'. Rather than
actively creating his own social world, man is pictured as passively
responding to external constraints. His actions are shaped by the needs of
social systems and the values, roles and norms which form a part of those
systems. Blumer rejects this view arguing that, 'the likening of human
group life to the operation of a mechanical structure, or to the functioning of a system seeking equilibrium, seems to me to face grave difficulties
in view of the formative and explorative character of interaction as the
participants judge each other and guide their own acts by that judgment'.

Although he is critical of those who see action as a predictable and standardized response to external constraints, Blumer accepts that action is
to some degree structured and routinized. He states that, 'In most situations in which people act towards one another they have in advance a firm
understanding of how to act and how other people will act'. However,
such knowledge offers only general guidelines for conduct. It does not
provide a precise and detailed recipe for action which is mechanically followed in every situation. Within these guidelines there is considerable
room for manoeuvre, negotiation, mutual adjustment and interpretation. Similarly, Blumer recognizes the existence of social institutions
and admits that they place limits on human conduct, but even in situations where strict rules prevail, there is still considerable room for human
initiative and creativity. Evidence in support of this view is presented in
the chapter on organizations and bureaucracy. (See Blau's research on
'unofficial practices, pp. 297–300.) Even when action appears particularly standardized and structured, this should not be taken as an indication
that actors are merely responding to external forces. Blumer argues that,
'The common repetitive behaviour of people in such situations should
not mislead the student into believing that no process of interpretation is
in play; on the contrary, even though fixed, the actions of the participating people are constructed by them through a process of interpretation'.
Thus standardized action is constructed by social actors, not by social
systems.

Much of Blumer's work has been concerned with developing an appropriate methodology for his view of human interaction. He rejects what he

regards as the simplistic attempts to establish causal relationships which characterize positivist methodology. As an example, Blumer refers to the proposition that industrialization causes the replacement of extended with nuclear families. He objects to the procedure of isolating variables and assuming one causes the other with little or no reference to the actor's view of the situation. He argues that data on the meanings and interpretations which actors give to the various facets of industrialization and family life are essential before a relationship can be established between the two factors. Blumer claims that many sociologists conduct their research with only a superficial familiarity with the area of life under investigation. This is often combined with a preoccupation for aping the research procedures of the natural sciences. The net result is the imposition of operational definitions on the social world with little regard for their relevance to that world. Rather than viewing social reality from the actor's perspective, many sociologists have attempted to force it into predefined categories and concepts. This provides little chance of capturing social reality but a very good chance of distorting it.

In place of such procedures Blumer argues that the sociologist must immerse himself in the area of life which he seeks to investigate. Rather than attempting to fit data into predefined categories, he must attempt to grasp the actor's view of social reality. This involves 'feeling one's way inside the experience of the actor'. Since action is directed by actors' meanings, the sociologist must 'catch the process of interpretation through which they construct their action'. This means he 'must take the role of the acting unit whose behaviour he is studying'. Blumer offers no simple solutions as to how this type of research may be conducted. However, the flavour of the research procedures he advocates is captured in the following quotation: 'It is a tough job requiring a high order of careful and honest probing, creative yet disciplined imagination, resourcefulness and flexibility in study, pondering over what one is finding, and a constant readiness to test and recast one's views and images of the area'.

Fred Davis

This section examines a typical piece of research conducted from an interactionist perspective. It provides specific illustrations for many of the general points made in the preceding sections. (For further applications of the interactionist approach see Chapter 5, pp. 207–15; Chapter 7, pp. 315–20; and Chapter 10, pp. 429–38.) In an article entitled, *Deviance Disavowal: The Management of Strained Interaction by the Visibly Handicapped*, Fred Davis examines interaction situations involving physically handicapped and 'normal' persons. Davis obtained his data from lengthy interviews with people who were blind, facially disfigured or crippled and confined to wheelchairs. He was concerned with interaction situations which lasted longer than a passing exchange but not long enough for close familiarity to develop. Such situations would include a conversation with a fellow passenger, getting to know someone at work and socializing at a party. The handicapped person wishes to present himself as 'someone who is merely different physically but not socially deviant'. He seeks to achieve ease and naturalness in his interaction with others since this will symbolize the fact that they have accepted his preferred definition of self, but his handicap poses a number of threats to the type of sociability he desires. This stems from the fact that he is defined as 'different', 'odd' and something other than normal by those who do not share his disability.

The first threat to sociability involves the possibility that others will become preoccupied with the handicap. The norms of everyday, casual sociability require an individual to act as if the other were a whole person rather than expressing concern or interest in a particular aspect of his person. However, there is a danger that the visible handicap will become the focal point of the interaction. Davis's respondents stated that the normal was unlikely to make explicit references to their handicap but it appeared to be 'uppermost in his awareness'. They sensed the normal's discomfort and felt it placed a strain on the interaction. In particular they noted 'confused and halting speech, the fixed stare elsewhere, the artificial levity, the compulsive loquaciousness, the awkward solemnity'. Such responses disrupted the smooth flow of interaction.

A second threat to sociability arises from the possibility that the handicap will lead to displays of emotion which exceed acceptable limits. Thus normals may be openly shocked, disgusted, pitying or fearful. Such emotional displays overstep what is usually considered appropriate and so place a strain on the interaction. Even if the normal manages to contain his emotion, sociability may be further threatened by what Davis terms the 'contradiction of attributes'. This involves an apparent contradiction between the normal attributes of the handicapped person such as his job, interests and other aspects of his appearance, and his handicap. This contrast often appears discordant to others and can result in remarks such as, 'How strange that someone so pretty should be in a wheelchair'. According to Davis's respondents, such remarks 'almost invariably cast a pall on the interaction and embarrass the recovery of smooth social posture'. Finally, sociability may be threatened by uncertainty concerning the ability of handicapped persons to participate in particular activities. For example, normals are unsure whether a blind person should be invited to the theatre or a crippled person asked to play a game of bowls. This uncertainty can place a strain on the interaction when the handicapped person is invited to participate in such activities. If he refuses the normal person will wonder whether he is simply being polite or whether his handicap actually prevents participation. Similarly, the handicapped person wonders whether the normal genuinely wants his company or is merely acting out of pity. Such uncertainties threaten to mar the ease and smoothness of the interaction process.

549

Having examined the threats that a visible handicap poses to the 'framework of rules and assumptions that guide sociability', Davis then looks at the way handicapped persons cope with these threats. He argues that the handicapped attempt to 'disavow deviance', to present themselves as normal people who happen to have a handicap. Davis identifies three stages in the process of 'deviance disavowal and normalization'. The first stage, 'fictional acceptance', follows the standard pattern of interaction when two people meet. There is a surface acceptance of the other which involves polite conversation and no apparent recognition of important differences between them. In the case of the visibly handicapped however, 'the interaction is kept starved at a bare subsistence level of sociability'. The handicapped person is treated like the poor relative at a wedding reception. Yet, he must maintain this polite fiction, no matter how 'transparent and confining it is', in order to move to the next stage which involves 'something more genuinely sociable'. If he exposed the polite fiction, the interaction might cease and the next stage would not be reached.

In order to move beyond 'fictional acceptance', the handicapped person must redefine himself in the eyes of others. He must project 'images, attitudes and concepts of self' which encourage the other to accept him as a normal person. Davis's respondents used a number of strategies to disavow deviance and project their desired self-image. For example they talked about their involvement in normal, everyday activities, joked about their disability to imply it was relatively insignificant and tried to give the impression that they were not offended by the unease of others. In this way they attempted to symbolize their normality.

Once others have accepted the handicapped person as normal, the relationship can then move to a third stage which Davis terms the 'institutionalization of the normalized relationship'. This can take two forms. In the first, the handicapped person is fully accepted into the world of normals who largely forget his disability. This can cause problems, however, since at certain times special consideration is needed for the handicap. Thus the handicapped person must achieve a delicate balance between 'special arrangements and understandings' and normal relationships. A second form of institutionalization involves a process whereby the normal person becomes rather like an adopted or honorary member of the handicapped group. In this way he vicariously shares the experiences and outlook of the handicapped and gains a 'strictly in-group license to lampoon and mock the handicap in a way that would be regarded as highly offensive were it to come from an uninitiated normal'. Once a normalized relationship is institutionalized the strains which previously beset the interaction process are largely removed.

Davis's study provides a classic example of the type of research which typifies symbolic interactionism. It focusses on small-scale face to face interaction. It portrays the complex process of role-taking and shows how interaction develops via a series of interpretive procedures. It emphasizes the importance of symbols and reveals how a phrase or a gesture can symbolize a set of attitudes. It illustrates the priority which interactionists assign to the concept of self. The handicapped are shown interacting with self, projecting images of self and managing the impressions of self which others receive. Davis's study subtly portrays the flexibility, creativity and mutual adjustment which interactionists see as the essence of human interaction.

Symbolic interactionism – a critique

Interactionists have often been accused of examining human interaction in a vacuum. They have tended to focus on small-scale face to face interaction with little concern for its historical or social setting. They have concentrated on particular situations and encounters with little reference to the historical events which led up to them or the wider social framework in which they occur. Since these factors influence the particular interaction situation, the scant attention they have received has been regarded as a serious omission. Thus in a criticism of Mead, Ropers argues that, 'The activities that he sees men engaged in are not historically determined relationships of social and historical continuity; they are merely episodes, interactions, encounters, and situations' (quoted in Meltzer, Petras and Reynolds, 1975, p. 97).

While symbolic interactionism provides a corrective to the excesses of societal determinism, many critics have argued that it has gone too far in this direction. Though they claim that action is not determined by structural norms, interactionists do admit the presence of such norms. However, they tend to take them as given rather than explaining their origin. Thus Fred Davis refers to the 'framework of rules and assumptions that guide sociability', in other words the norms of sociability. Yet he simply assumes their existence rather than attempting to explain their source. As William Skidmore comments, the interactionists largely fail to explain 'why people consistently choose to act in given ways in certain situations, instead of in all the other ways they might possibly have acted'. In stressing the flexibility and freedom of human action the interactionists tend to downplay the constraints on action. In Skidmore's view this is due to the fact that 'interactionism consistently fails to give an account of social structure'. In other words it fails to adequately explain how standardized normative behaviour comes about and why members of society are motivated to act in terms of social norms.

Similar criticisms have been made with reference to what many see as the failure of interactionists to explain the source of the meanings to which they attach such importance. As the chapters on education and deviance have shown, interactionism provides little indication of the origins of the meanings in terms of which individuals are labelled by teachers, police and probation officers. (See Chapter 5, pp. 214–15 and Chapter 10, pp. 437–8.) Critics argue that such meanings are not spontaneously created in interaction situations. Instead they are systematically generated by the social structure. Thus Marxists have argued that the meanings which operate in face to face interaction situations are largely the product of class relationships. From this viewpoint, interactionists have failed to explain the most significant thing about meanings: the source of their origin.

Symbolic interactionism is a distinctly American branch of sociology and to some this partly explains its shortcomings. Thus Leon Shaskolsky has argued that interactionism is largely a reflection of the cultural ideals of American society. He claims that, 'Symbolic interactionism has its roots deeply imbedded in the cultural environment of American life, and its interpretation of society is, in a sense, a "looking glass" image of what that society purports to be'. Thus the emphasis on liberty, freedom and individuality in interactionism can be seen in part as a reflection of America's view of itself. Shaskolsky argues that this helps to explain why the interactionist perspective finds less support in Europe since there is a greater awareness in European societies of the constraints of power and class domination. By reflecting American ideals, Shaskolsky argues that interactionism has failed to face up to and take account of the harsher realities of social life. Whatever its shortcomings however, many would agree with William Skidmore that, 'On the positive side, it is clearly true that some of the most fascinating sociology is in the symbolic interactionist tradition'.

Ethnomethodology

Ethnomethodology is the most recent of the four theoretical perspectives examined in this chapter. The term was coined by the American sociologist Harold Garfinkel who is generally regarded as its founder. Garfinkel's book, *Studies in Ethnomethodology*, which provided the initial framework for the perspective, was published in 1967. Roughly translated, ethnomethodology means the study of the methods used by people. It is concerned with examining the methods and procedures employed by members of society to construct, account for and give meaning to their social world. Ethnomethodologists draw heavily on the European tradition of phenomenological philosophy and in particular acknowledge a debt to the ideas of the philosopher–sociologist Alfred Schutz (1899–1959). Many ethnomethodologists begin with the assumption that society exists only in so far as members perceive its existence. (The term member replaces the interactionist term actor.) With this emphasis on members' views of social reality, ethnomethodology is generally regarded as a phenomenological approach. Ethnomethodology is a developing perspective which contains a diversity of viewpoints. The following account provides a brief and partial introduction.

Ethnomethodology and the problem of order

One of the major concerns of sociology is the explanation of social order. From the results of numerous investigations it appears that social life is ordered and regular and that social action is systematic and patterned. Typically the sociologist has assumed that social order has an objective reality. His research has apparently indicated that it actually exists. He then goes on to explain its origin, to provide causal explanations for its presence. Thus from a functionalist perspective, social order derives ultimately from the functional prerequisites of social systems which require its presence as a necessary condition of their existence. Social action assumes its systematic and regular nature from the fact that it is governed by values and norms which guide and direct behaviour. From a Marxian perspective social order is seen as precarious but its existence is recognized. It results from the constraints imposed on members of society by their position in the relations of production and from the reinforcement of these constraints by the superstructure. From an interactionist perspective, social order results from interpretive procedures employed by actors in interaction situations. It is a 'negotiated order' in that it derives from meanings which are negotiated in the process of interaction and involves the mutual adjustment of the actors concerned. The net result is the establishment of social order, of an orderly, regular and patterned process of interaction. Although the above perspectives provide very different explanations for social order, they nevertheless agree that some form of order actually exists and that it therefore has an objective reality.

Ethnomethodologists either suspend or abandon the belief that an actual or objective social order exists. Instead they proceed from the assumption that social life appears orderly to members of society. Thus in the eyes of members their everyday activities seem ordered and systematic but this order is not necessarily due to the intrinsic nature or inherent qualities of the social world. In other words it may not actually exist. Rather it may simply appear to exist because of the way members perceive and interpret social reality. Social order therefore becomes a convenient fiction, an appearance of order constructed by members of society. This appearance allows the social world to be described and explained and so made knowable, reasonable, understandable and 'accountable' to its members. The methods and accounting procedures used by members for creating a sense of order form the subject matter of ethnomethodological enquiry. Zimmerman and Wieder state that the ethnomethodologist is 'concerned with how members of society go about the task of *seeing, describing*, and *explaining* order in the world in which they live'.

This view of social order may be illustrated by Atkinson's research on suicide described in the previous chapter (pp. 498–501). Coroners are in the business of producing order. They are presented with a series of ambiguous and equivocal deaths, required to provide an explanation for them and to define them as suicide or non-suicide. They are therefore asked to construct order by categorizing and classifying deaths and providing acceptable explanations for those deaths. Atkinson argues that in this way coroners make 'otherwise disordered and potentially senseless events ordered and sensible'. However, the coroners' construction of order does not necessarily reflect the existence of an objective order. Thus deaths categorized as suicide may have little or nothing in common. They may simply be given the appearance of similarity by the interpretive procedures and methods of reasoning employed by coroners. If this is so, it makes little sense for sociologists to regard suicide statistics as 'facts' and then proceed to examine the causes of suicide. Suicide is a member's construction rather than an objective reality. The job of the sociologist is not to explain suicide as if it actually existed but to examine the methods and procedures employed to categorize deaths as suicide. More generally, sociologists should not regard social order as a fact but rather as an appearance of order constructed by members. The job of the sociologist then becomes the discovery of the methods and accounting procedures used by members to construct the appearance of order.

The above points will now be illustrated and developed by examining two studies conducted from an ethnomethodological perspective.

Harold Garfinkel – an experiment in counselling

Garfinkel argues that members employ the 'documentary method' to make sense and account for the social world and to give it an appearance of order. This method consists of selecting certain aspects of the infinite number of features contained in any situation or context, of defining them in a particular way and seeing them as evidence of an underlying pattern. The process is then reversed and particular instances of the underlying pattern are then used as evidence for the existence of the pattern. In Garfinkel's words, the documentary method 'consists of treating an actual appearance as "the document of", as "pointing to", as "standing on behalf of" a presupposed underlying pattern. Not only is the underlying pattern derived from its individual documentary evidences, but the individual documentary evidences, in their turn, are interpreted on the basis of "what is known" about the underlying pattern. Each is used to elaborate the other'. For example, in the case of Atkinson's study of coroners, those deaths defined as suicide were seen as such by reference to an underlying pattern. This pattern is the coroner's commonsense theory of suicide. However, at the same time, those deaths defined as suicide were seen as evidence for the existence of the underlying pattern. In this way particular instances of the pattern and the pattern itself are mutually reinforcing and are used to elaborate each other. Thus the documentary method can be seen as 'reflexive'. The particular instance is seen as a reflection of the underlying pattern and vice versa. Garfinkel argues that social life is 'essentially reflexive'. Members of society are constantly referring aspects of activities and situations to presumed underlying patterns and confirming the existence of those patterns by reference to particular instances of their expression. In this way members produce accounts of the social world which not only make sense of and explain but actually constitute that world. Thus in providing accounts of suicide, coroners are actually producing suicide. Their accounts of suicide constitute suicide in the social world. In this respect accounts are a part of the things they describe and explain. The social world is therefore constituted by the methods and accounting procedures in terms of which it is identified, described and explained. Thus the social world is constructed by its members by the use of the documentary method. This is what Garfinkel means when he describes social reality as 'essentially reflexive'.

Garfinkel claims to have demonstrated the documentary method and its reflexive nature by an experiment conducted in a university department of psychiatry. Students were invited to take part in what was described as a new form of psychotherapy. They were asked to summarize a personal problem on which they required advice and then ask a counsellor a series of questions. The counsellor sat in a room adjoining the student; they could not see each other and communicated via an intercom. The counsellor was limited to responses of either 'yes' or 'no'. Unknown to the student, his advisor was not a counsellor and the answers he received were evenly divided between 'yes' and 'no', their sequence being predetermined in accordance with a table of random numbers.

In one case a student was worried about his relationship with his girlfriend. He was Jewish and she was a Gentile. He was worried about his parents' reaction to the relationship and the problems that might result from marriage and children. His questions were addressed to these concerns. Despite the fact that the answers he received were random, given without reference to the content of questions and sometimes contradicted previous answers, the student found them helpful, reasonable and sensible. Similar assessments of the counselling sessions were made by the other students in the experiment. From comments made by the students on each of the answers they received, Garfinkel draws the following conclusions. Students *made* sense of the answers where no sense existed; they imposed an order on the answers where no order was present. When answers appeared contradictory or surprising, the students assumed that the counsellor was unaware of the full facts of their case. The students constructed an appearance of order by using the documentary method. From the first answer they perceived an underlying pattern in the counsellor's advice. The sense of each following answer was interpreted in terms of the pattern and at the same time each answer was seen as evidence for the existence of the pattern. Thus the students' method of interpretation was reflexive. Not only did they produce an account of the counselling session but the account became a part of and so constituted the session. In this way the accounting procedure described and explained and also constructed and constituted social reality at one and the same time. Garfinkel claims that the counselling experiment highlights and captures the procedures that members are constantly using in their everyday lives to construct the social world.

This experiment can also be used to illustrate the idea of 'indexicality', a central concept employed by Garfinkel and other ethnomethodologists. Indexicality means that the sense of any object or activity is derived from its context, it is 'indexed' in a particular situation. As a result any interpretation, explanation or account made by members in their everyday lives is made with reference to particular circumstances and situations. Thus the students' sense of the counsellor's answers was derived from the context of the interaction. From the setting – a psychiatry department – and the information they were given, the students believed that the counsellor was what he claimed to be and that he was doing his best to give honest and sound advice. His answers were interpreted within the framework of this context. If identical answers were received to the same set of questions from a fellow student in a coffee bar, the change of context would probably result in a very different interpretation. Such responses from a fellow student may be seen as evidence that he had temporarily taken leave of his senses or was having a joke at his friend's expense or was under the influence of alcohol and so on. Garfinkel argues that the sense of any action is achieved by reference to its context. Members' sense of what is happening or going on depends on the way they interpret the context of the activity concerned. In this respect their understandings and accounts are indexical: they make sense in terms of particular settings.

Don H. Zimmerman – *The Practicalities of Rule Use*

Studies of bureaucracies, as Chapter 7 has indicated, have often been concerned with the nature of rules in bureaucratic organizations. The bureaucrat is usually seen as strictly conforming to formal rules or else acting in terms of a system of informal rules. In either case his behaviour is seen to be governed by rules. Zimmerman's study suggests an alternative perspective. Rather than seeing behaviour as governed by rules, he suggests that members employ rules to describe and account for their activity. Part of this activity may be in direct violation of a stated rule yet it is still justified with reference to the rule. This paradox will be explained shortly.

Zimmerman studied behaviour in a US Bureau of Public Assistance. Clients applying for assistance were assigned to caseworkers by receptionists. Officially, the assignment procedure was conducted in terms of a simple rule. If there were four caseworkers, the first four clients who arrived were assigned one to each caseworker. The next four clients were assigned in a similar manner, providing the second interview of the day for each caseworker and so on. However, from time to time the rule was broken. For example a particular caseworker may have had a difficult case and the interview may have lasted far longer than usual. In this situation a receptionist may have reorganized the assignment list and switched his next client to another caseworker.

Such rule violations were justified and explained by the receptionists in terms of the rule. In their eyes by breaking the rule they were conforming to the rule. This paradox can be explained by the receptionists' view of the intention of the rule. From their viewpoint, it was intended to keep clients moving with a minimum of delay so that all had been attended to at the end of the day. Thus violating the rule to ensure this outcome can be explained as following the rule. This was the way receptionists justified and explained their conduct to themselves and their fellow workers. By seeing their activity as conforming to a rule, they created an appearance of order. However, rather than simply being directed by rules, Zimmerman argues that the receptionists were constantly monitoring and assessing the situation and improvising and adapting their conduct in terms of what they saw as the requirements of the situation. Zimmerman claims that his research indicates that, 'the actual practices of using rules do not permit an analyst to account for regular patterns of behaviour by invoking the notion that these practices occur because members of society are following rules'. He argues that the use of rules by members to describe and account for their conduct 'makes social settings appear orderly for the participants and it is this *sense and appearance* of order that rules in use, in fact, provide and what the ethnomethodologists, in fact study'.

Zimmerman's research highlights some of the main concerns of ethnomethodology. It provides an example of the documentary method and illustrates the reflexive nature of the procedures used by members to construct an appearance of order. Receptionists interpret their activity as evidence of an underlying pattern – the intent of the rule – and they see particular actions, even when they violate the rules, as evidence of the underlying pattern.

Ethnomethodology and mainstream sociology

Garfinkel argues that mainstream sociology has typically portrayed man as a 'cultural dope' who simply acts out the standardized directives provided by the culture of his society. Garfinkel states that, 'By "cultural dope" I refer to the man-in-the-sociologist's society who produces the stable features of society by acting in compliance with preestablished and legitimate alternatives of action that the common culture provides'. In place of the 'cultural dope', the ethnomethodologist pictures the skilled member who is constantly attending to the particular, indexical qualities of situations, giving them meaning, making them knowable, communicating this knowledge to others and constructing a sense and appearance of order. From this perspective members construct and accomplish their own social world rather than being shaped by it.

Ethnomethodologists are highly critical of other branches of sociology. They argue that 'conventional' sociologists have misunderstood the nature of social reality. They have treated the social world as if it had an objective reality which is independent of members' accounts and interpretations. Thus they have regarded aspects of the social world such as suicide and crime as facts with an existence of their own. They have then attempted to provide explanations for these 'facts'. By contrast, ethnomethodologists argue that the social world consists of nothing more than the constructs, interpretations and accounts of its members. The job of the sociologist is therefore to explain the methods and accounting procedures which members employ to construct their social world. According to ethnomethodologists, this is the very job that mainstream sociology has failed to do.

Ethnomethodologists see little difference between conventional sociologists and the man in the street. They argue that the methods employed by sociologists in their research are basically similar to those used by members of society in their everyday lives. Members employing the documentary method are constantly theorizing, drawing relationships between activities and making the social world appear orderly and systematic. They then treat the social world as if it had an objective reality separate from themselves. Ethnomethodologists argue that the procedures of conventional sociologists are essentially similar. They employ the documentary method, theorize and draw relationships and construct a picture of an orderly and systematic social system. They operate reflexively like any other member of society. Thus when a functionalist sees behaviour as an expression of an underlying pattern of shared values, he also uses instances of that behaviour as evidence for the existence of the pattern. By means of their accounting procedures members construct a picture of society. In this sense the man in the street is his own sociologist. Ethnomethodologists see little to choose between the pictures of society which he creates and those provided by conventional sociologists.

Ethnomethodology – a critique

Ethnomethodology's criticism of mainstream sociology has been returned by those it has labelled as conventional or 'folk' sociologists. Its critics have argued that the members who populate the kind of society portrayed by ethnomethodologists appear to lack any motives and goals. As Anthony Giddens remarks, there is little reference to 'the pursuance of practical goals or interests'. What, for example, motivated the students in Garfinkel's counselling experiment or the receptionists in Zimmerman's study? There is little indication in the writings of ethnomethodologists as to why people want to behave or are made to behave in particular ways. Nor is there much consideration of the nature of power in the social world and the possible effects of differences in power on members' behaviour. As Gouldner notes, 'The process by which social reality becomes defined and established is not viewed by Garfinkel as entailing a process of struggle among competing groups' definitions of reality, and the outcome, the common sense conception of the world, is not seen as having been shaped by institutionally protected power differences'. Critics have argued that ethnomethodologists have failed to give due consideration to the fact that members' accounting procedures are conducted within a system of social relationships involving differences in power. Many ethnomethodologists appear to dismiss everything which is not recognized and accounted for by members of society. They imply that if members do not recognize the existence of objects and events, they are unaffected by them. But as John H. Goldthorpe pointedly remarks in his criticism of ethnomethodology, 'If for instance, it is bombs and napalm that are zooming down, members do not have to be oriented towards them in any particular way, or at all, in order to be killed by them'. Clearly members do not have to recognize certain constraints in order for their behaviour to be affected by them. As Goldthorpe notes, with reference to the above example, death 'limits interaction in a fairly decisive way'. Finally, the ethnomethodologists' criticism of mainstream sociology can be redirected to themselves. As Giddens remarks, 'any ethnomethodological account must display the same characteristics as it claims to discern in the accounts of lay actors'. Ethnomethodologists' accounting procedures therefore become a topic for study like those of conventional sociologists or any other member of society. In theory the process of accounting for accounts is never ending. Carried to its extreme, the ethnomethodological position implies that nothing is ever knowable. Whatever its shortcomings, however, ethnomethodology asks interesting questions.

This comment is equally applicable to sociology as a whole.

Bibliography

Aaronvitch, S.	*The Ruling Class* (Lawrence and Wishart, London, 1961)
Abel-Smith, B. and Townsend, P.	*The Poor and the Poorest* (G. Bell & Sons, London, 1965)
Aberle, D.	*A Note on Relative Deprivation Theory as Applied to Millenarian Movements and other Cult Movements* in Lessa and Vogt, 1965
Aginsky, B. W.	'A Pomo's Soliloquy' in *Every Man His Way: Readings in Cultural Anthropology* edited by A. Dundes (Prentice-Hall, Englewood Cliffs, 1968)
Albrow, M.	*Bureaucracy* (Pall Mall Press, London, 1970)
Alexandrov, G. F. *et al*	'The Urban Strata of Contemporary Capitalist Society' in *American and Soviet Society* edited by P. Hollander (Prentice-Hall, Englewood Cliffs, 1969)
Allen, V. L.	*The Sociology of Industrial Relations* (Longman, London, 1971)
Althusser, L.	*Ideology and Ideological State Apparatuses* in Cosin, 1972
Anderson, M.	'Family, Household and the Industrial Revolution' in *Sociology of the Family* edited by M. Anderson (Penguin Books, Harmondsworth, 1971)
Andry, R. G.	*Parental Affection and Delinquency* in Wolfgang, Savitz and Johnston, 1962
Arensberg, C. M. and Kimball, S. T.	*Family and Community in Ireland* 2nd edition (Harvard University Press, Cambridge, USA, 1968)
Aron, R.	*Social Class, Political Class, Ruling Class* in Bendix and Lipset, 1967 *Main Currents in Sociological Thought* vols 1 and 2 (Penguin Books, Harmondsworth, 1968 and 1970)
Atkinson, J. M.	*Societal Reactions to Suicide* in Cohen, 1971 *Discovering Suicide* (Macmillan, London, 1978)
Barber, B.	Some Problems in the Sociology of Professions *Daedalus*, vol 92 no 4, 1963 *Acculturation and Messianic Movements* in Lessa and Vogt, 1965
Barker, D. L. and Allen, S. (eds)	*Dependence and Exploitation in Work and Marriage* (Longman, London, 1976)

Barron, R. D. and
Norris, G. M.

Sexual Divisions and the Dual Labour Market in Barker and Allen, 1976

Bebel, A.

'Women and Socialism' in *Feminism: The Essential Historical Writings* edited by M. Schneir (Vintage Books, New York, 1972)

Becker, H. S.

Outsiders (The Free Press, New York, 1963)
Sociological Work (Transaction Books, New Brunswick, 1970)
Social-Class Variations in the Teacher–Pupil Relationship in Cosin, Dale, Esland and Swift, 1971
Personal Change in Adult Life in Cosin, Dale, Esland and Swift, 1971
'Labelling Theory Reconsidered' in *Deviance and Social Control* edited by P. Rock and M. McIntosh (Tavistock, London, 1974)

Beck, J., Jenks, C.,
Keddie, N. and
Young, M. F. D. (eds)

Worlds Apart: Readings for a Sociology of Education (Collier-Macmillan, London, 1976)

Bellah, R. N.

Religious Evolution in Lessa and Vogt, 1965
New Religious Consciousness and the Crisis in Modernity in Glock and Bellah, 1976

Bell, C. R.

Middle Class Families (Routledge & Kegan Paul, London, 1968)

Bell, N. W. and
Vogel, E. F. (eds)

A Modern Introduction to the Family revised edition (The Free Press, New York, 1968)

Bendix, R. and
Lipset, S. M. (eds)

Class, Status, and Power 2nd edition (Routledge & Kegan Paul, London, 1967)

Benet, M. K.

Secretary: An Enquiry into the Female Ghetto (Sidgwick & Jackson, London, 1972)

Benston, M.

The Political Economy of Women's Liberation in Glazer-Malbin and Waehrer, 1972

Berger, P. L.

Invitation to Sociology (Penguin Books, Harmondsworth, 1966)
'Religious Institutions' in *Sociology: An Introduction* edited by N. J. Smelser (John Wiley & Sons, New York, 1967)
The Sacred Canopy: Elements of a Sociological Theory of Religion (Doubleday, New York, 1967)
A Rumour of Angels: Modern Society and the Rediscovery of the Supernatural (Allen Lane, London, 1970)

Berger, P. L. and
Luckmann, T.

Sociology of Religion and Sociology of Knowledge in Robertson, 1969

Berger, P. L.,
Berger, B. and
Kellner, H

The Homeless Mind: Modernization and Consciousness (Penguin Books, Harmondsworth, 1974)

Sociology

Berlin, I.   *Karl Marx* 4th edition (Oxford University Press, Oxford, 1978)

Bernard, J.   *The Future of Marriage* (Penguin Books, Harmondsworth, 1976)

Bernbaum, G.   *Knowledge and Ideology in the Sociology of Education* (Macmillan, London, 1977)

Bernstein, B.   *Social Class and Linguistic Development: A Theory of Social Learning* in Halsey, Floud and Anderson, 1961
A Socio-Linguistic Approach to Social Learning in Worsley, 1970
Education Cannot Compensate for Society in Cosin, Dale, Esland and Swift, 1971
Language and Social Context in Giglioli, 1972

Béteille, A.   *Inequality Among Men* (Basil Blackwell, Oxford, 1977)

Béteille, A. (ed)   *Social Inequality* (Penguin Books, Harmondsworth, 1969)

Bettelheim, B.   *The Children of the Dream* (Thames & Hudson, London, 1969)

Beynon, H.   *Working for Ford* (Allen Lane, Harmondsworth, 1973)

Bierstedt, R.   *The Social Order* (McGraw-Hill, New York, 1963)

Birnbaum, N. and Lenzer, G. (eds)   *Sociology and Religion: A Book of Readings* (Prentice-Hall, Englewood Cliffs, 1969)

Blackburn, R. M. and Mann, M.   *Ideology in the Non-skilled Working Class* in Bulmer, 1975

Blackburn, R. M. and Stewart, A.   'Women, Work and the Class Structure' *New Society* vol 41 no 788, 1 September 1977

Blauner, R.   *Alienation and Freedom* (University of Chicago Press, Chicago, 1964)
Work Satisfaction and Industrial Trends in Modern Society in Worsley, 1972

Blau, P. M.   *The Dynamics of Bureaucracy* 2nd edition (University of Chicago Press, Chicago, 1963)
On the Nature of Organizations (John Wiley & Sons, New York, 1974)

Blau, P. M. and Meyer, M. W.   *Bureaucracy in Modern Society* 2nd edition (Random House, New York, 1971)

Blau, P. M. and Schoenherr, R. A.   *The Structure of Organizations* (Basic Books, New York, 1971)

Blood, R. O. Jr and Hamblin, R. L.   *The Effects of the Wife's Employment on the Family Power Structure* in Bell and Vogel, 1968

Blumer, H.   *Society as Symbolic Interaction* in Rose, 1962

	Symbolic Interactionism (Prentice-Hall, Englewood Cliffs, 1969)
Bodmer, W. F.	'Race and IQ: The Genetic Background' in *Race, Culture and Intelligence* edited by K. Richardson and D. Spears (Penguin Books, Harmondsworth, 1972)
Bordua, D.	*A Critique of Sociological Interpretations of Gang Delinquency* in Wolfgang, Savitz and Johnston, 1962
Bott, E.	*Family and Social Network* 2nd edition (Tavistock, London, 1971)
Bottomore, T. B.	*Classes in Modern Society* (George Allen & Unwin, London, 1965) *Elites and Society* (Penguin Books, Harmondsworth, 1966)
Bottomore, T. B. and Rubel, M. (eds)	*Karl Marx: Selected Writings in Sociology and Social Philosophy* (Penguin Books, Harmondsworth, 1963)
Boudon, R.	*Education, Opportunity and Social Inequality* (John Wiley & Sons, New York, 1974)
Bourdieu, P.	*Intellectual Field and Creative Project* in Young, 1971 *Systems of Education and Systems of Thought* in Young, 1971 *Cultural Reproduction and Social Reproduction* in Brown, 1973 *The School as a Conservative Force: Scholastic and Cultural Inequalities* in Eggleston, 1974
Bourdieu, P. and De Saint-Martin, M.	*Scholastic Excellence and the Values of the Educational System* in Eggleston, 1974
Bourdieu, P. and Passeron, J.	*Reproduction in Education, Society and Culture* (Sage Publications, London, 1977)
Bourne, R.	'The Snakes and Ladders of the British Class System' *New Society* vol 47 no 853, 8 February 1979
Bowlby, J.	*Forty-four Juvenile Thieves* (Tindall and Cox, London, 1946) *Child Care and the Growth of Love* (Penguin Books, Harmondsworth, 1953)
Bowles, S. and Gintis, H.	*Schooling in Capitalist America* (Routledge & Kegan Paul, London, 1976)
Braverman, H.	*Labor and Monopoly Capitalism* (Monthly Review Press, New York, 1974)
Brown, R. (ed)	*Knowledge, Education and Cultural Change* (Tavistock, London, 1973)
Budd, S.	*Sociologists and Religion* (Collier-Macmillan, London, 1973)
Bulmer, M. (ed)	*Working-Class Images of Society* (Routledge &

	Kegan Paul, London, 1975)
	Sociological Research Methods (Macmillan, London, 1977)
Burnham, J.	*The Managerial Revolution* (Putman & Co, London, 1943)
Burns, T.	*Leisure in Industrial Society* in Smith, Parker and Smith, 1973
Burns, T. (ed)	*Industrial Man* (Penguin Books, Harmondsworth, 1969)
Burns, T. and Stalker, G. M.	*The Management of Innovation* 2nd edition (Tavistock, London, 1966)
Butler, D. E. and Rose, R.	*The British General Election of 1959* (Frank Cass, London, 1960)
Butterworth, E. and Weir, D. (eds)	*The Sociology of Modern Britain* revised edition (Fontana, Glasgow, 1975)
Caplovitz, D.	*The Poor Pay More* (The Free Press, New York, 1963)
Caplow, T.	*The Sociology of Work* (McGraw-Hill, New York, 1954)
Carson, W. G.	*White-Collar Crime and the Enforcement of Factory Legislation* in Carson and Wiles, 1971
Carson, W. G. and Wiles, P. (eds)	*Crime and Delinquency in Britain* (Martin Robertson, London, 1971)
Chambliss, W. J.	*Functional and Conflict Theories of Crime* in Chambliss and Mankoff, 1976 *The State and Criminal Law* in Chambliss and Mankoff, 1976 *Vice, Corruption, Bureaucracy and Power* in Chambliss and Mankoff, 1976
Chambliss, W. J. and Mankoff, M.	*Whose Law? What Order?* (John Wiley & Sons, New York, 1976)
Chester, R.	*Divorce* in Butterworth and Weir, 1975
Child, J. and Macmillan, B.	*Managers and their Leisure* in Smith, Parker and Smith, 1973
Cicourel, A. V.	*The Social Organization of Juvenile Justice* (Heinemann, London, 1976)
Cicourel, A. V. and Kitsuse, J. I.	*The Educational Decision-Makers* (Bobbs-Merrill, Indianapolis, 1963) *The Social Organization of the High School and Deviant Adolescent Careers* in Cosin, Dale, Esland and Swift, 1971
Clayre, A.	*Work and Play* (Weidenfeld & Nicolson, London, 1974)

Clinard, M. B.	*Sociology of Deviant Behavior* 4th edition (Holt, Rinehart & Winston, New York, 1974)
Cloward, R. A. and Ohlin, L. E.	*Delinquency and Opportunity* (The Free Press, Glencoe, 1961)
Coates, K. and Silburn, R.	*Poverty: The Forgotten Englishmen* (Penguin Books, Harmondsworth, 1970)
Cohen, A. K.	*Delinquent Boys* (The Free Press, Glencoe, 1955) *Deviance and Control* (Prentice-Hall, Englewood Cliffs, 1966)
Cohen, D.	'R. D. Laing: The Divided Prophet' *New Society* vol 40 no 761, 5 May 1977
Cohen, S. (ed)	*Images of Deviance* (Penguin Books, Harmondsworth, 1971)
Cohn, N.	*The Pursuit of the Millennium* (Secker & Warburg, London, 1957)
Collins, R.	*Functional and Conflict Theories of Educational Stratification* in Cosin, 1972
Colquhoun, R.	*Values, Socialization and Achievement* in Beck, Jenks, Keddie and Young, 1976
Coon, C. S.	*The Hunting Peoples* (Jonathan Cape, London, 1972)
Cooper, D.	*The Death of the Family* (Penguin Books, Harmondsworth, 1972)
Coser, L. A.	*Masters of Sociological Thought* 2nd edition (Harcourt Brace Jovanovich, New York, 1977)
Coser, L. A. and Rosenberg, B. (eds)	*Sociological Theory: A Book of Readings* 4th edition (Macmillan, New York, 1976)
Cosin, B. R. (ed)	*Education: Structure and Society* (Penguin Books, Harmondsworth, 1972)
Cosin, B.R., Dale, I.R., Esland, G. M. and Swift, D. F. (eds)	*School and Society* (Routledge & Kegan Paul, London, 1971)
Craft, M. (ed)	*Family, Class and Education* (Longman, London, 1970)
Dahl, R. A.	*Who Governs?* (Yale University Press, New Haven, 1961) *Modern Political Analysis* (Prentice-Hall, Englewood Cliffs, 1963) *A Critique Of The Ruling Elite Model* in Urry and Wakeford, 1973
Dahrendorf, R.	*Class and Class Conflict in an Industrial Society* (Routledge & Kegan Paul, London, 1959)
Dale, R.	*Phenomenological Perspectives and the Sociology of the School* in Flude and Ahier, 1974

Sociology

Davis, F.   *Deviance Disavowal* in Lindesmith, Strauss and Denzin, 1975

Davis, K.   *Human Society* (Macmillan, New York, 1948)

Davis, K. and   *Some Principles of Stratification* in Bendix and
Moore, W. E.   Lipset, 1967

Deckard, B. S.   *The Women's Movement* (Harper & Row, New York, 1975)

Deming, W. E.   *On Errors in Surveys* in Franklin and Osborne, 1971

Dennis, N.   *Relationships* in Butterworth and Weir, 1975

Dennis, N.,   *Coal is our Life* (Eyre & Spottiswoode, London,
Henriques, F. and 1956)
Slaughter, C.

Deutscher, I.   *Asking Questions (and Listening to Answers)* in Bulmer, 1977

Djilas, M.   *The New Class* (Thames & Hudson, London, 1957)

Dobson, R. B.   *Social Status and Inequality of Access to Higher Education in the USSR* in Karabel and Halsey, 1977

Douglas, J. D. (ed) *Understanding Everyday Life* (Routledge & Kegan Paul, London, 1971)

Douglas, J. W. B. *The Home and the School* (MacGibbon & Kee, London, 1964)

Douglas, J. W. B., *All Our Future* (Peter Davies, London, 1968)
Ross, J. M. and
Simpson, H. R.

Douglas, M.   *Natural Symbols* (Barrie & Jenkins, London, 1970)

Dowse, R. E. and   *Political Sociology* (John Wiley & Sons, London,
Hughes, J. A.   1972)

Dumazedier, J.   *Towards a Society of Leisure* (Collier-Macmillan, London, 1967)

Durkheim, E.   *The Rules of Sociological Method* (The Free Press, New York, 1938)
                   The Division of Labour in Society (The Free Press, New York, 1947)
                   Professional Ethics and Civic Morals (Routledge & Kegan Paul, London, 1957)
                   Moral Education (The Free Press, Glencoe, 1961)
                   The Elementary Forms of the Religious Life (Collier Books, New York, 1961)
                   Suicide: A Study in Sociology (Routledge & Kegan Paul, London, 1970)

Dye, T. R. and   *The Irony of Democracy* 3rd edition (Duxbury Press,
Zeigler, L. H.   North Scituate, 1975)

Eames, E. and   *Urban Poverty in a Cross-Cultural Context* (The Free
Goode, J. G.   Press, New York, 1973)

Eisenstadt, S. N.	*The Protestant Ethnic Thesis* in Robertson, 1969
Elcock, H.	*Political Behaviour* (Methuen, London, 1976)
Eggleston, J. (ed)	*Contemporary Research in the Sociology of Education* (Methuen, London, 1974)
Engels, F.	*The Origin of the Family, Private Property and the State* (Lawrence & Wishart, London, 1972) *On the History of Early Christianity* in Birnbaum and Lenzer, 1969
Essien-Udom, E. U.	*Black Nationalism: A Search for an Identity in America* (Dell, New York, 1962)
Etzioni, A.	*Modern Organizations* (Prentice-Hall, Englewood Cliffs, 1964)
Etzioni, A. (ed)	*A Sociological Reader on Complex Organizations* 2nd edition (Holt, Rinehart & Winston, New York, 1969)
Eysenck, H.	*Crime and Personality* (Routledge & Kegan Paul, London, 1964) *Race, Intelligence and Education* (Temple Smith, London, 1971)
Feeley, D.	'The Family' in *Feminism and Socialism* edited by L. Jenness (Pathfinder Press, New York, 1972)
Field, F.	'What is Poverty?' *New Society* vol 33 no 677, 25 September 1975
Field, M. G.	'Workers (and Mothers): Soviet Women Today' in *Women in the Soviet Union* edited by D.R.Brown (Teachers College Press, New York, 1968)
Filmer, P., Phillipson, M., Silverman, D. and Walsh, D.	*New Directions in Sociological Theory* (Collier-Macmillan, London, 1972)
Firestone, S.	*The Dialectic of Sex* (Paladin, London, 1972)
Fletcher, R.	*The Family and Marriage in Britain* (Penguin Books, Harmondsworth, 1966)
Flude, M.	*Sociological Accounts of Differential Educational Attainment* in Flude and Ahier, 1974
Flude, M. and Ahier, J. (eds)	*Educability, Schools and Ideology* (Croom Helm, London, 1974)
Franklin, B. J. and Osborne, H. W. (eds)	*Research Methods* (Wadsworth, Belmont, 1971)
Friedl, E.	*Women and Men: An Anthropological View* (Holt, Rinehart & Winston, New York, 1975)
Friedman, N. L.	*Cultural Deprivation: A Commentary on the Sociology of Knowledge* in Beck, Jenks, Keddie and Young, 1976

Gallie, D.

In Search of the New Working Class (Cambridge University Press, Cambridge, 1978)

Gans, H. J.

The Negro Family: Reflections on the Moynihan Report in Rainwater and Yancey, 1967
Culture and Class in the Study of Poverty: An Approach to Anti-Poverty Research in Moynihan, 1968
Poverty and Culture: Some Basic Questions about Methods of Studying Life-Styles of the Poor in Townsend, 1970
More Equality (Pantheon, New York, 1973)

Garfinkel, H.

Studies in Ethnomethodology (Prentice-Hall, Englewood Cliffs, 1967)

Gerth, H. H. and
Mills, C. W.

Character and Social Structure (Harcourt Brace, New York, 1953)

Gerth, H. H. and
Mills, C. W. (eds)

From Max Weber, Essays in Sociology (Routledge & Kegan Paul, London, 1948)

Gibbons, D. C. and
Jones, J. F.

The Study of Deviance (Prentice-Hall, Englewood Cliffs, 1975)

Gibbs, J.

'Issues in Defining Deviant Behaviour' in *Theoretical Perspectives on Deviance* edited by R. A. Scott and J. D. Douglas (Basic Books, New York, 1972)

Giddens, A.

'Power' in the Recent Writings of Talcott Parsons in Worsley, 1970
The Class Structure of the Advanced Societies (Hutchinson, London, 1973)
Studies in Social and Political Theory (Hutchinson, London, 1977)

Giglioli, P. P. (ed)

Language and Social Context (Penguin Books, Harmondsworth, 1972)

Gladwin, T.

Poverty USA (Little Brown, Boston, 1967)

Glasner, P.

The Sociology of Secularisation (Routledge & Kegan Paul, London, 1977)

Glass, D. V. (ed)

Social Mobility in Britain (Routledge & Kegan Paul, London, 1954)

Glass, D. V. and
Hall, J. R.

Social Mobility in Britain: A Study of Intergenerational Changes in Status in Glass, 1954

Glazer-Malbin, N. and
Waehrer, H. Y. (eds)

Woman in a Man-Made World (Rand McNally, Chicago, 1972)

Glock, C. Y.

Religion and the Face of America (University of California Press, Berkeley, 1958)

Glock, C. Y. and
Bellah, R. N. (eds)

The New Religious Consciousness (University of California Press, Berkeley, 1976)

Glock, C. Y. and

Religion and Society in Tension (Rand McNally,

	Chicago, 1965)
Stark, R.	*Dimensions of Religious Commitment* in Robertson, 1969
Gluckman, M.	*Preface* in Bott, 1971
Goffman, E.	*Asylums* (Penguin Books, Harmondsworth, 1968)
Goldthorpe, J. H.	*Social Stratification in Industrial Society* in Bendix and Lipset, 1967 'Review Article: A Revolution in Sociology?' *Sociology* vol 7 no 3, September 1973 'Correspondence: A Rejoinder to Benson' *Sociology* vol 8 no 1, January 1974 *Social Mobility and Class Structure in Modern Britain* (Clarendon Press, Oxford, 1980)
Goldthorpe, J. H. and Llewellyn, C.	'Class Mobility in Modern Britain: Three Theses Examined' *Sociology* vol 11 no 2, May 1977 'Class Mobility' *British Journal of Sociology* vol 28 no 3, September 1977
Goldthorpe, J. H., Lockwood, D., Bechhofer, F. and Platt, J.	*The Affluent Worker: Industrial Attitudes and Behaviour* (Cambridge University Press, Cambridge, 1968) *The Affluent Worker: Political Attitudes and Behaviour* (Cambridge University Press, Cambridge, 1968) *The Affluent Worker in the Class Structure* (Cambridge University Press, Cambridge, 1969)
González, N. L.	'Toward a Definition of Matrifocality' in *Afro-American Anthropology* edited by N. E. Whitten Jr and J. F. Szwed (The Free Press, New York, 1970)
Goode, W. J.	*World Revolution and Family Patterns* (The Free Press, New York, 1963) *A Sociological Perspective on Marital Dissolution* in Anderson, 1971
Gordon, D. M.	*Class and the Economics of Crime* in Chambliss and Mankoff, 1976
Gorz, A.	'Work and Consumption' in *Towards Socialism* edited by P. Anderson and R. Blackburn (Collins, London, 1965)
Goss, M. E. W.	*Influence and Authority among Physicians in an Outpatient Clinic* in Etzioni, 1969
Gough, K.	*An Anthropologist Looks at Engels* in Glazer-Malbin and Waehrer, 1972
Gouldner, A. W.	*Patterns of Industrial Bureaucracy* (The Free Press, Glencoe, 1954) *Wildcat Strike* (Routledge & Kegan Paul, London, 1957)

	The Coming Crisis of Western Sociology (Heinemann, London, 1971)
	Bureaucracy is Not Inevitable in Worsley, 1972
	For Sociology (Penguin Books, Harmondsworth, 1975)
Graham, E.	*The Politics of Poverty* in Roach and Roach, 1972
Graham, J. M.	*Amphetamine Politics on Capitol Hill* in Chambliss and Mankoff, 1976
Grant, W. and Marsh, D.	*The Confederation of British Industry* (Hodder & Stoughton, London, 1977)
Greer, G.	*The Female Eunuch* (Paladin, London, 1971)
Guttsman, W. L.	*The British Political Elite* Revised edition (MacGibbon and Kee, London, 1968)
	The British Political Elite and the Class Structure in Stanworth and Giddens, 1974
Hacker, A.	*The Social and Economic Power of Corporations* in Wrong and Gracey, 1967
	Power to do What? in Lopreato and Lewis, 1974
Hacker, H. M.	*Women as a Minority Group* in Glazer-Malbin and Waehrer, 1972
Halmos, P.	*The Personal Service Society* (Constable, London, 1970)
Hall, E. T.	*The Hidden Dimension* (Doubleday, New York, 1966)
	The Silent Language (Doubleday, New York, 1973)
Halsey, A. H.	*Government Against Poverty in School and Community* in Wedderburn, 1974
	The EPAs and their Schools in Eggleston, 1974
	Towards Meritocracy? The Case of Britain in Karabel and Halsey, 1977, (a)
	'Whatever Happened to Positive Discrimination' *The Times Educational Supplement* 21 January 1977, (b)
Halsey, A. H., Floud, J. and Anderson, C. A.	*Education, Economy and Society* (The Free Press, New York, 1961)
Hammersley, M. and Woods, P. (eds)	*The Process of Schooling* (Routledge & Kegan Paul, London, 1976)
Hannerz, U.	*Soulside: Inquiries into Ghetto Culture and Community* (Columbia University Press, New York, 1969)
Haralambos, M.	*Right On: From Blues to Soul in Black America* (Eddison Press, London, 1974)
Hargreaves, D. H.	*Social Relations in a Secondary School* (Routledge & Kegan Paul, London, 1967)

	Reactions to Labelling in Hammersley and Woods, 1976
Hargreaves, D. H., Hester, S. K. and Mellor, F. J.	*Deviance in Classrooms* (Routledge & Kegan Paul, London, 1975)
Harrington, M.	*The Other America: Poverty in the United States* (Penguin Books, Harmondsworth, 1963)
Harris, C. C.	*The Family* (George Allen & Unwin, London, 1969)
Harris, N.	*Beliefs in Society* (Penguin Books, Harmondsworth, 1971)
Hart, N.	*When Marriage Ends: A Study in Status Passage* (Tavistock, London, 1976)
Hazelrigg, L. E.	*Cross-National Comparisons of Father-to-Son Occupational Mobility* in Lopreato and Lewis, 1974
Heider, K. G.	*The Dugum Dani: A Papuan Culture in the Highlands of West New Guinea* (Wenner-Gren Foundation for Anthropological Research, New York, 1970)
Herberg, W.	*Protestant – Catholic – Jew* revised edition (Anchor Books, New York, 1960)
Herskovits, M. J.	*The Myth of the Negro Past* (Beacon Press, Boston, 1958)
Hewitt, C. J.	*Elites and the Distribution of Power in British Society* in Stanworth and Giddens, 1974
Hill, S.	*The Dockers* (Heinemann, London, 1976)
Horowitz, D.	*The Abolition of Poverty* in Roach and Roach, 1972
Howard, J. R.	'The Making of a Black Muslim' in *Race, Class and Power* 2nd edition edited by R. W. Mack (American Book Company, New York, 1963)
Hudson, K.	*The Place of Women in Society* (Ginn, London, 1970)
Hunter, F.	*Community Power Structure* (Anchor Books, New York, 1963)
Husén, T.	*Social Influences on Educational Attainment* (Organisation for Economic Co-operation and Development, Paris, 1975)
Hyman, H. H.	*The Value Systems of Different Classes* in Bendix and Lipset, 1967
Hyman, R.	*Strikes* (Fontana, London, 1972)
Illich, I.	*Deschooling Society* (Penguin Books, Harmondsworth, 1973)
	Medical Nemesis (Calder & Boyars, London, 1975)
Irwin, J.	*The Felon* (Prentice-Hall, Englewood Cliffs, 1970)

Sociology

James, E.	*America Against Poverty* (Routledge & Kegan Paul, London, 1970)
Jencks, C.	*Inequality: A Reassessment of the Effect of Family and Schooling in America* (Penguin Books, Harmondsworth, 1975)
Jensen, A. R.	*Educational Differences* (Methuen, London, 1973)
Jessop, B.	*Traditionalism, Conservatism and British Political Culture* (George Allen & Unwin, London, 1974)
Karabel, J. and Halsey, A. H. (eds)	*Power and Ideology in Education* (Oxford University Press, New York, 1977)
Kautsky, K.	*Foundations of Christianity* (Russell, New York, 1953)
Kaysen, C.	*The Corporation in Modern Society* (Harvard University Press, Cambridge, USA, 1959)
Keddie, N.	*Classroom Knowledge* in Young, 1971 *Tinker, Tailor . . . The Myth of Cultural Deprivation* (Penguin Books, Harmondsworth, 1973)
Kelsall, R. K.	*Recruitment to the Higher Civil Service* in Stanworth and Giddens, 1974
Kelsall, R. K., Poole, A. and Kuhn, A.	*Graduates: The Sociology of an Elite* (Methuen, London, 1972)
Kerr, C., Dunlop, J. T., Harbison, F. H. and Mayers, C. A.	*Industrialism and Industrial Man* (Heinemann, London, 1962)
Kerr, C. and Siegel, A.	'The Inter-industry Propensity to Strike' in *Industrial Conflict* edited by A. Kornhauser, R. Dubin and A. M. Ross (McGraw-Hill, New York, 1954)
Kincaid, J. C.	*Poverty and Equality in Britain: A Study of Social Security and Taxation* (Penguin Books, Harmondsworth, 1973)
Klein, V.	*Britain's Married Women Workers* (Routledge & Kegan Paul, London, 1965)
Klineberg, O.	'Race and IQ' *Courier* vol 24 no 10, November 1971
Kluckhohn, C.	'The Concept of Culture' in *The Policy Sciences* edited by D. Lerner and H. D. Lasswell (Stanford University Press, Stanford, 1951)
Kolko, G.	*The Triumph of Conservatism* (The Free Press, New York, 1963) *Railroads and Regulations* (Princeton University Press, Princeton, 1965)
Labov, W.	*The Logic of Nonstandard English* in Keddie, 1973
Laing, R. D.	*Self and Others* (Penguin Books, Harmondsworth, 1971)

	Series and Nexus in the Family in Worsley, 1972 *The Politics of the Family* (Penguin Books, Harmondsworth, 1976)
Laing, R. D. and Esterson, A.	*Sanity, Madness and the Family* (Penguin Books, Harmondsworth, 1970)
Lander, B.	*An Ecological Analysis of Baltimore* in Wolfgang, Savitz and Johnston, 1962
Lane, D.	*Politics and Society in the USSR* (Weidenfeld & Nicolson, London, 1970) *The Socialist Industrial State* (George Allen & Unwin, London, 1976)
Lane,T. and Roberts,K.	*Strike at Pilkingtons* (Fontana, London, 1971)
Laslett, P.	*Mean Household Size in England since the Sixteenth Century* in Laslett, 1972
Laslett, P. (ed)	*Household and Family in Past Time* (Cambridge University Press, Cambridge, 1972)
Lawton, D.	*Class, Culture and the Curriculum* (Routledge & Kegan Paul, London, 1975)
Leach, E. R.	*A Runaway World?* (BBC Publications, London, 1967)
Lemert, E. M.	*Human Deviance, Social Problems, and Social Control* 2nd edition (Prentice-Hall, Englewood Cliffs, 1972)
Lenin, V. I.	*Selected Works* (Lawrence & Wishart, London, 1969)
Lenski, G.	*The Religious Factor* revised edition (Anchor Books, New York, 1963)
Lessa, W. A. and Vogt, E. Z.	*Reader in Comparative Religion: An Anthropological Approach* 2nd edition (Harper & Row, New York, 1965)
Levy, M. J.	*The Structure of Society* (Princeton University Press, Princeton, 1952)
Lewis, O.	*Five Families* (Basic Books, New York, 1959) *The Children of Sanchez* (Random House, New York, 1961) *La Vida* (Random House, New York, 1966)
Lichtheim, G.	*Marxism* 2nd edition (Routledge & Kegan Paul, London, 1964)
Liebow, E.	*Tally's Corner* (Little Brown, Boston, 1967)
Lindesmith, A. R., Strauss, A. L. and Denzin, N. K. (eds)	*Readings in Social Psychology* 2nd edition (Dryden, Hinsdale, 1975)
Linton, R.	'Present World Conditions in Cultural Perspective' in *The Science of Man in World Crisis* edited by R.

	Linton (Columbia University Press, New York, 1945)
Lipset, S. M.	*Agrarian Socialism* (University of California Press, Berkeley, 1950) 'Political Sociology' in *Sociology Today* edited by R. K. Merton *et al* (Basic Books, New York, 1959) *Political Man* (Mercury Books, London, 1963)
Lipset, S. M., Trow, M. and Coleman, J.	*Union Democracy* (The Free Press, Glencoe, 1956)
Lipset, S. M. and Zetterburg, H. L.	'Social Mobility in Industrial Societies' in *Social Mobility in Industrial Society* edited by S. M. Lipset and R. Bendix (University of California Press, Berkeley, 1959)
Little, K.	*West African Urbanization* (Cambridge University Press, Cambridge, 1965)
Lockwood, D.	*The Blackcoated Worker* (George Allen & Unwin, London, 1958) *Some Remarks on 'The Social System'* in Worsley, 1970 *In Search of the Traditional Worker* in Bulmer, 1975 *Sources of Variation in Working Class Images of Society* in Bulmer, 1975
Lopreato, J. and Lewis, L. S.	*Social Stratification: A Reader* (Harper & Row, New York, 1974)
Luckmann, T.	*The Invisible Religion: The Transformation of Symbols in Industrial Society* (Macmillan, New York, 1967)
Lukes, S.	*Emile Durkheim: His Life and Work* (Allen Lane, London, 1973)
Lupton, T. and Wilson, C. S.	*The Social Background and Connections of 'Top Decision Makers'* in Urry and Wakeford, 1973
McClosky, H.	'Political Participation' in *International Encyclopedia of the Social Sciences* (Collier-Macmillan, New York, 1968)
McKenzie, R. T.	*Parties, Pressure Groups and the British Political Process* in R. Rose, 1969
McKenzie, R. T. and Silver, A.	*The Working Class Tory in England* in Worsley, 1972 *Angels in Marble* (Heinemann, London, 1968)
MacKenzie, W. J. M.	*Pressure Groups in British Government* in R. Rose, 1969
McLellan, D. (ed)	*Karl Marx: Selected Writings* (Oxford University Press, Oxford, 1977)
Maizels, J.	*Adolescent Needs and the Transition from School to Work* (Athlone Press, London, 1970)

Malinowski, B.	*Magic, Science and Religion and Other Essays* (Anchor Books, New York, 1954)
Mangin, W.	'Poverty and Politics in Cities of Latin America' in *Urban Poverty: Its Social and Political Dimensions* edited by W. Bloomberg Jr and H. J. Schmandt (Sage Publications, Beverly Hills, 1968)
Mankoff, M.	*Introduction to Perspectives on the Problem of Crime* in Chambliss and Mankoff, 1976
Manis, J. G. and Meltzer, B. N. (eds)	*Symbolic Interaction* 2nd edition (Allyn and Bacon, Boston, 1972)
Mannheim, K.	*Ideology and Utopia* (Routledge & Kegan Paul, London, 1948)
Mann, M.	*Consciousness and Action among the Western Working Class* (Macmillan, London, 1973)
Marcuse, H.	*One Dimensional Man* (Abacus, London, 1972)
Martin, D.	*A Sociology of English Religion* (Heinemann, London, 1967) *The Religious and the Secular* (Routledge & Kegan Paul, London, 1969)
Martin, F. M.	*Some Subjective Aspects of Social Stratification* in Glass, 1954
Marx, K.	See under Bottomore and Rubel, and McLellan
Matthews, M.	*Privilege in the Soviet Union* (George Allen & Unwin, London, 1978)
Matza, D.	*Delinquency and Drift* (John Wiley & Sons, New York, 1964)
Matza, D. and Sykes, G.	'Juvenile Delinquency and Subterranean Values' *American Sociological Review* vol 26 no 5, October 1961
Mead, G. H.	*Mind, Self and Society* edited by C. Morris (University of Chicago Press, Chicago, 1934)
Meier, G. M.	*Recent Indicators in International Poverty* in Roach and Roach, 1972
Meltzer, B. N., Petras, J. W. and Reynolds, L. T.	*Symbolic Interactionism* (Routledge & Kegan Paul, London, 1975)
Mencher, S.	*The Problem of Measuring Poverty* in Roach and Roach, 1972
Mennell, S.	*Sociological Theory* (Nelson, London, 1974)
Merton, R. K.	*Social Theory and Social Structure* Enlarged edition (The Free Press, New York, 1968)
Meyer, A. G.	*The Soviet Political System* (Random House, New York, 1965)

Michels, R.	*Political Parties* (The Free Press, Glencoe, 1949)
Midwinter, E.	'The Community School' in *Education and Deprivation* edited by J. Rushton and J. D. Turner (Manchester University Press, Manchester, 1975)
Milbrath, L.	*Political Participation* (Rand McNally, Chicago, 1965)
Miliband, R.	*The State in Capitalist Society* (Weidenfeld & Nicolson, London, 1969) *Politics and Poverty* in Wedderburn, 1974 *Marxism and Politics* (Oxford University Press, Oxford, 1977)
Miller, S. M. and Roby, P.	*Poverty: Changing Social Stratification* in Townsend, 1970 *The Future of Inequality* (Basic Books, New York, 1970)
Miller, W. B.	*Lower Class Culture as a Generating Milieu of Gang Delinquency* in Wolfgang, Savitz and Johnston, 1962 *The Elimination of the American Lower Class as National Policy: A Critique of the Ideology of the Poverty Movement of the 1960s* in Moynihan, 1968
Millett, K.	*Sexual Politics* (Doubleday, New York, 1970)
Mills, C. W.	*White Collar: The American Middle Classes* (Oxford University Press, New York, 1951) *The Power Elite* (Oxford University Press, New York, 1956)
Mitchell, J. J.	*Woman's Estate* (Penguin Books, Harmondsworth, 1971)
Mogey, J. M.	*Family and Neighbourhood* (Oxford University Press, Oxford, 1956)
Mooney, J.	*The Ghost-Dance Religion and the Sioux Outbreak of 1890* (Phoenix Books, Chicago, 1965)
Morgan, D. J. H.	*Social Theory and the Family* (Routledge & Kegan Paul, London, 1975)
Morton, D. C. and Watson, D. R.	'Compensatory Education and Contemporary Liberalism in the US: A Sociological View' in *Equality and City Schools* vol 2 edited by J. Raynor and J. Harden (Routledge & Kegan Paul, London, 1973)
Mosca, G.	*The Ruling Class* (McGraw-Hill, New York, 1939)
Mouzelis, N. P.	*Organisation and Bureaucracy* 2nd edition (Routledge & Kegan Paul, London, 1975)
Moynihan, D. P.	*The Negro Family: The Case for National Action* in Rainwater and Yancey, 1967
Moynihan, D. P. (ed)	*On Understanding Poverty* (Basic Books, New York, 1968)

Murdock, G. P.	*Social Structure* (Macmillan, New York, 1949)
Nash, R.	*Teacher Expectations and Pupil Learning* (Routledge & Kegan Paul, London, 1976)
National Advisory Commission	*Report of the National Advisory Commission on Civil Disorders* (Bantam Books, New York, 1968)
Neibuhr, H. R.	*The Social Sources of Denominationalism* (The World Publishing Company, New York, 1929)
Nisbet, R. A.	*The Sociological Tradition* (Heinemann, London, 1967)
Nordlinger, E. A.	'The Working-Class Tory' *New Society* vol 8 no 211, 13 October 1966 *Working-Class Tories* (MacGibbon & Kee, London, 1967)
Oakley, A.	*Housewife* (Allen Lane, London, 1974)
Ortner, S. B.	'Is Female to Male as Nature is to Culture?' in *Woman, Culture and Society* edited by M. Z. Rosaldo and L. Lamphere (Stanford University Press, Stanford, 1974)
Pareto, V.	*A Treatise on General Sociology* edited by A. Livingstone (Dover Publications, New York, 1963)
Parker, S.	*Work and Leisure* in Butterworth and Weir, 1970 *The Sociology of Leisure* (George Allen & Unwin, London, 1976)
Parkin, F.	*Middle-Class Radicalism* (Manchester University Press, Manchester, 1968) *Class Inequality and Political Order* (Paladin, St Albans. 1972) 'Review of "Class in a Capitalist Society" by J. Westergaard and H. Resler' *British Journal of Sociology* vol 28 no 1, March 1977
Parry, G.	*Political Elites* (George Allen & Unwin, London, 1969)
Parry, N. and Parry, J.	*The Rise of the Medical Profession* (Croom Helm, London, 1976) *Social Closure and Collective Social Mobility* in Scase, 1977
Parsons, T.	*The Structure of Social Action* (McGraw-Hill, New York, 1937) *The Social System* (The Free Press, New York, 1951) 'The Social Structure of the Family' in *The Family: Its Functions and Destiny* edited by R. N. Anshen (Harper & Row, New York, 1959) *Structure and Process in Modern Societies* (The Free Press, Chicago, 1960) *The School Class as a Social System* in Halsey, Floud

and Anderson, 1961
Essays in Sociological Theory (The Free Press, New York, 1964)
Religious Perspectives in Sociology and Social Psychology in Lessa and Vogt, 1965
'The Normal American Family' in *Man and Civilization: The Family's Search for Survival* edited by S. M. Farber (McGraw-Hill, New York, 1965)
Family and Church as 'Boundary' Structures in Birnbaum and Lenzer, 1969
Politics and Social Structure (The Free Press, New York, 1969)
The Evolution of Societies edited by J. Toby (Prentice-Hall, Englewood Cliffs, 1977)

Parsons, T. and Bales, R. F.	*Family, Socialization and Interaction Process* (The Free Press, New York, 1955)
Payne, G., Ford, G. and Robertson, C.	'A Reappraisal of Social Mobility in Britain' *Sociology* vol 11 no 2, May 1977
Pearce, F.	*Crimes of the Powerful* (Pluto Press, London, 1976)
Peters, B. G.	*The Politics of Bureaucracy* (Longman, New York, 1978)
Phillips, D. L.	*Knowledge From What?* (Rand McNally, Chicago, 1971) *Abandoning Method* (Jossey-Bass, San Francisco, 1973)
Phillipson, M.	*Theory, Methodology and Conceptualization* in Filmer, Phillipson, Silverman and Walsh, 1972
Pietrofesa, J. I. and Schlossberg, N. K.	*Counselor Bias and the Female Occupational Role* in Glazer-Malbin and Waehrer, 1972
Platt, J.	'Variations in Answers to Different Questions on Perceptions of Class' *Sociological Review* vol 19 no 3, August 1971
Poulantzas, N.	*The Problem of the Capitalist State* in Urry and Wakeford, 1973
President's Commission on Income Maintenance Programs	*Poverty Amid Plenty: The Report of the President's Commission of Income Maintenance Programs* (US Government Printing Office, Washington DC, 1969)
Rainwater, L.	*The Problem of Lower-Class Culture and Poverty-War Strategy* in Moynihan, 1968 *Behind Ghetto Walls* (Aldine, Chicago, 1970)
Rainwater, L. and Yancey, W. L. (eds)	*The Moynihan Report and the Politics of Controversy* (MIT Press, Cambridge, 1967)
Rapaport, R. and Rapaport, R.	*Dual-Career Families* (Penguin Books, Harmondsworth, 1971)

Reid, I.	*Social Class Differences* in Britain (Open Books, London, 1977)
Rein, M.	*Problems in the Definition and Measurement of Poverty* in Townsend, 1970
Rex, J.	*Capitalism, Elites and the Ruling Class* in Stanworth and Giddens, 1974
Roach, J. L. and Roach, J. K. (eds)	*Poverty: Selected Readings* (Penguin Books, Harmondsworth, 1972)
Roethlisberger,F.J.and Dickson, W. J.	*Management and the Worker* (Harvard University Press, Cambridge, USA, 1939)
Roberts,K.,Cook,F.G., Clark, S. C. and Semeonoff, E.	*The Fragmentary Class Structure* (Heinemann, London, 1977)
Robertson, R.	*The Sociological Interpretation of Religion* (Basil Blackwell, Oxford, 1970)
Robertson, R. (ed)	*Sociology of Religion* (Penguin Books, Harmondsworth, 1969)
Rose, A. M.	*The Power Structure: Political Process in American Society* (Oxford University Press, New York, 1967)
Rose, A. M. (ed)	*Human Behaviour and Social Processes* (Routledge & Kegan Paul, London, 1962)
Rosenfeld, E.	*Social Stratification in a 'Classless' Society* in Lopreato and Lewis, 1974
Rosen, H.	*Language and Class* 3rd edition (Falling Wall Press, Bristol, 1974)
Rosenthal, R. and Jacobson, L.	*Pygmalion in the Classroom* (Holt, Rinehart & Winston, New York, 1968)
Rose, R. (ed)	*Studies in British Politics* 2nd edition (Macmillan, London, 1969)
Ross, A. M. and Hartman, P. T.	*Changing Patterns of Industrial Conflict* (John Wiley & Sons, New York, 1960)
Rosser, R. and Harris, C.	*The Family and Social Change* (Routledge & Kegan Paul, London, 1965)
Rowbotham, S.	*Woman's Consciousness, Man's World* (Penguin Books, Harmondsworth, 1973)
Rubington, E. and Weinberg, M. S. (eds)	*Deviance: The Interactionist Perspective* 2nd edition (Macmillan, New York, 1973)
Runciman, W. G.	*Relative Deprivation and Social Justice* (Routledge & Kegan Paul, London, 1966)
Scase, R. (ed)	*Industrial Society: Class, Cleavage and Control* (George Allen & Unwin, London, 1977)
Schwartz, A. J.	'A Further Look at the "Culture of Poverty": Ten Caracas Barrios' in *Sociology and Social Research*

	vol 59, no 4, July 1975
Scott, H.	*Women and Socialism* (Allison & Busby, London, 1976)
Selznick, P.	*TVA and the Grass Roots* (Harper Torchbooks, New York, 1966)
Sharpe, S.	*Just Like a Girl: How Girls Learn to be Women* (Penguin Books, Harmondsworth, 1976)
Shaskolsky, L.	'The Development of Sociological Theory – A Sociology of Knowledge Interpretation' in *The Sociology of Sociology* edited by L. T. and J. M. Reynolds (McKay, New York, 1970)
Shaw, C. R. and McKay, H. D.	*Juvenile Delinquency and Urban Areas* (University of Chicago Press, Chicago, 1942)
Shiner, L.	'The Concept of Secularization in Empirical Research' in *Sociological Perspectives* edited by K. Thompson and J. Tunstall (Penguin Books, Harmondsworth, 1971)
Silverman, D.	*The Theory of Organisations* (Heinemann, London, 1970)
Skidmore, W.	*Theoretical Thinking in Sociology* (Cambridge University Press, Cambridge, 1975)
Smith, M. G.	*West Indian Family Structure* (University of Washington Press, Seattle, 1962)
Smith, M., Parker, S. and Smith, C.	*Leisure and Society in Britain* (Allen Lane, London, 1973)
Social Trends	*No 4 1973 No 8 1977* (Her Majesty's Stationery Office, London, 1973, 1977)
Spiro, M. E.	*Is the Family Universal? – The Israeli Case* in Bell and Vogel, 1968
Stacey, M.	*Tradition and Change: A Study of Banbury* (Oxford University Press, Oxford, 1960)
Stanworth, P. and Giddens, A. (eds)	*Elites and Power in British Society* (Cambridge University Press, Cambridge, 1974)
Stark, R. and Glock, C. Y.	*American Piety: The Nature of Religious Commitment* (University of California Press, Berkeley, 1968)
Sugarman, B.	*Social Class, Values and Behaviour in Schools* in Craft, 1970
Sussman, M. B. and Burchinal, L. G.	*The Kin Family Network in Urban-Industrial America* in Anderson, 1971
Sutherland, E. H.	*Is 'White Collar Crime' Crime?* in Wolfgang, Savitz and Johnston, 1962
	White Collar Crime (Holt, Rinehart & Winston, New York, 1960)

Sykes, G. M. and Matza, D.	*Techniques of Neutralization: A Theory of Delinquency* in Wolfgang, Savitz and Johnston, 1962
Talmon, Y.	*Pursuit of the Millennium: The Relations between Religious and Social Change* in Lessa and Vogt, 1965 *Sex-Role Differentiation in an Egalitarian Society* in Glazer-Malbin and Waehrer, 1972
Tausky, C.	*Work Organizations* (F. E. Peacock, Itasca, 1970)
Taylor, F. W.	*Scientific Management* (Harper & Row, New York, 1947)
Taylor, I., Walton, P. and Young, J.	*The New Criminology* (Routledge & Kegan Paul, London, 1973)
Taylor, L.	*Deviance and Society* (Michael Joseph, London, 1971)
Taylor, L. and Walton, P.	*Industrial Sabotage: Motives and Meanings* in Cohen, 1971
Thurow, L. C.	*Education and Economic Equality* in Karabel and Halsey, 1977
Tiger, L. and Fox, R.	*The Imperial Animal* (Secker & Warburg, London, 1972)
Tiger, L. and Shepher, J.	*Women in the Kibbutz* (Penguin Books, Harmondsworth, 1977)
Toffler, A.	*Future Shock* (Pan Books, London, 1971)
Torrey, J.	*Illiteracy in the Ghetto* in Keddie, 1973
Towler, R.	*Homo Religiosus: Sociological Problems in the Study of Religion* (Constable, London, 1974)
Townsend, P.	*Measures and Explanations of Poverty in High and Low Income Countries* in Townsend, 1970 *Poverty as Relative Deprivation* in Wedderburn, 1974
Townsend, P. (ed)	*The Concept of Poverty* (Heinemann, London, 1970)
Truman, D.	*The Governmental Process* (Knopf, New York, 1951)
Tumin, M. M.	*Some Principles of Stratification: A Critical Analysis* in Bendix and Lipset, 1967 *Social Stratification: The Forms and Functions of Social Inequality* (Prentice-Hall, Englewood Cliffs, 1967)
Tunstall, J.	*The Fishermen* (MacGibbon & Kee, London, 1962)
Tylor, E. B.	*Religion in Primitive Culture* (Peter Smith, Gloucester, 1970)
Urry, J. and Wakeford, J. (eds)	*Power in Britain* (Heinemann, London, 1973)
Vajda, M. and	*Family Structure and Communism* in Glazer-Malbin

Sociology

Heller, A.	and Waehrer, 1972
Valentine, C. A.	*Culture and Poverty* (University of Chicago Press, Chicago, 1968)
Valentine, C. A. and Valentine, B. L.	'Making the Scene, Digging the Action, and Telling it Like it is: Anthropologists at Work in a Dark Ghetto' in *Afro-American Anthropology* edited by N. E. Whitten Jr and J. F. Szwed (The Free Press, New York, 1970)
Veness, T.	*School Leavers* (Methuen, London, 1962)
Vernon, P. E.	*Intelligence and Cultural Environment* (Methuen, London, 1969)
Vogel, E. F. and Bell, N. W.	*The Emotionally Disturbed Child as the Family Scapegoat* in Bell and Vogel, 1968
Walsh, D.	*Functionalism and Systems Theory* in Filmer, Phillipson, Silverman and Walsh, 1972
Warwick, D.	*Bureaucracy* (Longman, London, 1974)
Weber, M.	*The Protestant Ethic and the Spirit of Capitalism* (Charles Scribner's Sons, New York, 1958)
	The Sociology of Religion (Beacon Press, Boston, 1963)
	See also under Gerth and Mills
Wedderburn, D.	'Workplace Inequality' *New Society* vol 15 no 393, 9 April 1970
Wedderburn, D. (ed)	*Poverty, Inequality and Class Structure* (Cambridge University Press, Cambridge, 1974)
Wedderburn, D. and Craig, C.	*Relative Deprivation in Work* in Wedderburn, 1974
Wedderburn, D. and Crompton, R.	*Workers' Attitudes and Technology* (Cambridge University Press, Cambridge, 1972)
Westergaard, J.	*Radical Class Consciousness: A Comment* in Bulmer, 1975
Westergaard, J. and Little, A.	*Educational Opportunity and Social Selection in England and Wales: Trends and Policy Implications* in Craft, 1970
Westergaard, J. and Resler, H.	*Class in a Capitalist Society* (Penguin Books, Harmondsworth, 1976)
Wesolowski, W.	*Some Notes on the Functional Theory of Stratification* in Bendix and Lipset, 1967
	The Notion of Strata and Class in Socialist Society in Béteille, 1969
Whyte, W. F.	*Street Corner Society* 2nd edition (University of Chicago Press, Chicago, 1955)
Wilensky, H. L.	*Work, Careers and Social Integration* in Burns, 1969

Wilensky, H. L. and Edwards, H.	*The Skidder: Ideological Adjustments of Downward Mobile Workers* in Lopreato and Lewis, 1974
Wiles, P. N. P.	*Criminal Statistics and Sociological Explanations of Crime* in Carson and Wiles, 1971
Williams, J. A. Jr	*Interviewer–Respondent Interaction* in Franklin and Osborne, 1971
Williamson, B.	*Continuities and Discontinuities in the Sociology of Education* in Flude and Ahier, 1974
Willmott, P. and Young, M.	*Family and Class in a London Suburb* (Routledge & Kegan Paul, London, 1960)
Wilson, B. R.	*Religion in a Secular Society* (C. A. Watts, London, 1966) *Religious Sects* (Weidenfeld & Nicolson, London, 1970) *Contemporary Transformations of Religion* (Oxford University Press, London, 1976)
Wolfgang, M. E., Savitz, L. and Johnston, N. (eds)	*The Sociology of Crime and Delinquency* (John Wiley & Sons, New York, 1962)
Worsley, P.	*The Trumpet Shall Sound* 2nd edition (MacGibbon & Kee, London, 1968)
Worsley, P. (ed)	*Modern Sociology: Introductory Readings* (Penguin Books, Harmondsworth, 1970) *Problems of Modern Society* (Penguin Books, Harmondsworth, 1972) *Introducing Sociology* 2nd edition (Penguin Books, Harmondsworth, 1977)
Wrong, D. H. and Gracey, H. L. (eds)	*Readings in Introductory Sociology* (Macmillan, New York, 1967)
Yablonsky, L.	*The Violent Gang* (Collier-Macmillan, New York, 1962)
Yeo-chi King, A.	'A Voluntarist Model of Organization' in *The British Journal of Sociology* vol 28 no 3, September 1977
Yinger, J. M.	*Religion, Society and the Individual* (Macmillan, New York, 1967)
Young, J.	*The Role of the Police as Amplifiers of Deviancy, Negotiators of Reality and Translators of Fantasy* in Cohen, 1971 *Foreword* in Pearce, 1976
Young, M.	*The Rise of the Meritocracy* (Penguin Books, Harmondsworth, 1961)
Young, M. and Willmott, P.	*Family and Kinship in East London* (Penguin Books, Harmondsworth, 1962) *The Symmetrical Family* (Penguin Books, Harmondsworth, 1975)

Sociology

Young, M. F. D.   *An Approach to the Study of Curricula as Socially Organized Knowledge* in Young, 1971

Young, M. F. D. (ed)   *Knowledge and Control* (Collier-Macmillan, London, 1971)

Zimmerman, D. H.   *The Practicalities of Rule Use* in Douglas, 1971

Zimmerman, D. H. and Wieder, D. L.   *Ethnomethodology and the Problem of Order* in Douglas, 1971

Author index

Sociology

Subject index